LOGOBOOK

Ed. Julius Wiedemann

LOGOBOOK

by Ludovic Houplain (H5)
co-director of the Oscar-winning
short animation film
LOGORAMA

TASCHEN

Contents
Inhalt
Contenu

Introduction
The Foundations
of Logorama
6

Einleitung
Logorama: Die Anfänge
12

Introduction
Les fondations
de Logorama
18

Essay
A Branded World
24

Die Welt als Marke
und als Logo
32

Le monde comme
marque et comme logo
40

User's Guide
Hinweise für die Benutzer
Guide de l'utilisateur
48

Logos
from # to Z
von # bis Z
de # à Z
49–745

Index
746

The Foundations of Logorama

I first thought about making a film entirely composed of logotypes after I made *The Child* (p. 8) for the French artist Alex Gopher. This film, which I made in 1999 with Antoine Bardou-Jacquet, represented our urban environment using nothing but words. Depicting Manhattan as just a mass of labels such as "building," "block," "bridge," and so on, the city and its inhabitants were turned into a vast typographical landscape. Moreover, by using different fonts and sizes the lettering shows immediately whether it's a new or used car, for example, or whether it was manufactured in the West or in Japan.

Soon after, our production company Midi-Minuit gave us the chance to work with Télépopmusik on another film, for an album called *Da Hoola*. I thought about different graphic approaches for it and as I looked at the CD cover realised that just as we had used typography in *The Child* we could try and do something similar using brand logos. I reckoned we'd be able to make a short film with only logos, since logos represent everything we see around us – people, fruit, buildings and so on. After that, logos became my Lego bricks. Based on this idea, I proposed a project to Télépopmusik which would set American and Russian logos against each other in a sort of Olympic Games, but the idea got no further than that.

However, the first seed had been planted, and for two years it continued to grow. Eventually, I asked my brother Cyril to work on some airport scenes using logos designed in the 1920s but this also didn't work, leaving the result too pictorial and too far removed from the feel of Pop Art. To talk about today's world we needed contemporary logos that can be easily recognised by everyone. In 2003, after winning the MTV Music Award for the Röyksopp video, H5 was asked by Dhani Harrison, George Harrison's son, to make a video for the title track for *Brainwashed*, his new album. He wanted an animation with a critical but nostalgic take on our consumer culture and after our first conversation, I thought this could be adapted and based on logos. Hervé de Crécy and I worked on the narrative, ensuring that it harmonised with both lyrics and music. We decided to set it in a generic US city, which we depicted in the form of a supermarket with streets like parallel aisles lined with shelves and the buildings as products on them with the logos of well-known brands. In the story, a hurricane suddenly tears through the city. All the well-ordered streets are devastated and the shop signs get all mixed up, creating unlikely visual associations and offering a strange, unnatural mix of things to buy. We wanted to create an apocalyptic landscape, and then have vegetation taking over this ravaged society. However, the project was scrapped when the record label objected to the use of real logos for legal reasons. But here we had laid the foundations of *Logorama*.

It became clear that no record company would want to make such a video, and as a film it could only exist as an artistic statement, not something simply made to order. We teamed up with Addict

Logorama, scene from the film, directed by H5 (Hervé de Crécy, François Alaux and Ludovic Houplain)

Films as co-producer, Mikros Image for post-production, and Autour de Minuit for their experience with short films. First of all we changed the setting from New Orleans, because of Hurricane Katrina, to Hollywood with all its clichés. If this was partly an homage, we could also now embrace and use all of Hollywood's cinematic codes. The idea wasn't born out of a sudden brainwave, but from a multitude of associations, observations and encounters, and we felt a real compulsion to get it made. Later on, François Alaux joined Hervé and me to help out with the enormous amount of work involved in directing the film.

Logos have fascinated me from an early age, and three vivid childhood memories may best explain this curiosity. The first is connected with my father. He was a racing driver and his environment was overloaded with logos – cars, uniforms, trackside, there wasn't an empty space. This was in the 1970s and motor racing was already saturated with sponsorship (p. 9). The second memory is from the same period and concerns the logo on the road sign for the supermarket chain Carrefour (p. 10). I was fascinated by the shape but couldn't make sense of it. I was attracted by the tricolor design reminiscent of the French flag, but quite baffled by the shape. The white letter "C" set against a blue and red background didn't mean much to a seven-year-old. On my way to school I used to wonder what it might mean; neither figurative nor abstract, but someone had designed it, so it had to mean something. The third memory is linked to my grandfather, whose factories were called LITA (p. 14) and later merged with Mazda. When visiting the factories at weekends, my brother and I realised how important their trademark was. There wasn't a letterhead, a box or a door unmarked by the company logo and subconsciously I became sure it too was part of the business, its very heart and soul. These three distinct memories showed me the power and impact logos can have even on children and how they can arouse interest, no matter if they are made up of lettering or drawings.

Logos are direct connections to corporate institutions but it isn't their aesthetic that makes them most identifiable, it's their level of exposure. A great logo which has poor exposure has very little chance of attracting attention, unlike a third-rate logo that is seen all round the world. We have been using logos ever since we started out as graphic designers, hijacking and adapting them to the needs of the French Touch label and the world of electronic music. From the outset, Antoine, Alex, Étienne de Crécy and I decided to handle the artists' image like a mass-market product you would find in a supermarket. The most spectacular example is the garish yellow cover of the *Super Discount* album (p. 15). The cover is a logo, the logo is a brand, the brand is an artist and the artist is a sound.

It was a revelation, the undeniable power of the logo and the brand. We felt like real graphic artists working in the retail sector and the other revelation was that graphic design can't just be restricted to

INTRODUCTION

the decorative aspect, it has to be the result of the discussions and experience behind it. Since then, we haven't stopped playing with the codes of multinational companies and brands, and *Logorama* was the climax of that process. But is the logo a bad symbol of the power of brands? I'm not so sure. A company logo can't be a bad thing in itself as it's only a visual element. Whether it's for Lehman Brothers or the RAF machine gun, it's not the logo's appearance that is the object of criticism, it's what it stands for, in terms of the philosophy behind the message it carries or the activities it represents. It can be detrimental to a company though if a logo gets over-used. The moment it reaches saturation point, when people see it every day and can't escape it, it becomes visual pollution – just think of commercial districts where there are more and more super-sized signs, each one more flamboyant than the one before (p.17).

The most challenging part of starting the film was to set up a database of logos, much like auditioning a cast. This meant profiling each logo according to the role it could play in the film, whether part of the scenery, a character, or a prop. Throughout the film, we kept on searching and looking out for logos, always with the idea that it wasn't about making a great movie but producing something that would resonate with the world around us. We also wanted to avoid falling into the trap of reducing it to an élitist exercise in visual stylistics. It should be aimed at a universal audience because it was a universal subject.

To achieve this, we had to distance ourselves from the habits of our original trade as graphic designers. On the contrary, we had to assume the role of directors, mixing a multitude of figurative or abstract forms to create landscapes and scenes from everyday life. From that point onwards there were no more logos, just actors and sets.

It took us a couple of years to build up this database. We first got hold of as many publications about logos as we could but found these only yielded about a hundred recurring examples, such as Mercedes, Coca-Cola and Michelin, chiefly from sports sponsorship, and a thousand-odd highly stylised logos that no one has ever heard of. An Internet search led me to a yearly compilation of American logos: *The Book of American Trade Marks*. I bought the 20 most recent issues and these contained a whole host of American trademarks which were much more suited to the film. Some dated back to the 1970s so I had to check these still existed, and at the same time find out whether they had developed visually so we could choose which ones to use in the film. Initial research was focused on internationally recognised brands, starting with the financial markets and prioritising companies listed on the New York Stock Exchange and NASDAQ. Then I did the same for all the G8 countries. Ultimately I think we used every possible source – everything from books on visual identity found in libraries to the financial sections of dailies like *Le Monde* and *The New York Times*.

left *The Child*, Alex Gopher, music video, 1999, directed by H5 (Antoine Bardou-Jacquet and Ludovic Houplain)

right *Circuit de Nevers Magny-Cours*, 1972, France, photo by Hervé Houplain

We didn't want our conception of the film to be governed by anything picturesque or pretty; it should be more like Pop Art, but with a subtle difference. Where Pop Art illustrates consumer society with images like Warhol's *Brillo Box* (p. 20), Ed Ruscha's *Standard Station* (p. 21) or Lichtenstein's *Blam* (p. 23), *Logorama* focuses on the image culture itself, where the product has become less visible than the brand. We aren't interested in the product, what intrigues us is the brand and the values it promotes. How do you explain the attraction of Hello Kitty (p. 26), a symbol that takes us straight back to the world of early childhood? The paradox of this famous brand is that, unlike Babar the elephant or Naruto the teenage ninja, it has nothing to back it up. There isn't any kids' story or cartoon behind the character. It's a remarkable masterpiece of marketing by Sanrio.

Returning to the film and the use of multinational logos, we wanted to direct them: push them around, combine them, amalgamate them, mix them up and mould them like modelling clay. Since these brands impose themselves upon us every day and via every possible means of communication, we decided it was *our* turn to impose our vision of the world on *them*, just to demonstrate that we had freedom of expression, which was even more important than any artistic aspect. That very freedom of expression scared the hell out of the English-speaking lawyers specialising in trademark law. But isn't taking risks in this over-legislated world the first step an artist should take before even thinking about aesthetic aspects?

I guess that we had seen probably around 50,000 logos by the end of the production period. One amongst various decisions was: should we include a logo's new form or hang on to the old one? When we went to Los Angeles to record the soundtrack, on the road from the airport to the city centre the new Pepsi logo (p. 28) took up the whole of the front of a building. But this teaser only existed in the USA, it hadn't arrived in Europe yet, and in the end it was the shape of the old version that persuaded us to stick with that. The same went for the Stop & Shop logo (p. 29), which had been given a makeover and turned into a cross between a basket of fruit and a bouquet of flowers. With some logos, we looked very closely at them before finally deciding to ditch them. We also performed a bit of "cosmetic surgery" on some of the more austere-looking logos, for example Walmart, Kraft Foods and Cheer, adding little touches such as flowers, sunshine and greenery. Throughout the making of *Logorama*, we also couldn't avoid realising the number of logos that had to be produced in 3D, which meant literally creating another dimension to add volume.

The film also features certain "vintage" logos, representing very small brands that are hard to identify. An example is the Cruz logo produced by an American design collective for a car-body maker. This was the perfect vehicle for two cops shaped like Michelin Man. We had imagined them

INTRODUCTION

Carrefour, logo, 1996, Carrefour SA, France, designed by Jacques Daniel and Etienne Thil

having an identifiable car, like *Starsky and Hutch*'s Ford Gran Torino or the Mercury driven by Sylvester Stallone in *Cobra*, but since no leading brand had the right sort of logo we had to turn to a little-known brand. It was also important to make sure all our logos were genuine, and we had to be absolutely sure of our sources.

After all this, we began making storyboards (p. 31) for the film so that our research kept geared to the action. Then we began our search for logos that would tell the story. This meant being very practical – we started with nothing and had to create a world made up entirely of logos. All the logos were classified under different headings, such as characters, animals, sets, objects, vehicles, and each heading had sub-headings, and so on. This produced a database of logos of different designs which together gave us all the visual elements we needed. There were also "special castings" for major logos. We were interested in their symbolic impact, their graphic form being secondary, and these logos mostly became signs or billboards in the film. Then we cast logotypes by shape. These were basic geometric forms we used as bricks to construct urban spaces and wide-angle shots of landscapes. The arc of a circle became a zigzag, a circle, or a sphere, which was then transformed into a planet. These simple shapes were ideal for creating a backdrop that allowed the audience to concentrate on the action in the foreground. The last heading was "picture words," such as the "sun" in Sun Microsystems or the name of a Milky Way chocolate bar. The direct symbolism of these brand names was, however, only used in moderation, with just brief appearances, to avoid the film becoming another version of *The Child*.

After several years of being immersed in the world of logos, I have come to realise that they follow fashion and artistic trends. Since the first logos appeared in the second half of the nineteenth century, they have had a history of borrowing from art movements, for example, the dropped initials of the Coca-Cola logo are borrowed from Art Nouveau (p. 34), while Renault (p. 34) asked Victor Vasarely, one of the founding fathers of Op Art, to give its logo a face-lift. Similarly the poster artist Cassandre designed the Yves Saint Laurent logo (p. 35), whilst Raymond Lœwy was responsible for the LU biscuits logo (p. 35). A logo aimed at the general public is a true graphic mirror of society. It is born, grows up, but is not allowed to grow old. It must be adapted to the aesthetics of the decades through which it operates so that it never becomes obsolete.

Making the film was also an opportunity for some unexpected encounters. Meeting Dhani Harrison at the start of the project, he invited us to his home outside London, which gave us some idea of what it must have felt like to be Beatles fans. It was great meeting David Fincher when we went to record the English voiceovers in Los Angeles. So too Andrew Kevin Walker, who wrote the screenplay for *Se7en*, and did the dialogue for us. Then there was our meeting with Thomas

"After several years of being immersed in the world of logos, I have come to realise that they follow fashion and artistic trends."

Bangalter of Daft Punk to work on the soundtrack, which was really interesting and helped us make up our minds whether to feature a number of different artists or opt for an original soundtrack with a single artist, in the style of someone like Michel Legrand. We settled on the first option, so sticking with the best that Hollywood entertainment had to offer. The Academy Award for Animated Short made all the learning and effort even more rewarding. A truly Hollywood experience.

Ludovic Houplain is the founder of H5, a multidisciplinary design studio established in 1996 in Paris, and co-director of the Oscar-winning short animation film *Logorama* in 2009. His inventive work for music and cultural institutions as well as luxury industry and advertising can be seen in association with big names like Air, Dior, Cannes Festival, Audi, Citroën, among others.

EINLEITUNG

Logorama: Die Anfänge

Auf die Idee, einen Film ausschließlich aus Logos zusammenzusetzen, kam ich, nachdem ich für den französischen Künstler Alex Gopher *The Child* (S. 8) gemacht hatte. Der Film, 1999 mit Antoine Bardou-Jacquet gedreht, bildet unsere urbane Umgebung ausschließlich aus Wörtern ab. Manhattan wird als Ansammlung von Substantiven wie etwa „building", „block", „bridge" („Gebäude", „Block", „Brücke") und so weiter dargestellt, die Stadt und ihre Bewohner werden also in eine gigantische typografische Szenerie verwandelt. Anhand unterschiedlicher Schrifttypen und Buchstabengrößen erkennt man zum Beispiel sofort, ob es sich um einen Neu- oder Gebrauchtwagen handelt, um ein westliches oder ein japanisches Modell.

Wenig später wurde es durch unsere Produktionsfirma Midi-Minuit möglich, mit Télépopmusik einen weiteren Film zu machen, und zwar für das Album *Da Hoola*. Ich entwickelte ein paar grafische Ideen, und angesichts des CD-Covers kam mir der Gedanke, dass wir etwas Ähnliches wie bei *The Child* machen könnten, allerdings mit Firmenlogos anstatt Typografie. So entstand weiter die Idee für einen richtigen Kurzfilm ausschließlich aus Logos. Schließlich repräsentieren Logos alles, was wir um uns her sehen – Menschen, Obst, Gebäude und so weiter. Logos wurden zu meinen Lego-Bausteinen. Ausgehend davon schlug ich Télépopmusik ein Projekt vor, in dem amerikanische und russische Logos quasi in einer Olympiade gegeneinander antreten sollten, doch das wurde nicht umgesetzt.

Aber die Idee war geboren, und sie reifte im Stillen zwei Jahre. Dann bat ich meinen Bruder Cyril, aus Logos der 1920er Jahre ein paar Flughafen-Szenen zu bauen. Allerdings funktionierte auch das nicht, das Ergebnis war zu bildlastig und hatte überhaupt nicht das Feeling von Pop-Art. Um etwas über das Heute zu sagen, muss man zeitgenössische Logos verwenden, die für jedermann sofort erkennbar sind. 2003, nachdem H5 für das Röyksopp-Video den MTV Music Award bekommen hatte, fragte Dhani Harrison, George Harrisons Sohn, wegen eines Videos für den Titelsong seines neuen Albums *Brainwashed* an. Ihm schwebte eine Animation mit einem kritischen und zugleich nostalgischen Blick auf unsere Konsumgesellschaft vor, und nach dem ersten Gespräch dachte ich mir, dass man diese Idee umgestalten und mit Logos umsetzen könnte. Hervé de Crécy und ich arbeiteten die Geschichte aus, so dass sie sowohl zum Text als auch zur Musik passte. Wir beschlossen, sie in einer typisierten amerikanischen Stadt anzusiedeln, der wir die Gestalt eines Supermarkts gaben; die Straßen waren von Regalen gesäumte Gänge, die Gebäude wurden durch bekannte Markenprodukte in den Regalen dargestellt. In der Geschichte fegt plötzlich ein Hurrikan durch die Stadt, die ordentlich angelegten Straßen werden herumgewirbelt, die Schriftzüge der Geschäfte geraten durcheinander, es entstehen ungewöhnliche visuelle Assoziationen, die eine widersinnige Mischung von Waren anbieten. Unsere Idee war, eine apokalyptische Landschaft zu schaffen, und diese zerstörte Stadt sollte dann von Vegetation

LOGORAMA: DIE ANFÄNGE

Logorama, digital sketch for the film, by Ludovic Houplain

überwuchert werden. Aber das Projekt zerschlug sich, weil das Plattenlabel es aus juristischen Gründen ablehnte, echte Logos zu verwenden. Das waren die Anfänge, aus denen sich *Logorama* entwickelte.

Allmählich wurde klar, dass kein Musiklabel ein solches Video machen würde und dass ein solcher Film nur als künstlerisches Werk entstehen konnte. Wir taten uns mit Autour de Minuit zusammen, wegen ihrer Erfahrung mit Kurzfilmen, die Co-Produktion übernahm Addict Films, die Post-Produktion Mikros Image. Zuerst einmal verlegten wir die Handlung, nachdem Hurrikan Katrina geschehen war, von New Orleans nach Hollywood mit all seinen Klischees. Das war zum Teil ein Tribut, außerdem konnten wir so auch die ganzen Hollywood eigenen filmischen Codes zitieren. Der Film war nicht das Ergebnis eines Geistesblitzes, sondern entstand aus einer Vielzahl von Assoziationen, Beobachtungen und Begegnungen heraus. Für uns wurde es regelrecht zum inneren Zwang, ihn zu machen. Später kam François Alaux dazu, um Hervé und mir bei der sehr aufwendigen Produktion des Films unter die Arme zu greifen.

Für Logos hatte ich mich schon als Kind begeistert. Vielleicht geht alles auf drei frühe Erinnerungen zurück. Die erste hat mit meinem Vater zu tun. Er war Rennfahrer, und seine Welt war mit Logos bepflastert (S. 9). Das war in den 70er Jahren, und Motorsportrennen waren schon ein großes Sponsor-Geschäft. Die zweite Erinnerung stammt aus derselben Zeit und betrifft das Logo der Supermarktkette Carrefour (S. 10). Ich fand die Form faszinierend, hatte aber keine Ahnung, was sie darstellen sollte. Mir gefiel das dreifarbige Muster, das an die französische Flagge erinnert, aber die Form verblüffte mich. Der weiße Buchstabe „C" vor dem blau-roten Hintergrund sagte mir als Siebenjährigem herzlich wenig. Auf dem Weg zur Schule fragte ich mich immer wieder, was es wohl bedeuten könnte; es war ja weder figürlich noch abstrakt, aber jemand hatte das entworfen, also musste es etwas bedeuten. Die dritte Erinnerung hängt mit meinem Großvater zusammen, dessen Fabriken LITA hießen (S. 14), die Marke ging später in Mazda auf. Wenn mein Bruder und ich am Wochenende die Fabriken besuchten, sahen wir überall, wie wichtig dieses Markenzeichen war. Kein Briefkopf, keine Schachtel, keine Tür ohne Firmenlogo, und unbewusst war ich überzeugt, dass es Teil der Firma war, eigentlich das Herz des Ganzen. Diese drei sehr lebhaften Erinnerungen führten mir vor Augen, welche Wirkung Logos selbst auf Kinder haben und welches Interesse sie wecken können, gleichgültig, ob sie auf Typografie oder Bildern aufbauen.

Logos sind direkte Verbindungen zu Unternehmen, ihr Identifikationspotenzial hat allerdings weniger mit ihrer Ästhetik zu tun als vielmehr mit der Häufigkeit ihres Auftretens. Ein tolles Logo, das selten zu sehen ist, wird keine große Aufmerksamkeit erregen, im Gegensatz zu einem drittklassigen Logo, dem man ständig begegnet. Seit wir als Grafikdesigner arbeiten, verwenden wir Logos, annektieren und verändern sie entsprechend den Bedürfnissen des Labels French Touch und der

EINLEITUNG

left *LITA*, logo, 1965, France, designed by Lark Publicité

right *Super Discount*, Étienne de Crécy, record album, 1997, designed by H5

Welt der elektronischen Musik. Von Anfang an beschlossen Antoine, Alex, Étienne de Crécy und ich, das Image der Musiker als Massenprodukt zu betrachten, als etwas, das man im Supermarkt findet. Das spektakulärste Beispiel dafür ist das grellgelbe Cover der CD *Super Discount* (S. 15). Das Cover ist ein Logo, das Logo ist eine Marke, die Marke ist ein Künstler, und der Künstler ist ein Sound.

Die unbestreitbare Macht des Logos und der Marke war eine Offenbarung. Wir kamen uns wie Grafikdesigner vor, die im Einzelhandel tätig waren. Die zweite Offenbarung war, dass grafisches Design sich nicht auf den dekorativen Aspekt beschränken lässt, es muss ein Ergebnis der zugrunde liegenden Diskussionen und Erfahrungen sein. Seitdem spielen wir ständig mit den Codes multinationaler Unternehmen und Marken, und *Logorama* war der Höhepunkt dieses Spiels. Aber sind Logos unbedingt ein negatives Symbol für die Macht der Marken? Ich bin mir nicht sicher. Ein Firmenlogo an sich kann nichts Böses sein, es ist lediglich ein visuelles Element. Ob es jetzt für Lehman Brothers oder das RAF-Maschinengewehr steht – fragwürdig ist ja nicht das Erscheinungsbild des Logos als vielmehr das, wofür es steht, sprich die Philosophie hinter der Botschaft, die es vermittelt, oder hinter den Handlungen, die es repräsentiert. Für ein Unternehmen kann es von Nachteil sein, wenn ein Logo allzu häufig verwendet wird. In dem Moment, in dem eine Übersättigung eintritt, wenn die Menschen es tagtäglich sehen und ihm nicht mehr entkommen können, wird es zu visueller Umweltverschmutzung – man denke nur an Geschäftsviertel, in denen immer mehr überdimensionale Reklametafeln hängen, eine schriller als die andere (S. 17).

Als wir mit dem Film begannen, bestand die größte Herausforderung zunächst darin, eine Datenbank von Logos aufzubauen. Das war wie das Vorsprechen der Darsteller. Es bedeutete, jedes Logo auf seine mögliche Rolle in dem Film hin zu untersuchen, sei es Teil der Kulisse, Figur oder Requisite. Wir suchten ständig weiter nach Logos, immer vor dem Hintergrund, dass es uns nicht darum ging, einen großartigen Film zu machen, sondern darum, etwas zu produzieren, das die Welt um uns her reflektierte. Außerdem wollten wir unbedingt vermeiden, dass der Film eine elitäre Übung in visuellem Stil würde – was leicht hätte passieren können. Unsere Zielgruppe war das Publikum weltweit, schließlich behandelte der Film ein weltumspannendes Thema. Zu dem Zweck mussten wir uns von den üblichen Gepflogenheiten unseres Berufs als Grafiker verabschieden und in die Rolle des Regisseurs schlüpfen, der eine Vielzahl figürlicher und abstrakter Formen verbindet und zu Landschaften und Szenen aus dem Alltag zusammensetzt. Von dem Punkt an gab es für uns keine Logos mehr, sondern nur noch Schauspieler und Kulissen.

Diese Datenbank aufzubauen dauerte rund zwei Jahre. Zuerst besorgten wir alle Bücher über Logos, die wir auftreiben konnten, stellten aber fest, dass wir damit auf höchstens hundert ständig wiederkehrende Beispiele wie Mercedes, Coca-Cola oder Michelin kamen, vorwiegend als Sponsoren

von Sportveranstaltungen, und gut tausend sehr stilisierte Logos, die kein Mensch kannte. Bei der Internetrecherche stieß ich dann auf ein Jahrbuch amerikanischer Logos: *The Book of American Trade Marks*. Davon kaufte ich die letzten zwanzig Ausgaben, und dort fanden wir eine Fülle amerikanischer Marken, die sich viel besser für den Film eigneten. Einige stammten noch aus den 70er Jahren, also musste ich recherchieren, ob es sie überhaupt noch gab, und auch überprüfen, ob sie visuell nicht weiterentwickelt worden waren. Erst dann konnten wir entscheiden, welche wir tatsächlich verwenden wollten. Ursprünglich suchten wir vor allem nach international genutzten Marken, ausgehend von den Finanzmärkten, und wählten vor allem Firmen, die an der New York Stock Exchange und am NASDAQ notiert waren. Dann machte ich dasselbe für alle G8-Staaten. Ich glaube, letztlich nutzten wir sämtliche nur denkbaren Quellen – von Büchern zum Thema visuelle Identität, die wir in Bibliotheken fanden, bis hin zu den Wirtschaftsseiten von Tageszeitungen wie *Le Monde* und *The New York Times*.

Kategorien wie „hübsch" oder „pittoresk" interessierten uns nicht, der Film sollte mehr in Richtung Pop-Art gehen, allerdings mit einem subtilen Unterschied. Während in der Pop-Art die Konsumgesellschaft illustriert wird, man denke etwa an Warhols *Brillo Box* (S. 20), Ed Ruschas *Standard Station* (S. 21) oder Lichtensteins *Blam* (S. 23), beschäftigt sich *Logorama* mit der Bildkultur an sich, in der das Produkt weitgehend hinter der Marke verschwindet. Uns geht es nicht um das Produkt, sondern um die Marke und die Werte, für die sie steht. Wie zum Beispiel erklärt sich der Reiz von Hello Kitty (S. 26), einem Symbol, das uns in die Welt der frühen Kindheit zurückversetzt? Das Paradoxe an dieser berühmten Marke ist, dass sie im Gegensatz zu Babar, dem Elefanten, oder zu Naruto, dem Teenage-Ninja, keinen Hintergrund hat, es gibt keine Kindergeschichte, keinen Cartoon dazu. Mit Hello Kitty ist Sanrio wirklich ein unglaublicher Marketing-Coup gelungen.

Um zum Film und der Verwendung multinationaler Logos zurückzukehren: Wir wollten sie wie ein Regisseur dirigieren, wollten sie herumschieben, verbinden, verschwimmen lassen, vermischen und wie Plastilinmasse verkneten. Schließlich drängen sich uns diese Marken jeden Tag in jedem nur denkbaren Medium auf – war es jetzt nicht einmal an der Zeit, ihnen unseren Blick auf die Welt aufzuoktroyieren? Nur um zu zeigen, dass bei uns Meinungsfreiheit herrscht. Das war uns wichtiger als jeder künstlerische Aspekt. Allerdings versetzte genau diese Meinungsfreiheit Anwälte in englischsprachigen Ländern, die auf Markenrecht spezialisiert waren, in Angst und Schrecken. Aber sollte der erste Schritt eines Künstlers in unserer überregulierten Wert nicht genau darin bestehen, Risiken einzugehen, und zwar noch vor jedem Gedanken an ästhetische Aspekte?

Bis zum Ende der Produktionszeit hatten wir etwa 50.000 Logos gesehen. Eine der vielen notwendigen Entscheidungen war, ob wir die neue Version eines Logos übernehmen oder doch eher bei der alten bleiben sollten. Als wir für die Auf-

„Nachdem ich mehrere Jahre in der Welt der Logos gelebt hatte, war mir klar geworden, dass sich diese der Mode und den Kunstströmungen anpassen."

nahme des Soundtracks nach Los Angeles fuhren, prangte auf dem Weg vom Flughafen in die Stadt auf einer Gebäudefassade großformatig das neue Pepsi-Logo (S. 28). Aber den Teaser gab es zu der Zeit nur in den USA, in Europa war er noch nicht bekannt, und letztlich überzeugte uns die Form der alten Version, es bei ihr zu belassen. Dasselbe gilt für das Logo von Stop & Shop (S. 29), dem ein Re-Design verpasst worden und das zu einer Verbindung von Obstkorb und Blumenstrauß geworden war. Manche Logos sahen wir uns sehr genau an, ehe wir sie auswählten. Einige der eher strengen Logos unterzogen wir einer gewissen „Schönheitsoperation", etwa die von Walmart, Kraft Foods und Cheer, ergänzten sie um ein paar Blumen, ein bisschen Sonnenschein oder etwas Grünzeug. Im Lauf der Produktionszeit von *Logorama* wurde uns auch zunehmend bewusst, wie viele Logos wir dreidimensional darstellen mussten, was ja buchstäblich bedeutete, eine weitere Dimension zu entwickeln.

Im Film kommen auch einige „klassische" Logos vor, die sehr kleine, wenig bekannte Marken repräsentieren. Ein Beispiel ist etwa das Cruz-Logo, das ein amerikanisches Design-Kollektiv für einen Karosseriebauer entworfen hatte. Es war genau das richtige Fahrzeug für die Bullen in Form zweier Michelinmännchen. Eigentlich hatten wir gedacht, dass sie in einem eindeutig identifizierbaren Wagen sitzen würden, etwa im Ford Gran Torino wie in *Starsky and Hutch* oder in dem Mercury, den Sylvester Stallone in *Cobra* (dt. Titel *Die City Cobra*) fährt. Aber da kein führender Autohersteller das für uns passende Logo hatte, mussten wir auf eine eher unbekannte Marke zurückgreifen. Außerdem war es uns wichtig sicherzustellen, dass all unsere Logos authentisch waren, unsere Quellen mussten also hieb- und stichfest sein.

Schließlich machten wir die ersten Storyboards (S. 31), damit unsere Recherche auch an der Handlung ausgerichtet blieb. Dann legten wir fest, welche Logos diese Geschichte erzählen sollten. Da war sehr viel praktischer Sinn gefragt: Wir fingen mit nichts an und mussten eine Welt schaffen, die ausschließlich aus Logos bestand. Dafür ordneten wir sie verschiedenen Kategorien zu, etwa Figuren, Tieren, Kulissen, Gegenständen und Fahrzeugen. Jede Kategorie hatte Unterkategorien, die weiter unterteilt wurden. So erhielten wir schließlich eine Datenbank von Logos unterschiedlicher Machart, die uns alle notwendigen visuellen Elemente lieferte. Für große Logos veranstalteten wir ein „Special Casting": Uns interessierte ihre symbolische Wirkung, die grafische Form war eher zweitrangig. Solche Logos verwendeten wir im Film vor allem als Tafeln oder Schilder. Dann besetzten wir Logos nach ihrer Form, einfache geometrische Figuren zum Beispiel als Ziegelsteine, um urbane Räume und Weitwinkelaufnahmen von Landschaften zu gestalten. Ein Kreisbogen wurde zu einer Zickzacklinie, einem ganzen Kreis oder einer Kugel, die dann zu einem Planeten wurde. Aus diesen einfachen Formen ließ sich wunderbar ein Hintergrund bauen, der es den Zuschauern ermöglichte, sich auf die Action im Vordergrund zu konzentrieren.

LOGORAMA: DIE ANFÄNGE

Breezewood, Pennsylvania, USA, Edward Burtynsky, 2008

Die letzte Kategorie hieß „Bildwort", zum Beispiel die „Sonne" in Sun Microsystems oder der Name des Schokoriegels Milky Way. Die direkte Symbolik dieser Markennamen verwendeten wir allerdings eher zurückhaltend, sie erschienen nur kurz, damit der Film kein Aufguss von *The Child* wurde.

Nachdem ich mehrere Jahre in der Welt der Logos gelebt hatte, war mir klar geworden, dass sich diese der Mode und den Kunstströmungen anpassen. Seit in der zweiten Hälfte des 19. Jahrhunderts die ersten Logos entstanden sind, haben sie sich immer wieder freizügig der jeweils vorherrschenden Kunstrichtung angepasst. So sind zum Beispiel die tiefer gesetzten Initialen des Coca-Cola-Logos dem Jugendstil entlehnt (S. 34), und Renault beauftragte Victor Vasarely, einen der Gründungsväter der Op-Art, mit der Überarbeitung seines Logos (S. 34). Ähnlich entwarf der Designer und Bühnenbildner Cassandre das Logo für Yves Saint Laurent (S. 35), Raymond Lœwy war für das Logo des Keksfabrikanten LU verantwortlich (S. 35). Eine Bildmarke, die die allgemeine Öffentlichkeit ansprechen soll, ist im wahrsten Sinn des Wortes ein grafischer Spiegel der Gesellschaft. Das Logo wird geboren, es wächst heran, aber es darf nie altern. Es muss sich den ästhetischen Bedingungen der unterschiedlichen Jahrzehnte anpassen, in denen es seine Funktion erfüllen soll, ohne je obsolet zu werden.

Durch die Arbeit an *Logorama* lernte ich auch ein paar Leute kennen, deren Bekanntschaft ich sonst nie gemacht hätte. Ganz zu Anfang des Projekts trafen wir mit Dhani Harrison zusammen, der uns zu sich außerhalb von London einlud; in seinem Haus bekamen wir eine Ahnung davon, was es bedeuten muss, ein Beatles-Fan zu sein. David Fincher begegneten wir, als wir für die Aufnahme des englischen Voiceovers nach Los Angeles reisten. Andrew Kevin Walker kennen zu lernen war auch famos, er hatte das Drehbuch für *Se7en* verfasst, für uns schrieb er den Dialog. Außerdem begegneten wir Thomas Bangalter von Daft Punk, der für den Soundtrack verantwortlich war. Das war ausgesprochen interessant und half uns auch bei der Entscheidung, ob wir eine Reihe unterschiedlicher Musiker haben wollten oder doch einen völlig neuen Soundtrack von einem einzigen Musiker, jemanden in der Art von Michel Legrand. Wir entschieden uns dann für die erste Variante, also für das Beste, was die Unterhaltungsindustrie von Hollywood zu bieten hatte. Letztlich hat sich die ganze Arbeit und Mühe dann noch richtig gelohnt – wir bekamen den Academy Award als Bester Animierter Kurzfilm. Eine typische Hollywood-Story eben!

Ludovic Houplain ist der Gründer von H5, einem multidisziplinären Design-Studio, 1996 in Paris gegründet. Er ist einer der Regisseure des Oscarprämierten animierten Kurzfilms *Logorama* im Jahr 2009. Seine überaus kreative Arbeit für Musik- und Kulturinstitutionen sowie für Luxusgüter und in der Werbung zeigt sich an seiner Zusammenarbeit mit großen Namen wie Air, Dior, das Festival von Cannes, Audi und Citroën.

Les fondations de Logorama

La première fois que j'ai eu l'idée de faire un film entièrement composé de logos, c'était après avoir fait *The Child* pour l'artiste français Alex Gopher. Ce film, que j'ai réalisé en 1999 avec Antoine Bardou-Jacquet, recréait notre environnement urbain uniquement à l'aide de mots (p. 8). Les éléments de Manhattan y sont représentés par leurs désignations, comme « immeuble », « pâté de maisons », « pont », etc. La ville et ses habitants deviennent un vaste paysage typographique. De plus, grâce à l'utilisation de différentes polices et tailles de caractères, les lettres montrent immédiatement s'il s'agit d'une voiture récente ou ancienne, ou si elle a été fabriquée en Occident ou au Japon.

Peu après cela, notre société de production Midi-Minuit nous a donné l'opportunité de travailler avec Télépopmusik sur un autre film, pour un album intitulé *Da Hoola*. J'ai réfléchi à d'autres approches graphiques pour ce film, et j'étais en train de regarder la couverture du CD lorsque j'ai réalisé que, tout comme nous avions utilisé la typographie dans *The Child*, nous pouvions essayer de faire quelque chose de similaire avec des logos de marques. Je pensais que nous pourrions faire un court-métrage uniquement à partir de logos, puisque les logos représentent tout ce que nous voyons autour de nous – les gens, les fruits, les bâtiments, etc. Après cela, les logos sont devenus mes Lego. Sur la base de cette idée, j'ai proposé à Télépopmusik un projet où des logos américains affrontaient des logos russes dans une sorte de Jeux olympiques, mais l'idée n'est pas allée plus loin.

Néanmoins, la première graine avait été plantée, et elle a continué de pousser au cours des deux années suivantes. J'ai fini par demander à mon frère Cyril de travailler sur quelques scènes d'aéroport en utilisant des logos conçus dans les années 1920, mais cela n'a pas marché non plus, le résultat était trop pictural, et s'éloignait trop du pop art. Pour parler du monde d'aujourd'hui, il faut des logos modernes que tout le monde peut reconnaître facilement. En 2003, après le prix MTV Music Award de H5 pour le clip de Röyksopp, Dhani Harrison, le fils de George Harrison, demanda à H5 de faire un clip pour le morceau titre de son nouvel album, *Brainwashed*. Il voulait une animation avec un point de vue critique mais nostalgique sur notre culture de consommation, et après notre première conversation j'ai pensé que cela pourrait être adapté et basé sur les logos. Hervé de Crécy et moi-même avons travaillé sur le scénario, en veillant à ce qu'il soit en harmonie avec les paroles et la musique. Nous avons décidé de situer l'action dans une ville américaine générique, que nous avons représentée sous la forme d'un supermarché avec des rues parallèles comme les rayons d'un magasin, et les immeubles jouant le rôle des produits de marques connues rangés sur les étagères. Dans l'histoire, un ouragan dévaste la ville. Toutes les rues bien ordonnées sont saccagées et les enseignes des magasins se mélangent, ce qui crée des associations visuelles improbables et offre un mélange étrange et antinaturel de choses à acheter. Nous voulions créer un paysage apocalyptique, puis faire en sorte que

la végétation envahisse cette société ravagée. Mais le projet a été mis au rancart lorsque la maison de disques a refusé d'utiliser de vrais logos, pour des raisons juridiques. Mais nous avions posé les fondations de *Logorama*.

Il devint évident qu'aucune maison de disques ne voudrait faire cette vidéo, et sous forme de film le projet ne pouvait exister qu'en tant que prise de position artistique, et non simplement comme une commande. Nous avons monté une équipe avec Addict Films pour la coproduction, Mikros Image pour la postproduction et Autour de Minuit pour leur expérience des courts-métrages. Tout d'abord, à cause de l'ouragan Katrina, nous avons déplacé le décor de la Nouvelle-Orléans à Hollywood, avec tous ses clichés. C'était en partie pour rendre hommage à ce lieu, mais cela nous permettait aussi d'utiliser tous les codes du cinéma hollywoodien. L'idée n'était pas née d'un coup de génie, mais d'une multitude d'associations, d'observations et de rencontres, et nous ressentions un vrai besoin de la réaliser. Et puis François Alaux nous a rejoints pour faire face à la tâche titanesque de la réalisation du film.

Les logos m'ont toujours fasciné, et j'ai trois souvenirs d'enfance très vivaces qui expliquent sans doute cette curiosité. Le premier est lié à mon père. Il était pilote de course, et son environnement était surchargé de logos – voitures, combinaisons, côtés de la piste, il n'y avait pas un seul espace vierge. C'était dans les années 1970, et le monde de la course automobile était déjà saturé par les sponsors (p. 9). Le deuxième souvenir date de la même période, et concerne le logo sur un panneau d'affichage en bord de route pour la chaîne de supermarchés Carrefour. J'étais fasciné par cette forme, mais je n'arrivais pas à la comprendre. J'étais attiré par le dessin en trois couleurs, qui évoquait le drapeau français, mais j'étais assez déconcerté par la forme. La lettre « C » en blanc sur fond bleu et rouge ne signifiait pas grand-chose pour un petit garçon de sept ans. Sur le chemin de l'école, je me demandais ce que cela pouvait signifier. Ce n'était ni figuratif ni abstrait, mais si quelqu'un l'avait dessiné, cela devait bien vouloir dire quelque chose (p. 10). Le troisième souvenir est lié à mon grand-père, dont les usines s'appelaient LITA avant leur fusion avec Mazda. En visitant les usines le week-end avec mon frère, j'ai réalisé à quel point la marque commerciale était importante. Il n'y avait pas un en-tête de lettre, une boîte ou une porte qui ne portait pas le logo de la société, et inconsciemment j'étais convaincu que cela faisait partie intégrante de l'activité de l'entreprise, et même de son âme (p. 14). Ces trois souvenirs m'ont montré le pouvoir des logos, l'impact qu'ils peuvent avoir, même sur les enfants, et comment ils peuvent susciter l'intérêt, qu'ils soient faits de lettres ou d'images.

Les logos sont des connexions directes avec les institutions commerciales, mais ce n'est pas leur esthétique qui les rend identifiables, c'est leur degré de visibilité. Un bon logo qui est peu vu a très peu de chances d'attirer l'attention, contrairement à un logo médiocre que l'on peut voir partout dans le monde. Nous avons utilisé des logos dès le début

left *Brillo Box*, Andy Warhol, 1964, silkscreen on wood

right *Standard Station, Amarillo, Texas*, Ed Ruscha, 1963, oil on canvas

de nos carrières de graphistes, en les détournant et en les adaptant aux besoins de la maison de disques French Touch et du monde de la musique électronique. Dès le départ, Antoine, Alex, Étienne de Crécy et moi avons décidé de gérer l'image des artistes comme un produit de consommation de masse que l'on pourrait trouver dans un supermarché. L'exemple le plus spectaculaire est la couverture jaune criard de l'album *Super Discount* (p. 15). La couverture est un logo, le logo est une marque, la marque est un artiste et l'artiste est un son.

Cela a été une révélation, le pouvoir indéniable du logo et de la marque. Nous avions l'impression d'être de vrais graphistes travaillant dans le secteur de la distribution, et l'autre révélation était que le graphisme ne peut pas se limiter à l'aspect décoratif, il doit être le résultat des discussions et de l'expérience qui se trouvent derrière. Depuis lors, nous n'avons jamais arrêté de jouer avec les codes des entreprises et marques multinationales, et *Logorama* a été le point culminant de ce processus. Mais le logo est-il un mauvais symbole du pouvoir des marques ? Je n'en suis pas si sûr. Le logo d'une entreprise ne peut pas être quelque chose de mauvais en soi, car ce n'est qu'un élément visuel. Même si c'est le logo de Lehman Brothers ou de la mitraillette RAF, ce n'est pas l'apparence du logo qui est l'objet des critiques, c'est ce qu'il incarne, la philosophie derrière le message qu'il transmet ou les activités qu'il représente. Mais si un logo est trop utilisé, cela peut nuire à l'entreprise. Dès que le point de saturation est atteint, lorsque les gens le voient tous les jours et ne peuvent plus y échapper, il se transforme en pollution visuelle – prenez par exemple les quartiers commerciaux, où l'on trouve de plus en plus de panneaux géants, tous plus tape-à-l'œil les uns que les autres (p. 17).

Pour commencer le film, le plus difficile a été de mettre en place une base de données de logos, un peu comme auditionner des acteurs. Cela impliquait d'établir un profil pour chaque logo en fonction du rôle qu'il pourrait jouer dans le film, que ce soit en tant qu'élément du décor, personnage ou accessoire. Tout le long du film, nous avons continué de chercher et repérer des logos, toujours avec en tête l'idée qu'il ne s'agissait pas de faire un grand film, mais de produire quelque chose qui allait entrer en résonance avec le monde qui nous entourait. Nous voulions aussi éviter de tomber dans le piège qui consistait à réduire ce projet à un exercice élitiste de style visuel. Il devait s'adresser à un public universel, parce que c'était un projet universel. Pour ce faire, nous devions prendre du recul par rapport aux habitudes de notre métier de graphistes. Nous devions au contraire endosser un rôle de metteurs en scène, et mélanger une multitude de formes abstraites et figuratives pour créer des paysages et des scènes de la vie quotidienne. À partir de ce moment, il n'y avait plus de logos, seulement des acteurs et des décors.

Il nous a fallu deux ans pour bâtir cette base de données. Tout d'abord, nous nous sommes procuré autant de publications que possible sur le sujet des logos, mais nous avons réalisé que cela ne nous

donnait qu'une centaine d'exemples récurrents tels que Mercedes, Coca-Cola et Michelin, principalement issus du parrainage sportif, et un bon millier de logos très stylisés que personne n'avait jamais vus. Une recherche sur Internet m'a fait découvrir une compilation annuelle de logos américains : *The Book of American Trade Marks*. J'ai acheté les 20 éditions les plus récentes, et elles contenaient une foule de marques américaines qui correspondaient bien mieux au film. Certaines dataient des années 1970, alors j'ai dû vérifier qu'elles existaient toujours, et me renseigner sur leur éventuelle évolution visuelle pour que nous puissions choisir les versions que nous voulions utiliser dans le film. La recherche initiale était centrée sur les marques de renom international, en commençant par le marché financier et en privilégiant les sociétés figurant à la Bourse de New York et au NASDAQ. Puis j'ai fait la même chose pour tous les pays du G8. En fin de compte je pense que nous avons utilisé toutes les sources possibles – depuis des livres sur l'identité visuelle trouvés dans des bibliothèques jusqu'aux pages finance de quotidiens tels que *Le Monde* et *The New York Times*.

Nous ne voulions pas que notre conception du film soit gouvernée par des critères esthétiques trop classiques, il devait plutôt tendre vers le pop art, mais avec une différence subtile. Là où le pop art illustre la société de consommation avec des images telles que *Brillo Box* de Warhol (p. 20), *Standard Station* d'Ed Ruscha (p. 21) ou *Blam* de Lichtenstein (p. 23), *Logorama* traite de la culture de l'image elle-même, dans laquelle le produit est éclipsé par la marque. Nous ne nous intéressons pas au produit, ce qui nous intrigue, c'est la marque et les valeurs qu'elle défend. Comment expliquer l'attrait de Hello Kitty (p. 26), un symbole qui nous renvoie directement au monde de la petite enfance ? Le paradoxe de cette marque célèbre est que, contrairement à Babar l'éléphant ou Naruto le ninja adolescent, elle n'a rien sur quoi reposer. Il n'y a pas d'histoire pour les enfants ni de dessin animé derrière le personnage. C'est un remarquable chef-d'œuvre de marketing de la part de Sanrio.

Pour revenir au film et à l'utilisation de logos multinationaux, nous voulions les mettre en scène : les bousculer, les combiner, les amalgamer, les mélanger et les modeler comme de l'argile. Puisque ces marques s'imposent à nous chaque jour et par tous les moyens de communication possibles, nous avons décidé que c'était à *notre* tour de *leur* imposer notre vision du monde, rien que pour prouver que nous étions libres de nous exprimer, ce qui était encore plus important que n'importe quel critère artistique. Cette liberté d'expression donnait une peur bleue aux avocats anglophones spécialisés dans le droit des marques commerciales. Mais, dans ce monde où tout est matière à légiférer, un artiste ne se doit-il pas de prendre des risques avant même de penser aux critères esthétiques ?

Je crois qu'à la fin de la phase de production, nous avions probablement vu 50 000 logos. L'une des nombreuses décisions que nous avons dû prendre était : faut-il utiliser la nouvelle forme d'un

INTRODUCTION

« Après plusieurs années d'immersion dans le monde des logos, j'ai fini par réaliser qu'ils suivent des modes et des tendances artistiques. »

logo, ou garder l'ancienne ? Lorsque nous sommes allés à Los Angeles pour enregistrer la bande sonore, sur le trajet entre l'aéroport et le centre-ville le nouveau logo de Pepsi (p. 28) s'étalait sur toute la façade d'un immeuble. Mais cette version n'existait qu'aux États-Unis, elle n'était pas encore arrivée en Europe, et finalement c'est la forme de l'ancienne version qui nous a convaincus. La même chose est arrivée pour le logo de Stop & Shop (p. 29), qui avait été complètement relooké et s'était transformé en une sorte de croisement entre un panier de fruits et un bouquet de fleurs. Certains logos ont été examinés de près avant d'être finalement abandonnés. Nous avons aussi pratiqué un peu de « chirurgie esthétique » sur certains des logos les plus austères, par exemple Walmart, Kraft Foods et Cheer, en leur ajoutant de petites touches de fleurs, de soleil ou de verdure. Tout au long de la production de *Logorama*, nous nous sommes aussi rendu compte du nombre de logos qu'il fallait mettre en 3D, ce qui signifiait de leur ajouter une dimension supplémentaire pour leur donner du volume.

Le film comprend aussi certains logos « vintage » qui représentent de toutes petites marques difficiles à identifier. Par exemple, le logo Cruz, créé par un collectif de design américain pour un carrossier. C'était le véhicule idéal pour deux policiers en forme de bonhomme Michelin. Nous avions imaginé qu'ils auraient une voiture reconnaissable, comme la Ford Gran Torino de *Starsky et Hutch* ou la Mercury que Sylvester Stallone conduisait dans *Cobra*, mais comme aucune grande marque n'avait le genre de logo qu'il nous fallait, nous avons dû faire appel à une marque peu connue. Il fallait aussi veiller à ce que tous nos logos soient authentiques, et nous devions être absolument sûrs de nos sources.

Après tout cela, nous avons commencé à faire des story-boards (p. 31) pour le film afin que nos recherches restent axées sur l'action. Puis nous avons commencé à chercher des logos pour raconter l'histoire. Cela impliquait d'adopter une attitude très pragmatique : nous partions de rien, et devions créer un monde exclusivement composé de logos. Tous les logos étaient classés sous différentes catégories, par exemple personnages, animaux, décors, objets, véhicules, et chaque catégorie avait des sous-catégories, etc. Cela a généré une base de données de logos de différents styles, qui ensemble nous ont donné les éléments visuels dont nous avions besoin. Il y a aussi eu des « auditions spéciales » pour les logos particulièrement importants. Nous étions intéressés par leur impact symbolique, leur forme graphique était secondaire, et la plupart de ces logos sont devenus des enseignes ou des panneaux dans le film. Puis nous avons distribué les logos en fonction de leur forme. Il s'agissait des formes géométriques de base, que nous avons utilisées comme des briques pour construire les espaces urbains et les plans de paysages en grand-angle. Un arc de cercle devenait un zigzag, un cercle complet ou une sphère qui se transformait ensuite en planète. Ces formes simples étaient idéales pour créer une toile de

Blam, Roy Lichtenstein, 1962, oil on canvas, Yale University Art Gallery, USA

fond qui permettait au public de se concentrer sur l'action qui se déroulait au premier plan. La dernière catégorie était les « mots-images », comme le « soleil » de Sun Microsystems ou le nom d'une barre Milky Way (Voie lactée). Le symbolisme direct de ces noms de marque a cependant été utilisé avec modération, uniquement pour de brèves apparitions, pour éviter que le film ne se transforme en un dérivé de *The Child*.

Après plusieurs années d'immersion dans le monde des logos, j'ai fini par réaliser qu'ils suivent des modes et des tendances artistiques. Depuis que les premiers logos sont apparus dans la seconde moitié du XIXe siècle, ils ont pris l'habitude d'emprunter aux mouvements artistiques, par exemple les arabesques des majuscules du logo de Coca-Cola s'inspirent de l'Art nouveau (p. 34), tandis que Renault (p. 34) a demandé à Victor Vasarely, l'un des pères fondateurs de l'art optique, de rajeunir son logo. De la même façon, l'affichiste Cassandre a dessiné le logo Yves Saint-Laurent (p. 35), tandis que Raymond Lœwy est responsable du logo des biscuits LU (p. 35). Un logo qui s'adresse au public général est un vrai miroir graphique de la société. Il naît et grandit, mais n'a pas le droit de vieillir. Il doit s'adapter à l'esthétique des décennies qu'il traverse afin de ne jamais devenir obsolète.

La réalisation du film a aussi donné lieu à quelques rencontres inattendues. Lorsque nous avons rencontré Dhani Harrison au début du projet, il nous a invités chez lui dans la banlieue de Londres, ce qui nous a donné une idée de ce que les fans des Beatles ont pu ressentir. Nous avons beaucoup apprécié de rencontrer David Fincher lorsque nous sommes allés enregistrer les voix en anglais à Los Angeles. La rencontre avec Andrew Kevin Walker a aussi été un grand moment, car c'est lui qui avait écrit le scénario de *Se7en*, et il nous a écrit le dialogue de *Logorama*. Et puis nous avons rencontré Thomas Bangalter de Daft Punk pour travailler sur la bande sonore, ce qui a vraiment été très intéressant, et nous a aidés à décider entre faire figurer plusieurs artistes différents ou opter pour une bande originale composée par un seul artiste, dans le style de quelqu'un comme Michel Legrand. Nous avons choisi la première option, ce qui nous a permis de tirer parti du meilleur de ce que l'industrie hollywoodienne du divertissement avait à offrir. L'Oscar que nous avons reçu pour le meilleur court-métrage d'animation n'a fait qu'ajouter à la satisfaction que nous ont apportée tout cet apprentissage et tous ces efforts. Une véritable expérience hollywoodienne.

Ludovic Houplain est le fondateur d'H5, atelier de design multidisciplinaire monté à Paris en 1996, et le co-réalisateur du court-métrage d'animation *Logorama* (2009) qui a remporté un Oscar. Ses créations inventives dans le domaine de la musique, des institutions culturelles, de l'industrie du luxe comme de la publicité sont associées à de grands noms comme Air, Dior, le Festival de Cannes, Audi, Citroën entre autres.

A Branded World

We are no longer a society of mass consumption such as existed during the post-war boom years of the 1930s. A new model of consumer culture is in full swing: a society of hyper-consumption, the late-modern consumer version of our hyper-modern world.

The inexorable rise of brands and logos is the most obvious indicator of this phenomenon. Certainly throughout the 20th century many people sounded the alarm and frequently objected to the encroachment of advertising into public life, but the past few decades have seen logos explode into every aspect of our daily lives: they have become omnipresent, working their way into all the foundations and cracks of daily life, into every moment and everywhere we live. Brand names bombard us in the streets, in stations and stadiums, in malls and airports around the world. Logos gather in thickets at the entry points to our cities, while adverts are streamed on the Internet 24/7, 365 days a year. Beyond billboards and manufactured goods, logos now inhabit museums, contemporary art, novels, films and TV series by way of product placement.

Gone are the days of the discreet designer label – logos noisily announce their presence on T-shirts, baseball caps, glasses, footwear, bags, pens, watches, toothbrushes, even skin: brand names tattooed on bodies have turned human beings into walking ads. Born in the late 19th century with the advent of mass marketing and production, modern branding is spiralling out of control; logos overload our world through sponsorship deals, spin-offs and tie-ins, relationship marketing, mobile and online advertising. Some sources estimate that we are exposed to around 1,200 logos every day. Wherever we are and whatever we're doing, it is hard to escape the barrage of brands.

The age of hyper-consumption is instantly characterised by the unbridled commodification of our time and space, the ever-expanding universe of brands and logos. But there's more, because this quantitative explosion is accompanied by a qualitative shift. Amid the proliferation of products, publicity and logos, we are experiencing a new type of marketing with new aspirations. Brands are redefining their relationship with consumers in response to changing consumer attitudes. And this turbo-charged consumerism is being restructured by logos. In this it is not just brands that are multiplying exponentially, but a *brand culture*, which has established its grip on both commerce and our daily lives. The era of product worship decried by Marx has given way to the era of branding and the worship of logos.

A new brand culture

Branding originally consisted of images and slogans designed to raise product awareness. But its scope has changed. In our hyper-consumerist society, the product is now less important than the brand, and the image and values it projects. Brands have to work harder nowadays: it is no longer simply a case of sparking a memory or reaction, but

A BRANDED WORLD

Logorama, scene from the film, directed by H5 (Hervé de Crécy, François Alaux and Ludovic Houplain)

of telling a story, developing a concept, creating a core identity or brand personality that is instantly recognisable through product design, logo, packaging, store design, sponsorship and advertising. Today's big brands are like mini universes that sell a whole lifestyle. Their goal is not just to be recognised, but to engender love by establishing themselves as "lovemarks". To do this, brands go well beyond just the promotion of their products: starting from a mission statement, they create a myth, and build an image that transmits a range of social, aesthetic and ethical messages. Nike does not position itself as a manufacturer of running shoes but as a brand that aims to "make the world a better place through sports and fitness" (Phil Knight). Logos have become more than mere visual representations of a brand or corporation: loaded with cultural references, their design must express the values, aesthetic and spirit of the brand.

But the transformations that are taking place are also linked to the new relationships brands are forging with consumers. Although the anti-corporation movement has ignited fierce debate and led to a shift in attitude in some quarters, brands continue to offer an enormous attraction to the majority of consumers, and in a broader sense are playing a new role in buying habits. Social media networks are abuzz with brand junkies who, not content simply to buy a brand, will publicly announce their loyalty and invite their friends to join their "tribe". Parents will even name their children after brands. Twice as many visitors to New York go for the shopping than for the museums and galleries. The flagship Louis Vuitton store on the Champs Elysées in Paris (p. 36) is as popular with tourists as the Eiffel Tower. And the Congolese *sapeurs*, just like living embodiments of advertising, will bankrupt themselves to show off their designer gear.

It wasn't so long ago that fashion designers dictated our desires. Nowadays it's the brands themselves that set the trends. Our jeans are Diesels, our phones and mp3 players are iPhones and iPods, and our glasses are by Dior, Chanel or Armani. As hyper-consumers, when we buy branded goods we are actually buying into an image, a dream, a myth. Brands are no longer just labels: they start conversations, spark debates and create controversy, as with porno chic or Benetton ads (p. 43). Love them or hate them, they are the new obsessions of our hyper-modern age.

The allure of logos is no longer limited to social elites or those living in the West: it permeates all countries, cultures and demographics. The burgeoning black market for designer fakes bears witness to our collective addiction to luxury brands. Young people can name more fashion labels than they can name saints, poets or philosophers, and the average consumer knows some 5,000 brands. The cult of the brand is ravaging China, India and other emerging economies, and nowadays even the most disadvantaged members of society recognise and dream of buying luxury brands. Designer labels are no longer the sole preserve of the privileged elite. They are for everyone.

ESSAY

Hello Kitty, character, 1974, Sanrio Co., Ltd., Japan, designed by Yuko Shimizu

The proliferation of logos in our streets, stores and media has led to the democratisation of desire and brands across the world: it has become one of the cornerstones of our globalised culture.

Logomania and consumer individualism

While brands are profoundly restructuring their relationship with consumers, this is not to say that consumers have become more conformist and obsessed with appearances. In fact, the influence of the media, poorer quality products and the growing trend to over-fill our homes with "stuff" have led to an increase in consumer individualism, or a "me first" attitude manifested by unpredictable buying habits, a more personalised use of space, time and objects, and the disintegration of traditional class-based social structures. Paradoxically, in an era defined by the cult of the brand, consumer trends are increasingly characterised by this spirit of liberalism and hyper-individualism. The economically disadvantaged now aspire to luxury brands, while the affluent are happy to team low-cost items with designer labels. More and more, consumers are breaking free from conventional social stereotypes, while becoming increasingly impulsive and unpredictable.

At the same time, brands are exerting a greater influence on consumer choice, which is increasingly based on emotional or experiential responses. The class-driven imperative to buy products for the sake of "keeping up with the Joneses" is no longer central to the dynamics of consumption: rather than bowing to external social pressures, consumers are behaving with greater autonomy, and are buying what they want, when they want. Today's consumers are less interested in asserting their social status, and more focused on affirming their individuality; their purchasing decisions are far more likely to be made for private reasons that fulfil the need for personal gratification and sensory pleasure.

The age of hyper-merchandising and hyper-individualism is consequently characterised by what has been termed "aestheticised consumption". Buying a brand now involves going on a qualitative "journey": it is a way for consumers to inject excitement into their daily routine, live in the moment and fire their imaginations. But it is also a way of feeling good about themselves, of comparing themselves favourably to others and of standing out from the crowd, without necessarily acting out of a need to boost their self-esteem in the sense described by the economist and sociologist Thorstein Veblen. Although our addiction to "bling" testifies to the persistence of conspicuous consumption and our love of flashy status symbols, it is now underpinned by the narcissistic pleasure of seeing ourselves as special and different, and of developing a positive self-image, a mindset exploited by the famous L'Oréal catchphrase "Because I'm worth it" (p. 42).

Other phenomena, such as teenagers' obsession with brands and group conformism, appear to run counter to the trend towards individualism,

> "Logos have become more than mere visual representations of a brand or corporation: loaded with cultural references, their design must express the values, aesthetic and spirit of the brand."

authenticity and personal independence. In this case, logos help to reassure insecure teens by creating a "tribal" identity that appeals to their need to belong and to be accepted by their peers. But by buying into a logo they are also distinguishing themselves from their parents, defining themselves by their tastes and preferences, and exercising their right to join a group that, unlike their family unit or social class, they have actively chosen. In this context, the logo conveys both a "tribal" and a personal identity that is at once conformist and yet, by contrast, loaded with a sense of individuality.

This new-found individualism also informs a new way in which brands have become talked about. The Internet has become the perfect medium for hoaxers, hackers and satirists to poke fun at corporations, subverting ads and creating content that instantly goes viral across discussion forums, chat rooms, social networking sites and the blogosphere. This is proof that brands can just as easily be knocked down as built up, and treated with irreverence as well as with respect.

The film *Logorama* displays a similar sense of irony and detachment by aestheticising the already aestheticised world of the logo. In the tradition of Pop Art, everything is treated as art, down to the banal symbols of our everyday consumer society. For the first time on film, the world of the logo, normally associated with aggressive marketing techniques, is transformed into a work of art that induces a sense of aesthetic pleasure.

Pop Art dignified media images and mass-produced goods by making art out of materials considered to be worthless and ordinary. Warhol's portraits of Campbell's soup cans (p. 44) and popular cultural icons such as Marilyn Monroe (p. 45) are considered high art in their own right and imbued with a glittering aura. Conversely, *Logorama* treats logos with a playful sense of irony rather than enshrouding them with a rarefied aura that elevates them to cult status. Logos are introduced into the art of film, but it is an understated art that does not intimidate by its monumentality or take itself too seriously, and that does not worship its subject matter.

In *Logorama* everything is a logo, and yet nothing truly is. What exactly is a commercial logo? It is nothing more than a visual sign created to stimulate brand recognition, to inform and reassure consumers, and to encourage them to buy one product rather than another. The central importance of these functions within a market economy has led to the "fetishisation" of logos, and consequently protected by the law against all forms of pirating, they appear triumphantly on everything from buildings and letterheads to ad hoardings, websites, clothes and packaging. It is precisely this "logo-worship" that *Logorama* transgresses. Brands are treated ironically, and as aesthetic rather than cult objects, within a narrative that has intrinsic value outside of any commercial scope. The logos in *Logorama* no longer express the values or philosophy of a brand; they exist autonomously as

ESSAY

below *Pepsi*, logos before and after, PepsiCo, USA

opposite page *Stop & Shop*, logos before and after, The Stop & Shop Supermarket Co., USA

aesthetic objects that have been stripped of their function and can be freely appropriated.

The power of the brand: what next?

The growing power of brands has led many to criticise what has become known as "cultural fascism", or the Orwellian control of our mental and cultural space. Brands have become more than a name and logo designed to boost sales by generating publicity: they are complex communication systems that seek to govern every aspect of our daily lives from cradle to grave, to manipulate the way we see, think and behave by imposing their own vision of the world. In extreme cases, they become an end in themselves, a reason for living. While they may claim to celebrate openness and tolerance, in reality brands are engulfing our minds, emotions and social structures. Some have likened our hyper-modern economy to a totalitarian regime that wields absolute power.

While the rising power of brands is undeniable, it would be wrong to liken them to omnipotent Leviathans. Consumers have never been so mistrustful, impulsive and fickle; and despite their huge marketing budgets, brands can still fall out of favour with the buying public. Thanks to increased choice, budget options and the Internet, consumers also have more power to make informed decisions by shopping around. The spectre of the passive, helpless consumer who is brainwashed and manipulated by brands is at odds with the phenomena of price sensitivity, fading brand loyalty and the success of the low-cost sector. Under the yoke of "brand fascism", the power of *homo consumericus* is actually increasing, with consumers enjoying greater autonomy in their buying decisions, even as the power of logos continues to strengthen. The god-like omnipotence of marketing is a myth, because today's consumer infatuation with logos is also reflexive and fickle. The more brands saturate our lives, the more individuals keep their distance from them. Rather than worship at their altars, consumers worship brands from afar.

Critics of marketing point to the vaulting ambition of brands, which aim to infiltrate the minds and imaginations of the population like a totalitarian dictatorship. But let's be frank: likening the world of brands to "fascism" is unacceptable. Totalitarian ideology aims to construct a completely homogeneous, classless society in which tensions and divisions are replaced by shared interests, knowledge, norms, beliefs and opinions. Totalitarianism is an all-encompassing political project that hinges on unity, unanimity and uniformity. By contrast, the world of brands is pluralist, and relies on the competition that springs from a diversity of interests, norms, aesthetics and tastes. Brands do not seek to dictate our religious or political beliefs; they only seek to win market share from their competitors. And the values they celebrate are collective (human rights, respect for the environment, tolerance, pluralism), and borrowed from society rather than imposed on it. In this sense, the scope of brands is emphatically not totalitarian: it is essentially *limited*,

however much they may intrude on our daily lives or have the power to transform our ways of living.

Are brands in decline?

Do brands have a future? Amid the turbulence of the 1990s recession and the 2008 global economic crash, many observers diagnosed that brands were also in deep crisis. As Naomi Klein's *No Logo* became an international bestseller, brands were held responsible for the whole gamut of society's ills, from pollution and cancer to obesity and child exploitation. Armies of consumers declared that they had fallen out of love with brands, that brands did not improve their daily lives and no longer made them want to buy products. They refused to pay the inflated prices associated with brands, which resulted in brands losing their power and the rise of low-cost alternatives. Society has become mistrustful and disaffected with brands and consumerism: most consumers feel that brands no longer influence their buying decisions because they do not offer any real benefits. Consumers are adopting more sustainable buying habits, the consensus being that over-consumption does not make us happy.

But is this really a systemic crisis? If we are really growing disenchanted with brands, how do we explain the continued growth of the global luxury goods market, or the popularity of brand fan clubs? Sales of prestigious German car marques have never been so high. The demand for brands is not in decline: it is spreading across all walks of society.

And while some brands have been hit, others are attracting followers in increasing numbers: there is no general move away from investing in brands. The ebbing of brand loyalty is not synonymous with consumer indifference.

Modern consumers may well be savvy to marketing techniques, but it would be naïve to suggest that we are freely rejecting hyper-consumption for a simpler, more sustainable way of life. In our dystopian society, consumerism and brands continue to perform an essential function, fulfilling our need for pleasure and reward: consumerism has become a type of therapy, a form of escapism from our problems and fears. Just two months after the Fukushima disaster, sales of major French luxury brands in Japan had shot back up to their previous levels. If a catastrophe of this magnitude is unable to stem our rampant consumption of luxury brands, it is hard to imagine what else might do so in the future.

There is another reason to believe that brands are not an endangered species. Our addiction to them is inextricably linked to the disintegration of traditional social structures and to the consequent anxieties that characterise the age of hyper-consumption. With consumers feeling increasingly lost and confused in the battlefield of choice and imagery, it is brands that are charging to the rescue. The breakdown of class barriers and the trend towards individualism has led to a consumer confidence crash on which brands have been able to capitalise. Organic brands, for example, have made

huge gains in the light of the horror stories about food that are reported in the news. As conventions of taste and class are shattered, and as fashion becomes increasingly heterogeneous and accessible to all, brands act as a security blanket for consumers who no longer feel a sense of collective belonging. Our mistrust of brands, and more generally of institutional authorities, is undoubtedly part and parcel of the hyper-modern age, but in terms of consumerism it remains limited: in this climate of widespread uncertainty, we haven't heard the last from brands.

There is one final reason why brands continue to seduce us: they reflect the growing emphasis our culture places on quality of life. In our hyper-consumer society, physical comfort is in itself no longer enough. The focus on quantifiable elements such as functionality and convenience has shifted to something less tangible: the desire for greater emotional well-being, articulated through the quest to improve our environment from the inside out. Quality of life is the new frontier of today's pleasure-seeking, image-conscious, health-obsessed society. Our attraction to expensive brands is less a result of targeted marketing strategies, and more a reflection of the prevailing individualist aspiration to material happiness and better lifestyles. Could our hedonistic culture really be on the brink of collapse when we remain addicted to one of its most powerful symbols, the popular brand?

Quite the contrary. Consumerism is alive and well and brands continue to shape our world.

Despite growing environmental awareness and the downsized spending habits of "alternative" eco-consumers, the systematic commodification of our daily lives carries on apace. Brands reign supreme over a planet dominated by free-market economies.

At the end of *Logorama*, even a natural cataclysm cannot pulverise the power of the logo: as Hollywood is swallowed up by an earthquake, logos still twinkle from the last remaining pockets of land. And when the Earth is finally destroyed, they continue their unstoppable expansion into space: the final frontier. The message is clear. If there is no more planet Earth, there are thousands of other worlds on which logos could settle and learn how to exploit anew. Our planet may be under threat of extinction, but the brand, that quintessential symbol of our hyper-modern age, will triumph out of disaster.

The philosopher and sociologist **Gilles Lipovetsky** studies the societal and cultural changes driven by the communication and consumer society. He is the author of a dozen books about today's individualist, consumerist world which have been translated in 20 countries. He holds honorary doctorates from the University of Sherbrooke, Canada, and from the New Bulgarian University.

A BRANDED WORLD

left *Michelin*, logo with character "Monsieur Bibendum", 1889, France, designed by O'Galop, concept by Edouard Michelin

right *Logorama*, storyboard for the film

"In Logorama everything is a logo, and yet nothing truly is. What exactly is a commercial logo? It is nothing more than a visual sign created to stimulate brand recognition, to inform and reassure consumers, and to encourage them to buy one product rather than another."

ESSAY

Die Welt als Marke und als Logo

Wir sind nicht länger die Gesellschaft der Massenkonsumenten aus der Zeit des Wirtschaftswunders. Eine neue Form von Konsumkultur entwickelt sich: eine Gesellschaft des Hyperkonsums – in einer unserer Spätmoderne oder Hypermoderne entsprechenden Konsumrauschvariante.

Die Inflation der Marken und Logos führt uns das unmittelbar vor Augen. Sicher, zahlreiche Stimmen haben im Laufe des 20. Jahrhunderts auf die Überflutung des öffentlichen Raums mit Werbung hingewiesen und diese oft auch verurteilt. Doch alles weist darauf hin, dass wir längst in eine neue Phase eingetreten sind, so explosionsartig hat sich das Phänomen Werbung während der letzten Jahrzehnte ausgebreitet. Logos sind omnipräsent, sie suchen alle Flächen heim, dringen in sämtliche Ritzen des Alltags, tauchen ständig auf, an jedem Ort unseres Lebens – Markennamen auf allen großen Straßen der Metropolen, in den Bahnhöfen und Stadien, in den Hallen und Shops aller Flughäfen der Welt. Einfallstraßen wirken wie Pfade durch einen Logo-Dschungel. Auf Internetseiten erscheinen Marken an jedem Tag des Jahres rund um die Uhr. Logos sind nicht mehr nur auf Stadtwänden und den fertigen Produkten präsent: Sie machen sich in Museen breit, in der zeitgenössischen Kunst, in Romanen und über das Productplacement auch in Filmen und TV-Serien.

Die Zeit der diskreten Markenzeichen der Haute Couture ist längst vergangen: Logos bieten sich ostentativ auf T-Shirts dar, auf Mützen, Brillen, Schuhen, Taschen, Stiften, Armbanduhren, Zahnbürsten. Man sieht sogar mit kommerziellen Logos tätowierte Körper. Das in den letzten beiden Jahrzehnten des 19. Jahrhunderts geborene Universum der modernen Marke mit seinen Verpackungen und der breitenwirksamen Werbung ist mittlerweile in einer hypertrophen Spirale gefangen. Durch Sponsoring, Merchandising, Beziehungsmarketing, Onlinewerbung und gesponserte Links entwickelt sich eine mit Logos übersättigte Welt: Schätzungen zufolge sind wir jeden Tag rund 1.200 Logos ausgesetzt. Wo auch immer man sich aufhält, was auch immer man gerade tut, es wird immer schwieriger, um nicht zu sagen unmöglich, der allgegenwärtigen Wucht der Markensymbole zu entkommen.

Das Zeitalter des Hyperkonsums macht sich auf Anhieb durch die grenzenlose Einflussnahme auf unseren Lebensrhythmus und unsere Erfahrungswelt bemerkbar. Doch da ist noch mehr, denn parallel zu dieser quantitativen Explosion ist eine tatsächlich qualitative Veränderung feststellbar. Gerade heute entwickeln sich ein neues Branding (Markenfixierung), neue Ambitionen der Marken und zugleich ein neues Verhältnis der Konsumenten zu ihnen. Neben einem Überangebot an Produkten, einer Überfülle an Werbung und Logos, kommen ein neuer Typus des Marketings und ein anderer Konsumgeist auf, die einen von der Welt der Logos umstrukturierten Turbo-Konsumrausch herausbilden. In dieser Hinsicht breiten sich nicht nur die Marken unendlich aus, eine regelrechte Markenkultur hat sich des kommerziellen Universums wie auch des Alltagslebens bemächtigt. Die Ära

DIE WELT ALS MARKE UND ALS LOGO

Logorama, scene from the film, directed by H5 (Hervé de Crécy, François Alaux and Ludovic Houplain)

des von Marx angeprangerten Warenfetischismus ist zu einer Ära des Brandings geworden, Logofetischismus inbegriffen.

Eine neue Markenkultur

Ursprünglich ging es beim Branding darum, ein Produkte bekannt zu machen. Darüber sind wir schon lange hinaus. In der Welt des Hyperkonsums ist nicht mehr so sehr das Produkt als vielmehr die Marke von Bedeutung, ihre Vorstellungswelt, ihre Werte, ihr Weltbild. Es wird eine Geschichte erzählt, ein Konzept entwickelt, eine Markenidentität oder -figur geschaffen, erkennbar über Design, Logo, Verpackung, Architektur der Geschäfte, Sponsoring und Werbung. Heutzutage präsentiert sich jede wichtige Marke als Universum mit eigener Philosophie, besonderem Geist, Look, eigener Ästhetik. Es geht nicht mehr nur darum, bekannt, sondern geliebt zu werden, sich als *lovemark* zu etablieren. Eine Marke vermittelt eine Mission, schafft Legenden, prägt gesellschaftliche Werte. Nike begreift sich nicht als Sportschuhfabrikant, sondern als Marke, die danach strebt, „das Leben durch Sport und Fitness schöner zu machen" (Phil Knight).

Auch das Verhältnis des Konsumenten zur Marke verändert sich. Zwar existiert heute eine ganze Palette skeptischen Verhaltens und kritischer Diskussion gegenüber Marken, doch das verdeckt nicht deren ansteigende Anziehungskraft auf die meisten und in einem weiteren Sinne deren neue Rolle im Kaufverhalten. Soziale Netzwerke zählen mittlerweile die Fans einer Marke: Man gibt sich nicht mehr damit zufrieden, etwas zu kaufen, man spricht darüber, erklärt sich öffentlich verbunden und lädt seine Freunde ein, Mitglied des gleichen Stammes zu werden. Eltern schrecken nicht davor zurück, ihre Kinder nach Markennamen zu benennen. Nach New York kommen doppelt so viele Shopping- wie Kulturtouristen. Der Flagshipstore von Vuitton an den Champs-Elysées in Paris ist, genau wie der Eiffelturm, Touristenziel geworden (Sp. 36). Und die kongolesischen *Sapeurs*, regelrechte wandelnde Werbesäulen, treiben sich in den Ruin, um stolz ihre Markenklamotten präsentieren zu können.

Es ist noch nicht lange her, da konzentrierten sich alle Sehnsüchte auf den „letzten Schrei" einzelner Modekollektionen: Inzwischen ist und macht die Marke Mode – das Publikum träumt weniger von Mode als von Marken. Es wird nicht einfach eine Jeans gekauft, sondern eine Diesel. Man kauft kein Telefon und keinen Walkman, sondern ein iPhone oder einen iPod. Der Hyperkonsument kauft mit der Marke vor allem die mit ihr verbundene Vorstellungswelt, den Traum, den Mythos. Die Marken sind nicht mehr schlichte Etiketten eines Produkts, sie sind Gesprächsgegenstand und Diskussionsstoff, Skandalobjekt oder Stein des Anstoßes, wie z.B. Porno Chic oder Benetton-Kampagnen (S. 43), Objekt von Liebe oder von Abneigung: Es sind die neuen Fetische des hypermodernen Zeitalters.

Die Anziehungskraft des Logos beschränkt sich nicht mehr auf die gesellschaftlichen Eliten des Westens. Die explosive Vermehrung von Fälschungen zeugt vom Streben der Massen nach

ESSAY

below *Coca-Cola*, logo, 1887, USA, designed by Frank Mason Robinson

Renault, logo, 1972, France, designed by Victor Vasarely

opposite page *Yves Saint Laurent*, logo, 1963, France, designed by Cassandre

LU Biscuits, logo, 1957, France, designed by Raymond Lœwy

Luxusmarken. Junge Menschen sind eher in der Lage Modemarken zu benennen als die Namen von Heiligen, Dichtern oder Gelehrten, ein Konsument kennt im Durchschnitt rund 5.000 Markenbezeichnungen. Der Markenkult wütet in China, in Indien, in allen aufstrebenden Ländern: Selbst die Unterprivilegiertesten kennen heute die renommiertesten Marken und träumen davon, sie kaufen zu können. Das einfache Volk hat keine Hemmungen mehr vor Mode- und Luxusmarken: Marken und Logos sind nicht länger nur für „die da oben", sie sind für alle da. Straßen, Geschäfte, Medien – alles ist von Logos überflutet, auf dem gesamten Globus werden die Sehnsüchte nach Marken demokratisiert: Sie stellen einen Hauptbestandteil der Alltagskultur unseres Planeten dar.

Logomanie und Verbraucherindividualismus
Wenn wir sagen, dass die Marken das Verhältnis zum Konsum gründlich umgestalten, so bedeutet dies keineswegs die Entstehung eines konformistischen Konsumenten. Tatsächlich hat die Gesellschaft des Hyperkonsums eine individualistische Steigerung erfahren. Sie wird begleitet von desynchronisierten Aktivitäten, individualisierten Konsumpraktiken, persönlich zugeschnittener Nutzung von Raum, Zeit und Objekten und von einer Auflösung der Zwänge und des Schichtenspezifischen. Paradoxerweise ist diese Epoche der Markenverehrung auch eine Ära, die den Konsum in einen Prozess von Deregulierung und Hyperindividualisierung trägt. Die unterprivilegierten Klassen träumen von Luxusmarken und in den oberen Klassen gilt es nicht mehr als ehrenrührig, günstig einzukaufen und Preiswertes mit Luxus zu kombinieren. Mehr und mehr zeichnet sich ein Konsument ab, der von der Last der Konvention und der Klassentraditionen befreit ist, ein Konsument, der sich nomadisch und unvorhersehbar, unkoordiniert und dereguliert verhält.

Nun, da den Marken in der Kaufentscheidung eine gesteigerte Bedeutung zukommt, kristallisiert sich ein Konsumverhalten heraus, das emotional oder experimentell geprägt ist. Geld für soziales Repräsentieren auszugeben, steht nicht mehr im Mittelpunkt der Konsumdynamik: Markenerwerb genügt nicht länger dem sozialen Druck, sondern dem persönlichen Lustbedürfnis. Das neue Verhältnis zu Marken tendiert zur Abnabelung von der Kultur der Ehren- und Statusausgaben. Der Neu-Konsument kauft weniger, um seinen Platz in der sozialen Hierarchie zu demonstrieren, sondern eher um seine Individualität in Szene zu setzen, persönliche, hedonistische und spielerische Befriedigung zu erlangen, Empfindungen zu erproben und Erfahrungen zu sammeln.

Die hyperkommerzielle und hyperindividualistische Epoche ist also eine der Ästhetisierung von Konsum und Markenbezug. Von nun an hat der Kauf einer Marke eine ähnliche Wirkung wie eine anspruchsvolle Reise: Er belebt die Alltagsroutine, intensiviert den Moment und setzt unsere Fantasie in Gang. Und es ist eine Form, sich am sehr persönlichen Gefühl, ein „besonderer Mensch" zu sein, zu

erfreuen, ohne dass man dafür unbedingt um Wertschätzung buhlen und dem demonstrativen Konsum, wie ihn Thorstein Veblen beschrieb, huldigen müsste. Auch wenn das Bling-Bling den Fortbestand des Musters eines prahlerischen Konsums offenbart, so hat dies weniger mit einer Sehnsucht nach sozialer Überlegenheit zu tun, die unseren Gesellschaften der Anziehungskraft der Luxusmarken zugrunde liegt, sondern mehr mit einem narzisstischen Vergnügen am Gefühl der Distanz zum Gewöhnlichen: „L'Oréal, weil ich es mir wert bin" (S. 42).

Zweifellos stehen Phänomene wie die Besessenheit nach Logos bei Heranwachsenden dieser Dynamik der Individualisierung entgegen. In ihren Fällen dient das Logo dazu, sich gegenseitig einer „Stammesidentität"zu versichern: Es hat die Funktion eines Abzeichens, um von Gleichgesinnten anerkannt zu werden. Doch gleichzeitig trifft der Heranwachsende, indem er demonstrativ dieses oder jenes Logo herzeigt, eine Wahl, die ihn von der Welt seiner Eltern abhebt. Er unterstreicht seine Vorlieben und seinen Geschmack, die ihn definieren, er fordert damit eine frei gewählte statt durch gesellschaftliches oder familiäres Schicksal zugeteilte Zugehörigkeit ein. Das Logo drückt so Identität aus, sowohl im Sinne einer Stammeszugehörigkeit wie auch einer persönlichen Identität. Tatsächlich subjektiviert das demonstrativ getragene Logo: Jenseits des wuchernden Konformismus vermittelt es paradoxerweise die persönliche Aneignung eines sozialen Codes wie auch einen Willen zu Individualismus.

Diese Dynamik der Individualisierung findet sich wieder in der alltäglichen Diskussion zum Thema Marken. Im Internet haben Parodien von Werbung Hochkonjunktur; in Diskussionsforen, Blogs und in den sozialen Netzwerken häufen sich kritische Beiträge, umfunktionierte Spots und humoristische Schöpfungen von Amateuren. Die Marke ist nicht nur ein Objekt der Sehnsucht, sondern eine bedenkenswerte Angelegenheit, ein Thema, das man umfunktionieren und mit dem man spielen kann. Unser Verhältnis zu den Marken wird zunehmend reflexiver, spielerischer, ästhetischer. Derselbe distanzierte und ironische Umgang findet sich in dem Film *Logorama*, in dem die kommerzielle Ästhetik zugunsten eines im eigentlichen Sinne ästhetischen Endes umfunktioniert wird. *Logorama* ist die Ästhetisierung des bereits ästhetischen Universums der Logos und beschreitet dafür den von modernen zeitgenössischen Künstlern vorgezeichneten Weg. Die Filmemacher nehmen sich das Recht heraus, alles von einem ästhetischen Standpunkt aus zu behandeln und alles, kommerzielle Zeichen ausdrücklich inbegriffen, in ein Kunstwerk zu verwandeln. Die Pop-Art hat das Alltagsobjekt in den Ritterstand der Kunstwürdigkeit erhoben: *Logorama* geht einen Schritt weiter. Erstmalig wird das Universum des kommerziellen Logos filmisch zum Kunstwerk. Symbole, die oft mit kommerzieller Aggressivität verbunden werden, bereiten ästhetisches Vergnügen.

Die Pop-Art verlieh Medienbildern wie auch trivialen Wahren Glanz, schuf Kunst aus Dingen, die als unwürdig, gewöhnlich, wertlos erachtet wurden.

Und immerhin sind nun auch die Werke des Pop ihrerseits von der Aura großer Kunst umfangen: Die Campbell-Suppendosen (S. 44) hängen gleichwertig neben Porträts von Marilyn (S. 45), von Idolen und Bildnissen, die ihren Platz in der Hochkultur haben. Das ist in *Logorama* nicht der Fall, denn hier tritt das spielerisch-ironische Bild an die Stelle der auratischen Wahrnehmung und der kulturellen Betrachtung. Der Film verschafft dem Logo Eingang in die Filmkunst, doch es ist eine Kunst ohne erhobenen Zeigefinger. In *Logorama* ist alles Logo und zugleich nichts mehr nur Logo. Was ist ein kommerzielles Logo? Schlicht ein visuelles Zeichen, das der Wiedererkennung einer Marke dient, den Konsumenten informieren und ihm Sicherheit geben soll. Es soll ihn dazu anregen, eher diese als jene Marke zu kaufen. Diese entscheidende wirtschaftliche Funktion hat zu einer gewissen „Fetischisierung" des Logos geführt, das gesetzlich gegen alle Formen von Nachahmung geschützt ist und triumphierend an Fassaden, auf Briefköpfen, Werbeplakaten, Websites, Kleidungsstücken und Verpackungen prangt. Genau gegen diese Totemisierung des Logos geht *Logorama* an. Hier wird keinem Markenkult gehuldigt, sondern mit eben diesen Marken über eine Geschichte, die an sich schon jeglicher kommerzieller Perspektive entbehrt, ein ironisches und ästhetisches Spiel getrieben. In *Logorama* existieren die Logos auf autonome Weise, als souveräne ästhetische Objekte, die frei angepasst werden können: Logos in einer erzählenden und ästhetischen Rolle, ihrer eigentlichen Funktion entbunden.

Die Macht der Marken: Wie weit reicht sie?

Das neue Gewicht der Marken im Wirtschaftsleben hat eine Vielzahl an kritischen Beiträgen zum Phänomen des „kulturellen Faschismus" und Orwell'scher Kontrolle des geistigen und kulturellen Raums zur Folge. In der Tat lässt sich eine Marke nicht mehr rein auf einen Namen und ein Logo reduzieren: Sie ist ein Grundmuster, das sich mittels einer bestimmten Vorstellung der Welt und über Lebensmaximen anschickt, die Gesamtheit unseres Daseins zu steuern, Stück für Stück unsere Betrachtungs-, Denk- und Handlungsweisen umzugestalten, und zwar vom Anfang bis zum Ende unserer Existenz. Die großen Marken bieten Weltanschauungen, sie verändern Verhaltensweisen und die Organisation unseres Alltagslebens; in manchen extremen Fällen werden sie zum Daseinsgrund. Die Marken seien, obgleich sie Werte wie Offenheit und Toleranz preisen, in Wirklichkeit Instanzen, die das gesamte geistige, emotionale und soziale Universum des Einzelnen vereinnahmen. Eine neue totale Macht, „totalitär" sagen manche, drängt sich mit der wirtschaftlichen Hypermoderne auf.

Die wachsende Macht der Marken ist sicherlich kaum abzustreiten. Wir sollten das jedoch nicht mit einem omnipotenten Leviathan gleichsetzen. Denn so misstrauisch, unbeständig und wenig markentreu wie heute waren die Konsumenten noch nie. Trotz der beträchtlichen Budgets für Kampagnen müssen die Marken jederzeit mit dem Liebesentzug ihrer Konsumenten rechnen. Mag sein, dass die Macht der Marken wächst, die der Konsumenten je-

„Es geht nicht mehr nur darum, bekannt, sondern geliebt zu werden, sich als lovemark zu etablieren."

left Louis Vuitton flagship store, Champs-Elysées, 2005, Paris, photo by Stéphane Muratet

doch auchMittels Manipulation durch Branding soll es möglich sein, für jedes Gut einen hypnotisierten, passiven, hilflosen Konsumenten aufzubauen? Wie wären dann die zunehmende Preissensibilität, der Erfolg der Niedrigpreise und die Phänomene abnehmender Konsumentenbindung zu erklären? Vorgeblich unter dem „Faschismus der Marken" nimmt die Macht des *homo consumericus* zu. Die Macht der Logos wächst, doch zugleich wird die Autonomie des Konsumenten immer deutlicher. Die demiurgische Allmacht des Marketings ist ein Mythos, denn der von Logos begeisterte Neu-Konsument verhält sich gleichzeitig bedacht und nomadisch. Je omnipräsenter Marken sind, desto distanzierter zeigt sich der Einzelne. Unser zeitgenössisches markengesättigtes Universum ist von einem Fetischismus geprägt, der Abstand hält.

Die Verächter des Brandings führen die demiurgischen Ambitionen der Marken an, die sich nach Art totalitärer Systeme anschicken, Geist und Phantasie zu kolonisieren. Sagen wir es deutlich: Das Universum der Marken mit Faschismus zu vergleichen ist nicht akzeptabel. Die Ambition des Totalitären ist die Erschaffung einer Gesellschaft, die jeglicher Antagonismen, jeglicher Unterteilung, jeglicher Heterogenität – ob im Hinblick auf Klassen, Interessen, Wissen, Normen, Glauben oder Meinungen – entbehrt. Dem Totalitarismus liegt die politisch globalisierende Intention zugrunde. Die Welt der Marken hat nichts davon. Sie ist einem pluralistischen Universum wesensgleich, geprägt von einer Konkurrenz, die auf der Unterschiedlichkeit der Interessen und Normen, ästhetischen Vorstellungen und Geschmacksrichtungen basiert. Die Marken – um der Wirklichkeit dieser Welt und den Fakten der Geschichte gerecht zu werden – zielen nicht auf das Totale, sie wollen weder religiöse noch politische Überzeugungen beherrschen – sie wollen die Märkte erobern und dabei die Oberhand über ihre Konkurrenten gewinnen. Und wenn Marken Werte preisen, dann sind es eher jene, die einhellige Zustimmung finden (Menschenrechte, Respekt vor der Umwelt, Toleranz, Pluralismus) und die aus der Gesellschaft gegriffen sind, statt Werte, die ihr aufgezwungen werden. In diesem Sinne haben die Intentionen der Marken nichts Totalitäres: Sie sind ihrer Natur nach begrenzt.

Niedergang der Marken?

Hat die Anziehungskraft der Marken Zukunft? Unmittelbar nach der Krise der 1990er-Jahre und wieder nach dem Debakel der Finanzwelt 2008 sahen zahlreiche Beobachter die Marke in einer tiefen Krise stecken. Während *No Logo*, das Buch von Naomi Klein, einen Welterfolg feiert, werden die Marken für die Übel unserer Zeit verantwortlich gemacht: Umweltverschmutzung, Krebs, Fettleibigkeit, Kinderausbeutung. Viele Konsumenten erklären nun, Marken würden ihren Alltag nicht verbessern, sie nicht mehr zum Träumen bringen, ihre Kauflust nicht fördern. Sie weigern sich, den mit ihr verbundenen Mehrpreis zu bezahlen: eine Schwächung der Marken, eine wachsende Bedeutung der Billigprodukte. Unsere Epoche erlebt eine

ESSAY

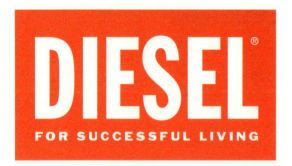

Steigerung des Argwohns und des Desinteresses sowohl den Marken gegenüber als auch dem Konsum im allgemeinen. Die Mehrheit der Verbraucher ist nun bereit, beim Kauf auf Nachhaltigkeit zu achten und meint übereinstimmend, unsere Konsumbulimie mache nicht glücklich. Aber handelt es sich wirklich um eine strukturelle und allgemeine Krise? Wie soll man den Gedanken einer Ernüchterung im Hinblick auf Marken bewerten, wenn weltweit ausgerechnet der Markt für Luxusgüter anhaltend wächst und sich zunehmend Fan-Clubs ausbreiten? Noch nie haben sich die Autos der deutschen Edelmarken so gut verkauft wie heute. Die Vorliebe für Marken schwindet nicht: sie weitet sich aus, erobert sämtliche gesellschaftlichen Schichten. Bestimmte Marken sind geschwächt, andere, die weiterhin immer mehr Aficionados gewinnen, nicht. Eine allgemeine Absetzbewegung der Investoren von Marken ist nicht zu erkennen. Die zunehmende Untreue gegenüber Marken ist nicht gleichbedeutend mit einer Indifferenz ihnen gegenüber.

Zu behaupten, die sich der Fallen des Marketings bewusste Konsumenten würden nun vernünftig, lehnten den Hyperkonsum, das Überflüssige und das Künstliche ab und bekehrten sich zu einer „freiwilligen Schlichtheit", ist wohl ziemlich naiv. In einer Gesellschaft, die die großen kollektiven Utopien über Bord geworfen hat, erfüllen Konsum und Marken eine nicht wegzudenkende Funktion der Traumbilder und der Kompensation: Konsumieren ist eine Art Therapie geworden, eine Möglich-

keit zu vergessen, was uns frustriert, uns wehtut, ängstigt. Zwei Monate nach dem Albtraum von Fukushima waren die Verkaufszahlen für die bekanntesten französischen Luxusprodukte in Japan wieder auf dem gleichen Niveau wie zuvor. Wenn die Nachfrage nach Luxusmarken nicht einmal nach einer solchen Katastrophe zurückgeht, ist weit und breit nicht erkennbar, was in naher Zukunft diesen Heißhunger stoppen könnte.

Ein anderer Grund lässt meinen, dass Marken ganz und gar nicht zu den aussterbenden Spezies gehören. Ihre Anziehungskraft heutzutage kann nämlich nicht getrennt werden vom Strukturverlust der Klassenkulturen, der neuen ästhetischen Ruhelosigkeit und den Angstgefühlen der Hyperkonsumgesellschaft gegenüber dem Konsumrausch. Konsumenten zeigen sich heute zunehmend unschlüssig, desorientiert und unsicher. Doch die Marke vermag den aus der Bahn geworfenen, im ästhetisch ansprechenden Warenangebot verlorenen Hyperkonsumenten wieder zu beruhigen. Die heutige zentrale Stellung der Marke ist eine Reaktion auf die Dynamik von Traditionsverlust und Individualisierung. Je weniger der Lebensstil durch Traditionen und Klassenbewusstsein ausgerichtet wird, desto stärker gewinnt die Logik der Logos an Boden. Je mehr Lebensmittelskandale für Nachrichten sorgen, desto häufiger greifen die Verbraucher zu Bio-Marken. Marken geben dem in der Überfülle des Angebots verlorenen Käufer Sicherheit. Sie liefert Orientierung, zerstreut Bedenken und bietet dem von alten Formen kollektiver Zuge-

left *Diesel*, logo with tagline, Diesel S.p.A., Italy

right *Emporio Armani*, logo, Giorgio Armani S.p.A., Italy

hörigkeit losgelösten Konsumenten eine Aufwertung des Egos: In einer Epoche weit verbreiteter Desorientierung haben die Marken noch lange nicht ihr letztes Wort gesprochen.

Letztes Argument: Logos bieten Halt bei der Suche nach Lebensqualität. In der Hyperkonsumgesellschaft genügt die praktische Bequemlichkeit nicht mehr: Nach dem quantitativen, sachgemäßen, funktionsgerechten Komfort der Anfangsphasen geht es nun um das Streben nach einem besseren Leben und gesteigertem Wohlbefinden. Davon zeugen der bewusstere Umgang mit dem Kulturerbe und mit Landschaftsräumen, der Gestaltung des Interieurs, der sensitiven und emotionalen Behaglichkeit, aber auch mit Qualitätsprodukten und -marken. Die Lebensqualität profiliert sich als neue Grenzlinie der Konsumgesellschaften. Nicht die Allmacht des Marketings triumphiert, sondern die Macht der hedonistischen, ästhetischen und gesundheitlichen Werte. Das Verführerische an teuren Marken heute: Sie verheißen Lebensqualität und persönliches Wohlergehen. Und eine Abkehr von der Kultur des Hedonismus ist nicht ersichtlich.

Wir leben nicht am Vorabend des Zusammenbruchs des Markenuniversums – ganz im Gegenteil. Weltweit breiten sich die Konsumleidenschaften und die allgemeine Kommerzialisierung von Lebensweisen aus. Wie ist die systematische Merkantilisierung von Erfahrungen ohne erweiterte Markenlogik vorstellbar? Weder die ökologischen Herausforderungen noch das neue maßvollere Konsumverhalten, auch nicht die „Alternativ-Konsumenten" werden es schaffen, die Flucht nach vorn zur Omnivermarktung von Lebensweisen zum Stillstand zu bringen. In einer Welt, die vom Wirtschaftsliberalismus dominiert wird, erringt die Kultur der Marke unweigerlich die Herrschaft über den gesamten Planeten. Genau daran lässt das Ende des Films *Logorama* denken – nicht einmal den schlimmsten Naturkatastrophen wird es gelingen, das Universum der Logos zu liquidieren. Auf einem kleinen von der Vernichtung Hollywoods verschonten Stückchen Land leuchten die Marken weiterhin auf. Und während die Erde verwüstet wird, setzen sie ihre unaufhaltsame Expansion fort, breiten sich im Kosmos aus, dem neuen Grenzbereich der Logos. Nach dem Planeten Erde können tausend andere den Logos als Basen dienen. Die bewohnbare Erde ist bedroht, nicht die Marken, diese triumphierenden Imperien hypermoderner Zeiten.

Forschungsschwerpunkt des Philosophen und Soziologen **Gilles Lipovetsky** ist die Frage, wie Gesellschaft und Kultur durch Kommunikation und Konsumverhalten geformt werden. Er ist Autor mehrerer Bücher über die heutige individualisierte und konsumorientierte Welt, und seine Werke wurden in 20 Sprachen übersetzt. Er ist Ehrendoktor der Universität von Sherbrooke in Kanada, und der Neuen Bulgarischen Universität.

Le monde comme marque et comme logo

Nous ne sommes plus dans la société de consommation telle qu'elle s'est constituée pendant les Trente Glorieuses. Une nouvelle figure de la civilisation consommationniste est en expansion : la société d'hyperconsommation, version consumériste de notre modernité, de notre hypermodernité.

L'inflation des marques et des logos en constitue l'aspect le plus observable. Au cours du XXe siècle, de nombreuses voix ont signalé et dénoncé l'envahissement de l'espace public par la publicité. Mais une étape nouvelle est franchie, tant le phénomène publicitaire a explosé au cours des dernières décennies, tant les logos sont omniprésents, envahissant tous les supports, s'immisçant dans tous les interstices du quotidien, tous les moments, tous les lieux de la vie. Les noms de marques s'affichent sur les grandes avenues des métropoles, dans les gares et les stades, dans les halls et les boutiques de tous les aéroports du monde. Les entrées de ville sont de véritables jungles de logos. Sur Internet les marques apparaissent 24h/24, 365 jours sur 365. Les logos sont présents sur les murs des villes et les produits manufacturés, mais aussi dans les musées, les œuvres d'art contemporain, les romans, les films et les séries télévisées au travers du *product placement*.

Le temps des griffes discrètes de la haute couture est révolu : les logos s'exhibent sur les tee-shirts, casquettes, lunettes, chaussures, sacs, stylos, bracelets-montres, brosses à dents. On voit des corps tatoués de logos commerciaux. L'univers de la marque moderne, né au cours des deux dernières décennies du XXe siècle avec le packaging et la publicité de grande ampleur, est pris dans une spirale hypertrophique. Avec le sponsoring, les produits dérivés, le marketing relationnel, le marketing mobile, la publicité online, les liens sponsorisés, un monde sursaturé de logos se développe : selon certaines estimations, nous serions exposés à quelque 1200 logos par jour. Où que l'on soit et quoi que l'on fasse, il devient difficile, voire impossible, d'échapper à la force de frappe des symboles de marques.

L'âge de l'hyperconsommation se signale par cette marchandisation des temps et expériences de la vie, cette excroissance de l'univers des marques et des logos. Mais parallèlement à cette explosion quantitative s'observe un changement qualitatif. Un nouveau branding se développe, ainsi que de nouvelles ambitions des marques et un nouveau rapport des consommateurs aux marques. Il y a prolifération des produits, surabondance des publicités et des logos, mais aussi avènement d'un type de marketing et d'un esprit consommationniste d'un nouveau genre, turbo-consumérisme restructuré par le monde des logos. Ce ne sont pas seulement les marques qui se diffusent à l'infini, c'est une *culture de marque* qui s'est emparée de l'univers commercial et de la quotidienneté. L'ère du fétichisme de la marchandise dénoncé par Marx est devenue l'ère du branding, du fétichisme des logos.

Une nouvelle culture de marque

A l'origine, le branding consistait en slogans et images destinés à faire connaître les produits. Mais

Logorama, scene from the film, directed by H5 (Hervé de Crécy, François Alaux and Ludovic Houplain)

dans le monde de l'hyperconsommation, l'important est moins le produit que la marque, son imaginaire, ses valeurs, sa vision du monde. Il ne s'agit plus de faire appel à la mémoire et aux réflexes, mais de raconter une histoire, de développer un concept, de créer une identité de marque reconnaissable à travers le design des produits, le logo, le packaging, l'architecture des magasins, le sponsoring, la publicité. Toute grande marque s'affirme comme un univers affichant une « philosophie », un look. Le but recherché n'est plus seulement de se faire connaître, mais d'être aimé comme une « lovemark ». Pour cela, les marques vont bien au-delà de la seule mise en valeur des produits : elles se construisent à partir d'une communication affirmant une « mission », forgeant une légende, un imaginaire social et esthétique, des messages de sens et d'éthique. Nike ne se positionne pas comme un fabricant de chaussures de sport, mais comme une marque qui ambitionne « d'embellir la vie par le sport et le fitness » (Phil Knight). Le logo est plus que la figure visuelle d'une marque ou d'une organisation : pénétré de référentiels culturels, son design exprime les valeurs, l'esthétique, l'esprit de la marque.

Mais le changement se lit dans le nouveau rapport qu'entretiennent les consommateurs avec les marques. Si la peur et le rejet des marques nourrissent un ensemble de pratiques et de discours critiques, cela ne masque pas l'attraction accrue qu'elles exercent sur le plus grand nombre et le nouveau rôle qu'elles jouent dans les comportements d'achat. L'heure est à la démultiplication des fans de marques sur les réseaux sociaux : on ne se contente plus d'acheter une marque, on aime déclarer son attachement à elle, on invite ses amis à devenir membre de la « tribu ». Des parents n'hésitent plus à donner des noms de marque à leurs enfants. Il y a deux fois plus de touristes qui vont à New York pour faire du shopping que pour visiter les musées. Le flagship Vuitton des Champs-Élysées à Paris est devenu une destination touristique comme la tour Eiffel (p. 36). Et les « sapeurs » congolais, véritables publicités vivantes, se ruinent pour exhiber leurs vêtements griffés.

Il y a peu encore, le « dernier cri » des collections de mode captait les désirs : maintenant, c'est la marque qui est et fait la mode : on fantasme moins sur la mode que sur les marques. On n'achète plus un jean, mais un Diesel. On n'achète plus un téléphone, mais un Iphone ou un Ipod. Une paire de lunettes ? Non : une monture Dior, Chanel ou Armani. L'hyperconsommateur achète la marque avec sa dimension d'imaginaire, de rêve, de mythe. Les marques ne sont plus de simples étiquettes de produit, elles sont objet de conversation et de débat, de scandale et de contestation, cf. le porno chic et les publicités Benetton (p. 43). Qu'on les adore ou qu'on les abhorre, ce sont les nouveaux fétiches de l'âge hypermoderne.

L'attraction du logo n'est plus circonscrite aux élites sociales de l'Occident : elle s'exerce dans toutes les nations, toutes les couches de la population, tous les âges. Ainsi, l'explosion de la contrefaçon signale la nouvelle aspiration des masses

ESSAY

aux marques de luxe. Les jeunes peuvent citer plus de marques de mode que de saints, de poètes ou de grands savants ; et un consommateur connaît quelque 5000 noms de marque. Le culte des marques fait des ravages en Chine, en Inde, dans les pays émergents : même les plus défavorisés connaissent et rêvent d'acheter les marques les plus prestigieuses. Finie l'ancienne inhibition des classes populaires envers les marques de mode et de luxe : les marques et les logos, ce n'est plus seulement pour les gens de « la haute » : c'est pour tous. Déferlement des logos dans les rues, dans les lieux de vente et les médias, démocratisation des désirs de marques sur tout le globe, qui constituent une des pièces majeures de la culture quotidienne planétaire.

Logomania et individualisme consommatoire
Dire que les marques restructurent le rapport à la consommation ne signifie pas l'avènement d'un consommateur conformiste et obsédé de « paraître ». Par les médias, l'offre en abîme des produits et du pluri-équipement des ménages, la société d'hyperconsommation a entraîné une escalade individualiste s'accompagnant d'activités désynchronisées, de pratiques de consommation individualisées, d'usages personnalisés de l'espace, du temps et des objets, d'une désorganisation des contraintes et modèles de classe. L'époque de l'idolâtrie des marques est celle où la consommation se trouve dans un processus de dérégulation et d'hyperindividualisation. Les classes défavorisées rêvent de marques de luxe, et dans les classes supérieures

il n'est plus infamant d'acheter en premier prix, de combiner low cost et marque de luxe. Un consommateur affranchi du poids des conventions et traditions de classe s'affirme, un consommateur dont les comportements sont plus nomades et imprévisibles, décoordonnés et dérégulés.

Au moment où les marques jouent un rôle accru dans les décisions des acheteurs s'affirme une consommation de type émotionnel. L'impératif de dépenser à des fins de représentation sociale n'est plus au centre de la dynamique de la consommation : on achète des marques non en raison d'une pression sociale de représentation, mais en fonction des moments et des envies. La nouvelle relation aux marques se détache de la culture de la dépense statutaire, centrée sur le désir d'affichage de la richesse. Le néo-consommateur achète moins pour rendre visible sa place dans la hiérarchie sociale que pour mettre en scène son individualité, obtenir des satisfactions privées, hédonistiques et ludiques, sensitives et expérientielles.

Ainsi, l'époque hypermarchande et hyperindividualiste est celle de l'esthétisation de la consommation et du rapport aux marques. L'achat d'une marque fonctionne comme un « voyage » de qualité : c'est une manière d'animer la routine des jours, d'intensifier le présent, de mettre en mouvement notre imaginaire. C'est une façon de jouir du sentiment intime d'être une « personne de qualité », de se comparer aux autres, de se détacher de la masse, sans que soient mobilisés la course à l'estime et le modèle de la consommation

LE MONDE COMME MARQUE ET COMME LOGO

left *L'Oréal*, advertising with Cybill Shepherd, 1991, McCann Erickson, L'Oréal USA, Inc.

right *United Colors of Benetton*, advertising, 1989, Oliviero Toscani, Benetton Group S.p.A., Italy

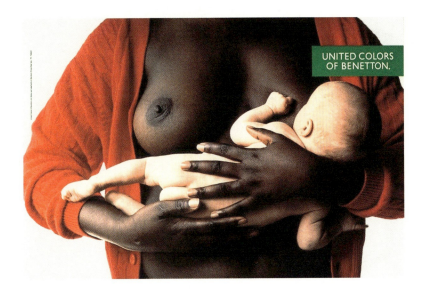

démonstrative chère à Veblen. Si le «bling-bling» révèle la persistance du modèle de la consommation ostentatoire et des passions du paraître social, c'est moins un désir de supériorité sociale qui sous-tend le tropisme vers les marques de luxe que le plaisir narcissique de sentir une distance avec le commun en s'offrant une image positive de soi pour soi: «L'Oréal, parce que je le vaux bien» (p. 42).

Certains phénomènes, comme l'obsession des logos chez les adolescents, semblent aller à contre-courant de cette dynamique, tant le conformisme de groupe l'emporte sur les désirs d'authenticité et de singularisation personnelle. Le logo sert à conforter ou à créer une identité «tribale», un sentiment d'appartenance à un groupe: il fonctionne comme moyen pour être reconnu par ses pairs. Mais, en arborant tel logo, l'adolescent fait un choix qui le distingue du monde de ses parents, il affirme des préférences, des goûts qui le définissent, il revendique une appartenance choisie et non plus reçue comme un destin social ou familial: le logo apparaît comme l'expression d'une identité à la fois «tribale» et personnelle. Le logo affiché est subjectivisant: par-delà le conformisme qui se déploie, il traduit l'appropriation personnelle d'un code social et d'une volonté d'individualité.

Cette dynamique d'individualisation se retrouve dans les nouvelles manières de s'exprimer au sujet des marques. Sur Internet plaisanteries, pastiches et parodies de publicités ont le vent en poupe; dans les forums de discussion, sur les blogs, sur les réseaux sociaux se multiplient les critiques des marques, les spots détournés, les créations humoristiques d'amateurs. La marque n'est pas seulement un objet de désir, mais un objet «bon à penser», à détourner, à «jouer». C'est de plus en plus un rapport réflexif, ludique, esthétique que nous entretenons avec les marques.

C'est pareille culture distanciée et ironique qu'exprime le film *Logorama*, où l'esthétique marchande des logos est détournée au profit d'une fin proprement esthétique. *Logorama*, c'est l'esthétisation de l'univers déjà esthétique des logos, empruntant la voie tracée par les artistes contemporains se donnant le droit de pouvoir tout traiter d'un point de vue esthétique, de tout transformer en œuvre d'art, y compris les signes explicitement commerciaux. Depuis le Pop Art, images médiatiques et objets de la consommation marchande quotidienne ont gagné leurs titres de noblesse artistique: *Logorama* prolonge cette démarche. Voilà, pour la première fois au cinéma, l'univers du logo commercial métamorphosé en œuvre d'art et procurant un plaisir esthétique avec des signes associés à l'agressivité marchande.

Les artistes Pop ont dignifié les images médiatiques ainsi que les choses triviales du commerce, ils ont entrepris de faire de l'art avec ce qui est jugé indigne, ordinaire, sans valeur. Les œuvres Pop n'en demeurent pas moins entourées de l'aura du grand art: les boîtes de soupe Campbell (p. 44) sont, à l'instar des portraits de Marilyn (p. 45), des idoles, des effigies installées dans les cimes du *high art*. Il n'en va pas ainsi avec *Logorama*, dans lequel l'image ludique-ironique se substitue à la

ESSAY

left *Campbell's Soup*, Andy Warhol, 1968, silkscreen prints

right *Marilyn*, Andy Warhol, 1964, silkscreen on canvas

perception et à la contemplation cultuelles. Le film fait entrer le logo dans l'art du cinéma, mais un art sans majuscules, sans monumentalité intimidante, sans dévotion ni climat sacral.

Dans *Logorama* tout est logo, et rien ne l'est vraiment. Qu'est-ce qu'un logo commercial ? Ce n'est qu'une image visuelle faite pour reconnaître une marque, informer et rassurer le consommateur, l'inciter à acheter celle-ci plutôt que celle-là. L'importance cruciale de ces fonctions dans l'économie marchande a conduit à une « fétichisation » du logo, lequel est protégé par le droit contre toutes contrefaçons et s'inscrit sur les façades de bâtiments, sur les papiers à en-tête, affiches publicitaires, sites web, vêtements, emballages de produits. C'est cette totémisation du logo que transgresse *Logorama* où ne s'exprime aucun culte des marques, mais un jeu ironique et esthétique avec celles-ci, au travers d'un récit valant pour lui seul hors de toute perspective commerciale. Dans *Logorama*, les logos n'expriment plus les valeurs ou la philosophie d'une marque ; ils existent de manière autonome à la manière d'objets esthétiques souverains, librement appropriables. Ce qui est donné à voir, ce ne sont plus les logos comme élément de symbolisation et de valorisation de la marque, mais leur indépendance vis-à-vis de celle-ci : des logos narratifs et esthétiques, défonctionnalisés.

Le pouvoir des marques : jusqu'où ?

Le poids nouveau des marques dans la vie économique a entraîné nombre de critiques, tournées vers ce qui est présenté comme un « fascisme culturel », un contrôle orwellien de l'espace mental et culturel. La marque ne se réduit plus à un nom et à un logo : elle est un dispositif qui, via une vision du monde et des maximes de vie, s'emploie à gouverner l'intégralité de nos existences, à remodeler nos façons de voir, de penser et d'agir du début à la fin de notre existence. Les grandes marques ne se contentent plus de la publicité pour booster les ventes : elles proposent des façons de voir le monde, elles changent les comportements et l'organisation de la vie quotidienne ; elles deviennent parfois raison de vivre, but de l'existence. Célébrant les valeurs d'ouverture et de tolérance, les marques seraient des instances qui phagocytent l'univers mental, émotionnel et social des individus. C'est un nouveau pouvoir total, « totalitaire » selon certains, qui s'impose avec l'hypermodernité marchande.

Le pouvoir grandissant des marques est peu contestable. Évitons toutefois de l'assimiler à un Léviathan omnipotent. Car jamais les consommateurs ne se sont montrés aussi méfiants, volatiles, infidèles aux marques. En dépit de budgets considérables affectés à la communication, les marques n'échappent pas aux cycles de désamour et de désaffection. Si les marques détiennent un pouvoir croissant, il en va de même des consommateurs qui, grâce à la diversification de l'offre marchande, au low cost, à Internet, peuvent arbitrer leurs achats en s'informant et en comparant les prix. Pouvoir de manipulation du branding, capable de fabriquer de toute pièce un consommateur

hypnotisé, passif, sans défense ? Comment comprendre alors la poussée de la sensibilité au prix, le succès du low cost, les phénomènes de défidélisation des consommateurs. Sous le prétendu « fascisme des marques », le pouvoir d'*homo consumericus* progresse. Plus il y a de puissance des logos, plus s'affirme l'autonomie du consommateur dans ses décisions d'achat. La toute-puissance démiurgique du marketing est un mythe, car le néoconsommateur épris de logos est aussi réflexif et nomade. A mesure que s'impose l'omniprésence des marques, les individus ont davantage de distance à leur égard. C'est un fétichisme distancié qui sous-tend l'univers contemporain saturé de marques.

Les contempteurs du branding mettent en avant les ambitions démiurgiques des marques, qui s'emploient à coloniser les esprits et les imaginaires à la manière des totalitarismes. Assimiler l'univers des marques au « fascisme » est inacceptable. L'ambition totalitaire réside dans le projet de construire une société délivrée de tout antagonisme, de toute division, de toute hétérogénéité, que ce soit en matière de classes, d'intérêt, de savoir, de normes, de croyances, d'opinions. C'est un projet politique global, inséparable de la visée de l'unité, de l'unanimité, de l'uniformité qui fait la singularité du totalitarisme. Rien de tel avec le monde des marques, univers pluraliste, concurrentiel, reposant sur la diversité des intérêts et des normes, des esthétiques et des goûts. Sans dessein total, les marques ne cherchent pas à gouverner les croyances religieuses et politiques, à dire la vérité du monde et de l'histoire ; elles cherchent à gagner des marchés et l'emporter sur leurs concurrents. Lorsqu'elles célèbrent des valeurs, ce sont plus des valeurs unanimistes (droits de l'homme, respect de l'environnement, tolérance, pluralisme) empruntées à la société que des visions du monde imposées à celle-ci. Le projet des marques n'a donc rien de totalitaire : il est essentiellement *limité*, quelle que soit leur intrusion dans le quotidien et leur puissance à transformer les modes de vie.

Déclin des marques ?

L'attractivité des marques a-t-elle un avenir ? Dans la foulée de la crise des années 1990 puis du crack financier de 2008, des observateurs ont diagnostiqué un état de crise profonde des marques. Tandis que le livre de Naomi Klein *No Logo* remporte un succès mondial, les marques sont rendues responsables des maux de notre temps : pollution, cancer, obésité, exploitation des enfants. Nombre de consommateurs déclarent que les marques n'améliorent pas leur quotidien, ne les font plus rêver, ne leur donnent plus envie d'acheter et refusent de payer l'excédent de prix lié à la marque : affaiblissement des marques et montée en puissance du low cost. L'époque serait témoin d'un mouvement de défiance et de désaffection, tant envers les marques qu'envers la consommation : pour la majorité des consommateurs la marque n'est pas un élément important lors d'un achat, parce qu'elle n'apporte aucun vrai « plus », ils sont prêts à adopter des habitudes d'achat durable et conviennent que notre boulimie de consommation ne donne pas le bonheur.

ESSAY

« Le logo est plus que la figure visuelle d'une marque ou d'une organisation : pénétré de référentiels culturels, il exprime par son design, les valeurs, l'esthétique, l'esprit de la marque. »

Mais s'agit-il d'une crise structurelle et générale ? Comment valider l'idée de désenchantement des marques au vu de l'essor continu du marché mondial du luxe ou des clubs de fans ? Jamais les grandes marques de voiture allemandes ne se sont aussi bien vendues. Le goût des marques ne décline pas : il se généralise, gagnant toutes les couches sociales, embrassant toute chose. Certaines marques sont fragilisées, d'autres non, qui attirent toujours plus d'aficionados : il n'y a aucun mouvement général de désinvestissement des marques. L'infidélité croissante aux marques n'est pas synonyme d'indifférence à celles-ci.

Dire que les consommateurs, désormais conscients des pièges du marketing, sont en passe de devenir raisonnables, de rejeter l'hyperconsommation, le superflu et l'artificiel, de se convertir à la « simplicité volontaire », c'est faire preuve de naïveté. Dans une société délestée des grandes utopies collectives, la consommation et les marques remplissent une fonction inéliminable de rêves et de compensation : consommer est devenu une forme de thérapie, une manière d'oublier ce qui nous frustre et nous angoisse. Deux mois après le cauchemar de Fukushima, les ventes des grandes marques de luxe françaises au Japon avaient retrouvé leur niveau antérieur. Si pareille catastrophe n'a pas réussi à faire fléchir la demande de marques de luxe, on voit mal ce qui pourrait arrêter la fringale de logos des consommateurs.

Une autre raison laisse à penser que la marque n'est pas une espèce menacée. Le tropisme contemporain envers les marques ne peut être séparé de la déstructuration des cultures de classe, des nouvelles anxiétés esthétiques et consuméristes de la société d'hyperconsommation. Ces phénomènes ont provoqué un état de désorientation, d'insécurité du consommateur. Et la marque vient rassurer l'hyperconsommateur déboussolé, perdu dans le surchoix marchand et esthétique. La place centrale contemporaine des marques est l'écho de la dynamique de détraditionnalisation et d'individualisation, de l'incertitude hypermoderne provoquée par l'évaporation des éthos de classe. Moins les styles de vie sont organisés par les traditions et consciences de classe, plus gagne la logique des logos. À mesure que les menaces alimentaires défraient la chronique, les marques bio sont plébiscitées. Quand les normes de classe du « bon goût » se brouillent, quand la mode est déhiérarchisée, décentrée, pluralisée en styles hétérogènes, la marque rassure l'acheteur perdu dans la profusion de l'offre. La marque apporte repères, sécurité, mais aussi valorisation de soi aux consommateurs détachés des anciennes formes d'appartenance collective. La défiance vis-à-vis des marques – et des autorités institutionnelles – est un processus consubstantiel à l'âge hypermoderne, mais en matière de consommation elle reste limitée : les marques sont loin d'avoir dit leur dernier mot dans une époque de désorientation généralisée.

Dernière raison. Le pouvoir d'attraction des logos ne s'explique pas seulement par les stratégies séductrices du branding : il répond à la montée d'une

Logorama, scene from the film, directed by H5 (Hervé de Crécy, François Alaux and Ludovic Houplain)

culture qui célèbre le référentiel de la quête de la qualité de vie, du mieux-vivre. Dans la société d'hyperconsommation, le confort technicien ne suffit plus : au confort quantitatif, fonctionnel, mécaniciste des premiers temps de la société de consommation a succédé la recherche de la qualité de vie et du mieux-être dont témoigne le succès du patrimoine, des paysages, de la décoration des intérieurs, du bien-être émotionnel, mais aussi des produits et marques de qualité. La qualité de vie s'impose comme la nouvelle frontière des sociétés consuméristes. Ce n'est pas la toute-puissance du marketing qui triomphe, mais la puissance des valeurs hédonistes, esthétiques et sanitaires. La séduction qu'exercent les marques les plus coûteuses traduit moins la persistance des stratégies distinctives que la diffusion sociale des aspirations individualistes aux bonheurs matériels et au bien-vivre. Qui peut penser que nous sommes à la veille d'un bouleversement capable d'entraîner l'éclipse de la culture hédoniste de la qualité de vie, dont l'une des manifestations est le goût des marques renommées ?

Nous ne sommes pas à la veille de l'effondrement de l'univers des marques. Au contraire. Partout sur le globe se répandent les passions consuméristes et la commercialisation généralisée des modes d'existence. Comment imaginer la marchandisation systématique des expériences sans l'extension de la logique des marques ? Ni les défis écologiques, ni les nouveaux modes de consommation plus sobres, ni les « alterconsommateurs » n'arrêteront la fuite en avant de l'omnimarchandisation des modes de vie. Dans un monde dominé par le libéralisme marchand, la culture des marques imposera son règne à toute la planète.

C'est ce que laisse à penser la fin du film *Logorama*, les plus grands cataclysmes naturels ne réussissant pas à liquider l'univers des logos. Sur l'ultime parcelle épargnée par le tremblement de terre qui engloutit Hollywood, les marques continuent de briller. La Terre est dévastée, mais les marques poursuivent leur irrésistible expansion, s'exportant dans le cosmos, nouvelle frontière des logos. Après la planète Terre, mille autres planètes pourront servir de bases d'exploitation aux logos. La Terre habitable est menacée, non les marques, ces empires triomphants des temps hypermodernes.

Philosophe et sociologue, **Gilles Lipovetsky** étudie les transformations sociétales et culturelles impulsées par la société de consommation et de communication. Auteur d'une douzaine de livres sur le monde individualiste et consumériste contemporain, traduits dans 20 pays, il est docteur *honoris causa* de l'Université de Sherbrooke, Canada et de la Nouvelle Université Bulgare.

USER'S GUIDE / HINWEISE FÜR DIE BENUTZER / GUIDE DE L'UTILISATEUR

Brand
Owner
Country, Year
Design
[Sector]

The logos are arranged in alphabetical order and are accompanied by a caption (see scheme above) that specifies the following information:
Brand denotes the product name, service, company or organisation that the logo represents.
Owner relates to the company, organisation or similar that currently owns the logo.
Country denotes where the logo owner is based.
Year indicates the date the logo first appeared in the public domain.
Design is for the name of the designer/design agency responsible for the logo's creation.
[Sector] describes the area of activity.
Play sign ▶ indicates logos that appear in the film *Logorama*.

Die Logos sind alphabetisch sortiert und werden in einer Legende (siehe Schema oben) durch diese Infos ergänzt:
Brand (Marke) gibt die Produktbezeichnung, Dienstleistung, Firma oder Organisation an, für die das Logo steht.
Owner (Eigentümer) bezieht sich auf Firmen, Organisationen o.Ä., denen das Logo aktuell gehört.
Country (Staat) nennt das Heimatland des Logo-Eigentümers.
Year (Jahr) verweist auf das Jahr der ersten Veröffentlichung des Logos.
Design steht für den Namen des Designers bzw. der Agentur, die für die Logo-Erstellung verantwortlich sind.
[Sector] (Sektor) beschreibt den Tätigkeitsbereich.
Das Wiedergabesymbol ▶ bezeichnet Logos, die im Film *Logorama* erscheinen.

Les logos sont présentés dans l'ordre alphabétique et sont accompagnés d'une légende (voir schéma ci-dessus) qui fournit les informations suivantes:
Brand (marque) indique le nom du produit, du service, de l'entreprise ou de l'organisme que le logo représente.
Owner (propriétaire) fait référence à l'entreprise, organisme ou autre qui est actuellement titulaire du logo.
Country (pays) précise le pays du propriétaire du logo.
Year (année) signale la date à laquelle le logo est apparu au public pour la première fois.
Design donne le nom du designer ou de l'agence de design responsable de la création du logo.
[Sector] (secteur) décrit le domaine d'activité.
Le symbole ▶ indique les logos qui apparaissent dans le film *Logorama*.

#-B

007 JAMES BOND

1 007 James Bond
   Danjaq LLC
   USA
   [Film]

2 1c
   1c Company
   Russia
   [Computer Software]

3 2Wire Inc
   USA
   [Consumer Electronics]

4 3Com
   Hewlett-Packard Company
   USA
   [Computer Technology]

5 3Com
   Hewlett-Packard Company
   USA, 2000
   Interbrand
   [Computer Technology]

6 3-IN-ONE
   WD-40 Company
   USA
   [Consumer Products]

7 3M
   3M Company
   USA, 1977
   Siegel+Gale
   [Industry]

8 3M MCS Warranty
   3M Company
   USA
   [Labelling, Standards & Certification]

9 3-Stjernet
   3-Stjernet A/S
   Denmark
   [Food & Beverage]

1 **3 Suisses**
 Groupe 3 Suisses International Group (Otto Group)
 France
 [Retail]

2 **4AD**
 Beggars Group
 UK, ca 1983
 V23: Vaughan Oliver
 [Music Industry]

3 **4A The Poker Suite**
 4A Poker e Giovanni Rossi
 Italy
 [Leisure & Entertainment]

4 **4-H**
 National Institute of Food and Agriculture (NIFA)
 USA
 Oscar Herman Benson
 [Foundations & Institutes]

5 **4th Centenary of the City of Rio de Janeiro**
 Brazil, 1964
 Aloísio Magalhães
 [Events]

6 **5* (Five Star)**
 Northern & Shell Network Ltd
 UK, 2011
 [Television Channel]

7 **5 Star Service**
 E.I. du Pont de Nemours and Company
 USA
 [Automotive]

7-ELEVEN

1 **7-Eleven**
7-Eleven Inc,
Seven & I Holdings Co. Ltd
USA, 1950s
[Retail]

2 **7-Eleven**
7-Eleven Inc,
Seven & I Holdings Co. Ltd
USA, 1960s
[Retail]

3 **7-Eleven**
7-Eleven Inc,
Seven & I Holdings Co. Ltd
USA
[Retail]

4 **7 Up (USA)**
Dr Pepper Snapple Group Inc
USA
[Food & Beverage]

5 **7 Up (International)**
PepsiCo Inc
USA, 2011
TracyLocke
[Food & Beverage]

6 **7x7 San Francisco**
McEvoy Group
USA
[Publications]

7 **9/11 Memorial**
National September 11
Memorial & Museum
USA, 2009
Landor Associates
[Galleries & Museums]

8 **13th Street Universal**
NBC Universal
USA
[Television Channel]

9 **20th Century Fox**
Twentieth Century Fox Film
Corporation, News Corporation
USA, 1935
Emil Kosa Jr
[Film Industry]

10 **21c Museum Hotel**
USA, 2006
Pentagram
[Hospitality; Galleries & Museums]

11 **24**
20th Century Fox Television,
Fox Entertainment Group
USA, 2001
[Television Series]

52

20000ST RECORDS

82nd Airborne Division

1   **33rd Degree Masonic Emblem**
    Freemasonry
    [Societies & Associations]

2   **64**
    SAS WD
    France, 1997
    [Apparel]

▶ 3 **76**
    ConocoPhillips Company
    USA
    [Automotive]

4   **82nd Airborne Division**
    United States Army
    USA, 1917
    [Defence]

5   **300**
    Warner Bros. Pictures
    USA, 1998
    Frank Miller
    [Film]

▶ 6 **411VM**
    GrindMedia LLC
    USA
    [Publications]

7   **555 East American Steakhouse**
    King's Seafood Company Inc
    USA
    [Food & Beverage]

▶ 8 **20000st Records**
    France, 1999
    H5: Antoine Bardou-Jacquet
    [Music Industry]

53

A&E NETWORK

1. **A&E Network**
   Arts & Entertainment Television Networks, Hearst Corporation, Disney-ABC Television Group
   USA
   [Television Network]

2. **A&M Records**
   A&M Records, Universal Music Group
   USA, 1962
   [Music Industry]

3. **A&P**
   The Great Atlantic & Pacific Tea Company
   USA
   Lippincott & Margulies
   [Retail]

4. **A&S**
   Allied Stores Corporation
   USA
   [Retail]

5. **AAA**
   Australian Automobile Association
   Australia
   [Societies & Associations]

6. **AAAA (Arte, Arquitectura, Antropologia y Autoritarismo)**
   Universidad Central de Venezuela
   Venezuela, 2007
   Santiago Pol
   [Education]

▶ 7. **AABS**
   Association for the Advancement of Baltic Studies
   USA
   [Societies & Associations]

8. **AAHA (American Animal Hospital Association)**
   USA
   [Societies & Associations]

9. **AAL (Aid Association for Lutherans)**
   USA
   [Societies & Associations]

10. **Aalborg White**
    Aalborg Portland A/S
    Denmark
    [Industrial Products]

1 **AAMA (American Amusement Machine Association)**
USA
[Societies & Associations]

2 **AAMCO Transmissions**
AAMCO, American Capital Strategies Ltd
USA
[Automotive]

3 **AARP**
USA
[Societies & Associations]

4 **AARP (formerly American Association of Retired Persons)**
USA, 2007
[Societies & Associations]

5 **ABA (American Bar Association)**
USA
[Societies & Associations]

6 **Abacus International Pte Ltd**
Singapore, 2006
Unreal
[Healthcare]

7 **Abadía Benedictina**
Venezuela, 2004
Álvaro Sotillo
[Agricultural]

8 **Abanka**
Abanka Vipa dd
Slovenia
[Financial Services]

9 **ABAV (Associação Brasileira de Agências de Viagens)**
Brazil
[Societies & Associations]

10 **ABB (Asea Brown Boveri)**
ABB Group
Switzerland
Pentagram
[Technology]

11 **Abba**
Sweden, 1976
Rune Söderqvist
[Music]

ABBEY

1 **Abbey**
Grupo Santander
UK, 2005
[Financial Services]

2 **Abbey National**
Abbey National plc
UK, 2001
[Financial Services]

3 **Abbey National**
Abbey National plc
UK
[Financial Services]

4 **Abbey Road Studios**
EMI Records Ltd
UK
Ed Lea
[Music Industry]

5 **Abbott Laboratories**
USA
[Pharmaceuticals]

6 **ABC (American Broadcasting Corporation)**
USA, 1962
Paul Rand
[Television Network]

7 **ABC (American Broadcasting Corporation)**
USA, 2007
Troika Design Group
[Television Network]

8 **ABC (Australian Broadcasting Corporation)**
Australia, 2002
[Broadcaster]

9 **ABC (Australian Broadcasting Corporation)**
Australia, 1975
Bill Kennard
[Broadcaster]

ABN AMRO

1 **ABCO Foods**
USA
[Food & Beverage]

2 **Abecip (Associação Brasileira das Entidades de Crédito Imobiliário e Poupança)**
Brazil, 1966
Ruben Martins
[Real Estate]

3 **Abercrombie & Fitch (A&F)**
Abercrombie & Fitch Co.
USA
[Apparel]

4 **AB InBev**
Anheuser-Busch InBev NV
Belgium, 2008
FutureBrand
[Food & Beverage]

5 **Abitibi Consolidated Inc**
Canada
[Paper Products]

6 **Ableton**
Ableton AG
Germany
[Computer Software]

▶ 7 **Ableton Live**
Ableton AG
Germany
[Computer Software]

8 **ABN (Algemene Bank Nederland)**
Netherlands, 1974
Allied International Designers
[Financial Services]

9 **ABN AMRO**
ABN AMRO Bank NV
Netherlands, 1991
Landor Associates
[Financial Services]

ABOB

accenture

1 abob (A Better Option Bag)
   A Better Option Brands
   Sweden
   [Consumer Products]

2 ABP
   Stichting Pensioenfonds ABP
   Netherlands
   [Financial Services]

3 ABS
   Cardo Flow Solutions AB
   Sweden
   [Industry]

4 Absolut Vodka
   V&S Group, Pernod Ricard SA
   Sweden
   [Wines, Beers & Spirits]

5 Absorba
   Poron SA, Groupe Zannier
   France
   [Apparel]

6 ABTCO
   KP & ABTCO Siding Products
   Canada
   [Home Furnishings]

7 Abu Garcia
   Pure Fishing Inc
   Sweden
   [Retail]

8 A Bug's Life
   Pixar Animation Studios,
   The Walt Disney Company
   USA, 1998
   [Film]

9 ABUS
   August Bremicker und Söhne KG
   Germany
   [Security & Safety]

10 Accenture
   Accenture plc
   Ireland, 2001
   Landor Associates
   [Professional Services]

ACE GROUP

1 **AccesRail**
AccesRail Inc
Canada
[Transport]

2 **Access Credit Card**
National Westminster Bank plc,
Midland Bank, Lloyds TSB,
The Royal Bank of Scotland plc
UK
[Financial Services]

3 **Acciona Airport Services**
Acciona SA
Spain
[Freight & Logistics]

4 **Accor**
Accor SA
France
[Hospitality]

5 **Accor**
Accor SA
France
[Hospitality]

6 **AC/DC**
Australia, 1977
Gerard Huerta
[Music]

7 **ACDelco**
ACDelco, General Motors
Company
USA
[Automotive]

8 **ACDelco**
ACDelco, General Motors
Company
USA
[Automotive]

9 **ACDSee**
ACD Systems International Inc
Canada
[Computer Software]

10 **Ace Beepers Inc**
USA
[Consumer Electronics]

11 **Ace Group**
ACE Ltd
Switzerland
Interbrand
[Financial Services]

59

1 **Ace Hardware**
Ace Hardware Corporation
USA
[Retail]

2 **Acela Express**
Amtrak, National Railroad
Passenger Corporation
USA, 2000
OH&CO, IDEO
[Transport]

3 **Acer**
Acer Inc
Taiwan, 1987
[Computer Technology]

4 **Acer**
Acer Inc
Taiwan, 2001
[Computer Technology]

5 **Acer**
Acer Inc
Taiwan, 2011
[Conglomerate]

6 **AchieveGlobal**
USA
[Retail]

7 **ACO**
ACO Systems Ltd
Canada
[Industrial Products]

8 **ACORN (Association of
Community Organizations
for Reform Now)**
USA
[Societies & Associations]

9 **ACR Systems**
ACR Systems Inc
Canada
[Information Technology]

1

2
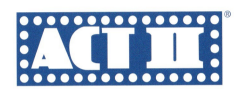

3

4

6

5

7

1   **ACT!**
    Symantec Corporation
    USA
    [Computer Software]

2   **ACT! by Sage**
    The Sage Group plc
    UK
    [Computer Software]

3   **Actifed**
    Warner-Lambert Company
    USA
    [Pharmaceuticals]

4   **Act II**
    ConAgra Foods Inc
    USA
    [Food & Beverage]

5   **Actionaid**
    South Africa, 2003
    CDT
    [Charity]

6   **Action Comics**
    DC Comics Inc, Time Warner
    USA, 1938
    Ira R. Schnapp
    [Publishing]

7   **Action for Blind People**
    UK
    [Charity]

8   **Action for children**
    UK
    [Charity]

9   **Action Man**
    Palitoy Ltd, Hasbro Inc
    UK
    [Toys, Games & Models]

10 **Activision**
    Activision Blizzard Inc,
    Vivendi SA
    USA
    [Computer & Video Games]

ACURA

1 **Acura**
Honda Motor Company Ltd
Japan, 1991
[Automotive]

2 **Acuson**
Siemens AG
USA
[Technology]

3 **Acuvue**
Vistakon, Johnson & Johnson Vision Care Inc
USA
[Healthcare]

4 **AC Verona**
Associazione Calcio Chievo Verona SrL
Italy
[Sport]

5 **Acxiom**
Acxiom Corporation
USA
[Marketing]

6 **AD**
Autodistribution International CVBA
Belgium
[Automotive]

▶ 7 **Adani**
Adani Advanced Analytical Instruments
Belarus
[Technology]

8 **Adaptec**
ADPT Corporation, PMC-Sierra
USA
[Computer Technology]

9 **Adata**
ADATA Technology Co. Ltd
Taiwan, 2010
[Computer Hardware]

10 **Ad Council**
Advertising Council
USA
[Advertising & Campaigns]

1 **Addict Films**
France, 2004
H5: Rachel Cazadamont
[Film Industry]

2 **Adecco**
Adecco SA
Switzerland
[Human Resources]

3 **Adelaide Bank**
Bendigo and Adelaide Bank
Australia
[Financial Services]

4 **AdeS**
Unilever plc/NV
Brazil
[Food & Beverage]

5 **AdForum**
AdForum, MayDream Inc
USA
[Advertising & Campaigns]

6 **adidas Sport Heritage**
adidas AG
Germany, 1972
Hans Fick
[Apparel]

7 **adidas Sport Performance**
adidas AG
Germany, 1990
Peter Moore
[Apparel]

8 **adidas Sport Style**
adidas AG
Germany, 2001
[Apparel]

9 **adidas Samba**
adidas AG
Germany, 2001
[Apparel]

ADIO FOOTWEAR

1 **Adio Footwear**
   Adio Footwear,
   Jarden Corporation
   USA
   [Footwear]

2 **Adler**
   Adlerwerke vorm. H. Kleyer AG.
   Germany
   [Consumer Products]

3 **ADMA (Aviation Distributors and Manufacturers Association)**
   USA
   [Societies & Associations]

4 **Admarc Southwest**
   USA
   [Design]

5 **Adobe**
   Adobe Systems Inc
   USA, 1982
   Marva Warnock
   [Computer Software]

▶ 6 **Adobe**
   Adobe Systems Inc
   USA, 1993
   [Computer Software]

7 **Adobe Acrobat**
   Adobe Systems Inc
   USA
   [Computer Software]

8 **Adobe Postscript**
   Adobe Systems Inc
   USA
   [Computer Software]

9 **ADP**
   Automatic Data Processing Inc
   USA
   [Information Technology]

10 **ADT Security Services**
   ADT Security Services,
   Tyco International Ltd
   Switzerland
   [Security & Safety]

11 **Advance Auto Parts**
   Advance Auto Parts Inc
   USA
   [Automotive]

AEG

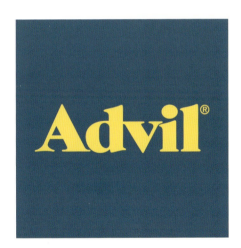

1. **Advanced Photo System**
   Eastman Kodak Company
   USA, 1990s
   [Imaging & Photographic]

2. **Advanta**
   Advanta Corporation
   USA
   [Financial Services]

3. **Advantage Rent-a-Car**
   Hertz Global Holdings Inc
   USA
   [Car Rental]

4. **Advantax Coporate Poperty Tax Solution**
   Advantax Group LLC
   USA
   [Financial Services]

5. **Advent Software**
   Advent Software Inc
   USA
   [Computer Software]

6. **Advil**
   Pfizer Inc
   USA
   [Pharmaceuticals]

7. **ADWEEK**
   Prometheus Global Media
   USA
   [Publications]

8. **AEG**
   AEG GmbH
   Germany, 1908
   Peter Behrens
   [Electronics]

9. **AEG**
   AEG GmbH
   Germany, 2000
   [Electronics]

AEGIS COMMUNICATIONS

1 **Aegis Communications**
Aegis Communications Group Inc, Essar Group
India
[Professional Services]

2 **Aegon NV**
Netherlands
[Financial Services]

3 **AEI**
Air Express International Corporation
USA
[Freight & Logistics]

4 **Aena (Aeropuertos Españoles y Navegación Aérea)**
Spain
[Aviation]

5 **Aer Lingus**
Aer Lingus Group plc
Ireland
[Airline]

6 **Aeroflot**
Aeroflot Russian Airlines
Russia
[Airline]

7 **Aerolíneas Argentinas**
Argentina, 2010
FutureBrand
[Airline]

8 **AeroMéxico**
Aerovías de México SA de CV
Mexico
[Airline]

9 **Aeromotive Inc**
USA
[Automotive]

10 **Aeroperú**
Empresa Nacional de Aeronavegación del Perú
Peru
[Airline]

11 **Aeroperú**
Empresa Nacional de Aeronavegación del Perú
Peru
[Airline]

AFTER EIGHT

Aftenposten

1. **Aéropostale**
Aéropostale Inc
USA
[Apparel]

2. **Aerosmith**
USA, 1971
Ray Tabano
[Music]

3. **Aetna Inc**
USA
[Financial Services]

4. **AFDEC (Association of Franchised Distributors of Electronic Components)**
UK
[Societies & Associations]

5. **Aflac Inc**
USA, 2004
FutureBrand
[Financial Services]

6. **AFP**
Agence France-Presse
France
[Media]

7. **African Gold**
UK
[Mining]

8. **Afri Cola**
Mineralbrunnen
Überkingen-Teinach AG
Germany
[Food & Beverage]

9. **AFTA (Australian Federation of Travel Agents Ltd)**
Australia
[Societies & Associations]

10. **Aftenposten**
Schibsted ASA
Norway
[Media]

11. **After Eight**
Nestlé SA
UK
[Food & Beverage]

67

AGA

 Agilent Technologies

Agip

agnès b.

1. **AGA**
   Linde Group
   Finland
   [Oil, Gas & Petroleum]

2. **AGC**
   Asahi Glass Co. Ltd,
   Mitsubishi Group
   Japan, 2007
   [Manufacturing]

3. **AGC**
   Asahi Glass Co. Ltd,
   Mitsubishi Group
   Japan
   [Manufacturing]

4. **Ageas**
   Ageas Insurance Ltd
   UK
   [Financial Services]

▶ 5. **AGFA**
   Agfa-Gevaert NV
   Belgium, 1984
   Schlagheck & Schultes
   [Imaging & Photographic]

6. **Aggro Berlin**
   Germany, ca 2001
   Specter
   [Music Industry]

7. **Agilent Technologies Inc**
   USA
   [Technology]

8. **AGIP (Azienda Generale Italiana Petroli)**
   AGIP SpA
   Italy, 1998
   Unimark: Bob Noorda
   [Retail]

9. **agnès b.**
   Société CMC
   France
   [Fashion]

10. **Agrigel**
    Toupargel-Agrigel SA
    France
    [Freight & Logistics]

AICHI BANK

1 **Agusta Westland**
Finmeccanica SpA, GKN plc
Italy/UK, ca 2000
[Aerospace]

2 **AGV**
AGV SpA, Dainese SpA
Italy
[Automotive]

3 **AGWAY**
Southern States Cooperative Inc
USA, 1964
[Agricultural]

4 **AHI**
Allied Holdings, Inc
USA
[Freight & Logistics]

5 **Ahlstrom**
Ahlstrom Corporation
Finland, 2001
Porkka & Kuutsa
[Paper Products]

6 **Ahold**
Koninklijke Ahold NV
Netherlands
[Retail]

7 **Aibo**
Sony Corporation
Japan
[Toys, Games & Models]

8 **aicep Portugal Global**
Portugal
[Government]

9 **Aichi Bank**
Japan
[Financial Services]

1 **AIG (American International Group) Inc**
  USA
  [Financial Services]

2 **AIGA (American Institute of Graphic Arts)**
  USA
  [Foundations & Institutes]

3 **Aigle**
  Aigle International SA
  France, 2005
  [Footwear]

4 **AIM Mail Centers**
  AIM Mail Centers Inc
  USA
  [Mail Services]

5 **AIM (AOL Instant Messenger)**
  AOL Inc
  USA, 1990s
  [Computer Software]

6 **AirAsia**
  AirAsia Bhd
  Malaysia
  [Airline]

7 **airBaltic**
  A/S Air Baltic Corporation
  Latvia, 2004
  [Airline]

8 **Airbus**
  Airbus SAS, European Aeronautic Defence and Space Company NV
  France, 2010
  [Aerospace]

9 **Airbus**
  Airbus SAS, European Aeronautic Defence and Space Company NV
  France, 1970
  [Aerospace]

1 **Air Canada**
Canada, 1960s
Stewart & Morrison: Hans Kleefeld
[Airline]

2 **Air Canada**
Canada, 2004
FutureBrand: Claude Salzberger
[Airline]

3 **Air China**
China International Airlines Company
China, 1988
Shao Xin, Han Meilin
[Airline]

4 **Airfield**
Airfield Walter Moser GmbH
Germany
[Apparel]

5 **Air France**
Air France-KLM SA
France, 1975
[Airline]

6 **Air France**
Air France-KLM SA
France, 2009
Brandimage
[Airline]

7 **Air India**
Air India Ltd
India
[Airline]

8 **Air India**
Air India Ltd
India, 1948
[Airline]

9 **Air India**
Air India Ltd
India, 2007
[Airline]

AIR JAMAICA

1

2

3

4

5

6

7

8

9

10

1 **Air Jamaica**
   Caribbean Airlines-Air Jamaica Transition Ltd
   Jamaica/Trinidad and Tobago
   Stewart & Morrison: Hans Kleefeld
   [Airline]

2 **Air Jamaica**
   Caribbean Airlines-Air Jamaica Transition Ltd
   Jamaica/Trinidad and Tobago
   [Airline]

3 **Air Jordan**
   Nike Inc
   USA, 1988
   Tinker Hatfield
   [Footwear]

4 **Air Lift**
   USA, 1949
   [Automotive]

5 **Air Liquide**
   L'Air Liquide SA
   France
   [Industry]

6 **Air Madagascar**
   Madagascar, 2004
   Peter Schmidt Group
   [Airline]

7 **Air Max**
   Nike Inc
   USA
   [Sporting Goods]

8 **Air New Zealand**
   New Zealand, 2006
   [Airline]

9 **AirPlus International Ltd**
   Lufthansa AirPlus Servicekarten GmbH
   Germany
   [Financial Services]

10 **Air Products**
   Air Products and Chemicals Inc
   USA
   [Industry]

1 **Airtel**
   Bharti Airtel Ltd
   India, 2010
   The Brand Union
   [Telecommunications]

2 **Airtronics**
   USA
   [Electronics]

3 **Airwalk**
   Airwalk International LLC,
   Collective Licensing
   International LLC
   USA
   [Sporting Goods]

4 **Airwell**
   Airwell Group
   France
   [Industry]

5 **Aiwa**
   Aiwa Corporation,
   Sony Corporation
   Japan, 2003
   [Consumer Electronics]

6 **Aixtron**
   Aixtron SE
   Germany
   [Technology]

7 **Ajax**
   Cameron International Corporation
   USA
   [Industry]

8 **Ajax**
   Phoenix Brands LLC
   USA
   [Household Products]

9 **Ajax Amsterdam**
   Amsterdamsche Football Club
   Ajax
   Netherlands, 1990
   Samenwerkende Ontwerpers:
   Andre Toet
   [Sport]

AJINOMOTO

1 **Ajinomoto**
Ajinomoto Co. Inc
Japan, 1999
[Food & Beverage]

2 **AJ Wright**
AJ Wright, The TJX Companies Inc
USA, 2009
[Retail]

▶ 3 **Akai**
Akai Sales Pte Ltd
Japan
[Consumer Electronics]

4 **Akbank**
Akbank TAS, Hacı Ömer Sabancı Holding AŞ
Turkey
[Financial Services]

5 **AKG Acoustics**
Austria, 1953
[Consumer Electronics]

6 **AKSA Energy**
AKSA Enerji Uretim AS, Kazancı Holding
Turkey
[Energy]

7 **AK Steel**
AK Steel Corporation
USA
[Industry]

8 **AkzoNobel**
Akzo Nobel NV
Netherlands, 1994
Wolff Olins
[Paints & Coatings]

▶ 9 **AkzoNobel**
Akzo Nobel NV
Netherlands, 2008
Saffron Brand Consultants, Martin Rijven, Pentagram
[Paints & Coatings]

10 **Alamo**
Enterprise Holdings Inc
USA
[Car Rental]

1. **Alaska Airlines**
USA
[Airline]

2. **Alaska Seafood**
Alaska Seafood Marketing Institute
USA
[Foundations & Institutes]

3. **Albert Heijn**
Albert Heijn BV
Netherlands, 1965
Allied International Designers
[Retail]

4. **Albertsons**
Albertsons LLC
USA
[Retail]

5. **Albi**
Albi GmbH & Co. KG
Germany
[Food & Beverage]

6. **Alcan Cable**
Alcan Products Corporation
USA
[Industrial Products]

7. **Alcatel-Lucent**
Alcatel-Lucent SA
France, 2006
Landor Associates
[Telecommunications]

▶ 8. **Alcoa**
Alcoa Inc
USA, 1999
Arnold Saks Associates
[Industry]

9. **Alesco**
Kansai Paint Co. Ltd
Japan
[Paints & Coatings]

10. **Alesis**
Alesis LP
USA
[Electronics]

ALEUTIAN CLASS

1 **Aleutian Class**
Grand Banks Yachts Ltd
USA
[Marine]

2 **Aleve**
Bayer Healthcare LLC
USA
Szylinski Associates
[Pharmaceuticals]

3 **Alfa Insurance**
Alfa Mutual Insurance Company
USA
[Financial Services]

4 **ALF (Animal Liberation Front)**
UK
[Political]

5 **Alfa Romeo**
Alfa Romeo Automobiles SpA,
Fiat SpA
Italy, 1992
Robilant Associati
[Automotive]

6 **alfi**
alfi GmbH
Germany, 2007
Baumann & Baumann
[Kitchenware]

7 **AlgarveShopping**
Portugal
[Retail]

8 **Algeco**
Algeco Scotsman
France
[Professional Services]

9 **Alien Skin Software**
Alien Skin Software LLC
USA, 1993
[Computer Software]

10 **Alienware**
Dell Inc
USA
[Computer & Video Games]

11 **Alinghi**
Société Nautique de Genève
Switzerland
[Sport]

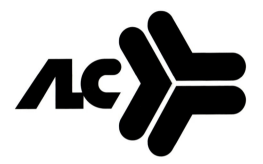

Allens Arthur Robinson

1 **Alitalia**
Compagnia Aerea Italiana SpA,
Air France-KLM SA
Italy, 1969
[Airline]

2 **Alitalia**
Compagnia Aerea Italiana SpA,
Air France-KLM SA
Italy, 2005
[Airline]

3 **AL-KO Kober**
Al-Ko Kober Ltd
UK
[Automotive]

4 **Allegheny Technologies Inc (ATI)**
USA
[Industry]

5 **Allegiance Telecom Inc**
USA
[Telecommunications]

6 **Alleman Cycle Plex**
USA
[Retail]

7 **Allen Lund**
Allen Lund Company Inc
USA
[Freight & Logistics]

8 **Allens Arthur Robinson**
Allens Arthur Robinson Group
Australia
[Professional Services]

9 **Allergan**
Allergan Inc
USA
[Pharmaceuticals]

10 **All-Glass Aquarium**
Aqueon (Central Garden
& Pet Company)
USA
[Pet Products]

ALLIANCE UNICHEM

1

2

3

4

5

6

7

8

9

10

1 **Alliance UniChem**
Alliance UniChem IP Ltd
UK
[Health & Beauty]

2 **Allianz**
Allianz SE
Germany, 1923
Karl Schulpig
[Financial Services]

3 **Allianz**
Allianz SE
Germany, 1999
Claus Koch
[Financial Services]

4 **Allied**
Allied Electronics Inc
USA
[Electronics]

5 **Allied Data Technologies**
Allied Data Technologies BV
Netherlands
[Telecommunications]

6 **Allied Gear**
Allied Gear & Machine Co. Inc
USA
[Tools & Machinery]

7 **Allied Van Lines**
SIRVA Inc
USA
[Transport]

8 **Allison Transmission**
The Carlyle Group LP,
Onex Corporation
USA
[Automotive]

9 **All News Channel**
CONUS Communications
USA
[Media]

10 **Allis-Chambers**
Allis-Chalmers Manufacturing Co.
USA
[Tools & Machinery]

ALOHA AIRLINES

1 **All Seasons Hotels**
Accor SA
France, 2011
W&Cie
[Hospitality]

2 **Allseating**
Canada, 1998
TAXI Toronto
[Office Supplies]

3 **Allstate Insurance**
The Allstate Corporation
USA
[Financial Services]

4 **Allstate Motor Club**
The Allstate Corporation
USA
[Financial Services]

5 **Allume Systems**
Allume Systems Inc
USA
[Computer Software]

6 **Almaty Financial District**
Capital Partners
USA, 2007
Pentagram
[Real Estate]

7 **Almay**
Revlon Inc
USA
[Personal Care]

8 **Almond Joy**
The Hershey Company
USA
[Food & Beverage]

9 **ALNO**
ALNO AG
Germany
[Home Furnishings]

10 **Aloha Airlines**
Aloha Airlines Inc
USA
[Airline]

1. **Alpego**
Alpego Srl
Italy
[Tools & Machinery]

2. **Alpina Eyewear & Helmets**
Alpina Sports GmbH
Germany
[Eyewear]

3. **Alpina Professional Helmets**
Alpina Sports GmbH
Germany
[Sporting Goods]

4. **Alpine**
Alpine Electronics of America Inc
USA
[Consumer Electronics]

▶ 5. **Alpine**
France
[Automotive]

6. **Alpinestars**
Alpinestars SpA
Italy
[Sporting Goods]

7. **Alpura**
Asociación Nacional
de Productores de Leche
Pura SA de CV
Mexico
[Food & Beverage]

8. **Alstom**
Alstom SA
France, 1998
CB'A
[Conglomerate]

9. **Altana**
Altana AG
Germany
[Chemicals & Materials]

10. **Altasfera**
L'Alco Grandi Magazzini SpA
Italy
[Retail]

AMA SUPERBIKE CHAMPIONSHIP

1 **AltaVista**
Yahoo! Inc
USA
[Internet]

2 **AltaVista**
Yahoo! Inc
USA
[Internet]

3 **Altec Lansing**
Altec Lansing Technologies Inc
USA
[Computer & Video Games]

4 **Alternative Bike Co.**
UK, ca 2010
[Bicycles]

5 **Altria**
Altria Group Inc
USA
[Tobacco]

6 **Alvis**
BAE Systems plc
UK
[Automotive]

7 **Alza**
Alza Corporation,
Johnson & Johnson
USA
[Pharmaceuticals]

8 **AMA Motocross Championship**
American Motorcyclist Association
USA
[Sporting Events]

9 **AMA Superbike Championship**
American Motorcyclist Association
USA
[Sporting Events]

AMAZON

1 **Amazon**
Amazon.com Inc
USA, 2000
Turner Duckworth: Anthony Biles
[Internet]

2 **Amazon Kindle**
Amazon.com Inc
USA, 2007
[Consumer Electronics]

3 **Amblin Entertainment**
Amblin Entertainment Inc
USA, 1982
[Film Industry]

4 **AMC (American Movie Classics)**
AMC Networks
USA, 2002
Trollbäck & Company
[Television Channel]

5 **AMC (American Movie Classics)**
AMC Networks
USA, 2007
[Television Channel]

6 **AMC Theatres (American Multi-Cinema)**
AMC Entertainment Inc,
Marquee Holdings Inc
USA
[Cinemas & Theatres]

7 **AMD**
Advanced Micro Devices Inc
USA
[Computer Hardware]

8 **Ameren**
Ameren Corporation
USA, 1998
Kiku Obata & Co.
[Utilities]

9 **American Airlines**
American Airlines Inc
USA, 1967
Massimo Vignelli
[Airline]

AMERICAN FAMILY INSURANCE

1 **American Cancer Society (ACS)**
   USA
   [Societies & Associations]

2 **American Century Investments**
   American Century Proprietary
   Holdings Inc
   USA
   [Financial Services]

3 **American Continental Corporation**
   USA, 1970s
   [Real Estate]

4 **American Diabetes Association**
   USA
   [Societies & Associations]

5 **American Electric Power (AEP)**
   USA
   [Energy]

6 **American Express**
   American Express Company
   USA, 1975
   Lippincott
   [Financial Services]

7 **American Family Insurance**
   American Family Mutual Insurance
   Company
   USA
   [Financial Services]

1 American Film Institute (AFI)
   USA, 1968
   [Foundations & Institutes]

2 American Film Institute (AFI)
   USA
   [Foundations & Institutes]

3 American Folk Art Museum
   USA, 2000
   Pentagram
   [Galleries & Museums]

4 American Heart Association (AHA)
   USA
   [Societies & Associations]

5 American Heart Association (AHA)
   USA
   Lippincott
   [Societies & Associations]

6 American Home Shield
   ServiceMaster
   USA
   [Retail]

7 American Hotel & Motel Association
   USA
   [Societies & Associations]

8 American Idol
   19 TV Ltd, FremantleMedia North America Inc
   USA, 2003
   [Television Programme]

9 American Israel Public Affairs Committee Anniversary
   American Israel Public Affairs Committee (AIPAC)
   USA, 1998
   Beth Singer Design
   [Societies & Associations]

10 American Motors Corporation (AMC)
   USA, 1970
   [Automotive]

AMERICA'S CREDIT UNIONS

1. **American Recording**
   American Recordings,
   Sony Music Entertainment Inc
   USA
   [Music Industry]

2. **American Red Cross (ARC)**
   USA
   [Charity]

3. **American Republic Insurance Company**
   USA, 1964
   Chermayeff & Geismar
   [Financial Services]

4. **American Revolution Bicentennial**
   American Revolution Bicentennial Administration (ARBA)
   USA, 1975
   Chermayeff & Geismar:
   Bruce Blackburn
   [Government]

5. **American Standard Brands**
   USA
   [Home Furnishings]

6. **American States Water Company (AWR)**
   USA
   [Utilities]

7. **American Stores Company**
   USA
   [Retail]

8. **America Online (AOL)**
   AOL Inc
   USA, 1991
   [Internet]

9. **America Online (AOL)**
   AOL Inc
   USA, 2006
   [Internet]

10. **America Online (AOL)**
    AOL Inc
    USA, 2009
    Wolff Olins
    [Internet]

11. **America's Credit Unions**
    Credit Union National Association
    USA, 1999
    [Financial Services]

AMERICA'S TIRE CO.

1 **America's Tire Co.**
The Reinalt-Thomas Corporation
USA
[Automotive]

2 **America Supports You**
United States Department of Defense
USA, 2004
[Defence]

3 **Americhem**
Americhem Inc
USA
[Chemicals & Materials]

4 **AmeriSuites**
Hyatt Hotels Corporation
USA
[Hospitality]

5 **Amersham**
Amersham plc
UK, 2001
Wolff Olins
[Pharmaceuticals]

6 **AMF**
AMF Bowling Centers Inc
USA
[Outdoor & Recreation]

7 **Amgen**
Amgen Inc
USA
[Pharmaceuticals]

8 **Amnesty International**
UK, 1961
Diana Redhouse
[Charity]

9 **Amoco**
Amoco Corporation
USA, 1970
[Industry]

10 **Amoeba Music Inc**
USA, 1990s
[Retail]

1

2

3

4
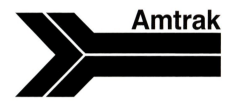

5

6

7

8

9

10

1 **Amora**
Unilever plc/NV
France
[Food & Beverage]

▸ 2 **ampm**
BP America Inc
USA
[Retail]

3 **AMRO Bank**
Netherlands, 1964
Theo Kurpershoek
[Financial Services]

▸ 4 **Amtrak**
National Railroad Passenger Corporation
USA, 1971
Lippincott & Margulies
[Transport]

5 **Amtrak**
National Railroad Passenger Corporation
USA, 2000
OH&CO: Brent Oppenheimer
[Transport]

6 **Analog Clothing**
The Burton Corporation
USA
[Apparel]

7 **Analog Devices**
Analog Devices Inc
USA
[Technology]

8 **Anchor Hocking**
The Anchor Hocking Company
USA, 1976
[Glass & Ceramics]

9 **Anchorman: The Legend of Ron Burgundy**
DreamWorks LLC
USA, 2004
[Film]

▸ 10 **Anco Diamonds**
American Superabrasives Corporation
USA
[Industry]

ANDA INC

1

2

ANDERSEN CONSULTING

3

4

5

6

ANDROID

7

8

9

10

11

1. **Anda Inc**
   USA, ca 1992
   [Pharmaceuticals]

2. **Andersen Consulting**
   USA
   [Professional Services]

3. **Andrews McMeel Universal**
   USA, 1985
   Chermayeff & Geismar:
   Steff Geissbuhler
   [Publishing]

4. **Andritz**
   Andritz Group
   Austria
   [Industry]

5. **Andritz KoneWood**
   Andritz Group
   Austria
   [Industry]

6. **Android**
   Google Inc
   USA
   Ascender Corporation
   [Computer Software]

7. **Android**
   Google Inc
   USA, 2007
   Irina Blok
   [Computer Software]

8. **Angry Birds**
   Rovio Entertainment Ltd
   Finland, 2009
   Rovio
   [Computer & Video Games]

9. **Anheuser-Busch**
   Anheuser-Busch Companies Inc,
   AB InBev
   USA
   [Industry]

10. **Animal Planet**
    Discovery Communications Inc
    USA, 2008
    Dunning Eley Jones
    [Television Channel]

11. **Anixter**
    Anixter Inc
    USA
    [Industry]

ANNE KLEIN

1 **Anne Klein**
JAG Footwear, Accessories
and Retail Corporation,
The Jones Group Inc
USA
[Apparel]

2 **ANPE (Agence Nationale pour l'Emploi)**
France
[Government]

3 **Anthro**
Anthro Corporation
USA
[Office Supplies]

4 **Appalachian League**
USA
[Sport]

5 **Apple Computer Co**
Apple Inc
USA, 1976
Ronald Wayne
[Computer Technology]

6 **Apple**
Apple Inc
USA
[Computer Technology]

7 **Apple**
Apple Inc
USA, 1977
Regis McKenna Advertising:
Rob Janoff
[Computer Technology]

8 **Apple**
Apple Inc
USA, 1998
[Computer Technology]

9 **Apple**
Apple Inc
USA, 1980s
[Computer Technology]

10 **Apple**
Apple Inc
USA, 2003
[Computer Technology]

11 **ara**
ara Shoes AG
Germany
[Footwear]

1 **Aracruz**
Aracruz Celulose SA
Brazil
[Paper Products]

2 **Arai**
Arai Helmet Ltd
Japan
[Motorsport]

3 **Aral**
Aral AG
Germany, 1972
[Retail]

4 **Aramark**
Aramark Corporation
USA, 1994
Schecter Interbrand
[Professional Services]

5 **Arca Racing**
Automobile Racing Club of America
USA
[Motorsport]

6 **Arcares**
Netherlands
[Healthcare]

7 **ArcelorMittal**
ArcelorMittal SA
Luxembourg
[Industrial Products]

8 **Arco**
BP plc
USA
[Oil, Gas & Petroleum]

9 **Arctic Blast**
J&J Snack Foods
USA
[Food & Beverage]

10 **Arena**
Arena Italia SpA
Germany, 1973
[Sporting Goods]

1 **Areva**
Areva SA
France
[Conglomerate]

2 **Argentina**
Ministry of Tourism
Argentina, 2006
Guillermo Brea & Associates:
Alejandro Luna, Carolina Mikalef
[Travel & Tourism]

3 **Argos**
Argos Ltd
UK, 1999
Interbrand Newell & Sorrell
[Retail]

4 **Argos**
Argos Ltd
UK, 2010
The Brand Union
[Retail]

5 **Ariba**
Ariba Inc
USA, 1990s
[Computer Software]

6 **Ariston**
Ariston Thermo SpA
Italy
[Heating & Cooling]

7 **Arla Foods**
Arla Foods amba
Sweden, Denmark, 2000
[Food & Beverage]

8 **Armani Exchange**
Giorgio Armani SpA
USA, 1991
[Retail]

9 **Armani Jeans**
Giorgio Armani SpA
Italy
[Fashion]

10 **Arm & Hammer**
Church & Dwight Co. Inc
USA
[Food & Beverage]

1 Army Black Knights
United States Military Academy at West Point
USA, 1994
[Sport]

2 Army Navy
USA
[Apparel]

3 ARP
ARP Instruments Inc
USA, 1970s
[Musical Instruments]

4 Arrow
Phillips-Van Heusen Corporation
USA, ca 1970
[Apparel]

5 Arsenal Football Club
UK, 2002
[Sport]

6 Arsenal Football Club
UK, 1930
[Sport]

7 Arte (Association Relative à la Télévision Européenne)
Groupe Arte
France/Germany, 2011
[Television Channel]

8 Art Institute of Chicago
USA, 2008
Pentagram: Abbott Miller
[Foundations & Institutes]

9 Asahi Breweries
Asahi Breweries Ltd
Japan
[Breweries]

10 Ashok Leyland
Ashok Leyland Ltd
India
[Automotive]

ASTRIUM

1

2

3

4
Associated British Foods plc

5

6

7

8

9

10

11

1 **Asics**
Asics Ltd
Japan
[Sporting Goods]

▶ 2 **Asics Tiger**
Asics Ltd
Japan
[Sporting Goods]

3 **A Special Wish Foundation**
USA
[Charity]

4 **Associated British Foods plc**
UK
[Food & Beverage]

5 **Associated Press**
USA, 1981
Associated Press
[Media]

6 **Assurant Inc**
USA, 2004
Carbone Smolan Agency
[Financial Services]

7 **Asterix**
Société Dargaud
France
Albert Uderzo
[Publications]

▶ 8 **Aston Martin**
Aston Martin Lagonda Ltd
UK, 1987
[Automotive]

9 **Astra**
SES SA
Luxembourg
[Satellite Television]

10 **AstraZeneca**
AstraZeneca plc
UK, 1999
Interbrand Newell & Sorrell
[Pharmaceuticals]

11 **Astrium**
EADS Space
France, 2000
Landor Associates
[Aerospace]

93

AT&T

1 **AT&T**
   AT&T Inc
   USA, 1983
   Yager & Associates: Saul Bass,
   Jerry Kuyper
   [Telecommunications]

2 **AT&T**
   AT&T Inc
   USA, 2005
   Interbrand
   [Telecommunications]

3 **Atari**
   Atari Interactive, Atari SA
   USA, 1972
   George Opperman
   [Computer & Video Games]

4 **Atari**
   Atari Interactive, Atari SA
   France, 2003
   [Consumer Electronics]

5 **Athens First**
   Synovus Bank
   USA
   [Financial Services]

6 **Athens Stock**
   Helex Group
   Greece
   [Financial Services]

7 **ATI**
   ATI Technologies Inc
   USA
   [Technology]

8 **Atlantic Records**
   Warner Music Group
   USA, 1966
   [Music Industry]

9 **Atlantic Records**
   Warner Music Group
   USA, 2005
   [Music Industry]

AUDI

1 **Atlas Copco AB**
   Sweden
   [Industrial Products]

2 **Atlas Fence**
   Atlas Fence Inc
   USA
   [Security & Safety]

3 **Atlas Schindler**
   Elevadores Atlas Schindler SA
   Brazil
   [Manufacturing]

4 **Atomic Skis**
   Atomic Austria GmbH
   Austria
   [Sporting Goods]

5 **Auchan**
   Groupe Auchan SA,
   Groupe Mulliez
   France
   [Retail]

6 **Audi NSU**
   Audi AG, Volkswagen Group
   Germany, 1969
   [Automotive]

7 **Audi**
   Audi AG, Volkswagen Group
   Germany, 1994
   Sedley Place
   [Automotive]

8 **Audi**
   Audi AG, Volkswagen Group
   Germany, 2009
   Rayan Abdullah
   [Automotive]

AUSTRALIA COUNCIL FOR THE ARTS

1 **Australia Council for the Arts**
Australia
[Government]

2 **Australian Made**
Australia Made Campaign Ltd
Australia, 1986
Ken Cato
[Labelling, Standards
& Certification]

3 **Autodesk**
Autodesk Inc
USA
[Computer Software]

4 **Autodesk**
Autodesk Inc
USA
[Computer Software]

5 **Autodesk Maya**
Autodesk Inc
USA
[Computer Software]

6 **Autogrill**
Autogrill SpA
Italy
[Retail]

7 **Automobile Club of Southern
California**
American Automobile
Association Inc
USA
[Societies & Associations]

▶ 8 **Auto Plus**
Editions Mondadori Axel Springer
France
[Publications]

9 **Autoroutes du Sud de la France
(ASF)**
France
[Transport]

▶ 10 **Auto Value Parts Stores**
USA
[Retail]

AXE

1
2
3
4

5
6
7 AVIREX U.S.A.

8
9

10 AVON
11
12

1 **Avaya**
   Avaya Inc
   USA
   [Telecommunications]

2 **Avenir SAS**
   France
   [Advertising & Campaigns]

3 **Aventis**
   Aventis SA
   France, 1999
   Corporate Branding
   [Pharmaceuticals]

4 **Avery**
   Avery Dennison Corporation
   USA, 1975
   Saul Bass & Associates
   [Office Supplies]

5 **Avid**
   Avid Technology Inc
   USA, 1980s
   [Computer Technology]

6 **Avid**
   Avid Technology Inc
   USA, 2009
   The Brand Union
   [Computer Technology]

7 **Avirex U.S.A**
   USA
   [Apparel]

▶ 8 **Avis Rent a Car**
   Avis Rent a Car System LLC,
   Avis Budget Group Inc
   USA
   [Car Rental]

9 **Aviva**
   Aviva plc
   UK, 2001
   Corporate Edge
   [Financial Services]

10 **Avon**
    Avon Products Inc
    USA
    [Health & Beauty]

11 **AXA**
    AXA SA
    France
    [Financial Services]

12 **Axe**
    Unilever plc/NV
    France
    [Personal Care]

BAA

1. **BAA (British Airport Authority)**
   BAA Ltd
   UK, 1986
   Lloyd Northover
   [Airline]

2. **Babcock**
   Babcock International Group PLC
   UK
   [Professional Services]

3. **Baby Milo**
   Bape (I.T. Group)
   Japan
   [Apparel]

4. **Bacardi**
   Bacardi Ltd
   Cuba, ca 1997
   [Wines, Beers & Spirits]

5. **Baek Sul**
   CJ Corp
   South Korea
   [Food & Beverage]

6. **Baidu**
   Baidu Inc
   China
   [Internet]

7. **Baileys Irish Cream**
   Diageo plc
   Ireland
   [Wines, Beers & Spirits]

8. **Ballard Power Systems**
   Ballard Power Systems Inc
   USA
   [Technology]

9. **Ball Corporation**
   USA
   [Manufacturing]

10. **Ball Park**
    Sara Lee Corporation
    USA
    [Food & Beverage]

11. **Ball Park**
    The Hillshire Brands Company
    USA
    [Food & Beverage]

BALTIC

BANANA REPUBLIC

BAND-AID

1 **Bally**
Bally Technologies Inc
USA, 1968
[Leisure & Entertainment]

2 **Baltic**
Baltic Centre for
Contemporary Art
UK, 1998
Henrik Nygren Design,
Greger Ulf Nilson
[Galleries & Museums]

3 **Ban**
KAO Brands Company
USA
[Personal Care]

4 **Banamex**
Grupo Financiero Banamex
SA de CV, Citigroup Inc
Mexico
Lippincott
[Financial Services]

5 **Banana Republic**
The Gap Inc
USA
[Retail]

6 **Banco del Pacifico**
Ecuador, 1972
Versus: Peter Mussfeldt
[Financial Services]

7 **Bandai**
Namco Bandai Co. Ltd,
Namco Bandai Holdings Inc
Japan
[Computer & Video Games]

8 **Band-Aid**
Johnson & Johnson
USA, 2006
[Personal Care]

9 **Bands of America**
Music for All Inc
USA
[Music]

BANG & OLUFSEN

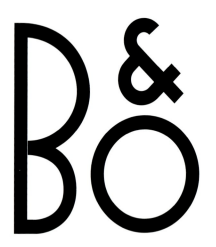

1. **Bang & Olufsen**
   Bang & Olufsen A/S
   Denmark
   [Consumer Electronics]

2. **BankBoston**
   USA
   [Financial Services]

3. **Bankgesellschaft Berlin**
   Germany
   [Financial Services]

4. **Bank of America**
   Bank of America Corporation
   USA, 1998
   Enterprise IG
   [Financial Services]

5. **Bank of Beijing**
   Bank of Beijing Co. Ltd
   China
   [Financial Services]

6. **Bank of China**
   Bank of China Ltd
   China
   [Financial Services]

7. **Bank of Montreal/
   Banque de Montréal**
   Canada, 1967
   Stewart & Morrison: Hans Kleefeld
   [Financial Services]

8. **Bank of the West**
   BNP Paribas SA
   USA
   [Financial Services]

9. **Bank Pekao**
   Bank Pekao SA
   Poland, 1997
   Mars & Venus
   [Financial Services]

1   **Banner Health**
    USA
    [Healthcare]

2   **Banner of Peace**
    Pax Cultura
    USA, 1931
    Nicholas Roerich
    [Societies & Associations]

3   **Banque Royale**
    Royal Bank of Canada
    Canada
    [Financial Services]

4   **Barack Obama Presidential Campaign**
    USA, 2007
    Sender
    [Political]

5   **Barbie**
    Mattel Inc
    USA, 1990
    [Toys, Games & Models]

6   **Barbie**
    Mattel Inc
    USA, 2004
    [Toys, Games & Models]

7   **Barbie**
    Mattel Inc
    USA, 1959/2009
    [Toys, Games & Models]

8   **Barbie**
    Mattel Inc
    USA, 1975
    [Toys, Games & Models]

9   **Barclaycard**
    Barclays plc
    UK, 2009
    The Brand Union
    [Financial Services]

10 **Barclays**
    Barclays plc
    UK, 1981
    John York
    [Financial Services]

▶11 **Barclays**
    Barclays plc
    UK, 2004
    Williams Murray Hamm
    [Financial Services]

BARCLAYS PREMIER LEAGUE

1 **Barclays Premier League**
The Football Association
Premier League Ltd
UK
[Sport]

2 **Barco**
Barco NV
Belgium
[Technology]

3 **BARD**
C.R. Bard Inc
USA
[Medical Devices]

4 **Barnes & Noble**
Barns & Noble Inc
USA
[Retail]

5 **Barneys New York**
USA, 1981
Chermayeff & Geismar:
Steff Geissbuhler
[Retail]

6 **BASF**
BASF SE
Germany, 2004
Interbrand Zintzmeyer & Lux
[Chemicals & Materials]

7 **Baskin-Robbins**
Baskin-Robbins Inc,
Dunkin' Brands Group Inc
USA, 1994
Lippincott & Margulies
[Restaurants & Bars]

8 **Baskin-Robbins**
Baskin-Robbins Inc,
Dunkin' Brands Group Inc
USA, 2006
[Restaurants & Bars]

BAUSCH + LOMB

1

2

3

4

5

6
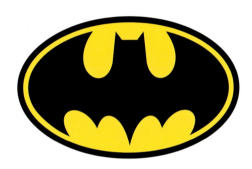

7

8
![Bausch & Lomb]

9
![BAUSCH + LOMB]

1 **Bassetti**
Vincenzo Zucchi SpA
Italy
[Fabrics & Textiles]

2 **Bata Shoes**
Bata Brands Sarl
Switzerland
[Footwear]

3 **Batavo**
BRF Brasil Foods SA
Brazil
[Food & Beverage]

4 **Batelco**
Bahrain Telecommunication Company BSC
Bahrain, 2010
FutureBrand
[Telecommunications]

5 **Batelco**
Bahrain Telecommunication Company BSC
Bahrain, 2010
FutureBrand
[Telecommunications]

6 **Batman**
DC Comics Inc, Warner Bros Entertainment Inc
USA
[Publications]

7 **Bauknecht**
Bauknecht Hausgeräte GmbH
Germany
[Home Appliances]

8 **Bausch + Lomb**
Bausch & Lomb Inc
USA, 2004
FutureBrand
[Eyewear]

9 **Bausch + Lomb**
Bausch & Lomb Inc
USA, 2010
Pentagram: Paula Scher, Lisa Kitschenberg
[Eyewear]

103

BAYER

1 **Bayer**
Bayer AG
Germany, 2002
Claus Koch
[Pharmaceuticals]

2 **Bayerischer Rundfunk (BR)**
Bayerischer Rundfunk
Germany, 1962
Richard Roth
[Broadcaster]

3 **Bayerischer Rundfunk (BR)**
Bayerischer Rundfunk
Germany, 1968
[Broadcaster]

4 **Bayerischer Rundfunk (BR)**
Bayerischer Rundfunk
Germany, 2007
[Broadcaster]

5 **Baygon**
S. C. Johnson & Son Inc
USA
[Agricultural]

▶ 6 **Baywatch**
Baywatch Production Company
USA, 1989
[Television Series]

7 **BBC (British Broadcasting Corporation)**
UK, 1997
Martin Lambie-Nairn
[Television Channel]

8 **BBDO**
BBDO, Omnicom Group
USA, 2012
[Advertising & Campaigns]

9 **Bburago**
May Cheong Group
Italy, 1976
[Toys, Games & Models]

10 **BBVA**
BBVA (Banco Bilbao Vizcaya Argentaria SA)
Spain
[Financial Services]

11 **BDNA**
USA, 2008
Pentagram
[Information Technology]

▶ 12 **Bear Stearns**
The Bear Stearns Companies Inc
USA
[Financial Services]

BENEFON

1

2

3

4

5

6

7

8

9

10

11

12

1 **Beghelli**
Beghelli SpA
Italy
[Technology]

2 **Behringer**
MUSIC Group IP Ltd
Germany
[Music Industry]

3 **Behrmann Motors**
Les Moteurs Reunis SA
Haiti
[Retail]

4 **Beiersdorf**
Beiersdorf AG
Germany
[Manufacturing]

5 **Bell Canada**
BCE Inc
Canada, 1994
Bell Canada
[Telecommunications]

6 **Bell System**
American Telephone
and Telegraph Company
USA, 1889
Angus S. Hibbard
[Telecommunications]

7 **Bell System**
AT&T (American Telephone
& Telegraph Company)
USA, 1921
[Telecommunications]

8 **Bell System**
AT&T (American Telephone
& Telegraph Company)
USA, 1964
[Telecommunications]

9 **Bell System**
AT&T Corporation
USA, 1969
Saul Bass & Associates
[Telecommunications]

10 **Bench**
Americana International Ltd
UK
[Apparel]

11 **Bendix**
Bendix Corporation
USA, 1966
Lippincott & Margulies
[Manufacturing]

12 **Benefon**
Benefon Oyj
Finland
[Telecommunications]

BENETTON

1 **Benetton**
Benetton Group SpA
Italy
[Fashion]

2 **Ben Hogan**
Calloway Golf Company
USA
[Sporting Goods]

3 **Benjamin Moore Paints**
Benjamin Moore & Co
USA
[Paints & Coatings]

4 **Ben & Jerry's**
Unilever plc/NV
USA
[Food & Beverage]

5 **Bennigan's**
Bennigan's Franchising Company LLC
USA, 1990s
[Restaurants & Bars]

6 **BenQ**
Qisda Corporation
Taiwan
[Consumer Electronics]

7 **Ben Sherman**
Ben Sherman Group Ltd
UK
[Apparel]

8 **Bentley**
Bentley Motors Ltd, Volkswagen Group
UK
[Automotive]

9 **Berjaya Air**
Berjaya Group
Malaysia
[Airline]

10 **Berlitz**
Berlitz Corporation
Japan, USA
[Education]

BEYERDYNAMIC

1 **Bertazzoni**
Bertazzoni SpA
Italy, 2007
Pentagram
[Kitchenware]

2 **Bertone**
Stile Bertone SpA
Italy
[Automotive]

3 **Best Buy**
Best Buy Co. Inc
USA, 1994
[Retail]

4 **Best Western**
Best Western International Inc
USA, 1993
[Hospitality]

5 **Betten**
Betten Trucks Inc
USA
[Automotive]

6 **Better Business Bureau (BBB)**
USA/Canada
[Societies & Associations]

7 **Better Business Bureau (BBB)**
USA/Canada
[Societies & Associations]

8 **Betty Crocker**
General Mills Inc
USA, 1950s
Lippincott
[Food & Beverage]

9 **Beyerdynamic**
Beyerdynamic GmbH & Co. KG
Germany
[Electronics]

BFGOODRICH TIRES

1 **BFGoodrich Tires**
Goodrich Corporation
USA
[Automotive]

2 **BFI Canada**
Progressive Waste Solutions Ltd
Canada
[Public Services]

3 **BHP**
Broken Hill Proprietary
Company Ltd
Australia
[Mining]

4 **BHS (British Home Stores)**
BHS Ltd
UK, 1995
[Retail]

5 **BIC**
Société BIC
France, 1962
Raymond Savignac
[Writing Products]

6 **Big Boy**
Big Boy Restaurants
International LLC
USA
Ben Washam
[Restaurants & Bars]

7 **Big Deal**
Var nv
Belgium
[Advertising & Campaigns]

8 **Big Kmart**
Sears Holdings Corporation
USA, 1997
[Retail]

9 **Big Websites**
South Africa
[Internet]

10 **Bild**
Axel Springer AG
Germany
[Publications]

1 **Billabong**
Billabong International Ltd
Australia
[Sporting Goods]

2 **Billboard**
Prometheus Global Media
USA
[Publications]

3 **Binatone**
Binatone Industries Ltd
UK
[Consumer Electronics]

4 **Bing**
Microsoft Corporation
USA, 2009
Razorfish
[Internet]

5 **Biohazard**
The Dow Chemical Company
USA, 1966
[Labelling, Standards & Certification]

6 **Biotherm**
L'Oréal SA
France
[Personal Care]

7 **Birds Eye**
Birds Eye Iglo Group Ltd (BEIG)
UK, 1940s
[Food & Beverage]

8 **Birkenstock**
Birkenstock Orthopädie GmbH & Co. KG
Germany
[Footwear]

9 **Bisquick**
General Mills Inc
USA, 2004
[Food & Beverage]

10 **Björk**
One Little Indian Records
UK, 1990s
[Music]

BLACKBERRY

1

2

3

4

5

6

7

8

9

1 **BlackBerry**
Research In Motion Ltd (RIM)
Canada
[Consumer Electronics]

2 **Black Crows**
France
Yorgo Tloupas
[Sporting Goods]

3 **Black & Decker**
Stanley Black & Decker Inc
USA, 2000
[Tools & Machinery]

4 **Blackwater**
Academi
USA
[Safety & Security]

5 **Blaupunkt**
Blaupunkt GmbH
Germany
[Consumer Electronics]

6 **Blimpie**
Kahala Corporation
USA, 2005
[Restaurants & Bars]

7 **Blimpie**
Kahala Corporation
USA, 2009
[Restaurants & Bars]

8 **Blizzard Entertainment**
Activision Blizzard Inc
USA
[Computer & Video Games]

9 **Blockbuster**
Blockbuster Inc
USA
Sandy Cook
[Retail]

1. **Blogger**
Google Inc
USA
[Internet]

2. **Bloomberg**
Bloomberg LP
USA
[Media]

3. **Bloomingdale's**
Macy's Inc
USA, 1975
Vignelli Associates
[Retail]

4. **Blue Band**
Unilever plc/NV
UK/Netherlands
[Food & Beverage]

5. **Blue Cross Animal Hospital**
Canada
[Charity]

6. **Blue Cross Blue Shield Association**
USA
[Societies & Associations]

7. **BlueScope Steel**
Australia
[Industrial Products]

8. **Blue Seal**
Kent Nutrition Group Inc
USA
[Pet Products]

9. **Blue Shield of California**
USA
[Healthcare]

10. **Bluetooth**
Bluetooth SIG
USA, 1998
[Technology]

1. **Bluewater**
Prudential plc,
Lend Lease Europe Ltd,
Lend Lease Retail Partnership,
Hermes Real Estate
UK, 1999
Minale Tattersfield
[Retail]

2. **Blu-ray Disc**
Blu-ray Disc Association
USA
[Consumer Electronics]

3. **bmi (British Midland International)**
International Airlines Group
UK
[Airline]

▶ 4. **BMW**
BMW AG
Germany, 1979
Franz Josef Popp
[Automotive]

5. **BMW Williams F1**
BMW AG, Williams Grand Prix
Engineering Ltd
Germany/UK, 2000
[Motorsport]

6. **BNI (Bahrain National Insurance)**
Bahrain National Holding Company
Bahrain
[Financial Services]

7. **BNP Paribas**
BNP Paribas SA
France
[Financial Services]

8. **Boards of Canada**
Warp Records Ltd
UK, 1990s
The Designers Republic
[Music]

BOISE CASCADE CORPORATION

1 **Bobcat**
Bobcat Company, Doosan Group
USA, ca 2007
[Industry]

2 **Boboli**
Bimbo Bakeries USA Inc
USA
[Food & Beverage]

3 **Boca Juniors**
Club Atletico Boca Juniors
Argentina, 2007
Diseño Shakespear
[Sport]

4 **Böckling**
Böckling GmbH & Co. KG
Germany
[Glass & Ceramics]

5 **Bodum**
Bodum AG
Denmark
[Kitchenware]

6 **Body Glove**
Body Glove International LLC,
Dive N' Surf Corporation
USA, 1960s
Bill Meistrell
[Sporting Goods]

7 **Boehringer Ingelheim**
Boehringer Ingelheim GmbH,
C.H. Boehringer Sohn AG & Co. KG
Germany, 1997
MetaDesign: Ole Schäfer
[Pharmaceuticals]

8 **Boeing**
The Boeing Company
USA, 1997
Rick Eiber
[Aerospace]

9 **Boffi SpA**
Italy
[Home Furnishings]

10 **Boise Cascade Corporation**
Boise Cascade Holdings LLC
USA, 2002
Siegel+Gale
[Paper Products]

BOLLÉ

1 **Bollé**
   Bushnell Outdoor Products Europe
   France
   [Eyewear]

2 **Bollinger**
   Bollinger Industries LP
   USA
   [Fitness & Wellbeing]

3 **Bombardier**
   Bombardier Inc
   Canada
   [Aerospace]

4 **Bombardier**
   Bombardier Inc
   Canada
   [Aerospace]

5 **Bonaqua**
   The Coca-Cola Company
   USA
   [Food & Beverage]

6 **BonBon-Land**
   BonBon-Land A/S
   Denmark
   [Theme Parks]

7 **Bondo**
   3M Company
   USA
   [Household Products]

8 **Book of Faith**
   Augsburg Fortress
   USA, 2008
   Spunk Design Machine
   [Foundations & Institutes]

9 **Books-A-Million**
   Books-A-Million Inc
   USA
   [Retail]

BORUSSIA DORTMUND

1 **Boost Mobile**
Sprint Nextel Corporation
USA
[Telecommunications]

2 **Boost Mobile**
Sprint Nextel Corporation
USA, 2008
Attik
[Telecommunications]

3 **Boots**
Boots UK Ltd,
Alliance Boots GmbH
UK, 1883
Jesse Boot
[Retail]

4 **Boots Healthcare International (BHI)**
Boots Group plc
UK
[Healthcare]

5 **Borden Foods**
Borden Food Corporation
USA
[Industry]

6 **Borders**
Borders Group Inc
USA
Lippincott
[Retail]

7 **Boréale**
Les Brasseurs du Nord
Canada
[Wines, Beers & Spirits]

8 **BorgWarner**
BorgWarner Inc
USA
[Automotive]

9 **Borland**
Borland Software Corporation,
Micro Focus International plc
USA
[Computer Software]

10 **Boron Gas Station**
Standard Oil of Ohio
USA
[Retail]

11 **Borussia Dortmund**
Ballspielverein Borussia 09 eV
Dortmund
Germany
SoDesign
[Sport]

1 **Bos**
Bos Auspuff GmbH
Germany
[Automotive]

2 **Bosal**
Bosal International SA/NV
Belgium
[Automotive]

▶ 3 **Bosch**
Robert Bosch GmbH
Germany, 2004
United Designers Network:
Erik Spiekermann
[Tools & Machinery]

▶ 4 **Bosch Service**
Robert Bosch GmbH
Germany, 1918
Robert Bosch
[Tools & Machinery]

5 **Bose**
Bose Corporation
USA, 1960s
[Consumer Electronics]

6 **Boss**
Boss Corporation, Roland Corporation
Japan, 1973
[Musical Instruments]

7 **Boston Acoustics**
D&M Holdings Inc
USA
[Consumer Electronics]

8 **Boston Whaler**
Boston Whaler Inc
USA
[Marine]

▶ 9 **Bouygues Telecom**
Bouygues SA
France
[Telecommunications]

10 **Bowne**
Bowne & Co. Inc,
RR Donnelley & Sons Company
USA
[Professional Services]

11 **Boy Scouts of America**
USA
[Societies & Associations]

BRASIL

1 **Boys & Girls Clubs of America (BGCA)**
USA, 1980
[Societies & Associations]

2 **BP**
BP plc
UK, 2000
Landor Associates
[Oil, Gas & Petroleum]

3 **Brabantia**
Brabantia Branding BV
Netherlands
[Household Products]

4 **Bradlees**
Bradlees Department Stores Inc
USA
[Retail]

5 **Braggin Waggon**
RFR Inc
USA
[Automotive]

6 **Brains**
SA Brain & Co. Ltd
UK
[Wines, Beers & Spirits]

7 **Brand Channel**
Brandchannel.com,
Interbrand/Omnicom Group
USA
[Television Channel]

8 **Brasil**
Embratur (Empresa Brasileira de Turismo)
Brazil, 2005
Kiko Farkas
[Travel & Tourism]

BRAUN

1 **Braun**
Braun GmbH
Germany, 1952
Wolfgang Schmittel
[Consumer Electronics]

2 **Bravo**
NBCUniversal Media LLC
USA, 2004
Open
[Television Channel]

3 **Breitling**
Breitling SA
Switzerland
[Watches & Jewelry]

4 **Brembo**
Brembo SpA
Italy
[Automotive]

▶ 5 **Bremykt**
Fjordland A/S
Norway
[Food & Beverage]

6 **Breyers**
Good Humor-Breyers USA,
Unilever plc/NV
USA
[Food & Beverage]

▶ 7 **Bridgestone**
Bridgestone Corporation
Japan, 2011
[Automotive]

8 **Brill**
HC Brill Company Inc
USA
[Food & Beverage]

BRITISH AMERICAN TOBACCO

1

2

3

4

5

6

7

8

1 **Brinks**
   Brink's Inc
   USA
   [Safety & Security]

2 **Brinks**
   Brink's Inc
   USA
   [Safety & Security]

3 **Bristol-Myers Squibb**
   Bristol-Myers Squibb Company
   USA, ca 1989
   [Pharmaceuticals]

4 **Brita**
   Brita GmbH
   Germany
   [Household Products]

5 **Britain**
   Visit Britain
   UK
   [Travel & Tourism]

6 **British Airways**
   British Airways plc
   UK, 1997
   Interbrand Newell & Sorrell
   [Airline]

7 **British Airways**
   British Airways plc
   UK, 1984
   Landor Associates
   [Airline]

8 **British American Tobacco**
   British American Tobacco plc
   UK
   [Tobacco]

BRITISH COUNCIL

1

2

3

4

5

6

7

8

9
Broil King

1   **British Council**
    UK
    [Charity]

2   **British Gas**
    British Gas plc
    UK, 2012
    CHI & Partners
    [Oil, Gas & Petroleum]

3   **British Rail**
    UK, 1965
    Design Research Unit:
    Gerry Barney
    [Transport]

4   **British Steel**
    British Steel plc
    UK
    [Industry]

5   **British Telecom**
    BT Group plc
    UK, 1980
    Banks & Miles
    [Telecommunications]

6   **British Waterways**
    UK, 2004
    Design Bridge
    [Conservation & Environment]

7   **Broadcom**
    Broadcom Corporation
    USA
    [Technology]

▶ 8 **Broan**
    Broan-NuTone LLC
    USA
    [Heating & Cooling]

9   **Broil King**
    Onward Manufacturing
    Company Ltd
    Canada
    [Kitchenware]

1 **Broncoway Software Solutions**
   Armenia
   [Computer Software]

2 **Brondi**
   Brondi SpA
   Italy
   [Consumer Electronics]

3 **Brother**
   Brother Industries Ltd
   Japan
   [Office Supplies]

4 **Browning**
   USA
   [Firearms]

5 **Bruno's Supermarkets**
   Southern Family Markets,
   C&S Wholesale Grocers
   USA
   [Retail]

6 **Brunswick**
   Brunswick Corporation
   USA
   [Conglomerate]

7 **Brussels Airlines**
   Belgium, 2007
   Hoet & Hoet
   [Airline]

8 **Brut**
   Unilever plc/NV
   USA
   [Personal Care]

9 **Bryant**
   Bryant Heating & Cooling
   Systems Inc
   USA
   [Heating & Cooling]

10 **Bryant Homes**
   Taylor Wimpey plc
   UK
   [Construction]

1   **BT**
    BT Group plc
    UK, 1991
    Wolff Olins
    [Telecommunications]

2   **BT – Connected World**
    BT Group plc
    UK, 2003
    Wolff Olins
    [Telecommunications]

3   **BTI (Battery Technology Inc)**
    USA
    [Electronics]

4   **Bticino**
    Legrand Group SA
    Italy
    [Consumer Electronics]

5   **BTMU**
    The Bank of Tokyo-Mitsubishi UFJ Ltd
    Japan
    [Financial Services]

6   **Bubble Tape**
    William Wrigley Jr. Company, Mars Inc
    USA
    [Food & Beverage]

7   **Buck Knives**
    Buck Knives Inc
    USA
    [Knives]

8   **Buck Knives**
    Buck Knives Inc
    USA
    [Knives]

BUGATTI

1 **Bud**
Anheuser-Busch InBev NV
USA
[Wines, Beers & Spirits]

2 **Budget Host Inn**
Budget Host Inns & Hotels
USA
[Hospitality]

3 **Budget Rent A Car**
Budget Rent A Car System Inc
USA
[Car Rental]

4 **Bud Light**
Anheuser-Busch InBev NV
USA
[Wines, Beers & Spirits]

5 **Budweiser**
Anheuser-Busch InBev NV
USA, 2011
[Wines, Beers & Spirits]

6 **Budweiser Budvar Brewery**
Budějovickým Budvarem NC
Czech Republic
[Breweries]

7 **Bugaboo**
Bugaboo International BV
Netherlands
[Baby Products]

8 **Bugatti**
Bugatti Automobiles SAS,
Volkswagen Group
France
[Automotive]

BULAVTO

1 BührmannUbbens
   The Netherlands, 2004
   TelDesign
   [Paper Products]

2 Buick
   General Motors Company
   USA, 1990s
   [Automotive]

3 Buick
   General Motors Company
   USA, 2002
   [Automotive]

4 BuildersSquare
   Builder's Square Inc
   USA
   [Internet]

5 Building One at Atlantic Yards
   Forest City Ratner Companies
   USA, 2008
   Pentagram
   [Real Estate]

6 BuiltGreen
   Canada
   [Labelling, Standards
   & Certification]

7 Buitoni
   Nestlé SA
   Italy
   [Food & Beverage]

8 Bulauto
   Bulauto JSC
   Bulgaria
   [Automotive]

BVLGARI

BULLOCK'S

BULOVA

1 **Bulgari**
Bulgari SpA, LVMH Moët
Hennessy Louis Vuitton SA
Italy
[Watches & Jewelry]

2 **Bull**
Bull SAS
France
[Computer Technology]

3 **Bullock's Department Store**
Macy's Inc
USA
[Retail]

4 **Bulova Watches**
Bulova Corporation
USA
[Watches & Jewelry]

5 **Bundesgartenschau
(Federal Garden Expo)**
Germany
Helmut Langer
[Events]

6 **Bundeswehr**
Federal Defence
Forces of Germany
Germany
[Defence]

7 **Bunn**
Bunn-O-Matic Corporation
Canada
[Kitchenware]

1

2

3

4

5
burdines

6
Burdines

1 **Bunn-O-Matic**
Bunn-O-Matic Corporation
Canada
[Kitchenware]

2 **Buongiorno**
Buongiorno SpA
Italy
[Design]

▶ 3 **Burberry**
Burberry Group plc
UK
[Fashion]

4 **Burberry**
Burberry Group plc
UK, 1901
[Fashion]

5 **Burdines**
Federated Department
Stores Inc
USA
[Retail]

6 **Burdines**
Federated Department
Stores Inc
USA
[Retail]

BURLINGTON COAT FACTORY

1 **Bureau Veritas**
   Bureau Veritas SA
   France, 1829
   Achille Deveria
   [Professional Services]

▶ 2 **Burger King**
   Burger King Holdings Inc
   USA, 1994
   [Food & Beverage]

3 **Burger King**
   Burger King Holdings Inc
   USA, 1999
   Sterling Brands
   [Restaurants & Bars]

4 **Burgopapers**
   Burgo Group SpA
   Italy
   [Paper Products]

5 **Burlington Coat Factory**
   Burlington Coat Factory
   Warehouse Corporation,
   Bain Capital LLC
   USA
   [Retail]

6 **Burlington Coat Factory**
   Burlington Coat Factory
   Warehouse Corporation,
   Bain Capital LLC
   USA
   [Retail]

BURLINGTON NORTHERN RAILROAD

1

2

3

4

5

6

7

1   **Burlington Northern Railroad**
    Burlington Northern Santa Fe
    Corporation, Berkshire
    Hathaway Inc
    USA
    [Transport]

2   **Burnham**
    U.S. Boiler Company Inc
    USA
    [Heating & Cooling]

3   **Burton**
    Burton Snowboards Inc
    USA
    [Sporting Goods]

4   **Busch**
    Anheuser-Busch Companies Inc,
    AB InBev
    USA
    [Wines, Beers & Spirits]

▶ 5 **BusinessWeek**
    Bloomberg LP
    USA
    [Media]

6   **Buster Brown**
    Brown Shoe Company Inc
    USA
    [Footwear]

7   **BUT**
    BUT International
    France
    [Retail]

1 **Butlins**
Bourne Leisure Ltd
UK, 1999
[Hospitality]

2 **Butlins**
Bourne Leisure Ltd
UK, 2010
[Leisure & Entertainment]

3 **Butterfly**
Germany
[Sport goods]

4 **Butternut Breads**
Hostess Brands Inc
USA
[Food & Beverage]

5 **Buy 'N Large**
WALL•E (film), Pixar Animation Studios, The Walt Disney Company
USA, 2008
[Film]

6 **Buzzcocks**
UK, 1977
Malcolm Garrett
[Music]

7 **BVD (Bradley, Voorhees & Day)**
Berkshire Hathaway Inc
USA
[Apparel]

C-D

C&A

1. **C&A**
   Cofra Holding AG
   Belgium/Germany, 2011
   Saffron Brand Consultants
   [Apparel]

2. **CA Computer Associates**
   Computer Associates Inc
   USA, 2001
   Landor Associates
   [Computer Software]

3. **CA**
   CA Technologies Inc
   USA, 2005
   Sequel Studio
   [Computer Software]

4. **CAA (Canadian Automobile Association)**
   Canada
   [Societies & Associations]

5. **Cabela's**
   Cabela's Inc
   USA, ca 1961
   [Retail]

6. **CablesOne**
   CablesOne Company
   Brunei
   [Professional Services]

7. **Cable & Wireless**
   Cable & Wireless Worldwide plc
   UK, 1986
   [Telecommunications]

8. **Cable & Wireless Communications**
   Cable & Wireless Communications plc
   UK, 2010
   Elmwood
   [Telecommunications]

9. **Cable & Wireless Worldwide**
   Cable & Wireless Worldwide plc
   UK, 2010
   TBD
   [Telecommunications]

10. **Cadbury**
    Kraft Foods
    UK
    [Food & Beverage]

CALGARY COWBOYS

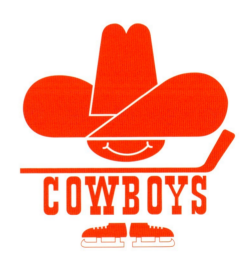

1 **Cadillac**
General Motors Company
USA, 1999
Anne-Marie LaVerge-Webb
[Automotive]

2 **Caesars Entertainment**
Hamlet Holdings
USA, 2010
[Leisure & Entertainment]

3 **Caesers Palace**
Caesars Entertainment
Corporation, Hamlet Holdings
USA, 1968
[Leisure & Entertainment]

4 **Café de Colombia**
Federación Nacional
de Cafeteros de Colombia
Colombia, ca 1981
DDB Worldwide
[Agricultural]

5 **Cailler of Switzerland**
Switzerland
[Food & Beverage]

6 **Caja Madrid**
Bankia SA
Spain
[Financial Services]

7 **Calberson**
SNCF Geodis
France
[Freight & Logistics]

8 **Cal Fed**
California Federal Bank
USA
[Financial Services]

9 **Calgary Cowboys**
World Hockey Association (WHA)
Canada, 1975
[Sport]

1 **California Academy of Sciences**
 USA, 2007
 Pentagram
 [Galleries & Museums]

2 **California Peaches, Plums, Nectarines**
 California Tree Fruit Agreement
 USA
 [Labelling, Standards & Certification]

3 **California Side Car Inc**
 USA
 [Automotive]

4 **California State Parks seal**
 California Department of Parks and Recreation
 USA
 [Outdoor & Recreation]

5 **California Water Service Co.**
 California Water Service Group
 USA
 [Utilities]

6 **Call 911 Emergency**
 National Emergency Number Association (NENA)
 USA
 [Societies & Associations]

7 **Callaway Golf**
 Callaway Golf Company
 USA
 [Sporting Goods]

8 **Callon Petroleum Company**
 USA
 [Oil, Gas & Petroleum]

9 **Caltex**
 Chevron Corporation
 USA, ca 1987
 [Industry]

1 **Caltrans**
California Department
of Transportation
USA, 1973
Dave Douglas
[Transport]

2 **Calvin Klein**
Calvin Klein Inc, PVH Corp
USA
[Fashion]

3 **ck Calvin Klein**
Calvin Klein Inc, PVH Corp
USA
[Fashion]

4 **Cam**
Cam SpA
Italy
[Baby Products]

5 **Camel**
R. J. Reynolds Tobacco Company
USA
[Tobacco]

6 **Campanile**
Louvre Hotels Group
France
[Hospitality]

7 **Campari**
Davide Campari-Milano SpA
Italy
[Wines, Beers & Spirits]

8 **Campbell's**
Campbell Soup Company
USA, ca 1900
[Food & Beverage]

CAMPER

1 **Camper**
Spain, 1981
[Footwear]

2 **Camping World**
Affinity Group Inc
USA
[Outdoor & Recreation]

3 **CAMPSA (Compañia Arrendataria del Monopolio del Petróleo SA)**
Spain
[Industry]

4 **Canada Dry**
Dr Pepper Snapple Group Inc
USA, 2009
[Food & Beverage]

5 **Canada Post**
Canada Post Corporation, Crown Corporation
Canada
[Mail Services]

6 **Canada Trust**
CT Financial Services Inc
Canada
[Financial Services]

7 **Canada Tsuga**
Japan/Canada
[Labelling, Standards & Certification]

8 **Canadian Airlines**
Canadian Airlines International Ltd
Canada, 1999
Landor Associates
[Airline]

▶ 9 **Canadian Natural**
Canadian Natural Resources Ltd
Canada
[Oil, Gas & Petroleum]

136

1 **Canadian Pacific Railway**
   Canadian Pacific Railway Ltd
   Canada
   [Transport]

2 **Canadian Paediatric Society**
   Canada
   [Societies & Associations]

3 **Canal+**
   Groupe Canal+, Vivendi SA
   France, 1995
   [Television Channel]

4 **CanalSat**
   Vivendi SA
   France, 2011
   Nude
   [Satellite Television]

5 **Canderel**
   The Merisant Company
   USA
   Team Créatif
   [Food & Beverage]

6 **Candia**
   France
   [Food & Beverage]

7 **Candy**
   Candy Group
   Italy
   [Home Appliances]

8 **Cannondale**
   Cannondale Bicycle Corporation
   USA
   [Bicycles]

9 **Canon**
   Canon Inc
   Japan, 1956
   [Consumer Electronics]

CANSON

1 **Canson**
France
[Paper Products]

2 **Canteen**
Canteen Vending,
Compass Group USA
USA
[Industrial Products]

3 **Canterbury**
Canterbury Ltd
UK
[Sporting Goods]

4 **Caparol**
Caparol Farben Lacke
Bautenschutz GmbH
Germany, 1984
Luigi Colani
[Paints and Coatings]

▶ 5 **Cap Gemini Ernst & Young**
Cap Gemini SA
France
[Professional Services]

6 **Capitol Records**
Capitol Music Group
USA
[Music Industry]

▶ 7 **Caradislac**
Car & Boat Media SAS
France, ca 2000
[Internet]

8 **Carambar**
Kraft Foods
France
[Food & Beverage]

9 **Cardinal Health**
Cardinal Health Inc
USA
[Healthcare]

CARNET

1. **Cargill**
Cargill Ltd
Canada, 1966
Sandgren & Murtha: Don Ervin
[Agricultural]

2. **Cargill**
Cargill Ltd
Canada, 2002
Franke+Fiorella: Craig Franke
[Agricultural]

3. **Cargolux**
Cargolux International Airlines SA
Luxembourg
[Airline]

4. **Carhartt**
Carhartt Inc
USA
[Apparel]

5. **Carlisle**
Carlisle Companies Inc
USA
[Conglomerate]

6. **Carlsberg**
Carlsberg Group
Denmark, 2011
Office
[Wines, Beers & Spirits]

7. **Carl's Jr.**
CKE Restaurants Inc
USA, 1997
[Food & Beverage]

8. **Carnation**
Nestlé SA
USA
[Food & Beverage]

9. **Carnet**
Promoción y Operación SA de CV
Mexico
[Financial Services]

CAROLCO

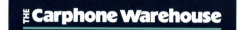

1 **Carolco**
Carolco Pictures Inc
USA
[Film Industry]

2 **Carphone Warehouse**
Carphone Warehouse Group plc
UK
[Retail]

3 **Carquest Auto Parts**
Carquest Corporation
USA
[Retail]

4 **Carré Bleu**
Blue Square International
France
[Construction]

5 **Carrefour**
Carrefour SA
France, 2009
Wolff Olins: Miles Newlyn
[Retail]

6 **Carrier**
Carrier Corporation,
United Technologies Corporation
USA
[Heating & Cooling]

7 **Cartier**
Cartier SA
France
[Watches & Jewelry]

8 **Cartier**
Cartier SA
France
[Watches & Jewelry]

9 **Cartoon Network**
Turner Broadcasting System Inc,
Time Warner
USA, 1992
[Television Channel]

CASTROL MOTOR OIL

Castle Alternative Invest AG

1 **Cartoon Network**
Turner Broadcasting System Inc,
Time Warner
USA, 2010
Brand New School, Cartoon Network
[Television Channel]

2 **CASA**
CASA International NV
Belgium
[Home Furnishings]

3 **Cash Station**
Star Networks Inc,
First Data Corporation
USA
[Financial Services]

4 **Casino Supermarkets**
Groupe Casino
France
[Retail]

5 **Casino Supermarkets**
Groupe Casino
France
[Retail]

6 **Casio**
Casio Computer Co. Ltd
Japan
[Consumer Electronics]

7 **Casterman**
Groupe Flammarion
Belgium
[Publishing]

8 **Castle Alternative Invest AG**
Castle Investment Companies
Switzerland
[Financial Services]

9 **Castrol Motor Oil**
BP plc
UK, 2006
[Automotive]

CAT

1 **CAT**
   Caterpillar Inc
   USA
   [Manufacturing]

2 **Cava**
   Canada, 2007
   Concrete
   [Restaurants & Bars]

3 **CBC (Canadian Broadcasting Corporation)**
   Canada, 1992
   Gottschalk+Ash
   [Television Network]

4 **CBR (Centraal Bureau Rijvaardigheidsbewijzen)**
   Netherlands
   [Security & Safety]

5 **CBRE (CB Richard Ellis)**
   CBRE Group Inc
   USA
   [Real Estate]

6 **CBS**
   CBS Broadcasting Inc
   USA, 1951
   William Golden
   [Television Network]

7 **CBTE (Central Brasileira dos Trabalhadores e Empreendedores)**
   Brazil
   [Societies & Associations]

8 **CCEBA (Centro Cultural de España en Buenos Aires)**
   Argentina, 2004
   Bernardo+Celis
   [Galleries & Museums]

9 **CCM**
   Reebok-CCM Hockey Inc
   Canada
   [Sport]

CENTREPOINT

1 **CCTV (Chinese Central Television)**
China
[Broadcaster]

2 **CDU (Christlich Demokratische Union Deutschlands)**
Germany, 2003
[Political]

3 **CE (Conformité Européenne)**
European Economic Area (EEA)
European Union, 1993
[Labelling, Standards & Certification]

4 **CEA (Commissariat Energie Atomique)**
France
[Energy]

5 **Celio***
Celio
France
[Retail]

6 **Celtic Football Club**
Celtic plc
UK, ca 1995
[Sport]

7 **CEMEX**
CEMEX SAB de CV
Mexico
[Construction]

8 **Center Parcs**
CenterParcs Europe NV
Netherlands, 1997
[Leisure & Entertainment]

9 **Central Bank**
Central Bancshares
USA
[Financial Services]

10 **Centrepoint**
UK
[Charity]

CENTRE POMPIDOU

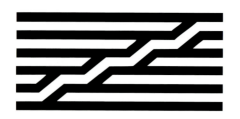

CERRUTI

1 **Centre Pompidou**
Centre national d'art et
de culture Georges Pompidou
France, 1977
Visual Design Association:
Jean Widmer
[Galleries & Museums]

2 **Century 21**
Century 21 Real Estate LLC,
Realogy Corporation
USA
[Real Estate]

3 **CEPSA (Compañía Española
de Petróleos SA)**
Spain
[Oil, Gas & Petroleum]

4 **Céréal**
Nutrition & Santé
France
[Food & Beverage]

5 **Cerner**
Cerner Corporation
USA, 1980s
[Information Technology]

6 **Cerutti**
Trinity Ltd, Li & Fung Group
France
[Apparel]

7 **Cerveza Zulia**
AmBev Venezuela
Venezuela
[Wines, Beers & Spirits]

8 **České dráhy**
České dráhy AS
Czech Republic
[Transport]

9 **Cessna**
Cessna Aircraft Company,
Textron Inc
USA
[Aerospace]

10 **Ceylon Tea**
Sri Lanka Tea Board
Sri Lanka
[Labelling, Standards
& Certification]

1. **CF Industries**
CF Industries Holdings Inc
USA
[Manufacturing]

2. **CFL**
Canadian Football League
Canada, 1970
[Sport]

3. **Chamberlain**
The Chamberlain Group,
The Duchossois Group
USA
[Household Products]

4. **Champion**
Federal-Mogul Corporation
USA
[Automotive]

5. **Champion**
HanesBrands Inc
USA
[Apparel]

6. **Champion International**
International Paper Company
USA
[Paper Products]

7. **Chanel**
Chanel SA
France, 1925
Coco Chanel
[Fashion]

8. **Changeman (Dengeki Sentai Changeman)**
Toei Co. Ltd
Japan
[Television Series]

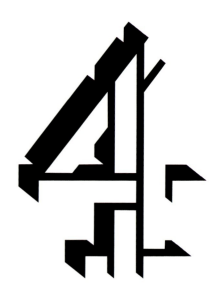

1. **Changhong**
   Sichuan Changhong Electric Co
   China
   [Consumer Electronics]

2. **Channel 4**
   Channel Four Television Corp.
   UK, 2005
   Rudd Studio
   [Broadcaster]

3. **Channel 5**
   Channel 5 Broadcasting Ltd,
   Northern & Shell Network Ltd
   UK, 1997
   Wolff Olins
   [Television Network]

4. **Channel 5**
   Channel 5 Broadcasting Ltd,
   Northern & Shell Network Ltd
   UK, 2011
   [Television Network]

5. **Chaparral Boats**
   Chaparral Boats Inc
   USA
   [Marine]

6. **Charles Schwab**
   The Charles Schwab Corporation
   USA
   [Financial Services]

7. **Chase**
   JPMorgan Chase Bank
   USA, 2006
   Sandstrom Design
   [Financial Services]

8. **CHC**
   CHC Helicopter
   Canada
   [Aerospace]

9. **Cheap Monday**
   Sweden, 2003
   Vår
   [Fashion]

10. **Cheerios**
    General Mills Inc
    USA
    [Food & Beverage]

CHEVROLET IMPALA

1 **Cheetos**
Frito-Lay North America Inc, PepsiCo Inc
USA, 2000s
[Food & Beverage]

2 **Chelsea Football Club**
Chelsea FC plc
UK
[Sport]

3 **Chemical Industries Association**
UK
[Societies & Associations]

4 **Chemigate**
Chemigate Oy
Finland
[Chemicals & Materials]

5 **CHEP (Commonwealth Handling Equipment Pool Organisation)**
Brambles Ltd
Australia
[Professional Services]

6 **Cherokee**
The Cherokee Group
USA
[Apparel]

7 **Cherry**
ZF Electronics Corporation
Germany
[Computer Hardware]

8 **Cherry Coke**
The Coca-Cola Company
USA
[Food & Beverage]

▶ 9 **Chevrolet**
General Motors Company
USA, 2004
[Automotive]

10 **Chevrolet Impala**
General Motors Company
USA
[Automotive]

CHEVRON

1 **Chevron**
Chevron Corporation
USA, 1960s
Lippincott & Margulies:
Raymond Poelvoorde
[Oil, Gas & Petroleum]

2 **Chicago Bulls**
USA, 1966
Theodore "Ted" W. Drake
[Sport]

3 **Chicago Cubs**
Family Trust of Joe Ricketts
USA
[Sport]

4 **Chicago Pneumatic**
USA
[Tools & Machinery]

5 **Chicago Rawhide**
SKF
Sweden
[Industrial Products]

6 **Chicago Tribune**
Tribune Company
USA
[Media]

7 **Chicco**
Artsana SpA
Italy
[Baby Products]

8 **Chi-Chi's**
Prandium Inc
USA
[Food & Beverage]

9 **Chick-fil-A**
Chick-fil-A Inc
USA, 1964
Louie Floyd Giglio Jr
[Restaurants & Bars]

1 **Children's Miracle Network**
USA
[Charity]

2 **Children's Miracle Network**
USA
[Charity]

3 **China Mobile 3G**
China Mobile Ltd
China, 2009
[Telecommunications]

4 **China Steel**
China Steel Corporation (CSC)
China
[Industry]

5 **China Telecom**
China Telecom Corp. Ltd
China
[Telecommunications]

6 **China Unicom**
China United Netcom (Hong Kong) Ltd
China, 2006
[Telecommunications]

7 **Chinon**
Chinon Industries Inc, Kodak Digital Product Center Japan Ltd
Japan
[Consumer Electronics]

8 **Chip Magazine**
Chip Holding GmbH
Germany
[Publications]

9 **Chips Ahoy!**
Nabisco, Kraft Foods Inc
USA
[Food & Beverage]

CHIQUITA

1   Chiquita
    Chiquita Brands International Inc
    USA, ca 1944
    Dik Browne
    [Agricultural]

2   Chocolate Skateboards
    The Chocolate Skateboard
    Company Inc
    USA
    [Sporting Goods]

3   CHODAI
    Chodai Co. Ltd
    Japan
    [Sporting Goods]

4   Choice Records
    France, 2000
    H5: Ludovic Houplain
    [Music Industry]

5   Chopard
    Le Petit-Fils de LU Chopard
    & Cie SA
    Switzerland
    [Watches & Jewelry]

6   Chris-Craft Boats
    Chris Craft Inc, Stellican Ltd
    USA
    [Marine]

7   Christian Aid
    UK, 2006
    johnson banks
    [Charity]

8   Christie
    Christie Digital Systems USA Inc
    USA
    [Technology]

9   Christie's
    Christies Inc
    USA/UK
    [Professional Services]

10 Christopher & Banks
    Christopher & Banks Inc
    USA
    [Retail]

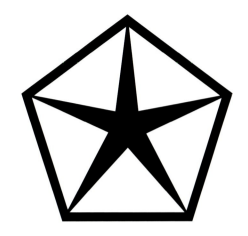

1 **C.H. Robinson Worldwide Inc**
USA
[Freight & Logistics]

2 **Chronicle Books**
McEvoy Group
USA
[Publishing]

▶ 3 **Chrysler**
Chrysler Group LLC
USA, 1962
Lippincott & Margulies:
Robert Stanley
[Automotive]

4 **Chrysler**
Chrysler Group LLC
USA, 2007
SVP Design: Trevor Creed
[Automotive]

5 **Chubb**
USA, 1968
Raymond Loewy
[Financial Services]

6 **Chubu Electric Power**
Chubu Electric Power Co. Inc
Japan
[Utilities]

7 **Chums**
Chums Inc
USA
Charles S. Anderson Design Co.
[Outdoor & Recreational]

8 **Chupa Chups**
Chupa Chups SAU,
Perfetti Van Melle SpA
Spain, 1969
Salvador Dalí
[Food & Beverage]

9 **CIA (Central Intelligence Agency)**
USA, 1950
[Government]

10 **CIB (Commercial International Bank)**
Egypt
[Financial Services]

11 **Ciba**
Ciba AG
Switzerland, ca 1997
Gottschalk+Ash: Stuart Ash
[Chemicals & Materials]

CIBA VISION

1

2

3

4

5

6

7

8

9

10

1 **Ciba Vision**
Ciba Vision Corporation,
Novartis AG
Switzerland
[Eyewear]

2 **CIC (Crédit Industriel et Commercial)**
France
[Financial Services]

3 **Cif**
Unilever plc/NV
France
[Household Products]

4 **Cigna**
Cigna Corporation
USA, 1993
Landor Associates: Lindon Leader
[Healthcare]

5 **Cigna**
Cigna Corporation
USA, 2011
BrandSinger, Jerry Kuyper Partners
[Healthcare]

6 **Cincom**
Cincom Systems Inc
USA
[Computer Software]

7 **CinéCinéma Channel**
Groupe Canal+, Vivendi SA
France, 2002
[Television Channel]

8 **Cinelli**
Gruppo Srl – Div. Cinelli
Italy, 1979
Italo Lupi
[Bicycles]

9 **Cinema for Peace Foundation**
Germany
[Foundations & Institutes]

10 **Cinemanía**
Editorial Televisa
Mexico, 2008
La fe ciega studio
[Publications]

CIRCLE

1

2

3

4

5

6

7

10

8

9

1 **Cinemax**
Home Box Office Inc,
Time Warner
USA, 1997
[Television Channel]

2 **Cinemax**
Home Box Office Inc,
Time Warner
USA, 2011
[Television Channel]

3 **Cinergy**
Cinergy Corporation
USA
[Energy]

4 **Cineworld**
Cineworld Group plc
UK, 2009
[Cinemas & Theatres]

5 **Cingular**
Cingular Wireless LLC
USA, 2000
VSA Partners
[Telecommunications]

6 **Cintas**
Cintas Corporation
USA
[Industrial Products]

7 **Cinzano**
Davide Campari-Milano SpA
Italy
[Wines, Beers & Spirits]

8 **CIO**
CXO Media Inc, IDG Enterprise
USA
[Publications]

9 **CIPEC (Canadian Industry
Program for Energy Conservation)**
Canada
[Conservation & Environment]

10 **Circle**
Circle Holdings plc
UK
[Healthcare]

153

CIRCLE K

1   **Circle K**
    Circle K Stores Inc
    USA, 1957
    [Retail]

2   **Cirrus**
    MasterCard Worldwide
    USA
    [Financial Services]

3   **Cirrus Logic**
    Cirrus Logic Inc
    USA
    [Technology]

4   **Cisco Systems**
    Cisco Systems Inc
    USA, 1996
    [Information Technology]

5   **Cisco Systems**
    Cisco Systems Inc
    USA, 2006
    Joe Finocchiaro, Jerry Kuyper
    [Information Technology]

6   **Citgo**
    Citgo Petroleum Corporation,
    Petróleos de Venezuela SA
    USA, 1965
    Lippincott & Margulies
    [Oil, Gas & Petroleum]

7   **Citibank**
    USA, 1970s
    Anspach Grossman Portugal:
    Gene Grossman
    [Financial Services]

8   **Citibank**
    Citigroup Inc
    USA, 1999
    Pentagram: Paula Scher
    [Financial Services]

9   **Citigroup**
    Citigroup Inc
    USA
    [Financial Services]

10 **Citizen**
    Citizen Holdings Co. Ltd
    Japan
    [Watches & Jewelry]

CITY NATIONAL BANK

1 **Citizen**
Citizen Holdings Co. Ltd
Japan
[Watches & Jewelry]

2 **Citizens Bank of Canada**
Canada
Herrainco
[Financial Services]

3 **Citrix**
Citrix Systems Inc
USA
[Computer Software]

4 **Citroën**
Automobiles Citroën,
PSA Peugeot Citroën
France, 1985
[Automotive]

5 **Citroën**
PSA Peugeot Citroën
France, 2009
Landor Associates
[Automotive]

6 **CityBus**
CitiBus Ltd
China
[Transport]

7 **City & Guilds**
City & Guilds of London Institute
UK
[Education]

8 **City Hopper**
UK, 2006
ICG
[Aviation]

▶ 9 **City National Bank**
City National Corporation
USA
[Financial Services]

CITY OF HOPE

1   **City of Hope**
    City of Hope National
    Medical Center
    USA
    [Healthcare]

2   **City of Melbourne**
    Australia, 2009
    Landor Associates
    [Places]

3   **City of Westminster College**
    UK
    Atelier Works
    [Education]

4   **CityRail**
    Rail Corporation New South Wales
    Australia, 2010
    [Transport]

5   **Citytv**
    Rogers Broadcasting Ltd,
    Rogers Communications Inc
    Canada
    [Television Network]

6   **City University of New York**
    USA, 2008
    Pentagram
    [Education]

7   **Civil Defense**
    United States Civil Defense
    USA, 1939
    N. W. Ayer: Charles T. Coiner
    [Defence]

8   **Civil Defense international sign**
    International Civil Defence
    Organisation (ICDO)
    Switzerland
    [Defence]

9   **Civitan International**
    USA
    [Societies & Associations]

156

1 **CJ (Cheil Jedang)**
CJ Group
South Korea
[Conglomerate]

2 **CKI**
Cheung Kong Infrastructure Holdings Ltd
China
[Utilities]

3 **Claire's**
Claire's Stores Inc, Apollo Global Management LLC
USA
[Retail]

4 **Clairol**
Procter & Gamble Co
USA
[Personal Care]

5 **Clairtone**
Clairtone Sound Corporation Ltd
Canada, ca 1967
Burton Kramer
[Consumer Electronics]

6 **Clan Campbell**
Ricard SA
UK
[Wines, Beers & Spirits]

7 **Clarion**
Clarion Co. Ltd
Japan
[Consumer Electronics]

8 **Clarion Hotels**
Choice Hotels International Inc
USA
[Hospitality]

9 **Clarks**
C and J Clark International Ltd
UK
[Footwear]

1 **Claro**
America Movil
Brazil, 2006
GAD
[Telecommunications]

2 **Clearly Canadian**
Clearly Canadian Beverage Corporation
Canada
[Food & Beverage]

3 **Cleveland Indians**
MLB Advanced Media LP
USA, 1980
[Sport]

4 **CLIA (Cruise Lines International Association)**
USA
[Societies & Associations]

5 **Cliché Skateboards**
France
[Sporting Goods]

6 **Clinique**
Clinique Laboratories LLC, Estée Lauder Companies Inc
USA
[Health & Beauty]

7 **Clopay**
Clopay Building Products Company Inc, Griffon Corporation
USA
[Household Products]

8 **Clorox**
The Clorox Company
USA, 1987
Greg Mitchell
[Household Products]

9 **Clorox**
The Clorox Company
USA, 2010
[Household Products]

10 **Closed Captioned**
National Captioning Institute
USA
[Labelling, Standards & Certification]

1 **Closed Captioned**
   USA, ca 1972
   WGBH-TV: Jack Foley
   [Labelling, Standards
   & Certification]

2 **Club Med**
   Club Méditerranée SA
   France
   [Travel & Tourism]

3 **CMAS (Confédération Mondiale
   des Activités Subaquatiques)**
   Italy
   [Societies & Associations]

4 **CMAS (Confédération Mondiale
   des Activités Subaquatiques)**
   Italy
   [Societies & Associations]

5 **CMC Markets**
   CMC Markets UK plc
   UK
   [Financial Services]

6 **CMI**
   CMI Corporation
   USA
   [Outdoor & Recreation]

7 **CMPC**
   Empresas CMPC SA
   Chile
   [Paper Products]

▶ 8 **CMT**
   Country Music Television
   USA, 1988
   [Television Channel]

9 **CMT**
   Country Music Television
   USA, 2004
   [Television Channel]

10 **CN (Canadian National Railway)**
    Canada, 1960
    Allan Fleming
    [Transport]

1 **CNBC**
NBCUniversal Media LLC
USA, 1997
[Media]

2 **c|net**
CBS Interactive, CBS Corporation
USA, 1994
[Internet]

3 **C-Netz**
DeTeMobil, Deutsche Bundespost Telekom AG
Germany, 1984
[Telecommunications]

4 **CNN (Cable News Network)**
Turner Broadcasting System Inc, Time Warner
USA, 1980
Toni Dwyer
[Television Network]

5 **Coach**
Coach Inc
USA
[Consumer Products]

6 **Coach**
Coach Inc
USA
[Consumer Products]

7 **Coach USA**
Stagecoach Group plc
USA
[Transport]

8 **Coastal**
Warren Unilube Inc
USA
[Automotive]

9 **Cobra**
Cobra USA Inc
USA
[Automotive]

COFFEE COMPANY

1 **Cobra Golf**
   Puma AG
   USA
   [Sporting Goods]

2 **Coca-Cola**
   The Coca-Cola Company
   USA, 1969
   Lippincott & Margulies
   [Food & Beverage]

3 **Coca-Cola (Coke)**
   The Coca-Cola Company
   USA, 1941
   Frank M. Robinson
   [Food & Beverage]

▶ 4 **Coca-Cola**
   The Coca-Cola Company
   USA, 2007
   Turner Duckworth
   [Food & Beverage]

5 **Coco's Bakery Restaurant**
   Coco's Bakery Restaurant Inc
   USA
   [Restaurants & Bars]

6 **Codan**
   Codan Forsikring A/S
   Denmark
   [Restaurants & Bars]

7 **Codarts**
   Netherlands, 2005
   75B
   [Education]

8 **Coffee Break Small Groups**
   Global Coffee Break,
   Christian Reformed Church
   in North America
   USA
   [Religious]

9 **CoffeeCompany**
   CoffeeCompany BV
   Netherlands
   [Restaurants & Bars]

161

COFLEXIP STENA OFFSHORE

1. **Coflexip Stena Offshore**
   France
   [Oil, Gas & Petroleum]

2. **Cogeco Inc**
   Canada
   [Media]

3. **Cognos**
   IBM
   USA
   [Computer Software]

4. **Coilhose Pneumatics**
   USA
   [Tools & Machinery]

5. **Coinstar**
   Coinstar Inc
   USA
   [Retail]

6. **Cointreau**
   Groupe Rémy Cointreau
   France
   [Wines, Beers & Spirits]

▶ 7. **Coldwell Banker**
   Coldwell Banker Real Estate LLC
   USA
   Ampersand Design
   [Real Estate]

8. **Coleco**
   Coleco Entertainment Corp
   USA
   [Computer & Video Games]

9. **Colegio de Arquitectos**
   Venezuela, 1977
   Álvaro Sotillo
   [Foundations & Institutes]

10. **Cole Haan**
    Nike Inc
    USA
    [Apparel]

COLOR QUICKCAM

1

2 3

4

5 6

7 8 9

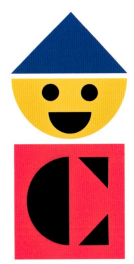

10

1 **Coleman**
Coleman Company Inc,
Jarden Corporation
USA
[Outdoor & Recreation]

2 **Coles Supermarkets**
Coles Supermarkets Australia
Pty Ltd, Wesfarmers Ltd
Australia, ca 2010
[Retail]

▶ 3 **Colgate**
Colgate-Palmolive Company
USA
[Personal Care]

4 **Colgate-Palmolive**
Colgate-Palmolive Company
USA
[Personal Care]

5 **Colonial**
Colonial Life & Accident Insurance
Company, Unum Group
USA
[Financial Services]

6 **Colorado Adventurewear**
Colorado Group Ltd
Australia
[Retail]

7 **Colorado Mammoth**
Kroenke Sports Enterprises LLC
USA, 2001
[Sport]

8 **Colorado State Rams**
Colorado State University
USA
[Sport]

9 **Colorforms**
University Games Corporation
USA, 1959
Paul Rand
[Toys, Games & Models]

10 **Color QuickCam**
Logitech International SA
USA
[Computer Technology]

163

COLORSYNC

1 ColorSync
   Apple Inc
   USA
   [Computer Technology]

2 Colt
   Colt's Manufacturing Company LLC
   USA
   [Firearms]

3 Colt Industries
   Colt Industries Inc
   USA
   [Paints & Coatings]

4 Columbia Business School
   Columbia University
   USA, 2007
   Pentagram: Michael Bierut
   [Education]

5 Columbia House
   Direct Brands Inc
   USA
   [Retail]

6 Columbia Pictures
   Columbia Pictures Industries Inc,
   Sony Pictures Entertainment Inc
   USA, 1976
   [Film Industry]

7 Columbia Sportswear
   Columbia Sportswear Company
   USA
   [Apparel]

8 Columbiettes
   The Affiliated Auxiliaries
   of the Knights of Columbus
   USA
   [Societies & Associations]

9 Columbus Clippers
   MLB Advanced Media LP
   USA
   [Sport]

10 Columbus Tubi
   Gruppo SpA
   Italy
   [Bicycles]

COMET

COMCAST

1   Com4Wheels
    Reifen Gundlach Inc
    Germany
    [Automotive]

2   Comair
    Delta Airlines Inc
    USA
    [Airline]

3   Comcast
    Comcast Corporation
    USA, 2007
    [Telecommunications]

4   Comcast
    Comcast Corporation
    USA, 1970s
    [Telecommunications]

5   Comdial
    Comdial Corporation
    USA
    [Telecommunications]

6   ComEd
    Commonwealth Edison Company,
    Exelon Corporation
    USA
    [Utilities]

7   Comedy Central
    Comedy Partners LLC,
    MTV Networks, Viacom Inc
    USA, 2000
    Imaginary Forces
    [Television Channel]

8   Comedy Central
    Comedy Partners LLC,
    MTV Networks, Viacom Inc
    USA, 2011
    The Lab
    [Television Channel]

9   Comerica Bank
    Comerica Inc
    USA
    [Financial Services]

10 Comet
    Comet Group plc
    UK, 2010
    Venturethree
    [Retail]

165

COMFORT INN

1

2

3

4

5

6

7

8

9

1 **Comfort Inn**
Choice Hotels International Inc
USA
[Hospitality]

2 **ComfortMind**
Canada
[Financial Services]

3 **Comfort Suites**
Choice Hotels International Inc
USA
[Hospitality]

4 **Commerce One**
Commerce One Inc
USA
[Internet]

5 **Commerzbank**
Commerzbank AG
Germany
[Financial Services]

6 **Commerzbank**
Commerzbank AG
Germany, 2009
MetaDesign
[Financial Services]

7 **Commodore-Amiga**
Commodore-Amiga Inc
USA, 1980s
[Computer Technology]

8 **Commodore**
Commodore International Ltd,
C=Holdings BV
Canada, 1985
[Computer Technology]

9 **Commonwealth Bank**
Commonwealth Bank of Australia
Australia
[Financial Services]

1 **Commsa**
   Grupo Industrial Monclova
   Mexico
   [Construction]

2 **Compact Disc**
   Koninklijke Philips Electronics NV
   Netherlands, 1982
   [Consumer Electronics]

3 **CompAir**
   Gardner Denver Inc
   UK
   [Industrial Products]

4 **Compaq**
   Compaq Computer Corporation
   USA, 1999
   Landor Associates
   [Computer Technology]

5 **CompUSA**
   Systemax Inc
   USA
   [Retail]

6 **ComputerLand**
   USA
   [Retail]

7 **Computerworld**
   International Data Group (IDG)
   USA
   [Publications]

8 **COMTEK**
   Russia, 2003
   [Events]

9 **ComTrade Group**
   Serbia
   [Information Technology]

CONAD

1 Conad (Consorzio Nazionale Dettaglianti)
Conad Soc. Coop
Italy
[Retail]

2 ConAgra Foods
ConAgra Foods Inc
USA
[Food & Beverage]

3 ConAgra Foods
ConAgra Foods Inc
USA, 2009
Bailey Lauerman
[Food & Beverage]

4 CONALEP (Colegio Nacional de Educación Profesional Técnica)
Mexico
[Education]

5 Condé Nast
Condé Nast, Advance Magazine Publishers Inc
USA
[Publishing]

6 Condor Earth Technologies Inc
USA
[Engineering]

7 Condor Flugdienst
Thomas Cook Group plc
Germany
[Airline]

8 conEdison
Consolidated Edison Inc
USA, 2000
Arnell Group
[Energy]

9 Conelsur
Transelec
Chile, 2007
Grupo Oxigeno
[Energy]

CONSERVATIVE PARTY

1   Conforms to BS5665
    BSI Group
    UK
    [Labelling, Standards
    & Certification]

2   Conley Corporation
    USA
    [Industrial Products]

3   Connectix
    Connectix Corporation
    USA
    [Computer Technology]

4   Conner
    Conner Peripherals Inc
    USA
    [Computer Hardware]

5   Connex
    Vodafone Romania
    Romania
    [Telecommunications]

▶ 6 Conoco
    Conoco Inc, ConocoPhillips
    Company
    USA
    [Oil, Gas & Petroleum]

7   ConocoPhillips
    ConocoPhillips Company
    USA
    [Oil, Gas & Petroleum]

8   Conrad Hotels
    Hilton Worldwide,
    The Blackstone Group
    USA
    [Hospitality]

9   Conservative Party
    UK, 2006
    Perfect Day
    [Political]

CONTADINA

1 **Contadina**
   Del Monte Foods
   USA
   [Food & Beverage]

2 **ConTel**
   ConTel Corporation
   USA
   [Telecommunications]

3 **Continental**
   Continental AG
   Germany
   [Automotive]

4 **Continental Airlines**
   United Continental Holdings Inc
   USA, 1991
   Lippincott & Margulies
   [Airline]

5 **Converse Inc**
   USA
   [Footwear]

6 **Co-op**
   Federated Co-operatives Ltd,
   TMC Distributing Ltd
   Canada
   [Retail]

7 **Coop Foodstore**
   Co-operative Group Ltd
   UK
   [Retail]

8 **Coopers Brewery**
   Coopers Brewery Ltd
   Australia
   [Breweries]

9 **Coopers Brewery**
   Coopers Brewery Ltd
   Australia
   [Breweries]

Coppertone

corbis

1 **Cooper Tires**
Cooper Tire & Rubber Company
USA, 1950s
[Automotive]

2 **Cooper Tires**
Cooper Tire & Rubber Company
USA, 2001
[Automotive]

3 **Coors**
Coors Brewing Company,
Molson Coors Brewing Company
Canada
[Wines, Beers & Spirits]

4 **Coors Light**
Coors Brewing Company,
Molson Coors Brewing Company
Canada
[Wines, Beers & Spirits]

5 **COPE (Cadena de Ondas Populares Españolas)**
Radio Popular
Spain
[Radio Stations]

6 **Copel (Companhia Paranaense de Energia)**
Brazil
[Utilities]

7 **Coppertone**
Merck & Co. Inc
USA
[Personal Care]

8 **Cora**
Cora SA
Belgium
[Retail]

9 **Coral (Tintas Coral)**
Akzo Nobel NV
Brazil
[Paints & Coatings]

10 **Corbis**
Corbis Corporation, Bill Gates
USA, 2004
Segura Inc: Carlos Segura
[Imaging & Photographic]

CORDURA

1. **Cordura**
   Invista, Koch Industries Inc
   USA
   [Fabrics & Textiles]

2. **Cordura Nylon**
   Invista, Koch Industries Inc
   USA
   [Fabrics & Textiles]

3. **CORE Business Technologies**
   USA
   [Information Technology]

4. **Corel**
   Corel Corporation
   USA, 1990s
   [Computer Software]

5. **Corel**
   Corel Corporation
   USA, 2001
   [Computer Software]

6. **Corelle**
   Corning Inc
   USA
   [Kitchenware]

7. **Corgi**
   Hornby Hobbies Ltd
   UK, 1984
   [Toys, Games & Models]

8. **Corgoň**
   Heineken Slovensko AS
   Slovakia
   [Wines, Beers & Spirits]

9. **Corian**
   E. I. du Pont de Nemours
   and Company
   USA
   [Chemicals & Materials]

CORNING

CORRIERE DELLA SERA

Corrugated Recycles

1 **Corinthians**
Sport Club Corinthians Paulista
Brazil
[Sport]

2 **Cormay**
PZ Cormay SA
Poland
[Manufacturing]

3 **Corning**
Corning Inc
USA
[Glass & Ceramics]

4 **Corona Extra**
Grupo Modelo SAB de CV
Mexico
[Wines, Beers & Spirits]

5 **Corporate Express**
Corporate Express NV,
Staples Inc
Netherlands, 1998
DG Design
[Office Supplies]

6 **Correos**
Sociedad Estatal Correos y
Telégrafos SA
Spain
[Mail Services]

7 **Correos Chile**
Chilean Government
Chile, 2008
Grupo Oxigeno
[Mail Services]

8 **Corriere della Sera**
RCS MediaGroup SpA
Italy
[Media]

9 **Corrugated Recycles**
Corrugated Packaging Council
USA
[Conservation & Environment]

1. **CORSA (Corvair Society of America)**
   USA
   [Societies & Associations]

2. **Corsair**
   Corsair Memory Inc
   USA
   [Computer Hardware]

3. **Corvette**
   General Motors Company
   USA, 1953
   Robert Bartholomew
   [Automotive]

4. **Corvette**
   General Motors Company
   USA
   [Automotive]

5. **Cosco Pacific**
   China Ocean Shipping (Group) Company
   China
   [Freight & Logistics]

6. **Cosmo Oil**
   Cosmo Oil Co. Ltd
   Japan
   [Oil, Gas & Petroleum]

7. **Cosmopolitan**
   Hearst Corporation
   USA
   [Publications]

8. **Costco Wholesale**
   Costco Wholesale Corporation
   USA, 2005
   [Retail]

COURTESY TRANSPORTATION

1 **Coteau du-Lac**
   City of Coteau du-Lac
   Canada
   [Places]

2 **Côte d'Or**
   Kraft Foods Inc
   Belgium
   [Food & Beverage]

3 **Cottee's**
   Asahi Breweries Inc
   Australia
   [Food & Beverage]

4 **Cotton Incorporated**
   USA
   [Societies & Associations]

5 **Cottonwood Valley**
   AtHomeNet Inc
   USA
   [Real Estate]

6 **Couche-Tard**
   Alimentation Couche-Tard Inc
   Canada, 1999
   [Retail]

7 **Country Inns & Suites**
   Carlson Rezidor Hotel Group
   USA
   [Hospitality]

▶ 8 **Courtesy Transportation**
     General Motors Company
     USA
     [Automotive]

▶ 9 **Courtesy Transportation**
     General Motors Company
     USA
     [Automotive]

COUTTS & CO

1 **Coutts & Co**
The Royal Bank of Scotland plc
UK
[Financial Services]

2 **Covercraft**
Covercraft Industries Inc
USA
[Automotive]

3 **Coverd**
Coverd Srl
Italy
[Construction]

4 **Cover Girl**
Procter & Gamble Co
USA
[Health & Beauty]

5 **CPC International (Corn Products International Inc)**
USA
[Food & Beverage]

6 **CPH**
Copenhagen Airports AS
Denmark
[Aviation]

7 **Cracker Jack**
Frito-Lay North America Inc, PepsiCo Inc
USA
[Food & Beverage]

8 **Crafted with Pride in USA**
Crafted With Pride in USA Council Inc
USA, ca 1984
[Societies & Associations]

9 **Craftsman**
KCD IP LLC
USA, 1927
[Tools & Machinery]

craigslist  CRANE

 # Crayola

1 **Craigslist**
Craigslist Inc
USA
[Internet]

2 **Cramo**
Cramo Finland Oy
Finland
[Professional Services]

3 **Crane**
Crane Co.
USA
[Conglomerate]

4 **Crane Plumbing**
Crane Plumbing Corporation
Canada
[Home Furnishings]

5 **Crayola**
Crayola LLC, Hallmark Cards Inc
USA, 1968
[Toys, Games & Models]

6 **Cray Research**
Cray Inc
USA
[Computer Technology]

7 **CRC Industries**
CRC Industries Inc
USA, 1958
[Chemicals & Materials]

8 **Cream Nightclub**
Cream Holdings Ltd
UK
Rob Petrie, Phil Sims
[Leisure & Entertainment]

9 **Creative**
Creative Technology Ltd
Singapore
[Consumer Electronics]

1 **Creative Commons**
 USA
 Creative Commons
 [Foundations & Institutes]

2 **Crédit Agricole**
 Crédit Agricole SA
 France, 1987
 [Financial Services]

3 **Crédit du Nord**
 Crédit du Nord SA
 France
 [Financial Services]

4 **Crédit Mutuel**
 Crédit Mutuel SA
 France
 [Financial Services]

5 **Credit Suisse**
 Credit Suisse Group AG
 Switzerland, 1997
 Wolff Olins
 [Financial Services]

6 **Credit Suisse**
 Credit Suisse Group AG
 Switzerland, 2005
 Enterprise IG
 [Financial Services]

7 **Credit Union**
 CBI Federal Credit Union
 USA
 [Societies & Associations]

8 **Crem Helado**
 Colombia
 [Food & Beverage]

9 **Crenlo**
 International Equipment
 Solutions LLC
 USA
 [Industrial Products]

1 **Crest**
Procter & Gamble Co
USA
[Personal Care]

2 **Cresta Swiss Bike**
Komenda AG
Switzerland
[Bicycles]

3 **Crestone International**
CedarCrestone Inc
USA
[Information Technology]

4 **Crime – Let's Bring It Down**
Home Office, UK Government
UK
[Government]

5 **Crisco**
The J.M. Smucker Company
USA
[Food & Beverage]

6 **CRKT (Columbia River Knife & Tool Inc)**
USA, 1990s
[Knives]

7 **Croatia**
Croatian National Tourist Board
Croatia
[Travel & Tourism]

8 **Crocodille**
Crocodille CR spol. s r.o.
Czech Republic
[Food & Beverage]

1 **Cross**
A.T. Cross Company
USA
[Writing Products]

2 **Cross**
A.T. Cross Company
USA
[Writing Products]

3 **CrossPad**
A.T. Cross Company, IBM
USA
[Consumer Electronics]

4 **Crown Audio**
Crown International, Harman International Industries
USA
[Consumer Electronics]

5 **Crown International**
Crown International, Harman International Industries
USA
[Electronics]

6 **Crown Cork & Seal Company**
Crown Holdings Inc
USA
[Industrial Products]

7 **Crown Pacific Partners LP**
USA
[Manufacturing]

8 **Crown Paints Ltd**
Hempel AS
UK
[Paints & Coatings]

▶ 9 **Cruise America Inc**
USA
[Car Rental]

10 **Nestlé Crunch**
Nestlé SA
Switzerland
[Food & Beverage]

11 **Cruz Roja Cubana**
Cuban Red Cross
Mexico, 1968
Félix Beltrán
[Charity]

1 **CSA (Canadian Standards Association)**
CSA Group
Canada
[Labelling, Standards & Certification]

2 **CSC (Computer Sciences Corporation)**
USA, 1987
Robert Miles Runyon
[Information Technology]

3 **CSC (Computer Sciences Corporation)**
USA, 2008
Interbrand
[Information Technology]

4 **C-SPAN (Cable-Satellite Public Affairs Network)**
National Cable Satellite Corporation
USA
[Television Network]

5 **CSX Corporation**
CSX Corporation Inc
USA, 2010
[Transport]

6 **CSX Intermodal**
CSX Intermodal Terminals Inc, CSX Corporation Inc
USA
[Transport]

7 **CTIC (Chicago Title Insurance Company)**
USA
[Financial Services]

8 **C-Tick**
Australian and New Zealand EMC (ANZEMC)
Australia
[Labelling, Standards & Certification]

9 **CTT Correios**
CTT Correios de Portugal SA
Portugal, 2004
Brandia Central
[Mail Services]

CUB FOODS

1 **Cub Foods**
SuperValu Inc
USA
[Retail]

2 **Cub Foods**
SuperValu Inc
USA
[Retail]

3 **Cuisinart**
Conair Corporation
USA
[Home Appliances]

4 **Culligan**
Culligan International Company
USA
[Food & Beverage]

5 **CultureBus**
San Francisco Municipal Transportation Agency
USA, 2008
Pentagram: Kit Hinrichs, Mo Woods
[Transport]

6 **Culver's**
Culver Franchising System Inc
USA
[Restaurants & Bars]

▶ 7 **Cummins Marine**
Cummins Inc
USA, 1962
Paul Rand
[Tools & Machinery]

8 **Cunard Line**
Carnival Corporation & plc
UK
[Travel & Tourism]

9 **Curragh**
Wesfarmers Curragh Pty Ltd
Australia
[Mining]

CZECH AIRLINES

1 **Curtis Mathes**
   Curtis Mathes Corporation
   USA
   [Retail]

2 **Curves**
   Curves International Inc
   USA
   [Health & Beauty]

3 **Cushman & Wakefield**
   Cushman & Wakefield Inc
   USA, 2007
   [Real Estate]

4 **CWS**
   CWS-boco International GmbH
   Germany
   [Professional Services]

5 **Cyber-shot**
   Sony Corporation
   Japan, ca 1996
   [Consumer Electronics]

6 **CYO (The Catholic Youth Organization)**
   USA
   [Societies & Associations]

7 **Cycle World**
   Bonnier Corporation
   USA
   [Publications]

8 **Cypress Hill**
   USA, ca 2001
   [Music]

9 **Czech Airlines (CSA)**
   Czech Republic
   [Airline]

D2 PRIVAT

1 **D2 Privat**
Mannesman Mobilfunk
Germany, 1990s
[Telecommunications]

2 **D&AD (Design & Art Direction)**
UK, 1962
Alan Fletcher
[Charities]

3 **D&AD (Design & Art Direction)**
UK, 2006
Rose
[Charities]

4 **DAB (Digital Audio Broadcasting)**
Koninklijke Philips Electronics NV
Netherlands
[Labelling, Standards
& Certification]

5 **Dacia**
Renault Deutschland AG
Germany
[Automotive]

6 **Dacia**
Renault Deutschland AG
Germany
[Automotive]

7 **Dacia**
Renault Deutschland AG
Germany
[Automotive]

8 **Daemar Inc**
Canada
[Manufacturer]

9 **Daewoo**
Daewoo Motors
South Korea
[Automotive]

1 **Daewoo Electronics**
South Korea
[Electronics]

2 **DAF (Van Doorne's Aanhanwagen Fabriek)**
Netherlands
[Automotive]

3 **DAF**
DAF Trucks NV, Paccar Inc
Netherlands
[Automotive]

4 **DAF**
MAS-DAF Makina Sanayi AŞ
Turkey
[Industrial Products]

5 **Daft Punk**
Virgin Records
France, 1997
Guy-Manuel de Homem-Christo
[Music]

6 **Dag Allemaal**
Magnet Magazines BV, Persgroep NV
Netherlands
[Publications]

7 **Daiei**
Daiei Inc
Japan
[Retail]

8 **Daihatsu**
Daihatsu Motor Co. Ltd
Japan
[Automotive]

9 **Dailymotion**
Dailymotion SA
France, 2005
[Internet]

1. **Daily's**
   Tri Star Energy LLC
   USA
   [Retail]

2. **Daimler**
   Daimler AG
   Germany, 2007
   Schindler Parent Identity,
   Underware
   [Automotive]

3. **Daimler-Benz Aerospace AG**
   Germany, ca 1995
   [Aerospace]

4. **DaimlerChrysler**
   DaimlerChrysler AG
   Germany, 1998
   [Automotive]

5. **Dainese**
   Dainese SpA
   Italy
   [Manufacturing]

6. **Dairy Crest**
   Dairy Crest Group plc
   UK
   [Food & Beverage]

7. **Dairy Queen (DQ)**
   International Dairy Queen Inc,
   Berkshire Hathaway Inc
   USA, 1960
   [Restaurants & Bars]

8. **Dairy Queen (DQ)**
   International Dairy Queen Inc,
   Berkshire Hathaway Inc
   USA, 2001
   [Restaurants & Bars]

9. **Dairy Queen**
   International Dairy Queen Inc,
   Berkshire Hathaway Inc
   USA, 2007
   [Restaurants & Bars]

1 **Daisytek**
   Daisytek Computers LLC
   United Arab Emirates
   [Retail]

2 **Daiwa Bank**
   Daiwa Bank Holdings Inc
   Japan
   [Financial Services]

3 **Daiwa House**
   Daiwa House Industry Co. Ltd
   Japan
   [Construction]

4 **DAK**
   DAK-Gesundheit
   Germany
   [Healthcare]

5 **Dakar Rally**
   Amaury Sports Organisation,
   Éditions Philippe Amaury
   France
   [Motorsport]

6 **Dakine**
   Billabong International Ltd
   USA
   [Apparel]

7 **Daktronics**
   Daktronics Inc
   USA
   [Electronics]

8 **Daler-Rowney**
   Daler-Rowney Ltd
   UK
   [Consumer Products]

9 **Dali (Danish Audiophile
   Loudspeaker Industries)**
   Dalis AS
   Denmark
   [Consumer Electronics]

10 **Dallas**
   City of Dallas
   USA
   [Places]

DALSA

1 **Dalsa**
Distribuidora de Aceros Laminados SA de CV
Mexico
[Retail]

2 **Dalum Papir**
Dalum Papir AS
Denmark
[Paper Products]

3 **Damart**
France
[Apparel]

4 **Damiani**
Damiani International BV
Italy
[Watches & Jewelry]

5 **Dana**
Dana Holding Corporation
USA
[Automotive]

6 **Danamon**
PT. Bank Danamon Indonesia
Indonesia, 2006
BD+A Design
[Financial Service]

7 **DAN (Divers Alert Network)**
Divers Alert Network Inc
USA
[Safety & Security]

8 **Danfoss**
Danfoss A/S
Denmark
[Heating & Cooling]

9 **Danisco**
Danisco A/S
Denmark
[Food & Beverage]

1 **Danish Crown**
Danish Crown AmbA
Denmark
[Food & Beverage]

2 **Danish Crown**
Danish Crown AmbA
Denmark
[Food & Beverage]

3 **Danka**
Konica Minolta Business Solutions USA Inc
USA
[Office Supplies]

4 **Danko Emergency Equipment Co**
USA
[Safety & Security]

5 **Danko Jones**
Canada
[Music]

6 **Danmarks Ishockey Union**
Denmark
[Sport]

7 **Danmønt**
Denmark
[Financial Services]

8 **Dannon**
The Dannon Company, Groupe Danone SA
USA
[Food & Beverage]

1 **Danone**
Groupe Danone SA
France, 1994
[Food & Beverage]

2 **Danone**
Groupe Danone SA
France
[Food & Beverage]

3 **Dan's Foods**
Associated Food Stores Inc
USA
[Retail]

4 **Danske Bank**
Danske Bank A/S
Denmark
[Financial Services]

5 **Dansk Squash**
Dansk Squash Forbund
Denmark
[Sport]

6 **Dantex**
Dantex SA
Poland
[Manufacturing]

7 **Danzka Vodka**
Belvédère Scandinavia A/S
Denmark
[Wines, Beers & Spirits]

8 **Dao Heng Bank**
Dao Heng Bank Group Ltd
China
[Financial Services]

1 **DAP**
DAP Products Inc
USA
[Household Products]

2 **Dark Dog**
Austria, ca 2001
[Food & Beverage]

3 **Dark Horse Comics**
USA
[Publishing]

4 **Darkstar**
Dwindle Distribution
USA
[Outdoor & Recreation]

5 **Darty**
KESA Electricals plc
France
[Retail]

6 **DAS**
DAS Legal Expenses
Insurance Company Ltd
UK
[Financial Services]

7 **Dasani**
The Coca-Cola Company
USA
[Food & Beverage]

8 **Dashboard Confessional**
USA
[Music]

DASSAULT SYSTÈMES

1 Dassault Systèmes
   Dassault Systèmes SA
   France
   [Aerospace]

2 DAT (Digital Audio Tape)
   Developed by Sony Corporation
   Japan, ca 1987
   [Consumer Products]

3 Data Cooler
   TITAN Technology Ltd
   Taiwan
   [Computer Hardware]

4 Data Copy
   Modo Papers
   Sweden
   [Paper Products]

5 Datacraft
   Dimension Data Holdings
   South Africa
   [Information Technology]

6 Data General
   Data General Corporation
   USA
   [Computer Technology]

7 Datamax-O'Neil
   Datamax-O'Neil Corporation,
   Dover Corporation
   USA, 2009
   [Manufacturing]

8 Datamonitor
   Datamonitor Group
   UK
   [Marketing]

9 Data Return
   Terremark Worldwide Inc,
   Verizon Communications Inc
   USA
   [Information Technology]

10 Datex Ohmeda
   General Electric Company
   USA
   [Healthcare]

1 **Daum**
France
[Glass & Ceramics]

2 **David Beckham**
adidas AG
UK, 2004
Eric Vellozzi
[Sporting Goods]

3 **Davidoff**
Davidoff & Cie SA
Switzerland
[Tobacco]

4 **Davidoff Cognac**
Davidoff & Cie SA
Switzerland
[Wines, Beers & Spirits]

5 **David Sunflower Seeds**
ConAgra Foods Inc
USA
[Food & Beverage]

6 **Davis Cup**
International Tennis Federation
UK
[Sporting Events]

7 **Davis Entertainment**
USA, 1985
[Film Industry]

8 **DaVita**
DaVita Inc
USA, 2003
IE Design+Communications
[Healthcare]

1 **Davos**
   Davos Destinations-Organisation
   Switzerland
   [Travel & Tourism]

2 **Dawn**
   Procter & Gamble Co
   USA
   [Household Products]

3 **Dayco**
   Dayco Products LLC
   USA
   [Industrial Products]

4 **Days Inn**
   Days Inn Worldwide Inc,
   Wyndham Hotel Group
   USA, 2007
   [Hospitality]

5 **Daytona International Speedway**
   International Speedway
   Corporation
   USA
   [Motorsport]

6 **DB (Deutsche Bahn)**
   Deutsche Bahn AG
   Germany, 1993
   Kurt Weidemann
   [Transport]

7 **DB Schenker**
   Schenker AG, Deutsche Bahn AG
   Germany
   [Freight & Logistics]

8 **DBA (Disk Brakes Australia)**
   Disk Brakes Australia Pty Ltd
   Australia
   [Automotive]

1 **D B Wilson**
D B Wilson & Co. Ltd
UK
[Automotive]

2 **dbx**
dbx Inc, Harman International Industries Inc
USA, 1971
[Consumer Electronics]

3 **DC Card**
DC Card Co. Ltd
Japan
[Financial Services]

4 **DC Comics (bullet logo)**
DC Comics Inc, Time Warner
USA, 1976
Milton Glaser
[Publishing]

5 **DC Comics (spin logo)**
DC Comics Inc, Time Warner
USA, 2005
Brainchild Studios: Josh Beatman
[Publishing]

6 **DC Comics**
DC Comics Inc, Time Warner
USA, 2012
Landor Associates
[Publishing]

7 **DC Shoes**
DC Shoes Inc
USA, ca 1993
[Footwear]

8 **DD TV**
Direct Digital Television
Romania
[Television Channel]

9 **DEA (Deutsche Erdöl AG)**
RWE Dea AG
Germany
[Oil, Gas & Petroleum]

DEAD SEA WORKS LTD.

1

2

3

4 5 6

7 8

1   Dead Sea Works Ltd
    Israel Chemicals Ltd
    (ICL Fertilizers)
    Israel
    [Chemicals & Materials]

2   Dean Foods
    Dean Foods Company
    USA
    [Food & Beverage]

3   Dean Foods
    Dean Foods Company
    USA
    [Food & Beverage]

4   De Beers
    De Beers Group
    South Africa, 2002
    The Partners: Michael Paisley,
    Rob Holloway
    [Mining]

5   debitel
    debitel AG
    Germany
    [Telecommunications]

6   De Boeck
    Group de Boeck
    Belgium, 2004
    Sign*
    [Publishing]

7   Debrett's
    Debrett's Limited
    UK
    The Partners
    [Publishing]

8   de Buyer
    de Buyer Industries SAS
    France
    [Kitchenware]

1 **Decathlon**
Decathlon SA
France
[Retail]

2 **Deceuninck**
Deceuninck NV
Belgium
[Construction]

3 **Decleor Paris**
Laboratoires Decleor SAS
France
[Health & Beauty]

4 **De Dietrich**
De Dietrich Process Systems Group
France
[Industrial Products]

5 **Dedon**
Dedon GmbH
Germany
[Home Furnishings]

6 **Deer Valley Resort**
Germany
[Places]

7 **Deezer**
Blogmusik SAS
France
[Internet]

8 **Definitive Techology**
Definitive Technology Inc
USA
[Consumer Electronics]

1. **Def Jam**
Def Jam Recordings,
Universal Music Group
USA
[Music Industry]

2. **Deflecta-Shield**
Lund International Inc
USA
[Automotive]

3. **Defra (Department for Environment, Food and Rural Affairs)**
HM Government
UK, 1990s
[Government]

4. **De Fursac**
France, 2009
H5: Fleur Fortuné
[Fashion]

5. **Deft**
Deft Inc
USA
[Paints & Coatings]

6. **Degussa-Hüls**
Degussa-Hüls AG
Germany
[Chemicals & Materials]

7. **DekaBank**
Germany
[Financial Services]

8. **Dekra**
Dekra eV
Germany
[Labelling, Standards & Certification]

9. **De La Rue**
De La Rue plc
UK
[Printing Services]

10. **Delco Electronics**
Delco Electronics Corporation
USA
[Automotive]

11. **Delco Systems**
Delco Electronics Corporation
USA
[Automotive]

1 **Delcourt**
  France
  [Publishing]

2 **Delhaize America**
  Delhaize Group SA/NV
  USA
  [Retail]

3 **Delhaize Group**
  Delhaize Group SA/NV
  Belgium
  [Retail]

4 **Delicious**
  AVOS Systems Inc
  USA, 2008
  [Internet]

5 **Dell**
  Dell Inc
  USA, 1994
  [Computer Technology]

▶ 6 **Dell**
  Dell Inc
  USA, 2009
  Dell Global Creative
  [Computer Technology]

7 **Dellorto**
  Dell'orto SpA
  Italy
  [Automotive]

DELL PHARMACY

1 **Dell Pharmacy**
Dell Chemists (1975) Ltd
Canada
[Healthcare]

2 **Del Monte Foods**
KKR & Co. LPO, Vestar Capital Partners, Centerview Partners
USA, 1990
[Food & Beverage]

3 **Deloitte**
Deloitte Touche Tohmatsu Limited
UK
The Brand Union
[Professional Services]

4 **DeLorean**
DeLorean Motor Company (DMC)
USA
[Automotive]

5 **DeLorean Motor Company (DMC)**
USA
[Automotive]

6 **Delta Airlines**
Delta Airlines Inc
USA, 2000
Landor Associates
[Airline]

7 **Delta Airlines**
Delta Airlines Inc
USA, 2007
Lippincott Mercer
[Airline]

8 **Delta Card**
Visa Inc
USA
[Financial Services]

1   **Del Taco**
    Del Taco Holdings Inc
    USA, 1992
    [Restaurants & Bars]

2   **Delta Dore**
    Groupe Delta Dore
    France
    [Technology]

3   **Delta Electricity**
    Australia
    [Energy]

4   **Delta Faucet**
    Delta Faucet Company,
    Masco Corporation
    USA, 2001
    Pentagram: Woody Pirtle
    [Home Appliances]

5   **Delta Faucet**
    Delta Faucet Company,
    Masco Corporation
    USA, 2001
    Pentagram: Woody Pirtle
    [Home Appliances]

6   **Delta Lloyd Bank**
    Delta Lloyd Group NV
    Netherlands
    [Financial Services]

7   **Del Valle**
    The Coca-Cola Company
    USA
    [Food & Beverage]

DEMECO

1 **Demeco**
Demeco SAS
France
[Freight & Logistics]

2 **Demko**
UL International Demko A/S
Denmark
[Labelling, Standards
& Certification]

3 **Democratic Party**
US Democratic Party
USA, 2010
[Political]

▶ 4 **Democratic Party**
US Democratic Party
USA
[Political]

5 **Democratic Party**
US Democratic Party
USA
[Political]

6 **DeNA**
DeNA Co. Ltd
Japan
[Internet]

7 **Dend Media Services**
Netherlands
[Internet]

8 **De Nederlandsche Bank**
De Nederlandsche Bank NV
Netherlands
[Financial Services]

9 **De Nederlandsche Bank**
De Nederlandsche Bank NV
Netherlands
[Financial Services]

DENTYNE

1 **DenizBank**
DenizBank AŞ
Turkey
[Financial Services]

2 **Deniz Yollari**
Türkiye Denizcilik İşletmeleri AŞ
Turkey
[Marine]

3 **Denmark**
Visit Denmark
Denmark
[Travel & Tourism]

4 **Denny's**
Denny's Corporation
USA
[Restaurants & Bars]

5 **Denon**
D&M Holdings Inc
Japan
[Consumer Electronics]

6 **Denso**
Denso Corporation
Japan
[Automotive]

7 **DentsCare**
FGM/Dentscare Ltda
Brazil
[Healthcare]

8 **Dentyne**
Cadbury Adams USA LLC,
Kraft Foods Inc
USA
[Food & Beverage]

9 **Dentyne**
Cadbury Adams USA LLC,
Kraft Foods Inc
USA
[Food & Beverage]

DENVER MATTRESS CO.

1 Denver Mattress Co.
   Furniture Row LLC
   USA
   [Retail]

2 Depa Fysiko Aerio
   Gas Supply Company
   of Thessaloniki SA
   Greece
   [Utilities]

3 Département du Val de Marne
   Conseil général du Val-de-Marne
   France
   [Places]

4 Department of Commerce (seal)
   United States Department
   of Commerce
   USA, 1913
   [Government]

5 Department of Energy (seal)
   United States Department
   of Energy
   USA, 1977
   [Government]

6 Department of Health & Human
   Services (logo)
   United States Department
   of Health & Human Services
   USA
   [Government]

7 Department of Justice – Office
   of Justice Programs (logo)
   USA
   [Government]

8 De Persgroep
   De Persgroep NV
   Belgium
   [Media]

1 **Depom**
Depom Depolama
Loj.Hiz.Ltd.Şti
Turkey
[Safety & Security]

2 **Depression Alliance**
UK
[Charity]

3 **Deputación de Pontevedra**
Spain
[Places]

4 **Der Grüne Punkt**
Der Grüne Punkt, Duales
System Deutschland GmbH
Germany
[Labelling, Standards
& Certification]

5 **Descente**
Descente Ltd
Japan, ca 1957
[Sporting Goods]

6 **Desert Group**
United Arab Emirates
[Construction]

7 **Designer Depot**
Hudson's Bay Company
Canada, ca 2004
[Retail]

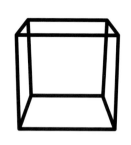

1 **Design Exchange (DX)**
   Canada
   [Galleries & Museums]

2 **Design Museum**
   UK
   [Galleries & Museums]

3 **Design Museum**
   UK, 2003
   Graphic Thought Facility
   [Galleries & Museums]

4 **Design Museum Shop**
   UK, 2007
   Build
   [Retail]

5 **Detroit Diesel**
   Detroit Diesel Corporation,
   Daimler AG
   USA
   [Oil, Gas & Petroleum]

6 **Detroit Institute of Arts**
   USA, 2008
   Pentagram
   [Galleries & Museums]

1 **Detroit Pistons**
National Basketball Association (NBA)
USA
[Sport]

2 **Detroit Red Wings**
USA, ca 1982
[Sport]

3 **Detroit Regional Chamber**
USA
[Societies & Associations]

4 **Deutsche Bank**
Deutsche Bank AG
Germany, 1974
Stankowski & Duschek:
Anton Stankowski
[Financial Services]

5 **Deutsche Börse**
Deutsche Börse AG
Germany, 1995
Stankowski & Duschek
[Financial Services]

6 **Deutsche Messe AG**
Germany, (mark) 1947
Paul Rademacher
[Places]

7 **Deutsche Nationalbibliothek**
Germany, 2007
Claus Koch
[Foundations & Institutes]

8 **Deutsche Post**
Deutsche Post AG
Germany, 1998
Nitsch Design
[Mail Services]

DEUTSCHES ZENTRUM

1. **Deutsches Zentrum**
   Ecuador, 2007
   Helou Design
   [Foundations & Institutes]

2. **Deutz**
   Deutz AG
   Germany
   [Manufacturing]

3. **Devon**
   Devon Energy Corporation
   USA
   [Oil, Gas & Petroleum]

4. **DeVry University**
   DeVry Inc
   USA
   [Education]

5. **DeWalt**
   Stanley Black & Decker Inc
   USA
   [Tools & Machinery]

6. **Dewar's**
   Bacardi & Company Limited
   UK
   [Wines, Beers & Spirits]

7. **Dexia**
   Dexia NV/SA
   Belgium
   [Financial Services]

8. **DFCG (Association Nationale des Directeurs Financiers et de Contrôle de Gestion)**
   France
   [Societies & Associations]

9. **DGC (Directors Guild of Canada)**
   Canada
   [Societies & Associations]

10. **DGOF (Deutsche Gesellschaft für Online-Forschung eV)**
    Germany, 2007
    Enorm
    [Societies & Associations]

1 **DHCC (Deployment Health Clinical Center)**
United States Department of Defence
USA, ca 2001
[Government]

2 **DHL Express**
Deutsche Post AG
Germany, 2003
Nitsch Design
[Mail Services]

3 **Dia (Distribuidora Internacional de Alimentacion SA)**
Spain, 2008
[Retail]

4 **Diadora**
Geox SpA
Italy
[Apparel]

5 **Diageo**
Diageo plc
UK, 1997
Wolff Olins
[Wines, Beers & Spirits]

6 **Diakonie (Diakonische Werk der Evangelischen Kirche in Deutschland eV)**
Germany
[Societies & Associations]

7 **Dial**
The Dial Corporation,
Henkel AG & Co. KGaA
USA
[Personal Care]

8 **Dial**
The Dial Corporation,
Henkel AG & Co. KGaA
USA, 2000
[Personal Care]

9 **Dialogic Corporation**
Canada, ca 2006
[Technology]

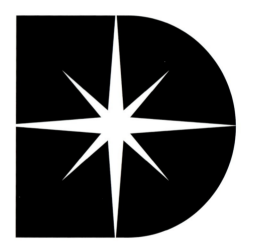

1 **Diamond Alloy**
  UK
  [Automotive]

2 **DiamondCluster**
  DiamondCluster International Inc
  USA
  [Professional Services]

3 **Diamond Shamrock**
  Valero Energy Corporation
  USA
  [Oil, Gas & Petroleum]

4 **Diamond Snow Ploughs**
  Meyer Products LLC
  USA
  [Tools & Machinery]

5 **Diamondtraxx**
  France
  H5: Yorgo Tloupas
  [Music Industry]

6 **Diana Ferrari**
  Fusion Retail Brands Pty Ltd
  Australia
  [Apparel]

7 **Diapar**
  France
  [Retail]

1 **Diane von Fürstenberg (DVF)**
USA
Fabien Baron
[Fashion]

2 **DICE (Digital Illusions Creative Entertainment)**
EA Digital Illusions CE AB
Sweden, ca 2008
[Computer & Video Games]

3 **Dickies**
Williamson-Dickie Manufacturing Company
USA
[Apparel]

4 **Dickson**
Dickson-Constant Sarl
France
[Home Furnishings]

5 **Diebold**
Diebold Inc
USA
[Manufacturing]

6 **Diebold**
Diebold Inc
USA
[Manufacturing]

7 **DieHard**
KCD IP LLC
USA
[Automotive]

8 **Diehl**
Diehl Stiftung & Co. KG
Germany
[Aerospace]

▶ 9 **Diesel**
Diesel SpA
Italy
[Apparel]

▶ 10 **Diesel**
Diesel SpA
Italy
[Apparel]

DIET COKE

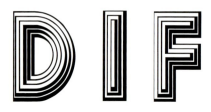

1 **Diet Coke**
The Coca-Cola Company
USA, 2007
[Food & Beverage]

2 **Diet Dr Pepper**
Dr Pepper Snapple Group Inc
USA, ca 1987
[Food & Beverage]

3 **Diet Snapple**
Dr Pepper Snapple Group Inc
USA, 2000
[Food & Beverage]

4 **DIF (Sistema Nacional para el Desarrollo Integral de la Familia)**
Mexico
[Societies & Associations]

5 **Digg**
Digg Inc
USA
[Internet]

6 **Digimagen**
Venezuela, 2003
Ají Pintao: Mariana Núñez
[Film Industry]

7 **DiGiorno Pasta**
Nestlé SA
USA
[Food & Beverage]

8 **Digital**
Digital Equipment Corporation
USA
[Computer Technology]

1 **Digital 8**
developed by Sony Corporation
Japan, 1999
[Consumer Electronics]

2 **Digital Data Storage (DDS)**
Sony Corporation
Japan
[Labelling, Standards
& Certification]

3 **Digital Emoticon**
Carnegie Mellon University
USA, 1982
Scott Fahlman
[Graphic Design]

4 **Digital Radio Plus
(DAB+) Australia**
Digital Radio Plus
Australia
[Radio Stations]

5 **Digital River**
Digital River Inc
USA
[Computer Software]

6 **Dilo Group**
Dilo Machines GmbH
Germany
[Manufacturing]

7 **Dillard's**
Dillard's Inc
USA
[Retail]

8 **DIM**
DIM SAS
France
[Apparel]

9 **Dime (Dime Savings
Bank of Williamsburgh)**
USA
[Financial Services]

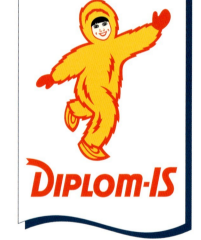

Dior

1 **Dimensional Fund Advisors**
USA
[Financial Services]

2 **Dimension Data**
Dimension Data Holdings plc
South Africa, ca 1983
[Information Technology]

3 **Dimplex**
GDC Group Ltd,
Glen Dimplex Group
UK
[Heating & Cooling]

4 **Diners Club**
Diners Club International
USA
[Financial Services]

5 **Dior**
Christian Dior SA
France
[Fashion]

6 **Diplom-Is mascot (Eskimonika)**
Diplom-Is A/S
Norway
[Food & Beverage]

DISCOUNT TIRE CO. INC.

1 **Direct 8**
Groupe Canal+SA
France, 2007
[Television Channel]

2 **Directbouw BV**
Netherlands
[Construction]

3 **Direct Print**
Kyocera Corporation
Japan
[Computer Software]

4 **Direct Stream Digital (DSD)**
Sony Corporation, Koninklijke
Philips Electronics NV
Japan/Netherlands
[Labelling, Standards
& Certification]

5 **DirecTV**
DirecTV Inc
USA, 2005
[Satellite Television]

6 **Dirt Devil**
TTI Floor Care North America,
Techtronic Industries
Company Ltd
USA
[Household Products]

7 **Di Sandro**
Sandro Magli & C. SAS
Italy
[Footwear]

8 **Discman**
Sony Corporation
Japan, 2000
[Consumer Electronics]

▶ 9 **Discount Tire Co. Inc.**
The Reinalt-Thomas Corporation
USA
[Retail]

215

1. **Discovery Channel**
Discovery Communications Inc
USA, 1987
[Television Channel]

2. **Discovery Channel**
Discovery Communications Inc
USA, 2009
[Television Channel]

3. **Discovery Cove**
SeaWorld Parks & Entertainment Inc
USA
[Aquariums & Zoos]

4. **Disc Tarra**
Tarra Group
Indonesia
[Retail]

5. **Dish Network**
Dish Network Corporation
USA, 2012
[Satellite Television]

6. **DISK (Türkiye Devrimci İşçi Sendikaları Konfederasyonu)**
Turkey
[Societies & Associations]

7. **Disney Channel**
Disney-ABC Television Group, The Walt Disney Company
USA, 2002
Razorfish
[Television Channel]

8. **Disney Channel**
Disney-ABC Television Group, The Walt Disney Company
USA
Razorfish
[Television Channel]

9. **Disney Channel**
Disney-ABC Television Group, The Walt Disney Company
USA, 1987
[Television Channel]

1 **Disston Tools**
Disston Company
USA
[Tools & Machinery]

2 **Distress Centres of Toronto**
Canada
[Charity]

3 **Ditch Witch**
The Charles Machine Works Inc
USA
[Tools & Machinery]

4 **Diversey**
Diversey Inc
USA, 2010
[Chemicals & Materials]

5 **Divo TV**
Russia
[Satellite Television]

6 **DivX**
DivX Inc, Rovi Corporation
USA
[Consumer Electronics]

7 **Dixie Cup**
Koch Industries Inc
USA, 1969
Saul Bass
[Household Products]

8 **Dixon**
Emerson & Renwick Ltd
Dixon Division
UK
[Tools & Machinery]

1 **Dixons**
Dixons Retail plc
UK
[Retail]

2 **DJ Hero**
Activision Blizzard Inc, Vivendi SA
USA, 2009
[Computer & Video Games]

3 **djuice**
Telenor Group
Norway, 2006
Wolff Olins
[Telecommunications]

4 **djuice**
Telenor Group
Norway
[Telecommunications]

5 **DKNY (Donna Karan New York)**
LVMH Moët Hennessy
Louis Vuitton SA
USA, 1989
Arnell Group: Peter Arnell
[Apparel]

6 **DKNY Eyes**
LVMH Moët Hennessy
Louis Vuitton SA
USA
[Eyewear]

7 **DKV (Deutsche Krankenversicherung AG, Ergo Versicherungsgruppe AG)**
Germany, 2003
MetaDesign
[Financial Services]

8 **D-Link**
D-Link Corporation
Taiwan
[Information Technology]

9 **DLR (Deutsches Zentrum für Luft- und Raumfahrt eV)**
Germany
[Aerospace]

10 **dm-drogerie markt**
dm-drogerie markt GmbH & Co. KG
Germany
[Retail]

DODGE VIPER

1 dm-drogerie markt
   dm-drogerie markt GmbH & Co. KG
   Germany, 2000
   Landor Associates
   [Retail]

2 DMSB-Streckensicherungs-Staffel
   Deutscher Motor Sport Bund eV
   Germany
   [Motorsport]

3 DNA
   DNA Oy
   Finland
   [Telecommunications]

4 DnB NOR
   DNB ASA
   Norway, 2003
   Scandinavian Design Group
   [Financial Services]

5 DNV (Det Norske Veritas)
   Norway, 1993
   [Foundations & Institutes]

6 Do buckle up
   USA
   [Safety & Security]

7 Dodge
   Chrysler Group LLC
   USA, 1993
   [Automotive]

8 Dodge
   Chrysler Group LLC
   USA, 1962
   [Automotive]

9 Dodge Viper
   Chrysler Group LLC
   USA, 1992
   [Automotive]

DOĞAN HOLDING

1 **Doğan Holding**
Doğan Sirketler Grubu Holding AS
Turkey
[Conglomerate]

2 **Dogs Trust**
UK
[Charities]

3 **Doimo Salotti**
Doimo Salotti SpA
Italy
[Home Furnishings]

4 **Do It Best**
Do It Best Corporation
USA
[Retail]

5 **Do-it-center**
USA
[Retail]

6 **DoKaSch**
DoKaSch GmbH
Germany
[Transport]

7 **Dolby**
Dolby Laboratories Inc
USA, 2008
Turner Duckworth
[Labelling, Standards
& Certification]

8 **Dolby Surround**
Dolby Laboratories Inc
USA
[Labelling, Standards
& Certification]

1 **Dolce & Gabbana**
Italy
[Fashion]

2 **Dole**
Dole Food Company Inc
USA, 1986
Landor Associates
[Food & Beverage]

3 **Dollar Rent A Car**
Dollar Thrifty Automotive Group
USA
[Car Rental]

4 **Dolly Madison Bakery**
Hostess Brands Inc
USA
[Food & Beverage]

5 **Dolphin Cruise Line**
Premier Cruise Lines
USA
[Travel & Tourism]

6 **Dolphin Safe**
U.S. Department of Commerce
USA, 1990
[Labelling, Standards
& Certification]

7 **Dolphin Square**
Mantilla Ltd
UK, 2006
ico Design
[Real Estate]

DOMESTOS

1 **Domestos**
Unilever plc/NV
USA, ca 2002
[Household Products]

2 **Dometic**
Dometic Group
Sweden
[Outdoor & Recreational]

3 **Dominion**
Dominion Resources Inc
USA
[Energy]

▶ 4 **Domino's Pizza**
Domino's Pizza Inc
USA, 1997
[Restaurants & Bars]

▶ 5 **Domino Sugar**
Domino Foods Inc, American
Sugar Refining Inc
USA
[Food & Beverage]

DOREL HOME PRODUCTS

1   **Dommelsch**
    Dommelsch Bierbrouwerij,
    Anheuser-Busch InBev NV
    Netherlands
    [Breweries]

2   **Dom Pérignon**
    Moët & Chandon
    France
    [Wines, Beers & Spirits]

3   **Donau**
    CTP Donau
    South Africa
    [Office Supplies]

4   **Dongfeng Motor Corporation**
    China
    [Automotive]

5   **Don Smallgoods**
    George Weston Foods Ltd
    Australia
    [Food & Beverage]

6   **Doorstep Dairy**
    USA
    [Food & Beverage]

7   **Doosan**
    Doosan Group
    South Korea
    Lippincott
    [Conglomerate]

8   **Doral**
    R. J. Reynolds Tobacco
    Company
    USA
    [Tobacco]

9   **Dorel Home Products**
    Dorel Home Furnishings,
    Dorel Industries Inc
    USA
    [Home Furnishings]

DORITOS

1

2

3

4

5

6

7

8

1 **Doritos**
Frito-Lay North America Inc, PepsiCo Inc
USA, 1964
[Food & Beverage]

2 **Doritos**
Frito-Lay North America Inc, PepsiCo Inc
USA, 1980s
[Food & Beverage]

3 **Doritos**
Frito-Lay North America Inc, PepsiCo Inc
USA, 1990s
[Food & Beverage]

4 **Doritos**
Frito-Lay North America Inc, PepsiCo Inc
USA, 2000
[Food & Beverage]

5 **Dorling Kindersley (DK)**
Penguin Group, Pearson plc
UK, 2003
Pentagram
[Publishing]

6 **Dorma**
Dorma Holding GmbH & Co. KGaA
Germany
[Construction]

7 **Dos Pinos**
Milk Producers Cooperative dos Pinos RL
Costa Rica
[Food & Beverage]

8 **Double Coffee**
AS DC Holding
Latvia, 2002
[Restaurants & Bars]

1 **Douglas**
Parfümerie Douglas GmbH
Germany
[Retail]

2 **Douwe Egberts**
Douwe Egberts Koninklijke Tabaksfabriek-Koffiebranderijen-Theehandel NV, Sara Lee Corporation
Netherlands
[Food & Beverage]

3 **Douwe Egberts**
Douwe Egberts Koninklijke Tabaksfabriek-Koffiebranderijen-Theehandel NV, Sara Lee Corporation
Netherlands
[Food & Beverage]

4 **Douwe Egberts**
Douwe Egberts Koninklijke Tabaksfabriek-Koffiebranderijen-Theehandel NV, Sara Lee Corporation
Netherlands
[Food & Beverage]

5 **Dove**
Unilever plc/NV
USA, ca 2003
[Personal Care]

6 **Dove**
Mars Inc
USA
[Food & Beverage]

7 **Dove**
Mars Inc
USA
[Food & Beverage]

8 **Dover**
Dover Corporation
USA
[Conglomerate]

1 **Dovre**
Dovrepeisen A/S
Norway
[Home Appliances]

2 **Dovre**
Dovre-JBS A/S
Norway, 2008
Norges Kreative Fagskole
[Apparel]

3 **Dow Chemical**
The Dow Chemical Company
USA, 1898
M. B. Johnson
[Chemicals & Materials]

4 **Dow Jones**
Dow Jones & Company Inc
USA, 1997
Belk Mignogna Associates
[Financial Services]

5 **Dow Jones Interactive**
Dow Jones & Company Inc
USA
[Financial Services]

6 **Downer Engineering**
Downer EDi Ltd
Australia
[Engineering]

7 **DPD (Deutscher Paket Dienst)**
Deutscher Paket Dienst GmbH
& Co. KG
Germany
[Mail Services]

1 **DQS (Deutsche Gesellschaft zur Zertifizierung von Managementsystemen)**
DQS Holding GmbH
Germany
[Labelling, Standards & Certification]

2 **DR (Danmarks Radio)**
Danish Broadcasting Corporation
Denmark, 1964
Connie Linck
[Broadcaster]

3 **DragonAir**
Hong Kong Dragon Airlines Ltd
China, 1985
[Airline]

4 **Dragon Alliance**
USA
[Eyewear]

5 **Dragon Ball Z**
Shueisha Inc
Japan
Funimation Productions
[Publications]

6 **Draka**
Draka Holding NV
Netherlands
[Manufacturing]

7 **Drake**
R.L. Drake Holdings LLC
USA
[Satellite Television]

8 **Drake's**
Hostess Brands Inc
USA
[Food & Beverage]

1 **Drakkar Noir**
Guy Laroche
France, ca 1982
[Personal Care]

2 **Drambuie**
Drambuie Liqueur Company Ltd
UK
[Wines, Beers & Spirits]

3 **Drano**
S.C. Johnson & Son Inc
USA
[Household Products]

4 **Draper**
Draper Inc
USA
[Manufacturing]

5 **Draw-Tite**
Cequent Performance Products Inc
USA
[Automotive]

6 **Drayton Windows**
Drayton Windows Ltd
UK
[Construction]

7 **Dreamcast**
SEGA Corporation
Japan, 1998
[Computer & Video Games]

8 **DreamWorks Records**
Universal Music Group
USA, 1996
Roy Lichtenstein
[Music Industry]

1 **DreamWorks Animation**
DreamWorks Animation SKG Inc
USA
Steven Spielberg,
Dennis Muren, Robert Hunt
[Film Industry]

2 **Dresdner Bank**
Germany, 2005
Claus Koch
[Financial Services]

3 **Dreyer's Grand Ice Cream**
Dreyer's Grand Ice Cream
Holdings Inc, Nestlé SA
USA, 1998
[Food & Beverage]

4 **Dristan**
Pfizer Inc
USA
[Pharmaceuticals]

5 **Driving Force**
The Driving Force Inc
Canada
[Car Rental]

6 **Dr. Oetker**
Dr. August Oetker KG
Germany
[Food & Beverage]

7 **Dronco**
Dronco AG
Germany
[Tools & Machinery]

DR PEPPER

1 **Dr Pepper**
Dr Pepper Snapple Group Inc
USA, 1968
[Food & Beverage]

2 **Dr Pepper**
Dr Pepper Snapple Group Inc
USA, 1997
[Food & Beverage]

3 **Dr. Scholl's**
SSL International plc,
Reckitt Benckiser plc
UK
[Footwear]

4 **Drug Emporium**
Drug Emporium Inc
USA
[Retail]

5 **Dryden Flight Research Center**
USA, 1998
[Aerospace]

6 **DSA (Direct Selling Association)**
USA
[Societies & Associations]

7 **DSB (Danske Statsbaner)**
Danish Ministry of Transport
Denmark
[Transport]

8 **DSM**
Koninklijke DSM NV
Netherlands
[Chemicals & Materials]

9 **DSME (Daewoo Shipbuilding & Marine Engineering)**
Daewoo Shipbuilding & Marine Engineering Co. Ltd
South Korea
[Industry]

1. **DSP (Demokratik Sol Parti)**
   Turkey
   [Political]

2. **Dsquared2**
   Italy, 1998
   Giovanni Bianco Studio 65
   [Fashion]

3. **DSS (Digital Satellite System)**
   DirecTV Inc
   USA
   [Satellite Television]

4. **DSW (Designer Shoe Warehouse)**
   DSW Inc
   USA
   [Retail]

5. **DTS**
   DTS Inc
   USA, 2007
   [Labelling, Standards & Certification]

6. **DTS Digital Surround**
   DTS Inc
   USA, 1991
   [Labelling, Standards & Certification]

7. **Duarig**
   Duarig SA
   France, 2000s
   [Sporting Goods]

DUBAI

1 **Dubai**
Dubai Department of Tourism
and Commerce Marketing
Dubai
[Travel & Tourism]

2 **Dubai Cares**
United Arab Emirates
[Charity]

3 **Dubai Ports Authority**
United Arab Emirates
[Marine]

4 **Dubai Sports Council (DSC)**
United Arab Emirates, ca 2005
[Sport]

5 **Dubbles**
[Music]

6 **Ducati**
Ducati Motor Holding SpA
Italy, 1967
[Automotive]

7 **Ducati**
Ducati Motor Holding SpA
Italy, 1987
[Automotive]

8 **Ducati**
Ducati Motor Holding SpA
Italy, 2008
[Automotive]

9 **Ducati**
Ducati Motor Holding SpA
Italy
[Automotive]

DUN & BRADSTREET

1 Duck Records
Duck Records Ltd
UK, ca 1982
[Music Industry]

2 Ducks Unlimited
USA
[Conservation & Environment]

3 Dudson
Dudson Ltd
UK
[Glass & Ceramics]

4 Dufferin Concrete
Holcim (Canada) Inc
Canada
[Construction]

5 Duke Energy
Duke Energy Corporation
USA
[Energy]

6 Duke Realty
Duke Realty Corporation
USA
[Real Estate]

7 Dulux
Akzo Nobel NV
UK
[Paints & Coatings]

8 Dun & Bradstreet Inc
USA, 1996
Landor Associates
[Information Technology]

233

1 **Duncan Aviation**
Duncan Aviation Inc
USA, 1989
Mitchell Mauk
[Aviation]

2 **Dundee Leeds**
Dundee Corporation
Bermuda
[Financial Services]

3 **Dunhill**
British American Tobacco plc
UK
[Tobacco]

4 **Dunhill Clothiers**
USA, 1947
Paul Rand
[Apparel]

5 **Dunhill London**
Alfred Dunhill Ltd
UK
[Luxury Goods]

6 **Duni**
Duni AB
Sweden
[Paper Products]

7 **Dunkin' Donuts**
Dunkin' Brands Inc
USA, 2002
[Restaurants & Bars]

8 **Dunkin' Donuts**
Dunkin' Brands Inc
USA, 2006
[Restaurants & Bars]

1 **Dunlopillo**
Hilding Anders Group
UK
[Consumer Products]

2 **Dunlop Tyres**
The Goodyear Tire & Rubber Company, Sumitomo Rubber Industries Ltd
UK, 1962
Design Research Unit
[Automotive]

3 **Dunlop Tyres**
The Goodyear Tire & Rubber Company, Sumitomo Rubber Industries Ltd
UK
[Automotive]

4 **Duplo**
The LEGO Group
Denmark
[Toys, Games & Models]

5 **Duplo**
The LEGO Group
Denmark, 2004
[Toys, Games & Models]

6 **DuPont**
E. I. du Pont de Nemours and Company
USA
[Chemicals & Materials]

7 **Duracell**
Procter & Gamble Co
USA, 1964
Lippincott
[Household Products]

8 **Duran Group**
Duran Group GmbH
Germany
[Glass & Ceramics]

DURASWITCH

1 **Duraswitch**
Esterline Technologies Corporation
USA
[Technology]

2 **Durex**
Reckitt Benckiser plc
UK
[Personal Care]

3 **Durham Bulls**
Minor League Baseball Properties
USA, 1998
[Sport]

4 **Dusit Hotels & Resorts**
Dusit International
Thailand
[Hospitality]

5 **Dustbane**
Dustbane Products Ltd
Canada
[Industrial Products]

6 **Dust-Off**
Cargill Ltd
Canada
[Industrial Products]

7 **DutchBird**
DutchBird BV
Netherlands, 2000
[Airline]

8 **DV (Digital Video)**
Sony Corporation
Japan, 1994
[Labelling, Standards & Certification]

9 **DVD**
DVD Format/Logo Licensing Corporation, DVD FLLC
Japan, 1990s
[Labelling, Standards & Certification]

10 **DVD+RW Alliance**
USA
[Societies & Associations]

11 **DVTK 1910**
Diósgyőr-Vasgyári Testgyakorlók Köre
Hungary
[Sport]

1. **DWP (Digital Water Pavilion)**
   Zaragoza Municipality
   Spain, 2008
   studio FM milano
   [Places]

2. **Dyflex**
   Dyflex Co. Ltd
   Japan
   [Chemicals & Materials]

3. **Dynamic Zone**
   Netherlands
   [Advertising & Campaigns]

4. **Dynamite**
   Dynamite Food
   Handelsgesellschaft mbH
   Germany
   [Food & Beverage]

5. **Dynamo Kyiv**
   FC Dynamo Kyiv
   Ukraine
   [Sport]

6. **Dyneff**
   Dyneff SAS, Rompetrol
   Group NV
   France
   [Energy]

7. **Dyneff**
   Dyneff SAS, Rompetrol
   Group NV
   France, 2008
   [Energy]

8. **Dynegy**
   Dynegy Inc
   USA
   Will Ayres
   [Energy]

9. **Dysan**
   Dysan Corporation
   Canada, 1970s
   [Data Storage]

10. **Dyson**
    Dyson Ltd
    UK
    [Household Products]

E-G

EADS

1. **EADS (European Aeronautic Defence and Space Command NV)**
   Netherlands, 2000
   [Defence]

2. **EA (Electronic Arts)**
   Electronic Arts Inc
   USA, 2006
   [Computer & Video Games]

3. **EA Games**
   Electronic Arts Inc
   USA
   [Computer & Video Games]

4. **EA Sports**
   Electronic Arts Inc
   USA, 1999
   [Computer & Video Games]

5. **Eagle Broadband Inc**
   USA
   [Internet]

6. **Eagle Records**
   Eagle Rock Entertainment
   UK
   [Music Industry]

7. **Eastman**
   Eastman Chemical Company
   USA
   [Chemicals & Materials]

8. **Easton**
   Easton-Bell Sports Inc
   USA
   [Sporting Goods]

9. **Eastpak**
   VF Corporation
   USA
   [Manufacturing]

10. **East West Bancorp**
    East West Bancorp Inc
    USA
    [Financial Services]

EAT.

∉BEL

EBONY ecco®

1 **East West Records**
Warner Music Group
USA, 1990
Laurence Dunmore
[Music Industry]

2 **EasyJet**
EasyJet plc
UK, 1995
[Airline]

3 **EAT.**
EAT. The Real Food Co. Ltd
UK, 2002
Pentagram
[Restaurants & Bars]

4 **Eaton Corporation**
Eaton SRL
Italy
[Industrial Products]

5 **Ebara**
Ebara Corporation
Japan
[Industry]

6 **eBay**
eBay Inc
USA, 1995
Bill Cleary
[Internet]

7 **eBay**
eBay Inc
USA, 2012
Lippincott
[Internet]

8 **Ebel**
MGI Luxury Group SA
Switzerland
[Watches & Jewelry]

9 **Ebony**
Johnson Publishing Company Inc
USA
[Publications]

10 **ECCO**
ECCO Sko AS
Denmark
[Footwear]

1 **Eckerd**
Eckerd Corporation
USA
[Retail]

2 **Eckō unltd.**
Iconix Brand Group Inc,
MEE Direct LLC
USA
[Fashion]

3 **Eckrich**
Armour-Eckrich Meats LLC
USA
[Food & Beverage]

4 **Ecolab**
Ecolab Inc
USA
[Chemicals & Materials]

5 **Eddy Merckx Cycles**
Belgium, 2011
[Bicycles]

6 **Edelbrock**
Edelbrock LLC
USA
[Automotive]

7 **Edel Music**
Edel AG
Germany
[Music Industry]

8 **Eden Foods**
Eden Foods Inc
USA
[Food & Beverage]

9 **EDF**
EDF Group
France, 2005
Plan Créatif: Vanessa
van Steelandt, Patrick
Le Mahec, Sophie Tchérakian
[Utilities]

E! ENTERTAINMENT TELEVISION

1 **Edinaya Rossiya/United Russia**
Russia
[Political]

2 **Edison International**
USA, 1996
[Utilities]

3 **Editora Abril**
Editora Abril SA,
Grupo Abril
Brazil
[Publishing]

4 **Editorial Andina**
Chile, 1974
Mario Fonseca
[Publishing]

5 **Edox**
Edox & Vista SA
Switzerland
[Watches & Jewelry]

6 **Ed Tel (Edmonton Telephones Corporation)**
Canada
[Telecommunications]

7 **Educación es camino**
Ecuador, 2009
Latinbrand
[Education]

8 **Education First**
Education First Ltd
UK
[Education]

9 **E! Entertainment Television**
E! Entertainment Television,
NBCUniversal
USA, 1990
[Television Channel]

1. **Effect Energy Drink**
   MBG International Premium BrandsGmbH
   Germany
   [Food & Beverage]

2. **Effer**
   Effer SpA (CTE Group)
   Italy
   [Tools & Machinery]

3. **EgyptAir**
   Egypt Air Holding Company
   Egypt
   [Airline]

4. **EgyptAir**
   Egypt Air Holding Company
   Egypt, 2008
   [Transport]

5. **Ehrmann**
   Ehrmann AG
   Germany
   [Food & Beverage]

6. **Eiffage Construction**
   Eiffage SA
   France
   [Construction]

7. **Eiki**
   Eiki International Inc
   Japan
   [Consumer Electronics]

8. **Einstein Bros. Bagels**
   Einstein Noah Restaurant Group Inc
   USA, ca 1995
   [Restaurants & Bars]

9. **Eircom**
   Eircom Group Ltd
   Ireland
   [Telecommunications]

ELECTRIC

1 **Eizo**
   Eizo Nanao Corporation
   Japan
   [Technology]

2 **Eker**
   Eker Süt Ürünleri Gıda San. ve
   Ticaret AŞ
   Turkey
   [Food & Beverage]

3 **Ekoland**
   Poland
   [Societies & Associations]

4 **ELAC**
   ELAC Electroacustic GmbH
   Germany
   [Consumer Electronics]

5 **Elan**
   Elan d.o.o.
   Slovenia
   [Sporting Goods]

6 **Elco**
   Elco Vayonis SA
   Greece
   [Heating & Cooling]

7 **El Corte Ingles**
   El Corte Inglés SA
   Spain
   [Retail]

8 **Electric**
   Electric Visual Llc
   USA, 2000
   [Eyewear]

ELECTROHOME

ELECTROHOME

⊟ Electrolux

electronics boutique

1 **Electrohome**
Bluetronics Group, Circus World
Displays Ltd
Canada
[Consumer Electronics]

▶ 2 **Electrolux**
AB Electrolux
Sweden, 1962
Carlo L. Vivarelli
[Home Appliances]

3 **Electronic Cash (EC)**
Zentraler Kreditausschuss
Germany
[Financial Services]

▶ 4 **Electronics Boutique**
EB Games, GameStop Corporation
USA
[Retail]

5 **Electronorte**
Centrais Elétricas do Norte do
Brasil SA
Brazil
[Utilities]

6 **Elektra Records**
Elektra Entertainment Group Inc,
Warner Music Group
USA
[Music Industry]

7 **Elektra Records**
Elektra Entertainment Group Inc,
Warner Music Group
USA
[Music Industry]

8 **Elektro Helios**
AB Electrolux
Sweden
[Home Appliances]

1 **Element Skateboards**
Billabong International
USA
[Sporting Goods]

2 **Elf Service Stations**
Total SA
France
[Retail]

3 **Elle**
Hachette Filipacchi Médias SA, Lagardère Active
France
[Publications]

4 **Elliott Aviation**
Elliott Aviation Inc
USA
[Aviation]

5 **Elmer's**
Elmer's Products Inc
USA
[Consumer Products]

6 **e.l.m leblanc**
France
[Heating & Cooling]

7 **Elpida**
Elpida Memory Inc
Japan
[Technology]

8 **El Pollo Loco**
El Pollo Loco Inc
USA, 1975
[Restaurants & Bars]

ELSA

EMBASSY SUITES

HOTELS

1 ELSA
   ELSA Technology Inc
   Germany/Taiwan
   [Computer Hardware]

2 Embarq
   Embarq Corporation
   USA, 2006
   [Telecommunications]

3 Embassy Suites Hotels
   Hilton Worldwide
   USA
   [Hospitality]

4 Embassy Television
   USA, 1982
   [Media]

5 Embraer
   Embraer SA
   Brazil
   [Aerospace]

6 Emco
   Emco Maier GmbH
   Austria
   [Tools & Machinery]

7 Emerald City Press
   USA, 2007
   Pentagram
   [Retail]

1 **Emerica**
Sole Technology Inc
USA
[Footwear]

2 **Emerson**
Emerson Electric Co.
USA
[Conglomerate]

3 **Emerson Electronics**
BlueTronics Group
USA
[Consumer Electronics]

4 **Emerson Electronics**
BlueTronics Group
USA
[Consumer Electronics]

5 **EMI**
EMI Group Ltd, Citigroup Inc
UK
[Music Industry]

6 **EMI-Capitol Music**
EMI Group Ltd, Citigroup Inc
USA
[Music Industry]

7 **Emirates Airlines**
The Emirates Group
United Arab Emirates, 1999
[Airline]

8 **Emirates Group**
The Emirates Group
United Arab Emirates, 1999
[Airline]

EMPORIO ARMANI

1 **Emporio Armani**
Giorgio Armani SpA
Italy
[Fashion]

2 **ENAV**
ENAV SpA
Italy
[Aviation]

3 **Endeavor Talent Agency**
USA
[Professional Services]

4 **Energie Thun**
Energie Thun AG
Switzerland
[Utilities]

5 **Energizer**
Energizer Holdings Inc
USA, 1996
[Consumer Products]

6 **Energizer**
Energizer Holdings Inc
USA
[Consumer Products]

7 **Energy**
Klipsch Group Inc
Canada
[Consumer Electronics]

8 **Energy Star**
U.S. Environmental Protection Agency, U.S. Department of Energy
USA
[Government]

ENTENMANN'S

1 **Energy Trust**
Energy Trust of Oregon Inc
USA
[Energy]

2 **Engen**
Engen Petroleum Ltd
South Africa
[Oil, Gas & Petroleum]

3 **English National Opera**
UK, 1991
CDT: Mike Dempsey
[Music]

▶ 4 **Enjoi Skateboarding**
Globe International Ltd
USA
[Sporting Goods]

5 **Enkes**
Enkes Marine BV
Netherlands
[Marine]

▶ 6 **Enron**
Enron Corporation
USA, 1996
Paul Rand
[Conglomerate]

7 **Entenmann's**
Bimbo Bakeries USA Inc
USA
[Food & Beverage]

8 **Entenmann's**
Bimbo Bakeries USA Inc
USA
[Food & Beverage]

ENTERPRISE PRODUCTS PARTNERS

1 **Enterprise Products Partners LP**
USA
[Energy]

▶ 2 **Enterprise Rent-A-Car**
Enterprise Holdings Inc
USA, 1989
[Car Rental]

3 **Enterprise Rent-A-Car**
Enterprise Holdings Inc
USA, 2010
[Transport]

4 **Environmental Choice Program**
Environment Canada
Canada
[Conservation & Environment]

5 **e.on**
E.ON AG
Germany
[Utilities]

6 **EPA**
U.S. Environmental Protection Agency
USA
[Government]

7 **EPA**
EPA Neue Warenhaus AG
Switzerland
[Retail]

1 **Epic Records**
Sony Music Entertainment Inc
USA, 1979
[Music Industry]

2 **Epic Records**
Sony Music Entertainment Inc
USA, 1960s
[Music Industry]

3 **Epic Records**
Sony Music Entertainment Inc
USA, ca 1992
[Music Industry]

4 **Epic Records**
Sony Music Entertainment Inc
USA, 1970s
[Music Industry]

5 **Epic Records**
Sony Music Entertainment Inc
USA, 2011
[Music Industry]

6 **Epilepsy Foundation**
Epilepsy Foundation of America
USA
[Societies & Associations]

7 **E-Plus**
E-Plus Service GmbH & Co. KG
Germany
[Telecommunications]

8 **E-Plus**
E-Plus Service GmbH & Co. KG
Germany
[Telecommunications]

▶ 9 **Epson**
Seiko Epson Corporation
Japan
[Consumer Electronics]

EQUAL OPPORTUNITY HOUSING

1 **Equal Opportunity Housing**
Office of Fair Housing and Equal Opportunity (U.S. Department of Housing and Urban Development)
USA, 1988
[Government]

2 **Equifax**
Equifax Inc
USA
[Financial Services]

3 **ERA**
ERA Franchise Systems LLC
USA
[Real Estate]

4 **Eram**
Chaussures Eram SARL
France
[Footwear]

5 **Erdemir**
Ereğli Demir ve Çelik Fabrikaları TAŞ
Turkey
[Industrial Products]

6 **Erdgas/Natural Gas**
Verband der Schweizerischen Gasindustrie (VSG)
Switzerland
[Energy]

7 **Erector**
Meccano/Erector Sets
France
[Toys, Games & Models]

8 **Ericsson**
Telefonaktiebolaget LM Ericsson
Sweden, 1982
AID: Terry Moore
[Telecommunications]

ESCADA

1   **Erie Insurance**
    Erie Insurance Group
    USA
    [Financial Services]

2   **Ernst & Young**
    Ernst & Young Global Ltd
    UK
    [Professional Services]

3   **Erreà**
    Erreà Sport SpA
    Italy
    [Sporting Goods]

4   **ESA (European Space Agency)**
    France
    [Aerospace]

5   **ESA (European Space Agency)**
    France
    [Aerospace]

6   **ESAB (Electric Welding Limited company)**
    Sweden
    [Manufacturing]

7   **ESB**
    Electricity Supply Board (ESB)
    Ireland
    [Utilities]

8   **Escada**
    Escada SE
    Germany
    [Fashion]

ESPAÑA

ESPRIT

1   España
    Instituto de Turismo de España,
    Turespaña
    Spain, 1983
    Joan Miró
    [Travel & Tourism]

2   ESPN
    ESPN Inc
    USA, 1985
    [Television Network]

3   ESPRIT
    Esprit Holdings Ltd
    USA, 1979
    John Casado
    [Fashion]

4   Esquire
    Hearst Corporation
    USA
    [Publications]

5   ESRB Rating – Adults Only (AO)
    ESRB (Entertainment Software
    Rating Board)
    USA, 1994
    [Labelling, Standards
    & Certification]

6   Essar Steel
    Essar Group
    India
    [Industry]

7   Esselte
    Esselte Corporation
    USA
    [Office Supplies]

8   Esselte
    Esselte Corporation
    USA
    [Office Supplies]

9   Essilor
    Essilor International SA
    France
    [Eyewear]

1 **Esso**
Exxon Mobil Corporation
USA, 1923
[Oil, Gas & Petroleum]

2 **Esso Girl**
Exxon Mobil Corporation
Canada
[Oil, Gas & Petroleum]

3 **Estathè**
Ferrero SpA
Italy
[Food & Beverage]

4 **Estée Lauder**
Estée Lauder Companies Inc
USA
[Health & Beauty]

5 **Estes**
Estes-Cox Corporation
USA
[Toys, Games & Models]

6 **Estonia**
Visit Estonia, Estonian
Tourist Board
Estonia
[Travel & Tourism]

7 **Etam**
Etam Group
France
[Apparel]

ETAP ACCOR HOTELS

1 **ETAP Accor Hotels**
Accor SA
France, 1996
[Hospitality]

2 **ETAP Accor Hotels**
Accor SA
France, 2002
[Hospitality]

3 **Etnies**
Sole Technology Inc
USA
[Apparel]

4 **Eurocard**
Eurocard International NV
Belgium
[Financial Services]

5 **Eurocopter**
Eurocopter SAS, European Aeronautic Defence and Space Company NV
France
[Aerospace]

6 **Eurocopter**
Eurocopter SAS, European Aeronautic Defence and Space Company NV
France, 2012
[Aerospace]

7 **Euroleague Basketball**
Spain, 2005
Sockeye Creative
[Sport]

8 **Euronews**
SOCEMIE (Societé Opératrice de la Chaîne Européenne Multilingu d'Information Euronews)
France/European Union, 2008
FFL
[Television Channel]

258

1 **Europcar**
Europcar, Eurazeo SA
France
[Car Rental]

2 **European Patent Office**
European Union
[Professional Services]

3 **Euro RSCG Worldwide**
USA
[Marketing]

4 **EuroSpar**
Spar International
Netherlands
[Retail]

5 **Eurosport**
Groupe TF1
France, 2011
[Television Network]

6 **Eurostar**
Eurostar International Ltd
UK, 2011
SomeOne
[Transport]

7 **Eurovia SA**
Vinci Group
France
[Construction]

8 **Eurovision Song Contest**
European Broadcasting Union
Switzerland, 2004
[Television Programme]

1 **Eva Air**
EVA Airways Corporation,
The Evergreen Group
Taiwan
[Airline]

2 **Evans Drumheads**
D'Addario & Company Inc
USA
[Music]

▶ 3 **Eveready**
Eveready Battery Company Inc,
Energizer Holdings Inc
USA
[Consumer Products]

4 **Everex**
Everex, First International
Computer Inc of Taiwan
Taiwan
[Computer Technology]

5 **Evergreen Rehabilitation**
USA
[Healthcare]

▶ 6 **Evian**
Groupe Danone SA
France
[Food & Beverage]

7 **Evinrude**
Evinrude Outboard Motors
USA
[Marine]

8 **Exabyte**
Exabyte Corporation
USA
[Information Technology]

▶ 9 **Exel**
Exel Inc, Deutsche Post AG
USA, 1992
[Freight & Logistics]

1 **Exel**
Exel Inc, Deutsche Post AG
USA, 2000
[Freight & Logistics]

2 **Exercare**
Exercare Corporation
USA
[Fitness & Wellbeing]

3 **Expedia**
Expedia Inc
USA
[Internet]

4 **Expedia.com**
Expedia Inc
USA, 2010
[Internet]

5 **Exxon**
Exxon Mobil Corporation
USA, 1972
Raymond Loewy
[Oil, Gas & Petroleum]

6 **Eye – The International Review of Graphic Design**
Eye Magazine Ltd
UK
[Publications]

7 **E-Z Mart**
E-Z Mart Inc
USA, 1970s
[Retail]

8 **E-Z Mart**
E-Z Mart Inc
USA
[Retail]

1 **Fabco-Air**
Fabco-Air Inc
USA
[Industrial Products]

2 **Faber and Faber**
Faber and Faber Ltd
UK
Pentagram
[Publishing]

3 **Faber Bygg A.S.**
Norway
[Construction]

4 **Faber-Castell**
Faber-Castell AG
Germany
[Writing Products]

5 **Fabergé**
Fabergé Ltd, Pallinghurst Resources Ltd
USA
[Personal Care]

6 **Facebook**
Facebook Inc
USA, 2005
Cuban Council: Joe Kral, Peter Markatos
[Internet]

7 **Facebook (icon)**
Facebook Inc
USA
Future Farmers: Linda Leow
[Internet]

8 **Facet**
Motor Components LLC
USA
[Industrial Products]

9 **Facom**
Facom SAS, Stanley Black & Decker Inc
France
[Tools & Machinery]

1 **Fa Cosmetics**
Henkel AG & Co. KGaA
Germany
[Health & Beauty]

2 **Factiva**
Dow Jones & Company
USA, 2011
[Internet]

3 **Factory 2-U**
National Stores Inc
USA
[Retail]

4 **Factory Records**
UK, ca 1978
Peter Saville
[Music Industry]

5 **Faena**
Faena Hotel + Universe
Argentina, 2004
Tholön Kunst
[Hospitality]

6 **FAG**
Schaeffler Technologies
GmbH & Co. KG
Germany
[Automotive]

7 **Fage**
Fage SA
Greece
[Food & Beverage]

8 **Fagor**
Fagor Electrodomésticos
S.Coop, Mondragon Corporation
Spain
[Home Appliances]

FAIRCHILD

1

2

3

4

5

6

7

8

9

1 **Fairchild**
Fairchild Semiconductor Corporation
USA
[Industrial Products]

▶ 2 **Fairfield Inn**
Marriott International Inc
USA
[Hospitality]

3 **Fairtrade**
Fairtrade Labelling Organizations International eV
Germany
[Labelling, Standards & Certification]

4 **Fairwinds Credit Union**
USA
[Financial Services]

5 **Falck**
Falck A/S
Denmark
[Professional Services]

6 **FalconJet**
France
[Aerospace]

7 **Falcon Ladder**
Falcon MFG
Canada
[Manufacturing]

8 **Falken**
Falken Tire Corporation
USA
[Automotive]

9 **Fallen**
Fallen Footwear
USA
[Footwear]

1 **Familon**
Finlayson & Co. Oy
Finland
[Home Furnishings]

2 **Family Dollar**
Family Dollar Stores Inc
USA
[Retail]

3 **Family Dollar**
Family Dollar Stores Inc
USA, 2008
[Retail]

4 **Family Fare Supermarkets**
Spartan Stores Inc
USA
[Retail]

5 **Family Inns of America**
Family Inns of America Inc
USA
[Hospitality]

6 **Family Motor Coach Association (FMCA)**
USA
[Societies & Associations]

7 **Famous Footware**
Brown Shoe Company Inc
USA, 2005
[Retail]

8 **Fanatic**
Fanatic Snowboards
Germany, 2005
3Deluxe
[Sporting Goods]

FANDANGO

1 Fandango
Fandango Corporation,
NBCUniversal
USA
[Television Channel]

2 Fannie Mae
Federal National Mortgage
Association (FNMA)
USA
[Financial Services]

3 Fanta
The Coca-Cola Company
USA, 1980s
[Food & Beverage]

4 Fanta
The Coca-Cola Company
USA, 1980
[Food & Beverage]

5 Fanta
The Coca-Cola Company
USA, 2000
[Food & Beverage]

6 Fanta
The Coca-Cola Company
USA, 2009
Office
[Food & Beverage]

7 fapa (Friends and
Player Alliance)
2011
[Internet]

8 Fapinha
Fapinha Mini Veículos
e Motores Ltda
Brazil
[Automotive]

9 FaraEditore
Italy
[Publishing]

1 **Farallon Computing**
Netopia Inc, Motorola Inc
USA
[Telecommunications]

2 **Farberware**
Meyer Corporation
USA
[Kitchenware]

3 **Fargo Electronics**
Fargo Electronics Inc
USA
[Electronics]

4 **Farm Bureau**
American Farm Bureau Federation
USA
[Societies & Associations]

5 **Farm Bureau Co-op**
Universal Cooperatives Inc
USA
[Societies & Associations]

6 **Farmer John**
USA
[Food & Beverage]

7 **Farmers Insurance**
Farmers Insurance Group
of Companies
USA
[Financial Services]

8 **Farm Family**
Farm Family Casualty
Insurance Company
USA
[Financial Services]

9 **Farmland Industries**
Smithfield Foods Inc
USA
[Marketing]

FARM QUALITY ASSURED NORTHERN IRELAND

1 **Farm Quality Assured Northern Ireland**
The Livestock & Meat Commission of Northern Ireland
UK
[Labelling, Standards & Certification]

2 **Farnell Electronics**
Premier Farnell UK Ltd
UK
[Electronics]

3 **Fashion TV**
FTV BVI Ltd
France, 2009
[Television Channel]

4 **Fassi**
Fassi Gru SpA
Italy
[Tools & Machinery]

5 **Fast Company**
Fast Company Inc
USA, 1995
[Publications]

6 **Fastpuppy**
Canada, 1999
[Internet]

7 **Fastsigns**
Fastsigns International Inc
USA
[Printing Services]

▶ 8 **Fatboy Slim**
UK
[Music]

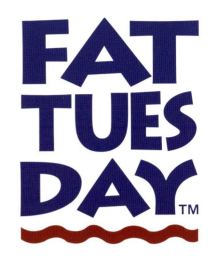

1 **FatCow Web Hosting**
FatCow Inc
USA
[Internet]

2 **Fat Tuesday**
David Briggs Enterprises Inc
USA
[Restaurants & Bars]

3 **Faurecia**
Faurecia, PSA Peugeot Citroën
France
[Automotive]

4 **Fay's Drug**
Rite Aid Corporation
USA
[Retail]

5 **Fazer**
Oy Karl Fazer AB
Finland
[Food & Beverage]

6 **FC Bayern München**
Fußball-Club Bayern München eV
Germany
SoDesign
[Sport]

7 **FC Dallas**
USA, 2005
[Sport]

8 **FC Dietikon**
Switzerland
[Sport]

F.C. KØBENHAVN

f c u k

1 F.C. København
Parken Sport & Entertainment AS
Denmark
[Sport]

2 FC Steaua Bucuresti
Fotbal Club Steaua Bucuresti
Romania, 2003
[Sport]

3 fcuk
French Connection Group plc
UK
TBWA: Trevor Beattie
[Apparel]

4 FDA (Food & Frug Administration)
United States Department of
Health & Human Services
USA
[Government]

5 FDIC (Federal Deposit Insurance
Corporation)
USA, 1974
[Political]

6 FDJ (La Française des Jeux)
France
[Leisure & Entertainment]

7 FDR (Roosevelt-Campobello
International Park)
USA
[Galleries & Museums]

8 FEAD (European Federation
of Waste Management
and Environmental Services)
Belgium
Helmut Langer
[Foundations & Institutes]

9 Fechaduras Brasil
Brazil, 1987
Alexandre Wollner
[Home Appliances]

1 **Fedders**
Fedders Corporation
USA
[Heating & Cooling]

2 **Federal Express**
FedEx Corporation
USA, 1974
Richard Runyon
[Mail Services]

3 **Federal-Mogul**
Federal-Mogul Corporation
USA
[Automotive]

4 **Federal Reserve Bank of Boston**
USA
[Financial Services]

5 **Federal Signal**
Federal Signal Corporation
USA
[Manufacturing]

6 **Federated Investors**
Federated Investors Inc
USA
[Financial Services]

7 **FedEx Express**
FedEx Corporation
USA, 1994
Landor Associates: Lindon Leader
[Mail Services]

8 **FedEx Home Delivery**
FedEx Corporation
USA
[Mail Services]

9 **FedEx Kinko's**
FedEx Office Print & Ship
Services Inc, FedEx Corporation
USA
[Retail]

FEED NOVA SCOTIA

1 **Feed Nova Scotia**
UK
[Charity]

2 **FEHB (Federal Employees Health Benefits)**
U.S. Office of Personnel Management
USA
[Government]

3 **Fein Electronic Tools**
C. & E. Fein GmbH
Germany, 1920s
[Tools & Machinery]

4 **Feintool**
Feintool International Holding AG
Germany
[Technology]

5 **Felina**
Felina GmbH
Germany
[Apparel]

6 **Felissimo**
Felissimo Corporation
Japan
[Retail]

7 **Fellowes**
Fellowes Inc
USA
[Office Supplies]

1 **Fel-Pro**
Federal-Mogul Corporation
USA
[Automotive]

2 **Fenco Truck Accessories**
USA
[Automotive]

3 **Fender**
Fender Musical Instruments Corporation
USA
[Musical Instruments]

4 **Fendi**
Fendi Srl, LVMH Moët Hennessy Louis Vuitton SA
Italy
[Fashion]

5 **Fenwick**
Pure Fishing Inc
USA
[Outdoor & Recreational]

6 **Feodora**
Feodora Chocolade GmbH & Co. KG
Germany, 1910
Princess Feodora
[Food & Beverage]

7 **Ferco**
Ferco International SAS
France
[Construction]

8 **Ferma**
Ferma SA
France
[Telecommunications]

1 **Fermax**
Fermax Electronica SAU
Spain
[Electronics]

2 **Ferrarelle**
Ferrarelle SpA
Italy
[Food & Beverage]

3 **Ferrari**
Ferrari SpA
Italy, 1947
[Automotive]

4 **Ferrero**
Ferrero SpA
Italy
[Food & Beverage]

5 **Ferrioni**
Ferrioni SA de CV
Mexico
[Apparel]

6 **Ferro**
Ferro Corporation
USA
[Chemicals & Materials]

7 **Ferrous**
Ferrous Resources do Brasil
Brazil, 2007
Hardy Design: Mariana Hardy
[Industry]

8 **Festina**
Festina Lotus SA
Switzerland
[Automotive]

1 **Festo**
Festo AG & Co. KG
Germany
[Manufacturing]

2 **FFBB (Fédération Française de Basketball)**
France, 2010
Graphèmes
[Sport]

3 **FFS (Fédération Française de Ski)**
France
[Sport]

4 **FFT (Fédération Française de Tennis)**
France
[Sport]

5 **FiA (Fédération Internationale de l'Automobile)**
France
[Motorsport]

6 **Fiac (Foire Internationale d'Art Contemporain)**
France
M/M Paris
[Marketing]

7 **FIAIP (Federazione Italiana Agenti Immobiliari Professionali)**
Italy
[Societies & Associations]

8 **Fiat**
Fiat SpA
Italy, 1967
Jean Reiwald, Armin Vogt
[Automotive]

FIAT

1   **Fiat**
    Fiat SpA
    Italy, 2011
    Robilant Associati
    [Automotive]

2   **Fiatagri**
    Fiat SpA
    Italy
    [Tools & Machinery]

3   **FICO**
    Fair Isaac Corporation
    USA
    [Financial Services]

4   **Fiction Records**
    Universal Music Group
    UK
    [Music Industry]

5   **Fida Film**
    Fida Film Yapim Dagitim
    Ve Reklamcilik AS
    Turkey
    [Cinemas & Theatres]

6   **Fidelity Bank**
    Fidelity Southern Corporation
    USA
    [Financial Services]

7   **Fidelity Investments**
    FMR LLC
    USA
    [Financial Services]

8   **Fidelstone Mortgage Company**
    USA
    [Financial Services]

FIFA WORLDCUP ARGENTINA 1978

1   **Fideuram Vita**
    Fideuram Vita SpA
    Italy
    [Financial Services]

2   **Fido Dido**
    Fido Dido Inc
    USA, 1985
    Joanna Ferrone, Sue Rose
    [Graphic Design]

3   **Fields Department Store**
    FHC Holdings Ltd
    Canada
    [Retail]

4   **Fiery**
    Electronics for Imaging Inc
    USA
    [Imaging & Photographic]

5   **Fiesta Inn**
    Grupo Posadas SA de CV
    Mexico
    [Hospitality]

6   **FIFA (Fédération Internationale de Football Association)**
    Switzerland
    [Sporting Events]

7   **FIFA World Cup Mexico 1970**
    FIFA
    Mexico
    [Sporting Events]

8   **FIFA World Cup Argentina 1978**
    FIFA
    Argentina
    [Sporting Events]

FIFA WORLDCUP ESPAÑA 1982

1. **FIFA World Cup España 1982**
   FIFA
   Spain
   [Sporting Events]

2. **FIFA World Cup Mexico 1986**
   FIFA
   Mexico
   [Sporting Events]

3. **FIFA World Cup Italia 1990**
   FIFA
   Italy
   [Sporting Events]

4. **FIFA World Cup USA 1994**
   FIFA
   USA, 1991
   Pentagram: Michael Gericke
   [Sporting Events]

5. **FIFA World Cup France 1998**
   FIFA
   France, 1994
   ADSA
   [Sporting Events]

6. **FIFA World Cup South Korea/ Japan 2002**
   FIFA
   South Korea/Japan, 1999
   [Sporting Events]

7. **FIFA World Cup Germany 2006**
   FIFA
   Germany, 2002
   Whitestone, abold
   [Sporting Events]

8. **FIFA World Cup South Africa 2010**
   FIFA
   South Africa, 2006
   [Sporting Events]

9. **FIFA World Cup Brasil 2014**
   FIFA
   Brazil, 2010
   Africa
   [Sporting Events]

1 **Fil (Festival Intercâmbio de Linguagens)**
Brazil, 2008
Laboratório Secreto:
Marcelo Martinez
[Events]

2 **Fila**
Fila Ltd
Italy
[Sporting Goods]

3 **Fila**
Fila Ltd
Italy
[Sporting Goods]

4 **Filene's Basement**
Syms Corporation
USA
[Retail]

5 **Fill'er Up**
USA
[Retail]

6 **Film4**
Channel Four Television Corporation
UK, 2006
[Television Channel]

7 **Filmax**
Sociedad General de Derechos Audiovisuales SA
Spain
[Film Industry]

8 **Film Council**
UK Film Council (UKFC)
UK
[Foundations & Institutes]

FILMPLUS

1 **Filmplus, Forum für Filmschnitt und Montagekunst (Forum for film editing)**
Filmplus gemeinnützige UG
Germany
[Societies & Associations]

2 **Filtri Tecnocar**
Sofegi Filtration SpA
Italy
[Automotive]

3 **Fina**
Total SA
Belgium, 1972
[Oil, Gas & Petroleum]

4 **Findus**
Findus Group, Lion Capital LLP
Sweden, 2001
[Food & Beverage]

5 **Fine Line Features**
New Line Cinema, Warner Bros. Entertainment Inc
USA, 1991
Woody Pirtle
[Film Industry]

6 **Fine Living**
Scripps Networks Interactive
USA, 2002
[Television Channel]

7 **Finland**
Visit Finland, Finnish Tourist Board
Finland
[Travel & Tourism]

8 **Finnair**
Finnair Oy
Finland, 2000
SEK & Grey
[Airline]

9 **Finnair**
Finnair Oy
Finland, 2010
SEK & Grey
[Airline]

10 **Finn Crisp**
VAASAN Group
Finland
[Food & Beverage]

1 **Finnish Road Administration**
Finland
[Government]

2 **Firefox 3.5**
Mozilla Corporation
USA, 2009
The Iconfactory: Anthony Piraino,
Jon Hicks, Stephen Horlander
[Internet]

3 **Firehawk**
Bridgestone Firestone LLC
USA
[Automotive]

4 **Fire Kills**
UK Government
UK
[Safety & Security]

5 **FIREloc**
U.S. Chemical Storage LLC
USA
[Construction]

6 **Fireman's Fund**
Fireman's Fund Insurance
Company, Allianz SE
USA
[Financial Services]

7 **Fireseal**
Essve Produkter AB
Sweden
[Industrial Products]

8 **Firestone**
Bridgestone Firestone LLC
USA
[Automotive]

9 **Firestone**
Bridgestone Firestone LLC
USA
[Automotive]

FIREWIRE

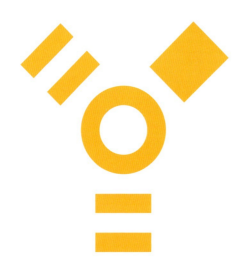

1 **FireWire**
developed by Apple Inc
USA
[Computer Hardware]

2 **Fireye**
Fireye Inc, UTC Fire & Security Company
USA
[Security & Safety]

3 **First American Real Estate**
First American Financial Corporation
USA
[Financial Services]

4 **Firstar Bank**
USA
[Financial Services]

5 **First Citizens Bank**
First-Citizens Bank & Trust Company
USA
[Financial Services]

6 **First Data**
First Data Corporation
USA
[Financial Services]

7 **First Data**
First Data Corporation
USA, 2008
VSA Partners
[Financial Services]

8 **First Federal Bank of California**
USA
[Financial Services]

1   **FirstGroup**
    FirstGroup plc
    UK
    [Transport]

2   **First Hawaiian Bank**
    USA
    [Financial Services]

3   **First Horizon**
    First Horizon National
    Corporation
    USA
    [Financial Services]

▶ 4 **First Interstate BanK**
    First Interstate Bancorp
    USA
    [Financial Services]

5   **FirstMerit**
    FirstMerit Corporation
    USA
    [Financial Services]

6   **First Union**
    Wachovia Corporation
    USA
    [Financial Services]

7   **Fischer**
    Fischer Sports GmbH
    Austria
    [Sporting Goods]

8   **Fisher & Paykel**
    Fisher & Paykel Appliances Ltd
    New Zealand
    [Home Appliances]

FISHERMAN'S FRIEND

1 **Fisherman's Friend**
   Lofthouse of Fleetwood Ltd
   UK
   [Food & Beverage]

2 **Fisher-Price**
   Mattel Inc
   USA, 1984
   [Toys, Games & Models]

3 **Five Chefs**
   Russia
   [Food & Beverage]

4 **Five Franklin Place (ffp)**
   USA, 2008
   Pentagram: Luke Hayman
   [Real Estate]

5 **Fixot**
   France
   [Publisher]

6 **Fjällräven**
   Fjällräven AB
   Sweden
   [Outdoor & Recreational]

7 **Fjellman**
   Fjellman Press AB
   Sweden
   [Tools & Machinery]

8 **Flamingo**
   Caesars Entertainment Corp
   USA
   [Leisure & Entertainment]

9 **Flap Jack Restaurants**
   USA
   [Food & Beverage]

1 **FleetBoston Financial**
Bank of America
USA
[Financial Services]

2 **Fleet One**
Fleet One Holdings LLC
USA
[Financial Services]

3 **FLENI (Fundación para la Lucha contra las Enfermedades Neurológicas de la Infancia)**
Argentina
[Foundations & Institutes]

4 **Fletcher Building**
Fletcher Building Ltd
New Zealand
[Construction]

5 **Flex**
American Media Inc
USA, 1983
[Publications]

6 **Flex-a-lite**
Flex-a-lite Consolidated
USA
[Heating & Cooling]

7 **Flextronics**
Flextronics International Ltd
Singapore
[Electronics]

FLICKR

1 **flickr**
Yahoo! Inc
USA
[Internet]

2 **Florida Gulf Coast University**
USA
[Education]

3 **Florida Ice & Farm Co**
Costa Rica
[Food & Beverage]

4 **Flos**
Flos SpA
Italy, 1990s
[Home Furnishings]

5 **Flowserve**
Flowserver Corporation
USA
[Industries]

6 **Flybe**
Flybe Group plc
UK, 2004
[Airline]

7 **Fly Emirates**
The Emirates Group
United Arab Emirates
[Airline]

8 **FlyerTalk**
Internet Brands Inc
USA
[Internet]

1 **flyerwire.de**
flyerwire GmbH
Germany
[Printing Services]

2 **FMC**
FMC Corporation
USA
[Chemicals & Materials]

3 **FMI Truck Sales & Service**
USA
[Retail]

4 **Fnac (Fédération Nationale d'Achats des Cadres)**
France
[Retail]

5 **Foex**
Foex Indexes Ltd
Finland
[Professional Services]

6 **Fog City Records**
USA
[Music Industry]

7 **Fokker**
Netherlands
[Aviation]

8 **Folgers Coffee**
The J.M. Smucker Company
USA
[Food & Beverage]

FOLIATEC

1 **Foliatec**
FOLIATEC Böhm GmbH
& Co. Vertriebs KG
Germany
[Automotive]

2 **Folkpartiet liberalerna/
Liberal People's Party**
Sweden
[Political]

3 **Fona**
F Group AS
Denmark
[Retail]

4 **FONATUR (Fondo Nacional
de Fomento al Turismo)**
Mexico
[Travel & Tourism]

5 **Fondation Abbé Pierre pour
le logement des défavorisés**
France
[Foundations & Institutes]

6 **Fondation de France**
France
[Foundations & Institutes]

7 **Fonos Exhaust**
Tenneco Inc
Spain
[Automotive]

8 **Fontys University
of Applied Sciences**
Netherlands
[Education]

FOOD LION

FoodBusiness*news*

Fonzies
Kraft Foods Italia Srl
Italy
[Food & Beverage]

Food and Agriculture Organization (FAO)
Food and Agriculture Organization of the United Nations
Italy
[Societies & Associations]

Food Basics
Metro Inc
Canada
[Retail]

FoodBusiness News
Sosland Publishing Co.
USA
[Publications]

Fooding
LeFooding.com, Mmm! Sarl
France
[Publications]

Foodland Ontario
Ontario Ministry of Agriculture, Food & Rural Affairs
Canada
The Watt Group
[Government]

Food Lion
Food Lion LLC,
Delhaize Group SA/NV
USA
[Retail]

FOOD STANDARDS AGENCY

1 Food Standards Agency
HM Government
UK
[Government]

▶ 2 Food Town Supermarkets
Seaway Foodtown Inc
USA
[Retail]

3 Foohy
Sanford LP, Newell Rubbermaid Inc
USA
[Writing Products]

▶ 4 Foot Locker
Foot Locker Inc
USA
[Retail]

5 Forbes
Forbes Media LLC
USA
[Publications]

6 Forbo
Forbo International SA
Switzerland
[Manufacturing]

7 Force Financial
Force Financial LLC
USA
[Financial Services]

▶ 8 Ford
Ford Motor Company
USA
The Partners
[Automotive]

FORMULA 1

1 **Ford Motor Company**
Ford Motor Company
USA
[Automotive]

2 **Ford Sponsored Auctions**
Ford Motor Company
USA
[Automotive]

3 **Ford Trucks**
Ford Motor Company
USA, 2001
[Automotive]

4 **Foreca**
Foreca Ltd
Finland
[Media]

5 **Foreign Autopart**
Autopart International Inc
USA
[Automotive]

6 **Forge Consulting**
Forge Consulting LLC
USA
[Professional Services]

7 **For us the living**
USA
[Music]

8 **Formica**
Formica Corporation,
Fletcher Building Ltd
UK
[Chemicals & Materials]

9 **Formula 1**
Formula One Licensing BV
UK, 1994
Carter Wong Tomlin
[Motorsport]

FIA

1 FIA – Formula 1 World Championship
   Formula One Licensing BV
   Netherlands, 1997
   [Sporting Events]

2 **Forney**
   Forney LLC
   USA
   [Industrial Products]

3 **Fortis**
   Fortis NV/SA
   Belgium/Netherlands, 2006
   TBD
   [Financial Services]

4 **Fortum**
   Fortum Oyj
   Finland
   [Utilities]

5 **Fortune**
   Time Inc
   USA
   [Publications]

6 **Fossil**
   Fossil Inc
   USA
   [Watches & Jewelry]

7 **Foster's**
   Foster's Group Ltd
   Australia
   [Wines, Beers & Spirits]

8 **Foster's Group**
   Foster's Group Ltd
   Australia, 2011
   [Breweries]

1 **Foster Wheeler**
Foster Wheeler AG
Switzerland
[Conglomerate]

2 **Fostex**
Foster Electric Co. Ltd
Japan
[Consumer Electronics]

3 **Foundation Skateboards**
Foundation Skateboard Company
USA
[Outdoor & Recreational]

4 **Four Winns**
Four Winns LLC
USA
[Marine]

5 **Fox**
Twentieth Century Fox Film Corporation
USA, 1999
[Film Industry]

6 **Fox Kids**
Fox Entertainment Group Inc
USA
[Television Network]

7 **Fox Racing Shox**
FOX Factory Inc
USA
[Automotive]

8 **Fox Records**
BMG (Bertelsmann Music Group), 20th Century Fox/Fox Films
USA, 1990s
[Music Industry]

FOX SMART ESTATE AGENCY

1 **FOX Smart Estate Agency**
   FOX Smart Estate Agency
   Network Ltd
   Cyprus
   [Real Estate]

2 **Fox Sports Net (FSN)**
   Fox Sports Interactive Media LLC
   USA, 1999
   [Television Channel]

3 **Fox Sports Net (FSN)**
   Fox Entertainment Group Inc
   USA, 2008
   [Television Network]

4 **FP Diesel**
   Federal-Mogul Corporation
   USA
   [Automotive]

5 **Frabosk**
   Frabosk Casalinghi SAS
   Italy
   [Kitchenware]

6 **Fram**
   France
   [Travel & Tourism]

7 **Fram Filters**
   Fram Group IP LLC
   USA
   [Automotive]

8 **Framesi**
   Framesi SpA
   Italy
   [Health & Beauty]

1 **France**
French Government Tourist Office
France, 2009
[Travel & Tourism]

2 **France Loisirs**
France Loisirs SAS
France
[Publishing]

3 **France Telecom**
France Telecom SA
France, 2000
Landor Associates
[Telecommunications]

4 **France Telecom**
France Telecom SA
France
[Telecommunications]

5 **France Télévisions**
France Télévisions SA
France, 2008
[Broadcaster]

6 **France 2**
France Télévisions SA
France, 2000s
[Broadcaster]

7 **France 3**
France Télévisions SA
France, 2000s
[Broadcaster]

8 **Franck Kava**
Franck dd
Croatia
[Food & Beverage]

FRANCO-AMERICAN

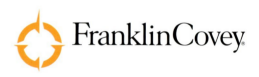

1. **Franco-American**
Campbell Soup Company
USA
[Food & Beverage]

2. **Frangelico Liqueur**
Davide Campari-Milano SpA
Italy
[Wines, Beers & Spirits]

3. **Franke**
Franke Artemis Management AG
Switzerland
[Conglomerate]

4. **Frankenheim**
Brauerei Ausschank
Wielandstrasse Ein Unternehmen
der Altbier Düsseldorf GmbH
Germany
[Breweries]

5. **Franklin Computer**
Franklin Electronic Publishers Inc
USA
[Consumer Electronics]

6. **FranklinCovey**
Franklin Covey Co.
USA
[Education]

7. **Franklin Mills**
Simon Property Group Inc
USA
[Retail]

8. **Frank Parsons**
Frank Parsons Company,
TSRC Inc
USA
[Office Supplies]

9. **Frank's RedHot**
Reckitt Benckiser LLC
USA
[Food & Beverage]

1 **Fraternal Order of Eagles International (F.O.E.)**
   USA
   [Societies & Associations]

2 **Fraunhofer Society**
   Fraunhofer-Gesellschaft zur Förderung der angewandten Forschung eV
   Germany, 2009
   [Societies & Associations]

3 **Fred & Friends**
   Easy Aces Inc
   USA
   [Toys, Games & Models]

4 **Freddie Mac**
   Federal Home Loan Mortgage Corporation (FHLMC)
   USA
   [Financial Services]

5 **Fred Meyer**
   Fred Meyer Inc
   USA, 1999
   [Retail]

6 **Fred Perry**
   Fred Perry Ltd
   UK
   [Apparel]

7 **Freedent**
   William Wrigley Jr. Company
   USA, 1970s
   [Food & Beverage]

FREENET

1 **Freenet**
Freenet AG
Germany
[Telecommunications]

2 **Freesat**
British Broadcasting Corporation, ITV plc
UK
[Satellite Television]

3 **Freeview**
Freeview Australia Ltd
Australia, 2008
[Digital Television]

4 **Freeview**
DTV Services Ltd
UK, 2006
999 Design
[Digital Television]

5 **Freidig Moto-Active**
Freidig Moto-Active GmbH
Germany
[Motorsport]

6 **Freightliner Trucks**
Daimler Trucks North America LLC
USA
[Automotive]

▶ 7 **French's**
Reckitt Benckiser plc
USA, 1921
[Food & Beverage]

8 **Fresenius Medical Care**
Fresenius Medical Care AG & Co. KGaA
USA
[Healthcare]

1 **Freshfields Bruckhaus Deringer**
Freshfields Bruckhaus Deringer LLP
UK, 2000
Gottschalk+Ash
[Professional Services]

2 **Freudenberg**
Freudenberg & Co. KG
Germany
[Conglomerate]

3 **Frico**
Frico AB
Sweden
[Heating & Cooling]

4 **Friendly's**
Friendly's Ice Cream LLC
USA
[Restaurants & Bars]

5 **Friends**
Warner Bros. Entertainment Inc,
Time Warner
USA, 1994
[Television Series]

6 **Friends of the Earth**
Friends of the Earth International
USA, 2001
[Charity]

7 **Friendster**
Friendster Sdn. Bhd
Malaysia, 2009
Yello
[Internet]

8 **FrieslandCampina**
Koninklijke FrieslandCampina NV
Netherlands, 2009
[Food & Beverage]

FRIESLAND COBERCO DAIRY FOODS

1 **Friesland Coberco Dairy Foods**
Koninklijke Friesland Foods NV
Netherlands
[Food & Beverage]

2 **Friesland Foods**
Koninklijke Friesland Foods NV
Netherlands, 2004
[Food & Beverage]

3 **Frigidaire**
Electrolux International Company
USA, 1955
[Home Appliances]

4 **Frigidaire**
Electrolux International Company
USA, 2009
[Home Appliances]

5 **Frisch's**
Frisch's Restaurants Inc
USA
[Restaurants & Bars]

6 **Friskies**
Nestlé SA
USA
[Pet Products]

7 **Frïs Vodka**
Denmark
[Wines, Beers & Spirits]

8 **Frito Lay**
Frito-Lay North America Inc,
PepsiCo Inc
USA, ca 1985
[Food & Beverage]

  **Fritz Hansen &**

 **FRONTIER AIRLINES**

1 **Frito Lay**
Frito-Lay North America Inc, PepsiCo Inc
USA, 1997
Landor Associates
[Food & Beverage]

2 **Fritos**
Frito-Lay North America Inc, PepsiCo Inc
USA, 2004
[Food & Beverage]

3 **Fritz Hansen**
Denmark
[Home Furnishings]

4 **Frontier Biscuits**
Frontier Biscuits Factory Pvt Ltd
India
[Food & Beverage]

5 **Frontier Airlines**
Frontier Airlines Inc
USA
[Airline]

6 **Frontier Silicon**
Frontier Silicon Ltd
UK
[Technology]

7 **Frost Bank**
USA
[Financial Services]

8 **Fruité**
France
[Food & Beverage]

FRUIT OF THE LOOM

1 **Fruit of the Loom**
Berkshire Hathaway Inc
USA
[Apparel]

2 **Frye**
The Frye Company (LF USA)
USA
[Footwear]

3 **FSB**
Franz Schneider Brakel
GmbH + Co KG
Germany
[Home Appliances]

4 **FSC**
(Forest Stewardship Council)
Germany
[Conservation & Envrionment]

5 **FSG**
(Facility Solutions Group)
USA
[Electronics]

6 **FSI**
FLIR Systems Inc
USA
[Imaging & Photographic]

7 **Fuchs**
Fuchs Petrolub AG
Germany
[Chemicals & Materials]

8 **Fuchs**
Otto Fuchs KG
Germany, 1999
[Automotive]

1 **Fuelman**
Fleetcor LLC
USA
[Financial Services]

2 **Fuji**
Fuji Co. Ltd
Japan
[Retail]

3 **Fuji Bank**
The Fuji Bank Ltd
Japan
[Financial Services]

4 **Fuji Bikes**
Advanced Sports International
USA
[Bicycles]

5 **Fujifilm**
Fujifilm Holdings Corporation
Japan, 1992
[Imaging & Photographic]

6 **Fujifilm**
Fujifilm Holdings Corporation
Japan, 2006
[Imaging & Photographic]

7 **Fuji Heavy Industries**
Fuji Heavy Industries Co. Ltd
Japan
[Conglomerate]

8 **Fuji Television Network Inc**
Japan
[Television Network]

9 **Fujitsu**
Fujitsu Ltd
Japan, 1989
[Information Technology]

FUKUDA DENSHI

1 **Fukuda Denshi Global Network**
   Fukuda Denshi Co. Ltd
   Japan
   [Medical Devices]

2 **Full**
   YPF
   Argentina, 2005
   Rubén Fontana
   [Oil, Gas & Petroleum]

3 **Full Sail University**
   USA
   [Education]

4 **Funai**
   Funai Electric Co. Ltd
   Japan
   [Consumer Electronics]

5 **Fundación Alfredo Armas Alfonso**
   Venezuela, 1994
   Álvaro Sotillo
   [Foundations & Institutes]

6 **Fundación Cultural de la Ciudad de México**
   Mexico, 2008
   Gabriela Rodríguez Studio
   [Foundations & Institutes]

7 **Funika**
   Funika Ltd
   Turkey
   [Fabrics & Textiles]

1 **Funke Gerber**
Funke-Dr.N.Gerber
Labortechnik GmbH
Germany
[Manufacturing]

2 **Furnas**
Eletrobas Furnas, Centrais
Elétricas SA
Brazil
[Utilities]

3 **Furukawa**
Furukawa Industrial SA
Brazil
[Industrial Products]

4 **Fußball-Bundesliga**
DFL Deutsche Fußball Liga GmbH
Germany
[Sport]

5 **Futbol Club Barcelona**
Spain
[Sport]

6 **Futuremark Corporation**
Finland
[Computer Software]

7 **FWA**
Favourite Website Awards
UK, 2003
Dual
[Internet]

8 **FWT Studios**
UK
[Information Technology]

9 **FX**
FX Networks LLC
USA, 1997
[Television Channel]

Gaffel Kölsch

GAGGENAU

GAGOSIAN GALLERY

GALAXY

1 **Gadoua**
Gadoua Bakery Ltd
Canada
[Food & Beverage]

2 **GAF**
GAF Materials Corporation
USA
[Construction]

3 **Gaffel Kölsch**
Gaffel Becker & Co. oHG
Germany
[Wines, Beers & Spirits]

4 **Gaggenau**
Gaggenau Hausgeräte GmbH
Germany
[Home Appliances]

5 **Gagosian Gallery**
USA
[Galleries & Museums]

6 **Galaxy Technology**
Galaxy Microsystems Ltd
China
[Computer Technology]

7 **Galbani**
Egidio Galbani SpA,
Groupe Lactalis
Italy
[Food & Beverage]

1 **Gallina Blanca**
Gallina Blanca Star SAU
Spain
[Food & Beverage]

2 **Gallup**
Gallup Inc
USA
[Professional Services]

3 **Galp Energia**
Portugal, 2003
[Oil, Gas & Petroleum]

4 **Gama**
The Game Manufacturers Association
USA
[Societies & Associations]

5 **Gambero Rosso**
Gambero Rosso Holding SpA
Italy
[Publishing]

6 **Game Boy**
Nintendo Co. Ltd
Japan, 1989
[Computer & Video Games]

7 **Gamma**
Intergamma BV
Netherlands
[Retail]

1. **Gammon Skanska**
   China
   [Construction]

2. **Gannett Co. Inc**
   USA, 1979
   Young & Rubicam, Matsuo Yasamura & Associates
   [Media]

3. **Gap**
   The Gap Inc
   USA, 1986
   [Apparel]

4. **Gardenburger**
   Kellogg Company
   USA
   [Food & Beverage]

5. **Gardner Bender**
   Actuant Corporation
   USA
   [Tools & Machinery]

6. **Gardner Denver Inc**
   USA
   [Industrial Products]

7. **Garlock Sealing Technologies**
   The Garlock Family of Companies
   USA
   [Chemicals & Materials]

GAS AS INTERFACE

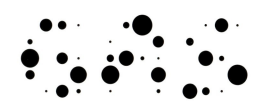

1 **Garmin**
   Garmin Ltd
   USA, 2006
   [Technology]

2 **Garnier**
   L'Oréal Group
   France
   [Health & Beauty]

3 **Garrard**
   Garrard Engineering &
   Manufacturing Company Ltd
   UK
   [Consumer Electronics]

4 **Gartmore**
   Gartmore Group Ltd
   UK, 2002
   Corporate Edge
   [Financial Services]

5 **Gart Sports**
   Gart Sports Company
   USA
   [Sporting Goods]

6 **Garuda Indonesia**
   PT Garuda Indonesia
   (Persero) Tbk
   Indonesia, 2009
   [Airline]

7 **Gary Fisher**
   Trek Bicycle Corporation
   USA
   [Bicycles]

8 **Gas As Interface**
   GAS As Interface Co. Ltd
   Japan
   [Design]

1 **Gas Blue Jeans**
Diana Srl
Italy
[Apparel]

2 **Gascogne Wood**
Gascogne Wood Products SAS
France
[Home Furnishing]

3 **Gas Natural Fenosa**
Gas Natural SDG SA
Spain, 2010
[Utilities]

4 **Gasunie**
NV Nederlandse Gasunie
Netherlands
[Energy]

5 **Gates Corporation**
Tomkins Ltd
USA
[Industrial Products]

6 **Gateway**
Gateway Inc, Acer Inc
USA
[Computer Technology]

7 **Gateway**
Gateway Inc, Acer Inc
USA, 2002
Arnell Group
[Computer Hardware]

8 **Gateway**
Gateway Inc, Acer Inc
USA
[Computer Technology]

GAYLORD

1   **Gateway Safety Inc**
    USA
    [Security & Safety]

2   **Gatorade**
    PepsiCo Inc
    USA, 1973
    [Food & Beverage]

3   **Gatorade**
    PepsiCo Inc
    USA, 1991
    [Food & Beverage]

4   **Gatorade**
    PepsiCo Inc
    USA, 2009
    [Food & Beverage]

5   **GATX Corporation**
    USA
    [Freight & Logistics]

6   **Gaumont Film Company**
    France, ca 2004
    [Film Industry]

7   **Gautier Cognac**
    Cognac Gautier
    France
    [Food & Beverage]

8   **Gaylord Hauser**
    Modern Products Inc
    USA
    [Food & Beverage]

9   **Gaylord Container Corporation**
    USA
    [Manufacturing]

GAYLORD PALMS

1 **Gaylord Palms Resort & Convention Center**
Gaylord Entertainment Company
USA
[Hospitality]

2 **Gaz de France**
France, 1987
[Utilities]

3 **Gaz de France**
France
[Utilities]

4 **Gaz Naturel**
Association Suisse de l'Industrie Gazière (ASIG)
Switzerland
[Societies & Associations]

5 **Gazprom JSC**
Russia
[Oil, Gas & Petroleum]

▶ 6 **GE**
General Electric Company
USA, 2004
Wolff Olins
[Industry]

7 **GEA**
GEA Group AG
Germany
[Conglomerate]

8 **Gebrit**
Geberit International AG
USA
[Industrial Products]

GEMEENTE ALMERE

GEF

GEFFEN

GEHL　　GEICO　　GEJOHNSON

GELCO

Gemeente Almere

1　GEF (Global Environment Facility)
USA
[Societies & Associations]

2　Geffen Records
Interscope Geffen A&M,
Universal Music Group
USA, 1980
Saul Bass
[Music Industry]

3　Gehl
Gehl Company
USA
[Tools & Machinery]

4　Geico Direct
Geico Insurance Agency Inc
USA
[Financial Services]

5　GE Johnson Construction
Company
USA
[Construction]

6　Gelco (General Equipment
Leasing Corporation)
USA
[Professional Services]

7　Gemeente Almere
Local authority of the city
of Almere
Netherlands
[Government]

1. **Gemeente Breda**
   Local authority of the city of Breda
   Netherlands
   [Government]

2. **Gemeente Uden**
   Local authority of the city of Uden
   The Netherlands, 2004
   Nies & Partners
   [Government]

3. **Gencorp Inc**
   USA
   [Manufacturing]

4. **Genelec Oy**
   Finland
   [Electronics]

5. **Genentech Inc**
   Roche Group
   USA
   [Pharmaceuticals]

6. **Generac Power Systems**
   Generac Holdings Inc
   USA, 2009
   [Manufacturing]

7. **General Cable Corporation**
   USA, 1969
   [Manufacturing]

8. **General Cinema Corporation**
   USA, 1980s
   [Cinemas & Theatres]

GENERAL NUTRITION CENTERS

General Dynamics

1 **General Dynamics Corporation**
   USA
   [Defence]

2 **Generalitat Valenciana**
   Autonomous Community
   of Valencia
   Spain
   [Places]

3 **General Mills**
   General Mills Inc
   USA, 2001
   [Food & Beverage]

4 **General Mills**
   General Mills Inc
   USA, 1928
   [Food & Beverage]

5 **General Monitors**
   USA
   [Safety & Security]

▶ 6 **General Motors (GM)**
   General Motors Company
   USA
   [Automotive]

7 **General Nutrition Centers (GNC)**
   General Nutrition Centers Inc
   USA
   [Retail]

315

GENERAL PAINT

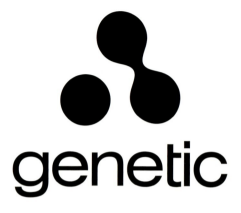

1 **General Paint**
Comex Group
Canada
[Paints & Coatings]

2 **General Tire**
Continental Tire North America Inc
USA, 1960s
[Automotive]

3 **Genetic Skateboard Products**
USA
[Sporting Goods]

4 **Genie**
Terex Corporation
USA
[Tools & Machinery]

5 **Gentek Building Products Inc**
USA
[Construction]

6 **Gentry Living Color Inc**
USA, 1993
Paul Rand
[Paints & Coatings]

7 **Genuine Parts Company (GPC)**
USA
[Automotive]

8 **Geobrugg**
Geobrugg AG
Switzerland
[Safety & Security]

9 **George Fischer**
Georg Fischer Piping Systems Ltd
Switzerland
[Industrial Products]

GERRY WEBER

1 **George Foreman**
Russell Hobbs Inc,
Spectrum Brands Inc
USA
[Kitchenware]

2 **Georgia-Pacific LLC**
Koch Industries Inc
USA
[Paper Products]

3 **Georgia Power**
Southern Company
USA
[Utilities]

4 **Gepe**
Gepe Produkte AG
Switzerland, 1955
Göran Pettersson, Per Lindström
[Imaging & Photographic]

5 **Gerber**
Fiskar Brands Inc
USA, 2005
[Knives]

6 **Gerber Systems**
USA
[Computer Software]

7 **Gerry Weber**
Gerry Weber International AG
Germany, 1990s
[Fashion]

8 **Gervais**
Nestlé SA
Switzerland
[Food & Beverage]

1
2
3

4 gettyimages®

5 GF FERRÉ

6

7

8 GIANNI VERSACE

1 **Getinge**
Getinge AB
Sweden
[Professional Services]

2 **GetLiveMusic.com**
Canada
[Music Industry]

3 **Get London Reading**
Booktrust
UK, 2008
KentLyons
[Advertising & Campaigns]

4 **Getty Images**
Getty Images Inc
USA, 2000
Pentagram
[Imaging & Photographic]

5 **GF Ferré**
Gianfranco Ferré SpA
Italy
Winkreative
[Fashion]

6 **GHI (Group Health Incorporated)**
EmblemHealth Companies
USA
[Financial Services]

7 **Ghostbusters**
Columbia Pictures Industries Inc
USA, 1984
Dan Aykroyd (concept)
[Film]

8 **Gianni Versace**
Gianni Versace SpA
Italy
[Fashion]

1   **Giant**
    Giant Manufacturing Co. Ltd
    Taiwan
    [Bicycles]

    Giant-Carlisle
    Giant Food Stores LLC
    USA
    [Retail]

    Giant Eagle Inc
    USA
    [Retail]

4   **Giant Food**
    Giant Food Inc
    USA, 1963
    [Retail]

5   **Giant Food**
    Giant of Maryland LLC
    USA, 2008
    [Retail]

6   **Giants**
    New York Giants
    USA, 1976
    [Sport]

7   **Gibson**
    Gibson Guitar Corporation
    USA, ca 1947
    [Musical Instruments]

8   **Gig Ant Promotion**
    Poland
    [Music Industry]

GIGABYTE TECHNOLOGY

1. **Gigabyte Technology**
Gigabyte Technology Co. Ltd
Taiwan
[Computer Hardware]

2. **G.I. Joe**
Hasbro Inc
USA
[Toys, Games & Models]

3. **Gilera**
Piaggio & Co. SpA
Italy
[Automotive]

4. **Gillette**
Procter & Gamble Co
USA
[Personal Care]

5. **Giochi Preziosi**
Giochi Preziosi SpA
Italy
[Toys, Games & Models]

6. **Giorgio Armani**
Giorgio Armani SpA
Italy
[Fashion]

7. **Girl Scouts of the USA**
USA, 1977
Saul Bass
[Societies & Associations]

8. **Giroflex**
Stoll Giroflex AG
Switzerland
[Office Supplies]

9. **Gitanes**
Imperial Tobacco Group plc
France
[Tobacco]

GLACÉAU

1 **Gitem**
Euronics Group
France
[Retail]

2 **Givenchy**
LVMH Moët Hennessy
Louis Vuitton SA
France
[Fashion]

3 **Givi**
GIVI Srl
Italy
[Automotive]

4 **GKN Automotive**
GKN plc
UK
[Automotive]

5 **G&K Services**
G&K Services Inc
USA
[Professional Services]

6 **GLAAD (Gay & Lesbian Alliance Against Defamation)**
USA, 2010
Lippincott
[Societies & Associations]

7 **Glacéau**
The Coca-Cola Company
USA
[Food & Beverage]

1 Glad
The Glad Products Company,
The Clorox Company,
Procter & Gamble Co
USA
[Household Products]

2 Glade
S.C. Johnson & Son Inc
USA
[Household Products]

3 Glade
S.C. Johnson & Son Inc
USA
[Household Products]

4 Gladwork
Russia
[Office Supplies]

5 Glass Recycles
Glass Packaging Institute
USA
[Labelling, Standards
& Certification]

6 Glendale Community College
USA
[Education]

7 Glengarry Highland Games
Canada
[Sporting Events]

8 Glico
Ezaki Glico Co. Ltd
Japan, 1992
[Food & Beverage]

1 **Glidden Paint**
Akzo Nobel NV
USA
[Paints & Coatings]

2 **Global Crossing**
Global Crossing Ltd
Bermuda
[Telecommunications]

3 **Global Reporting Initative (GRI)**
Netherlands
[Conservation & Environment]

4 **Global Television Network**
Shaw Communications
Canada
[Television Network]

5 **Global Van Lines**
Global Van Lines Inc
USA
[Transport]

6 **Globetrotter**
Globetrotter Ausrüstung
Denart & Lechhart GmbH
Germany, ca 1985
[Outdoor & Recreation]

7 **Glock Perfection**
Glock GmbH
Austria
[Firearms]

8 **Glunz & Jensen**
Glunz & Jensen A/S
Denmark
[Industrial Products]

GLYNWED PIPE SYSTEMS

1 **Glynwed Pipe Systems**
Aliaxis Group
UK
[Industrial Products]

2 **GMAC (General Motors Acceptance Corporation)**
Ally Financial Inc
USA
[Financial Services]

3 **Gmail**
Google Inc
USA, 2010
Google
[Internet]

4 **GMC**
General Motors Company
USA
[Automotive]

▶ 5 **GMC Truck**
General Motors Company
USA
[Automotive]

6 **GMPTE (Transport for Greater Manchester)**
UK
[Government]

7 **GMR Group**
India
[Conglomerate]

8 **GN ReSound Group**
Denmark
[Healthcare]

1 **Go Airlines**
UK, 1998
Wolff Olins: Joseph Mitchell
[Airline]

2 **Go! Express & Logistics**
Go! General Overnight Service (Germany) GmbH
Germany
[Mail Services]

3 **GoVideo**
TCL Corporation
USA
[Consumer Electronics]

4 **GO Voyages**
GO Voyages SAS
France
[Travel & Tourism]

5 **GOAL (German Operating Aircraft Leasing GmbH & Co. KG)**
Germany
[Aviation]

6 **Goaliath Kicker**
Germany, 2005
Machbar
[Sporting Goods]

7 **Godfather's Pizza**
USA
[Restaurants & Bars]

8 **Godiva Chocolatier**
Godiva Chocolatier Inc,
Yıldız Holding
Belgium, 1993
Pentagram: Michael Bierut
[Food & Beverage]

9 **Godiva Chocolatier**
Godiva Chocolatier Inc,
Yıldız Holding
Belgium
[Food & Beverage]

GOETHE-INSTITUT

1 Goethe-Institut
Germany
[Foundations & Institutes]

2 Gola
Jacobson Group
UK
[Sporting Goods]

3 Golden Corral
Golden Corral Corporation
USA, ca 1978
[Restaurants & Bars]

4 Golden Toast
Arbeitsgemeinschaft
Golden Toast eV
Germany
[Food & Beverage]

5 Golden West Financial Corporation
USA
[Financial Services]

6 Goldman Sachs
The Goldman Sachs Group Inc
USA
[Financial Services]

7 Gold Peak Group
Gold Peak Industries (Holdings) Ltd
China
[Electronics]

GOODMAN MANUFACTURING

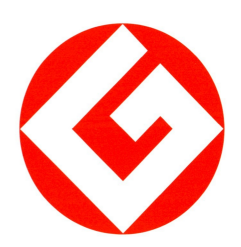

1 **Gold's Gym**
Gold's Gym International Inc
USA
[Fitness & Wellbeing]

2 **Gold Star Chili**
Gold Star Chili Inc
USA
[Restaurants & Bars]

3 **Gonera Property**
Gonera & Company Sp. z o.o.
Poland
[Real Estate]

4 **Good Design Award**
Japan Industrial Design
Promotion Organization
Japan
[Design]

5 **Good Humor**
Unilever plc/NV
USA, 1960s
[Food & Beverage]

6 **Good Humor**
Unilever plc/NV
USA, 2003
[Food & Beverage]

▶ 7 **Goodman Manufacturing**
Goodman Global Group Inc
USA
[Heating & Cooling]

GOODRICH

1 **Goodrich**
Goodrich Corporation
USA, 2001
Kass Uehling
[Aerospace]

2 **Goodwill Industries International**
USA, 1968
Joseph Selame
[Charity]

3 **Goodyear**
The Goodyear Tire
& Rubber Company
USA, 1900
[Automotive]

4 **Google**
Google Inc
USA, 1999
Ruth Kedar
[Internet]

5 **Google (browser icon)**
Google Inc
USA, 1999
Ruth Kedar
[Internet]

6 **Google Chrome**
Google Inc
USA, 2011
Office, Google Creative Lab
[Internet]

7 **Google Earth**
Google Inc
USA, 2010
[Internet]

8 **Goo Software**
Goo Software Ltd
UK
Jon Hicks
[Computer Software]

1 **Gordon's Gin**
Diageo plc
UK
[Wines, Beers & Spirits]

2 **Gore-Tex**
W. L. Gore & Associates Inc
USA
[Fabrics & Textiles]

3 **Gorillaz**
Daman Albarn, Jamie Hewlett
UK, 1998
Jamie Hewlett
[Music]

4 **Goshawk Insurance**
Goshawk Insurance Holdings plc
UK
[Financial Services]

5 **Gotham Books**
Penguin Group
USA, 2003
Eric Baker, Eric Strohl
[Publishing]

6 **Government of Saskatchewan**
Canada
[Government]

7 **Goya**
Goya Foods Inc
USA
[Food & Beverage]

1 **GQ**
Condé Nast, Advance Magazine Publishers Inc
USA, 1990s
[Publications]

2 **Graber**
Spring Window Fashions LLC
USA
[Home Furnishings]

3 **Graber**
Spring Window Fashions LLC
USA
[Home Furnishings]

4 **Graceland Universtity**
USA
[Education]

5 **Graco**
Newell Rubbermaid Inc
USA
[Baby Products]

6 **Graco**
Newell Rubbermaid Inc
USA
[Baby Products]

7 **Gradiente**
Gradiente Eletronica SA
Brazil
[Consumer Electronics]

8 **Graham**
Graham Sourcing LLC
USA
[Professional Services]

9 **Grainger**
W. W. Grainger Inc
USA
[Industry]

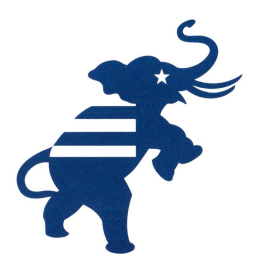
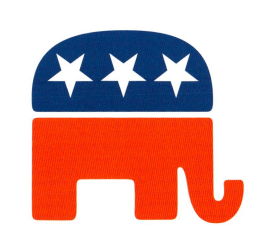

1 **Gramercy Pictures**
PolyGram Filmed Entertainment,
Universal Pictures
USA
[Film Industry]

2 **GRAND-AM Road Racing**
USA
[Motorsport]

3 **Grandcell**
Grand Battery Technologies
(Australia) Pty Ltd
Australia
[Consumer Products]

4 **Grand Eagle**
Grand Eagle Companies Inc
USA
[Engineering]

5 **Grand Old Party (GOP)**
Republican Party
USA
[Political]

6 **Grand Old Party (GOP)**
Republican National Convention
Republican Party
USA, 2008
[Political]

▶ 7 **Grand Old Party (GOP)**
Republican Party
USA
[Political]

1. **Grand Royal Records**
   Beastie Boys
   USA, 1992
   [Music Industry]

2. **Grand Union**
   C&S Wholesale Grocers
   USA, 1980s
   [Retail]

3. **Granini**
   Eckes-Granini Group GmbH
   Germany
   [Food & Beverage]

4. **Gran Turismo**
   Polyphony Digital Inc, Sony Computer Entertainment Inc
   Japan
   [Political]

5. **Grant Thornton**
   Grant Thornton International Ltd
   UK, 2008
   Pentagram: Angus Hyland
   [Professional Services]

6. **Gras Savoye**
   Gras Savoye SA
   France
   [Financial Services]

7. **Grasshöpper**
   Big Rock Brewery
   Canada
   [Wines, Beers & Spirits]

GREAT LAKES CHEMICAL CORPORATION

Grayson Mitchell Inc
USA
[Transport]

Grease
Paramount Pictures Corporation
USA, 1978
[Film]

Grease 2
Paramount Pictures Corporation
USA, 1982
[Film]

4 **Grease Monkey**
Grease Monkey International Inc
USA
[Automotive]

5 **Great Eastern Group**
Singapore/Malaysia
[Financial Services]

6 **Greater Atlantic Bank**
Greater Atlantic Financial Corporation
USA
[Financial Services]

7 **Greater Union**
Australian Theatres,
Village Roadshow-Amalgamated Holdings Ltd
Australia
[Cinemas & Theatres]

8 **Great Lakes Chemical Corporation**
Chemtura Corporation
USA
[Chemicals & Materials]

GREAT WESTERN BANK

1 Great Western Bank
   USA
   [Financial Services]

2 Great West Life
   Assurance Company
   USA
   [Financial Services]

3 GReddy
   Trust Co. Ltd
   Japan
   [Automotive]

4 Greece
   Greek National Tourism
   Organisation (GNTO)
   Greece
   [Travel & Tourism]

5 Green Burrito
   Carl Karcher Enterprises Inc
   USA
   [Restaurants & Bars]

6 Green Canteen
   Blum Enterprises
   USA, 2008
   Pentagram
   [Restaurants & Bars]

7 Green Chemistry Challenge
   United States Environmental
   Protection Agency
   USA, 1990s
   [Conservation & Environment]

8 Green Cross for Safety
   National Safety Council
   USA
   [Safety & Security]

GREENLEE

Green Day – American Idiot
Reprise Records
USA, 2004
Chris Bilheimer
[Music]

Green Giant
General Mills Inc
USA, 1986
[Food & Beverage]

Green Giant
General Mills Inc
USA, 2009
[Food & Beverage]

4 **Green Hills**
Green Hills Software Inc
USA
[Computer Software]

5 **Greenland Home Rule**
Government of Greenland
Greenland, 2004
Bysted
[Government]

6 **Green Lantern**
DC Comics Inc
USA
[Publications]

7 **Greenlee**
Greenlee Textron Inc
USA
[Tools & Machinery]

335

GREENLEE LIGHTING

1 **Greenlee Lighting**
Greenlee Lighting Inc
USA
[Manufacturing]

2 **Green Mountain Coffee Roasters Inc**
USA
[Food & Beverage]

3 **Green Mountain Energy Company**
USA
[Energy]

4 **Greenpeace**
Netherlands
[Conservation & Environment]

5 **GreenPoint Financial Corp.**
USA
[Financial Services]

6 **greenSand**
Olivine Group BV
Netherlands
[Chemicals & Materials]

7 **Greyhound Lines Inc**
USA
[Transport]

8 **Griffin Radiator**
Griffin Thermal Products LLC
USA
[Heating & Cooling]

9 **Griffin Technology**
USA
[Computer Technology]

Grohe
Grohe AG
Germany
[Household Products]

Grolsch
Koninklijke Grolsch NV
Netherlands
[Breweries]

Groove Armada
UK
Zip
[Music]

Group 4 Falck
UK
[Safety & Security]

Group 4 Securicor
G4S plc
UK, 2005
Stylus Design
[Safety & Security]

Groupama
Groupama SA
France
[Financial Services]

Group Janssens
Belgium
[Safety & Security]

GROUPON

1. **Groupon**
   Groupon Inc
   USA, 2008
   [Internet]

2. **Grubb & Ellis Company**
   USA, 2009
   [Real Estate]

3. **Grundfos**
   Grundfos Holding A/S
   Denmark, 2001
   [Industrial Products]

4. **Grundig**
   Grundig AG
   Germany
   [Consumer Electronics]

5. **Gruner + Jahr**
   Gruner + Jahr GmbH & Co. KG
   Germany
   [Publishing]

6. **Grupo Bimbo**
   Grupo Bimbo SAB de CV
   Mexico
   [Food & Beverage]

7. **Grupo Ken**
   Grupo Ken Construcciones
   SA de CV
   Mexico
   [Construction]

8. **Grupo Prasa**
   Grupo PRA SA
   Spain
   [Construction]

GT BICYCLES

Grupo Tampico
Grupo Tampico SA de CV
Mexico
[Conglomerate]

Grupo Uniradio
Grupo Uniradio SA de CV
Mexico
[Radio Stations]

GS Battery
GS Yuasa Corporation
Japan
[Automotive]

4   **GSA**
US General Services
Administration
USA
[Government]

5   **GSK**
GlaxoSmithKline plc
UK, 2001
FutureBrand
[Pharmaceuticals]

▶ 6 **GSM**
Global System for Mobile
Communications
UK
[Labelling, Standards
& Certification]

7   **GSN (Game Show Network)**
DirecTV Inc,
Sony Pictures Television Inc
USA, 2008
Buster Design, Stun Creative
[Television Network]

8   **GT Bicycles**
Dorel Industries Inc
USA
[Bicycles]

339

GTE

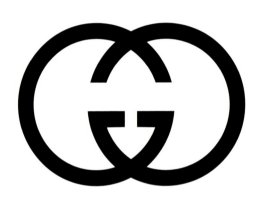

1   **GTE Corporation**
    USA
    [Telecommunications]

2   **GTL**
    GTL Infrastructure Ltd
    India
    [Telecommunications]

3   **Guaranty Bank and Trust Company**
    USA
    [Financial Services]

4   **Guardian Insurance**
    The Guardian Life Insurance Company of America
    USA
    [Financial Services]

5   **Guardian Media Group plc (GMG)**
    UK
    [Media]

6   **Gucci**
    Gucci Group, PPP Group
    Italy, 1933
    Gucci family
    [Fashion]

7   **Gucci**
    Gucci Group, PPP Group
    Italy, 1933
    Gucci family
    [Fashion]

8   **Geurlain**
    Guerlain SA
    France
    [Health & Beauty]

GUESS

GUGGENHEIM

1 **Guerrilla Games**
Sony Computer Entertainment Inc
Netherlands, 2004
[Computer & Video Games]

2 **Guess**
Guess Inc
USA
[Fashion]

3 **Guggenheim**
Solomon R. Guggenheim
Foundation (SRGF)
USA, 2009
Pentagram: Abbott Miller,
John Kudos
[Foundations & Institutes]

4 **GuideOne Insurance**
GuideOne Mutual Insurance
Company
USA
[Financial Services]

5 **Guigoz**
Laboratoires Guigoz SAS
France
[Baby Products]

6 **Guinness**
Diageo plc
Ireland, 1997
[Wines, Beers & Spirits]

7 **Guinness**
Diageo plc
Ireland, 2005
[Wines, Beers & Spirits]

GUITAR HERO

1 Guitar Hero
Activision Blizzard Inc, Vivendi SA
USA, 2005
[Computer & Video Games]

2 Gulf Air
Bahrain
[Airline]

3 Gulf Oil
Gulf Oil LP
USA, ca 1936
[Oil, Gas & Petroleum]

4 Gulf Oil
Gulf Oil LP
USA, ca 1920
[Oil, Gas & Petroleum]

▶ 5 Gulf Oil
Gulf Oil LP
USA, 1960
[Oil, Gas & Petroleum]

6 Gunica
The Gunica Company
South Korea
[Toys, Games & Models]

7 G-Unit Clothing Company
USA
[Fashion]

342

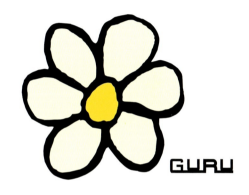

Gunk
Radiator Specialty Company
USA
[Automotive]

Gunnebo Fastening
Gunnebo Industries AB
Sweden
[Industrial Products]

Guoco Group
Guoco Group Ltd
China
[Financial Services]

4 **Guru**
BRFL Italia Srl
Italy
[Fashion]

5 **Gustavsberg**
Villeroy & Boch Gustavsberg AB
Sweden
[Home Furnishings]

6 **Guy Cotten SA**
France
[Apparel]

7 **GVB Amsterdam**
CFP NV
Netherlands, 1970
[Transport]

8 **GWDG (Gesellschaft für wissenschaftliche Datenverarbeitung mbH)**
Germany
[Information Technology]

H-L

H&M

1 **H&M**
H&M Hennes & Mauritz AB
Sweden
[Retail]

2 **H&R Block**
H&R Block Inc
USA, 2000
[Financial Services]

3 **haacon**
haacon hebetechnik GmbH
Germany
[Tools & Machinery]

4 **Häagen-Dazs**
General Mills Inc
USA
[Food & Beverage]

5 **Habitat**
Habitat Retail Ltd,
Home Retail Group plc
UK, 2002
Andy Stevens, Paul Neal
[Retail]

6 **Hachette Livre**
Lagardère Publishing
France
[Publishing]

7 **Hägglunds Drives**
Hägglunds Drives AB
Sweden
[Marine]

8 **Haglöfs**
Haglöfs Scandinavia AB
Sweden
[Outdoor & Recreational]

9 **Hahne**
C. Hahne Mühlenwerke
GmbH & Co. KG
Germany
[Food & Beverage]

10 **Haier**
Haier Group
China
[Consumer Electronics]

11 **Hakuto**
Hakuto Co. Ltd
Japan
[Conglomerate]

HANJIN

1 **Halifax**
   Bank of Scotland plc,
   Lloyds Banking Group plc
   UK, 1980s
   [Financial Services]

2 **Halliburton**
   USA
   [Oil, Gas & Petroleum]

3 **Hallmark**
   Hallmark Cards Inc
   USA, 1949
   Hallmark: Andrew Szoeke
   [Consumer Products]

4 **Hamilton**
   Hamilton International Ltd,
   The Swatch Group Ltd
   USA/Switzerland
   [Watches & Jewelry]

5 **Hammerson**
   Hammerson plc
   UK
   [Real Estate]

6 **Hampton**
   Hilton Worldwide
   USA
   [Hospitality]

7 **Hancock Bank**
   Hancock Holding Company
   USA
   [Financial Services]

8 **Handy Bag**
   Groupe Mellita
   France
   [Household Products]

9 **Hanes**
   HanesBrands Inc
   USA
   [Apparel]

10 **Hanjin**
   Hanjin Group
   South Korea
   [Conglomerate]

347

HANKOOK

1 **Hankook**
Hankook Tire
South Korea
[Automotive]

2 **Hankook**
Hankook Tire
South Korea
[Automotive]

3 **Hansaplast**
Beiersdorf AG
Germany
[Personal Care]

4 **Hard Rock Café**
Seminole Tribe of Florida
USA, 1971
Alan Aldridge
[Restaurants & Bars]

5 **Haribo Boy**
Haribo GmbH & Co. KG
Germany
[Food & Beverage]

6 **Haribo**
Haribo GmbH & Co. KG
Germany
[Food & Beverage]

7 **Harken**
Harken Inc
USA
[Marine]

8 **Harley-Davidson**
H-D Michigan LLC
USA, 1965
[Automotive]

9 **HarperCollins Publishers**
HarperCollins, News Corporation
USA
Chermayeff & Geismar
[Publishing]

HASSELBLAD

HASSELBLAD

Harpic
Reckitt Benckiser plc
UK
[Household Products]

Harris Bank
BMO Harris Bank NA
USA
[Financial Services]

Harrods
Qatar Investment Authority
UK, 1967
Minale Tattersfield:
Brian Tattersfield
[Retail]

4 **Harry Potter**
Warner Bros. Entertainment Inc
USA, 2001
[Film]

5 **Harry's**
Barilla France SAS
France
[Food & Beverage]

6 **Hasbro**
Hasbro Inc
USA, 1980s
[Toys, Games & Models]

7 **Hasbro**
Hasbro Inc
USA, 2009
[Toys, Games & Models]

8 **Hasselblad**
Victor Hasselblad AB
Sweden
[Imaging & Photographic]

349

HÄSTENS

1 **Hästens**
 Sweden, 2001
 Stockholm Design Lab, TEArk
 [Consumer Products]

2 **Hauri**
 Hauri Inc
 South Korea
 [Computer Software]

3 **Havaianas**
 São Paulo Alpargatas SA
 Brazil
 [Footwear]

4 **Havas**
 France
 [Advertising & Campaigns]

5 **Hawaiian Airlines**
 Hawaiian Airlines Inc
 USA, 1993
 Lindon Leader
 [Airline]

6 **Hayward Pool Products**
 Hayward Industries Inc
 USA
 [Manufacturing]

7 **Hazama Corporation**
 Vietnam
 [Construction]

8 **HBO**
 Home Box Office Inc,
 Time Warner
 USA, 1981
 [Television Network]

9 **HDCD (High Definition Compatible Digital)**
 Microsoft Corporation
 USA
 [Labelling, Standards & Certification]

10 **Head**
 Head NV
 USA
 [Sporting Goods]

11 **Hebrew National**
 ConAgra Foods Inc
 USA
 [Food & Beverage]

Hecho en México
(Made in Mexico)
Mexico
[Labelling, Standards
& Certification]

Hecht's
Federated Department
Stores Inc
USA
[Retail]

Hefty
Pactiv Corporation
USA
[Household Products]

4 Heidelberg Technology
Heidelberger
Druckmaschinen AG
Germany
[Engineering]

5 Heidmar
Heidmar Inc
USA
[Freight & Logistics]

▶ 6 Heineken
Heineken International
Netherlands, 1999
Edenspiekermann
[Wines, Beers & Spirits]

▶ 7 Heinz
H. J. Heinz Company Inc
USA
[Food & Beverage]

8 Helgeland Holding
Helgeland Holding A/S
Norway
[Industrial Products]

9 Helicopter Association
International (HAI)
USA
[Societies & Associations]

10 Helicraft
Helicraft Ltee
Canada
[Transport]

HELLA

1 **Hella**
Hella KGaA Hueck & Co
Germany
[Automotive]

2 **Hellboy**
Dark Horse Comics
USA
Mike Mignola
[Publications]

3 **Hellenic Post (Elta)**
Hellenic Post SA
Greece
[Mail Services]

4 **Heller**
Heller Joustra SA
France
[Toys, Games & Models]

5 **Heller**
ITW Heller GmbH
Germany
[Tools & Machinery]

6 **Hello**
France
[Toys, Games & Models]

7 **Hello Kitty**
Sanrio Co. Ltd
Japan, 1974
Yuko Shimizu (character)
[Toys, Games & Models]

8 **Helly Hansen**
Altor Equity Partners
Norway
[Apparel]

9 **Helvetia**
Helvetia Group
Switzerland, 2006
[Financial Services]

10 **Hemköp**
Axfood AB
Sweden, 2004
Happy F&B,
Forsman & Bodenfors
[Retail]

HERSHEY'S

1. **Herbalife**
Herbalife International
USA
[Health & Beauty]

Hercules Offshore
Hercules Offshore Inc
USA
[Oil, Gas & Petroleum]

Hering
Cia Hering SA
Brazil
[Retail]

4. **Herman Miller**
Herman Miller Inc
USA, 1999
[Office Supplies]

5. **Hermès**
Hermès International SA
*France, 1945
(based on a drawing by)
Alfred de Dreux*
[Luxury Goods]

6. **Hermle**
Hermle Uhrenmanufaktur GmbH
Germany
[Watches & Jewelry]

7. **Hero**
Hero MotoCorp,
Hero Cycles Ltd
India
[Automotive]

8. **Heron. The coral Island**
Australia
[Places]

9. **Hershey's**
The Hershey Company
USA
[Food & Beverage]

10. **Herta**
Nestlé SA
Germany
[Food & Beverage]

HERTZ

1   Hertz Rent-A-Car
    The Hertz Corporation
    USA, 1978
    [Car Rental]

2   Hertz Rent-A-Car
    The Hertz Corporation
    USA, 2009
    Landor Associates
    [Car Rental]

3   Hess
    Hess Corporation
    USA
    [Oil, Gas & Petroleum]

4   Hettich
    Hettich Holding GmbH & Co. oHG
    Germany
    [Home Furnishings]

5   HFC (Household Finance Corporation)
    HSBC Finance Corporation
    USA
    [Financial Services]

6   HGCA
    Agriculture and Horticulture Development Board (AHDB)
    UK
    [Agricultural]

7   Hi
    Koninklijke KPN NV
    Netherlands
    [Telecommunications]

8   Hiab (Hydrauliska Industri AB)
    Cargotec Corporation
    Finland, 1971
    [Manufacturing]

9   Higashi-Nippon Bank
    Higashi-Nippon Bank Ltd
    Japan
    [Financial Services]

10 Hill's
    Hill's Pet Nutrition Inc,
    Colgate-Palmolive Company
    USA
    [Pet Products]

Hills Department Store
USA
[Retail]

Hillshire Farm
Sara Lee Corporation
USA, 2004
[Food & Beverage]

Hilo Hattie
Pomare Inc
USA
[Retail]

4 **Hilti**
Hilti Corporation
Liechtenstein
[Construction]

5 **Hilton Hotels & Resorts**
Hilton Worldwide
USA, 1998
Enterprise IG: Gene Grossman
[Hospitality]

6 **Hiper Bompreço**
Bompreço SA, Wal-Mart Stores Inc
Brazil
[Retail]

7 **Hirobo Limited**
Japan
[Toys, Games & Models]

8 **His Master's Voice (HMV)**
HMV Group plc
UK, 2007
[Music Industry]

9 **Historia**
Astral Media Inc, Shaw Media
Canada, 2010
Fred Dompierre, Nicolas Ménard
[Television Channel]

HITACHI

1   **Hitachi**
    Hitachi Ltd
    Japan
    [Conglomerate]

2   **Hi-Tec**
    Hi-Tec Sports plc
    UK
    [Footwear]

3   **HLN (Headline News)**
    Turner Broadcasting System Inc,
    Time Warner
    USA, 2008
    Digital Kitchen: Brian Bowman,
    Ben Grube
    [Television Network]

4   **Hobart**
    Hobart Corporation,
    Illinois Tool Works Inc
    USA
    [Manufacturing]

5   **HOBAS Engineering GmbH**
    Austria
    [Manufacturing]

6   **Hobie**
    Hobie Cat Company
    USA
    [Marine]

7   **Hoechst**
    Hoechst AG
    Germany
    [Chemicals & Materials]

8   **Hoegaarden**
    Anheuser-Busch InBev NV
    Netherlands
    [Breweries]

9   **Holden**
    GM Holden Ltd
    Australia, 1994
    [Automotive]

10 **Holiday Inn**
    British InterContinental Hotels
    Group (IHG)
    USA, 2007
    [Hospitality]

▶ 11 **Holiday Inn Express**
    InterContinental Hotels Group
    UK, 2007
    Interbrand
    [Hospitality]

HOMEWOOD SUITES

Holiday on Ice
Stage Entertainment Group
Netherlands
[Leisure & Entertainment]

Holland Cup
Euro-Sportring
Netherlands
[Sporting Events]

Holley
Holley Performance Products Inc
USA
[Industrial Products]

5 Hollister Co.
Abercrombie & Fitch Co.
USA, 2000
[Apparel]

5 Hollywood Chewing Gum
Cadbury France
France
[Food & Beverage]

6 Hollywood Records
Disney Music Group
USA, 1995
[Music Industry]

7 HomeAway
HomeAway Inc
USA
[Hospitality]

8 Home Credit Bank
Home Credit BV
Netherlands
[Financial Services]

9 Home Satellite Sales & Service
USA
[Satellite Television]

10 Homewood Suites
Hilton Worldwide
USA
[Hospitality]

357

HONDA

1. **Honda Automobiles**
   Honda Motor Company Ltd
   Japan
   Miles Newlyn
   [Automotive]

2. **Honda Powersports**
   Honda Motor Company Ltd
   Japan
   Miles Newlyn
   [Automotive]

▶ 3. **Honda Powersports**
   Honda Motor Company Ltd
   Japan
   [Automotive]

4. **Honeywell**
   Honeywell International Inc
   USA
   [Conglomerate]

5. **Hong Kong Sports Development Board**
   China
   [Government]

▶ 6. **Hoover**
   The Hoover Company
   USA, ca 1940
   Raymond Loewy
   [Food & Beverage]

7. **Horizon Healthcare**
   Horizon Healthcare Services Inc
   USA
   [Healthcare]

8. **Hornby**
   Hornby plc
   UK, ca 1996
   [Toys, Games & Models]

9. **Hot Key Books**
   Bonnier Publishing
   UK
   [Publishing]

▶ 10. **Hot Wheels**
   Mattel Inc
   USA, 1968
   Rick Irons
   [Toys, Games & Models]

1 **Hoya**
   Hoya Corporation
   Japan
   [optical products]

2 **HP**
   Hewlett-Packard Company
   USA, 2000
   [Information Technology]

3 **HP**
   Hewlett-Packard Company
   USA, 2008
   [Computer Technology]

4 **HP OpenView**
   Hewlett-Packard Company,
   HP Software Division
   USA
   [Computer Software]

5 **HRC (Honda Racing Corporation)**
   Honda Motor Company Ltd
   Japan, 1982
   [Motorsport]

6 **HSBC**
   HSBC Holdings plc
   UK, 1999
   Henry Steiner
   [Financial Services]

7 **HSLS (Hrvatska socijalno liberalna stranka/Croatian Social Liberal Party)**
   Croatia, ca 1999
   [Political]

8 **HTC**
   HTC Corporation
   Taiwan, 2009
   Figtree
   [Telecommunications]

9 **Huawei**
   Huawei Technologies Co. Ltd
   China
   [Telecommunications]

10 **Huawei**
   Huawei Technologies Co. Ltd
   China, 2006
   [Telecommunications]

HUBER GRUPPE

1. **Huber Gruppe**
MHM Holding GmbH
Germany
[Paints & Coatings]

2. **Hudson's Bay Company**
Hudson's Bay Trading Company LP
Canada, 2009
Arcade Agency
[Retail]

3. **Huggies**
Kimberly-Clark Corporation
USA
[Baby Products]

4. **Hugo Boss**
Hugo Boss AG, Valentino Fashion Group SpA
Germany
[Fashion]

5. **Human**
USA
[Music Industry]

6. **Human Rights Campaign Foundation (HRCF)**
USA
[Political]

7. **Human Rights Campaign (HRCF)**
USA, 1995
Stone Yamashita
[Political]

8. **Hummer**
General Motors Company
USA, 1992
[Automotive]

9. **Humpty Dumpty**
Old Dutch Foods Ltd
Canada
[Food & Beverage]

1. **Hungry Jack**
The J.M. Smucker Company
USA, ca 1967
[Food & Beverage]

2. **Hungry Jack's**
Hungry Jack's Pty Ltd,
Competitive Foods Australia
Pty Ltd
Australia
[Restaurants & Bars]

3. **Hungry Tiger Press**
USA
[Publishing]

4. **Huntington**
Huntington Bancshares Inc
USA, 2010
[Financial Services]

5. **Hurricane**
Hurricane Exploration plc
UK
[Oil, Gas & Petroleum]

6. **Husky Energy**
Husky Energy Inc
Canada
[Energy]

7. **Husqvarna**
Husqvarna AB
Sweden, 1972
[Tools & Machinery]

8. **Hustler**
Larry Flynt Publications
USA, 1974
[Publications]

9. **Hyatt**
Hyatt Corporation
USA, 1990
Landor Associates
[Hospitality]

10. **Hyster**
Hyster Company
USA
[Manufacturing]

11. **HYT Radios**
Shenzhen Science
and Technology Company
Australia
[Telecommunications]

12. **Hyundai**
Hyundai Motor Company
South Korea
[Automotive]

IAB

1. IAB (Interactive Advertising Bureau)
   USA, 2008
   Pentagram: Michael Bierut
   [Advertising & Campaigns]

2. IAFF (International Association of Fire Fighters)
   USA
   [Societies & Associations]

3. IAG Insurance Australia Group (IAG)
   Insurance Australia Group Ltd
   Australia
   [Financial Services]

4. IAI (Israel Aerospace Industries) Ltd
   Israel
   [Aerospace]

5. IAMS
   Procter & Gamble Co
   USA
   [Pet Products]

6. IATA (International Air Transport Association)
   Canada
   [Societies & Associations]

7. IATSE (International Alliance of Theatrical Stage Employees)
   USA/Canada
   [Societies & Associations]

8. Ibanez Guitars
   Hoshino Gakki Group
   Japan
   [Musical Instruments]

9. Iberia Airlines
   Iberia Líneas Aéreas de España SA, International Consolidated Airlines Group SA
   Spain
   [Airline]

10. Ibis Hotels
    Accor SA
    France, 2011
    W&Cie
    [Hospitality]

1 **IBM**
   USA, 1956
   Paul Rand
   [Computer Technology]

2 **IBM**
   USA, 1972
   Paul Rand
   [Technology]

3 **IBM Smarter Planet**
   IBM
   USA, 2008
   Studio Intraligi, Ogilvy
   [Technology]

4 **ICA**
   ICA Sverige AB
   Sweden
   [Retail]

5 **ICA (Industria Chimica Adriatica) SpA**
   ICA Group
   USA
   [Paints & Coatings]

6 **Citrix ICA (Independent Computer Architecture)**
   Citrix Systems Inc
   USA
   [Computer Software]

7 **ICA (Institute of Contemporary Arts)**
   UK
   [Foundations & Institutes]

8 **I Can't Believe It's Yogurt (ICBIY)**
   Yogen Früz
   USA
   [Restaurants & Bars]

9 **ICBC (Industrial and Commercial Bank of China Ltd)**
   China
   [Financial Services]

10 **ICC (Instituto Cidades Criativas)**
   Brazil
   [Societies & Associations]

ICC BERLIN

ICEBERG

1 ICC Berlin (Internationale
   Congress Centrum Berlin)
   Messe Berlin GmbH
   Germany
   [Places]

2 ICE
   Grupo ICE
   Cosat Rica
   [Utilities]

3 Iceberg
   Gilmar SpA
   Italy
   [Fashion]

4 Ice Cream for America
   International Ice Cream
   Association
   USA
   [Advertising & Campaigns]

5 Icelandair
   Icelandair Group ehf
   Iceland
   [Airline]

6 Iceland Express
   Eignarhaldsfélagið Fengur hf
   Iceland
   [Airline]

7 ICI (Imperial Chemical Industries)
   Akzo Nobel NV
   UK, 1987
   Wolff Olins
   [Chemicals & Materials]

8 ICL (International Computers Ltd)
   UK
   [Computer Technology]

9 ICOM
   ICOM Inc
   Japan
   [Consumer Electronics]

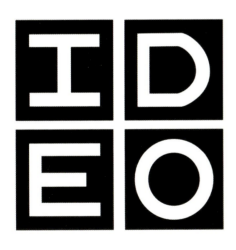

1 **ICS**
ICS, Blount Inc
USA
[Tools & Machinery]

2 **Idacorp**
Idacorp Inc
USA
[Utilities]

3 **Idealease**
Idealease Inc
USA
[Transport]

4 **Ideal Standard International**
Australia
[Home Furnishings]

5 **IDEO**
IDEO Inc
USA, 1991
Paul Rand
[Design]

6 **IDEO**
IDEO Inc
USA, 1997
Pentagram: Michael Bierut
[Design]

7 **IDI (Industrial Developments International) Inc**
USA
[Real Estate]

8 **Idols**
19 TV Ltd/FremantleMedia North America Inc
USA
[Television Series]

9 **IEA (Institute of Economic Affairs)**
UK
[Foundations & Institutes]

10 **IEEE**
Institute of Electrical and Electronics Engineers
USA, 1963
[Foundations & Institutes]

1 IER
Groupe Bolloré
France
[Freight & Logistics]

2 iF
iF International Forum
Design GmbH
Germany
[Design]

3 IF (Instituto Federal Goiano)
Brazil
[Education]

4 IFAW (International Fund for Animal Welfare)
Canada
[Charity]

5 IFC (Independent Film Channel)
AMC Networks
USA, 2001
[Television Network]

6 IFIA (International Fence Industry Service Association)
USA
[Societies & Associations]

7 Ifor Williams Trailers Ltd
UK
[Manufacturing]

8 Ifremer (Institut français de recherche pour l'exploitation de la mer)
France
[Foundations & Institutes]

9 IFS Defence
Industrial and Financial Systems (IFS AB)
Sweden
[Computer Software]

10 IGA (Interessengemeinschaft der Abschlepp- und Pannendienstunternehmer eV)
Germany
[Societies & Associations]

IGA Supermarkets
Independent Grocers Alliance
USA
[Retail]

Iglo
Birds Eye Iglo Group Ltd (BEIG)
Belgium, 1983
[Food & Beverage]

Igloo
Igloo Products Corp.
USA
[Household Products]

4 **IG Metall**
Industrial Union of Metal Workers
Germany
[Societies & Associations]

5 **Igol France**
Igol France SA
France
[Chemicals & Materials]

6 **Igol Lubrifiants**
Igol France SA
France, 2000
[Chemicals & Materials]

Iguana Cerveza
Cervecería y Maltería Quilmes
Argentina
[Wines, Beers & Spirits]

8 **IHI Corporation**
Japan
[Industry]

9 **IHK (Industrie- und Handelskammer)**
Germany
[Societies & Associations]

10 **IHS Engineering**
IHS Inc
USA
[Publishing]

1 **IIA (The Institute of Internal Auditors)**
USA
[Foundations & Institutes]

2 **IIJ**
Internet Initiative Japan Inc
Japan
[Internet]

3 **IKEA**
IKEA International Group
Sweden, 1943
[Retail]

4 **IKKS Group**
France
[Apparel]

5 **IKON Office Solutions Inc**
Ricoh Americas Corp
USA
[Computer Software]

6 **Ikusi**
IKUSI – Ángel Iglesias SA
Spain
[Technology]

7 **Iles de Paix**
Islands of Peace ASBL
Belgium
[Foundations & Institutes]

8 **Ilford Photo**
Harman Technology Ltd
UK, ca 1966
Design Research Unit
[Imaging & Photographic]

9 **i.LINK**
Sony Corporation
Japan
[Labelling, Standards & Certification]

10 **Illy**
illycaffè SpA
Italy, 1996
James Rosenquist
[Food & Beverage]

Ilmia
HAKOTOWI GmbH Berlin
Germany
[Footwear]

I Love New York
New York State Department of Economic Development, Empire State Development Corporation
USA, 1977
Milton Glaser
[Places]

I Love New York More Than Ever
USA, 2001
Milton Glaser
[Places]

4 **ILVA**
ILVA A/S
Denmark
[Retail]

5 **The Image Bank**
Getty Images Inc
USA
[Imaging & Photographic]

6 **IMAX**
IMAX Corporation
Canada
[Film Industry]

7 **IMI International**
Spain
[Heating & Cooling]

8 **Imperial Tobacco**
Imperial Tobacco Group plc
UK
[Tobacco]

9 **Imperial War Museum**
UK
Minale Tattersfield: Paul Astbury
[Galleries & Museums]

10 **Impregilo**
Impregilo SpA
Italy
[Construction]

IMPRESA

1 impresa
Impresa Sociedade Gestora de Participações Sociais SA
Portugal
[Conglomerate]

2 IMSS (Instituto Mexicano del Segura Social)
Mexico, 1992
[Government]

3 INC (Instituto Nacional de Cultura)
Ministry of Culture
Peru
[Government]

4 INCM
Imprensa Nacional-Casa da Moeda SA
Portugal
[Printing Services]

5 Inco
Inco Ltd
Canada
[Mining]

6 Independent Bank
Independent Bank Corporation
USA
[Financial Services]

7 Independent Insurance Agent
Independent Insurance Agents & Brokers of America Inc
USA, 2010
[Financial Services]

8 Independent Pictures
Switzerland
[Societies & Associations]

9 Indesit Company
Italy, 1998
Wolff Olins
[Home Appliances]

10 Indiana Fever
WNBA Enterprises LLC
USA, 2000
[Sport]

Indiana Jones
Paramount Pictures Corporation
USA, 1981
[Film]

Indian Pacific
Great Southern Rail
Australia
[Transport]

Indy Racing League LLC
USA
[Motorsport]

4 **InfantSEE**
American Optometric Association
USA
[Healthcare]

5 **Infiniti**
Nissan Motor Company Ltd
Japan, 2004
Lippincott Mercer
[Automotive]

6 **Infogrames**
Infogrames Entertainment SA
France
[Computer & Video Games]

7 **InfoWorld**
InfoWorld Media Group Inc (IDG)
USA
[Publications]

8 **ING**
ING Groep NV
Netherlands, 1991
[Financial Services]

9 **Ingles Markets Inc**
USA
[Retail]

10 **Ingram Micro Inc**
USA
[Electronics]

INNOCENT

1 **Innocent**
Innocent Drinks Ltd
UK, 1999
Gravy (aka David Streek),
Deepend
[Food & Beverage]

2 **In-N-Out Burger**
In-N-Out Burgers Inc
USA
[Restaurants & Bars]

3 **Insight**
Insight Propaganda
& Marketing Ltda
Brazil
[Design]

4 **Instagram**
Burbn Inc
USA, 2011
[Computer Software]

5 **Instituto Cervantes**
Spain, international
[Foundations & Institutes]

6 **Instituto Estudios Gráficos de Chile**
Asimpres
Chile, 2007
Vicente Larrea
[Foundations & Institutes]

7 **Instituto Terra e Memória**
Portugal
[Foundations & Institutes]

8 **Intel**
Intel Corporation
USA, 2006
FutureBrand: Sylvia Chu,
Rebecca Cobb, Ana Gonzalez,
Isabella Ossott
[Technology]

9 **Intel**
Intel Corporation
USA, 1968
[Technology]

10 **Intel Inside**
Intel Corporation
USA, 2003
[Technology]

11 **Interac Inc**
Canada
[Societies & Associations]

INTERNATIONAL PAINT

INTERNATIONAL
FILM FESTIVAL
ROTTERDAM

1   **InterContinental Hotels**
    InterContinental Hotels Group plc
    UK
    [Hospitality]

2   **Interfilm Berlin**
    Interfilm-Berlin Management GmbH
    Germany
    [Film Industry]

3   **International Airlines Group**
    International Consolidated Airlines Group SA
    UK/Spain, 2011
    Bostock & Pollitt
    [Aviation]

4   **International Boston Seafood Show**
    Diversified Business Communications
    USA
    [Events]

5   **International Environmental**
    LSB Industries Inc
    USA
    [Industrial Products]

6   **International Film Festival Rotterdam**
    Netherlands, 2008
    75B
    [Events]

7   **International Harvester Company**
    USA
    [Agricultural]

8   **International Paint**
    AkzoNobel NV
    UK
    [Paints & Coatings]

INTERNATIONAL PAPER COMPANY

1 **International Paper Company**
USA, 1961
Lester Beall Associates
[Paper Products]

2 **International Trucks**
Navistar International Corporation
USA
[Automotive]

▶ 3 **Internet Explorer**
Microsoft Corporation
USA
[Computer Software]

4 **Intershop**
Intershop Communications AG
Germany, USA
[Internet]

▶ 5 **Interview**
Interview Inc
USA, 1969
Andy Warhol
[Publication]

6 **In the City Entertainment Inc**
Canada
[Film Industry]

7 **Intramuros (International Design Magazine)**
Intramuros SA
France, 2010
H5: Rachel Cazadamont
[Publications]

8 **Intuit**
Intuit Inc
USA, 2008
[Computer Software]

9 **Invesco**
Invesco Ltd
Bermuda/USA
[Financial Services]

10 **Iomega**
EMC Corporation
USA
[Computer Hardware]

IRELAND

1 **Iowa Hawkeyes**
University of Iowa
USA, 1979
[Sport]

2 **Iowa Public Television (IPTV)**
Iowa Public Broadcasting Board
USA
[Television Network]

3 **iPhone**
Apple Inc
USA, 2007
[Telecommunications]

4 **Ippon**
Russia
[Consumer Electronics]

5 **IPSSA (Independent Pool and Spa Association Inc)**
USA
[Societies & Associations]

6 **IPWEA (Institute of Public Works Engineering Australia)**
Australia
[Foundations & Institutes]

7 **IranAir**
Iran National Airlines Corporation
Iran, 1962
[Airline]

8 **IRB (International Rugby Board)**
Ireland
[Sport]

9 **IR Bobcat**
Ingersoll Rand plc
USA
[Industry]

10 **Ireland**
Tourism Ireland Ltd
Ireland
[Travel & Tourism]

375

1 **IRFU (Irish Rugby Football Union)**
Ireland
[Sport]

2 **Iris Ohyama Inc**
Japan
[Consumer Products]

3 **Irisbus**
Irisbus IVECO
France
[Automotive]

4 **Irma**
Irma A/S
Denmark
[Retail]

5 **IRS (Internal Revenue Service)**
Department of the Treasury
USA
[Government]

6 **I.R.S. Records (International Record Syndicate)**
USA, 1979
[Music Industry]

7 **Irving Oil Ltd**
Canada
[Oil, Gas & Petroleum]

8 **Irving Oil**
Irving Oil Ltd
Canada, 2004
[Oil, Gas & Petroleum]

9 **Irving Texas**
Irving Convention & Visitors Bureau
USA
[Travel & Tourism]

10 **Irwin Financial**
Irwin Financial Corporation
USA, 1990
Paul Rand
[Financial Services]

Irwin Financial
Irwin Financial Corporation
USA, 1999
Chermayeff & Geismar:
Steff Geissbuhler
[Financial Services]

Irwin Tools
Newell Rubbermaid Inc
USA
[Tools & Machinery]

Irwin Toy Limited
Canada
[Toys, Games & Models]

4 **ISE – In Sink Erator**
Emerson Electric Co.
USA
[Home Appliances]

5 **Island Records**
Universal Music Group
USA
[Music Industry]

6 **ISN (Instituto de Servicios a la Nación)**
Ecuador
Diego Corrales
[Foundations & Institutes]

7 **ISO (International Organization for Standardization)**
Switzerland
[Labelling, Standards & Certification]

8 **Isocor**
USA
[Internet]

9 **Israel Police**
Israeli Ministry of Public Security
Israel
[Public Services]

10 **ISS**
ISS World Services A/S
Denmark
[Professional Services]

ISS

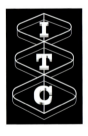

1 **ISS (International Service System)**
   UK
   [Professional Services]

2 **ISSF (International Shooting Sport Federation)**
   Germany
   [Societies & Associations]

3 **Ista**
   USA
   [Energy]

4 **Isuzu**
   Isuzu Motors Ltd
   Japan
   [Automotive]

5 **Italia 1**
   Mediaset SpA
   Italy
   [Television Channel]

6 **Italian Trade Commission**
   Italian Institute for Foreign Trade (ICE)
   Italy
   [Foundations & Institutes]

7 **ITC (Incorporated Television Company)**
   UK, 1973
   [Television Network]

8 **I Teach Nyc**
   USA, 2008
   Pentagram
   [Foundations & Institutes]

9 **ITN (Independent Television News)**
   Independent Television News Ltd
   UK, 2000s
   [Media]

ITT

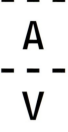

ITT
ITT Corporation
USA
[Conglomerate]

ITT
ITT Corporation
USA, 1998
Landor Associates
[Conglomerate]

iTunes
Apple Inc
USA, 2006
[Internet]

4 **iTunes**
Apple Inc
USA, 2010
[Internet]

5 **IUAV (Istituto Universitario
di Architettura di Venezia)**
Iuav University of Venice
Italy, 2002
Phillipe Apeloig
[Education]

6 **Ivar's**
Ivar's Inc
USA
[Restaurants & Bars]

7 **IVECO**
IVECO SpA, Fiat Industrial SpA
Italy
[Automotive]

8 **Ivory**
Procter & Gamble Co
USA, 2011
Wieden+Kennedy
[Personal Care]

9 **Iwatsu**
Iwatsu Electric Co. Ltd
Japan
[Electronics]

1. **J&B**
   Diageo plc
   UK
   [Wines, Beers & Spirits]

2. **Jack Daniel's**
   Jack Daniel Distillery, Lem Motlow, Prop. Inc, Brown-Forman Corporation
   USA
   [Wines, Beers & Spirits]

3. **Jack in the Box**
   Jack in the Box Inc
   USA, 1980
   [Restaurants & Bars]

4. **Jack in the Box**
   Jack in the Box Inc
   USA, 2009
   Duffy & Partners
   [Restaurants & Bars]

5. **Jackson Hole Realty**
   USA
   [Real Estate]

6. **Jack Wolfskin**
   Jack Wolfskin GmbH & Co. KGaA
   Germany, 1980s
   [Outdoor & Recreation]

7. **Jacobs**
   Kraft Foods Deutschland
   Germany
   [Food & Beverage]

8. **Jacuzzi**
   Jacuzzi Inc
   USA
   [Home Appliances]

9. **Jaeger**
   Paul Jaeger GmbH & Co. KG
   Germany
   [Paints & Coatings]

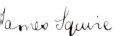

1 **Jaguar**
Jaguar Cars Ltd, Tata Motors Ltd
UK, 2002
The Partners: Greg Quinton,
Steve Owen, Helen Cooley
[Automotive]

2 **JAL (Japan Airlines)**
Japan Airlines Co. Ltd
Japan, 2011
[Airline]

3 **James Squire**
Malt Shovel Brewery Pty Ltd
Australia
[Breweries]

4 **Jamie Oliver**
Jamie Oliver Enterprises Ltd
UK
SEA Design
[Food & Beverage]

5 **Jams Music Center**
Brazil
[Music Industry]

6 **Janus Capital**
Janus Capital Group Inc
USA, 2003
Templin Brink Design:
Joel Templin, Gaby Brink
[Financial Services]

7 **Japan**
Japan National Tourism
Organization
Japan
[Travel & Tourism]

8 **Japan Information Processing
Service Ltd**
Japan
[Information Technology]

9 **Jarman Award**
Film London
UK, 2009
KentLyons: Jon Cefai
[Events]

10 **JAS (Japanese Agricultural
Standards)**
Government of Japan
Japan
[Labelling, Standards
& Certification]

1 **JAS (Japanese Agricultural Standards)**
Government of Japan
Japan
[Labelling, Standards & Certification]

2 **Jason Industrial Inc**
Megadyne Group
USA
[Industrial Products]

3 **Jatronic**
Jatronic A/S
Norway
[Electronics]

4 **Java**
Oracle Corporation
USA
[Computer Technology]

5 **Jayco**
Jayco Inc
USA
[Automotive]

6 **JBL**
Harman International Industries Inc
USA, 1968
Arnold Wolf
[Consumer Electronics]

7 **J/Boats**
J/Boats Inc
USA
[Marine]

8 **JCB**
J C Bamford Excavators Ltd
UK, 1953
Leslie Smith
[Tools & Machinery]

9 **JCB Brand Partner**
JCB Co. Ltd
Japan
[Financial Services]

2 **JC Penney**
J.C. Penney Company Inc
USA, 2012
Brand Advisors: Tom Suiter
[Retail]

JC Penney
J.C. Penney Company Inc
USA, 2011
Luke Langhus
[Retail]

JC Penney
J.C. Penney Company Inc
USA, 1969
Unimark International
[Retail]

4 **Jean Paul Gautier website**
France
[Fashion]

5 **Jeep**
Jeep, Chrysler Group LLC
USA
[Automotive]

6 **Jeep**
Jeep, Chrysler Group LLC
USA
[Automotive]

7 **Jeep**
Jeep, Chrysler Group LLC
USA
[Automotive]

8 **Jell-O**
Kraft Foods Inc
USA, 2006
[Food & Beverage]

9 **Jenn-Air Brand Home Appliances**
Whirlpool Corporation
USA
[Home Appliances]

1 **Jeppesen**
Jeppesen Sanderson Inc
USA, 2008
[Information Technology]

2 **Jernbanverket**
Norwegian National Rail Administration
Norway
[Government]

3 **Jersey Mike's Subs**
Jersey Mike's Franchise Systems Inc
USA
[Restaurants & Bars]

4 **Jessica**
Jessica Cosmetics International Inc
USA
[Health & Beauty]

5 **JET**
ConocoPhillips Company
USA
[Retail]

6 **Jet Airways**
Jet Airways (India) Ltd
India, 1993
Lintas: KV Sridhar (mark)
[Airline]

7 **Jet Aviation**
General Dynamics Corporation
Switzerland
[Airline]

8 **JetBlue Airways**
JetBlue Airways Corporation
USA, 2009
[Airline]

9 **Jetset Travel**
Stella Travel Services Pty Ltd
Australia
[Travel & Tourism]

JOE MOBILE

Jewel
The Jewel Companies Inc
USA, 1979
[Retail]

Jewson
Jewson Ltd
UK
[Retail]

JICA
Japan International Cooperation Agency
Japan
[Foundations & Institutes]

4 **Jif**
The J.M. Smucker Company
USA
[Food & Beverage]

5 **Jiffy**
Jiffy Products International BV
Netherlands
[Household Products]

6 **Jiffy Lube**
Jiffy Lube International Inc
USA, 1970s
[Retail]

7 **Jil Sander**
Jil Sander AG
Germany
[Fashion]

8 **Jim Beam**
Beam Inc
USA
[Wines, Beers & Spirits]

9 **Jive Records**
RCA Music Group
USA
[Music Industry]

10 **JK Harris & Company**
JK Harris & Company LLC
USA
[Financial Services]

11 **Joe Mobile**
SFR SA
France, 2012
[Telecommunications]

385

JOHN DEERE

1. **John Deere**
Deere & Company
USA, 2000
[Tools & Machinery]

2. **John Dickinson**
John Dickinson & Co. (WI) Ltd
UK
[Consumer Products]

3. **John F. Kennedy Presidential Library and Museum**
USA, 1964
Chermayeff & Geismar
[Galleries & Museums]

4. **Johnnie Walker**
Diageo plc
UK, 1908
Tom Browne
[Wines, Beers & Spirits]

5. **Johnny Lightning**
Learning Curve Brands Inc
USA
[Toys, Games & Models]

6. **Johnny Loco**
Johnny Loco International BV
Netherlands
[Outdoor & Recreation]

7. **Johnny's Pizza House**
Johnny's Pizza House Inc
USA
[Restaurants & Bars]

8. **John Player Special (JPS)**
Imperial Tobacco Group plc
UK
[Tobacco]

9. **John Sands**
John Sands (Australia) Ltd
Australia
[Consumer Products]

10. **Johns Manville**
Johns Manville, Berkshire Hathaway Inc
USA
[Household Products]

JOSÉ CUERVO

Johnson Controls
Johnson Controls Inc
USA, 1974
Byron Osterweil Associates:
Milt Kass
[Industry]

Johnson Controls
Johnson Controls Inc
USA, 2007
Lippincott
[Industry]

3 **Johnson & Johnson**
Johnson & Johnson
USA, 1886
James Wood Johnson
[Pharmaceuticals]

4 **Johnson's**
Johnson & Johnson Consumer
Companies Inc
USA
[Baby Products]

5 **Jones Lang LaSalle**
Jones Lang LaSalle Inc
USA
[Financial Services]

6 **Jonny Cupcakes Inc**
USA
[Apparel]

7 **Jonsson**
The Jonsson Group
South Africa
[Apparel]

8 **José Cuervo**
Tequila Cuervo SA de CV
Mexico
[Wines, Beers & Spirits]

JØTUL

1. Jøtul
Jøtul AS
Norway
[Heating & Cooling]

2. Jōvan
Coty US LLC
USA, 1972
[Health & Beauty]

3. JPM
ASSA ABLOY Group
France
[Safety & Security]

4. J-POWER
J-POWER Electric Power Development Co. Ltd
Japan
[Energy]

5. JR (Japan Rail)
Japan Railways Group
Japan
[Transport]

6. JSE
Johannesburg Stock Exchange Ltd
South Africa
[Financial Services]

7. JSF
Japan Securities Finance Co. Ltd
Japan
[Financial Services]

8. J-Sky
Japan Telecom Co. Ltd
Japan
[Telecommunications]

9. JTI (Japan Tobacco)
Japan Tobacco Inc
Japan
[Tobacco]

10. Juicy Fruit
William Wrigley Jr. Company
USA
[Food & Beverage]

1. **Jumbo**
Companhia Portuguesa de Hipermercados SA
Portugal
[Retail]

2. **Jungheinrich**
Jungheinrich AG
Germany
[Manufacturing]

Junker Group
Germany
[Tools & Machinery]

4. **Junkers**
Bosch Thermotechnik GmbH
Germany
[Heating & Cooling]

5. **Junkers**
Junkers Flugzeug- und Motorenwerke AG (JFM)
Germany
[Aviation]

6. **Jupiler**
Piedboeuf Brewery,
Anheuser-Busch InBev NV
Belgium
[Wines, Beers & Spirits]

7. **Jurassic Park**
Universal Pictures
USA, 1993
Chip Kidd (concept)
[Film]

8. **Just Do It**
Nike Inc
USA, 1988
Wieden+Kennedy:
Dan Wieden (concept)
[Sporting Goods]

9. **JVC**
Victor Company of Japan Ltd, JVC Kenwood Holdings Inc
Japan
[Consumer Electronics]

K2

1 **K2**
K2 Inc, Jarden Corporation
USA
[Sporting Goods]

2 **Kagawa Bank**
Kagawa Bank Ltd
Japan
[Financial Services]

3 **Kalles Kaviar**
Abba Seafood AB
Sweden
[Food & Beverage]

4 **Kamaz**
Kamaz Inc
Russia
[Automotive]

5 **Kambly**
Kambly SA Spécialités
de Biscuits Suisses
Switzerland
[Food & Beverage]

6 **Kamps**
Kamps GmbH
Germany
[Food & Beverage]

7 **Kanal 5 Danmark**
ProSiebenSat.1 Media AG
Denmark, 2004
[Television Channel]

8 **Kaneka**
Kaneka Americas Holding Inc
Japan
[Chemicals & Materials]

9 **Kanematsu Corporation**
Japan
[Conglomerate]

10 **KangaROOS**
KangaROOS International Ltd
USA
[Footwear]

Kangol
kangolstore.com
UK
[Apparel]

Kappa
BasicNet SpA
Italy, 1969
[Sporting Goods]

Karl Lagerfeld
Karl Lagerfeld Retail BV
Netherlands
[Fashion]

4 **Karlsberg**
The Karlsberg Group
Germany
[Wines, Beers & Spirits]

5 **Kashi Company**
USA
[Food & Beverage]

6 **Kaufland**
Kaufland Warenhandel
GmbH & Co. KG
Germany
[Retail]

7 **Kawasaki**
Kawasaki Heavy Industries Ltd
Japan
[Conglomerate]

8 **Kawasaki Steel Corporation**
Japan
[Industrial Products]

9 **KB Banki**
Kaupthing Banki HF
Iceland
[Financial Services]

KBE

1 KBE Fenstersysteme
profine GmbH
Germany
[Manufacturing]

2 Keane
Keane Inc
USA
[Information Technology]

3 Keds
Collective Brands Inc
USA
[Footwear]

4 Keebler
Kellogg Company
USA
Raphael Boguslav
[Food & Beverage]

5 Keeneland
Keeneland Association Inc
USA
[Places]

6 KEF
KEF Electronics Ltd
UK
[Consumer Electronics]

7 Keiper
Keiper Group
Germany
[Automotive]

8 Keiyo Bank
Keiyo Bank Ltd
Japan
[Financial Services]

9 Kellogg's
Kellogg Company
USA, 1906
Will Keith Kellogg
[Food & Beverage]

Kelvinator
AB Electrolux
Sweden
[Home Appliances]

KEM Playing Cards
The United States Playing Card Company, Jarden Corporation
USA
[Toys, Games & Models]

Kendall Motor Oil
ConocoPhillips Company
USA
[Automotive]

4 **Ken Garff Automotive Group**
USA
[Retail]

5 **Kenko Ball**
Nagase-Kenko Corp.
Japan
[Sporting Goods]

6 **Kennametal**
Kennametal Inc
USA
[Industrial Products]

7 **Kenner**
Hasbro Inc
USA
[Games & Models]

8 **Kensington**
Kensington Computer Group, ACCO Brands Corporation
USA
[Computer Technology]

9 **Kent**
Berner UK Ltd
UK
[Automotive]

10 **Kent**
British American Tobacco plc
UK
[Tobacco]

KENT

1   **Kent**
    Kent Nutrition Group Inc
    USA
    [Pet Products]

2   **Kenwood**
    Kenwood Corporation
    Japan
    [Consumer Electronics]

3   **Kenwood**
    Kenwood Corporation
    Japan
    [Consumer Electronics]

4   **KENZO**
    KENZO SA
    France
    [Fashion]

5   **Kerr-McGee**
    Kerr-McGee Corporation
    USA
    [Oil, Gas & Petroleum]

6   **Kerrygold**
    Irish Dairy Board
    Ireland, 1980
    Fanstone Group
    [Food & Beverage]

7   **Kesko**
    Kesko Corporation
    Finland
    [Retail]

8   **Kettle Chips**
    Diamond Foods Inc
    USA
    [Food & Beverage]

9   **KeyBank**
    KeyCorp
    USA
    [Financial Services]

10 **KeyCreator**
    Kubotek USA Inc
    USA
    [Computer Software]

Keyence
Keyence Corporation
Japan
[Technology]

Keystone
Grupo Keystone
Brazil
[Imaging & Photographic]

KFC
Yum! Brands Inc
USA, 1991
Schecter & Luth
[Restaurants & Bars]

4 **KFC**
Yum! Brands Inc
USA, 1997
Landor Associates
[Restaurants & Bars]

5 **Kia Motors**
Kia Motors Corporation
South Korea
[Automotive]

6 **Kid Knowledge**
Knowing Science LLC
USA, 2009
Danne Design:
[Education]

7 **Kidp (Korean Institute of Design Promotion)**
South Korea
[Foundations & Institutes]

8 **Kidsafe**
The Child Accident Prevention Foundation of Australia
Australia
[Foundations & Institutes]

9 **Kiehl's**
L'Oréal Group
USA
[Health & Beauty]

KIKKOMAN

1

2

3

4

5

6

7

8

9

10

1 **Kikkoman**
Kikkoman Corporation
Japan, 2008
[Food & Beverage]

2 **Killer 7**
Capcom Co. Ltd
Japan, 2005
[Computer & Video Games]

3 **Killer Loop**
Bencom Srl
Italy
[Apparel]

4 **Kimberly-Clark**
Kimberly-Clark Corporation
USA
[Personal Care]

5 **Kimco Realty Corporation**
USA
[Real Estate]

6 **Kinder**
Ferrero SpA
Germany, 1967
[Food & Beverage]

7 **Kingsway Exhibitions**
UK
[Design]

8 **Kintek**
Kintek Srl
Italy
[Tools & Machinery]

9 **Kipling**
VF Europe BVBA
Belgium, 1987
[Eyewear]

10 **Kiss**
USA, 1973
Ace Frehley
[Music]

Kitaco
Kitaco Co. Ltd
Japan
[Automotive]

KitchenAid
Whirlpool Corporation
USA
[Home Appliances]

Kitemark
British Standards Institution,
BSI Group
UK, 1903
[Labelling, Standards & Certification]

4 **Kit Kat**
Nestlé SA
USA
[Food & Beverage]

5 **Kity**
Atelier Des Boiseux/Kity
France
[Tools & Machinery]

6 **Kiwi**
France
[Sporting Goods]

7 **KiX**
General Mills Inc
USA
[Food & Beverage]

8 **Klabin**
Brazil, 1979
Alexandre Wollner
[Paper Products]

9 **Klauke**
Gustav Klauke GmbH,
Textron Inc
Germany
[Industrial Products]

10 **Klaukol**
Parex Group
Argentina
[Chemicals & Materials]

KLEBER

1

2

3

4
Klipsch

5

6

7

8

1 Kleber
   Michelin Tyre plc
   UK
   [Automotive]

2 Kleenex
   Kimberly-Clark Corporation
   USA, 2008
   Sterling Brands
   [Personal Care]

3 Klein
   Theo Klein GmbH
   Germany
   [Toys, Games & Models]

4 Klipsch
   Klipsch Group Inc
   USA
   [Consumer Electronics]

5 KLM Royal Dutch Airlines
   Koninklijke Luchtvaart
   Maatschappij NV
   Netherlands, 1991
   Henrion, Ludlow & Schmidt:
   Chris Ludlow
   [Airline]

6 Klondike
   Good Humor-Breyers,
   Unilever plc/NV
   USA
   [Food & Beverage]

▶ 7 Kmart
   Sears Holdings Corporation
   USA, 1990
   [Retail]

8 KMB (Kowloon Motor Bus)
   Kowloon Motor Bus Company Ltd,
   Transport International
   Holdings Ltd
   China
   [Transport]

K'Nex
K'Nex LP Group
USA
[Toys, Games & Models]

K&N Filters
K&N Engineering Inc
USA
[Automotive]

Knight Frank
Knight Frank LLP
UK
[Real Estate]

Knights Inn
Knights Franchise Systems Inc,
Wyndham Worldwide Corporation
USA
[Hospitality]

Knipex
KNIPEX-Werk C. Gustav Putsch KG
Germany
[Tools & Machinery]

Knirps
Knirps Licence Corporation
GmbH & Co. KG
Germany
[Consumer Products]

Knoll
Knoll Pharmaceuticals
Germany
[Pharmaceuticals]

Knorr
Unilever plc/NV
UK/Netherlands
[Food & Beverage]

KNOWLEDGE NETWORK

1 Knowledge Network
Knowledge Network Corporation
Canada
[Broadcaster]

2 KNVB
Royal Dutch Football Association
The Netherlands
SoDesign
[Sport]

3 KOA
Kampgrounds of America Inc
USA
[Outdoor & Recreation]

4 Kobelco
Kobe Steel Group
Japan
[Industry]

5 Kobe Sportswear
Kobe Sportswear Inc
Canada
[Apparel]

6 Koçbank
Koç Holding AŞ
Turkey
[Financial Services]

7 Koch Industries
Koch Industries Inc
USA
[Conglomerate]

▶ 8 Kodak
Eastman Kodak Company
USA, 1971
Peter J. Oestreich
[Imaging & Photographic]

9 Kodak
Eastman Kodak Company
USA, 2006
Brand Integration Group
[Imaging & Photographic]

400

Kodak Colorwatch system
Eastman Kodak Company
USA
[Labelling, Standards
& Certification]

Kogas
Korea Gas Corporation
South Korea
[Utilities]

Kohl's
Kohl's Corporation
USA, 1985
[Retail]

4 **Ko-ken**
Ko-Ken Tool Co. Ltd
Japan
[Tools & Machinery]

5 **Kokuyo**
Kokuyo Co. Ltd
Japan
[Office Supplies]

6 **KölnTicket**
Derticketservice.de
GmbH & Co. KG
Germany
Helmut Langer
[Retail]

7 **Kolon**
Kolon Industries Inc
South Korea
[Chemicals & Materials]

8 **Komatsu**
Komatsu Ltd
Japan
[Tools & Machinery]

KONAMI

1 **Konami**
   Konami Corporation
   Japan, 1986
   [Computer & Video Games]

2 **Konami**
   Konami Corporation
   Japan, 2003
   [Computer & Video Games]

3 **Kone**
   Kone Oyj
   Finland, 1999
   [Manufacturing]

4 **Konica**
   Konica Corporation
   Japan
   [Imaging & Photographic]

5 **Konica Minolta**
   Konica Minolta Holdings Inc
   Japan, 2003
   [Imaging & Photographic]

6 **König Pilsener**
   König-Brauerei GmbH
   Germany
   [Wines, Beers & Spirits]

7 **Kookaï**
   Kookaï SA
   France, 1983
   [Fashion]

8 **Kool**
   Reynolds American Inc
   USA, 1933
   [Tobacco]

9 **Kool-Aid**
   Kraft Foods Inc
   USA
   [Food & Beverage]

Korean Air
Korean Air Lines Co. Ltd
South Korea
[Airline]

Korg
Korg Corporation
Japan
[Musical Instruments]

K par K
KPARK SAS
France
[Home Furnishings]

4 **KPMG**
Netherlands
Interbrand
[Professional Services]

5 **KPN**
Royal KPN NV
Netherlands, 2004
Studio Dumbar
[Telecommunications]

6 **KPN**
Royal KPN NV
Netherlands, 2006
Studio Dumbar
[Telecommunications]

7 **Kraft**
Kraft Foods Inc
USA
[Food & Beverage]

8 **Kraft Foods**
Kraft Foods Inc
USA, 2009
Nitro Group, Kraft, Genesis,
Landor Associates
[Conglomerate]

9 **Krispy Kreme**
Krispy Kreme Doughnuts Inc
USA, 1937
Benny Dinkins
[Food & Beverage]

1. **Kroger**
   The Kroger Company
   USA
   [Retail]

2. **Krohne**
   Krohne Messtechnik GmbH
   Germany
   [Technology]

3. **Krüger**
   Krüger GmbH & Co. KG
   Germany
   [Food & Beverage]

4. **Krups**
   Germany
   [Home Appliances]

5. **Krylon**
   Krylon Products Group,
   Sherwin-Williams Company
   USA
   [Paints & Coatings]

6. **K-Salat**
   Rieber & Søn Danmark AS
   Denmark, 2001
   [Food & Beverage]

7. **K-Swiss**
   K-Swiss Inc
   USA, 1966
   [Footwear]

8. **KTM**
   KTM Sportmotorcycle AG
   Austria
   [Outdoor & Recreation]

9. **Kubota**
   Kubota Tractor Corporation
   Japan
   [Manufacturing]

10. **Kumutu**
    Kumutu Inc
    USA
    [Outdoor & Recreation]

Kungsörnen
Kungsörnen AB
Sweden, 2001
[Food & Beverage]

Kuno Moser
Kuno Moser GmbH
Germany
[Personal Care]

Kuoni
Kuoni Group
Switzerland
[Travel & Tourism]

4 **Kurita**
Kurita Water Industries Ltd
Japan
[Chemicals & Materials]

5 **K-Way**
BasicNet SpA
Italy
[Apparel]

6 **KYB**
KYB Corporation
Japan
[Automotive]

7 **Kyocera**
Kyocera Corporation
Japan, 1982
Mitsuo Hosokawa
[Electronics]

8 **Kyodo Card**
Kyodo Credit Service Co. Ltd
Japan
[Financial Services]

9 **Kyosho**
Kyosho Corporation
Japan
[Toys, Games & Models]

10 **Kyowa**
Kyowa Hakko Kirin Co. Ltd
Japan
[Pharmaceuticals]

LABATT BLUE

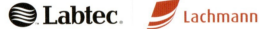

1. **Labatt Blue**
   Labatt Brewing Company Ltd,
   Anheuser-Busch InBev NV
   Canada
   [Wines, Beers & Spirits]

2. **Labatt Ice**
   Labatt Brewing Company Ltd,
   Anheuser-Busch InBev NV
   Canada
   [Wines, Beers & Spirits]

3. **Labatt's**
   Labatt Brewing Company Ltd,
   Anheuser-Busch InBev NV
   Canada
   [Wines, Beers & Spirits]

4. **Labels**
   France
   [Music Industry]

5. **Labour Party**
   UK
   [Political]

6. **Labrador Records**
   Sweden
   [Music Industry]

7. **Labtec**
   Labtec Inc, Logitech
   International SA
   USA
   [Computer Technology]

8. **Lachmann**
   Brazil
   Ana Couto Branding & Design
   [Freight & Logistics]

9. **LaCie**
   LaCie Ltd
   USA/France, 1995
   Neil Poulton
   [Computer Hardware]

Lacoste
France, 1930s
Robert George
[Apparel]

Lacsa
Lineas Aéreas Costarricenses SA, Grupo TACA
Costa Rica
[Airline]

Lada
JSC AvtoVAZ
Russia
[Automotive]

LADWP (Los Angeles Department of Water and Power)
USA
[Utilities]

Lady Remington
Spectrum Brands Inc
USA
[Personal Care]

Lady Speed Stick
The Mennen Company, Colgate-Palmolive Company
USA
[Personal Care]

Lafarge
Lafarge SA
France
[Construction]

La Flor del Itapebí Editorial
Uruguay, 1996
Marcos Larghero
[Publishing]

Lafuma
Groupe Lafuma
France
[Outdoor & Recreation]

LA GEAR

LAGERFELD

LAMY   LA NACION

1. **LA Gear**
   ACI International
   USA
   [Footwear]

2. **Lagerfeld**
   Karl Lagerfeld
   Germany
   [Fashion]

3. **La Laitière**
   Nestlé SA
   France
   [Food & Beverage]

4. **Lalique**
   France
   [Luxury Goods]

5. **Lamborghini**
   Automobili Lamborghini SpA,
   Audi AG
   Italy
   [Automotive]

6. **Lambretta**
   Lambretta Srl, Lambretta
   Consortium
   Italy
   [Automotive]

7. **Lamy**
   C Joseph Lamy GmbH
   Germany
   [Writing Products]

8. **La Nacion**
   Argentina, 2000
   Rubén Fontana
   [Media]

9. **Lancel**
   Lancel Sogedi SA
   France
   [Luxury Goods]

10. **Lancia**
    Lancia Automobiles SpA, Fiat
    Italy, 2007
    Robilant Associati
    [Automotive]

LANVIN

1 **Lancôme Paris**
L'Oréal SA
France
[Health & Beauty]

2 **Lancôme Paris**
L'Oréal SA
France
[Health & Beauty]

3 **Landini**
Argo Tractors SpA
Canada
[Automotive]

4 **Land Rover**
Jaguar Land Rover Group, Tata Motors Ltd
UK, 1986
Tatham Pearce: David Pearce
[Automotive]

5 **Lange**
Skis Rossignol SA
France
[Sporting Goods]

6 **Langnese**
Unilever plc/NV
Germany, 1960s
[Food & Beverage]

7 **Langnese**
Unilever plc/NV
Germany
[Food & Beverage]

8 **Lanover**
Brazil, 1966
Alexandre Wollner
[Fabrics & Textiles]

▶ 9 **Lanvin**
Jeanne Lanvin SA
France
[Fashion]

10 **La Poste**
La Poste SA
France
[Mail Services]

LA POSTE

1. **La Poste/De Post Group**
   Belgium, 2008
   Sign*
   [Mail Services]

2. **La Prairie**
   La Prairie Group (Beiersdorf AG)
   Switzerland
   [Health & Beauty]

3. **La Quinta Inn**
   LQ Management LLC,
   The Blackstone Group
   USA
   [Hospitality]

4. **La Quinta Inns & Suites**
   LQ Management LLC,
   The Blackstone Group
   USA
   [Hospitality]

5. **La Repubblica**
   Gruppo Editoriale L'Espresso SpA
   Italy, ca 1976
   [Media]

6. **Lāse 2007**
   Latvia
   [Sporting Events]

7. **La Sept (Société d'édition de programmes de télévision)**
   France, 1989
   Étienne Robial, Mathias Ledoux
   [Television Channel]

8. **Laser**
   Performance Sailcraft Pty. Ltd
   Australia
   [Marine]

9. **LaserDisc**
   LaserVision Association
   USA, 1981
   [Labelling, Standards
   & Certification]

10. **LaserDisc**
    Pioneer Corporation
    Japan, 1990s
    [Consumer Electronics]

1 **Lasmo (London and Scottish Marine Oil)**
Eni Lasmo plc
UK
[Oil, Gas & Petroleum]

2 **Las Vegas Magazine**
Greenspun Media
USA, 2006
Pentagram
[Publications]

3 **Laurent-Perrier**
Laurent-Perrier Group SA
France
[Wines, Beers & Spirits]

4 **La Vache quit Rit**
Groupe Bel
France, 1990s
[Food & Beverage]

5 **Lavazza**
Luigi Lavazza SpA
Italy, 1992
[Food & Beverage]

6 **LA X...Press**
USA
[Publications]

7 **Lay's**
Frito-Lay North America Inc, PepsiCo Inc
USA, 2003
[Food & Beverage]

8 **Leading Edge**
Leading Edge Hardware Products Inc
USA
[Computer Technology]

9 **LeapFrog**
LeapFrog Enterprises Inc
USA
[Toys, Games & Models]

LEAR CORPORATION

1 **Lear Corporation**
   USA
   [Automotive]

2 **Learjet**
   Bombardier Aerospace,
   Bombardier Inc
   Canada
   [Aerospace]

3 **Learning Tree International**
   Learning Tree International Inc
   USA
   [Education]

4 **Le Bon Marché**
   Le Bon Marché Maison Aristide
   Boucicaut SA
   France
   [Retail]

5 **Leclerc**
   E.Leclerc
   France
   [Retail]

6 **Le Coq Sportif**
   France, 2009
   [Sporting Goods]

7 **Le Cube**
   France
   [Places]

8 **Lee**
   VF Corporation
   USA
   [Apparel]

9 **Lee**
   VF Corporation
   USA
   [Apparel]

Lee Cooper
Lee Cooper Brands,
Red Diamond Holdings Sàrl
UK
[Apparel]

Leer
Truck Accessories Group LLC
USA
[Automotive]

Leerdammer
Bel Leerdammer BV
Netherlands
[Food & Beverage]

4 **Lee's Sandwiches**
Lee's Sandwiches International inc
USA
[Restaurants & Bars]

5 **Le Figaro**
Groupe Le Figaro,
Dassault Group SA
France
[Media]

▶ 6 **Left 4 Dead**
Turtle Rock Studios,
Valve Corporation
USA, 2008
[Computer & Video Games]

7 **Legacy Recordings**
Sony Music Entertainment Inc
USA, 1990
[Music Industry]

8 **Legal & General**
Legal & General Group plc
London
[Financial Services]

9 **Legal Sea Foods**
USA
[Restaurants & Bars]

LEGAMBIENTE

1
2
3
4

5

6
7

8

9

10 **LEICA**

1 **Legambiente (League for the Environment)**
Italy
[Conservation & Environment]

2 **Legendary Pictures Inc**
USA, ca 2000
[Film Industry]

3 **Legend Group**
Lenovo Group Ltd
China
[Computer Technology]

4 **L'eggs**
HanesBrands Inc
USA, 1969
Herb Lubalin Associates:
Roger Ferriter
[Apparel]

▶ 5 **LEGO**
The LEGO Group
Denmark, 1998
[Toys, Games & Models]

6 **Legrand**
Legrand Group SA
France
[Electronics]

7 **LeHA**
Leha GmbH
Germany
[Food & Beverage]

8 **Lehman Brothers**
Lehman Brothers Holdings Inc
USA
[Financial Services]

▶ 9 **Leica**
Leica Camera AG
Germany, 1995
Stankowski & Duschek
[Imaging & Photographic]

▶ 10 **Leica**
Leica Camera AG
Germany
[Imaging & Photographic]

Le Monde

lenovo 联想

LE PETIT MARSEILLAIS

Le Point

4 **Leiner**
Leiner Health Products Inc
USA
[Healthcare]

Le Livre de Poche
Librairie Générale Française,
Hachette Livre
France
[Publishing]

Le Monde
La Vie-Le Monde Group
France
[Media]

4 **Lenovo Group**
Lenovo Group Ltd
China
[Computer Technology]

5 **Lenoxx Sound**
Lenoxx Electronics Corporation
USA
[Consumer Electronics]

6 **Leonidas Pralines**
Confiserie Leonidas SA
Belgium
[Food & Beverage]

7 **Le Petit Marseillais**
Johnson & Johnson Santé
Beauté France SAS
France, 1989
[Personal Care]

8 **Le Point**
PPR SA
France
[Media]

9 **Leprino Foods**
Leprino Foods Company
USA
[Food & Beverage]

LE PROGRÈS

1 **Le Progrès**
   L'est Républicain
   France
   [Media]

2 **L'Equipe**
   Amaury Group
   France
   [Media]

3 **Le Robert**
   Dictionnaires Le Robert
   France
   [Publications]

4 **Leroy-Somer**
   Emerson Electric Co.
   France
   [Industrial Products]

5 **Lesjöfors AB**
   Sweden
   [Industrial Products]

6 **Lete**
   Lete SpA
   Italy
   [Food & Beverage]

7 **Le Tour de France**
   Amaury Sports Organisation
   France
   Joël Guenoun
   [Sporting Events]

8 **Le Tour de France**
   Amaury Sports Organisation
   France
   [Sporting Events]

9 **Letraset**
   Letraset Ltd
   UK
   [Printing Services]

10 **Leucadia National Corporation**
   USA
   [Conglomerate]

Levi's
Levi Strauss & Co
USA, 1936
[Apparel]

Levi's Store
Levi Strauss & Co
USA
[Retail]

Levitz
Levitz Furniture Inc
USA
[Retail]

4 **Lexjet Corporation**
USA
[Imaging & Photographic]

5 **Lexmark**
Lexmark International Inc
USA, 1994
[Computer Hardware]

6 **L'Express**
Groupe Express-Roularta SA
France
[Media]

7 **Lexus**
Toyota Motor Corporation
Japan, 2002
Siegel+Gale
[Automotive]

8 **LFP (Ligue de Football Professionnel)**
France
[Sport]

9 **LG**
LG Corporation
South Korea, 2008
[Conglomerate]

10 **Libbey**
Libbey Glass Inc
USA
[Glass & Ceramics]

1 **Libby's**
Corlib Brand Holding Ltd
USA
[Food & Beverage]

2 **Libération**
France
[Media]

3 **Liberty**
Liberty Ltd
UK
[Retail]

4 **Liberty Mutual**
Liberty Mutual Group
USA
[Financial Services]

5 **Lidl**
Lidl Stiftung & Co. KG
Germany
[Retail]

6 **Liebherr Group**
Liebherr-International
Deutschland GmbH
Switzerland
[Industrial Products]

7 **Lieken Urkorn**
Lieken Brot- und
Backwaren GmbH
Germany
[Food & Beverage]

8 **Life**
See Your World LLC
USA, 1936
[Media]

9 **Life Savers**
Wrigley Company
USA, 1999
[Food & Beverage]

1 **Lifetime Television**
A&E Television Networks LLC
USA, 2008
[Television Channel]

2 **Light**
Brazil, 1966
Aloísio Magalhães
[Energy]

3 **Light**
Brazil, 1998
eg.design
[Energy]

4 **Lightstorm Entertainment**
Lightstorm Entertainment Inc
USA
[Film Industry]

5 **Lillian Vernon**
Lillian Vernon Corporation
USA, 2005
Fry
[Retail]

6 **Lilly**
Eli Lilly and Company
USA
[Pharmaceuticals]

7 **Lincoln**
Ford Motor Company
USA
[Automotive]

8 **Lincoln Electric**
The Lincoln Electric Company
USA
[Automotive]

9 **Linde**
The Linde Group
Germany, 2004
Peter Schmidt Group
[Industry]

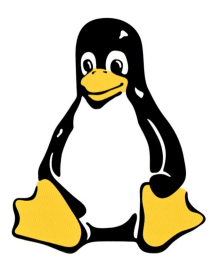

1 **Lindt**
Lindt & Sprüngli AG
Switzerland
[Food & Beverage]

2 **Linens 'n Things**
Linens 'n Things Inc
USA
[Retail]

3 **LinkedIn**
LinkedIn Corporation
USA, 2003
[Internet]

4 **Linkin Park**
USA
[Music]

5 **Linotype**
Linotype GmbH, Monotype Imaging Inc
USA
[Manufacturing]

▶ 6 **Linux mascot (Tux the Penguin)**
Linux
USA, 2006
Larry Ewing
[Computer Technology]

7 **Linux Powered**
Linux
USA
[Computer Technology]

8 **Linux Professional Institute**
Linux
USA
[Computer Technology]

9 **Lionsgate**
Lionsgate Entertainment Corporation
USA, 1997
[Film Industry]

LITTLE CHEF

LISTERINE

1 **Lippert-Unipol GmbH**
Germany
[Tools & Machinery]

2 **Lipton**
Unilever plc/NV
UK/Netherlands, ca 1890
[Food & Beverage]

3 **Lipton Ice Tea**
Unilever plc/NV
UK/Netherlands
[Food & Beverage]

4 **Liquid Audio**
Liquid Audio Inc
USA
[Software]

5 **Liqui Moly**
Liqui Moly GmbH
Germany
[Chemicals & Materials]

6 **Lisbon Aquarium**
Oceanário de Lisboa
Portugal, 1998
Chermayeff & Geismar
[Places]

7 **Listerine**
Johnson & Johnson
USA
[Personal Care]

8 **Lita**
France, 1965
Lark Publicité
[Automotive]

9 **Little Brown & Company**
Little, Brown & Company,
Hachette Book Group USA
USA, 2009
Lance Hidy
[Publishing]

10 **Little Chef**
RCapital Partners LLP
UK
Venturethree
[Restaurants & Bars]

11 **Little Chef**
RCapital Partners LLP
UK
[Restaurants & Bars]

421

LITTLE LEAGUE BASEBALL

1 **Little League Baseball**
Little League Baseball Inc
USA
[Sport]

2 **Little Red Door**
Little Red Door Cancer Agency
USA, 2004
Essex Two
[Charity]

3 **Little Tikes**
The Little Tikes Company, MGA Entertainment Inc
USA
[Toys, Games & Models]

4 **Little Trees**
Car-Freshner Corporation
USA, 1952
Julius Sämann
[Consumer Products]

5 **Litton Industries**
Northrop Grumman Corporation
USA
[Defence]

6 **Litton Industries**
Northrop Grumman Corporation
USA
[Defence]

7 **Litt's Treetops Shooting Ground**
DJ Litt Firearms Ltd
UK
[Outdoor & Recreation]

8 **Live Aid**
UK, 1985
Bob Geldof, Steve Maher
[Charity]

9 **Liverpool Football Club**
Liverpool LFC, Fenway Sports Group
UK
[Sport]

10 **Liz Claiborne**
J.C. Penney Company Inc
USA
[Fashion]

LKAB

L.L.Bean

LLOYD'S

1. **LKAB (Luossavaara-Kiirunavaara Aktiebolag)**
   Sweden
   [Mining]

2. **L!–Lance!**
   Brazil
   [Media]

3. **L.L. Bean**
   LL Bean Inc
   USA
   Pentagram
   [Retail]

4. **Lloyd's**
   Lloyd's of London
   UK
   [Financial Services]

5. **Lloyd's**
   Lloyd's of London
   UK
   [Financial Services]

6. **Lloyds TSB**
   Lloyds TSB Bank plc
   UK
   [Financial Services]

7. **Lockheed Martin**
   USA, 1997
   Anspach Grossman Enterprise:
   Gene Grossman
   [Conglomerate]

8. **Lock-Right**
   Richmond Gear & Machine Co. Inc
   USA
   [Automotive]

LOCTITE CORPORATION

1 **Loctite Corporation**
   USA
   [Aerospace]

2 **Loeb**
   Metro Inc
   Canada
   [Retail]

3 **Logica plc**
   UK
   [Professional Services]

4 **Logitech**
   Logitech International SA
   Switzerland, 1988
   Frog Design: Timothy Stebbing
   [Computer Technology]

5 **Logorama**
   France, 2008
   H5: Ludovic Houplain
   [Film]

6 **Lokomotiv Yaroslavl**
   Russian Railways
   Russia, 2000
   [Sport]

7 **London Stock Exchange plc**
   London Stock Exchange Group
   UK
   [Financial Services]

8 **Lonely Planet**
   Lonely Planet Publications Pty Ltd
   Australia
   [Publishing]

9 **Lone Star**
   Lone Star Brewing Company,
   Pabst Brewing Company
   USA
   [Wines, Beers & Spirits]

10 **LongHorn Steakhouse**
   Darden Restaurants Inc
   USA
   [Restaurants & Bars]

Long John Silver's
Long John Silver's Inc
USA, 2011
[Restaurants & Bars]

Lonsdale
Lonsdale Sports Ltd
UK
[Sporting Goods]

Look
Look Cycle International
France, 1980s
[Bicycles]

4 **Loon Mountain Resort**
USA
[Places]

▶ 5 **Looptroop Rockers**
Sweden
[Music]

6 **Looza**
Tropicana Looza Benelux BVBA,
PepsiCo Inc
Belgium
[Food & Beverage]

7 **Lord**
Lord Corporation
USA, 1970s
[Chemicals & Materials]

8 **Lord Abbettt**
Lord Abbett & Co. LLC
USA
[Financial Services]

9 **L'Oréal**
L'Oréal SA
France
[Personal Care]

LORUS

1. **Lorus**
   Seiko Watch Corporation
   Japan
   [Watches & Jewelry]

2. **Los Angeles Dodgers**
   USA
   [Sport]

3. **Los Angeles Dodgers**
   (cap insignia)
   Los Angeles Dodgers
   USA, 1958
   [Sport]

4. **Los Angeles Lakers**
   Turner Digital Basketball Services Inc, NBA Media Ventures LLC
   USA, 2002
   [Sport]

5. **Los Angeles Lakers**
   Turner Digital Basketball Services Inc, NBA Media Ventures LLC
   USA, 2011
   [Sport]

6. **Los Angeles Times**
   Tribune Company
   USA
   [Media]

7. **Los Angeles Zoo**
   City of Los Angeles
   USA
   [Aquariums & Zoos]

8. **Loterie Nationale**
   Belgium
   [Leisure & Entertainment]

9. **Loto**
   France, ca 1976
   [Leisure & Entertainment]

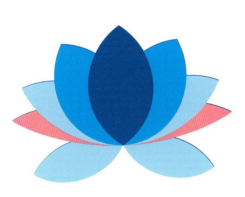

LOT Polish Airlines
Polskie Linie Lotnicze LOT SA
Poland, 1978
Roman Duszek, Andrzej Zbrożek
[Airline]

Lotto (Deutsche Lotterie)
Germany
[Leisure & Entertainment]

Lotto (Lotterie Nationale)
Belgium
[Leisure & Entertainment]

Lottomatica
Lottomatica Group SpA
Italy
[Leisure & Entertainment]

Lotto Sport Italia
Lotto Sport Italia SpA
Italy, 1970s
[Leisure & Entertainment]

Lotus
International Business Machines Corporation (IBM)
USA, 1980s
[Computer Software]

Lotus
Lotus Cars Ltd, Lotus Group plc
UK, 1952
[Automotive]

Lotus Software
IBM
USA
[Computer Software]

Louis Dreyfus
Louis Dreyfus Holding BV
Netherlands
[Conglomerate]

LOUISVILLE CARDINALS

1 **Louisville Cardinals**
University of Louisville
USA
[Sport]

2 **LOVE**
Museum of Modern Art
USA, 1964
Robert Indiana
[Advertising & Campaign]

3 **Lowe**
Lowe and Partners
UK, 2003
Carter Wong Tomlin
[Advertising & Campaigns]

4 **Löwenbräu**
Löwenbräu AG
Germany
[Wines, Beers & Spirits]

5 **Lowe's Foods**
Lowe's Food Stores Inc
USA
[Food & Beverage]

6 **Lowe's Home Improvement Warehouse**
Lowe's Companies Inc
USA, 1997
[Retail]

7 **LP (Louisiana-Pacific)**
Louisiana-Pacific Corporation
USA, 1973
[Construction]

8 **LPS**
LPS laboratories, Illinois Tool Works Inc
USA, ca 1961
[Industrial Products]

9 **L&Q Group (London & Quadrant Housing)**
UK
[Real Estate]

10 **LSI Logic**
LSI Corporation
USA
[Technology]

LTR Germany
DRUCK & TEMPERATUR
Leitenberger GmbH
Germany
[Industrial Products]

Lucas
TRW Automotive Holdings Corp
UK
[Automotive]

Lucasfilm
Lucasfilm Ltd
USA
[Film Industry]

4 **Lucas Oil**
Lucas Oil Products Inc
USA
[Automotive]

5 **Lucent Technologies**
Lucent Technologies Inc
USA
[Telecommunications]

6 **Luckyfish**
Innovative Dining Goup
USA, 2007
Pentagram
[Restaurants & Bars]

7 **Lucky Strike**
British American Tobacco plc
USA, 1940
Raymond Loewy
[Tobacco]

8 **Lufthansa**
Deutsche Lufthansa AG
Germany, 1969
Otl Aicher
[Airline]

9 **LuK**
Schaeffler Gruppe
Germany
[Manufacturing]

LUKOIL

1 **Lukoil**
OJSC Lukoil
Russia
[Oil, Gas & Petroleum]

2 **LU (Lefèvre-Utile)**
Kraft Foods Inc
France, 1957
Raymond Loewy
[Food & Beverage]

3 **LU (Lefèvre-Utile)**
Kraft Foods Inc
France, ca 1998
Euro RSCG
[Food & Beverage]

4 **LU (Lefèvre-Utile)**
Kraft Foods Inc
France, 2011
Dragon Rouge
[Food & Beverage]

5 **Lund International**
USA
[Automotive]

6 **Lustucru**
Lustucru Frais SAS
France
[Food & Beverage]

7 **Lutheran Brotherhood**
Thrivent Financial for Lutherans
USA, 1976
[Financial Services]

8 **Lux**
Unilever plc/NV
UK
[Personal Care]

9 **Luxair**
Luxair SA
Luxembourg
[Airline]

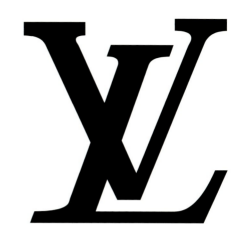

Luxo ASA
Norway
[Design]

Luxottica
Luxottica Group SpA
Italy
[Eyewear]

LV Louis Vuitton
LVMH Moët Hennessy
Louis Vuitton SA
France, 1854
Louis Vuitton
[Luxury Goods]

4 **LVMH**
LVMH Moët Hennessy
Louis Vuitton SA
France
[Luxury Goods]

5 **Lycos**
Ybrant Digital Ltd
USA
[Internet]

6 **Lycra**
Invista, Koch Industries Inc
USA
[Fabrics & Textiles]

7 **Lyonnaise des Eaux**
Lyonnaise des Eaux SA,
GDF Suez SA
France
[Utilities]

8 **Lyso+Form**
Lysoform Disinfektion AG
Switzerland
[Household Products]

9 **Lysol**
Reckitt Benckiser plc
USA, 2010
[Household Products]

M-Q

M&M'S

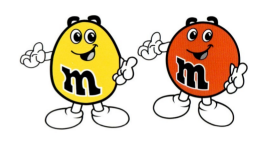

1 M&M's
Mars Inc
USA
[Food & Beverage]

2 M&M's
Mars Inc
USA, 1972
[Food & Beverage]

3 M6 (Metropole Television)
Groupe M6
France
[Television Channel]

4 Maac (Museo Antropologico
y de Arte Contemporaneo)
Banco Central del Ecuador
Ecuador, 2000
Versus: Peter Mussfeldt
[Galleries & Museums]

5 Maalox
Novartis International AG
Switzerland
[Pharmaceuticals]

6 Mac
Apple Inc
USA, 1997
Apple: Tom Hughes, John Casado
[Computer Technology]

7 MacGregor Golf
MacGregor Golf, Golfsmith
International Holdings Inc
USA
[Sporting Goods]

8 Macintosh
Apple Inc
USA, 1984
[Computer Technology]

9 Mackenzie Financial
Mackenzie Financial Corporation
Canada
[Financial Services]

MACWORLD

Mack Trucks
Mack Trucks Inc, AB Volvo
USA, 1921
[Automotive]

MacLaren
UK
Baby Products

Macmahon
Macmahon Holdings Ltd
Australia
[Mining]

4 **Mac Papers**
Mac Papers Inc
USA
[Office Supplies]

5 **Macromedia**
Macromedia Inc
USA, 1997
[Computer Software]

6 **Macromedia Flash 5**
Macromedia Inc
USA
[Computer Software]

7 **Mac's Convenience Stores**
Alimentation Couche-Tard Inc
Canada, 1999
[Retail]

8 **Mac Tools**
Stanley Black & Decker Inc
USA
[Tools & Machinery]

9 **MacWEEK**
Ziff Davis Holdings Inc
USA
[Publications]

10 **Macworld**
Mac Publishing LLC, IDG
USA, 1990s
[Publications]

435

MACY'S

1 **Macy's**
Macy's Inc
USA
[Retail]

2 **MAD**
Time Warner
USA, ca 1955
[Publications]

3 **Madame Tussauds**
Merlin Entertainments Group Ltd
UK
[Galleries & Museums]

4 **Made in America**
USA
[Labelling, Standards
& Certification]

5 **Made in NY**
The City of New York Mayor's
Office of Film, Theatre &
Broadcasting
USA, 2003
Rafael Esquer
[Advertising & Campaigns]

6 **Made in USA Brand**
Made in USA Brand LLC
USA
[Labelling, Standards
& Certification]

7 **Mademoiselle**
Condé Nast, Advance Magazine
Publishers Inc
USA
[Publications]

8 **Madison Square Garden**
Madison Square Garden Inc
USA
[Venues]

▶ 9 **Maersk Seeland**
AP Moller, Maersk Group
Denmark
[Freight & Logistics]

10 **Maestrani Swiss Chocolate**
Maestrani Schweizer
Schokoladen AG
Switzerland, 1990
[Food & Beverage]

Maestro
MasterCard Worldwide
USA
[Financial Services]

Mafka
JSC Mafka
Russia
[Food & Beverage]

Maggi
Nestlé SA
Switzerland
[Food & Beverage]

4 **Maggi**
Nestlé SA
Switzerland
[Food & Beverage]

5 **Magic Software**
Magic Software Enterprises Ltd
Israel
[Computer Software]

6 **Magic Chef**
CNA International Inc, MC Appliance Corporation
USA
[Home Appliances]

7 **Magimix**
France
[Kitchenware]

8 **Mag-Lite**
Mag Instruments Inc
USA
[Consumer Products]

9 **Magnavox**
Philips Electronics North America Corporation
USA
[Consumer Electronics]

MAGNETI MARELLI

1. **Magneti Marelli**
Magneti Marelli SpA
Italy
[Automotive]

2. **Magnum**
Unilever plc/NV
UK, 2006
[Food & Beverage]

3. **Magnum Magnetics**
Magnum Magnetics Corporation
USA
[Chemicals & Materials]

4. **Mahle**
Mahle GmbH
Germany
[Automotive]

5. **Maille**
Unilever plc/NV
France
[Food & Beverage]

6. **Majesty Cruise Line**
Dolphin Cruise Line
Norway
[Travel & Tourism]

7. **Major League Baseball**
USA, 1969
Jerry Dior
[Sport]

8. **Makita**
Makita Corporation
Japan, 1991
Makita
[Tools & Machinery]

9. **Mako Marine**
Mako Marine International Inc
USA
[Marine]

10. **Makro**
Metro AG
Netherlands, 2000s
[Retail]

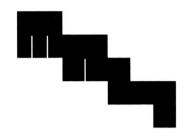

Malaco
Leaf Sverige AB
Sweden, 2000s
[Food & Beverage]

Maldives
Maldives Marketing & Public Relations Corporation (MMPRC)
Maldives, 2011
Quo Keen
[Travel & Tourism]

Malibu Rum
Pernod Ricard SA
Barbados
[Wines, Beers & Spirits]

Mali (Museo de Arte de Lima)
Peru, 2004
Studioa
[Galleries & Museums]

Mallard
Fleetwood RV Inc
USA
[Automotive]

Malmö Högskola
Sweden, 1998
[Education]

Malta
Malta Tourism Authority
Malta
[Travel & Tourism]

Maltesers
Mars Inc
USA
[Food & Beverage]

Mamie Nova
SNC Nova
France
[Food & Beverage]

MAMMOUTH

1 **Mammouth**
Groupe Auchan SA
France
[Retail]

2 **Mammut**
Mammut Sports Group AG
Switzerland
[Sporting Goods]

3 **Mango**
Mango Group
Spain
[Apparel]

4 **MAN SE**
Germany
[Automotive]

5 **Manpower**
ManpowerGroup
USA, 2006
Wolff Olins: Luke Gifford
[Professional Services]

6 **Manulife Financial Corporation**
Canada
[Financial Services]

7 **Mapal Inc**
USA
[Tools & Machinery]

8 **Mapei**
Mapei SpA
Italy
[Paints & Coatings]

9 **Mapfre**
Mapfre SA
Spain
[Financial Services]

10 **Marabout**
Éditions Marabout
France
[Publishing]

MARKET SYSTEM

MARC JACOBS

MarketingWeek

1   **Marantz**
    D&M Holdings inc
    USA
    [Consumer Electronics]

2   **Marathon**
    Marathon Petrolium Corporation
    USA
    [Oil, Gas & Petroleum]

3   **Marathon Equipment**
    Marathon Equipment Comapany
    USA
    [Tools & Machinery]

4   **Marchal**
    SEV-Marchal
    France
    [Automotive]

5   **Marchesan**
    Marchesan Implementos e
    Máquinas Agrícolas TATU SA
    Brazil
    [Tools & Machinery]

6   **Marc Jacobs**
    Marc Jacobs International LLC
    USA
    [Fashion]

7   **Marcus Theatres**
    Marcus Corporation
    USA
    [Cinemas & Theatres]

8   **Maret**
    Maret Pharmaceuticals Inc,
    Essential Therapeutics Inc
    USA
    [Pharmaceuticals]

9   **Mariner**
    E P Barrus Ltd
    UK
    [Marine]

10 **Marketing Week**
    Centaur Media plc
    UK
    [Publications]

11 **Market System**
    CSU CardSystem SA
    Brazil
    [Financial Services]

MARKS & SPENCER

1 **Marks & Spencer**
Marks & Spencer plc
UK, 2000
[Retail]

2 **Marks & Spencer**
Marks & Spencer plc
UK, 2007
[Retail]

3 **Marlboro**
Altria Group Inc, Philip Morris International
USA
[Tobacco]

4 **Marlette Homes**
USA
[Manufacturing]

5 **Marmite**
Unilever plc/NV
UK
[Food & Beverage]

6 **Marmitek**
Marmitek BV
Netherlands
[Consumer Electronics]

7 **Marmot**
Marmot Mountain LLC
USA
[Outdoor & Recreation]

8 **Marriott**
Marriott International Inc
USA
[Hospitality]

9 **Mars**
Mars Inc
UK
[Food & Beverage]

10 **Mars Inc**
USA
[Food & Beverage]

442

MARUTI SUZUKI

1. **Mars Supermarkets Inc**
   USA, ca 2002
   [Retail]

   Marsh Supermarkets
   USA
   [Retail]

2. **Marshall**
   Marshall Amplification plc
   UK, 1960s
   [Music Industry]

3. **Marshalls**
   Marshalls Inc
   USA
   [Retail]

4. **Marshall Thundering Herd**
   Marshall University
   USA
   [Sport]

5. **Martinair**
   Martinair Holland NV
   Netherlands
   [Airline]

6. **Martini**
   Martini & Rossi
   Italy, 1929
   [Wines, Beers & Spirits]

7. **Martin-Senour Paints**
   The Sherwin-Williams Company
   USA
   [Household Products]

8. **Marui**
   Marui Co. Ltd
   Japan
   [Retail]

9. **Maruti Suzuki**
   Maruti Suzuki India Ltd,
   Suzuki Motor Corporation
   India, 2011
   [Automotive]

MARVEL COMICS

1 **Marvel Comics**
Marvel Worldwide Inc
USA, 2000s
[Publishing]

2 **Mary Kay Cosmetics**
Mary Kay Inc
USA
[Health & Beauty]

3 **Maryland-National Capital Park and Planning Commission (M-NCPPC)**
USA
[Government]

4 **Masco**
Masco Corporation
USA
[Construction]

5 **Maserati**
Maserati SpA, Fiat SpA
Italy, 1914
Mario Maserati
[Automotive]

6 **Massachusetts Credit Union League Inc**
USA
[Financial Services]

7 **Massey Ferguson**
AGCO Corporation
USA, 1958
[Tools & Machinery]

8 **Massive Music**
Massive Music BV
Amsterdam
[Music Industry]

▶ 9 **MasterCard**
MasterCard Worldwide
USA, 1997
Interbrand
[Financial Services]

▶ 10 **Matchbox**
Mattel Inc
USA
[Toys, Games & Models]

MAXELL

match.com

Matiz

matrox

Matsushita®

Match.com
IAC/InterActiveCorp
USA
[Internet]

Daewoo Matiz
GM Korea Company
South Korea
[Automotive]

Matrox
Matrox Electronic Systems Inc
Canada
[Computer Hardware]

4 **Matsushita**
Matsushita Electric Industrial Co. Ltd
Japan
[Electronics]

5 **Mattel**
Mattel Inc
USA, 1959
Elliot Handler
[Toys, Games & Models]

6 **Mattel**
Mattel Inc
USA, 1970
[Toys, Games & Models]

7 **Matter**
Fabric
UK, 2008
Pentagram
[Leisure & Entertainment]

8 **Mavi**
Turkey
[Apparel]

9 **MAW (Masters at Work)**
USA
[Music]

10 **Maxell**
Hitachi Maxell Ltd
Japan
[Consumer Electronics]

MAXTOR

1 **Maxtor**
Maxtor Corporation,
Seagate Technology LLC
USA
[Computer Hardware]

2 **Maxwell House**
Kraft Foods Inc
USA, 2005
[Food & Beverage]

▶ 3 **Maya Complete**
Autodesk Inc
USA
[Computer Software]

4 **Maya Ediciones**
Ecuador
Azuca Ingenio Gráfico:
Diego Corrales
[Publishing]

5 **Maybach**
Maybach-Motorenbau GmbH
Germany
[Automotive]

6 **Maybelline New York**
L'Oréal SA
USA
[Health & Beauty]

7 **Maytag**
Maytag Corporation, Whirlpool Corporation
USA
[Home Appliances]

8 **Mazda**
Mazda Motor Corporation
Japan, 1997
Rei Yoshimara
[Automotive]

9 **MB (Milton Bradley)**
Milton Bradley Company,
Hasbro Inc
USA
[Toys, Games & Models]

10 **MBK**
MBK Europe,
Yamaha Motor Europe NV
France
[Automotive]

MBT (Master Builders Technologies)
MBT Holding AG, BASF SE
Switzerland
[Chemicals & Materials]

McAfee Security
McAfee Inc, Intel Corporation
USA
[Computer Software]

McCain Foods
McCain Foods Ltd
Canada
[Food & Beverage]

4 **McCormick**
McCormick & Company Inc
USA
[Food & Beverage]

5 **McCulloch**
McCulloch Motors Corporation
USA
[Tools & Machinery]

6 **McDonald's**
McDonald Corporation
USA, 1962
Jim Schindler
[Restaurants]

▶ 7 **McDonald's**
McDonald Corporation
USA, 1968
[Restaurants & Bars]

8 **McDonald's**
McDonald Corporation
USA, 2003
Heye & Partner
[Restaurants & Bars]

9 **McDonald's Drive Thru**
McDonald Corporation
USA
[Restaurants & Bars]

MCDONNELL DOUGLAS

1 **McDonnell Douglas**
McDonnell Douglas Corporation
USA, 1967
[Aerospace]

2 **MCI Worldcom**
MCI Inc, Verizon
Communications Inc
USA, 1995/2003
Interbrand
[Telecommunications]

3 **McKesson HBOC**
McKesson Corporation
USA
[Pharmaceuticals]

4 **McKesson HBOC**
McKesson Corporation
USA
[Pharmaceuticals]

5 **MD Walkman**
Sony Corporation
Japan
[Consumer Electronics]

6 **Measurex**
Measurex Corporation
USA
[Computer Technology]

7 **MECA Group**
Sweden/Norway
[Automotive]

8 **Meccano**
France
[Toys, Games & Models]

9 **Mechel**
Russia
[Industrial Products]

10 **Medeco**
ASSA ABLOY Group AB
USA
[Manufacturing]

11 **Medima**
Medima GmbH
Germany
[Apparel]

MERALCO

Medtronic Inc
USA
[Medical Devices]

MEF (Maskinentrepreneurenes Forbund)
Norway
[Societies & Associations]

Mega Bloks
Mega Brands Inc
Canada
[Toys, Games & Models]

4 **Meiji**
Meiji Dairies Corporation
Japan, 1971
Yusaku Kamekura
[Food & Beverage]

5 **Meinl Percussion**
Roland Meinl Musikinstrumente GmbH & Co. KG
Germany
[Musical Instruments]

6 **Melitta**
Melitta Kaffee GmbH
Germany
[Food & Beverage]

7 **Memorex**
Imation Corporation
USA
[Consumer Electronics]

8 **Meneba**
meneba BV
Netherlands
[Manufacturing]

9 **Mentos**
Perfetti Van Melle SpA
Netherlands
[Food & Beverage]

10 **Meralco**
Manila Electric Company
Philippines
[Utilities]

MERCEDES-BENZ

1 **Mercedes-Benz**
Mercedes-Benz, Daimler AG
Germany, 1988
Kurt Weidemann
[Automotive]

2 **Merck**
Merck & Co. Inc
USA
Chermayeff & Geismar: Audrey Kraus, Steff Geissbuhler
[Pharmaceuticals]

3 **Merck**
Merck & Co. Inc
USA, 1991
Chermayeff & Geismar: Audrey Kraus, Steff Geissbuhler
[Pharmaceuticals]

4 **Merck**
Merck & Co. Inc
USA
Chermayeff & Geismar: Audrey Kraus, Steff Geissbuhler
[Pharmaceuticals]

5 **Merck**
Merck KGaA
Germany
[Pharmaceuticals]

6 **Mercosur (Mercado Común del Sur)**
Argentina/Brazil/Paraguay/Uruguay/Venezuela
[Government]

7 **Mercury**
Altera Corporation
USA
[Electronics]

8 **Mercury Insurance Group**
USA
[Financial Services]

9 **Mercury Records**
Universal Music Group
UK
[Music Industry]

Meredith
Meredith Corporation
USA, 2009
Lippincott
[Conglomerate]

Merrill Lynch
Merrill Lynch & Co. Inc, Bank of America Corporation
USA, 1974
King Casey
[Financial Services]

Mervyns
Mervyns LLC
USA
[Retail]

Merz
Merz Pharma GmbH & Co. KGaA
Germany
[Pharmaceuticals]

Messerschmitt
Messerschmitt AG
Germany
[Aerospace]

Metallica
USA, 1980s
James Hetfield
[Music]

MetLife
MetLife Inc
USA
[Financial Services]

Metro Cash & Carry
Metro AG
Germany
[Retail]

Metro International
Luxembourg
[Media]

METRO-GOLDWYN-MAYER

1. **Metro-Goldwyn-Mayer**
MGM Holdings Inc
USA, 1957
[Film Industry]

2. **Met-Rx**
Met-Rx Inc
USA
[Fitness & Wellbeing]

3. **Mexico**
Mexico Tourism Board
Mexico
[Travel & Tourism]

4. **Mexico City Metro**
Sistema de Transporte Colectivo
Mexico, 1969
Lance Wyman
[Transport]

5. **Meyer**
Meyer Corporation
USA
[Kitchenware]

6. **MG**
MG Motor UK Ltd, Shanghai Automotive Industry Corporation, SAIC Group
UK, 1924
[Automotive]

7. **MGM Grand**
MGM Resorts International
USA
[Hospitality]

8. **MGM Grand**
MGM Resorts International
USA
[Hospitality]

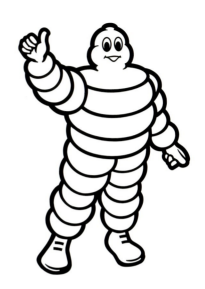

Michelin Man (aka Bibendum)
Michelin SCA
France, 1998
[Automotive]

Michelin Man (aka Bibendum)
Michelin SCA
France, 1998
[Automotive]

Michelin
Michelin SCA
France
[Automotive]

▶ 4 **Michelin Man (aka Bibendum)**
Michelin SCA
France, 1998
[Automotive]

▶ 5 **Michelin Man (aka Bibendum)**
Michelin SCA
France, 1998
[Automotive]

▶ 6 **Michelin Man (aka Bibendum)**
Michelin SCA
France, 1998
[Automotive]

▶ 7 **Michelin XAS**
Michelin SCA
France
[Automotive]

MICHELOB

1 **Michelob**
Anheuser-Busch InBev NV
USA
[Wines, Beers & Spirits]

2 **Michelob Lager**
Anheuser-Busch InBev NV
USA
[Wines, Beers & Spirits]

3 **Microchip Technology Inc**
USA
[Technology]

4 **Micro Machines**
Hasbro Inc
USA
[Toys, Games & Models]

5 **Micron**
Micron Technology Inc
USA
[Technology]

6 **Microsoft**
Microsoft Corporation
USA, 1987
Scott Baker
[Computer Technology]

7 **Midas**
Midas International Corporation
USA
[Automotive]

8 **Midwest Airlines**
USA
[Airline]

9 **Miele**
Miele & Cie KG
Germany
[Home Appliances]

Miko
Unilever plc/NV
France, 1980s
[Food & Beverage]

Miko
Unilever plc/NV
France, 2003
[Food & Beverage]

Mikros Image
Mediacontech SpA
France
[Film Industry]

4 Milca Soda Roja
Nicaragua
[Food & Beverage]

5 Milk
Canada
[Food & Beverage]

6 Milka
Kraft Foods inc
Switzerland
[Food & Beverage]

▶ 7 Milky Way
Mars Inc
USA
[Food & Beverage]

8 Miller
MillerCoors LLC, SABMiller plc,
Molson Coors Brewing Company
USA
Brian Collins
[Wines, Beers & Spirits]

9 Miller
Miller Electric Mfg Co
USA
[Tools & Machinery]

MILLIPORE

1 **Millipore**
EMD Millipore, EMD Chemicals, Merck KGaA
USA, 2011
[Pharmaceuticals]

2 **Mills**
Wallace Mills Architect
USA
[Design]

3 **Millward Brown**
Kantar, WPP plc
UK
[Professional Services]

4 **Milwaukee**
Milwaukee Electric Tool Corporation
USA
[Tools & Machinery]

5 **Mind**
UK, 2004
Glazer
[Charity]

6 **Mind the Gap**
UK
Brahm
[Cinemas & Theatres]

7 **Mini**
BMW
UK, 2001
Interbrand Zintzmeyer & Lux
[Automotive]

8 **MiniDisc**
Sony Corporation
Japan, 1992
[Consumer Electronics]

9 **Ministério da Saúde**
Brazil, 2004
OZ Design: Ronald Kapaz
[Government]

10 **Mini Stop**
Aeon Co. Ltd
Japan
[Restaurants & Bars]

Ministry of Sound
MSHK Group Ltd
UK, 1991
Marc Woodhouse, Justin Berkman
[Venues]

Minol
Total SA
Germany, 1950s
[Retail]

Minute Maid
The Coca-Cola Company
USA
Duffy & Partners
[Food & Beverage]

4 **Minuteman Press**
Minuteman Press International Inc
USA
[Publishing]

5 **Minuteman Press**
Minuteman Press International Inc
USA
[Publishing]

6 **Miracle-Ear Inc**
USA
[Medical Device Technology]

7 **Miramax Films**
Miramax Film Corporation,
Filmyard Holdings LLC
USA
[Film Industry]

8 **Miramax Home Entertainment**
Miramax Film Corporation
(Filmyard Holdings LLC)
USA, 1994
[Film Industry]

9 **Miro**
Miro Marketing + Service GmbH
Germany
[Marketing]

MISS AMERICA

1 Miss America
   Miss America Organization
   USA
   [Events]

2 Mission
   Mission Foods Corporation
   USA
   [Food & Beverage]

3 Miss Universe
   Miss Universe Organization,
   NBC Universal, Donald Trump
   USA
   [Events]

4 Mister Donut
   Allied Domecq plc
   USA
   [Restaurants & Bars]

5 Mister Minit
   Belgium, 1990s
   [Retail]

▶ 6 Mister Minit mascot (Fred)
   Belgium, ca 1964
   [Retail]

7 Mistral
   Mistral International BV
   Netherlands
   [Outdoor & Recreation]

8 Mistral Paints
   Mistral Paints sro
   Czech Republic
   [Paints & Coatings]

9 MIT (Massachusetts Institute
   of Technology)
   USA
   [Education]

10 MIT (Massachusetts Institute
   of Technology)
   USA, 2003
   Tim Blackburn, Matthew Carter
   [Education]

1. **MIT Press**
Massachusetts Institute of
Technology (MIT)
USA, 1960s
Muriel Cooper
[Publishing]

2. **Mita**
Mita Industrial Co. Ltd, Kyocera
Document Solutions Corporation
Japan
[Office Supplies]

3. **Mitel Networks**
Mitel Networks Corporation
Canada
[Telecommunications]

4. **Mitre**
Mitre Sports International Ltd,
Pentland Group
UK, 2001
[Sporting Goods]

5. **Mitsubishi**
Mitsubishi Group
Japan
[Conglomerate]

6. **Mitsubishi Chemical**
Mitsubishi Chemical Corporation
Japan
[Chemicals & Materials]

7. **Mitsui Sumitomo**
Mitsui Sumitomo Insurance
Group Holdings Inc
Japan
[Financial Services]

8. **Mitsukoshi**
Mitsukoshi Ltd, Isetan Mitsukoshi
Holdings Ltd
Japan
[Retail]

9. **Mitsumi**
Mitsumi Electric Co. Ltd
Japan
[Electronics]

10. **Mitutoyo**
Mitutoyo Corporation
Japan
[Technology]

1. **Miu Miu**
Prada SpA
Italy
[Fashion]

2. **Miwon**
PT Miwon Indonesia
Indonesia
[Food & Beverage]

3. **Mizuno**
Mizuno Corporation
Japan, 1983
[Sporting Goods]

4. **MK2**
France
[Film Industry]

5. **MKE Ankaragücü**
Turkey
[Sport]

6. **MLC Services**
Meat and Livestock
Commercial Services Ltd
UK, ca 2006
[Professional Services]

7. **MLS (Multiple Listing Service)**
USA
[Real Estate]

8. **MMEM (MM Electrical Merchandising)**
Metal Manufactures Ltd
Australia
[Retail]

9. **Mobil**
Exxon Mobil Corporation
USA, 1900s
[Retail]

10. **Mobil**
Exxon Mobil Corporation
USA, 1965
Chermayeff & Geismar
[Retail]

MOMIJI FINANCIAL GROUP

MoMA

Momiji Financial Group

Moblime Muebles
Ecuador, 2006
Helou Design
[Home Furnishings]

Moderaterna
Moderatera samlingspartiet
Sweden, ca 2003
[Political]

Modern Times Group (MTG)
Modern Times Group MTG AB
Sweden, 1995
[Media]

4 **Moen**
Moen Inc
USA
[Home Appliances]

5 **Moët & Chandon**
France
[Wines, Beers & Spirits]

6 **Mohawk**
Mohawk Industries Inc
USA
[Home Furnishings]

7 **Moldavkabel**
Moldavkabel ZAO
Moldavia
[Industrial Products]

8 **Moleskin**
Moleskin Srl
Italy, ca 1997
[Writing Products]

9 **Molson**
Molson Coors Brewing Company
Canada
[Wines, Beers & Spirits]

10 **Molson Export Ale**
Molson Coors Brewing Company
Canada
[Wines, Beers & Spirits]

11 **MoMa (Museum of Modern Art)**
USA
[Galleries & Museums]

12 **Momiji Financial Group**
The Momiji Bank Ltd
Japan
[Financial Services]

461

1. **Momo**
Momo Srl
Italy
[Automotive]

2. **Mona**
Campina Nederland BV
Netherlands
[Food & Beverage]

3. **Monarch**
Monarch Group
UK, 1980s
[Airline]

4. **Moncler**
Moncler Group
France
[Apparel]

5. **Mondadori Informatica**
Arnoldo Mondadori Editore SpA
Italy
[Publishing]

6. **Mondex**
Mondex International Ltd,
MasterCard Worldwide
UK
[Financial Services]

7. **Mondi**
Mondi Group
South Africa
[Paper Products]

8. **Moneo**
Moneo Payment Solutions
France
[Financial Services]

9. **Monogram**
Revell-Monogram Inc
USA, 1991
[Toys, Games & Models]

MONTEDISON

MONTEDISON

Monopoly
Hasbro Inc
USA
[Toys, Games & Models]

Monopoly
Hasbro Inc
UK, 2008
[Toys, Games & Models]

Monsanto
The Monsanto Company
USA
[Industry]

Monsanto
The Monsanto Company
USA, 2003
[Industry]

Monster
Monster Worldwide Inc
USA
[Internet]

Monster Cable
Monster Cable Products Inc
USA
[Consumer Electronics]

Montblanc
Montblanc International GmbH
Germany, 1913
[Luxury Goods]

Monte
Zott SE & Co. KG
Germany
[Food & Beverage]

Montedison
Montecatini Edison SpA
Italy, ca 1966
[Conglomerat]

MONTREAL METRO

Morgan Stanley

Morningstar

1. **Montreal Metro/Métro de Montréal**
   Société de transport de Montréal/
   Montreal Transit Corporation
   Canada
   [Transport]

2. **Moog Music**
   Moog Music Inc
   USA
   [Musical Instruments]

3. **Mooks Clothing Co.**
   Pacific Brands
   Australia
   [Apparel]

4. **Moore Wallace**
   Moore Wallace Inc, RR Donnelley
   USA
   [Professional Services]

5. **Mopar**
   Chrysler Group LLC
   USA, 1964
   [Automotive]

6. **Morel**
   Morel Ltd
   Israel
   [Consumer Electronics]

7. **More Th>n**
   RSA Insurance Group plc
   UK, 2000
   johnson banks
   [Financial Services]

8. **Morgan Stanley**
   USA, 2001
   Landor Associates
   [Financial Services]

9. **Moriwaki Engineering**
   Moriwaki Engineering Co. Ltd
   Japan
   [Automotive]

10. **Morningstar**
    Morningstar Inc
    USA, 1991
    Paul Rand
    [Professional Services]

Morocco
Moroccan National Tourist Office
Morocco
[Travel & Tourism]

Morphy Richards
Morphy Richards,
Glen Dimplex Group
UK, 1985
Lloyd Northover
[Home Appliances]

Mosaid
Mosaid Technologies Inc
USA
[Professional Services]

4 **Motel 6**
Accor SA
USA/Canada
[Hospitality]

5 **Mothercare**
Mothercare plc
UK
[Retail]

6 **Mothers**
Mothers Polishes Waxes
Cleaners Inc
USA
[Consumer Products]

7 **Motion Picture Association
of America Inc (MPAA)**
USA
[Societies & Associations]

8 **Motobécane**
Motobecane USA
France, 1970s
[Automotive]

9 **Moto Guzzi**
Piaggio & Co. SpA
Italy
[Automotive]

MOTOR

1 **Motor**
Motor Entertainment GmbH
Germany
[Music Industry]

2 **MotorCities**
MotorCities National Heritage Area
USA
[Places]

3 **Motorola**
Motorola Inc
USA, 1955
Zeke Ziner
[Telecommunications]

4 **Motown Records**
Motown Record Corporation,
Universal Music Group
USA
[Music Industry]

5 **Motown Records**
Motown Record Corporation,
Universal Music Group
USA, 1965
[Music Industry]

6 **Motul SA**
France
[Chemicals & Materials]

7 **Moulinex**
Groupe SEB
France
[Home Appliances]

Mounds
The Hershey Company
USA
[Food & Beverage]

Mountain Dew
PepsiCo Inc
USA, 2005
[Food & Beverage]

MountSnow
USA
[Outdoor & Recreation]

4 **Mövenpick**
Nestlé SA
Switzerland, 1999
Conran Design Group
[Food & Beverage]

5 **Mövenpick**
Nestlé SA
Switzerland
[Food & Beverage]

6 **Mozilla Corporation**
USA
[Internet]

7 **Mozilla Foundation**
USA, ca 2003
[Foundations & Institutes]

8 **MP3.com**
CBS Interactive Music Group, CBS Radio Inc
USA
[Internet]

▶ 9 **Mr. Clean**
Procter & Gamble Co
USA, 1958
Tatham-Laird & Kudner: Ernie Allen
[Household Products]

MR. COFFEE

1 **Mr. Coffee**
Jarden Consumer Solutions
USA
[Kitchenware]

2 **MRC Polymers**
MRC Polymers Inc
USA
[Chemicals & Materials]

3 **Mr. Jardinage**
France
[Retail]

4 **Mrs. Fields Cookies**
Mrs. Fields' Original Cookies Inc
USA
[Retail]

5 **Ms.**
Feminist Majority Foundation
USA
[Publications]

6 **MSA (Mine Safety Appliance) Corporation**
USA
[Safety & Security]

7 **MSAS**
USA, 1999
[Freight & Logistics]

8 **MSG Network**
MSG Holdings LP
USA, 2006
[Television Network]

9 **MSI**
Micro-Star International Co. Ltd
Taiwan, 2009
[Computer Technology]

10 **MSN**
Microsoft Corporation
USA, 1999
[Internet]

11 **MSN**
Microsoft Corporation
USA, 2010
Microsoft
[Internet]

MSNBC
MSNBC Interactive News LLC,
MSNBC.com
USA, 2007
[Internet]

MTA New York City Transit (NYCT)
Metropolitan Transportation
Authority of the State
of New York (MTA)
USA
[Transport]

3 **MTC**
SSTL India
India
[Telecommunications]

4 **MTV**
MTV Networks, Viacom Inc
USA, 1981
Manhattan Design: Pat Gorman,
Frank Olinsky, Patti Rogoff
[Television Channel]

5 **MTV2**
MTV Networks, Viacom Inc
USA, 2006
[Television Channel]

6 **MTV2 Sunset**
MTV Networks, Viacom Inc
USA
[Television Channel]

7 **MTX Audio**
Mitek Corporation
USA
[Consumer Electronics]

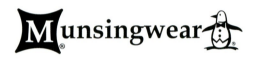

1 **Mueller's**
American Italian Pasta Company,
Ralcorp Holdings Inc
USA
[Food & Beverage]

2 **Muji**
Ryohin Keikaku Co. Ltd
Japan
[Retail]

3 **Müller**
Unternehmensgruppe
Theo Müller
Germany
[Food & Beverage]

4 **Multicanal**
Multicanal SA, Grupo Clarin SA
Argentina, 1996
Chermayeff & Geismar:
Steff Geissbuhler
[Television Channel]

5 **Munsingwear**
Perry Ellis International Group
Holdings Ltd
USA
[Apparel]

▶ 6 **Murata**
Murata Manufacturing Co. Ltd
USA, ca 1947
[Electronics]

7 **Murphy Oil Corporation**
USA
[Oil, Gas & Petroleum]

8 **Murphy's Irish Stout**
Murphy Brewery Ireland
Ireland
[Wines, Beers & Spirits]

9 **Muse**
UK, 1998
[Music]

MUSEUM FÜR FILM UND FERNSEHEN

MUSEE OLYMPIQUE
LAUSANNE

MUSEO DE PALPA

MUSEON

DEUTSCHE
KINEMATHEK
**MUSEUM
FÜR FILM UND
FERNSEHEN**

MUSEU **CIÊNCIA** E **VIDA**

Musée d'Orsay
France
[Galleries & Museums]

Musée Olympique
(Olympic Museum)
Switzerland
[Galleries & Museums]

Museo del Niño
UNICEF Ecuador
Ecuador, 2009
Latinbrand
[Galleries & Museums]

4 Museo de Palpa
Peru, 2003
Ideo Comunicadores
[Galleries & Museums]

5 Museon
Netherlands, 2003
Faydherbe & De Vringer
[Galleries & Museums]

6 Museu Ciência e Vida
Fundação CECIERJ
Brazil, 2009
Tecnopop
[Galleries & Museums]

7 Museum für Film und Fernsehen
Germany, 2006
Pentagram
[Galleries & Museums]

1 Museum of Arts and Design
   USA, 2008
   Pentagram
   [Galleries & Museums]

2 Museum of Chinese in America
   USA, 2011
   Pentagram: Michael Bierut,
   Yve Ludwig
   [Galleries & Museums]

3 Museum of Sex
   USA
   Pentagram
   [Galleries & Museums]

4 Museum of the Moving Image
   (MoMI)
   USA, 2011
   karlssonwilker
   [Galleries & Museums]

5 Museumsinsel Berlin
   Germany
   Baumann & Baumann
   [Galleries & Museums]

6 Mustang Survival
   Canada
   [Safety & Security]

7 Mute Records
   UK
   [Music Industry]

8 Muzak
   Muzak Holdings LLC
   USA, 1997
   Pentagram
   [Music Industry]

MYSQL

MX 1 – FIM Motocross World Championship
FIM (Fédération Internationale de Motocyclisme)
Switzerland
[Sporting Events]

My First Thomas & Friends
Gullane Entertainment Inc
UK, 1990s
[Toys, Games & Models]

Mylan Inc
USA
[Pharmaceuticals]

MYOB (Mind Your Own Business)
MYOB Ltd
Australia
[Computer Software]

MySpace
Specific Media LLC
USA, 2003
[Internet]

Myspace (launch logo)
Specific Media LLC
USA, 2010
[Internet]

Myspace
Specific Media LLC
USA, 2010
[Internet]

MySQL
Oracle Corporation
USA
Priority Advertising:
Renne Angelvuo
[Computer Technology]

NAA

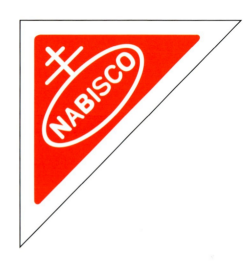

1 **NAA (North American Aviation)**
   USA
   [Aerospace]

2 **Nabisco**
   Kraft Foods Inc
   USA
   Bernhardt Fudyma Design Group
   [Food & Beverage]

3 **Nady Systems**
   Nady Systems Inc
   USA
   [Electronics]

4 **Naftal Algerie**
   Sonatrach SpA
   Algeria
   [Oil, Gas & Petroleum]

5 **NAHB (National Association of Home Builders)**
   USA
   [Societies & Associations]

6 **NAHI (National Association of Home Inspectors Inc)**
   USA
   [Societies & Associations]

7 **NAIT (The Northern Aberta Institute of Technology)**
   Canada
   [Education]

8 **Nakamichi**
   Nakamichi Corporation Ltd
   Japan
   [Consumer Electronics]

9 **Naked Music**
   Naked Music Recordings
   USA
   [Music Industry]

10 **Nalco**
   Nalco Holding Company
   USA
   [Industry]

Nalley Foods
Foods Group LLC
USA
[Food & Beverage]

Nampak
Nampak Ltd
South Africa
[Manufacturing]

Nanni Diesel
Italy
[Marine]

Nanya Technology
Nanya Technology Corporation
USA
[Technology]

Napa Auto Parts
National Automotive Parts
Association (NAPA)
USA
[Societies & Associations]

Napster
Best Buy Co. Inc
USA
[Internet]

NARPM (National Association of Residential Property Managers)
USA
[Societies & Associations]

NARS Cosmetics
Shiseido Americas Corporation
USA
[Health & Beauty]

NASA

1. NASA (National Aeronautics and Space Administration)
   USA, 1976
   Danne & Blackburn
   [Government]

2. NASA (National Aeronautics and Space Administration)
   USA, 1959
   James Modarelli
   [Government]

3. NASCAR (National Association for Stock Car Auto Racing)
   USA
   [Societies & Associations]

4. NASDAQ
   The Nasdaq Stock Market Inc
   USA
   [Financial Services]

5. Nasha Gazeta
   Latvia
   [Media]

6. Nathan's Famous
   Nathan's Famous Inc
   USA
   [Restaurants & Bars]

7. National Academy for Nuclear Training (NANT)
   Nuclear Energy Institute
   USA
   [Education]

8. National Arts Centre (Ottawa)
   Canada, 1967
   Design Collaborative
   [Venues]

9. National Bank van België (National Bank of Belgium)
   Belgium
   [Financial Services]

10. National Baseball Hall of Fam and Museum
    USA
    [Galleries & Museums]

National Blood Service
NHS Blood and Transplant
UK
[Healthcare]

National Captioning Institute Inc
USA
[Foundations & Institutes]

National Car Rental
Enterprise Holdings
USA
[Car Rental]

4 **National Center for Missing and Exploited Children (NCMEC)**
USA
[Foundations & Institutes]

5 **National Express**
National Express Group plc
UK
[Transport]

6 **National Gallery of Art**
USA
[Museums & Galleries]

NATIONAL GEOGRAPHIC

1 **National Geographic**
National Geographic Society
USA
Chermayeff & Geismar
[Societies & Associations]

2 **National Institutes of Health (NIH)**
United States Department of Health and Human Services
USA, 1976
[Foundations & Institutes]

3 **National Instruments**
National Instruments Corporation
USA
[Computer Technology]

4 **National Leasing**
National Leasing Group Inc
Canada
[Financial Services]

5 **National Library of Australia**
Australia
[Foundations & Institutes]

6 **National Linen Service**
National Linen and Uniform Service LLC
USA
[Fabrics & Textiles]

7 **Nationallotterie**
Belgium
[Leisure & Entertainment]

8 **National Lottery Commission**
UK
[Government]

9 **National Maritime Museum (Darling Harbour)**
Australian National Maritime Museum
Australia
[Galleries & Museums]

10 **National Mutual**
Australia
[Financial Services]

11 **National Notary Association (NNA)**
USA
[Societies & Associations]

NATIONAL TRUST

National Park Foundation (NPF)
USA
[Foundations & Institutes]

National Park Service (NPS)
USA, 1966
Chermayeff & Geismar
[Government]

National Park Service (NPS)
United States Department
of the Interior
USA, 1951/2001
[Government]

National Rifle Association
of America (NRA)
USA, 1871
[Societies & Associations]

National Semiconductor
National Semiconductor
Corporation
USA
[Technology]

National Sign Systems
USA
[Imaging & Photographic]

National Stonewall Democrats
USA
[Political]

National Theatre
The Royal National Theatre
UK, 1971
Ian Dennis, FHK Henrion
[Cinemas & Theatres]

National Trust
The National Trust for Places of
Historic Interest or Natural Beauty
UK, 1980s
David Gentleman
[Foundations & Institutes]

479

NATIONWIDE BUILDING SOCIETY

1 **Nationwide Building Society**
UK, 1994
[Financial Services]

2 **Nationwide Insurance**
Nationwide Mutual Insurance Company
USA
[Financial Services]

3 **Nationwide**
Nationwide Mutual Insurance Company
USA
[Financial Services]

4 **Natixis**
France
[Financial Services]

5 **NATO**
North Atlantic Treaty Organization
Belgium
[Defence]

▶ 6 **NATSN (North American Truck Stop Network)**
USA/Canada
[Retail]

7 **Natural Gas**
Verband der Schweizerischen Gasindustrie (VSG)
Switzerland
[Oil, Gas & Petroleum]

8 **NaturFoods**
Russia
[Food & Beverage]

9 **NatWest**
National Westminster Bank plc
UK, 2003
The Partners
[Financial Services]

10 **Nautibel (Belgian Federation of Watersports)**
Nautibel vzw
Belgium
[Societies & Associations]

11 **Navistar**
Navistar International Corpora
USA
[Automotive]

Navitar
Navitar Inc
USA
[Technology]

Navistar
Navistar International Corporation
USA
[Automotive]

Navy Federal
Navy Federal Credit Union
USA
[Financial Services]

Naya
Naya Waters Inc
Canada
[Food & Beverage]

NBA (National Basketball Association)
USA, 1969
Siegel+Gale
[Sport]

NBC
National Broadcasting Company
USA, 1975
[Broadcaster]

NBC
National Broadcasting Company
USA, 1986
Chermayeff & Geismar:
Steff Geissbuhler
[Broadcaster]

NCC Construction
NCC AB
Sweden
[Construction]

NCIS
CBS Corporation
USA
[Television Series]

NCR

1. **NCR**
NCR Corporation
USA
[Technology]

2. **NCR**
NCR Corporation
USA, 1996
Saul Bass
[Technology]

3. **NDR (Norddeutscher Rundfunk)**
Germany, 2001
[Broadcaster]

4. **Neal's Yard Remedies**
UK, 2001
Turner Duckworth
[Retail]

5. **NEC**
NEC Corporation,
Sumitomo Group
Japan, 1992
Landor Associates
[Electronics]

6. **Nederlandse Spoorwegen**
Netherlands Government
Netherlands, 1968
Gert Dumbar, Gert-Jan Leuvelink
[Transport]

7. **Nedlloyd**
Netherlands
[Freight & Logistics]

8. **NeilPryde**
NeilPryde Ltd
China
[Sporting Goods]

9. **Nelvana**
Nelvana Ltd
Canada, 2004
[Film Industry]

10. **Nemi Forsikring**
Nemi Forsikring A/S
Norway
[Financial Services]

11. **Nemko**
Norges Elektriske Materiellkontroll
Norway
[Professional Services]

NESTLÉ WATERS

Neos
Neos SpA
Italy
[Airline]

Neo Synthetic Oil
Neo Corporation
USA
[Automotive]

Nerco
Nerco Inc
USA
[Mining]

Nescafé
Nestlé SA
Switzerland
[Food & Beverage]

NESN (New England Sports Network)
Fenway Sports Group
USA
[Food & Beverage]

Nespresso
Nestlé Nespresso SA
Switzerland
[Food & Beverage]

Nestlé
Nestlé SA
Switzerland
[Food & Beverage]

Nestlé
Nestlé SA
Switzerland
[Food & Beverage]

Nestlé Food Services
Nestlé SA
Switzerland
[Food & Beverage]

Nestlé Waters
Nestlé SA
Switzerland
[Food & Beverage]

NET

1. **NET**
Net Serviços de Comunicação SA
(Organizações Globo)
Brazil
[Telecommunications]

2. **NetApp**
NetApp Inc
USA, 2008
[Data Storage]

3. **Netdecisions**
Nertdecisions Group
UK, ca 1998
[Information Technology]

4. **Netflix**
Netflix Inc
USA, 1997
[Video-on-Demand]

5. **Netgear**
Netgear Inc
USA
[Computer Hardware]

6. **Netigy**
Netigy Corporation
USA
[Professional Services]

7. **Netkey**
NCR Netkey Inc
USA
[Computer Software]

8. **Netopia**
Motorola Mobility Inc
USA
[Telecommunications]

9. **Netscape**
Netscape Communications,
AOL Inc
USA
[Internet]

10. **Netto**
Dansk Supermarked A/S
Denmark
[Retail]

11. **Network Appliance**
Network Appliance Inc
USA
[Data Storage]

NEWCASTLE UNITED FOOTBALL CLUB

1. **Network Solutions**
Network Solutions LLC,
VeriSign Inc.
USA, 1990s
[Internet]

2. **Network Solutions**
Network Solutions LLC,
General Atlantic
USA, 2009
Pappas Group
[Internet]

3. **NetWorld Interop**
UBM LLC
USA
[Events]

4. **Neutrogena**
Neutrogena Corporation,
Johnson & Johnson
USA
[Personal Care]

5. **Nevada Bell**
Nevada Bell Telephone Company,
Pacific Bell
USA
[Telecommunications]

6. **Nevada Power Company**
NV Energy Inc
USA
[Utilities]

7. **Nevada Tele.Com**
Energis Communications Ltd
UK
[Telecommunications]

8. **Nevskoe**
JSC Baltika Breweries,
Carlsberg Group
Russia, 1990s
[Wines, Beers & Spirits]

9. **Neways**
Neways International
USA
[Marketing]

10. **New Balance**
New Balance Athletic Shoe Inc
USA
[Footwear]

11. **Newcastle United Football Club**
Newcastle United FC Ltd
UK
[Sport]

485

NEW ERA

1. **New Era**
New Era Cap Co
USA
[Apparel]

2. **New Era**
New Era Cap Co
USA
[Apparel]

3. **New Holland Construction**
CNH Global NV
USA
[Tools & Machinery]

4. **New Jersey Cardinals**
USA, 1994
[Sport]

5. **New Line Home Entertainment**
New Line Film Productions Inc
USA, 1990
[Film Industry]

6. **New Man**
France, 1969
Raymond Loewy
[Apparel]

7. **New National Theatre Tokyo**
Japan
[Cinemas & Theatres]

8. **Newport**
Lorillard Tobacco Company Inc
USA, 1957
[Tobacco]

9. **Newport Boats**
USA
[Retail]

10. **New Riders Publishing**
Pearson Education
USA
[Publishing]

11. **News Corporation**
USA
[Media]

News of the World
News International Ltd
UK, 1984
[Media]

Newsvine Inc
USA
[Media]

Newsweek
Sidney Harman
USA
Jim Parkinson
[Media]

4   **Newton**
Apple Inc
USA, ca 1993
[Computer Hardware]

5   **Newton Investment Management**
UK
[Financial Services]

6   **New York City Ballet**
New York City Ballet (NYCB)
USA, 2008
Pentagram: Paula Scher
[Cinemas & Theatres]

7   **New York Life**
New York Life Insurance Company
USA, 1964
Lippincott & Margulies:
Raphael Boguslav
[Financial Services]

8   **New York Post**
News Corporation
USA
[Media]

9   **New York Yankees**
Yankee Global Enterprises LLC
USA, 1970s
[Sport]

10 **New York Yankees (Cap logo)**
Yankee Global Enterprises LLC
USA
[Sport]

11 **Nexans**
Nexans SA
France
[Manufacturing]

NEXT COMPUTER

1 NeXT Computer
NeXT Software Inc
USA, 1986
Paul Rand
[Computer Technology]

2 Nextel Communications
Sprint Nextel Corporation
USA, 2011
Landor Associates
[Telecommunications]

3 NFB/ONF (National Film Board of Canada/Office national du film du Canada)
Canada, 2002
Paprika Communications
[Film Industry]

4 NFL (National Football League)
USA, 2008
[Sport]

5 NFL Players (National Football League Players Association)
USA, ca 2006
[Societies & Associations]

6 NFPA International
National Fire Protection Association (NFPA)
USA
[Societies & Associations]

7 NGA (National Gallery of Australia)
Australia
[Galleries & Museums]

8 NGA (National Glass Association)
USA
[Societies & Associations]

9 NGK
NGK Spark Plug Co. Ltd
Japan
[Automotive]

10 NHRA (National Hot Rod Association)
USA/Canada
[Societies & Associations]

11 NHS (National Health Service)
UK, 1990
Moon Brand: Richard Moon
[Healthcare]

1 **Niasi**
Niasi Indústria de Cosméticos Ltda
Brazil
[Health & Beauty]

NIBCO Inc
USA
[Industrial Products]

Nichibutsu
Nihon Bussan Co. Ltd
Japan
[Computer & Video Games]

4 **Nichirei**
Nichirei Corporation
Japan
[Food & Beverage]

5 **Nickelodeon**
MTV Networks, Viacom Inc
USA, 1984
Fred/Alan Inc: Tom Corey, Scott Nash
[Television Channel]

6 **Nicoletti**
Italy
[Home Furnishings]

7 **Nidar**
Norway
[Food & Beverage]

8 **Nidwaldner Kantonalbank**
Switzerland
[Financial Services]

9 **Niigita Institute of Technology**
Japan
[Education]

NIKE

1 **Nike**
Nike Inc
USA, 1971
Carolyn Davidson
[Sporting Goods]

2 **Nike**
Nike Inc
USA, 1978
[Sporting Goods]

3 **Niki**
NIKI Luftfahrt GmbH
Austria
[Airline]

4 **Nikkalite**
Nippon Carbide Industries (USA) Inc
USA
[Manufacturing]

5 **Nikkei**
Nikkei Inc
Japan
[Media]

6 **Nikkei BP**
Nikkei Business Publications Inc
Japan
[Publishing]

7 **Nikko**
Nikko Co. Ltd
Japan
[Toys, Games & Models]

8 **Nikko Hotels International**
Ocura Hotels & Resorts
Japan
[Hospitality]

9 **Nikon**
Nikon Corporation
Japan, 2003
[Imaging & Photographic]

Nilfisk Advance
Nilfisk-Advance A/S
Denmark
[Manufacturing]

Nilla Wafers
Nabisco, Kraft Foods Inc
USA
[Food & Beverage]

Ninja Tune Records
Ninja Tune Records Ltd
UK, ca 1994
Kevin Foakes
[Music Industry]

4 **NIN (Nine Inch Nails)**
USA, 1989
Trent Reznor, Gary Talpas
[Music]

▶ 5 **Nintendo 64**
Nintendo Co. Ltd
Japan, 1996
[Computer & Video Games]

▶ 6 **Nintendo**
Nintendo Co. Ltd
Japan, 2006
[Computer & Video Games]

7 **Nippon Express**
Nippon Express Co. Ltd
Japan
[Freight & Logistics]

8 **Nipponkoa Insurance**
Japan
[Financial Services]

9 **Nippon Paint**
Nipponpaint Co. Ltd
Japan
[Paints & Coatings]

NIPPON SANSO

1 **Nippon Sanso**
Japan
[Oil, Gas & Petroleum]

2 **Nirvana**
USA, 1989
Lisa Orth
[Music]

3 **Nishi-Nippon Bank**
The Nishi-Nippon Bank Ltd
Japan
[Financial Services]

4 **Nissan**
Nissan Motor Company Ltd
Japan, 1984
[Automotive]

5 **Nissan**
Nissan Motor Company Ltd
Japan, 2000
FutureBrand
[Automotive]

6 **Nissay**
Nippon Life Insurance Company
Japan
[Financial Services]

▶ 7 **Nissin**
Nissin Foods Holdings Co. Ltd
Japan
[Food & Beverage]

8 **Nissin**
Nissin Brake Ohio Inc
USA
[Automotive]

9 **Nitta Corporation**
Japan
[Industrial Products]

NOKIA

Nittaku
Nippon Takkyu Co. Ltd
Japan
[Sporting Goods]

Nitto Denko
Nitto Denko Corporation
Japan
[Manufacturing]

Nivea
Beiersdorf AG
Germany, 1993
[Personal Care]

Nixxo
Nixxo Telecom
USA
[Telecommunications]

NKK Group
Japan
[Industrial Products]

NMMA (National Marine Manufacturers Association)
USA
[Societies & Associations]

NOBI (Norsk Betongindustri)
Norway
[Chemicals & Materials]

NOK
NOK Corporation
Japan
[Industry]

Nokia
Nokia Corporation
Finland, 1990s
[Telecommunications]

NOLTE KÜCHEN

1 **Nolte Küchen**
Nolte Küchen GmbH & Co. KG
Germany
[Design]

2 **Nomaï**
Nomaï SA
France
[Data Storage]

3 **Nomura**
Nomura Holdings Inc
Japan
[Financial Services]

4 **Noranda**
Noranda Inc
Canada
[Mining]

5 **Norbert Dentressangle**
France
[Freight & Logistics]

6 **Nordica**
Tecnica Group SpA
Italy
[Sporting Goods]

7 **Nordic Aluminium**
Nordic Aluminium Oyj
Finland
[Industrial Products]

8 **Norelco**
Koninklijke Philips Electronics NV
USA
[Consumer Products]

9 **Norges Dykkeforbund/
Norwegian Diving Federation**
Norway
[Societies & Associations]

NorgesGruppen
NorgesGruppen ASA
Norway
[Retail]

NORTHEAST UTILITIES SYSTEM

Norges Ischockeyforbund
Norway
[Sport]

Noritake
China
[Kitchenware]

Nor Lines
Nor Lines AS
Norway
[Freight & Logistics]

Norman
Norman ASA
Norway
[Computer Software]

Norquip
Canada
[Professional Service]

Norske Skog
Norske Skogindustrier ASA
Norway
[Paper Products]

Nortec
Hamburg Messe und
Congress GmbH
Germany
[Events]

Nortel
Nortel Networks Corporation
USA, 1995
Siegel+Gale
[Telecommunications]

North American
North American Van Lines Inc
USA
[Freight & Logistics]

Northeast Utilities System
Northeast Utilities
USA
[Utilities]

495

NORTHERN FOODS

1. **Northern Foods**
   2 Sisters Food Group
   UK
   [Food & Beverage]

2. **Northern Trust**
   Northern Trust Corproation
   USA
   [Financial Services]

3. **Northpine**
   Northpine Ltd
   New Zealand
   Scenario Communications:
   Jason Saunders
   [Manufacturing]

4. **North Sails**
   North Marine Group
   USA
   [Marine]

5. **Northstar at Tahoe**
   Northstar California
   USA
   [Outdoor & Recreation]

6. **NorthwesTel**
   NorthwesTel Inc
   USA
   [Telecommunications]

7. **Norton**
   Norton Motorcycles Ltd
   UK, 1913
   James Lansdowne Norton
   [Automotive]

8. **Norton Antivirus**
   Symantec Corporation
   USA
   [Computer Software]

9. **Norton Bear-Tex**
   Saint-Gobain Abrasives Inc
   USA
   [Household Products]

10. **Norton Triumph**
    Norton Villiers Triumph
    UK, 1970s
    [Automotive]

11. **Norton Utilities**
    Symantec Corporation
    USA
    [Computer Software]

12. **Norwest Corporation**
    USA, 1980s
    [Financial Services]

NTB

Norwich Union
Aviva plc
UK
[Financial Services]

NOS
Nitrous Oxide Systems Inc, Holley Performance Products Inc
USA
[Chemicals & Materials]

Nova Scotia
Province of Nova Scotia, Department of Economic and Rural Development and Tourism
Canada
[Travel & Tourism]

4 **Novell**
Novell Inc, The Attachmate Group
USA, 1996
Frankfurt Balkind
[Computer Software]

5 **Novo Nordisk**
Nordisk AS
Denmark
[Pharmaceuticals]

6 **NRJ**
Astral Media Inc
Canada
[Radio Stations]

7 **NSA (National Speakers Association)**
USA
[Societies & Associations]

8 **NSB Group**
Canada
[Retail]

9 **NSI (National Service Industries)**
USA
[Industrial Products]

10 **NSTA (National Safe Transit Association)**
USA
[Societies & Associations]

11 **NTB (National Tire & Battery)**
TBC Corporation
USA
[Automotive]

497

1 **NTPC (National Thermal Power Corporation)**
NTPC Ltd
India
[Energy]

2 **NTT Communications (Nippon Telegraph and Telephone) Corporation**
Japan
[Telecommunications]

3 **NTT DoCoMo**
NTT DoCoMo Inc
Japan, 2008
[Telecommunications]

4 **NTT Verio**
Verio Inc, NTT Communications Corporation
USA, 2000
[Internet]

5 **Nucor**
Nucor Corporation
USA
[Industry]

6 **Nutella**
Ferrero SpA
Italy
[Food & Beverage]

7 **Nuvelo**
Nuvelo Inc
USA
[Pharmaceuticals]

8 **Nuxe**
Laboratoire Nuxe
France
[Health & Beauty]

NVF
The Dutch Film Distributors'
Association
Netherlands, 2003
SoDesign
[Societies & Associations]

Nvidia
Nvidia Corporation
USA, 2006
[Computer Technology]

3 **NWA (Northwest Airlines)**
Northwest Airlines Inc
USA, 2003
TrueBrand: John Dieffenbach,
Vince Carra
[Airline]

4 **NYC (New York City)**
NYC & Company Inc
USA, 2007
Wolff Olins
[Places]

5 **NYCE (New York Cash Exchange)**
The New York Currency Exchange
USA, 1984
Siegel+Gale
[Financial Services]

6 **Nykredit**
Nykredit Holding A/S
Denmark, 1990
Bysted
[Financial Services]

7 **NYLC**
USA, 1999
Amster Yard
[Fashion]

8 **NYSE (New York Stock Exchange)**
USA, 2000
Landor Associates
[Financial Services]

O2

1 **O2**
Telefónica UK Ltd
UK, 2002
Lambie-Nairn
[Telecommunications]

2 **OAG**
UBM Aviation
UK
[Information Technology]

3 **Oakley**
Oakley Inc, Luxottica Group SpA
USA
[Eyewear]

4 **Oakwood**
Oakwood Worldwide
USA
[Hospitality]

5 **Oase**
Oase GmbH
Germany
[Manufacturing]

6 **Oasis**
Oasis Merchandising Ltd
UK, 1994
Microdot Creative: Brian Cannon
[Music]

7 **o.b.**
McNeil-PPC Inc
USA
[Personal Care]

8 **Obayashi**
Obayashi Corporation
Japan
[Construction]

9 **Obey Giant**
USA, 1989
Shepard Fairey
[Apparel]

OB Lager
Oriental Brewery Co. Ltd
South Korea
[Wines, Beers & Spirits]

Oblicore
Oblicore Inc
USA
[Computer Software]

OCB
Groupe Bolloré
France
[Tobacco]

Océ
Océ NV
Netherlands, 1982
Baer Cornet
[Restaurants & Bars]

Oceanico
Oceanico Group
Portugal
[Real Estate]

Ocean Spray
Ocean Spray Cranberries Inc
USA
[Food & Beverage]

Octanorm
Octanorm Vertriebs GmbH
Germany
[Professional Services]

Oddfellows
Grand United Order of Oddfellows Friendly Society
UK
[Societies & Associations]

Oddrane
Norway
[Societies & Associations]

1 Odyssey
Odyssey Ltd
Russia
[Freight & Logistics]

2 Odell Brewing Co.
USA
tbd agency
[Breweries]

3 Oenobiol
Laboratoire Oenobiol SA
France
[Health & Beauty]

4 Oerlikon
Oerlikon Corporation AG
Switzerland
[Manufacturing]

5 OFF!
S.C. Johnson & Son Inc
USA
[Personal Care]

6 Office Depot
Office Depot Inc
USA, 2002
[Office Supplies]

7 OfficeMax
OMX Inc
USA, 1980s
[Office Supplies]

8 Offley Porto
Portugal
[Wines, Beers & Spirits]

9 Offshore Logistics Inc
USA
[Freight & Logistics]

OKUMA

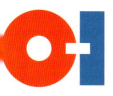

Öhlins
Öhlins Racing AB
Sweden
[Automotive]

Ohtsu
Falken Tire Corporation HQ
USA
[Automotive]

O-I
Owens Illinois Inc
USA
[Glass & Ceramics]

Oil & Gas Journal
PennWell Petroleum Group
USA
[Publications]

Oil of Olaz
Procter & Gamble GmbH
Germany
[Health & Beauty]

Okamura
Okamura Corporation
Japan
[Office Supplies]

Okasan Securities
Okasan Securities Group Inc
Japan, 1991
Paul Rand
[Financial Services]

Oki
Oki Electric Industry Co. Ltd
Japan
[Office Supplies]

Okuma
Okuma Corporation
Japan
[Tools & Machinery]

503

OK USED CARS

1. **OK Used Cars**
   USA
   [Retail]

2. **Oldcastle**
   Oldcastle Inc
   USA
   Suzi Godson
   [Construction]

3. **Old Navy**
   Gap Inc
   USA
   [Apparel]

4. **Oldsmobile**
   General Motors Company
   USA
   [Automotive]

5. **Oldsmobile**
   General Motors Company
   USA, 1981
   [Automotive]

6. **Old Spice**
   Procter & Gamble Co
   USA, 2008
   [Personal Care]

7. **Old Style Beer**
   Pabst Brewing Company
   USA
   [Wines, Beers & Spirits]

8. **Olidata**
   Olidata SpA
   Italy
   [Computer Technology]

9. **Olin**
   Olin Corporation
   USA
   [Chemicals & Materials]

OLYMPIC GAMES ATLANTA 1996

Olivetti
Olivetti SpA
Italy, 1970
Walter Ballmer
[Computer Technology]

OLN
Rogers Media Inc
Canada, 2011
[Television Channel]

Oloid
Oloid AG
Switzerland
[Industry]

4 Olympic Airways
Greece, 1960s
[Airline]

5 Olympic Paints & Stains
PPG Architectural Finishes Inc
USA
[Paints & Coatings]

6 Olympic Games Tokyo 1964
Japan, 1964
[Sporting Events]

7 Olympic Games Mexico 1968
Mexico
Lance Wyman
[Sporting Events]

8 Olympic Games Los Angeles 1984
USA, 1980
Robert Miles Runyon Associates
[Sporting Events]

9 Olympic Games Barcelona 1992
Spain, 1992
Josep Maria Trias
[Sporting Events]

10 Olympic Games Atlanta 1996
USA, 1992
Landor Associates
[Sporting Events]

OLYMPIC GAMES SYDNEY 2000

1. **Olympic Games Sydney 2000**
   Australia, 2000
   FHA Image Design
   [Sporting Events]

2. **Olympic Games Athens 2004**
   Greece, 2001
   Wolff Olins, Red Design
   [Sporting Events]

3. **Olympic Games Beijing 2008**
   China
   Guo Chunning
   [Sporting Events]

4. **Olympic Games London 2012**
   UK, 2007
   Wolff Olins
   [Sporting Events]

5. **Olympic Games Rio 2016**
   Brazilian Olympic Committee
   Brazil, 2010
   Tatil Design
   [Sporting Events]

6. **Olympic symbol**
   International Olympic Committee
   Switzerland, 1913
   Pierre de Coubertin
   [Sport]

7. **Olympic Winter Games Salt Lake City 2002**
   USA
   [Sporting Events]

8. **Olympic Winter Games Torino 2006**
   Italy
   [Sporting Events]

9. **Olympic Winter Games Vancouver 2010**
   Canada, 2005
   Elena Rivera MacGregor
   [Sporting Events]

Olympique de Marseille (OM)
Olympique de Marseille SASP
France
[Sport]

Olympus
Olympus Corporation
Japan, 2001
[Consumer Electronics]

Omaha Paper
Omaha Paper Company
USA
[Paper Products]

OMC Card
OMC Card Inc
Japan
[Financial Services]

Omega
Omega SA, The Swatch Group
Switzerland
[Watches & Jewelry]

Omer DeSerres
Omer DeSerres Inc
Canada
[Retail]

Omni Hotels
Omni Hotels Corporation
USA
[Hospitality]

OmniPage Pro
Nuance Communications Inc
USA
[Computer Software]

OmniSky Corporation
USA
[Information Technology]

1 **Omni Television**
Rogers Communications Inc
Canada
[Television Network]

2 **Omron**
Omron Corporation
Japan
[Consumer Electronics]

3 **OMS**
OMS Online Marketing Service
GmbH & Co. KG
Germany
[Marketing]

4 **Onan**
Cummins Inc
USA
[Tools & Machinery]

5 **One**
London Eastern Railway Ltd,
National Express Group plc
UK, 2004
Lawrence Pierce
[Transport]

▶ 6 **O'Neill**
O'Neill Inc
USA
[Outdoor & Recreation]

7 **One Laptop per Child Foundation**
USA, 2007
Pentagram
[Foundations & Institutes]

8 **Oneok**
Oneok Inc
USA
[Utilities]

9 **Onitsuka Tiger**
ASICS Ltd
Japan
[Footwear]

Onkyo
Onkyo Corporation
Japan
[Consumer Electronics]

Oops! Express
Oops! Inc
Canada
[Retail]

Opel
Adam Opel AG, General Motors Company
Germany, 1987
[Automotive]

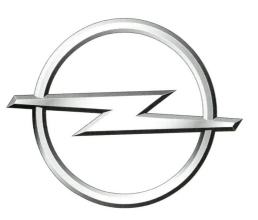

Opel
Adam Opel AG, General Motors Company
Germany, 2002
[Automotive]

Open Road
Sirius XM Radio
USA
[Radio Station]

OpenText
OpenText Corporation
Canada
[Computer Software]

Opera
Cicli Pinarello SpA
Italy
[Bicycles]

Op (Ocean Pacific)
Iconix Brand Group Inc
USA
[Apparel]

Oppo
Royal KPN NV
The Netherlands, 2004
Studio Dumbar
[Electronics]

OPRAH!

1 **Oprah!**
Oprah Winfrey
USA, 2004
Essex Two
[Television Series]

2 **Optimal**
Optimal AG & Co. KG
Germany
[Automotive]

3 **Optimist International**
USA
[Societies & Associations]

4 **Opus**
The Opus Group
USA
[Real Estate]

5 **Oracle**
Oracle Corporation
USA
[Computer Technology]

6 **Oral-B**
Procter & Gamble Co
USA
[Personal Care]

7 **Orange**
France Telecom SA
France, 1994
Wolff Olins
[Telecommunications]

8 **Orange County Convention Center (OCCC)**
USA
[Places]

Orange Julius
Orange Julius of America Inc
USA
[Restaurants & Bars]

Orangina
Suntory Holdings Ltd,
Dr Pepper Snapple Group Inc
Japan/USA, 2010
[Food & Beverage]

Orangina
Suntory Holdings Ltd,
Dr Pepper Snapple Group Inc
Japan/USA, 2007
[Food & Beverage]

4 **Oranjeboom**
United Dutch Breweries BV
Netherlands
[Wines, Beers & Spirits]

5 **Orbea**
Orbea S. Coop
Spain
[Bicycles]

6 **Orbis**
Orbis Tecnologia Eléctrica SA
Spain
[Electronics]

7 **Oreck**
Oreck Corporation
USA
[Household Products]

8 **Ore-Ida**
Ore-Ida Potato Products Inc,
H. J. Heinz Company Inc
USA
[Food & Beverage]

1 **O'Reilly Auto Parts**
O'Reilly Automotive Inc
USA
[Retail]

2 **Oreo**
Nabisco, Kraft Foods Inc
USA, 1987
[Food & Beverage]

3 **Oreo**
Nabisco, Kraft Foods Inc
USA, 2004
[Food & Beverage]

4 **Original Source**
PZ Cussons Ltd
UK
[Personal Care]

5 **Orion**
Daimler AG
USA
[Automotive]

6 **Orion Home Video**
Orion Pictures Corporation
USA, 1980s
[Film Industry]

7 **Orix**
ORIX Corporation
Japan
[Financial Services]

8 **Orkin**
Rollins Inc
USA
[Professional Services]

Orlando Museum of Art (OMA)
USA, 2008
Push
[Galleries & Museums]

Orlen
PKN Orlen SA
Poland, 2000
Henryk Chyliński
[Oil, Gas & Petroleum]

Oro Azul Tequila
Agave Tequila Productores (AT)
Mexico
[Wines, Beers & Spirits]

Oroweat
Bimbo Bakeries USA Inc
USA
[Food & Beverage]

Oscar de la Renta
USA, 1960s
Oscar de la Renta
[Fashion]

Oscar Meyer
Kraft Foods Inc
USA, 2010
[Food & Beverage]

OSCE (Organization for Security and Co-operation in Europe)
Austria
[Government]

Osco Drug
SuperValu Inc
USA
[Retail]

OSG

OSG Tap & Die
OSG Tap & Die Inc
USA
[Tools & Machinery]

OshKosh B'gosh Inc
USA
[Apparel]

OSRAM
OSRAM AG
Germany, 1919
[Manufacturing]

Osuna Nursery
USA
[Professional Services]

OTC
SPX Corporation
USA
[Tools & Machinery]

OTE
Hellenic Telecommunications Organization AE
Greece
[Telecommunications]

Otis
Otis Elevator Company
USA
[Manufacturing]

OTP Bank
Hungary
[Financial Services]

Ottakringer Brewery
Ottakringer Brauerei AG
Austria
[Manufacturing]

Outback Steakhouse
Bloomin Brands INC
USA
[Restaurants]

Outokumpu
Outokumpu Group
Finland
[Industrial Products]

Overture Services
Yahoo! Inc
USA
[Internet]

Owens Corning
Owens Corning Corporation
USA
[Manufacturing]

Oxelo
Decathlon
UK, 2008
Pentagram
[Sport]

Oxiteno
Oxiteno, Ultrapar Participações
Brazil, 2005
FutureBrand BC&H
[Conglomerate]

Oxxo
Fomento Económico Mexicano
SAB de CV (FEMSA)
Mexico, 1970s
[Retail]

Oxxio
Netherlands
[Utilities]

Oxy Petroleum
Occidental Petroleum
Corporation (Oxy)
USA
[Oil, Gas & Petroleum]

1 P4 Ogilvy
Star Communications Holding
Panama
[Advertising & Campaigns]

2 P&G
Procter & Gamble Co
USA, 1941
Lipson Alport Glass & Associates
[Consumer Products]

3 P&L (Pratt & Lambert)
The Sherwin-Williams Company
USA
[Paints & Coatings]

4 P&O Cruises
Carnival Corporation & PLC
UK/USA
[Travel & Tourism]

5 Pabst Brewing Company
USA
[Breweries]

6 Paccar
Paccar Inc
USA
[Automotive]

7 PacifiCare
UnitedHealth Group Inc
USA
[Healthcare]

8 Pacific Bell
Pacific Bell Telephone Company, AT&T California
USA, 1984
[Telecommunications]

9 Pacific Gas and Electric Company (PG&E)
PG&E Corporation
USA
[Utilities]

10 Package Steel Building Systems
Package Industries Inc
USA
[Industry]

Pacon™

Paddington
Walk

Packard Bell
Packard Bell BV, Acer Inc
Netherlands, 2003
[Computer Technology]

Packard Bell
Packard Bell BV (Acer Inc)
Netherlands, 2009
Acer
[Computer Technology]

Packeteer
Blue Coat Systems Inc
USA, 1996
[Information Technology]

4 **Pac-Man**
Namco Bandai Games Inc
Japan, 1980
[Computer & Video Games]

5 **Pacon Corporation**
USA
[Writing Products]

6 **PADI (Professional Association of Diving Instructors)**
USA, 1966
Ralph Erickson
[Societies & Associations]

7 **Paddington Walk**
Paddington Basin
UK
ico Design
[Real Estate]

1 **Pago**
Pago International GmbH
Germany
[Food & Beverage]

2 **Paint USA**
Intex DIY Inc
USA
[Paints & Coatings]

3 **Pakistan International Airlines (PIA)**
Pakistan International Airlines Corporation
Pakistan
[Airline]

4 **Palace Amusement Co. (1921) Ltd**
Jamaica
[Cinemas & Theatres]

5 **Pall**
Pall Corporation
USA
[Industrial Products]

6 **Palm**
Palm Inc
USA, 2005
Turner Duckworth
[Computer Technology]

7 **Palmolive**
Colgate-Palmolive Company
USA
[Personal Care]

8 **PalmOne**
PalmOne Inc
USA, 2004
[Computer Hardware]

9 **Palomino**
C&A, Cofra Holding AG
Belgium/Germany
[Apparel]

10 **Pampers**
Procter & Gamble Co
USA, 2001
[Baby Products]

Pan Am
Pan American World Airways
USA
[Airline]

Panametrics
General Electric Company
USA
[Industrial Products]

Panasonic
Panasonic Corporation
Japan, 2007
[Consumer Electronics]

Panavision
Panavision Inc
USA
[Film Industry]

Panda Embroidery
USA
[Apparel]

Panda Express
Panda Restaurant Group Inc
USA
[Restaurants & Bars]

Panda Software
Panda Security
Spain, 1990
[Computer Software]

Panini Comics
Panini SpA
Italy
[Publishing]

Pantech
Pantech Corporation
South Korea
[Telecommunications]

PANTONE

paper products

1 **Pantone**
X-Rite Inc
USA
[Imaging & Photographic]

2 **Pantone Hexachrome**
X-Rite Inc
USA
[Imaging & Photographic]

3 **Paper Mate**
Sanford LP, Newell Rubbermaid Inc
USA
[Writing Products]

4 **Paper Products Design**
Paper Products Design GmbH
Germany
[Paper Products]

5 **Papier Recyclé**
France
[Labelling, Standards & Certification]

6 **Papyrus AB**
Sweden
[Paper Products]

7 **Paramount Pictures**
Paramount Pictures Corporation
USA, 1974
[Film Industry]

8 **Paraboot**
Richard-Pontvert SA
France
[Footwear]

9 **Parental Advisory Explicit Content**
Recording Industry Association of America (RIAA)
USA, ca 2000
[Labelling, Standards & Certification]

Parexel
Parexel International
USA
[Pharmaceuticals]

Paris Match
Hachette Filipacchi Médias SA,
Lagardère Active
France, ca 1949
[Publications]

Paris Première
Groupe M6
France, 2009
SlooDesign
[Television Channel]

4 **Paris Saint-Germain Football Club**
Paris Saint-Germain Football SASP
France
Étienne Robial
[Sport]

5 **Parker**
Parker Pen Company,
Newell Rubbermaid Inc
USA
[Writing Products]

6 **Parker**
Parker Hannifin Corporation
USA
[Technology]

7 **Parker Games**
Hasbro Inc
USA
[Toys, Games & Models]

8 **Park Inn**
The Carlson Rezidor Hotel Group
USA, 2010
[Hospitality]

9 **Park Inn International**
Olympus Hospitality Group
USA
[Hospitality]

1 **Park Plaza**
PPHE Hotel Group Ltd,
Carlson Rezidor Hotel Group
Netherlands, 2001
[Hospitality]

2 **Parmalat**
Parmalat SpA, Groupe Lactalis
Italy
[Manufacturing]

3 **Partek**
Partek Oy Ab
Finland, 1998
Lloyd Northover
[Manufacturing]

4 **Parti Socialiste/
Socialist Party**
France
[Political]

5 **Partido Socialista/
Socialist Party**
Portugal
[Political]

6 **Pasquier**
Brioche Pasquier
France
[Food & Beverage]

7 **Pathé**
Pathé SA
France, 1998
Landor Associates:
Margaret Youngblood
[Film Industry]

8 **Pathé**
Pathé SA
France
[Film Industry]

9 **Pathé Records**
France, 1900s
[Music Industry]

 Paulmann

Paul Smith

1. **Pato Pampo**
   Argentina
   [Apparel]

2. **Patta**
   Netherlands
   [Apparel]

3. **Pattex**
   Henkel Central Eastern Europe GmbH
   Austria
   [Consumer Products]

4. **Paulaner**
   Paulaner Brauerei GmbH & Co. KG
   Germany
   [Breweries]

5. **Paulmann Lighting**
   Canada
   [Home Furnishings]

6. **Paul Smith**
   Paul Smith Ltd
   UK
   Zena
   [Fashion]

7. **Payne**
   Carrier Corporation
   USA
   [Heating & Cooling]

8. **PayPal**
   PayPal, eBay Inc
   USA
   Chad Hurley
   [Financial Services]

9. **PBS (Public Broadcasting Service)**
   USA, 1984
   Chermayeff & Geismar
   [Broadcaster]

1 **PCC (Power Corporation of Canada)**
Canada
[Conglomerate]

2 **PC Week**
Ziff Inc
USA
[Publications]

3 **Peace Corps**
Peace Corps, United States Government
USA, 1961
[Government]

4 **Peace Symbol**
Original usage: Campaign for Nuclear Disarmament (CND)
UK, 1958
Gerald Holtom
[Graphic Design]

5 **Peak Performance**
IC Companys A/S
Sweden
[Sporting Goods]

6 **Pearl**
Pearl Musical Instrument Company
Japan
[Musical Instruments]

7 **Pearson**
Pearson plc
UK
[Publishing]

8 **Peavey**
Peavey Electronics Corporation
USA, ca 1965
Hartley Peavey
[Consumer Electronics]

9 **PECO Energy**
Exelon Corporation
USA
[Oil, Gas & Petroleum]

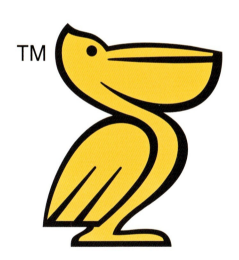 

PECSA
Peru
[Oil, Gas & Petroleum]

Pediatric Palliative Care Institute
USA
Essex Two
[Health & Safety]

Peerless Tyre Co
USA
[Automotive]

PEFC (Programme for the Endorsement of Forest Certification)
PEFC International
Switzerland
[Conservation & Environment]

Pekao Leasing
Bank Pekao SA
Poland, 1990s
[Financial Services]

Pelforth
Pelforth Brewery,
Heineken International
France
[Wines, Beers & Spirits]

Pelforth
Pelforth Brewery
(Heineken International)
France
[Wines, Beers & Spirits]

Pelikan
Pelikan Holding AG
Switzerland, 2003
[Writing Products]

PEMEX
Petróleos Mexicanos
Mexico, 1989
[Oil, Gas & Petroleum]

PEM

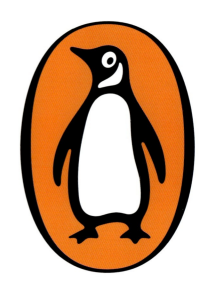

PEM (Plant Engineering & Maintenance)
Annex Business Media
Canada
[Publications]

Pemsa Cable Management Systems
Pemsa International
Spain
[Industrial Products]

Pen Club Venezuela
Venezuela, 2009
Ariel Pintos
[Societies & Associations]

Penguin
UK, 2005
Pentagram: Angus Hyland
[Publishing]

Penn
Head NV
USA
[Sporting Goods]

Pennzoil
SOPUS Products
USA
[Automotive]

Penske
Penske Corporation
USA
[Transport]

Pentax
Pentax Ricoh Imaging Coporation
Japan
[Imaging & Photographic]

Pentel
Pentel Co. Ltd
Japan
[Writing Products]

Penthouse
FriendFinder Networks
USA
[Publications]

People
Time Inc
USA
[Publications]

Peoples Energy
Peoples Gas
USA
[Utilities]

Pep Boys Auto
The Pep Boys – Manny, Moe & Jack
USA
[Automotive]

Pepe Jeans
Pepe Jeans SL
UK, 1992
[Apparel]

Pepsi
PepsiCo Inc
USA, 2003
[Food & Beverage]

Pepsi
PepsiCo Inc
USA, 2008
Arnell Group
[Food & Beverage]

Pepsi Center (aka The Can)
USA, 1999
[Places]

PepsiCo
PepsiCo Inc
USA, 2002
Landor Associates
[Food & Beverage]

Pepsi-Cola
PepsiCo Inc
USA, 1940
[Food & Beverage]

1. **Perkin Elmer**
PerkinElmer Inc
USA
[Technology]

2. **Perma Press**
Perma Press AB
Sweden
[Manufacturing]

3. **Pernod Ricard**
Pernod Ricard SA
France
[Wines, Beers & Spirits]

4. **Peroni**
Peroni Brewery, Birra Peroni
Italy
[Wines, Beers & Spirits]

5. **Perrier**
Nestlé SA
France
[Food & Beverage]

6. **Perry Sport**
Perry Sport BV
Netherlands
[Retail]

7. **Pershing**
Pershing LLC, The Bank of New York Mellon Corporation
USA
[Financial Services]

8. **Persil**
Henkel AG & Co. KGaA, Unilever plc/NV
Germany/UK
[Household Products]

9. **Persol**
Luxottica Group SpA
Italy
[Eyewear]

1 **Perumtel**
PT Telekomunikasi Indonesia Tbk
Indonesia, 1974
[Telecommunications]

2 **Petco**
Petco Animal Supplies Inc
USA
[Pet Products]

3 **Peterbilt**
Peterbilt Motors Company, Paccar Inc
USA
[Automotive]

4 **Peter Kaiser**
Peter Kaiser GmbH
Germany
[Footwear]

5 **Peter Paul**
Peter Paul Candy Manufacturing Company, The Hershey Company
USA
[Food & Beverage]

6 **Peterson**
Peterson Manufacturing Company
USA
[Automotive]

7 **Petit Bateau**
Groupe Yves Rocher
France
[Apparel]

8 **Petrobras**
Petróleo Brasileiro SA
Brazil, 1970
Aloísio Magalhães
[Oil, Gas & Petroleum]

9 **Petrobras**
Petróleo Brasileiro SA
Brazil, 1958
[Oil, Gas & Petroleum]

PETRO-CANADA

1

2

3

4

5

6

7

8

9

10
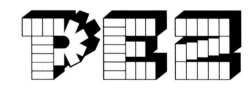

1. **Petro-Canada**
   Petro-Canada, Crown Corporation
   Canada
   Interbrand
   [Oil, Gas & Petroleum]

2. **PetroChina**
   PetroChina Company Ltd
   China, 2004
   [Oil, Gas & Petroleum]

3. **Petróleos de Venezuela SA (PDVSA)**
   Venezuela, 1975
   Jesús Emilio Franco
   [Oil, Gas & Petroleum]

4. **Petrom**
   OMV Petrom SA
   Romania
   [Oil, Gas & Petroleum]

5. **Petronas**
   Petroliam Nasional Berhad
   Malaysia
   [Oil, Gas & Petroleum]

6. **Petroplus**
   Petroplus Holdings AG
   Switzerland
   [Oil, Gas & Petroleum]

7. **Petro Rabigh**
   Rabigh Refining & Petrochemical Co.
   Saudi Arabia, 2007
   [Oil, Gas & Petroleum]

8. **Peugeot**
   Peugeot SA
   France, 1998
   [Automotive]

9. **Peugeot**
   Peugeot SA
   France, 2010
   BETC Design
   [Automotive]

▶ 10. **PEZ candy/dispensers**
   PEZ
   Austria, ca 1927
   [Food & Beverage]

Pfaff
VSM Group AB
Germany
[Tools & Machinery]

Pferd
August Rüggeberg GmbH
& Co. KG
Germany
[Tools & Machinery]

Pfizer
Pfizer Inc
USA, 2009
Siegel+Gale
[Pharmaceuticals]

4   **PG – Parental Guidance
    Suggested –MPAA Movie Rating**
    Motion Picture Association
    of America Inc (MPAA)
    USA
    [Labelling, Standards
    & Certification]

5   **Pharmacia**
    Pharmacia Corp
    UK, 2000
    Landor Associates
    [Pharmaceuticals]

6   **Philadelphia Cream Cheese**
    Kraft Foods Inc
    USA, 2008
    [Food & Beverage]

7   **Philco Argentina**
    Philco Argentina SA, Grupo
    Newsan
    Argentina
    [Consumer Electronics]

8   **Philco Brazil**
    SAC Philco
    Brazil
    [Consumer Electronics]

9   **Philco US**
    Philips Electronics North
    America Corporation
    USA
    [Consumer Electronics]

PHILIP MORRIS INTERNATIONAL

1   Philip Morris International (PMI)
    USA/Switzerland
    [Tobacco]

2   Philippine Stock Exchange
    Philippines
    [Financial Services]

▶ 3 Philips
    Koninklijke Philips Electronics NV
    Netherlands, 1995
    [Electronics]

4   Phillies
    The Philadelphia Phillies
    USA
    [Sport]

▶ 5 Phillips 66
    ConocoPhillips Company
    USA, 1959
    [Retail]

6   PHLX (Philadelphia Stock Exchange)
    USA
    [Financial Services]

7   Photodisc
    Getty Images Inc
    USA
    [Imaging & Photographic]

8   Perma Press
    Perma Press AB
    Italy
    [Automotive]

9   Picard
    Picard Surgelés
    France
    [Food & Beverage]

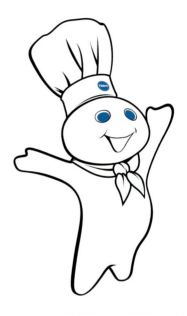

Picasa
Google Inc
USA
[Computer Software]

Citroën Picasso
Automobiles Citroën,
PSA Peugeot Citroën
France
[Automotive]

Pier 1 Imports Inc
USA
[Retail]

4   Pierce
Pierce Manufacturing Inc
USA
[Safety & Security]

5   Piggly Wiggly
Southern Family Markets, C&S
Wholesale Grocers
USA
[Retail]

6   Pikolin
Pikolin SA
Spain
[Manufacturing]

7   Pillsbury
The Pillsbury Company,
General Mills Inc
USA
[Food & Beverage]

8   Pillsbury Doughboy
The Pillsbury Company,
General Mills Inc
USA, 1965
Leo Burnett: Rudy Perz,
Martin Nodell
[Food & Beverage]

9   Pilot Pen
Pilot Corporation
Japan
[Writing Products]

10 PING
Karsten Manufacturing
Corporation
USA
[Sporting Goods]

PININFARINA

1 **Pininfarina**
Pininfarina SpA
Italy
[Automotive]

2 **Pink Floyd (The Wall)**
UK, 1979
Gerald Scarfe
[Music]

3 **Pinnacle Systems**
Avid Technology Inc
USA
[Film Industry]

4 **Pinterest**
Pinterest Inc
USA
[Internet]

5 **Pioneer**
Pioneer Corporation
Japan, 1998
[Consumer Electronics]

6 **PIP (Postal Instant Press)**
Postal Instant Press Inc
USA
[Printing Services]

7 **Piper Aircraft**
Piper Aircraft Inc, Imprimis
USA
[Aerospace]

8 **Piper Cub**
Piper Aircraft Corporation
USA, 1938
[Aviation]

9 **Piperlime**
Gap Inc
USA, 2006
Pentagram
[Fashion]

10 **Pirelli**
Pirelli & C. SpA
Italy, 1945
[Automotive]

PLANTERS

  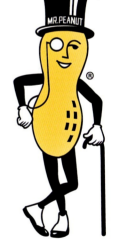

Pitney Bowes
Pitney Bowes Inc
USA
[Computer Technology]

Pixar
Pixar Animation Studios
USA, ca 1995
[Film Industry]

Piz Buin
Cilag GmbH International,
Division Greiter
Switzerland
[Personal Care]

▶ 4 **Pizza Hut**
Pizza Hut Inc, Yum! Brands Inc
USA, 1967
Lippincott & Margulies
[Restaurants & Bars]

5 **Pizza Hut**
Pizza Hut Inc, Yum! Brands Inc
USA, 1999
[Restaurants & Bars]

6 **Plan B Skateboards**
USA
[Sporting Goods]

7 **Planet Hollywood**
Planet Hollywood
International Inc
USA
[Restaurants & Bars]

8 **Plannja**
Plannja AB
Sweden
[Industrial Products]

▶ 9 **Planters**
Kraft Foods Inc
USA
[Food & Beverage]

▶ 10 **Planters mascot (Mr. Peanut)**
Kraft Foods Inc
USA, 1914–16
Antonio Gentile
[Food & Beverage]

535

PLASTICS USA

1
2
3
4

5

6

7

8

9

10

1 **Plastics USA**
USA
[Chemicals & Materials]

2 **Plastimo**
Navimo Group
France
[Marine]

3 **Plâtres Lambert**
Gyproc, Saint-Gobain
Construction Products
Belgium NV SA
Belgium
[Industrial Products]

4 **Plaxo**
Plaxo Inc
USA
[Internet]

5 **Playboy**
USA, 1953
Art Paul
[Publications]

6 **Playboy**
USA, 1953
Art Paul
[Publications]

7 **Play.com**
Play Ltd
UK
[Internet]

8 **Play-Doh**
Hasbro Inc
USA
[Toys, Games & Models]

9 **Playmobil**
Geobra Brandstätter
GmbH & Co. KG
Germany
[Toys, Games & Models]

10 **Playskool**
Playskool Corporation,
Hasbro Inc
USA
[Toys, Games & Models]

1 **PlayStation**
Sony Computer Entertainment Inc
Japan, 1994
Manabu Sakamoto, Sony
[Computer & Video Games]

2 **PlayStation 2**
Sony Computer Entertainment Inc
Japan, 2000
[Computer & Video Games]

3 **PlayStation 3**
Sony Computer Entertainment Inc
Japan
[Computer & Video Games]

4 **Playtex**
Playtex Products Inc,
Energizer Holdings Inc
USA
[Apparel]

5 **Plus**
Picture Licensing Universal System
USA, 2005
Pentagram
[Societies & Associations]

6 **Plus**
Plus Retail BV
Netherlands
[Retail]

7 **Plus**
Visa Inc
USA
[Financial Services]

8 **Plymart**
Ply Marts Inc
USA
[Retail]

9 **PMU**
France
[Leisure & Entertainment]

1. **PO (Petrol Ofisi)**
   OMV Petrol Ofisi AS
   Turkey
   [Oil, Gas & Petroleum]

2. **PocketCard**
   USA, 1999
   Segura Inc: Carlos Segura,
   Tnop Wangsillapakun
   [Financial Services]

3. **Pohjola**
   Pohjola Insurance Ltd
   Finland
   [Financial Services]

4. **Point.P**
   France
   [Construction]

5. **Pokémon**
   Pokémon Company
   Japan
   [Computer & Video Games]

6. **Polar**
   Polar Electro Oy
   Finland
   [Fitness & Wellbeing]

7. **Polar Ice Vodka**
   Corby Distilleries Ltd
   Canada
   [Wines, Beers & Spirits]

8. **Polaris**
   Polaris Industries
   USA
   [Automotive]

9. **Polaroid**
   Polaroid Corporation,
   PLR IP Holdings LLC
   USA, ca 1976
   Paul Giambarba
   [Imaging & Photographic]

10. **Polaroid**
    Polaroid Corporation,
    PLR IP Holdings LLC
    USA
    Paul Giambarba
    [Imaging & Photographic]

1. **Polar Pilsen**
Empresas Polar
Venezuela
[Wines, Beers & Spirits]

2. **Polartec**
Polartec LLC, Chrysalis Capital Partners
USA, 1997
Jorgensen Quint
[Fabrics & Textiles]

3. **Pôle emploi**
France, ca 2008
[Government]

4. **Police Fédérale/ Federale Politie**
Belgium, 2003
Hoet & Hoet
[Safety & Security]

▶ 5. **Police Sunglasses**
De Rigo SpA
Italy
[Eyewear]

6. **Polizei Hamburg**
Germany, 2004
Peter Schmidt Group
[Safety & Security]

7. **Pollo Rico**
Molinos de Nicaragua SA
Nicaragua
[Food & Beverage]

8. **Polo Jeans Company**
Ralph Lauren Corporation
USA
[Fashion]

9. **Polo Sur**
Les Yeux Wines
Argentina, 2008
Boldrini & Ficcardi
[Food & Beverage]

pomona
POND'S

Pont-Aven School of Contemporary Art

popular science

PORTER ◆ CABLE

PORSCHE

1. **Polskie Radio**
Polskie Radio SA
Poland, 2004
Studio P: Andrzej Pągowski
[Broadcaster]

2. **Polydor Records**
Universal Music Group
Germany
[Music Industry]

3. **Pomona**
Groupe Pomona
France
[Freight & Logistics]

4. **Pond's**
Unilever plc/NV
UK/Netherlands
[Personal Care]

5. **Pont-Aven School of Contemporary Art**
USA, 2008
Pentagram
[Education]

6. **Pontiac**
General Motors Company
USA, 2006
[Automotive]

7. **Pop**
USWC (Union Sky Wine Company Limited)
China
[Wines, Beers & Spirits]

8. **Popular Science**
Bonnier Corporation
USA
[Publications]

9. **Porsche**
Porsche Automobil Holding SE
Germany
[Automotive]

10. **Porter-Cable**
Porter-Cable, The Black & Decker Corporation
USA
[Tools & Machinery]

POSTEN AB

Porto Cruz
CEPP
Portugal
[Wines, Beers & Spirits]

Port-O-Let
Port-O-Let International Inc
USA
[Industry]

Porto Seguro
Porto Seguro Seguros SA
Brazil
[Financial Services]

4 **Posca**
Mitsubishi Pencil Co UK Ltd
Japan
[Writing Products]

5 **POSCO**
Pohang Iron and Steel
Company (POSCO)
South Korea
[Industry]

6 **Post**
Post Holdings Inc
USA
[Food & Beverage]

7 **Postbank**
Deutsche Postbank AG
Germany
[Financial Services]

8 **Postbank NV**
Netherlands
[Financial Services]

9 **Post Danmark**
Post Danmark A/S
Denmark, 1993
Studio Dumbar, Kontrapunkt
[Mail Services]

10 **Posten AB**
Posten AB,
PostNorden AB
Sweden
[Mail Services]

541

POSTGRESQL

1

2

3

4

5

6

7

8

9

10

1. **PostgreSQL**
   PostgreSQL Global Development Group
   USA
   [Computer Software]

2. **Post-It**
   3M Company
   USA
   [Consumer Products]

3. **Post Office Ltd**
   UK
   [Mail Services]

4. **Potlach Corporation**
   USA
   [Agricutural]

5. **Chocolat Poulain**
   Cadbury France
   France
   [Food & Beverage]

6. **Powell Peralta**
   USA
   [Sporting Goods]

7. **Powell Peralta**
   USA
   [Sporting Goods]

8. **Powerade**
   The Coca-Cola Company
   USA
   [Food & Beverage]

9. **PowerBar**
   Nestlé SA
   USA
   [Food & Beverage]

10. **Powerflush Ltd**
    UK
    [Heating & Cooling]

PowerPC
IBM
USA, 1992
[Computer Technology]

POW-MIA (Prisoners of War/ Missing in Action)
National League of POW/MIA Families
USA
William Graham Wilkin III
[Foundations & Institutes]

Pöyry
Pöyry PLC, Vantaa
Finland
[Engineering]

4 **PPSEC Accredited**
Private Post Secondary Education Commission
Canada
[Education]

5 **Prada**
Prada SpA
Italy
[Fashion]

6 **Praktiker**
Praktiker Bau-und Heimwerkermärkte Holding AG
Germany, 1978
[Retail]

7 **Pramac Group**
Pramac Group SpA
Italy
[Electronics]

8 **Pratt & Whitney Canada**
United Technologies Corporation
Canada
[Aerospace]

9 **Preciosa**
Preciosa AS
Czech Republic
[Glass & Ceramics]

PRECISION LOCKER

Prestone

PRIMARK

1 **Precision Locker Company**
USA
[Safety & Security]

2 **Premier Cruise Lines**
Premier Cruises
USA
[Travel & Tourism]

3 **Premier League**
The Football Association
Premier League Ltd
UK
[Sport]

4 **Premier Research Group**
USA
[Healthcare]

5 **Prestone**
Prestone Products Corporation,
FRAM Group IP LLC
USA
[Automotive]

6 **Pret A Manger**
Pret A Manger (Europe) Ltd
UK, ca 1986
[Restaurants & Bars]

7 **Prevent Child Abuse America**
USA
[Societies & Associations]

8 **Primark**
Primark Stores Ltd,
Associated British Foods plc
Ireland
[Retail]

9 **Primedia**
Primedia Ltd
South Africa
[Media]

Prince
Prince Sports Inc
USA
[Sporting Goods]

Princess Cruises
Carnival Corporation & PLC
USA
[Travel & Tourism]

Princeton University Art Museum
USA, 2005
Pentagram
[Galleries & Museums]

Princeton University Press
Princeton University
USA, 2007
Chermayeff & Geismar
[Publishing]

Principal Financial
Principal Financial Group Inc
USA
Lippincott
[Financial Services]

Pringles
Diamond Foods Inc
USA, 1996
[Food & Beverage]

Pringles
Diamond Foods Inc
USA, 2002
[Food & Beverage]

Pringles
Diamond Foods Inc
USA
[Food & Beverage]

Prinsel
Mexico
[Baby Products]

PRITT

1

2

3

4

5
Prospect Park  Alliance

6
PRO-TEC

7

8

9

1   **Pritt**
    Henkel AG & Co. KGaA
    Germany
    [Consumer Products]

2   **Progress Energy**
    USA
    [Utilities]

3   **ProSieben**
    ProSiebenSat.1 Digital GmbH
    Germany, 1994
    [Television Channel]

4   **ProSiebenSat.1**
    ProSiebenSat.1 Media AG
    Germany
    [Conglomerate]

5   **Prospect Park Alliance**
    USA
    [Conservation & Environment]

6   **Pro-tec**
    Vans Inc
    USA
    [Sporting Goods]

7   **Protective Life Corporation**
    USA
    [Financial Services]

8   **Protest Boardwear**
    Dekker Olifanta BV
    Netherlands
    [Apparel]

9   **Proton**
    Proton Holdings Bhd
    Malaysia
    [Automotive]

1. **Prudential Insurance Company of America**
Prudential Financial Inc
USA, 1990
Siegel+Gale
[Financial Services]

2. **PSL (Polskie Stronnictwo Ludowe/ Polish People's Party)**
Poland
[Political]

3. **PTT Post**
Netherlands
[Mail Services]

4. **Public Enemy**
USA, 1986
Carlton Douglas Ridenhour
(aka Chuck D)
[Music]

5. **Publicis Groupe**
France
[Advertising & Campaigns]

6. **Publix**
Publix Super Markets Inc
USA
[Retail]

7. **Puffin Books**
Penguin Group, Pearson plc
UK, 2003
Pentagram
[Publishing]

8. **Puget**
France
[Food & Beverage]

9. **Pukka-Pies**
Pukka-Pies Ltd
UK
[Food & Beverage]

Pulco
Orangina Schweppes France
France
[Food & Beverage]

Pull-Ups
Kimberly-Clark Worldwide Inc
USA
[Baby Products]

Pull-Ups
Kimberly-Clark Worldwide Inc
USA
[Baby Products]

Pulp
UK
[Music]

Pulsar
Seiko Watch Corporation
of America (SCA)
USA
[Watches & Jewelry]

Puma
Puma SE
Germany, 1967
Lutz Backes
[Sporting Goods]

Pumas de la UNAM
(Club Universidad Nacional AC)
Mexico
[Sport]

Pumper Nic
Argentina, 1980s
[Restaurants & Bars]

Pump Records
Dino Entertainment
USA
[Music Industry]

Purina
Purina Mills LLC,
Land O'Lakes Inc
USA
[Pet Products]

Purolator Courier
Purolator Courier Ltd
Canada
[Mail Services]

Purolator
Purolator Courier Ltd
Canada
[Automotive]

Putoline Oil
Netherlands
[Automotive]

Putzmeister
Putzmeister Concrete
Pumps GmbH
Germany
[Industrial Products]

PYE
Pye Ltd, Koninklijke Philips
Electronics NV
UK
[Electronics]

Pyrex
Corning Inc, Arc International
USA
[Glass & Ceramics]

Q8

1 **Q8**
Kuwait Petroleum Corporation
Kuwait, 1986
Wolff Olins
[Retail]

2 **Qantas**
Qantas Airways Ltd
Australia, 2008
[Airline]

3 **Qatar Airways**
Qatar Airways QCSC,
Government of Qatar
Qatar, 2006
[Airline]

4 **Qiagen**
Qiagen NV
Netherlands
[Technology]

5 **QinetiQ**
Qinetiq Group plc
UK
[Defence]

6 **QLogic**
QLogic Corporation
USA
[Computer Hardware]

7 **Q Magazine**
Bauer Verlagsgruppe GmbH
UK, 1986
[Publications]

8 **Qooq**
société Unowhy
France
[Internet]

9 **QR Queensland Rail**
Queensland Government
Australia, 2010
Cornwall Design
[Transport]

10 **QSC Audio**
QSC Audio Products LLC
USA, 2002
[Electronics]

QUANTUM

1 **QSound Labs**
QSound Labs Inc
Canada
[Technology]

2 **Quadriga**
Austria
[Financial Services]

3 **Quaker Oats**
Quaker Oats Company,
Pepsico Inc
USA, 1957
Haddon Sundblom
[Food & Beverage]

4 **Quaker Oats**
Quaker Oats Company,
PepsiCo Inc
USA, 1971
Saul Bass
[Food & Beverage]

▶ 5 **Quaker Oats**
Quaker Oats Company,
PepsiCo Inc
USA, 2010
Wallace Church
[Food & Beverage]

6 **Quaker State**
(SOPUS Products) Pennzoil
Quaker State Company
USA
[Automotive]

7 **Quaker State**
SOPUS Products,
Pennzoil Quaker State Company
USA
[Automotive]

8 **Qualibat**
France
[Construction]

9 **Qualcomm**
Qualcomm Inc
USA
[Telecommunications]

10 **Quality Hotel**
Singapore
[Hospitality]

11 **Quantum Corporation**
USA
[Data Storage]

QUARK

1. **Quark**
Quark Inc
USA, 2005
SicolaMartin (Young & Rubicam)
[Computer Software]

2. **Quark**
Quark Inc
USA, 2006
Quark
[Computer Software]

3. **Quasar**
Quasar Electronics Inc
USA
[Electronics]

4. **Quebramar**
Portugal
[Apparel]

5. **Queen**
UK, 1970s
Freddie Mercury
[Music]

6. **Quelle**
Quelle GmbH
Germany
[Retail]

7. **Que Publishing**
Pearson Education,
Pearson plc
USA
[Publishing]

8. **Quercetti**
Quercetti & C. SpA
Italy
[Toys, Games & Models]

9. **Questar**
Questar Corporation
USA, 1998
[Oil, Gas & Petroleum]

10. **Quick**
SA Quick Restaurants
France
[Restaurants & Bars]

QWEST

Quick Brake
OJD Quick Brake ApS
Denmark
[Automotive]

Quick Chek
Quick Chek Food Stores Inc
USA, 2008
Lippincott
[Retail]

Quick meals
Russia
Alexey Shelepov
[Food & Beverage]

4 **QuickTime**
Apple Inc
USA
[Computer Technology]

5 **Quik Print**
USA
[Printing Services]

6 **Quiksilver**
Quiksilver Inc
USA
[Outdoor & Recreation]

7 **Quiksilver**
Quiksilver Inc
USA
[Outdoor & Recreation]

8 **Quito**
Municipality of Quito
Ecuador, 2009
[Places]

9 **Qume**
Wyse Technology Inc
USA
[Consumer Electronics]

10 **QVC**
QVC, Liberty Media Corporation
USA, 2007
[Television Channel]

11 **Qwest**
Qwest Communications International Inc
USA, 1998
Enterprise IG
[Telecommunications]

R-T

RABOBANK

1 **Rabobank**
Rabobank Groep NV
Netherlands, 2010
Edenspiekermann
[Financial Services]

2 **RAC**
RAC plc
UK, 1997
North
[Automotive]

3 **Radeberger**
Dr. August Oetker KG
Germany
[Wines, Beers & Spirits]

4 **Radioactive (Hazard symbol)**
USA
[Labelling, Standards & Certification]

5 **Radio-Québec**
Canada
[Radio Stations]

6 **RadioShack**
RadioShack Corporation
USA, 1996
Landor Associates
[Retail]

7 **Radisson Hotels**
The Carlson Rezidor Hotel Group
USA
[Hospitality]

8 **Radura**
Netherlands, 1960s
[Labelling, Standards & Certification]

9 **RAF (Red Army Faction)**
Baader-Meinhof Group
Germany
[Political]

Raid
S.C. Johnson & Son Inc
USA
[Household Products]

Rainforest Alliance Certified
Rainforest Alliance
USA
[Labelling, Standards & Certification]

Rain-X
SOPUS Products,
Royal Dutch Shell plc
Netherlands
[Automotive]

RAI (Resource America Inc)
USA
[Financial Services]

Raisio Group
Finland
[Food & Beverage]

Ralliart
Ralliart Inc, Mitsubishi Motors Corporation
Japan, 1984
[Motorsport]

Rally's
Checkers Drive-In Restaurants Inc
USA
[Restaurants & Bars]

Ralph Lauren
Ralph Lauren Corporation
USA
[Fashion]

Ralphs
The Kroger Company
USA
[Retail]

1 **RAM Golf**
Ram Golf Corporation
USA
[Sporting Goods]

2 **Rammstein**
Rammstein GbR
Germany, 2001
Dirk Rudolph
[Music]

3 **Ramones**
USA, 1970s
Arturo Vega
[Music]

4 **Randalls**
Safeway Inc
USA
[Retail]

5 **Rand Merchant Bank**
FirstRand Bank Ltd
South Africa
[Financial Services]

6 **Randstad**
Randstad Holding NV
Netherlands, 1967
Total Design: Ben Bos
[Professional Services]

7 **Randy's Donuts**
USA, 1950
[Restaurants & Bars]

8 **RATP Group (Régie Autonome des Transports Parisiens)**
France
[Transport]

9 **Ravensburger**
Ravensburger AG
Germany, 1974
[Toys, Games & Models]

Rawlings
Rawlings Sporting Goods
Company Inc, Jarden Corporation
USA
[Sporting Goods]

Ray-Ban
Luxottica Group SpA
Italy
[Eyewear]

Raybestos
Affinia Group
USA, 1900s
[Automotive]

4 **Ray Cook Golf**
RockBottomGolf.com
USA
[Sporting Goods]

5 **Rayovac**
Rayovac Corporation
USA, 2002
[Consumer Products]

6 **Raytheon**
Raytheon Company
USA
[Defence]

7 **RBB**
Rundfunk Berlin-Brandenburg
Germany, 2003
DMC Group
[Broadcaster]

8 **RBC (Royal Bank of Canada)**
RBC Financial Group
Canada, 2001
[Financial Services]

9 **RBK**
Reebok International Ltd,
adidas AG
UK, 2006
Arnell Group
[Sporting Goods]

RBS (Royal Blind Society)
UK
[Societies & Associations]

RCA
RCA Trademark Management SA, Technicolor SA
USA, 1969
[Music Industry]

RCA (Nipper the dog)
RCA Corporation
USA, 1977
[Music Industry]

RCA Records
Sony Music Entertainment Inc
USA, 1988
[Music Industry]

RDS Radio Data System
European Broadcasting Union, British Broadcasting Corporation, National Association of Broadcasters
UK/USA
BBC
[Labelling, Standards & Certification]

Reading Matters
UK
Brahm
[Charity]

Reading Rainbow
Public Broadcasting Service (PBS)
USA, 1983
[Broadcaster]

Real,-
Metro AG
Germany
[Retail]

Real California Cheese
California Milk Producers Advisory Board
USA
[Labelling, Standards & Certification]

RealChat Software
USA
[Computer Software]

RECKITT BENCKISER

REAL SIMPLE

Republic steel

RECKITT BENCKISER

Real Madrid Club de Fútbol
Spain, 2001
[Sport]

RealPlayer
RealNetworks Inc
USA
[Computer Software]

Real Simple
Time Inc
USA, 2000
[Publications]

Realtor
National Association of Realtors
USA
[Societies & Associations]

Realty World
Realty World Inc
USA
[Real Estate]

Rearden Commerce
Rearden Commerce Inc
USA
[Computer Software]

Rebasa
Refractarios Basicos SA de CV
Mexico
[Industrial Products]

Rebublic Steel
USA
[Industrial Products]

Reckitt Benckiser
Reckitt Benckiser plc
UK, 1999
[Consumer Products]

Reckitt Benckiser
Reckitt Benckiser plc
UK, 2009
The Workroom
[Consumer Products]

RECLAIM THE MEDIA

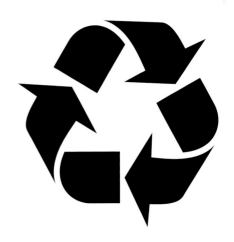

1 **Reclaim the Media**
  USA
  [Political]

2 **Record**
  Cofina Media
  Portugal, 2003
  [Media]

3 **Record Makers**
  France , 2000
  Alexandre Courtes
  [Music Industry]

4 **Record Town**
  Trans World Entertainment
  Corporation
  USA
  [Retail]

5 **Recycle**
  UK
  Gardiner Richardson
  [Labelling, Standards
  & Certification]

6 **Recycling Symbol**
  USA, 1970
  Gary Anderson
  [Labelling, Standards
  & Certification]

7 **Redbook**
  Hearst Corporation
  USA
  [Publications]

8 **Red Bull**
  Red Bull GmbH
  Thailand/Austria
  [Food & Beverage]

9 **Red Crescent**
  International Red Cross
  and Red Crescent Movement
  Switzerland
  [Foundations & Institutes]

10 **Red Cross**
   International Red Cross
   and Red Crescent Movement
   Switzerland, 1863
   Guillaume-Henri Dufour,
   Henry Dunant, Louis Appia
   [Foundations & Institutes]

RED RIVER SUPPLY

1. Red Crystal
   (the third Protocol emblem)
   Magen David Adom, International Red Cross and Red Crescent Movement
   Israel, 2005
   [Foundations & Institutes]

   reddit
   Condé Nast Digital, Advance Magazine Publishers Inc
   USA
   [Internet]

3. red dot design award
   red dot GmbH & Co. KG
   Germany
   [Design]

4. Rede Globo
   Organizações Globo
   Brazil, 2008
   Hans Donner
   [Media]

5. Red Hat (Shadowman logo)
   Red Hat Inc
   USA, 1990s
   [Computer Software]

6. Red Hot Chilli Peppers
   (Star of Affinity logo)
   Bravado International Group Merchandising Services Inc
   USA
   Anthony Kiedis
   [Music]

7. Redken
   L'Oréal SA
   USA
   [Health & Beauty]

8. Red Lion Hotels
   Red Lion Hotels Corporation
   USA
   [Hospitality]

9. Redman Homes
   Redman Homes Inc
   USA
   [Construction]

10. Red River Supply
    Red River Supply Inc
    USA
    [Retail]

RED ROOF INN

1 **Red Roof Inn**
Citigroup Global Special Situations Group, Westbridge Hospitality Fund LP
USA
[Hospitality]

2 **Redskins**
Washington Redskins
USA, 1970
[Sport]

3 **Red Star of David**
Magen David Adom, International Red Cross and Red Crescent Movement
Israel
[Foundations & Institutes]

4 **Red Stripe**
Desnoes & Geddes Ltd, Diageo plc
Jamaica
[Wines, Beers & Spirits]

5 **Reebok**
Reebok International Ltd, Adidas AG
UK, 1986
[Sporting Goods]

6 **Reebok**
Reebok International Ltd, Adidas AG
UK, 2008
[Sporting Goods]

7 **Reed**
Reed Specialist Recruitment Ltd
UK
[Professional Services] Company

8 **Refco**
Refco Inc
USA
[Financial Services]

9 **Regions Bank**
Regions Financial Corporation
USA
[Financial Services]

10 **Registered Trademark**
U.S. Patent and Trademark Office
USA
[Labelling, Standards & Certification]

REI
Recreational Equipment Inc
USA
[Outdoor & Recreation]

Reka
Swiss Travel Fund, Reka Cooperative
Czech Republic
[Financial Services]

Reliance
Reliance Group
India, 2006
Landor Associates
[Conglomerate]

Reliance Life Insurance
Reliance Life Insurance Company Limited
India
[Financial Services]

Rema 1000
Reitangruppen AS
Norway
[Retail]

Remington
Spectrum Brands Inc
USA
[Personal Care]

Remington
Remington Arms Company LLC
USA
[Firearms]

Renault
Renault SA
France, 2007
[Automotive]

Renfe
Renfe Operadora
Spain, 1972
[Rail Transport]

Renk
Renk AG, MAN SE
Germany
[Automotive]

Rent-2-Own
USA, 1980s
[Retail]

RENT-A-WRECK

1 **Rent-A-Wreck**
Rent-A-Wreck of America Inc,
JJF Management Services
USA
[Car Rental]

2 **rent.com**
eBay Inc
USA, ca 2005
[Internet]

3 **Renu**
Bausch & Lomb Inc
USA, 2010
Pentagram: Paula Scher
[Personal Care]

4 **Reprise Records**
Warner Music Group (WMG)
USA, 1960s
[Music Industry]

5 **Repsol**
Repsol YPF SA
Spain
[Oil, Gas & Petroleum]

6 **Republic Services**
Republic Services Inc
USA
[Professional Services]

7 **Residence Inn by Marriott**
Marriott International Inc
USA
[Hospitality]

8 **Restricted (MPAA Movie Rating)**
Motion Picture Association
of America Inc (MPAA)
USA
[Labelling, Standards
& Certification]

9 **Retail Motor Industry
Federation (RMI)**
UK
[Societies & Associations]

10 **Reuters**
Thomson Reuters Corporation
UK
[Media]

11 **Revell**
Revell-Monogram Inc
USA, 2007
[Toys, Games & Models]

RFU ENGLAND RUGBY

REVLON

Revere Ware
World Kitchen LLC
USA
[Kitchenware]

Revigrés
Revigrés Lda
Portugal
[Glass & Ceramics]

Revlon
Revlon Inc, MacAndrews & Forbes Holdings Inc, FMR LLC
USA
Pentagram
[Health & Beauty]

Revlon Professional
The Colomer Group, Revlon Inc
USA
[Health & Beauty]

Revo
Luxottica Group SpA
Italy
[Eyewear]

Rexel
Rexel Group
France
[Electronics]

Rex Regional Express
Regional Express Pty Ltd
Australia, 2002
[Airline]

Rexton
SsangYong Motor Company
South Korea
[Automotive]

Reynolds Metals Company
Reynolds Group Holdings
USA
[Consumer Products]

RFM
France
[Radio Stations]

RFU England Rugby
UK
[Sport]

Rheem
Rheem Manufacturing Company
USA
[Oil, Gas & Petroleum]

Rhiga Royal Hotels
Rhiga Royal Hotels
Japan
[Hospitality]

Rhino Records
Rhino Entertainment Company, Warner Music Group
USA
[Music Industry]

Rhodia
Rhodia SA
France
[Chemicals & Materials]

RIAA
Recording Industry Association of America
USA
[Music Industry]

Ribogojstvo Goričar
Ribogojstvo Goričar d.o.o.
Slovenia
Borut Bizjak
[Food & Beverage]

Ricard
Ricard SA
France
[Beers & Spirits]

Richemont
Compagnie Financière Richemont SA
Switzerland
[Luxury Goods]

Ricoh
Ricoh Company Ltd
Japan
[Electronics]

RICS (Royal Institution of Chartered Surveyors)
UK
[Foundations & Institutes]

Riders
VF Corporation
USA
[Apparel]

Ridgid
Emerson Electric Company
USA
[Tools & Machinery]

Rieger
Rieger Kfz-Kunststoffteile, Design und Tuning GmbH
Germany
[Automotive]

Rieker
Rieker Holding AG
Germany/Switzerland
[Footwear]

Rifle
Super Rifle SpA
Italy
[Apparel]

Rīgas piena kombināts
Rīgas Piena kombināts JSC
Latvia
[Food & Beverage]

Riken
Michelin SCA
France
[Automotive]

Rimowa
Rimowa GmbH
Germany
[Consumer Products]

Rio 2007
XV Pan American Games Rio 2007
Brazil, 2003
Dupla Design
[Sporting Events]

Rio Offices
Brazil, 2004
Bruno Richter
[Real Estate]

Rip Curl
Rip Curl International Pty Ltd
Australia
[Sporting Goods]

Rita's
Rita's Franchise Company
USA
[Food & Beverage]

RITE AID

1 **Rite Aid**
Rite Aid Corporation
USA
[Retail]

2 **Ritter Sport**
Alfred Ritter GmbH & Co. KG
Germany
[Food & Beverage]

3 **Ritz Carlton Hotels**
The Ritz-Carlton Hotel Company LLC
USA
Cesar Ritz
[Hospitality]

4 **Ritz Crackers**
Nabisco, Kraft Foods Inc
USA
[Food & Beverage]

5 **Rivella**
Rivella AG
Switzerland, 2007
[Food & Beverage]

6 **Rizla+**
Imperial Tobacco Group plc
France
[Tobacco]

7 **RKO Pictures
(Radio-Keith-Orpheum)**
USA
[Film Industry]

8 **RM**
Rietze Automodelle GmbH & Co. KG
Germany
[Toys, Games & Models]

9 **RMN (Réunion des Musées Nationaux)**
France
[Galleries & Museums]

10 **R.M. Williams**
R.M. Williams Pty Ltd
Australia
[Apparel]

11 **RNN (Regional News Network)**
Regional News Network Compa
USA
[Television Network]

12 **Road Demon**
High Performance Industries Inc
USA
[Automotive]

Roadmaster Bike
Pacific Cycle Inc,
Dorel Industries Inc
USA
[Bicycles]

Roadmaster Drivers School
UK
[Education]

Roads Service
Department for Regional Development
UK
[Transport]

Robinson
TUI.com GmbH
Germany
[Outdoor & Recreation]

RoC
Johnson & Johnson Santé
Beauté France SAS
France
[Personal Care]

Roces
Roces Srl
Italy
[Sporting Goods]

Rochdale
The Netherlands, 2003
SoDesign
[Real Estate]

Roche
F. Hoffmann-La Roche Ltd,
Roche Holding AG
Switzerland
[Pharmaceuticals]

Roche Bobois
Roche Bobois International SAS
France
[Home Furnishings]

Rock and Roll – Hall of Fame and Museum
USA
[Galleries & Museums]

ROCKEFELLER CENTER

Rockefeller Center
Tishman Speyer Properties
USA, 1985
Chermayeff & Geismar
[Places]

Rocket Comics
Dark Horse Comics Inc
USA
[Publications]

Rockford Fosgate
Rockford Corporation
USA
[Consumer Electronics]

Rock 'n' Roll High School
USA, 1979
[Film]

Rock Oil
Rock Oil Ltd
UK
[Chemicals & Materials]

Rockport Publishers
Quarto Group Inc
USA
[Publishing]

Rockstar Games
Rockstar Games Inc,
Take-Two Interactive Software Inc
USA
[Computer & Video Games]

Rockwell
Rockwell International
USA
Saul Bass (original mark)
[Conglomerate]

Rockwell Automation
USA, 2001
[Industrial Products]

Rockwell Collins
Rockwell Collins Inc
USA, 2006
BrandLogic: Randell Holder,
Fredy Jaggi, Gene Grossman
[Aerospace]

Rocky
Rocky Brands Inc
USA
[Footwear]

Rodeway Inn
Choice Hotels International Inc
USA
[Hospitality]

Röd Press
Sweden
[Publications]

Rogers
Rogers Communications Inc
Canada
[Media]

Rohn and Haas
Rohn and Haas Company,
The Dow Chemical Company
USA
[Chemicals & Materials]

Roland
Roland Corporation
Japan
[Musical Instruments]

Rolex
Rolex SA
Switzerland
[Watches & Jewelry]

Rollei
Rollei GmbH
Germany
[Imaging & Photographic]

Rollerblade
Nordica, Tecnica Group
Italy
[Outdoor & Recreation]

Rolling Stone
Wenner Media LLC
USA, 1977
Jim Parkinson
[Publications]

Rollitos
Frito-Lay North America Inc,
PepsiCo Inc
USA
[Food & Beverage]

ROLLS-ROYCE

1 **Rolls-Royce**
Rolls-Royce Group plc
UK
Tatham Pearce
[Aerospace]

2 **Rolodex**
Newell Rubbermaid Inc
USA
[Office Supplies]

3 **Romi**
Indústrias Romi
Brazil, 1972
Cauduro Martino
[Tools & Machinery]

4 **Romika**
Josef Seibel Group
Germany
[Footwear]

5 **Ronald McDonald**
McDonalds Corporation
USA, ca 1967
Barry Klein
[Restaurants & Bars]

6 **Ronald McDonald**
McDonalds Corporation
USA, ca 1967
Barry Klein
[Restaurants & Bars]

7 **Ronald McDonald House Charities**
McDonalds Corporation
USA
[Charity]

8 **Ronson**
Zippo Manufacturing Company
USA
[Manufacturing]

9 **Roots**
Roots Canada Ltd
Canada
[Apparel]

10 **Ropa Siete Leguas**
Ropa Siete Leguas SA de CV
Mexico
[Apparel]

11 **ros.gov.uk**
Registers of Scotland
UK, 2009
RR Donnelley
[Government]

Roskilde Bank
Denmark
[Financial Services]

Rossignol
Skis Rossignol SA
France, 2008
[Outdoor & Recreation]

Ross River Parkway
Townsville City Council
Australia
[Places]

Rotary International
USA, 1923
[Societies & Associations]

5 **Rotel**
Japan
[Consumer Electronics]

6 **Ro Theater**
Netherlands, 2009
75B
[Cinemas & Theatres]

7 **Roto**
Roto Frank AG
Germany, 2008
[Manufacturing]

8 **Rotork**
Rotork plc
UK
[Industrial Products]

9 **Roto-Rooter**
Roto-Rooter Group Inc
USA
[Domestic Services]

1. **Rotovision**
UK
[Publishing]

2. **Rotring**
Rotring, Newell Rubbermaid Inc
Germany, 1965
[Writing Products]

3. **Rover**
Jaguar Land Rover plc,
Tata Motors Ltd
UK
[Automotive]

4. **Rowenta**
Groupe SEB
Germany
[Consumer Electronics]

5. **Royal**
Kraft Foods Inc
Spain
[Food & Beverage]

6. **Royal Air Force**
UK, 1947
[Defence]

7. **Royal Canin**
Royal Canin SAS, Mars Inc
France
[Pet Products]

8. **Royal Caribbean International**
Royal Caribbean Cruises Ltd
Norway/USA
[Travel & Tourism]

9. **Royal Life Saving Society**
Australia
[Societies & Associations]

Royal Mail
Royal Mail Holdings plc
UK, 1990
[Mail Services]

Royal Wear
France
[Apparel]

Royco
Unilever plc/NV
South Africa
[Food & Beverage]

RSA
EMC Corporation
USA
[Computer Technology]

RT (Russia Today)
Russian International News Agency, RIA Novosti
Russia, ca 2009
[Television Channel]

RTL
RTL Group SA
Germany, 1992
GRFX/Novocom
[Television Channel]

RTL
RTL Nederland, RTL Group
Netherlands, 2005
[Television Channel]

RTL 4
RTL Nederland, RTL Group
Netherlands, 2005
[Television Channel]

RTL 7
RTL Nederland, RTL Group
Netherlands, 2010
OOQ
[Television Channel]

RTL GROUP

1 **RTL Group**
RTL Group SA
Luxembourg
[Conglomerate]

2 **RTL Z**
RTL Group SA
Belgium
[Television Programme]

3 **Rubbermaid**
Newell Rubbermaid Inc
USA
[Consumer Products]

4 **Ruger**
Sturm, Ruger & Company Inc
USA
[Firearms]

5 **Run–D.M.C.**
USA
[Music]

6 **Rural Centro**
Brazil
[Agricultural]

7 **Rush**
Pac West Distributing Inc
USA
[Freight & Logistics]

8 **Russell Athletic**
Russell Brands LLC
USA
[Sporting Goods]

9 **Russell Athletic**
Russell Brands LLC
USA
[Sporting Goods]

10 **Russian Football Union**
Russia
[Sport]

11 **Russian Post**
Russia
[Mail Services]

Russian Railways
Russia, 2007
[Transport]

Ruud
Ruud Heating, Cooling
& Water Heating
USA
[Heating & Cooling]

Ruukki
Rautaruukki Oyj
Finland
[Construction]

4 **RWE**
RWE AG
Germany, 2008
Jung von Matt
[Utilities]

5 **RWS Rotweill**
RUAG Ammotec GmbH
Germany
[Firearms]

6 **Rx**
USA
[Labelling, Standards
& Certification]

7 **Ryanair**
Ryanair Ltd
Ireland
[Airline]

8 **Ryba Ve Vodě**
Czech Republic, 2009
Jan Sabach Design
[Internet]

9 **Ryco Filters**
GUD Automotive Pty Ltd
Australia
[Automotive]

▶ 10 **Ryobi**
Ryobi Ltd
Japan
[Manufacturing]

S-BAHN

1. S-Bahn
Deutsche Bahn AG
Germany, 1930s
[Transport]

2. S-Bahn
ÖBB-Holding AG (SBB)
Austria
[Transport]

3. S7 Airlines
OJSC Siberia Airlines
Russia, 2005
Landor Associates
[Airline]

4. S&H Green Stamps
The Sperry and Hutchinson Company Inc
USA
[Retail]

5. S&H greenpoints
The Sperry and Hutchinson Company Inc
USA
[Retail]

6. Saab
Saab Automobile AB, Swedish Automobile NV
Sweden, 2000
[Automotive]

7. Saab-Scania
Saab-Scania AB
Sweden, 1984
Carl Frederik Reuterswärd
[Automotive]

8. Saatchi & Saatchi
Saatchi & Saatchi plc
UK
Saatchi & Saatchi
[Advertising & Campaigns]

9. Sabena
Sabena World Airlines
Belgium
[Airline]

10. SABMiller
SABMiller plc
UK
[Breweries]

SAGE

Sachs
ZF Sachs AG
Germany
[Automotive]

Saeco
Saeco International Group SpA
Italy
[Household Products]

Safeco Insurance
Safeco Insurance Company
of America
USA
[Financial Services]

Safe Place
National Safe Place
USA
[Societies & Associations]

Safescan
Netherlands
[Safety & Security]

Safety-Kleen
Safety-Kleen Systems Inc
USA
[Automotive]

Safeway
Safeway Inc
USA, ca 1999
[Retail]

Safeway
Safeway Inc
USA, 2005
[Retail]

SafeWay Hydraulics Inc
USA
[Industrial Products]

Sage
The Sage Group plc
UK
[Computer Software]

SAGEM

S A K S
F I F T H
A V E N U E

1 **SAGEM** (Société d'Applications Générales de l'Électricité et de la Mécanique)
France
[Telecommunications]

2 **Sagres Cerveja**
Sociedad Central de Cervejas e Bebidas SA, Heineken NV
Portugal
[Wines, Beers & Spirits]

3 **SAIC** (School of the Art Institute of Chicago)
USA
[Education]

4 **SAI Global**
SAI Global Ltd
Australia
[Professional Services]

5 **Sainsbury's**
J. Sainsbury plc
UK, 1999
M&C Saatchi
[Retail]

6 **Saint-Gobain**
Saint-Gobain SA
France
[Construction]

7 **Säkerhetspartner**
Säkerhetspartner AB
Sweden
[Security & Safety]

8 **Saks Fifth Avenue**
Saks Inc
USA, 1973
Vignelli Associates
[Retail]

9 **Saks Fifth Avenue**
Saks Inc
USA, 2007
Pentagram
[Retail]

SALTON SALTON INC

1 **Saku**
Saku Õlletehase AS
Estonia
[Breweries]

2 **Saldus Celinieks**
Saldus Celinieks Ltd
Latvia
[Construction]

3 **Salewa**
Oberalp SpA AG
Italy, 1979
[Outdoor & Recreational]

4 **Salisbury House**
Salisbury House of Canada Ltd
Canada
[Restaurants & Bars]

5 **Salitos Tequila**
Salitos Brewing Company
Panama
[Wines, Beers & Spirits]

6 **Sallie Mae**
Sallie Mae Inc
USA
[Financial Services]

7 **Salling Bank**
Salling Bank A/S
Denmark
[Financial Services]

8 **Salomon**
Salomon Group,
Amer Sports Oyj
France
[Sporting Goods]

9 **Salt Lake City Weekly**
Copperfield Publishing Inc
USA
[Media]

10 **Salton**
Salton Appliances (1985) Corp
Canada
USA
[Home Appliances]

SALVATORE ROBUSCHI

1 **Salvatore Robuschi**
Salvatore Robuschi & C. Srl
Italy
[Manufacturing]

2 **SAM**
SAM Group Holding AG
Switzerland
[Financial Services]

3 **Samro**
Samro SA
France
[Automotive]

4 **Samsøe & Samsøe**
Denmark
[Apparel]

5 **Samsonite**
Samsonite Corporation
USA
[Consumer Products]

6 **Samsung**
Samsung Group
South Korea, 1993
Lippincott & Margulies
[Conglomerate]

7 **Sanborns**
Grupo Sanborns SA de CV
Mexico
[Retail]

8 **SanDisk**
SanDisk Corporation
USA
[Computer Technology]

9 **SanDisk**
SanDisk Corporation
USA, 2007
MetaDesign
[Computer Technology]

10 **Sanford**
Sanford LP,
Newell Rubbermaid Inc
USA
[Writing Products]

SANWA BANK

Sanford Limited
New Zealand
[Food & Beverage]

San Francisco Chronicle
Hearst Corporation
USA
[Media]

Sanistal
Denmark
[Retail]

Sankyo America Inc
USA
[Manufacturing]

5 **Sansui**
Sansui Electric Co. Ltd
Japan
[Electronics]

6 **Santa Cruz Skateboards**
NHS Inc
USA
[Outdoor & Recreation]

7 **Santa Cruz Skateboards**
NHS Inc
USA, 1973
Jim Phillips
[Outdoor & Recreation]

8 **Santa Fe (The Atchison, Topeka and Santa Fe Railway)**
USA
[Transport]

9 **Santander**
Grupo Santander
Spain
Landor Associates
[Financial Services]

10 **Sanwa Bank**
Japan
[Financial Services]

585

1. **Sanyo**
   Sanyo Electric Co. Ltd
   Japan, 1970s
   [Electronics]

2. **Sanyo**
   Sanyo Electric Co. Ltd
   Japan, 1987
   [Electronics]

3. **São Paulo Petróleo**
   Brazil, 1986
   Alexandre Wollner
   [Oil, Gas & Petroleum]

4. **SAP**
   SAP AG
   Germany, ca 2000
   Frog Design
   [Computer Software]

5. **SAP**
   SAP AG
   Germany, 2011
   [Computer Software]

6. **SAPEC Agro**
   SAPEC Agro SA
   Portugal
   [Agricultural]

7. **Sappi**
   Sappi Ltd
   South Africa
   [Paper Products]

8. **Saputo**
   Saputo Inc
   Canada
   [Food & Beverage]

9. **Sara Lee**
   Sara Lee Corporation
   USA
   [Food & Beverage]

10. **Sarar**
    Sarar Giyim Sanayii Fabrika
    Turkey
    [Fashion]

SAUER DANFOSS

Sargent
Sargent Aerospace & Defense Inc
USA
[Aerospace]

Sarotti
Germany, 2004
Peter Schmidt Group
[Food & Beverages]

SAS
Scandinavian Airlines
Sweden, 1998
Stockholm Design Lab, TEArk
[Airline]

Sat.1
ProSiebenSat.1 Media AG
Germany, 2008
[Television Channel]

Sata
Brazil, 2003
PVDI Design
[Aviation]

Sata International
Groupo Sata
Portugal
[Airline]

Saturn
Saturn LLC, General Motors Company
USA, 1987
[Automotive]

Saturn
Media Saturn Holding, Metro AG
Germany, 1999
KMSTeam: Bruno Marek, Peta Kobrow
[Retail]

Saudi Arabian Airlines
Saudi Arabia, 2006
[Airline]

Sauer Danfoss
USA
[Manufacturing]

1. **Saunier Duval**
Vaillant GmbH
France
[Heating & Cooling]

2. **Sauter**
FagorBrandt SAS
France
[Home Appliances]

3. **Savin**
Savin Corporation,
Ricoh Company Ltd
Japan
[Office Supplies]

4. **Sav-On Drugs**
Osco Drug, Supervalu Inc
USA
[Retail]

5. **Saxo Bank**
Denmark
[Financial Services]

6. **Saxon Mutual Funds**
Mackenzie Financial Corporation
Canada
[Financial Services]

7. **SBAC (The Society of British Aerospace Companies)**
UK
[Societies & Associations]

8. **Sbarro**
Sbarro Inc/MidOcean Partners
USA
[Restaurants & Bars]

SBB CFF FFS
(Schweizerische Bundesbahnen)
Switzerland, 1978
Josef Müller-Brockmann,
Peter Spalinger
[Transport]

SBC
SBC Communications Inc
USA, 1995
[Telecommunications]

SCA Móveis
SCA Indústria de Móveis Ltda
Brazil
[Home Furnishings]

SCA (Svenska Cellulosa
Aktiebolaget)
Sweden, 1990
Pentagram
[Paper Products]

SCALA
SCALA Inc
USA
[Computer Software]

Scanbox Entertainment
Scanbox Entertainment Group A/S
Denmark
[Film Industry]

Scandale
France
[Apparel]

Scania
Scania AB
Sweden, 1995
[Automotive]

1. **Scarab**
Wellcraft LLC
USA
[Marine]

2. **Scarlets**
Scarlets Regional Ltd
UK
[Sport]

3. **Schering-Plough**
Schering-Plough Corporation
USA
[Pharmaceuticals]

4. **Schindler**
Schindler Management AG
Switzerland, 2006
[Industrial Products]

5. **Schindler**
The Schindler Group
Switzerland
[Manufacturing]

6. **Schlumberger**
Schlumberger Ltd
USA/France/Netherlands
[Professional Services]

7. **Schmidt**
Schmidt Beer
USA
[Wines, Beers & Spirits]

8. **Schneebergbahn**
Niederösterreichische
Schneebergbahn GmbH
Austria
[Transport]

9. **Schnucks**
USA
[Retail]

Schöffel
Schöffel Sportbekleidung GmbH
Germany
[Apparel]

Schott
Schott Boral dd
Croatia
[Glass & Ceramics]

Schuco
DICKIE Spielzeug GmbH & Co. KG
Germany
[Toys, Games & Models]

Schüco
Schüco International KG
Germany, 2003
Peter Schmidt Group
[Construction]

Schunk
Schunck GmbH & Co. KG
Germany
[Technology]

Schwalbe
Ralf Bohle GmbH
Germany
[Bicycles]

Schwartz
McCormick & Company Inc
Canada
[Food & Beverage]

Schwarzkopf
Henkel AG & Co. KGaA
Germany, 1937 (mark)
[Health & Beauty]

Schweizer Fernsehen
Switzerland, 2005
Dunning Eley Jones
[Television Network]

Schweppes
Dr Pepper Snapple Group Inc
UK
[Food & Beverage]

SCHWINN

1 **Schwinn**
Schwinn Bicycle Company
USA, ca 1940
[Bicycles]

2 **Schwinn**
Schwinn Bicycle Company
USA
[Bicycles]

3 **Schwinn Cycling**
Schwinn Bicycle Company
USA
[Fitness & Wellbeing]

4 **Schwinn (quality seal)**
Schwinn Bicycle Company
USA
[Labelling, Standards
& Certification]

5 **Science Museum**
UK, 2010
johnson banks: Michael Johnson,
Kath Tudball, Miho Aishima
[Galleries & Museums]

6 **Sci-Fi Channel**
NBCUniversal LLC
USA
[Television Channel]

7 **Scion**
Toyota Motor Corporation
USA
[Automotive]

8 **SC Johnson Wax**
S.C. Johnson & Son Inc
USA
[Household Products]

9 **Scorpion**
Fiat SpA
Italy
[Automotive]

10 **Scotch**
3M Company
USA
[Consumer Products]

Scotiabank
Bank of Nova Scotia
Canada
[Financial Services]

Scotland
Visit Scotland
UK
[Travel & Tourism]

Scott Sports
Scott Sports SA
Switzerland
[Bicycles]

Scott Products
Kimberly-Clark Worldwide Inc
USA
[Paper Products]

Scottish Arts Council
UK, 2001
Graven Images: Janice Kirkpatrick
[Foundations & Institutes]

Scottish Citylink
Scottish Citylink Coaches Ltd
UK
[Transport]

Scottish Equitable
Scottish Equitable plc
UK
[Financial Services]

SCOTTISH POWER

SCREAM

[scrubs]

1. **ScottishPower**
ScottishPower PLC
UK, 1990
[Utilities]

2. **Scotts Lawn Products**
Scotts Miracle-Gro Company
USA
[Household Products]

3. **Scotts Lawn Service**
Scotts Miracle-Gro Company
USA
[Professional Services]

4. **Scouts Canada**
Canada
[Societies & Associations]

5. **Scrabble**
Hasbro Inc
USA
[Toys, Games & Models]

6. **Scream (film)**
Woods Entertainment
USA, 1996
[Film]

7. **Screen Gems**
Sony Pictures Entertainment Inc
USA, 1966
Chermayeff & Geismar
[Film Industry]

8. **Scribner**
Simon & Schuster Inc
USA
[Publishing]

9. **Scrubs**
NBC (National Broadcasting Company)
USA, 2001
[Television Series]

10. **Scubapro**
Johnson Outdoors Inc
USA
[Marine]

11. **SD Card**
SD Card Association
USA
[Consumer Electronics]

SDGE (San Diego Gas & Electric)
Sempra Energy
USA
[Utilities]

SDP (Socijaldemokratska Partija Hrvatske/Social Democratic Party of Croatia)
Croatia
[Political]

Seagate
Seagate Technology LLC
USA, 2002
Landor Associates
[Computer Hardware]

Seagram's
Seagram Company Ltd, Pernod Ricard SA
Canada
[Wines, Beers & Spirits]

Sea Grant Oregon
National Oceanic and Atmospheric Administration, U.S. Department of Commerce
USA
[Education]

Sealed Air
Sealed Air Corporation
USA
[Chemicals & Materials]

Sealy
Sealy Corporation
USA
[Household Products]

Sears
Sears Holdings Corporation
USA
[Retail]

Sears
Sears Holdings Corporation
USA, 2004
[Retail]

SEAT

1. **Seat**
   Seat SA
   Spain
   Enterprise IG
   [Automotive]

2. **Seattle's Best Coffee**
   Starbucks Corporation
   USA, 2010
   Creature
   [Restaurants & Bars]

3. **SeaWorld**
   SeaWorld Parks & Entertainment,
   The Blackstone Group
   USA
   [Aquariums & Zoos]

4. **Secom**
   Secom Co. Ltd
   Japan
   [Safety & Security]

5. **Sector No Limits**
   Morellato SpA
   Italy
   [Watches & Jewelry]

6. **Securitas**
   Securitas AB
   Sweden
   [Professional Services]

7. **Securitas**
   Securitas AG
   Switzerland
   [Safety & Security]

8. **Seed Media Group**
   Seed Media Group LLC
   USA, 2005
   Sagmeister Inc: Stefan Sagmeister,
   Matthias Ernstberger
   [Media]

9. **See's Candies**
   See's Candy Shops Inc
   USA
   [Food & Beverage]

1. **SEGA**
SEGA Corporation
Japan
[Computer & Video Games]

2. **SEGA Saturn (Western logo)**
SEGA Corporation
Japan, 1995
[Computer & Video Games]

3. **SEGD (Society for Environmental Graphic Design)**
USA, 2009
Pentagram: Michael Gericke
[Societies & Associations]

4. **Seiko**
Seiko Holdings Corporation
Japan
[Watches & Jewelry]

5. **Seiko Instruments**
Seiko Instruments Inc, Seiko Holdings Corporation
Japan
[Electronics]

6. **Selectour Voyages**
France
[Travel & Tourism]

7. **Self**
Condé Nast, Advance Magazine Publishers Inc
USA
[Publications]

8. **Selfridges & Co**
Selfridges Retail Ltd
UK
[Retail]

9. **Selga**
Rexel
Sweden
[Freight & logistics]

10. **Selkirk**
Selkirk Corporation
USA/Canada
[Heating & Cooling]

11. **SEM**
SEM Products Inc
USA
[Paints & Coatings]

12. **Semcon**
Semcon AB
Sweden
[Automotive]

SENCO

1   **Senco**
    Senco Brands Inc
    USA
    [Tools & Machinery]

2   **Seneca**
    Seneca Foods Corporation
    USA
    [Food & Beverage]

3   **Senior Corps**
    Senior Corps, US Government
    USA
    [Government]

4   **Sennheiser**
    Sennheiser Electronic
    GmbH & Co. KG
    Germany
    [Electronics]

5   **SensoNor**
    SensoNor A/S,
    Infineon Technologies AG
    Norway
    [Technology]

6   **Senstar Stellar**
    USA
    [Safety & Security]

7   **Sentry Insurance**
    Sentry Group
    USA
    [Financial Services]

8   **Sentry Insurance**
    Sentry Group
    USA
    [Financial Services]

9   **SentrySafe**
    John D. Brush & Co
    USA
    [Manufacturing]

10 **Sequent Computer
    Systems Inc**
    USA
    [Computer Technology]

SETI INSTITUTE

Serie A
Lega Nazionale Professionisti
Serie AP
Italy, 2010
[Sport]

Serie A TIM
Lega Nazionale Professionisti
Serie AP
Italy, 2009
[Sport]

Serta
Serta Mattress Company
USA
[Household Products]

4 **Servior**
Luxembourg
[Healthcare]

5 **ServiStar**
American Hardware & Supply,
ServiStar
USA
[Retail]

▶ 6 **Servpro**
Servpro Industries Inc
USA
[Professional Services]

▶ 7 **Sesame Street**
Sesame Workshop
USA, 1998
[Television Programme]

8 **SES (Société Européenne des Satellites)**
SES SA
Luxembourg, 2011
MetaDesign
[Telecommunications]

9 **SETI Institute (Search for Extra Terrestrial Intelligence)**
USA, 1998
Turner Duckworth
[Foundations & Institutes]

599

1 **Severin**
Severin Elektrogeräte GmbH
Germany
[Home Appliances]

2 **Severstal**
OAO Severstal
Russia
[Industry]

3 **Sex Pistols**
UK, 1976
Jamie Reid
[Music]

4 **SFMOMA (San Francisco Museum of Modern Art)**
USA
[Galleries & Museums]

5 **SG Cowen**
Société Générale SA
USA, ca 1998
[Financial Services]

6 **SGI**
Silicon Graphics International Corporation
USA, 2009
[Computer Technology]

7 **SGL Carbon Group**
SGL Carbon AG
Germany
[Chemicals & Materials]

8 **Shaq (Shaquille O'Neal/ Payless Shoes TWisM)**
Collective Brands Inc
USA, 2005
Design Ranch: Michelle Sonderegger, Ingred Sidie, Michelle Martinowicz, Tad Carpenter
[Footwear]

9 **Shark Energy Drink**
Osotspa Co. Ltd
Thailand
[Food & Beverage]

Sharp
Sharp Corporation
Japan
[Consumer Electronics]

Sharpie
Newell Rubbermaid Inc
USA, 1964
[Writing Products]

Shaw
The Shaw Group Inc
USA
[Construction]

Shaw Communications
Shaw Communications inc
Canada, 1997
[Telecommunications]

Shaw's
SuperValu Inc
USA
[Retail]

SHCP (Secretaria de Hacienda Y credito Publico)
Finance Ministry
Mexico
[Government]

Sheaffer
BIC Corporation
USA
[Writing Products]

Shelby Cobra
AC Cars Group Ltd
UK
[Automotive]

Shell
Royal Dutch Shell plc
Netherlands/UK, 1971
Raymond Loewy
[Oil, Gas & Petroleum]

Shell Helix
Royal Dutch Shell plc
Netherlands/UK
[Automotive]

SHELTER

1	2

Shelter

SHIMANO

1 **Shelter**
UK, 2003
johnson banks
[Charity]

2 **Sheraton Hotels & Resorts**
Starwood Hotels and Resorts Worldwide Inc
USA
[Hospitality]

3 **Sherwin-Williams**
Sherwin-Williams Company
USA
[Paints & Coatings]

4 **Shimadzu**
Shimadzu Corporation
Japan
[Technology]

5 **Shimano**
Shimano Inc
USA
[Outdoor & Recreation]

6 **Shinkin Central Bank (SCB)**
Japan
[Financial Services]

7 **Shinko**
Image Pro International Inc
USA
[Imaging & Photographic]

8 **Shinko Shoji**
Shinko Shoji Co. Ltd
Japan
[Electronics]

9 **Shinsegae**
Shinsegae Corporation
South Korea
[Retail]

10 **Shinsei Bank**
Shinsei Bank Ltd
Japan
[Financial Services]

Silverstone
Octagon Motorsport
UK, 2003
Carter Wong Tomlin
[Sporting Events]

Simca (Société Industrielle de Mécanique et Carrosserie Automobile)
France
[Automotive]

Simmons
Simmons Bedding Company
USA, 1998
[Household Products]

Simple Signs
The Plastic Lumber Company Inc
USA
[Imaging & Photographic]

Sin City
Dark Horse Comics
USA, ca 1991
[Publications]

Sinclair
Sinclair Oil Corporation
USA
[Oil, Gas & Petroleum]

Singapore Airlines
Singapore, 1987
[Airline]

Singer
Singer Sewing Company
USA
[Tools & Machinery]

1 **Sinochem Corporation**
Sinochem Group
China
[Conglomerate]

2 **Sire Records**
Warner Music Group (WMG)
USA, 1960s
[Music]

3 **Sirius Satellite Radio**
Sirius XM Radio Inc
USA
[Radio Stations]

4 **Sirius XM Radio**
Sirius XM Radio Inc
USA
[Radio Stations]

5 **Sirloin Stockade**
Stockade Companies LLC
USA
[Restaurants & Bars]

6 **Sisley**
Bencom Srl
Italy, 1996
[Fashion]

7 **SITA**
Belgium
[Transport]

8 **Sixt**
Germany
[Car Rental]

9 **Skandia**
Skandia International,
Old Mutual plc
Sweden
[Financial Services]

Skandia
Skandia International,
Old Mutual plc
Sweden, 2008
[Financial Services]

Skanska
Skanska AB
Sweden
[Construction]

Skate America
USA
[Sporting Goods]

SKF
(Svenska Kullagerfabriken)
SKF AB
Sweden
[Manufacturing]

Skil
Robert Bosch Tool Corporation
USA
[Tools & Machinery]

Skillbond
Skillbond Direct Ltd
UK
[Medical Devices]

SkinCeuticals
L'Oréal Group
USA
[Personal Care]

Skippy
Unilever plc/NV
USA
[Food & Beverage]

Skittles
William Wrigley Jr. Company,
Mars Inc
USA
[Food & Beverage]

Skoal
Skoal Tobacco, US Smokeless
Tobacco Company
USA
[Tobacco]

ŠKODA

Škoda
Škoda Auto, Volkswagen Group
Czech Republic, 1994
[Automotive]

Škoda
Škoda Auto, Volkswagen Group
Czech Republic, 2011
[Automotive]

Skol
Anheuser-Busch InBev NV
Brazil
[Wines, Beers & Spirits]

SKS Germany
Germany
[Tools & Machinery]

Skullcandy
USA
[Consumer Electronics]

Sky Channel
British Sky Broadcasting Group plc
UK, 2010
Miles Newlyn
[Television Channel]

Skype
Skype Communications Sàrl,
Microsoft Corporation
Luxembourg
[Internet]

Skype icon
Skype Communications Sàrl,
Microsoft Corporation
Luxembourg
[Internet]

SkyTeam
Netherlands
[Transport]

SkyWest Airlines
SkyWest Airlines Inc
USA
[Airline]

Slazenger
Dunlop Slazenger International Ltd
UK
[Sporting Goods]

Sleep Inn
Choice Hotels International Inc
USA
[Hospitality]

Slick 50
SOPUS Products, Royal Dutch Shell plc
USA
[Automotive]

Slim-Fast
Unilever plc/NV
USA, 1970s
[Food & Beverage]

Slim-Fast
Unilever plc/NV
USA
[Food & Beverage]

Slim Jim
ConAgra Foods Inc
USA
[Food & Beverage]

Sloggi
Inter-Triumph Marketing-GmbH
Germany
[Apparel]

SLOVAKIA

Slovakia
Slovakia Tourist Board
Slovakia
[Travel & Tourism]

Slovnaft
Slovnaft as
Slovakia
[Oil, Gas & Petroleum]

Slow Food
Italy
[Societies & Associations]

S-Mart
Mexico
[Retail]

Smart
Daimler AG
Germany, 1994
[Automotive]

Smart
Daimler AG
Germany
[Automotive]

Smart & Final
Smart & Final Inc
USA
[Retail]

Smead
The Smead Manufacturing
Company Inc
USA
[Manufacturing]

Smead
The Smead Manufacturing
Company Inc
USA
[Manufacturing]

Smeg
Smeg Group SpA
Italy
[Home Appliances]

Smiley
World Smile Corporation
USA, 1963
Harvey Ball
[Design]

Smint
Perfetti Van Melle SpA
Spain
[Food & Beverage]

Smirnoff
Diageo plc
Russia
[Wines, Beers & Spirits]

Smirnoff
Diageo plc
Russia
[Wines, Beers & Spirits]

Smithkline Beecham
SmithKline Beecham plc
UK
[Pharmaceuticals]

Smith & Nephew
Smith & Nephew plc
UK, 2003
Wolff Olins
[Medical Devices]

Smith & Wesson
Smith & Wesson Holding Corporation
USA
[Firearms]

Smiths
Smiths Group plc
UK
[Technology]

1 **Smithsonian**
Smithsonian Institution
USA, 1997
Chermayeff & Geismar
[Foundations & Institutes]

2 **SMM**
SMM/Hamburg Messe und Congress GmbH
Germany
[Marine]

3 **SNAP (Supplemental Nutrition Assistance Program)**
U.S. Department of Agriculture
USA
[Government]

4 **Snapixel**
USA
[Internet]

5 **Snap-on**
Snap-on Inc
USA
[Tools & Machinery]

6 **Snapple**
Dr Pepper Snapple Group Inc
USA, 2000
[Food & Beverage]

7 **Snapple**
Dr Pepper Snapple Group Inc
USA, 2008
CBX
[Food & Beverage]

8 **SNCF (Société Nationale des Chemins de fer français)**
France, 1986
Roger Tallon
[Transport]

9 **SNCF (Société Nationale des Chemins de fer français)**
France, 2005
Carré Noir
[Transport]

10 **SNCM (Société Nationale Maritime Corse Méditerranée)**
France
[Transport]

SOHIO

SOFITEL
SOFTSHEEN·CARSON

1 **Snickers**
Mars Inc
USA, 2003
[Food & Beverage]

Snickers Workwear
Snickers Workwear, Hultafors Group
Sweden
[Apparel]

Snickers Workwear
Snickers Workwear, Hultafors Group
Sweden
[Apparel]

4 **SoBe Grape Grog**
South Beach Beverage Company, PepsiCo Inc
USA
[Food & Beverage]

5 **Sobey's**
Sobey's Inc
Canada
[Retail]

6 **SOCAR**
State Oil Company of Azerbaijan Republic
Azerbaijan
[Oil, Gas & Petroleum]

7 **Sodexo**
Sodexo SA
France, 2008
W&Cie
[Professional Services]

8 **Sofitel**
SO Luxury HMC Sarl, Accor Group
France
[Hospitality]

9 **Softsheen-Carson**
L'Oréal Group
USA
[Health & Beauty]

10 **Softub**
Softub Inc
USA
[Household Products]

11 **Sogo**
Sogo Co. Ltd
Japan
[Retail]

12 **Sohio (Standard Oil of Ohio)**
BP plc
USA
[Oil, Gas & Petroleum]

SOKKIA

Sokkia
Sokkia Co. Ltd
Japan
[Industrial Products]

Sol
Heineken International
Netherlands
[Wines, Beers & Spirits]

SOLA
Carl Zeiss Inc
Australia
[Eyewear]

Solectron
Solectron Corporation
USA
[Electronics]

Solidarnosc
Poland, 1980
Jerzy Janiszewski
[Political]

Solid Waste
City of Tampa Department of
Solid Waste & Environment
Program Management
USA
[Public Services]

Somfy
SOMFY SAS
France
[Home Furnishings]

Sonangol
Sonjangol EP
Angola, 2004
Oil, Gas & Petroleum

Sonion
Sonion A/S
Denmark
[Medical Devices]

Sonofon
Sonofon Holding A/S
Denmark
[Telecommunications]

Sony
Sony Corporation
Japan, 1973
Yasuo Kuroki
[Consumer Electronics]

Sony Entertainment Television
Sony Pictures Television Inc
USA, 2008
[Television Channel]

Sony Ericsson
Sony Ericsson Mobile Communications AB
UK, 2001
Takuya Kawagoi
[Telecommunications]

Sony Music
Sony Corporation of America
USA
[Music Industry]

Sony Music
Sony Music Entertainment Inc, Sony Corporation of America
USA, 2009
[Music Industry]

Sony Pictures
Sony Pictures Entertainment Inc
Japan
[Film Industry]

It's a Sony
Sony Corporation
Japan, 1982
[Consumer Electronics]

Sorel
Columbia Sportswear Company
Canada
[Apparel]

Sotheby's International Realty
Sotheby's International Realty Affiliates LLC
UK
[Real Estate]

SOURCE

1 **Source Records**
   France, 2006
   M/M Paris
   [Music Industry]

2 **Southern Miss Golden Eagles**
   The University of Mississippi
   USA
   [Sport]

3 **South Africa**
   South African Tourist Board
   South Africa
   [Travel & Tourism]

4 **South African Airways**
   Government of South Africa
   South Africa
   [Airline]

5 **Southern Californian Gas Company (SoCalGas)**
   Sempra Energy
   USA
   [Utilities]

6 **Southern Company**
   USA
   Lippincott
   [Utilities]

7 **South Park**
   Comedy Partners LLC,
   MTV Networks, Viacom Inc
   USA, 1997
   Trey Parker, Matt Stone
   [Television Series]

8 **SouthTrust Bank**
   SouthTrust Corporation
   USA
   [Financial Services]

9 **Southwest Airlines**
   Southwest Airlines Co
   USA
   [Airline]

1 **Southwestern Bell Telephone**
USA
[Telecommunications]

2 **Soya Kaas**
Soy Kaas Inc
USA, 1980s
[Food & Beverage]

3 **SP. (Socialistische Partij/ Socialist Party)**
Netherlands, 2006
Thonik
[Political]

4 **SPA**
SA Spadel NV
Belgium
[Food & Beverages]

5 **Space Camp**
U.S. Space & Rocket Center, Alabama Space Science Exhibit Commission
USA
[Galleries & Museums]

6 **Spalding**
Spalding Sports, Russell Brands LLC
USA
[Sporting Goods]

7 **Spar**
Spar International
Netherlands, 1968
Raymond Loewy
[Retail]

8 **Sparco**
Sparco SpA
Italy
[Automotive]

SPARKASSEN-FINANZGRUPPE

Sparkassen-Finanzgruppe
Deutscher Sparkassen- und
Giroverband eV
Germany
[Financial Services]

Spar Nord
Spar Nord Bank A/S
Denmark
[Financial Services]

Speakman
Speakman Company
USA
[Home Appliances]

Specialized
Specialized Bicycle
Components Inc
USA
[Bicycles]

Speedo
Speedo International Ltd,
Pentland Group plc
Australia
[Sporting Goods]

Speedo
Speedo International Ltd,
Pentland Group plc
Australia
[Sporting Goods]

Speed Stick
The Mennen Company,
Colgate-Palmolive Company
USA
[Personal Care]

Speedy
Speedy Muffler King
Canada
[Automotive]

S. Pellegrino
Nestlé SA
Italy, 1999
Minale Tattersfield
[Food & Beverage]

Spencer Gore Developments
Spencer Gore Developments (Pty) Ltd
South Africa
[Construction]

Spescom
Spescom Ltd
South Africa, 1970s
[Information Technology]

Spies Hecker
Spies Hecker GmbH
Germany
[Paints & Coatings]

Spike TV
Viacom International Inc
USA, 2003
[Television Channel]

SPIN
SPIN Media LLC
USA, 1985
[Publications]

Spitfire
USA
[Sporting Goods]

Sports Car Club of America (SCCA)
USA
[Societies & Associations]

Sports Illustrated
Time Warner Inc
USA
[Publications]

Sports Illustrated for Kids
Time Warner
USA, 1989
[Publications]

Spot
Spot LLC
Ireland
[Telecommunications]

Spotify
Spotify AB, Spotify Ltd
Sweden/UK
Christian Wilsson,
Rasmus Andersson
[Internet]

SRG SSR

Spray 'n Wash
Reckitt Benckiser LLC
USA
[Household Products]

Sprint
Sprint Nextel Corporation
USA, 2005
Lippincott Mercer
[Telecommunications]

Sprite
The Coca-Cola Company
USA, 1994
[Food & Beverage]

Sprite
The Coca-Cola Company
USA, 2009
[Food & Beverage]

SPVM
Service de police de la Ville
de Montréal
Canada, 2008
[Public Services]

Square-Enix
Square Enix Holdings Co. Ltd
Japan
[Computer & Video Games]

Squirt
Dr Pepper Snapple Group Inc
USA, ca 2002
[Food & Beverage]

SRG
SRG SSR
Switzerland, 1985
[Television Channel]

SRG SSR (Schweizerische
Radio- und Fernsehgesellschaft/
Société suisse de radiodiffusion)
SRG SSR
Switzerland, 2011
Dunning Penney Jones
[Broadcaster]

SSAB
SSAB Swedish Steel AB
Sweden
[Industrial Products]

Ssang Yong
SsangYong Motor Company
South Korea
[Automotive]

ST
STMicroelectronics NV
Switzerland
[Technology]

Stabilo
Schwan-Stabilo Group
Germany
[Writing Products]

Staedtler
Staedtler Mars GmbH & Co. KG
Germany, 2005
Staedtler
[Writing Products]

Stagecoach Group
Stagecoach Group plc
UK
[Transport]

Stainmaster
Invista, Koch Industries Inc
USA
[Home Furnishings]

Standard Bank
The Standard Bank of South Africa
Ltd, Standard Bank Group
South Africa
[Financial Services]

Standard Chartered Bank
UK
[Financial Services]

STARGATE SG-1

Standard Life plc
UK
[Financial Services]

Standard & Poor's
Standard & Poor's Financial Services LLC, The McGraw Hill Companies
USA
Lippincott
[Financial Services]

Stanley
Stanley Black & Decker Inc
USA
[Tools & Machinery]

Staples
Staples Inc
USA
[Office Supplies]

Star Networks
Star Networks Inc, First Data Corporation
USA
[Financial Services]

Star Alliance
Star Alliance Services GmbH
Germany
[Transport]

Starbucks
Starbucks Corporation
USA
Heckler Associates: Terry Heckler
[Restaurants & Bars]

Starbucks
Starbucks Corporation
USA, 2011
Lippincott, Starbucks in-house design team
[Restaurants & Bars]

Star Channel
Greece
[Television Network]

Stargate SG-1
Metro-Goldwyn-Mayer Inc
USA
[Television Series]

625

STAR GOLD

1. **Star Gold (US)**
Satellite Television Asian Region (STAR), News Corporation
India, 2011
[Television Channel]

2. **Starkey**
Starkey Laboratories Inc
USA
[Medical Devices]

3. **Starline Inc**
USA
[Consumer Products]

4. **Staropramen**
Pivovary Staropramen a.s.
Czech Republic
[Wines, Beers & Spirits]

5. **Starter**
Iconix Brand Group Inc
USA
[Apparel]

6. **Star Trek**
CBS Corporation
USA, 1966
[Television Series]

7. **Star Trek – The Next Generation**
CBS Corporation
USA, 1987
[Television Series]

8. **Star Trek**
CBS Corporation
USA
[Television Series]

9. **Star Trek – Voyager**
CBS Corporation
USA, 1995
[Television Series]

10. **Star Wars**
Lucasfilm Ltd
USA, 1976
Suzy Rice
[Film]

11. **Star Wars – The Empire Strikes Back**
Lucasfilm Ltd
USA, 1980
[Film]

Starz
Starz Entertainment LLC
USA
Darwin, Design & Image Communications
[Television Channel]

State Bank of India
India, 1971
Shekhar Kamat
[Financial Services]

State Farm
State Farm Mutual Automobile Insurance Company
USA
[Financial Services]

Statoil
Statoil ASA
Norway
[Oil, Gas & Petroleum]

Statoil
Statoil ASA
Norway, 2009
Scandinavian Design Group
[Oil, Gas & Petroleum]

Stazione Zoologica Anton Dohrn of Naples
Ministero dell'Istruzione dell'Università e della Ricerca
Italy
[Foundations & Institutes]

STCP (Sociedade de Transportes Colectivos do Porto)
Portugal
[Transport]

Steel Recycling Institute
USA
[Foundations & Institutes]

Steelmark
American Iron and Steel Institute
USA, 1960
[Industry]

Steelcase
Steelcase Inc
USA
[Office Supplies]

Steel Dynamics Inc
USA
[Industrial Products]

STEFANEL

STEFANEL

1. **Stefanel**
Stefanel SpA
Italy
[Fashion]

2. **Steiff**
Margarete Steiff GmbH
Germany
[Toys, Games & Models]

3. **Steinberg GmbH**
Germany
[Computer Software]

4. **Steinway**
Steinway & Sons
USA
[Musical Instruments]

5. **Stella McCartney**
Gucci Group
UK
Winkreative
[Fashion]

6. **Stena**
Stena AB
Sweden
[Transport]

7. **Stena**
Stena Metall AB
Sweden
[Conservation & Environment]

8. **Stentofon**
Zenitel NV
Norway
[Safety & Security]

9. **ST Ericsson**
Switzerland
[Technology]

10. **Stern**
Gruner + Jahr GmbH & Co. KG
Germany
[Publications]

628

STOP & SHOP

  (Stoli)

Stihl
Andreas Stihl AG & Company
Germany
[Tools & Machinery]

Stikk
Kosovo ICT Association
Kosovo, 2009
projectGRAPHICS
[Information Technology]

Stimorol
Kraft Foods Inc
Denmark
[Food & Beverage]

4 **St. Ivel**
Dairy Crest Group plc
UK
[Food & Beverage]

5 **STM (Société de transport de Montréal/Montreal Transit Corporation)**
Canada, 2009
Sid Lee
[Transport]

6 **StockLogos**
USA
[Imaging & Photographic]

7 **Stoli Razberi**
Soyuzplodimport
Russia
[Wines, Beers & Spirits]

8 **Stone Island**
Sportswear Company SpA
Italy, 1980s
[Apparel]

9 **Stop Aids Now!**
Aids Fonds, Hivos, ICCO, Cordaid, Oxfam Novib
Netherlands, 2000
[Charity]

10 **Stop & Shop**
The Stop & Shop Supermarket Company, Koninklijke Ahold NV
USA
[Retail]

11 **Stop & Shop**
The Stop & Shop Supermarket Company, Koninklijke Ahold NV
USA, 2008
[Retail]

629

Storage USA
Extra Space Storage LP/SUSA
Partnership LP
USA
[Storage]

Stork
Stork BC
Netherlands
[Aerospace]

STP
USA
Armored AutoGroup Inc
[Automotiv]

StrategicNova
StrategicNova Inc
Canada
[Financial Services]

Street Fighter II
Capcom Co. Ltd
Japan, 1991
[Computer & Video Games]

Stroh's
Pabst Brewing Company
USA
[Wines, Beers & Spirits]

Strukton
Strukton Groep
Netherlands
[Construction]

Studio Ghibli
Studio Ghibli Inc
Japan
[Film Industry]

StumbleUpon
StumbleUpon Inc
USA
[Internet]

StumbleUpon
StumbleUpon Inc
USA
[Internet]

Stüssy
Stüssy Inc
USA, 1980
Shawn Stussy
[Apparel]

STV (Scottish TV)
SMG Television
UK, 2009
Bruce Dunlop & Associates
[Television Channel]

Subaru
Fuji Heavy Industries Co. Ltd
Japan
[Automotive]

Subaru/Fuji Heavy Industries
Fuji Heavy Industries Co. Ltd
Japan, 1953
[Automotive]

Subway
Doctor's Associates Inc
USA, 1968
[Restaurants & Bars]

Subway
Doctor's Associates Inc
USA, 2002
[Food & Beverage]

Sucrets
Insight Pharmaceuticals LLC
USA
[Pharmaceuticals]

Sulake
Finland
[Internet]

Sümerbank
Turkey
[Financial Services]

Sumo + Compal
Sumo + Compal SA
Portugal
[Food & Beverage]

Sunbeam
Sunbeam Products Inc, Jarden Corporation
USA
[Consumer Electronics]

SUNCHIPS

1 SunChips
   Frito-Lay North America Inc,
   PepsiCo Inc
   USA, 1991
   [Food & Beverage]

2 Suncor Energy
   Suncor Energy Inc
   Canada
   [Energy]

3 Sundance Channel
   AMC Networks
   USA, 2008
   Tender: Dean Di Simone
   [Television Channel]

4 Sunflower Children
   USA
   [Charity]

5 Sunkist
   Sunkist Growers Inc
   USA
   [Agricultural]

6 Sunkist
   Sunkist Growers Inc, Dr Pepper
   Snapple Group Inc
   USA, 1990s
   [Food & Beverage]

7 Sunkist
   Sunkist Growers Inc,
   Dr Pepper Snapple Group Inc
   USA, 2010
   [Food & Beverage]

8 Sun Microsystems
   Oracle America Inc
   USA, 1990s
   [Computer Technology]

9 Sunoco
   Sunoco Inc
   USA, ca 2000
   [Oil, Gas & Petroleum]

10 Sunsilk
   Unilever plc/NV
   UK/Netherlands, 2008
   [Personal Care]

11 Sun Sports
   Fox Sports Regional Networks,
   Fox Entertainment Group Inc
   USA, ca 2004
   [Television Channel]

1 **SunTrust**
SunTrust Banks Inc
USA
[Financial Services]

2 **Suomi Mutual**
Finland
[Financial Services]

3 **Super 8 Motels**
Super 8 Hotels Inc,
Wyndham Hotel Group
USA, 2008
[Hospitality]

4 **Super 8 Motels**
Super 8 Hotels Inc,
Wyndham Hotel Group
USA, 1982
[Hospitality]

5 **SuperAmerica**
Marathon Ashland Petroleum LLC
USA
[Retail]

6 **Super Best**
Dagrofa AS
Denmark
[Retail]

7 **Super Bock**
União Cervejeira SA, Unicer
Portugal
[Wines, Beers & Spirits]

8 **Super by Dr. Nicholas Perricone**
Perricone MD
USA
Concrete: Diti Katona
[Health & Beauty]

9 **Superdry**
SuperGroup plc
UK
[Apparel]

10 **Superdry**
SuperGroup plc
UK, ca 2004
[Apparel]

11 **Super Famicom**
Nintendo Co. Ltd
Japan, 1990
[Computer & Video Games]

Superga
Superga SpA
Italy, 1999
Brunazzi & Associati:
Giovanni Brunazzi
[Footwear]

Superior Essex Inc
USA
[Industrial Products]

Superloc
U.S. Chemical Storage LLC
USA
[Construction]

Superman
DC Comics Inc, Time Warner
USA
[Publications]

Superman
DC Comics Inc, Time Warner
USA, 1960s
Curt Swan
[Publications]

Superman: Ride of Steel
DC Comics Inc, Time Warner, Six Flags Entertainment Corporation
USA
[Theme Parks]

Super Mario Bros (Mushroom Kingdom)
Nintendo Co. Ltd
Japan
[Toys, Games & Models]

Super Nintendo Entertainment System
Nintendo Co. Ltd
Japan, 1991
[Computer & Video Games]

SuperValu
SuperValu Inc
USA
[Retail]

Supra Vit
Kendi Droujestvo S Ogranitchena Otgovornost
Bulgaria
[Pharmaceuticals]

Supreme
USA
[Apparel]

Surcouf
Surcouf SAS
France
[Retail]

SureFire
SureFire LLC
USA
[Consumer Electronics]

Suzuken
Suzuken Co. Ltd
Japan
[Healthcare]

Suzuki
Suzuki Motor Corporation
Japan
[Automotive]

Svit (Swiss Real Estate Association)
Switzerland
[Societies & Associations]

Swann-Morton
Swann-Morton Ltd
UK
[Medical Devices]

Swarovski
Swarovski AG
Austria, 1988
[Watches & Jewelry]

S.W.A.T.
Columbia Pictures Industries Inc
USA, 2003
[Film]

Swatch
The Swatch Group Ltd
Switzerland
[Watches & Jewelry]

SWEET'N LOW

1 **Sweet'n Low**
Cumberland Packing Corporation
USA, 1950s
[Food & Beverage]

2 **Swiss Army Brands Ltd**
Victorinox Swiss Army
Brands Inc
Switzerland
Gerard Huerta
[Consumer Products]

3 **Swisscom**
Swisscom AG
Switzerland, 1997
[Telecommunications]

4 **Swisscom**
Swisscom AG
Switzerland, 2008
Moving Brands
[Telecommunications]

5 **Swiss Hutless**
New Swiss Hutless
International AG
Switzerland
[Sporting Goods]

6 **Swiss International Airlines**
Swiss International Airlines AG
Switzerland, 2002
Winkreative
[Airline]

7 **Swiss International Airlines**
Swiss International Airlines AG
Switzerland, 2011
[Airline]

8 **Swiss Life**
Swiss Life Ltd
Switzerland, 2006
MetaDesign
[Financial Services]

9 **Swiss Paraplegic Centre**
Switzerland
[Foundations & Institutes]

10 **Swiss Paraplegics Foundation**
Switzerland
[Foundations & Institutes]

Swiss Re

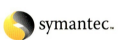

Swiss Re
Swiss Reinsurance Company Ltd
Switzerland
[Financial Services]

Switzerland
Swiss National Tourist Office
Switzerland
[Travel & Tourism]

Syfy
NBCUniversal
USA, 2009
Landor Associates
[Television Channel]

Sylvania
Havells Sylvania
Germany
[Manufacturing]

Symantec
Symantec Corporation
USA, 1990
[Computer Software]

Symantec
Symantec Corporation
USA, ca 2001
Interbrand
[Computer Software]

Symantec
Symantec Corporation
USA, 2010
[Computer Software]

Syngenta
Syngenta AG
Switzerland, 2000
Interbrand Zintzmeyer & Lux
[Agricultural]

SyQuest
SYQT Inc
USA
[Computer Hardware]

Sysco
Sysco Corporation
USA, ca 1970
[Distribution]

Sysco
Sysco Corporation
USA, 2008
[Professional Services]

TAB

1 **TaB**
The Coca-Cola Company
USA
[Food & Beverage]

2 **Tabasco**
McIlhenny Company
USA
[Food & Beverage]

3 **TACA Airlines**
(Transportes Aéreos del Continente Americano)
TACA SA, AviancaTaca Holding SA
El Salvador
[Airline]

4 **TACA Airlines**
(Transportes Aéreos del Continente Americano)
TACA SA, AviancaTaca Holding SA
El Salvador, 2008
Lippincott
[Airline]

5 **Taco Bell**
Yum! Brands Inc
USA, 1994
[Restaurants & Bars]

6 **Tact Precision**
Tact Precision Industrial Co. Ltd, Tekman Group Ltd
Taiwan
[Electronics]

7 **taggen4life**
Germany
[Apparel]

8 **Tag Heuer**
LVMH Moët Hennessy Louis Vuitton SA
Switzerland
[Conglomerate]

1 **Taishin Bank**
Taishin International Bank,
Taishin Financial Holding Co. Ltd
Taiwan, 1992
[Financial Services]

2 **Taisho Pharmaceutical**
Taisho Pharmaceutical Co. Ltd,
Taisho Pharmaceutical
Holdings Co. Ltd
Japan
[Pharmaceuticals]

3 **Taiwan Business Bank**
Taiwan Business Bank Co. Ltd
Taiwan
[Financial Services]

4 **Taiwan Cooperative Bank**
Taiwan
[Financial Services]

5 **Taiwan – The Heart of Asia**
Taiwan Tourism Bureau
Taiwan, 2011
Winkreative
[Travel & Tourism]

6 **Tajan**
Tajan SA
France
[Professional Services]

7 **Takara Bio**
Takara Bio Inc,
Takara Holdings Inc
Japan
[Pharmaceuticals]

8 **Takeda**
Takeda Pharmaceutical
Company Ltd
Japan
[Pharmaceuticals]

9 **Take-Two**
Take-Two Interactive Software Inc
USA
[Computer & Video Games]

10 **Talbot**
Peugeot SA
France
[Automotive]

TALENS

Talens
Royal Talens BV, Sakura Color Products Corporation
Netherlands
[Consumer Products]

TalkTalk
TalkTalk Telecom Ltd
UK, 2006
[Telecommunications]

Tama Drums
Hoshino Gakki Co. Ltd
Japan, ca 1974
[Musical Instruments]

Tambour
Tambour Ltd,
Granite Hacarmel Invest Ltd
Israel
[Paints & Coatings]

Tamiya
Tamiya Inc
Japan
[Toys, Games & Models]

Tampax
Procter & Gamble Co
USA, 2000s
[Personal Care]

Tamron
Tamron Co. Ltd
Japan
[Imaging & Photographic]

Tandem
Tandem Computer Inc
USA
[Computer Technology]

Tandy
Tandy Corporation
USA
[Retail]

Tang
Kraft Foods Inc
USA, 1999
[Food & Beverage]

 TASCAM

Taniguchi
Taniguchi Ink Corporation of America
USA
[Imaging & Photographic]

Tapflo
Tapflo AB
Sweden, 1980s
[Industrial Products]

TAP Pharmaceuticals
TAP Pharmaceutical Products Inc
USA
[Pharmaceuticals]

TAP Portugal
Transportes Aéreos Portugueses, SGPS SA
Portugal
[Airline]

Target
Target Corporation
USA, 2004
[Retail]

Target
Target Corporation
USA, 1980
[Retail]

Tartan Yachts
USA
[Marine]

Tartex
Tartex + Dr. Ritter GmbH, Wessanen Group
Germany
[Food & Beverage]

Tascam
Teac Corporation
Japan
[Consumer Electronics]

Tata Steel
Tata Steel Ltd
India, 1999
Wolff Olins
[Industry]

TATE

Tate
UK, 1999
Wolff Olins
[Galleries & Museums]

Tate & Lyle
Tate & Lyle plc
UK
[Agricultural]

Tatneft
Russia
[Oil, Gas & Petroleum]

Tatonka
Tatonka GmbH
Germany
[Outdoor & Recreational]

Tatra
Tatra AS
Czech Republic
[Automotive]

Taurus Film
Kirch Group
Germany
[Media]

Taurus Firearms USA
Taurus International
Manufacturing Inc,
Forjas Taurus SA
Brazil
[Firearms]

Tax Free Shopping
European Union
[Travel & Tourism]

Taylor Label
Canada
[Paper Products]

TaylorMade
TaylorMade-Adidas Golf Comp
USA
[Sporting Goods]

TBN (Trinity Broadcasting Network)
USA
[Television Network]

TCBY (The Country's Best Yogurt)
Mrs. Fields Famous Brands LLC
USA, 2010
Struck, Axiom
[Restaurants & Bars]

Tchibo
Tchibo GmbH
Germany
[Food & Beverage]

TCi Tire Centers
Tci Tires LLC, Michelin SA
USA
[Automotive]

TD (Toronto-Dominion Bank)
TD Bank Financial Group
Canada, 1969
[Financial Services]

TDG
Norbert Dentressangle SA
UK
[Freight & Logistics]

TDK
TDK Corporation
Japan
[Electronics]

TDS Tele Data System
Tele Data System, spol. sr.o.
Czech Republic
[Information Technology]

TEAC
TEAC Corporation
Japan
[Electronics]

TECATE

Technics

Tecate
Cuauhtémoc-Moctezuma
Brewery, Heineken NV
Mexico
[Wines, Beers & Spirits]

Tecatel
Tecatel SA
Spain
[Electronics]

TechCrunch (TC)
AOL Inc
USA, 2011
Code & Theory
[Internet]

Tech Data
Tech Data Corporation
USA
[Technology]

Technicolor
Technicolor Motion Picture
Corporation
USA
[Film Industry]

Technicolor
Technicolor SA
France, 2010
Gyro:HSR, Technicolor
[Film Industry]

Technics
Panasonic Corporation
USA
[Consumer Electronics]

Technisub
Aqua Lung International
Italy
[Marine]

Tecumseh
Tecumseh Products Company
USA
[Industrial Products]

TED (Technology Entertainment and Design)
TED Conferences LLC,
Sapling Foundation
USA
[Events]

1 **Tefal**
Groupe SEB
France
[Kitchenware]

2 **T-Fal**
T-Fal USA, Groupe SEB
USA
[Kitchenware]

3 **Teijin Limited**
Japan
[Chemicals & Materials]

4 **Tein**
Tein Inc
Japan
[Automotive]

5 **Teksid**
Teksid SpA
Italy
[Industrial Products]

6 **Tektronix**
Tektronix Inc,
Danaher Corporation
USA
[Industrial Products]

▶ 7 **Telcel**
Radiomovil Dipsa SA de CV,
América Móvil SAB de CV
Mexico
[Telecommunications]

8 **Tele2**
Tele2 AB
Sweden, 2007
[Telecommunications]

9 **Tele Atlas**
Tele Atlas NV
Netherlands
[Information Technology]

TELECHECK

1   TeleCheck
    First Data Corporation
    USA
    [Financial Services]

2   Telecom Italia
    Telecom Italia SpA
    Italy, 2003
    [Telecommunications]

3   Telecom New Zealand
    Telecom New Zealand Ltd
    New Zealand, 2009
    Designworks
    [Telecommunications]

4   Teledyne
    Teledyne Technologies Inc
    USA, ca 2000
    [Conglomerate]

5   Teleflora
    Teleflora LLC
    USA
    [Consumer Products]

6   Teleflora
    Teleflora LLC
    USA
    [Consumer Products]

7   Teleflorist
    British Teleflower Service Ltd,
    Teleflora LLC
    UK
    [Consumer Products]

8   Telefónica
    Telefónica SA
    Spain, 1998
    FutureBrand
    [Telecommunications]

9   TeleFood
    Food and Agriculture Organization
    of the United Nations
    Italy, ca 1997
    [Foundations & Institutes]

10 Telefunken
    Telefunken Licenses GmbH
    Germany
    [Consumer Electronics]

TELENOR

TELEFUNKEN

Telefunken
Telefunken Licenses GmbH
Germany
[Consumer Electronics]

Telekom Deutschland
Deutsche Telekom AG
Germany
Interbrand
[Telecommunications]

Telekom Slovenije
Telekom Slovenije dd
Republic of Slovenia
[Telecommunications]

Telekom Srbija
Telekom Srbija ad
Serbia, ca 1997
[Telecommunications]

Telemadrid
Televisión Autonómica
de Madrid SA
Spain
[Television Channel]

Telemarketing Store
Telemarketing SA
Greece
[Marketing]

Telemundo
NBCUniversal Media LLC
USA, 1992
Chermayeff & Geismar: Steff
Geissbuhler, Robert Matza
[Television Network]

Telemundo
NBCUniversal Media LLC
USA, 1999
[Television Network]

Telenor
Telenor Group
Norway, 2006
Wolff Olins: Keshen Teo
[Telecommunications]

647

TELEWEST

KRAKÓW

1 **Telewest**
Telewest Communications plc
UK, 1980s
[Telecommunications]

2 **Telewizja 3 Krakow**
Telewizja Polska SA
Poland
[Broadcaster]

3 **Telex**
Bosch Security Systems Inc,
Robert Bosch LLC
USA
[Consumer Electronics]

4 **Telfort**
Telfort BV, Royal KPN NV
Netherlands, 1996
[Telecommunications]

5 **Telfort**
Telfort BV, Royal KPN NV
Netherlands, 2010
VBAT
[Telecommunications]

6 **Telkom**
Telkom SA Ltd
South Africa
[Telecommunications]

7 **Telkom Indonesia**
PT Telekomunikasi Indonesia Tbk
Indonesia, 2009
[Telecommunications]

8 **TelkomVision**
Indonesia
[Digital Television]

9 **Tellabs Inc**
USA
[Telecommunications]

10 **Tempstar**
International Comfort
Products LLC
USA
[Heating & Cooling]

1. **Tenneco**
Tenneco Inc
USA, 1990s
Lippincott & Margulies
[Oil, Gas & Petroleum]

2. **Tenneco**
Tenneco Inc
USA, 1995
Lippincott & Margulies
[Oil, Gas & Petroleum]

3. **Tennis Australia**
Australia
[Sport]

4. **Tenzing**
Tenzing Communications Inc
USA
[Telecommunications]

5. **TEPCO**
Tokyo Electric Power Co. Ltd
Japan
[Utilities]

6. **Teradyne**
Teradyne Inc
USA
[Electronics]

7. **Terasaki**
Terasaki Electric Europe Co. Ltd
Japan
[Electronics]

8. **Termignoni**
Termingnoni SpA
Italy
[Automotive]

9. **Ternium**
Ternium SA
Luxembourg
[Industrial Products]

10. **Terra Networks**
Terra Networks SA, Telefónica SA
Spain
FutureBrand
[Internet]

1 **Terumo**
Terumo Corporation
Japan
[Medical Devices]

2 **Tesa**
Tesa SE, Beiersdorf AG
Germany, 1990
[Consumer Products]

3 **Tesco**
Tesco plc
UK, 1996
[Retail]

4 **Tesco**
Tesco Corporation
USA
[Tools & Machinery]

5 **Tesla**
Tesla Motors Inc
USA
[Automotive]

6 **Tetra Pak**
Tetra Laval
Switzerland, 1992
Toni Manhart, Jörgen Haglind
[Industry]

7 **Teuco**
Teuco Guzzini SpA
Italy
[Home Furnishings]

8 **Teva**
Deckers Outdoor Corporation
USA
[Footwear]

9 **Texaco**
Chevron Corporation
USA, 1981
[Oil, Gas & Petroleum]

1 **Texas Instruments**
Texas Instruments Inc
USA
[Technology]

2 **Texas Motor Speedway**
Speedway Motorsports Inc
USA, 1990s
[Motorsport]

3 **Texas State Aquarium**
USA
[Aquariums & Zoos]

4 **Textron**
Textron Inc
USA
[Conglomerate]

5 **Tex-Tryk**
Tex-Tryk A/S
Denmark
[Apparel]

6 **TF1 (Télévision Française 1)**
Groupe TF1
France
[Television Channel]

7 **T.G.I. Friday's**
T.G.I. Friday's Inc, Carlson
USA, 1965
[Restaurants & Bars]

8 **Thai Airways**
Thai Airways International
Thailand, 2005
Interbrand
[Airline]

9 **Thales**
Thales SA
France, 2000
Euro RSCG
[Electronics]

10 **Thames & Hudson**
Thames & Hudson Ltd
UK, 1999
The Partners
[Publishing]

11 **Thames & Kosmos**
Thames & Kosmos LLC
USA, ca 2001
[Publishing]

THAMES VALLEY HOUSING

1 **Thames Valley Housing**
Thames Valley Housing Association
UK
[Societies & Associations]

2 **Thames Valley Housing**
Thames Valley Housing Association
UK
[Societies & Associations]

3 **Thames Water**
Thames Water Utilities Ltd
UK
[Utilities]

4 **The Atlantic**
Atlantic Media Company
USA, 2008
Pentagram: Michael Bierut, Luke Hayman, Joe Marianek, Ben King
[Publications]

5 **The Bank of New York**
USA, 2005
Lippincott Mercer
[Financial Services]

6 **The Bank of New York**
USA
[Financial Services]

7 **The Barn Markets**
Canada
[Retail]

8 **The Beatles**
UK, 1963
Ivor Arbiter
[Music]

9 **The Black Book**
The Black Book Inc
USA
[Publications]

10 **The Body Shop**
The Body Shop International plc
L'Oréal SA
UK
[Retail]

11 **The Body Shop**
The Body Shop International plc
L'Oréal SA
UK, 2008
[Health & Beauty]

The Bond Market Association
USA, 1998
Chermayeff & Geismar: Steff Geissbuhler
[Societies & Associations]

The Box
MTV Networks, Viacom Inc
USA, 1980s
[Television Channel]

The Box
Channel Four Television Corporation, Bauer Media Group
UK, 2005
[Television Channel]

The Brand Distillery
The Brand Distillery Ltd
UK, 2004
Aloof Design
[Retail]

The Building Box
Reno-Depot Inc
Canada
[Retail]

The Cellar
Marshall Field & Company, Macy's Inc
USA
[Retail]

The Championships Wimbledon
All England Lawn Tennis and Croquet Club (AELTC)
UK
[Sporting Events]

The Cheesecake Factory
TCF Co. LLC
USA
[Restaurants & Bars]

The Chemical Brothers
UK
[Music]

The Children's Medical Center
The Children's Medical Center of Dayton
USA
[Healthcare]

The Clash
UK, ca 1977
[Music]

The Clorox Company
The Clorox Company
USA, 2010
[Household Products]

The Coffee Bean & Tea Leaf
International Coffee & Tea LLC
USA
[Restaurants & Bars]

The Co-operative
Co-operative Group Ltd
UK, 2007
Pentagram
[Retail]

The Cooper Union
The Cooper Union for the Advancement of Science and Art
USA, 2009
Doyle Partners
[Education]

The Daily Telegraph
News Ltd
Australia
[Media]

The Daily Telegraph
Telegraph Media Group
UK
[Media]

The Denver Public Library
USA
[Foundations & Institutes]

The Dorchester Collection
UK, 2006
Pentagram: John Rushworth
[Hospitality]

The Economist
The Economist Group
UK
[Publications]

THE GREATER BOSTON FOOD BANK

The Electric Company
Children's Television Workshop
USA
[Television Series]

The Exchange
ACCEL/Exchange
Canada/USA, 1970s
[Financial Services]

The Finals
USA
[Sporting Goods]

The Football League
UK, 2004
[Sport]

The Franklin Mint
TFM LLC
USA
[Manufacturing]

The Gillette Company
Procter & Gamble Co
USA, 1993
Lippincott & Margulies
[Personal Care]

The Glass House
(The Philip Johnson Glass House)
National Trust for Historic Preservation
USA, 2008
Pentagram
[Foundations & Institutes]

The Global Fund
The Global Fund to Fight AIDS, Tuberculosis and Malaria
Switzerland
[Financial Services]

The Godfather
Paramount Pictures Corporation
USA, 1969
S. Neil Fujita
[Film]

The Greater Boston Food Bank
USA
[Charity]

655

THE GREEN BURRITO

THE HUFFINGTON POST

The Green Burrito
Carl Karcher Enterprises Inc
USA
[Restaurants]

The Green Hornet
USA, 1966
[Television Series]

The Greene Turtle
USA
[Restaurants & Bars]

The Guardian
Guardian Media Group plc (GMG)
UK, 2005
Mark Porter, Paul Barnes,
Christian Schwartz
[Media]

The Hartford
The Hartford Financial Services
Group Inc
USA
[Financial Services]

The History Channel
A&E Television Networks LLC
USA, 1995
[Television Channel]

The Home Depot
Homer TLC Inc
USA, 1978
[Retail]

The Huffington Post
The Huffington Post Media Group,
AOL Inc
USA
[Media]

The Ink Well
USA
[Printing Services]

The Ivy League
Council of Ivy Group Presidents
USA
[Education]

THE NELSON-ATKINS MUSEUM OF ART

The Met
ropolitan
Opera

The
Nelson-Atkins
Museum
of Art

The Japan Research
Institute Limited
Japan
[Foundations & Institutes]

The Kennedy Center
The John F. Kennedy Center
for the Performing Arts
USA
[Venues]

The Land Registry
UK Government
UK, 2003
North
[Government]

4 The Lung Association
Canada
[Societies & Associations]

5 The Mac Store
USA
[Retail]

6 The Metropolitan Opera
USA, 2006
Pentagram: Paula Scher, Julia
Hoffmann
[Music]

7 The Movie Channel
Showtime Networks Inc, CBS
Corporation
USA, 2006
[Television Channel]

8 The National Lottery
Camelot UK Lotteries Ltd
UK
[Leisure & Entertainment]

9 The Nelson-Atkins Museum of Art
USA
[Galleries & Museums]

THE NEW YORKER

1 The New Yorker
Condé Nast, Advance Magazine Publishers Inc
USA, 1925
Rea Irvin
[Publications]

2 The New York Times
The New York Times Company
USA
[Media]

3 The New York Times Company
USA
[Media]

▶ 4 The North Clothing
UK
[Apparel]

▶ 5 The North Face
The North Face Inc,
VF Corporation
USA, 1968
[Outdoor & Recreation]

6 The Oakland Press
Journal Register Company
USA
[Media]

7 The Open University
UK
[Education]

▶ 8 The Phone House
Carphone Warehouse Group plc
UK
[Retail]

9 The Pickup Guy
USA
[Automotive]

The Pirate Bay
Sandryds Handel AB
Sweden
[Internet]

The Public Theater
USA, 2008
Pentagram: Paula Scher
[Cinemas & Theatres]

Thermax
Thermax Ltd
India
[Heating & Cooling]

4 **Thermo Electron Corporation**
USA
[Technology]

5 **Thermo Pride**
Thermo Products LLC
USA
[Heating & Cooling]

6 **Thermos**
Thermos LLC
USA
[Consumer Products]

7 **The Rolling Stones**
UK, 1971
John Pasche
[Music]

8 **The Royal Parks**
Department for Culture,
Media and Sport
UK, 1996
Moon Brand: Richard Moon,
Ceri Webber, Andy Locke
[Outdoor & Recreation]

9 **The Ryland Group Inc**
USA, 1960s
[Construction]

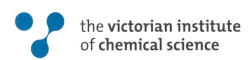

THE WALL STREET JOURNAL.

1 **The Salvation Army**
   UK, ca 1915
   [Religious]

2 **The Schwan Food Company**
   USA
   [Food & Beverage]

3 **The Simpsons**
   Fox Broadcasting Company
   USA, ca 1989
   Matt Groening
   [Television Series]

4 **The Sims Online**
   Maxis; Electronic Arts Inc
   USA, ca 2002
   [Computer & Video Games]

5 **The Store**
   The Store Corporation Bhd
   Malaysia
   [Retail]

6 **The Sun**
   News International Ltd
   UK, 1980s
   [Media]

7 **The Twilight Zone**
   CBS Broadcasting Inc
   USA, 1959
   Joe Messerli
   [Television Series]

8 **The Victorian Institute of Chemical Science**
   Australia, 2006
   Dale Harris
   [Foundations & Institutes]

9 **The Wall Street Journal**
   Dow Jones & Company,
   News Corporation
   USA
   [Media]

The Warriors
Paramount Pictures Corporation
USA, 1997
[Film]

The Washington Post
The Washington Post Company
USA
[Media]

The Weather Channel
NBC Universal LLC,
The Blackstone Group,
Bain Capital LLC
USA
[Television Channel]

The White House
The United States Government
USA
[Places]

The Who
UK, 1964
Brian Pike
[Music]

Thimble Sourcing
Peru, 2007
Ideo Comunicadores
[Fashion]

Thomas Cook
Thomas Cook Group plc
UK, 2001
[Travel & Tourism]

Thomas Cook
Thomas Cook Group plc
UK
[Travel & Tourism]

Thomas & Friends
HIT Entertainment Ltd,
Fisher-Price Inc
UK, 2002
[Television Series]

THOMSON

1 **Thomson**
Thomson SA
France
[Professional Services]

2 **Thomson Reuters**
Thomson Reuters Corporation
USA, 2008
Interbrand
[Media]

3 **Thomy**
Nestlé SA
Switzerland
[Food & Beverage]

4 **Thor**
Royal Unibrew A/S
Denmark
[Wines, Beers & Spirits]

5 **Thrasher**
High Speed Productions Inc
USA, 1981
[Publications]

6 **Three**
Hutchison 3G UK Limited
UK
[Telecommunications]

7 **Thule**
Thule Group
Sweden
[Manufacturing]

8 **Thunderbird**
Mozilla Corporation
USA, 2011
[Internet]

9 **THX**
THX Ltd, Lucasfilm Ltd
USA, ca 1983
[Film Industry]

TOKYO DOME CORPORATION

1 **Toblerone**
   Kraft Foods Inc
   Switzerland, 1908 (wordmark)
   [Food & Beverage]

2 **Tochigi Bank**
   Tochigi Bank Ltd
   Japan
   [Financial Services]

3 **Todini**
   Todini Costruzioni Generali SpA
   Itlay
   [Construction]

4 **Tofutti**
   Tofutti Brands Inc
   USA
   [Food & Beverage]

5 **Togu**
   TOGU Gebr. Obermaier OHG
   Germany
   [Health & Fitness]

6 **Tohatsu**
   Tohatsu Corporation
   Japan
   [Manufacturing]

7 **Tokio Marine Nichido**
   Tokio Marine Holdings Inc
   Japan
   [Financial Services]

8 **Tokio Marine Nichido**
   Tokio Marine Holdings Inc
   Japan
   [Financial Services]

9 **Toko**
   Toko-Swix Sport AG
   Switzerland
   [Sporting Goods]

10 **Tokyo Dome Corporation**
   Japan
   [Venues]

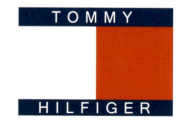

1. **Tokyo Electron (TEL)**
Tokyo Electron Ltd
Japan
[Technology]

2. **Tokyo Gas**
Tokyo Gas Co. Ltd
Japan
[Utilities]

3. **Tokyo Steel**
Tokyo Steel Co. Ltd
Japan
[Industry]

4. **Tokyo Stock Exchange**
Tokyo Stock Exchange Group Inc
Japan
[Financial Services]

5. **Tokyu Corporation**
TVR Motors Company Ltd
Japan
[Transport]

6. **Tokyu Hands**
Tokyu Hands Inc
Japan
[Retail]

7. **Tokyu Hotels**
Tokyu Group
Japan
[Hospitality]

8. **Tombow**
Tombow Pencil Co. Ltd
Japan
[Writing Products]

9. **Tom Ford**
Tom Ford International LLC
USA
[Fashion]

10. **Tommy Hilfiger**
Tommy Hilfiger Licensing LLC, PVH Corp
USA
[Fashion]

1 Tom Tailor
Tom Tailor GmbH,
Tom Tailor Holding AG
Germany
[Apparel]

2 TomTom
TomTom NV
Netherlands, 2007
TBWA\Neboko: Matthew Harvey
[Automotive]

3 Tomy
Tomy Co. Ltd
Japan, ca 1979
[Toys, Games & Models]

4 Tomy
Tomy Co. Ltd
Japan
[Toys, Games & Models]

5 Tonka
Hasbro Inc
USA
[Toys, Games & Models]

6 Toothfriendly International
Switzerland
[Healthcare]

7 Topcon
Topcon Positioning Systems Inc
USA
[Technology]

8 Tornado
AB Electrolux
France
[Home Appliances]

9 Toro
The Toro Company
USA
[Industrial Products]

10 Toronto Blue Jays
Rogers Communications Inc
Canada, 2004
[Sport]

TORONTO PEARSON

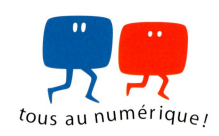

1 **Toronto Pearson**
Greater Toronto Airport Authority
Canada, 2011
Ove Design and Communications
[Travel & Tourism]

2 **Toronto Zoo**
City of Toronto
Canada, 2004
Hambly & Woolley:
Barbara Woolley
[Aquariums & Zoos]

3 **Toshiba**
Toshiba Corporation
Japan
[Electronics]

4 **Tosoh**
Tosoh Corporation
Japan
[Chemicals & Materials]

5 **Total**
Total SA
France, 1982
[Oil, Gas & Petroleum]

▶ 6 **Total**
Total SA
France, 2003
A&Co Paris: Laurent Vincenti
[Oil, Gas & Petroleum]

7 **Totaline**
Carrier Corporation
USA
[Heating & Cooling]

8 **Tottenham Hotspur Football Club**
ENIC International Ltd
UK, 2006
[Sport]

9 **Touchstone Home Entertainment**
Walt Disney Motion Pictures Group
USA
[Film Industry]

10 **Tous au numerique!**
France Télé Numérique
France
[Digital Television]

1 **Towa**
Towa Corporation
Japan
[Technology]

2 **Tower Records**
Tower.com Inc
USA
[Retail]

3 **ToyBiz**
Charan Industries Inc
Canada, ca 1988
[Toys, Games & Models]

4 **Toy Machine**
Toy Machine Blood Sucking Skateboard Company
USA
[Sporting Goods]

5 **Toyobo**
Toyobo Co. Ltd
Japan
[Fabrics & Textiles]

▶ 6 **Toyota**
Toyota Motor Corporation
Japan
[Automotive]

7 **Toys "R" Us**
Toys "R" Us-Delaware Inc
USA, 2007
[Retail]

8 **TracFone**
TracFone Inc, América Móvil SAB de CV
USA
[Telecommunications]

▶ 9 **TradingPost**
Telstra Corporation Ltd
Australia
[Internet]

1 **Tragon**
Tragon Corporation
USA, 2008
Pentagram
[Marketing]

2 **Trammell Crow Company**
CB Richard Ellis Group Inc
USA
[Real Estate]

3 **Trane**
Trane Inc, Ingersoll-Rand plc
USA
[Heating & Cooling]

4 **Transamerica**
Transamerica Corporation
USA
[Financial Services]

5 **Transamerica**
Transamerica Corporation
USA
[Financial Services]

6 **Transformers:
Revenge of the Fallen**
Paramount Pictures Corporation
USA, 2009
[Film]

7 **Transport for London (TfL)**
Greater London Authority
UK
[Transport]

8 **Trappey's**
Trappey's Fine Foods Inc,
B&G Foods Inc
USA
[Food & Beverage]

9 **Travel Channel**
Scripps Networks LLC
USA, 2011
Loyalkaspar
[Television Channel]

10 **Travel Channel (UK)**
Travel Channel International Ltd
UK, 2000
[Television Channel]

11 **Travelers Insurance**
The Travelers Companies
USA
[Financial Services]

1. **Travel of America**
USA
[Travel & Tourism]

2. **Travis Perkins**
Travis Perkins plc
UK
[Construction]

3. **Trebruk**
Trebruk AB, Arctic Paper AB
Sweden
[Paper Products]

4. **Trek**
Trek Bicycle Corporation
USA
[Bicycles]

5. **Trekstor**
Trekstor GmbH & Co. KG
Germany
[Consumer Electronics]

6. **Tribune**
Tribune Company
USA
[Media]

7. **Trico**
Trico Corporation,
Kohlberg & Company LLC
USA
[Automotive]

8. **Triple O's**
White Spot Ltd
Canada
[Restaurants & Bars]

9. **Triple-S**
Triple-S Management Corporation
Puerto Rico
[Financial Services]

10. **Triton**
Triton Systems of Delaware LLC
USA
[Manufacturing]

11. **Triumph International**
Triumph Global Sales AG
Switzerland
[Apparel]

TRIUMPH MOTORCYCLES

1 **Triumph Motorcycles**
   Triumph Motorcycles Ltd
   UK, 2005
   [Automotive]

2 **Trix**
   General Mills Inc
   USA
   [Food & Beverage]

3 **Troika**
   Switzerland
   [Watches & Jewelry]

4 **Trojan**
   Church & Dwight Co. Inc
   USA
   [Personal Care]

5 **Tropical**
   Cia. Tropical de Hotéis
   Brazil, 1966
   Ruben Martins
   [Travel & Tourism]

▶ 6 **Tropicana**
   Tropicana Products, PepsiCo Inc
   USA
   [Food & Beverage]

7 **T. Rowe Price**
   T. Rowe Price Investment Services Inc
   USA
   [Financial Services]

8 **True Value**
   True Value Company
   USA, 2006
   [Retail]

9 **Trusted Choice**
   Trusted Choice Inc
   USA
   [Financial Services]

10 **Tryg**
   Tryg plc
   Denmark
   [Financial Services]

11 **TSE (Turkish Standard Institution)**
   Turkey
   [Labelling, Standards & Certification]

TURNER

1 **TSX (Toronto Stock Exchange)**
Canada
[Financial Services]

2 **Tuborg Beer**
Carlsberg A/S
Denmark
[Wines, Beers & Spirits]

3 **Tudor**
Rolex SA
Switzerland
[Watches & Jewelry]

4 **TUI**
TUI AG
Germany, 2001
Interbrand Zintzmeyer & Lux
[Travel & Tourism]

5 **tumblr.**
Tumblr Inc
USA
[Internet]

6 **Tumi**
Tumi Inc
USA
[Consumer Products]

7 **Tune**
Tune Group Sdn Bhd
Malaysia
[Conglomerate]

8 **Tungsram**
General Electric Company
Hungary
[Consumer Products]

9 **Tupperware**
Tupperware Brands Corporation
USA
[Consumer Products]

10 **Turkish Airlines**
Turkey, 2010
[Airline]

▶ 11 **Turner**
Turner Broadcasting System Inc,
Time Warner
USA, 1987
[Broadcaster]

TURNER CLASSIC MOVIES

Twinkie

1 **Turner Classic Movies (TCM)**
Turner Broadcasting System Inc,
Time Warner
USA
[Television Channel]

2 **TU Wien**
Vienna University of Technology
Austria
[Education]

3 **TV2**
TV2 Cultura São Paulo
Brazil, 1968
Cauduro Martino
[Television Channel]

4 **TV Food Network**
Scripps Networks Interactive
USA, 1993
[Television Channel]

5 **TV Guide**
TV Guide Online Holdings LLC
USA, 2003
[Publications]

6 **TV Land**
MTV Networks, Viacom Inc
USA, 2009
[Television Channel]

7 **TVP**
Telewizja Polska SA
Poland, 2003
Loża A5
[Television Channel]

8 **TVR (Televiziunea Română)**
Societatea Română de Televiziune
Romania, 2004
English & Pockett
[Broadcaster]

9 **TWA (Trans World Airlines)**
Transworld Corporation
USA
Raymond Loewy
[Airline]

10 **Twigs**
Elememt Skateboards
USA
[Sporting Goods]

11 **Twinkie**
Hostess Brands Inc
USA
[Food & Beverage]

TYSON FOODS

1 **Twitter**
Twitter Inc
USA, 2010
[Internet]

2 **Twitter**
Twitter Inc
USA, 2007
Simon Oxley
[Internet]

3 **TXU**
Energy Future Holdings Corporation
USA, ca 1998
[Energy]

4 **TXU Energy**
Energy Future Holdings Corporation
USA, 2010
[Utilities]

5 **Tyco Electronics**
Tyco International Ltd
Switzerland/USA
[Electronics]

6 **Tyco Electronics**
Tyco International Ltd
Switzerland/USA, 2007
Interbrand: Daniel Sim, Curt Munger
[Electronics]

7 **Tyco Toys**
Mattel Inc
USA
[Toys, Games & Models]

8 **Type Directors Club (TDC)**
USA, 1994
Gerard Huerta
[Societies & Associations]

9 **Type Tested**
Standards Australia
Australia
[Labelling, Standards & Certification]

10 **Tyr**
Tyr Sport Inc
USA
[Sporting Goods]

11 **Tyson Foods**
Tyson Foods Inc
USA
[Food & Beverage]

677

U-Z

U

1. U
   Système U
   France
   [Retail]

2. U&lc. (Upper and lower case)
   USA, 1973
   Herb Lubalin
   [Publications]

3. UBI Banca
   Unione di Banche Italiene ScpA
   Italy, 2007
   [Financial Services]

▶ 4. UBS
   UBS AG
   Switzerland, 1998
   Interbrand Zintzmeyer & Lux
   [Financial Services]

5. UCB Pharma
   (Union Chimique Belge)
   UCB SA
   Belgium
   [Pharmaceuticals]

6. UCLA (University of California, Los Angeles)
   USA
   [Education]

7. UCSF (University of California San Francisco)
   USA, 2007
   [Education]

8. UEFA Champions League
   UEFA (Union of European Football Associations)
   Switzerland, 1992
   [Sporting Events]

1 **UFA**
UFA Film & TV Produktion GmbH
Germany
[Film Industry]

2 **UFA**
Universum Film AG, UFA Film & TV Produktion GmbH
Germany
[Film Industry]

3 **UGC Cinémas**
France
[Cinemas & Theatre]

4 **U-Haul**
U-Haul International Inc (AMERCO)
USA
[Car Rental]

5 **Uher**
Uher Informatik GmbH
Germany
[Electronics]

6 **UHU**
UHU GmbH & Co. KG
Germany
[Consumer Products]

7 **UKWA**
United Kingdom Warehousing Association
UK, 2009
[Societies & Associations]

8 **UL Classification Mark**
Underwriters Laboratories Inc
USA/Canada, ca 1903
[Labelling, Standards & Certification]

9 **Ülker**
Ülker Bisküvi Sanayi AŞ, Yildiz Holding
Turkey
[Food & Beverage]

10 **Ultragaz**
Brazil, 1977
Alexandre Wollner
[Oil, Gas & Petroleum]

11 **Ultragaz**
Grupo Ultra
Brazil
[Oil, Gas & Petroleum]

ULTRAMAR

1 **Ultramar**
Valero Energy Corporation
Canada
[Oil, Gas & Petroleum]

2 **UMAX**
UMAX Technologies Inc
Taiwan
[Computer Technology]

3 **UMB Financial Corporation**
USA
[Financial Services]

4 **Umbro**
Nike Inc
UK, 1992
[Sporting Goods]

5 **UMP (Union for a Popular Movement)**
France
[Political]

6 **UMWA (United Mine Workers of America)**
USA
[Societies & Associations]

7 **UNCF (United Negro College Fund) Inc**
USA
[Foundations & Institutes]

8 **Uncle Ben's**
Mars Inc
USA
[Food & Beverage]

9 **Under Armour**
Under Armour Inc
USA
[Apparel]

UNICEF

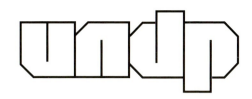

1 **Underground**
Transport for London (TfL)
UK, ca 1919
Edward Johnston
[Transport]

2 **UNDP (United Nations Development Programme)**
USA
[Foundations & Institutes]

3 **UNESCO**
United Nations Educational, Scientific and Cultural Organization
France
[Foundations & Institutes]

4 **Unibanco**
União de Bancos Brasileiros SA, Itaú Unibanco Holding SA
Brazil
[Financial Services]

5 **Unibank**
Denmark
[Financial Services]

6 **UNICEF**
United Nations Children's Fund
USA
[Foundations & Institutes]

1 UniCredit Banca Mobiliare (UBM)
UniCredit SpA
Italy, ca 2000
[Financial Services]

2 UniCredit Group
UniCredit SpA
Italy
[Financial Services]

3 Unifrutti
Chile, 1982
Alex Gonzales
[Food & Beverage]

4 Unilever
Unilever plc/NV
UK/Netherlands
[Conglomerate]

5 Unilever
Unilever plc/NV
UK/Netherlands, 2005
Wolff Olins: Miles Newlyn
[Conglomerate]

6 Unimed
Brazil
[Healthcare]

7 Union Bank of California
USA
[Financial Services]

8 Union Carbide
Union Carbide Corporation,
The Dow Chemical Company
USA
[Chemicals & Materials]

9 Union Central
Union Central Life Insurance Company
USA
[Financial Services]

UNITAU

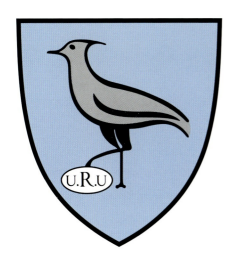

1. **Unión de Rugby del Uruguay**
Uruguay
[Sport]

2. **Union Pacific**
Union Pacific Railroad Company
USA, 1969
[Transport]

3. **UNIQA**
UNIQA Versicherungen AG
Austria
[Financial Services]

4. **Uniqlo**
Uniqlo Co. Ltd
Japan, 2007
Kashiwa Sato
[Fashion]

5. **Uni Records**
Universal Music Group
USA, 1967
[Music Industry]

6. **Uniroyal**
Michelin North America Inc
USA
[Automotive]

7. **UniSA (University of South Australia)**
Australia
[Education]

8. **Unisys**
Unisys Corporation
USA
[Computer Technology]

9. **Unitau (Universidade de Taubaté)**
Brazil
[Education]

UNITED AIRLINES

1 **United Airlines**
United Air Lines Inc, United Continental Holdings Inc
USA, 1974
Saul Bass
[Airline]

2 **United Artists**
United Artists Corporation, MGM Holdings Inc
USA, 1987
[Film Industry]

3 **United Artists Records**
United Artists Music and Record Group (UAMARG)
USA, ca 1970
[Music Industry]

▶ 4 **United Colors of Benetton**
Benetton Group SpA
Italy, 1995
Vignelli Associates
[Retail]

5 **United Financial Group**
Russia
[Financial Services]

6 **United Fire Group**
United Fire & Casualty Company
USA
[Financial Services]

7 **United International Pictures**
United International Pictures BV
USA, 2001
[Film Industry]

8 **United Nations (UN)**
USA, 1946
Oliver Lincoln Lundquist, Donal McLaughlin
[Foundations & Institutes]

UNITED TELECOM

1   **United Pageant International Corporation**
    Taiwan
    [Textile business activities]

2   **United Rentals**
    United Rentals Inc
    USA, 1997
    [Construction]

3   **United Space Alliance (USA)**
    USA, 1990s
    [Aerospace]

4   **United States Coast Guard**
    United States Coast Guard (USCG)
    USA, 1968
    Raymond Loewy
    [Defence]

5   **United States Lines**
    USA
    [Travel & Tourism]

6   **United States Postal Service (USPS)**
    United States Postal Service
    USA, 1993
    [Mail Services]

7   **United States Space Foundation**
    USA
    [Foundations & Institutes]

8   **United Technologies**
    United Technologies Corporation
    USA
    [Conglomerate]

9   **United Telecom**
    USA, ca 1972
    [Telecommunications]

687

UNITED UTILITIES

1. **United Utilities**
United Utilities Group plc
UK
[Utilities]

2. **United Utilities**
United Utilities Group plc
UK
[Utilities]

3. **United Way of America**
USA, 2004
FutureBrand: David Weinberger
[Foundations & Institutes]

4. **Universal Studios**
NBCUniversal LLC
USA
[Film Industry]

5. **University of Cambridge**
UK
[Education]

6. **University of Oxford**
UK
[Education]

7. **Univision**
Univision Communications Inc
USA, 1989
Chermayeff & Geismar:
Tom Geismar, Steff Geissbuhler
[Television Network]

8. **Unocal (Union Oil Company of California)**
Unocal Corporation
USA
[Oil, Gas & Petroleum]

9. **Unum**
Unum Group
USA, 2007
The Gate Worldwide
[Financial Services]

688

1 **Unza**
Wipro Unza Holdings Ltd
Malaysia
[Health & Beauty]

2 **UOB**
United Overseas Bank Ltd
Singapore
[Financial Services]

3 **UPC (Universitat Politècnica de Catalunya, BarcelonaTech)**
Spain
[Education]

4 **Up & Go**
Sanitarium (Australian Health and Nutrition Association Ltd)
Australia
[Food & Beverage]

5 **UpJohn**
The Upjohn Company
USA
[Pharmaceuticals]

6 **UPM**
UPM-Kymmene Oyj
Finland, 1996
[Paper Products]

7 **UPN**
United Paramount Network, CBS Corporation
USA, 1995
[Television Network]

8 **UPN**
United Paramount Network, CBS Corporation
USA, 2002
[Television Network]

9 **Uponor**
Uponor Oyj
Finland
[Heating & Cooling]

10 **Upper Crust**
SSP Group Ltd
UK
[Restaurants]

UPS

URBAN OUTFITTERS

1. **UPS**
   United Parcel Service Inc
   USA, 2003
   FutureBrand
   [Mail Services]

2. **UPSA Laboratories**
   UPSA (Union Pharmacologique Scientifique Appliquee) Laboratories
   France
   [Pharmaceuticals]

3. **Urban Decay Cosmetics**
   USA
   [Health & Beauty]

4. **Urban Outfitters**
   Urban Outfitters Inc
   USA
   [Retail]

5. **URSA**
   URSA Insulation, Uralita
   Spain, 2004
   Peter Schmidt Group
   [Construction]

6. **USA Cycling**
   USA, 2005
   Goodby Silverstein & Partners: Rich Silverstein
   [Societies & Associations]

7. **USAir**
   US Airways Inc
   USA, 1989
   SBG Partners
   [Airline]

8. **U.S. Air Force**
   United States Air Force
   USA, 2000
   Siegel+Gale
   [Defence]

9. **US Airways**
   US Airways Inc
   USA, 1997
   Deskey Associates: Luxon Carrá
   [Airline]

10. **USA Network**
    NBCUniversal Media LLC
    USA, 2005
    Peloton Design: Sean Serio
    [Television Channel]

U.S. FIGURE SKATING

1   USA Today
    Gannett Company Inc
    USA, 1982
    [Media]

2   U.S. Bank
    US Bancorp
    USA
    [Financial Services]

3   USB (Universal Serial Bus)
    USB Implementers Forum Inc
    USA
    [Labelling, Standards &
    Certification]

4   USB (Universal Serial Bus)
    USB Implementers Forum Inc
    USA
    [Labelling, Standards &
    Certification]

5   US Cellular
    United States Cellular Corporation,
    TDS Inc
    USA
    [Telecommunications]

6   US Concrete Inc
    USA
    [Industrial Products]

7   USF&G
    The St Paul Companies Inc
    USA, ca 1981
    [Financial Services]

8   U.S. Figure Skating
    United States Figure Skating
    Association
    USA, 2003
    [Sport]

U.S. GRADE A

1 **U.S. Grade A**
U.S. Department of Commerce
USA
[Labelling, Standards & Certification]

2 **Usimunas**
Usiminas SA
Brazil
[Industrial Products]

▶ 3 **U.S. Mail**
United States Postal Service
USA, 1970
Raymond Loewy
[Mail Services]

4 **US Oncology**
US Oncology Inc, McKesson Corporation
USA
[Healthcare]

▶ 5 **U.S. Robotics**
USRobotics Corporation, Platinum Equity
USA
[Computer Technology]

6 **US Sailing**
United States Sailing Association
USA
[Societies & Associations]

7 **USS (U.S. Steel)**
United States Steel Corporation
USA
[Industry]

1　**USSB (United States Satellite Broadcasting)**
United States Satellite Broadcasting Company Inc
USA, 1996
Paul Rand
[Satellite Television]

2　**USTA**
USTA (United States Tennis Association)
USA, 2006
USTA, Siegel+Gale
[Societies & Associations]

3　**USX**
USX Corporation
USA, 1991
[Industry]

4　**UTA (United Talent Agency)**
USA, 2011
Siegel+Gale
[Professional Services]

5　**UTAH Life Elevated**
Utah Office of Tourism
USA, 2006
[Travel & Tourism]

6　**Utica Boilers**
ECR International
USA
[Heating & Cooling]

▶ 7　**Utz**
Utz Quality Foods Inc
USA
[Food & Beverage]

8　**UUNET**
MCI WorldCom, Verizon Business
USA, 1990s
[Internet]

V2 MUSIC

1 V2 Music
V2 Music Ltd
UK
[Music Industry]

2 V8 Vegetable Juice
Campbell Soup Company
USA
[Food & Beverage]

3 V33 Group
France
[Paints & Coatings]

4 V&A
Victoria & Albert Museum
UK, 1989
Alan Fletcher
[Galleries & Museums]

5 V&S (Vin & Spirit)
V&S Group, Pernod Ricard SA
Sweden
[Wines, Beers & Spirits]

6 Vacheron Constantin
Compagnie Financière
Richemont SA
Switzerland
[Watches & Jewelry]

7 Vagle Elektro
Vagle Elektro Installasjon A/S
Norway
[Professional Services]

8 Vaio
Sony Corporation
Japan, 1996
Manabu Sakamoto
[Computer Technology]

9 Vaja
Vaja Corp.
USA
RDYA
[Consumer Products]

10 VAK
France
[Security & Safety]

VAN DE KAMP'S

1 **Val d'Isère**
Val d'Isère Tourist Office
France
[Travel & Tourism]

2 **Valeo**
Valeo SA
France, 2004
[Automotive]

3 **Valley Irrigation**
Valmont Industries Inc
USA
[Engineering]

4 **Vallourec**
Vallourec SA
France
[Manufacturing]

5 **Valspar**
Valspar Corporation
USA, 2011
[Paints & Coatings]

6 **Valve Corporation**
USA
[Computer & Video Games]

7 **Valvoline**
Ashland Inc
USA
[Automotive]

8 **Van Camp's**
ConAgra Foods Inc
USA
[Food & Beverage]

9 **Van de Kamp's**
Pinnacle Foods Group LLC
USA
[Food & Beverage]

VAN HALEN

1 **Van Halen**
   USA, 1978
   Dave Bhang
   [Music]

2 **Van Heusen**
   PVH Corp, Phillips-Van Heusen Corporation
   USA
   [Apparel]

3 **Van Hool NV**
   Belgium
   [Automotive]

4 **Van Houten**
   Barry Callebaut Group
   Sweden
   [Food & Beverage]

5 **Vanity Fair**
   Condé Nast, Advance Publications Inc
   USA, 1983
   [Publications]

6 **Vans**
   Vans Inc, VF Corporation
   USA, 1960s
   [Apparel]

7 **Vans "Off the Wall"**
   Vans Inc, VF Corporation
   USA
   [Apparel]

8 **Vänsterpartiet/Left Party**
   Sweden
   [Political]

9 **Vantex**
   Fashion Fair LLC, Johnson Publishing Company Inc
   USA, 1988
   [Health & Beauty]

10 **Vårdförbundet**
   Sweden, 1999
   Stockholm Design Lab
   [Health & Safety]

VATTENFALL

1 **Varefakta Kontrolleret**
   Sweden, 2011
   [Labelling, Standards & Certification]

2 **Varefakta Kontrolleret**
   Sweden
   [Labelling, Standards & Certification]

3 **Variety**
   Reed Business Information, Reed Elsevier plc/NV
   USA, 1905
   [Publications]

4 **Variflex**
   Variflex Inc, Bravo Sports Corporation
   USA
   [Sporting Goods]

5 **Varig**
   VRG Linhas Aéreas, Gol Linhas Aéreas Inteligentes SA
   Brazil, 2007
   [Airline]

6 **Varilux**
   Essilor International SA
   France, 2009
   [Eyewear]

7 **Varta**
   Varta Microbattery GmbH
   Germany
   [Consumer Products]

8 **Vaseline**
   Unilever plc/NV
   UK/Netherlands, 2007
   [Personal Care]

9 **Vassallo**
   Industrias Vassallo Inc
   Puerto Rico
   [Chemicals & Materials]

▶ 10 **Vat Motor Oil**
   VatOil
   Netherlands
   [Automotive]

11 **Vattenfall**
   Vattenfall AB
   Sweden
   [Energy]

697

VAUDE

1 **Vaude**
Vaude Sport GmbH & Co. KG
Germany
[Sporting Goods]

2 **Vauxhall**
Vauxhall Motors,
General Motors UK Ltd
UK, 1990s
[Automotive]

3 **Vauxhall**
Vauxhall Motors,
General Motors UK Ltd
UK, 2009
[Automotive]

4 **VBB (Verkehrsverbund Berlin-Brandenburg)**
Germany
[Societies & Associations]

5 **VDE**
VDE Association for Electrical, Electronic and Information Technologies eV
Germany
[Societies & Associations]

6 **Vectorpile.com**
[Internet]

7 **Veer**
Corbis Corporation
USA
[Imaging & Photographic]

8 **Veer**
Corbis Corporation
USA
[Imaging & Photographic]

9 **Velbon**
Velbon Tripod Co. Ltd
Japan
[Imaging & Photographic]

10 **Velux**
VKR Holding A/S
Denmark
[Household Products]

11 **Velveeta**
Kraft Inc
USA, 1990s
[Food & Beverage]

1 **Venturi**
Venturi Automobiles SA
France, 1989
[Automotive]

2 **Venturi**
Venturi Automobiles SA
France
[Automotive]

3 **Veolia**
Veolia Environnement SA
France, 2005
[Utilities]

4 **Verbatim**
Verbatim Americas LLC
USA
[Computer Technology]

5 **VeriFone**
VeriFone Holdings Inc
USA
[Financial Services]

6 **Verio**
Verio Inc
USA
[Internet]

7 **Veritas**
Veritas Software Corp
USA
[Computer Software]

8 **Verizon**
Verizon Communications Inc
USA, 2000
Landor Associates, DeSola Group
[Telecommunications]

9 **Verkade**
Netherlands
[Food & Beverage]

1 **Vermeer**
Vermeer Corporation
USA
[Industrial Products]

2 **Vermeer**
Vermeer Corporation
USA
[Industrial Products]

3 **Vermont American**
Robert Bosch Tool Corporation
USA
[Tools & Machinery]

4 **Versace**
Gianni Versace SpA
Italy
[Fashion]

5 **Vertigo**
Mercury Records,
Universal Music UK
UK, 1969
Linda Glover
[Music Industry]

6 **Vertu**
UK
[Telecommunications]

7 **Verve**
Verve Records,
Universal Music Group
USA, 1956
[Music Industry]

8 **Veryeri Makina**
Turkey
[Tools & Machinery]

9 **Vespa**
Piaggio & Co. SpA
Italy
[Automotive]

10 **Vestax**
Vestax Corporation
Japan, 1970s
[Consumer Electronics]

1   **Vetropack**
    Vetropack Holding Ltd
    Switzerland
    [Glass & Ceramics]

2   **Vetta**
    Acumen Inc
    USA
    [Sporting Goods]

3   **Veuve Clicquot Ponsardin**
    LVMH Moët Hennessy
    Louis Vuitton SA
    France
    [Wines, Beers & Spirits]

4   **VF**
    VF Corporation
    USA
    [Apparel]

5   **VGH**
    VGH Versicherungen
    Germany
    [Financial Services]

6   **VH1**
    MTV Networks, Viacom Inc
    USA, 2003
    [Television Channel]

7   **VHS (Video Home System)**
    developed by JVC Kenwood
    Holdings Inc, Victor Company
    of Japan Ltd
    Japan, 1976
    [Consumer Electronics]

8   **Via**
    Via Rail Canada
    Canada
    [Transport]

9   **Viacom**
    Viacom Inc
    USA, 1990
    [Conglomerate]

10 **Viacom**
    Viacom Inc
    USA, 2006
    [Conglomerate]

11 **Viasat**
    Modern Times Group MTG AB
    Sweden
    [Satellite Television]

12 **Viasat**
    Modern Times Group MTG AB
    Sweden
    [Satellite Television]

VIBE

1. **Vibe**
   InterMedia Partners LLC
   USA, 1990s
   [Publications]

2. **Vice**
   Vice Media Inc
   Canada/USA
   [Publications]

3. **Vice City**
   (Grand Theft Auto: Vice City)
   Rockstar Games Inc
   UK
   [Computer & Video Games]

4. **Viceroy**
   Grupo Munreco SL
   Spain
   [Watches & Jewelry]

5. **Vichy Laboratoires**
   L'Oréal SA
   France
   [Health & Beauty]

6. **Vichy Pastilles**
   Cadbury plc
   France
   [Food & Beverage]

7. **Vickers plc**
   UK
   [Engineering]

8. **Vicks**
   Procter & Gamble Co
   USA
   [Pharmaceuticals]

9. **Vicks**
   Procter & Gamble Co
   USA
   [Pharmaceuticals]

10. **Vicson**
    Vicson Bekaert
    Venezuela
    [Industry]

11. **Victa**
    Briggs & Stratton Corporation
    Australia
    [Tools & Machinery]

1 **Victoria Bitter (VB)**
Carlton & United Beverages,
Foster's Group
Australia
[Wines, Beers & Spirits]

2 **Victoria's Secret**
Limited Brands
USA
[Apparel]

3 **Victorinox**
Victorinox AG
Switzerland, 2009
[Knives]

4 **Victory Motorcycles**
Polaris Industries Inc
USA, 1997
[Automotive]

5 **Vidal Sassoon**
Procter & Gamble Co
UK
[Fashion]

6 **Vidikron**
Planar Systems Inc
USA
[Electronics]

7 **Vienna Beef**
Vienna Beef Inc
USA
[Food & Beverage]

8 **Viessman**
Viessmann Werke GmbH & Co. KG
Germany, 1960
Stankowski & Duschek:
Anton Stankowski
[Heating & Cooling]

VIKING

1

2

3

4

5

6

7

8

9

1 **Viking**
STIHL Ges.m.b.H
Austria, 1980s
[Tools & Machinery]

2 **Viking**
Office Depot International Ltd
UK, 2011
Lippincott
[Office Supplies]

3 **Viking**
Viking Group Inc
USA
[Security & Safety]

▶ 4 **Viking**
Viking Range Corporation
USA
[Home Appliances]

5 **Viking Tyres**
Viking International, Stepgrades Motor Accessories Ltd
UK
[Automotive]

6 **Viking Components Inc**
Viking Technology, Sanmina-SCI Corporation
USA, 1988
[Computer Technology]

7 **Vileda**
Vileda GmbH, Freudenberg Haushaltsprodukte KG
Germany
[Household Products]

8 **Village Cinemas**
Australian Theatres
Australia
[Cinemas & Theatres]

9 **Village Inn**
American Blue Ribbon Holdings LLC
USA
[Restaurants & Bars]

VIRGINIA SLIMS

1 **Villares**
Empresas Villares
Brazil, 1967
Cauduro Martino
[Industry]

2 **Villeroy & Boch**
Villeroy & Boch AG
Germany
[Glass & Ceramics]

3 **Vimeo**
Vimeo LLC
USA
[Internet]

4 **Vinci**
Vinci SA
France, 2000s
[Construction]

5 **Vinex International Wine Fair**
Luxembourg
Helmut Langer
[Wines, Beers & Spirits]

6 **Virb**
Virb LLC, Media Temple Inc
USA, 2007
[Internet]

7 **Virgin Atlantic Airways**
Virgin Group Ltd,
Singapore Airlines Ltd
UK, 2010
johnson banks, Virgin Atlantic
[Airline]

8 **Virgin Records**
EMI Group Ltd
UK
[Music Industry]

9 **Virginia Slims**
Altria Group Inc
USA
[Tobacco]

VIRU VALGE

1. **Viru Valge**
   AS Liviko Masina
   Estonia
   [Wines, Beers & Spirits]

2. **Visa**
   Visa Inc
   USA, 1993
   [Financial Services]

3. **Visa**
   Visa Inc
   USA, 2006
   Greg Silveria, Visa International Brand Management
   [Financial Services]

4. **Visine**
   Johnson & Johnson Healthcare Products, McNeil-PPC Inc
   USA
   [Pharmaceuticals]

5. **Visteon**
   Visteon Corporation
   USA, 1997
   Landor Associates
   [Automotive]

6. **Vitaminwater**
   Glacéau, The Coca-Cola Company
   USA
   [Food & Beverage]

7. **Vítkovice**
   Vítkovice Inc
   Czech Republic
   [Tools & Machinery]

8. **Vitra**
   Vitra AG
   Switzerland
   [Home Furnishings]

VIVIENNE WESTWOOD

1 **Vittel**
Nestlé SA
France
[Food & Beverage]

2 **Vittoria**
Vittoria SpA
Italy
[Automotive]

3 **VIV América Latina**
VNU Exhibitions Europe BV
Netherlands
[Events]

4 **Viva**
MTV Networks Europe Inc/
Viacom Networks Europe
Germany, 1993
[Television Channel]

5 **Viva**
MTV Networks Europe Inc/
Viacom Networks Europe
Germany, 2011
MTV Networks Europe
[Television Channel]

6 **Viva! Experiências**
Brazil, 2009
[Retail]

7 **Vivantes**
Germany, 2006
Pentagram
[Healthcare]

8 **Vivendi**
Vivendi SA
France, 2006
Carré Noir, Publicis
[Conglomerate]

9 **Vivendi Universal Games**
Vivendi SA
France, 2002
[Computer & Video Games]

10 **Vivienne Westwood**
Vivienne Westwood Ltd
UK
[Fashion]

707

VIVIR MEJOR

Vivitar

VOGELZANG

1. **Vivir Mejor**
Secretaria de Desarrollo Social (SEDESOL)
Mexico, 2008
[Government]

2. **Vivitar**
Vivitar Corporation
USA
[Imaging & Photographic]

3. **Vizir Ultra**
Procter & Gamble Co
USA
[Household Products]

4. **VM (Veenkoloniaal Museum in Veendam)**
Netherlands
[Galleries & Museums]

5. **VNB (Vermont National Bank)**
USA
[Financial Servicesv]

6. **VNG (Vereniging van Nederlandse Gemeenten)**
Netherlands
[Societies & Associations]

7. **VNU (Verenigde Nederlandse Uitgeverijen)**
VNU Group
Netherlands
[Publishing]

8. **Vodafone**
Vodafone Group plc
UK, 1997
Saatchi & Saatchi
[Telecommunications]

9. **Vodafone**
Vodafone Group plc
UK, 2005
Enterprise IG
[Telecommunications]

10. **Vodavi**
Vodavi Technology Inc
USA
[Telecommunications]

11. **Vogelzang**
Vogelzang International Corporation
USA
[Heating & Cooling]

VOGUE   VOITH

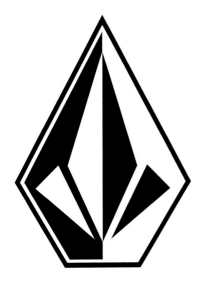

1 **Vogue**
   Condé Nast,
   Advance Publications Inc
   USA
   [Publications]

2 **Voith**
   Voith GmbH
   Germany
   [Industry]

3 **Vola**
   Vola A/S
   Denmark
   [Home Furnishings]

4 **Volant**
   Amer Sports Oyj
   USA
   [Sporting Goods]

5 **Volaris**
   Mexico, 2006
   Ideograma: Carl Forssell,
   Mariana Leegi,
   Juan Carlos Fernández
   [Airline]

6 **Volcom**
   Volcom Stone Inc
   USA
   [Apparel]

7 **VolgaTelecom**
   VolgaTelecom OJSC
   Russia, 2002
   [Telecommunications]

8 **VolkerWessels**
   VolkerWessels NV
   Netherlands
   [Construction]

VÖLKL

1 **Völkl**
Völkl Group, Jarden Corporation
Germany
[Sporting Goods]

2 **Volksbank**
Volksbank AG
Austria
[Financial Services]

3 **Volksbühne**
Volksbühne am Rosa-Luxemburg-Platz
Germany, 1992
Bert Neumann
[Cinemas & Theatres]

4 **Volunteers of America**
USA
[Charity]

5 **Volvic**
Groupe Danone
France
[Food & Beverage]

6 **Volvo**
Volvo Trademark Holding AB, Zhejiang Geely Holding Group
Sweden
[Automotive]

7 **Volvo GM Canada Heavy Truck**
Volvo GM Heavy Truck Corporation
USA, 1988
[Automotive]

1 **Von Dutch**
Von Dutch Originals LLC, Groupe Royer SA
USA, ca 1950
Kenny Howard (aka Von Dutch)
[Apparel]

2 **Von Roll Group**
Von Roll Holding AG
Switzerland
[Energy]

3 **Vons**
The Vons Companies Inc, Safeway Inc
USA
[Retail]

4 **Von Zipper**
Billabong International Ltd
USA
[Eyewear]

5 **Voortman**
Voortman Cookies Ltd
Canada
[Food & Beverage]

6 **Votorantim**
Votorantim Group
Brazil, 1999
FutureBrand BC&H
[Conglomerate]

VOX

1 **Vox**
   RTL Group SA
   Luxembourg
   [Television Channel]

2 **Vox Footwear**
   USA
   [Footwear]

3 **VPAR**
   Red Group Ltd
   UK, 2008
   SViDesign
   [Sport]

4 **VR**
   VR Group
   Finland, 2009
   [Transport]

5 **VR Cargo**
   VR Group
   Finland
   [Freight & Logistics]

6 **Vredestein**
   Apollo Vredestein BV
   Netherlands
   [Automotive]

7 **Vtech**
   Video Technology Ltd
   China
   [Consumer Electronics]

8 **VTG-LEHNKERING AG**
   Germany
   [Freight & Logistics]

9 **VTR**
   VTR Banda Ancha (Chile) SA
   Chile
   [Telecommunications]

1. **Vuarnet**
Sporoptic Pouilloux SA
France
[Eyewear]

2. **Vueling**
International Airlines Group
Spain, 2004
Saffron Brand Consultants
[Airline]

3. **Vulcain**
Manufacture des montres
Vulcain S.A.
Switzerland
[Watches & Jewelry]

4. **Vulcan**
Vulcan Materials Company
USA
[Construction]

5. **Vulco**
Vulco Développement SA
France
[Automotive]

6. **VW**
Volkswagen AG
Germany, 2000
MetaDesign
[Automotive]

7. **VW (Promotion)**
Volkswagen AG
Germany
[Automotive]

8. **Výtahy VMC s.r.o.**
Czech Republic
[Industrial Products]

1 **Wachovia**
Wachovia Corporation
USA
[Financial Services]

2 **Wacom**
Wacom Co. Ltd
Japan
[Computer Technology]

3 **Wacom**
Wacom Co. Ltd
Japan, 2007
Wolff Olins
[Computer Technology]

4 **Wagner**
WAGNER-Group
Germany
[Tools & Machinery]

5 **Wagner Brake Products**
USA
[Automotive]

6 **Waldenbooks**
Walden Book Company Inc,
Borders Group
USA, 1979
Gerard Huerta
[Retail]

7 **Walgreens**
Walgreen Co.
USA, 1901
[Retail]

8 **Walker Exhaust Systems**
Tenneco Inc
USA
[Automotive]

9 **Walkers**
Frito-Lay North America Inc,
PepsiCo Inc
UK
[Food & Beverage]

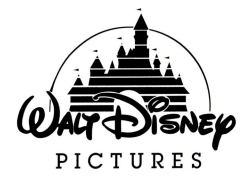

1 **Walkman**
Sony Corporation
Japan
Hiroshige Fukuhara
[Consumer Electronics]

2 **Wallkö**
Wall-Thürmer A/S
Denmark
[Tools & Machinery]

3 **Wall of Sound**
UK
[Music Industry]

4 **Walmart**
Wal-Mart Stores Inc
USA, 1992
Don Watt
[Retail]

5 **Walmart**
Wal-Mart Stores Inc
USA, 2008
Lippincott
[Retail]

6 **Walt Disney Pictures**
The Walt Disney Company
USA, 1985
[Film Industry]

7 **Walt Disney Records**
The Walt Disney Company
USA
[Music Industry]

8 **Walter**
Walter's Produce Inc
USA
[Food & Beverage]

9 **Waltham**
The Waltham Centre
for Pet Nutrition
UK
[Pet Products]

10 **Walther**
Carl Walther GmbH
Germany
[Firearms]

WARBURG PINCUS

1 **Wanadoo**
Orange SA, France Telecom SA
France, 1990s
[Internet]

2 **Wander**
Wander AG, Associated British Foods plc
Switzerland
[Food & Beverage]

3 **Wang**
Wang Laboratories Inc
USA, ca 1976
[Computer Technology]

4 **Wanit Fulgurit**
Etex Group
Germany, 2007
[Construction]

5 **Wanted by the FBI**
Federal Bureau of Investigation
USA
[Security & Safety]

6 **Warburg Pincus**
Warburg Pincus LLC
USA
[Financial Services]

7 **Warcraft**
Blizzard Entertainment Inc
USA
[Computer & Video Games]

8 **Waring Products**
Conair Corporation
USA
[Kitchenware]

9 **Warn**
Warn Industries Inc
USA
[Tools & Machinery]

WATCHMEN

Warner Brothers
Warner Bros. Entertainment Inc,
Time Warner
USA
[Film Industry]

Warner Chilcott
Warner Chilcott plc
Ireland
[Pharmaceuticals]

Warner Music Group
Access Industries Inc
USA, 1972
Saul Bass
[Music Industry]

Warp Records
Warp Records Ltd
UK, 1989
The Designers Republic:
Ian Anderson
[Music Industry]

Warteck Invest
Warteck Invest AG
Switzerland
[Real Estate]

Wasa
Wasabröd AB,
Barilla Alimentare SpA
Sweden
[Food & Beverage]

Washington Mutual
Washington Mutual Inc
USA
[Financial Services]

Watabe Wedding
Watabe Wedding Corporation
Japan
[Professional Services]

Watchmen
DC Comics Inc, Time Warner
USA, 1986
[Publications]

WATERMAN

1. **Waterman**
Waterman SA, Newell Rubbermaid Inc
France
[Writing Products]

2. **Wattyl**
The Wattyl Group
Australia
[Paints & Coatings]

3. **Wausau Paper**
Wausau Paper Corporation
USA, 2004
[Paper Products]

4. **Wawa**
Wawa Inc
USA
[Retail]

5. **WCVB-TV Channel 5**
Hearst Television Inc
USA, 1971
Wyman & Cannon: Lance Wyman
[Television Channel]

6. **Weathermatic**
Weathermatic Inc
USA
[Technology]

7. **WD-40**
WD-40 Company
USA
[Consumer Products]

8. **WEA (Warner-Elektra-Atlantic)**
Warner Music Group (WMG)
USA
[Music Industry]

9. **Weber**
Weber-Stephen Products LLC
USA
[Household Products]

10. **Weber**
Magneti Marelli Powertrain SpA, Fiat SpA
Italy
[Automotive]

Wedgwood
KPS Capital Partners LP
UK, 2000
The Partners
[Glass & Ceramics]

Weed Eater
Husqvarna Consumer
Outdoor Products (HCOP)
USA
[Tools & Machinery]

Weeder Sheeter
Bold Advertising Products
USA
[Tools & Machinery]

Wega
Sony Corporation
Germany
[Consumer Electronics]

Wega
Wega Srl
Italy, 1980s
[Manufacturing]

WEG Electric
WEG SA
Brazil
[Industrial Products]

Wegener
Koninklijke Wegener NV,
Mecom Group plc
Netherlands
[Publishing]

Wegmans
Wegmans Food Markets Inc
USA, 2008
[Retail]

WeightWatchers
Weight Watchers International Inc
USA
[Fitness & Wellbeing]

Weiler
Weiler Corporation
USA
[Industrial Products]

Weil-McLain
Weil-McLain Inc
USA
[Manufacturing]

Weinbrenner
Weinbrenner Shoe Company Inc,
Bata Brands Sarl
USA, 1980s
[Footwear]

Weiss Technik
Weiss Umwelttechnik GmbH
Germany
[Industrial Products]

Wella
Wella AG, Procter & Gamble Co
Germany, 1993
Klaus Koch Corporate
Communications
[Health & Beauty]

Wellcraft
Wellcraft LLC
USA
[Marine]

Wells Fargo
Wells Fargo Bank NA,
Wells Fargo & Company
USA
[Financial Services]

1   Wells Lamont
    Marmon Group, Berkshire
    Hathaway Inc
    USA
    [Apparel]

2   Wembley Stadium
    Wembley National Stadium Ltd
    UK, 2010
    Bulletproof
    [Venues]

▶ 3 Wendy's
    The Wendy's Company
    USA, 1969
    [Restaurants & Bars]

4   Wenger
    Wenger Corporation
    USA
    [Music Industry]

5   Werkraum Wartek PP
    Switzerland
    [Venues]

6   Werner
    Werner Co.
    USA
    [Manufacturing]

7   Wernli
    Wernli AG
    Switzerland
    [Food & Beverage]

8   WeSC (We are the
    Superlative Conspiracy)
    Sweden
    [Apparel]

9   Wesfarmers
    Wesfarmers Ltd
    Australia
    [Conglomerate]

1. **West Bend**
West Bend Housewares LLC
USA
[Home Appliances]

2. **Westbound**
USA
SightTwo
[Music Industry]

3. **Westbrae Natural**
The Hain Celestial Group Inc
USA
[Food & Beverage]

4. **West Coast Choppers**
West Coast Choppers Inc (WCC)
USA
[Apparel]

5. **Western Digital**
Western Digital Corporation
USA, 2004
[Computer Hardware]

6. **Western Properties Trust**
USA
[Real Estate]

▶ 7. **Western Union**
The Western Union Company
USA
[Financial Services]

8. **Westfalia**
Germany
[Manufacturing]

▶ 9. **Westfield**
Westfield Group
Australia
[Retail]

1 **Westinghouse**
Westinghouse Electric Company LLC, CBS Corporation
USA, 1960
Paul Rand
[Utilities]

2 **Weston**
Weston Foods (Canada) Inc
Canada
[Food & Beverage]

3 **Westside Concrete Materials**
USA
[Chemicals & Materials]

4 **Wetterau Incorporated**
USA
[Food & Beverage]

5 **Weyerhaeuser**
Weyerhaeuser Company
USA
[Paper Products]

6 **WGBH-TV**
WGBH Educational Foundation
USA, 1977
Chermayeff & Geismar
[Broadcaster]

7 **Whale**
Munster Simms Engineering Ltd
UK
[Industrial Products]

8 **Wham-O**
Wham-O Inc
USA
[Toys, Games & Models]

WHATABURGER

1. Whataburger
   Whataburger Restaurants LP
   USA, 1967
   [Restaurants & Bars]

2. Whatcom Museum
   USA
   [Galleries & Museums]

3. What's On TV
   IPC Media, Time Inc
   UK, 2003
   [Publications]

4. Whelen
   National Association for Stock Car Auto Racing (NASCAR)
   USA, 2007
   [Motorsport]

5. Whirlpool
   Whirlpool Corporation
   USA, 2010
   [Home Appliances]

6. Whiskas
   Mars Inc
   USA
   [Pet Products]

7. White Castle
   White Castle Management Co.
   USA, 2003
   [Restaurants & Bars]

8. White Farm Equipment
   AGCO Corporation
   USA
   [Tools & Machinery]

9. Whitesnake
   UK
   Jim Gibson
   [Music]

WIELTON

1 **Whitman's**
Whitman's Candies Inc, Russell Stover Candies Inc
USA
[Food & Beverage]

2 **Whole Foods Market**
Whole Foods Market IP LP
USA, 1980s
[Retail]

3 **W Hotels**
Starwood Hotels and Resorts Worldwide Inc
USA, 1990s
[Hospitality]

4 **Who Wants to be a Millionaire?**
Sony Pictures Television Inc
UK, 2010
[Television Series]

5 **WHSmith**
WHSmith plc
UK, 1990s
[Retail]

6 **Wick**
Procter & Gamble GmbH
Germany, 2008
[Pharmaceuticals]

7 **Wickes Inc**
USA
[Retail]

8 **Wide-Lite**
Koninklijke Philips Electronics NV, Atlanta Fulton County Recreation Authority
USA
[Industrial Products]

9 **Wide Span Sheds**
Australia
[Construction]

10 **Wielton**
Wielton SA
Poland
[Industrial Products]

1. **Wienerberger**
Wienerberger AG
Austria
[Manufacturing]

2. **Wienerschnitzel**
Galardi Group Inc
USA, 1978
Saul Bass
[Restaurants & Bars]

3. **Wiener's der Kaffee**
Wieners der Kaffee-Röster GmbH
Germany, 1985
[Restaurants & Bars]

4. **Wiener Städtische**
Wiener Städtische Versicherung AG
Austria
[Financial Services]

5. **Wiesbauer**
Wiesbauer Holding AG
Austria
[Food & Beverage]

6. **Wiha Tools**
Wiha Werkzeuge GmbH
Germany
[Tools & Machinery]

7. **Wihuri**
Wihuri Oy
Finland
[Conglomerate]

8. **Wii**
Nintendo Co. Ltd
Japan, 2006
[Computer & Video Games]

9. **Wika**
WIKA Alexander Wiegand SE & Co. KG
Germany
[Technology]

1. **WikiLeaks**
Sweden, ca 2010
Metahaven
[Internet]

2. **Wikimedia**
Wikimedia Foundation Inc
USA, 2010
Wikimedia Foundation:
Philip Metschan
[Internet]

3. **Wikipedia**
Wikimedia Foundation Inc
USA, 2010
Wikimedia Foundation:
Philip Metschan
[Internet]

4. **Wild Side Vidéo**
France
[Video-on-Demand]

5. **Wilkinson Sword**
Energizer Holdings Inc
UK
[Personal Care]

6. **William Grant's**
William Grant & Sons Ltd
UK
[Wines, Beers & Spirits]

7. **William Lawson's**
Bacardi Global Brands Ltd
UK
[Wines, Beers & Spirits]

8. **Williams**
The Williams Companies Inc
USA
[Energy]

9. **Willy:s**
Willys AB, Axfood AB
Sweden
[Retail]

10. **Wilson**
Wilson Sporting Goods Company,
Amer Sports Oyj
USA
[Sporting Goods]

11. **Wilton**
Wilton Industries Inc
USA
[Kitchenware]

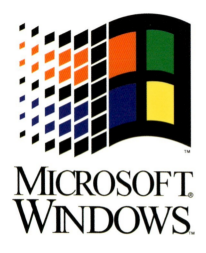

1 **Wimpy**
Famous Brands Ltd
UK, 1960s
[Restaurants & Bars]

2 **Winchester**
Winchester Repeating Arms
USA
[Firearms]

3 **Windows 1.0**
Microsoft Corporation
USA, 1985
[Computer Software]

4 **Windows 3.0**
Microsoft Corporation
USA, 1990
[Computer Software]

5 **Windows**
Microsoft Corporation
USA, 2001
[Computer Software]

6 **Windstopper**
W. L. Gore & Associates Inc
USA
[Fabrics & Textiles]

7 **Wingate Inn**
Wingate Inns International Inc
USA
Lippincott
[Hospitality]

8 **Winn-Dixie**
Winn-Dixie Stores Inc
USA, 2006
[Retail]

9 **Winsor & Newton**
ColArt Fine Art & Graphics Ltd
UK
[Retail]

WOLFENSTEIN

1

2

3

4

5

6

7

8

9

10

1 **Winston**
R. J. Reynolds Tobacco Company,
Reynolds American Inc
USA
[Tobacco]

2 **Wintershall**
Wintershall Holding AG
Germany
[Oil, Gas & Petroleum]

3 **WinWay**
WinWay Corporation
USA
[Computer Software]

4 **Wired**
Condé Nast, Advance
Magazine Publishers Inc
USA, 1994
John Plunkett, Barbara Kuhr
[Publications]

5 **Wired**
Condé Nast, Advance Magazine
Publishers Inc
USA
[Publications]

6 **Wirtschaftswoche**
Verlagsgruppe Handelsblatt
GmbH & Co. KG
Germany
[Publications]

7 **Wish-Bone**
Unilever plc/NV
USA
[Food & Beverage]

8 **WMF**
WMF AG Geislingen/Steige
Germany, 2006
Baumann & Baumann
[Kitchenware]

9 **WM Waste Management**
Waste Management Inc
USA
[Publications]

10 **Wolfenstein**
Activision Blizzard Inc
USA, ca 2009
[Computer & Video Games]

729

WOLFORD

1. **Wolford**
   Wolford AG
   Austria
   [Apparel]

2. **Wolf's Head**
   Wolf's Head Oil Company
   USA
   [Automotive]

3. **Wolters-Noordhoff**
   Wolters-Noordhoff BV
   Netherlands
   [Publishing]

4. **Wolverine**
   Wolverine World Wide Inc
   USA
   [Footwear]

5. **Wonderbra**
   HanesBrands Inc
   USA
   [Apparel]

6. **Wonder Bread**
   Hostess Brands Inc
   USA
   [Food & Beverage]

7. **Woolmark**
   Australian Wool Innovation Ltd
   Australia, 1964
   Francesco Saroglia
   [Labelling, Standards & Certification]

8. **Woolrich**
   Woolrich Inc
   USA
   [Apparel]

9. **Woolworth**
   F. W. Woolworth Company
   USA
   [Retail]

10. **Woolworths**
    Woolworths Ltd
    Australia
    [Retail]

WORLD HEALTH ORGANIZATION

1. Woolworths Group plc
   UK
   [Retail]

2. WordPress
   WordPress Foundation
   USA
   [Internet]

3. World Bank
   The World Bank
   USA
   [Financial Services]

4. WorldCat.org
   Online Computer Library Center Inc (OCLC)
   USA
   [Internet]

5. WorldCom
   WorldCom Inc
   USA, 2000
   Interbrand
   [Telecommunications]

6. World Customs Organization (WCO)
   Belgium, 1993
   [Government]

7. World Federation of the Sporting Goods Industry (WFSGI)
   Switzerland, ca 1978
   [Societies & Associations]

8. World Health Organization (WHO)
   United Nations
   Switzerland
   [Foundations & Institutes]

WORLD INDUSTRIES

Wrangler

WRIGLEY'S

WRIGHT TOOL

1 World Industries mascot (Flame Boy)
World Industries Inc
USA
[Outdoor & Recreation]

2 World Industries mascot (Wet Willy)
World Industries Inc
USA
[Outdoor & Recreation]

3 World of Concrete
Hanley Wood LLC
USA
[Events]

4 Worlds of Wonder (WoW)
Worlds of Wonder Inc
USA, 1980s
[Toys, Games & Models]

5 Worth
Rawlings Sporting Goods Company, Inc
USA
[Sporting Goods]

6 WPP
WPP plc
UK
[Advertising & Campaigns]

7 Wrangler
VF Corporation
USA
[Apparel]

8 Wright Tool
Wright Tool Company
USA
Sonnhalter
[Tools & Machinery]

9 Wrigley's
William Wrigley Jr. Company, Mars Inc
USA
[Food & Beverage]

WYSE TECHNOLOGY

1   Writers Guild of Canada
    Canada
    [Societies & Associations]

2   WSP Group plc
    UK
    [Engineering]

3   WTA (Women's Tennis Association)
    WTA Tour Inc
    USA
    [Sport]

4   Würth
    Adolf Würth GmbH & Co. KG
    Germany, 1983
    [Industrial Products]

5   Wu Tang Clan
    USA
    Allah Mathematics
    [Music]

▶ 6   WWF
    World Wide Fund for Nature
    Switzerland, 2000
    Samenwerkende Ontwerpers
    [Foundations & Institutes]

7   Wyeth
    Wyeth, Pfizer Inc
    USA, 2002
    Landor Associates
    [Pharmaceuticals]

8   Wyeth Lederle
    American Home Products Corporation (AHP)
    USA
    [Pharmaceuticals]

9   Wyndham Hotels & Resorts
    Wyndham Worldwide Corporation
    USA
    [Hospitality]

10 Wyse Technology
    USA
    [Computer Technology]

X-ACTO

1. **X-Acto**
Elmer's Products Inc
USA
[Office Supplies]

2. **Xantech**
Xantech LLC
USA
[Technology]

3. **Xantrex**
Xantrex Technology USA Inc
USA
[Electronics]

4. **Xaos Tools**
Xaos Tools Inc
USA
[Computer Software]

5. **Xbox**
Microsoft Corporation
USA
[Computer & Video Games]

6. **Xbox 360**
Microsoft Corporation
USA
[Computer & Video Games]

7. **Xerox**
Xerox Corporation
USA, 2008
Interbrand
[Imaging & Photographic]

8. **Xerox**
Xerox Corporation
USA, 1994
Landor Associates
[Imaging & Photographic]

9. **Xerox**
Xerox Corporation
USA
[Imaging & Photographic]

1 **X Games**
ESPN
USA
[Sporting Events]

2 **XL**
XL Group plc
UK, 2011
Venturethree
[Financial Services]

3 **XLO Electric**
Ultralink Products Inc
Canada
[Consumer Electronics]

4 **XM Satellite Radio**
Sirius XM Radio
USA
[Radio Stations]

5 **XO Communications**
XO Holdings Inc
USA
[Telecommunications]

6 **XTRA Corporation**
Berkshire Hathaway Inc
USA
[Car Rental]

7 **XX Special Lager**
Cuauhtémoc Moctezuma Brewery
Mexico
[Wines, Beers & Spirits]

8 **XXX Energy Drink**
XXX Energy Drink Inc
Netherlands
[Food & Beverage]

9 **Xypex**
Xypex Chemical Corporation
Canada
[Chemicals & Materials]

YACCO

1 **Yacco**
Yacco SA
France
[Automotive]

2 **Yahoo!**
Yahoo! Inc
USA, 1996
Organic: Kevin Farnham,
Geoff Katz; Yahoo!: David Shen
[Internet]

3 **Yakka Apparel Solutions**
Australia
[Apparel]

4 **Yale**
ASSA ABLOY Group AB
USA
[Consumer Products]

5 **Yale Materials**
Yale Materials Handling
Corporation
USA
[Tools & Machinery]

6 **Yale University**
USA
[Education]

7 **Yale Bulldogs**
Yale University Athletics
USA
[Sport]

8 **Yale University Press**
Yale University
USA, 1985
Paul Rand
[Publishing]

1 **Yamaguchi Bicycles**
Yamaguchi Bicycles Inc
USA
[Bicycles]

2 **Yamaha Corporation**
Japan, 1998
Rei Yoshimara
[Conglomerate]

3 **Yamaichi Electronics**
Yamaichi Electronics Co. Ltd
Japan
[Electronics]

4 **Yamalube**
Yamaha Motor Corporation USA
USA
[Automotive]

5 **Yamanouchi**
Yamanouchi Pharmaceutical Co. Ltd
Japan
[Pharmaceuticals]

6 **Yamato**
Germany
[Sporting Goods]

7 **Yara**
Yara International ASA
Norway
[Agricultural]

8 **Yard-Man**
MTD Products Inc
USA
[Household Products]

9 **Yashica**
JNC Datum Tech International Ltd
Japan
[Imaging & Photographic]

YASKAWA

Yaskawa
Yaskawa America Inc
USA
[Industrial Products]

Yellow Book
Yellow Book USA Inc
USA, 2008
[Publications]

Yellow Freight
Yellow Worldwide Inc
USA
[Freight & Logistics]

Yellow Pages
USA, 1962
Henry Alexander
[Publications]

YMCA (Young Men's
Christian Association)
USA, 2003
[Societies & Associations]

Yokogawa
Yokogawa Electric Corporation
Japan
[Technology]

Yokohama
Yokohama Rubber Company Ltd
Japan
[Manufacturing]

Yonden
Shikoku Electric Power Co. Inc
Japan, ca 1991
[Utilities]

Yonex
Yonex Co. Ltd
Japan, 1973
[Sporting Goods]

Yoplait
Yoplait Marques International SAS
France
[Food & Beverage]

Yoppi
Yoppi Hungary kft
Hungary
[Manufacturing]

York
Johnson Controls Inc
Canada
[Heating & Cooling]

Yorkshire Television
ITV plc
UK
[Television Channel]

Yoshimura
Yoshimura R&D of America Inc
USA
[Automotive]

Yoshinoya
Yoshinoya Holdings Co. Ltd
Japan
[Restaurants & Bars]

YouSendIt
YouSendIt Inc
USA
[Internet]

YouTube
YouTube LLC, Google Inc
USA, 2006
Chad Hurley
[Internet]

Y&R (Young & Rubicam)
USA
[Advertising & Campaigns]

Yukos Oil Company
Russia
[Oil, Gas & Petroleum]

Yum!
Yum! Brands Inc
USA, 2002
[Restaurants & Bars]

Yupo
Yupo Corporation
Japan
[Sporting Goods]

Yves Saint-Laurent
PPR SA
France, 1963
A. M. Cassandre
[Fashion]

1 **Zadig & Voltaire**
ZF France SAS
France
[Apparel]

2 **Zagato**
CPP Milan Srl
Italy
[Automotive]

3 **Zale Corporation**
USA
[Retail]

4 **Zales**
Zale Corporation
USA
[Retail]

5 **Zalf**
Gruppo Euromobil
Italy
[Home Furnishings]

6 **Zalman**
Zalman Tech Co. Ltd
USA
[Computer Hardware]

7 **Zanello**
Zanello SA
Argentina
[Manufacturing]

8 **Zanker**
Electrolux Hausgeräte
Vertriebs GmbH
Germany
[Home Appliances]

9 **Zanussi**
AB Electrolux
Italy
[Home Appliances]

10 **Zapata Corporation**
USA
[Oil, Gas & Petroleum]

1 **Zara**
INDITEX Group
Spain
[Retail]

2 **ZDF**
(Zweites Deutsches Fernsehen)
Germany
[Broadcaster]

3 **Zebco**
W.C. Bradley Co.
USA
[Outdoor & Recreation]

4 **Zebra Technologies**
USA
[Technology]

5 **Zeeman**
Zeeman textielSupers BV
Netherlands
[Retail]

6 **Zeiss**
Carl Zeiss AG
Germany, 1993
[Industrial Products]

7 **Zellers**
Hudson's Bay Company
Canada, 1975
[Retail]

8 **Zenetti Wheels**
Australia
[Automotive]

9 **Zenith Electronics**
Zenith Electronics,
LG Electronics
USA
[Consumer Electronics]

10 **Zenith**
LVMH Moët Hennessy
Louis Vuitton SA
Switzerland
[Watches & Jewelry]

11 **Zenji**
Activision Blizzard Inc,
Vivendi SA
USA
[Computer & Video Games]

ZEPPELIN

ZIG-ZAG

1 **Zeppelin**
France
[Marine]

2 **Zero Skateboards**
USA
[Sporting Goods]

3 **Zest**
Procter & Gamble Co
USA
[Personal Care]

4 **ZD (Ziff Davis Inc)**
USA
[Media]

5 **Zig-Zag**
Republic Technologies
International Company
France
[Consumer Products]

6 **Zimmer**
Zimmer Inc
USA
[Medical Devices]

7 **Ziploc**
S.C. Johnson & Son Inc
USA
[Consumer Products]

8 **Zippo**
Zippo Manufacturing Company
USA
[Consumer Products]

1 **Zirh International**
USA
[Personal Care]

2 **ZixCorp**
Zix Corporation
USA
[Information Technology]

3 **Zodiac Marine & Pool**
Zodiac International SASU
France
[Household Products]

4 **Zoomp**
Brazil
[Apparel]

5 **Zune**
Microsoft Corporation
USA
[Computer Hardware]

6 **Zurich**
Zurich Financial Services AG
Switzerland
[Financial Services]

7 **Zwillings J. A. Henckels**
Germany
[Knives]

8 **ZyLAB**
Zylab Technologies BV
Netherlands
[Information Technology]

INDEX

Company Index

#
1c Company, 50
2 Sisters Food Group
– Northern Foods, 496
2Wire Inc, 50
3M Company
– 3M, 50
– Bondo, 114
– Post-It, 542
– Scotch, 592
3-Stjernet A/S, 50
4A Poker e Giovanni Rossi
– 4A The Poker Suite, 51
4th Centenary of the City of Rio de Janeiro, 51
7-Eleven Inc, 52
19 TV Ltd/FremantleMedia North America Inc
– Idols, 365
20th Century Fox/ Fox Films
– Fox Records, 293
20th Century Fox Television
– 24, 52
21c Museum Hotel, 52
20000st Records, 53
(OCLC) Online Computer Library Center Inc
– WorldCat.org, 731
(PSL), 547
(SOPUS Products) Pennzoil Quaker State Company, 551
Tyco Toys, 677

A
AAHA (American Animal Hospital Association), 54
AAL (Aid Association for Lutherans), 54
Aalborg Portland A/S
– Aalborg White, 54
AAMA (American Amusement Machine Association), 55
AAMCO Transmissions, 55
AARP, 55

AARP (formerly American Association of Retired Persons), 55
ABA (American Bar Association), 55
Abacus International Pte Ltd, 55
Abadía Benedictina, 55
Abanka Vipa dd, 55
ABAV (Associação Brasileira de Agências de Viagens), 55
Abba, 55
Abba Seafood AB
– Kalles Kaviar, 390
Abbey National plc, 56
ABB Group
– ABB (Asea Brown Boveri), 55
Abbott Laboratories, 56
ABC (American Broadcasting Corporation), 56
ABC (Australian Broadcasting Corporation), 56
ABCO Foods, 57
Abecip (Associação Brasileira das Entidades de Crédito Imobiliário e Poupança), 57
AB Electrolux, 246
– Elektro Helios, 246
– Kelvinator, 393
– Tornado, 669
– Zanussi, 740
Abercrombie & Fitch Co., 57
– Hollister Co., 357
A Better Option Brands
– abob (A Better Option Bag), 58
AB InBev
– Anheuser-Busch, 88
– Busch, 128
Abitibi Consolidated Inc, 57
Ableton AG, 57
ABN (Algemene Bank Nederland), 57
ABN AMRO Bank NV, 57

AB Volvo
– Mack Trucks, 435
Academi
– Blackwater, 110
AC Cars Group Ltd
– Shelby Cobra, 601
ACCEL/Exchange
– The Exchange, 655
Accenture plc, 58
AccesRail Inc, 59
Access Industries Inc
– Warner Music Group, 717
Accessories and Retail Corporation
– Anne Klein, 89
Acciona SA
– Acciona Airport Services, 59
ACCO Brands Corporation
– Kensington, 393
Accor Group
– Sofitel, 615
Accor SA, 59
– All Seasons Hotels, 79
– ETAP Accor Hotels, 258
– Ibis Hotels, 362
– Motel 6, 465
AC/DC, 59
ACDelco, 59
ACD Systems International Inc
– ACDSee, 59
Ace Beepers Inc, 59
Ace Hardware Corporation
– Ace Hardware, 60
ACE Ltd, 59
Acer Inc
– Acer, 60
– Gateway, 310
– Packard Bell, 517
AchieveGlobal, 60
ACI International
– LA Gear, 408
ACORN (Association of Community Organizations for Reform Now), 60
ACO Systems Ltd, 60
ACR Systems Inc, 60
Actionaid, 61

Action for Blind People, 61
Action for children, 61
Activision Blizzard Inc
– Activision, 61
– Blizzard Entertainment, 110
– DJ Hero, 218
– Guitar Hero, 342
– Wolfenstein, 729
– Zenji, 741
Actuant Corporation
– Gardner Bender, 308
Acumen Inc
– Vetta, 701
Acxiom Corporation, 62
Adam Opel AG, 509
Adani Advanced Analytical Instruments
– Adani, 62
ADATA Technology Co. Ltd, 62
Addict Films, 63
Adecco SA, 63
AdForum, 63
adidas AG
– adidas Samba, 63
– adidas Sport Heritage, 63
– adidas Sport Performance, 63
– adidas Sport Style, 63
– David Beckham, 193
– RBK, 559
– Reebok, 564
Adio Footwear, 64
Adlerwerke vorm. H. Kleyer AG.
– Adler, 64
ADMA (Aviation Distributors and Manufacturers Association), 64
Admarc Southwest, 64
Adobe Systems Inc
– Adobe, 64
– Adobe Acrobat, 64
– Adobe Postscript, 64
Adolf Würth GmbH & Co. KG
– Würth, 733
ADPT Corporation

– Adaptec, 62
ADT Security Services, 64
Advance Auto Parts Inc, 64
Advanced Micro Devices Inc, 82
Advanced Sports International
– Fuji Bikes, 303
Advance Magazine Publishers Inc
– Condé Nast, 168
– GQ, 330
– Mademoiselle, 436
– reddit, 563
– Self, 597
– The New Yorker, 658
– Wired, 729
Advance Publications Inc
– Vanity Fair, 696
– Vogue, 709
Advanta Corporation, 65
Advantax Group LLC
– Advantax Coporate Property Tax Solution, 65
Advent Software Inc, 65
Advertising Council
– Ad Council, 62
AEG GmbH, 65
Aegis Communications Group Inc, 66
Aegon NV, 66
Aena (Aeropuertos Españoles y Navegación Aérea), 66
Aeon Co. Ltd
– Mini Stop, 456
Aer Lingus Group plc, 66
Aeroflot Russian Airlines, 66
Aerolíneas Argentinas, 66
Aeromotive Inc, 66
Aéropostale Inc, 67
Aerosmith, 67
Aerovías de México SA de CV
– AeroMéxico, 66
A&E Television Networks LLC
– Lifetime Television, 419
– The History Channel, 656

COMPANY INDEX

Aetna Inc, 67
AFDEC (Association of Franchised Distributors of Electronic Components), 67
Affinia Group
 - Raybestos, 559
Affinity Group Inc
 - Camping World, 136
Aflac Inc, 67
African Gold, 67
AFTA (Australian Federation of Travel Agents Ltd), 67
Agave Tequila Productores (AT)
 - Oro Azul Tequila, 513
AGCO Corporation
 - Massey Ferguson, 444
 - White Farm Equipment, 724
Ageas Insurance Ltd, 68
Agence France-Presse (AFP), 67
Agfa-Gevaert NV
 - AGFA, 68
Aggro Berlin, 68
Agilent Technologies Inc, 68
AGIP SpA, 68
Agriculture and Horticulture Development Board (AHDB)
 - HGCA, 354
AGV SpA, 69
Ahlstrom Corporation, 69
aicep Portugal Global, 69
Aichi Bank, 69
Aids Fonds
 - Stop Aids Now!, 629
AIGA (American Institute, 70
AIG (American International Group) Inc, 70
Aigle International SA, 70
AIM Mail Centers Inc, 70
AirAsia Bhd, 70
Airbus SAS, 70
Air Canada, 71
Air Express International Corporation (AEI), 71
Airfield Walter Moser GmbH, 71
Air France-KLM SA
 - Air France, 71
 - Alitalia, 77
Air India Ltd, 71
Air Lift, 72
Air Madagascar, 72
Air New Zealand, 72
Air Products and Chemicals Inc
 - Air Products, 72
Airtronics, 73
Airwalk International LLC, 73
Airwell Group, 73
Aiwa Corporation, 73
Aixtron SE, 73
Ajinomoto Co. Inc, 74
AJ Wright, 74
Akai Sales Pte Ltd, 74
Akbank TAS, 74
AKG Acoustics, 74
AKSA Enerji Uretim AS
 - AKSA Energy, 74
AK Steel Corporation, 74
Akzo Nobel NV
 - AkzoNobel, 74
 - Coral (Tintas Coral), 171
 - Dulux, 233
 - Glidden Paint, 323
 - ICI (Imperial Chemical Industries), 364
 - International Paint, 373
 - Sikkens, 606

Alabama Space Science Exhibit Commission
 - Space Camp, 619
Alaska Airlines, 75
Alaska Seafood Marketing Institute
 - Alaska Seafood, 75
Albert Heijn BV, 75
Albertsons LLC, 75
Albi GmbH & Co. KG, 75
Alcan Products Corporation
 - Alcan Cable, 75
Alcatel-Lucent SA, 75
Alcoa Inc, 75
Alesis LP, 75
Alfa Mutual Insurance Company, 76
ALF (Animal Liberation Front), 76
Alfa Romeo Automobiles SpA, 76
alfi GmbH, 76
Alfred Dunhill Ltd
 - Dunhill London, 234
Alfred Ritter GmbH & Co. KG
 - Ritter Sport, 570
AlgarveShopping, 76
Algeco Scotsman, 76
Aliaxis Group
 - Glynwed Pipe Systems, 324
Alien Skin Software LLC, 76
Alimentation Couche-Tard Inc
 - Couche-Tard, 175
 - Mac's Convenience Stores, 435
Al-Ko Kober Ltd, 77
Allegheny Technologies Inc (ATI), 77
Allegiance Telecom Inc, 77
Alleman Cycle Plex, 77
All England Lawn Tennis and Croquet Club (AELTC)
 - The Championships Wimbledon, 653
Allen Lund Company Inc, 77
Allens Arthur Robinson Group, 77
Allergan Inc, 77
Alliance Boots GmbH
 - Boots, 115
Alliance UniChem IP Ltd, 78
Allianz SE
 - Allianz, 78
 - Fireman's Fund, 281
Allied Data Technologies BV, 78
Allied Domecq plc
 - Mister Donut, 458
Allied Electronics Inc, 78
Allied Gear & Machine Co. Inc, 78
Allied Holdings Inc (AHI), 78
Allied Stores Corporation
 - A&S, 54
Allis-Chalmers Manufacturing Co.
 - Allis-Chambers, 78
Allseating, 79
Allume Systems Inc, 79
Ally Financial Inc
 - GMAC (General Motors Acceptance Corporation), 324
ALNO AG, 79
Aloha Airlines Inc, 79
Alpego Srl, 80
Alpina Sports GmbH

 - Alpina Eyewear & Helmets, 80
 - Alpina Professional Helmets, 80
Alpine, 80
Alpine Electronics of America Inc, 80
Alpinestars SpA, 80
Alstom SA, 80
Altana AG, 80
Altec Lansing Technologies Inc, 81
Altera Corporation
 - Mercury, 450
Alternative Bike Co., 81
Altor Equity Partners
 - Helly Hansen, 352
Altria Group Inc
 - Altria, 81
 - Marlboro, 442
 - Virginia Slims, 705
Alza Corporation, 81
Amaury Group
 - L'Equipe, 416
Amaury Sports Organisation
 - Dakar Rally, 187
 - Le Tour de France, 416
Amazon.com Inc
 - Amazon, 82
 - Amazon Kindle, 82
AmBev Venezuela
 - Cerveza Zulia, 144
Amblin Entertainment Inc, 82
AMC Entertainment Inc
 - AMC Theatres (American Multi-Cinema), 82
AMC Networks
 - AMC (American Movie Classics), 82
 - IFC (Independent Film Channel), 366
 - Sundance Channel, 632
Ameren Corporation, 82
America Movil
 - Claro, 158
América Móvil SAB de CV
 - Telcel, 645
 - TracFone, 671
Americana International Ltd
 - Bench, 105
American Airlines Inc, 82
American Automobile Association Inc
 - Automobile Club of Southern California, 96
American Blue Ribbon Holdings LLC
 - Village Inn, 704
American Cancer Society (ACS), 83
American Capital Strategies Inc
 - AAMCO Transmissions, 55
American Century Proprietary Holdings Inc
 - American Century Investments, 83
American Continental Corporation, 83
American Diabetes Association, 83
American Electric Power Companies Inc (AEP), 83
American Express Company
 - American Express, 83
American Family Mutual Insurance, 83
American Farm Bureau Federation, 267
American Hardware & Supply
 - ServiStar, 599

American Home Products Corporation (AHP)
 - Wyeth Lederle, 733
American Iron and Steel Institute
 - Steelmark, 627
American Italian Pasta Company
 - Mueller's, 470
American Media Inc
 - Flex, 285
American Motorcyclist Association
 - AMA Motocross Championship, 81
 - AMA Superbike Championship, 81
American Optometric Association
 - InfantSEE, 371
American Recordings, 85
American Red Cross (ARC), 85
American Republic Insurance Company, 85
American Revolution Bicentennial Administration (ARBA), 85
American Standard Brands, 85
American States Water Company (AWR), 85
American Stores Company, 85
American Sugar Refining Inc
 - Domino Sugar, 222
American Superabrasives Corporation
 - Anco Diamonds, 87
American Telephone and Telegraph Company
 - Bell System, 105
Americhem Inc, 86
Amersham plc, 86
Amer Sports Oyj
 - Salomon, 583
 - Volant, 709
 - Wilson, 727
AMF Bowling Centers Inc, 86
Amgen Inc, 86
Amnesty International, 86
Amoco Corporation, 86
Amoeba Music Inc, 86
A&M Records, 54
AMRO Bank, 87
Amsterdamsche Football Club Ajax
 - Ajax Amsterdam, 73
Amtrak
 - Acela Express, 60
Analog Devices Inc, 87
Anda Inc, 88
Andersen Consulting, 88
Andreas Stihl AG & Company
 - Stihl, 629
Andrews McMeel Universal, 88
Andritz Group
 - Andritz, 88
 - Andritz KoneWood, 88
Anheuser-Busch Companies Inc
 - Anheuser-Busch, 88
 - Busch, 128
Anheuser-Busch InBev NV
 - AB InBev, 57
 - Bud, 123
 - Bud Light, 123
 - Dommelsch, 223
 - Hoegaarden, 356
 - Jupiler, 389

 - Labatt Blue, 406
 - Labatt Ice, 406
 - Labatt's, 406
 - Michelob, 454
 - Michelob Lager, 454
 - Skol, 610
Anixter Inc, 88
Annex Business Media
 - PEM (Plant Engineering & Maintenance), 526
ANPE (Agence Nationale pour l'Emploi), 89
Anthro Corporation, 89
AOL Inc
 - AIM (AOL Instant Messenger), 70
 - America Online (AOL), 85
 - Netscape, 484
 - TechCrunch (TC), 644
 - The Huffington Post, 656
AP Moller, 436
Apollo Global Management LLC
 - Claire's, 157
Apollo Vredestein BV
 - Vredestein, 712
Appalachian League, 89
Apple Inc
 - Apple, 89
 - Apple Computer Co, 89
 - ColorSync, 164
 - FireWire, 282
 - iPhone, 375
 - iTunes, 379
 - Mac, 434
 - Macintosh, 434
 - Newton, 487
 - QuickTime, 553
Aqua Lung International
 - Technisub, 644
Aqueon (Central Garden & Pet Company)
 - All-Glass Aquarium, 77
Aracruz Celulose SA, 90
Arai Helmet Ltd, 90
Aral AG, 90
Aramark Corporation, 90
ara Shoes AG, 89
Arbeitsgemeinschaft Golden Toast eV, 326
Arcares, 90
ArcelorMittal SA, 90
Arc International
 - Pyrex, 549
Arctic Paper AB
 - Trebruk, 673
Arena Italia SpA, 90
Areva SA, 91
Argos Ltd, 91
Argo Tractors SpA
 - Landini, 409
Ariba Inc, 91
Ariston Thermo SpA, 91
Arla Foods amba, 91
Armour-Eckrich Meats LLC
 - Eckrich, 242
Army Navy, 92
Arnoldo Mondadori Editore SpA
 - Mondadori Informatica, 462
ARP Instruments Inc, 92
Arsenal Football Club, 92
artido Socialista, 522
Art Institute of Chicago, 92
Artsana SpA
 - Chicco, 148
Arts & Entertainment Television Networks
 - A&E Network, 54
Asahi Breweries Inc
 - Cottee's, 175

747

COMPANY INDEX

Asahi Breweries Ltd, 92
Asahi Glass Co. Ltd
– AGC, 68
A/S Air Baltic Corporation, 70
AS DC Holding
– Double Coffee, 224
Ashland Inc
– Valvoline, 695
Ashok Leyland Ltd, 92
Asia Pacific Breweries Ltd
– Tiger Beer, 663
Asics Ltd, 93
– Asics Tiger, 93
– Onitsuka Tiger, 508
Asimpres
– Instituto Estudios Gráficos de Chile, 372
AS Liviko Masina
– Viru Valge, 706
Asociación Nacional de Productores de Leche Pura
– Alpura, 80
A Special Wish Foundation, 93
ASSA ABLOY Group
– JPM, 388
ASSA ABLOY Group AB
– Medeco, 448
– Yale, 736
Associated British Foods plc, 93
– Primark, 544
– Wander, 716
Associated Food Stores Inc
– Dan's Foods, 190
Associated Press, 93
Association for the Advancement of Baltic Studies
– AABS, 54
Association Suisse de l'Industrie Gazière (ASIG)
– Gaz Naturel, 312
Associazione Calcio Chievo Verona SrL
– AC Verona, 62
Assurant Inc, 93
AS Tallink Grupp
– Silja Line, 606
Asterix
– Société Dargaud, 93
Aston Martin Lagonda Ltd, 93
Astral Media Inc
– Historia, 355
– NRJ, 497
AstraZeneca plc, 93
Atari Interactive, 94
Atari SA, 94
A.T. Cross Company
– Cross, 180
– CrossPad, 180
Atelier Des Boiseux/Kity
– Kity, 397
AtHomeNet Inc
– Cottonwood Valley, 175
ATI Technologies Inc
– ATI, 94
Atlanta Fulton County Recreation Authority
– Wide-Lite, 725
Atlantic Media Company
– The Atlantic, 652
Atlas Copco AB, 95
Atlas Fence Inc, 95
Atomic Austria GmbH
– Atomic Skis, 95
AT&T (American Telephone Telegraph Company)
– Bell System, 105
AT&T California

– Pacific Bell, 516
AT&T Corporation
– Bell System, 105
AT&T Inc, 94
Audi AG
– Audi, 95
– Audi NSU, 95
– Lamborghini, 408
Augsburg Fortress
– Book of Faith, 114
August Bremicker und Söhne KG
– ABUS, 58
August Rüggeberg GmbH & Co. KG
– Pferd, 531
Australia Council for the Arts, 96
Australia Made Campaign Ltd
– Australian Made, 96
Australian and New Zealand EMC (ANZEMC)
– C-Tick, 181
Australian Automobile Association
– AAA, 54
Australian National Maritime Museum, 478
Australian Theatres
– Greater Union, 333
– Village Cinemas, 704
Australian Wool Innovation Ltd
– Woolmark, 730
Autodesk Inc
– Autodesk, 96
– Autodesk Maya, 96
– Maya Complete, 446
Autodistribution International CVBA
– AD, 62
Automatic Data Processing Inc
– ADP, 64
Automobile Racing Club of America
– Arca Racing, 90
Automobiles Citroën, 155
– Citroën Picasso, 533
Automobili Lamborghini SpA
– Lamborghini, 408
Autonomous Community of Valencia
– Generalitat Valenciana, 315
Autopart International Inc, 291
Autoroutes du Sud de la France (ASF), 96
Auto Value Parts Stores, 96
Autrogrill SpA, 97
Avaya Inc, 97
Avenir SAS, 97
Aventis SA, 97
Avery Dennison Corporation
– Avery, 97
AviancaTaca Holding SA
– TACA Airlines (Transportes Aéreos del Continente Americano), 638
Avid Technology Inc
– Avid, 97
– Pinnacle Systems, 534
Avirex U.S.A, 97
Avis Budget Group Inc
– Avis Rent a Car, 97
Avis Rent a Car System LLC, 97
Aviva plc, 97
Avon Products Inc, 97
AVOS Systems Inc
– Delicious, 199
AXA SA, 97

Axel Springer AG
– Bild, 108
Axfood AB
– Hemköp, 352
– Willy:s, 727

B

BAA (British Airport Authority), Ltd, 98
Babcock International Group PLC, 98
Bacardi & Company Limited
– Dewar's, 208
Bacardi Global Brands Ltd
– William Lawson's, 727
Bacardi Ltd, 98
BAE Systems plc
– Alvis, 81
Bahrain National Holding Company
– BNI (Bahrain National Insurance), 112
Bahrain Telecommunication Company BSC
– Batelco, 103
Baidu Inc, 98
Bain Capital LLC
– Burlington Coat Factory, 127
– The Weather Channel, 661
Ballard Power Systems Inc, 98
Ball Corporation, 98
Ballspielverein Borussia 09 eV Dortmund, 115
Bally Technologies Inc, 99
Baltic Centre for Contemporary Art
– Baltic, 99
Banco Central del Ecuador
– Maac (Museo – Antropologico y de Arte Contemporaneo), 434
Banco del Pacifico, 99
Bang & Olufsen A/S, 100
BankBoston, 100
Bankgesellschaft Berlin, 100
Bankia SA
– Caja Madrid, 133
Bank of America
– FleetBoston Financial, 285
Bank of America Corporation, 100
– Merrill Lynch, 451
Bank of Beijing Co. Ltd, 100
Bank of China Ltd, 100
Bank of Montreal/Banque de Montréal, 100
Bank of Nova Scotia
– Scotiabank, 593
Bank of Scotland plc (Lloyds Banking Group plc)
– Halifax, 347
Bank Pekao SA, 100
– Pekao Leasing, 525
Banner Health, 101
Bape (I.T. Group)
– Baby Milo, 98
Barack Obama Presidential Campaign, 101
BarcelonaTech), 689
Barclays plc
– Barclaycard, 101
– Barclays, 101
Barco NV, 102
Barilla Alimentare SpA
– Wasa, 717
Barilla France SAS
– Harry's, 349
Barneys New York, 102

Barns & Noble Inc, 102
Barry Callebaut Group
– Van Houten, 696
BASF SE, 102
– MBT (Master Builders Technologies), 447
BasicNet SpA
– Kappa, 391
– K-Way, 405
Baskin-Robbins Inc, 102
Bata Brands Sarl
– Bata, 103
– Weinbrenner, 720
Bauer Media Group
– The Box, 653
Bauer Verlagsgruppe GmbH
– Q Magazine, 550
Bauknecht Hausgeräte GmbH, 103
Bausch & Lomb Inc, 103, 566
Bayer AG, 104
Bayer Healthcare LLC
– Aleve, 76
Bayerischer Rundfunk (BR), 104
Baywatch Production Company
– Baywatch, 104
BBC (British Broadcasting Corporation), 104
BBDO, 104
BBVA (Banco Bilbao Vizcaya Argentaria SA), 104
BCE Inc
– Bell Canada, 105
BDNA, 104
Beam Inc
– Jim Beam, 385
Beastie Boys, 332
Beggars Group
– 4AD, 51
Beghelli SpA, 105
Beiersdorf AG, 105
– Hansaplast, 348
– La Prairie, 410
– Nivea, 493
– Tesa, 650
Bel Leerdammer BV, 413
Belvédère Scandinavia A/S
– Danzka Vodka, 190
Bencom Srl
– Killer Loop, 396
– Sisley, 608
Bendigo and Adelaide Bank, 63
Bendix Corporation, 105
Benefon Oyj, 105
Benetton Group SpA
– Benetton, 106
– United Colors of Benetton, 686
Benjamin Moore & Co
– Benjamin Moore Paints, 106
Bennigan's Franchising Company LLC
– Bennigan's, 106
Ben Sherman Group Ltd
– Ben Sherman, 106
Bentley Motors Ltd
– Bentley, 106
Berjaya Group
– Berjaya Air, 106
Berkshire Hathaway Inc
– Burlington Northern Railroad, 128
– BVD (Bradley, Voorhees & Day), 129
– Dairy Queen (DQ), 186
– Fruit of the Loom, 302
– Wells Lamont, 721
– XTRA Corporation, 735

Berlitz Corporation, 106
Berner UK Ltd
– Kent, 393
Bertazzoni SpA, 107
Best Buy Co. Inc, 107
– Napster, 475
Best Western International Inc, 107
Betten Trucks Inc, 107
Better Business Bureau (BBB), 107
Beyerdynamic GmbH & Co. KG, 107
B&G Foods Inc
– Trappey's, 672
Bharti Airtel Ltd
– Airtel, 73
BHS (British Home Stores) Ltd, 108
BIC Corporation
– Sheaffer, 601
Big Boy Restaurants International LLC, 108
Big Deal
– Var nv, 108
Big Rock Brewery
– Grasshöpper, 332
Big Websites, 108
Billabong International
– Billabong International Ltd, 109
– Dakine, 187
– Element Skateboards, 247
– Von Zipper, 711
Bill Gates
– Corbis, 171
Bimbo Bakeries USA Inc
– Boboli, 111
– Entenmann's, 251
– Oroweat, 513
Binatone Industries Ltd, 109
Birds Eye Iglo Group Ltd (BEIG)
– Birds Eye, 109
– Iglo, 367
Birkenstock Orthopädie GmbH & Co. KG
– Birkenstock, 109
Birra Peroni, 528
Black Crows, 110
Blaupunkt GmbH, 110
Blizzard Entertainment Inc
– Warcraft, 716
Blockbuster Inc, 110
Blogmusik SAS
– Deezer, 197
Bloomberg LP, 111
– BusinessWeek, 128
Bloomin Brands INC
– Outback Steakhouse, 515
Blount Inc
– ICS, 365
Blue Coat Systems Inc
– Packeteer, 517
Blue Cross Animal Hospital, 111
Blue Cross Blue Shield Association, 111
BlueScope Steel, 111
Blue Shield of California, 111
Blue Square International
– Carré Bleu, 140
Bluetooth SIG, 111
Bluetronics Group
– Electrohome, 246
BlueTronics Group
– Emerson Electronics, 249
Blum Enterprises
– Green Canteen, 334
Blu-ray Disc Association, 112

748

COMPANY INDEX

BMG (Bertelsmann Music Group)
- Fox Records, 293

BMO Harris Bank NA
- Harris Bank, 349

BMW AG
- BMW, 112
- BMW Williams F1, 112

BNP Paribas SA, 112
- Bank of the West, 100

Bobcat Company, 113

Böckling GmbH & Co. KG, 113

Bodum AG, 113

Body Glove International LLC, 113

Boehringer Ingelheim GmbH, 113

Boffi SpA, 113

Boise Cascade Holdings LLC, 113

Bold Advertising Products
- Weeder Sheeter, 719

Bollinger Industries LP, 114

Bombardier Aerospace
- Learjet, 412

Bombardier Inc, 114
- Learjet, 412

Bompreço SA
- Hiper Bompreço, 355

BonBon-Land A/S, 114

Bonnier Corporation
- Cycle World, 183
- Popular Science, 540

Bonnier Publishing
- Hot Key Books, 358

Books-A-Million Inc, 114

Booktrust
- Get London Reading, 318

Boots Healthcare International (BHI), 115

Boots UK Ltd
- Boots, 115

Borden Food Corporation, 115

Borders Group
- Waldenbooks, 714

Borders Group Inc, 115

BorgWarner Inc, 115

Borland Software Corporation
- Borland, 115

Bosal International SA/NV, 116

Bos Auspuff GmbH, 116

Bosch Security Systems Inc
- Telex, 648

Bosch Thermotechnik GmbH
- Junkers, 389

Bose Corporation, 116

Boss Corporation, 116

Boston Whaler Inc, 116

Bourne Leisure Ltd
- Butlins, 129

Bouygues SA
- Bouygues Telecom, 116

Bowne & Co. Inc, 116

Boy Scouts of America, 116

Boys & Girls Clubs of America (BGCA), 117

BP America Inc
- ampm, 87

BP plc, 117
- Arco, 90
- Castrol Motor Oil, 141
- Sohio (Standard Oil of Ohio), 615

Brabantia Branding BV, 117

Bradlees Department Stores Inc
- Bradlees, 117

Braggin Waggon, 117

Brambles Ltd

– CHEP (Commonwealth Handling Equipment Pool Organisation), 147

Brandchannel.com
- Brand Channel, 117

Brauerei Ausschank Wielandstrasse Ein Unternehmen der Altbier Düsseldorf GmbH
- Frankenheim, 296

Braun GmbH, 118

Bravado International Group Merchandising Services Inc
- Red Hot Chilli Peppers (Star of Affinity logo), 563

Bravo Sports Corporation
- Variflex, 697

Brazilian Olympic Committee
- Olympic Games Rio 2016, 506

Breitling SA, 118

Brembo SpA, 118

BRF Brasil Foods SA
- Batavo, 103

BRFL Italia Srl
- Guru, 343

Bridgestone Corporation, 118

Bridgestone Firestone LLC
- Firehawk, 281
- Firestone, 281

Briggs & Stratton Corporation
- Victa, 702

Brink's Inc
- Brinks, 119

Brioche Pasquier, 522

Bristol-Myers Squibb Company, 119

Brita GmbH, 119

British Airways plc, 119

British American Tobacco plc
- British American Tobacco, 119
- Dunhill, 234
- Kent, 393
- Lucky Strike, 429

British Broadcasting Corporation
- Freesat, 298
- RDS Radio Data System, 560

British Council, 120

British Gas plc, 120

British InterContinental Hotels Group (IHG)
- Holiday Inn, 356

British Rail, 120

British Sky Broadcasting Group plc
- Sky Channel, 610

British Standards Institution
- Kitemark, 397

British Steel plc, 120

British Teleflower Service Ltd, 646

British Waterways, 120

Broadcom Corporation, 120

Broan-NuTone LLC, 120

Broken Hill Proprietary Company Ltd
- BHP, 108

Broncoway Software Solutions, 121

Brondi SpA, 121

Brother Industries Ltd, 121

Brown-Forman Corporation
- Jack Daniel's, 380

Browning, 121

Brown Shoe Company Inc
- Brown Shoe Company, 128
- Famous Footwear, 265

Brunswick Corporation, 121

Brussels Airlines, 121

Bryant Heating & Cooling Systems Inc
- Bryant, 121

BSI Group, 169
- Kitemark, 397

BT Group plc
- British Telecom, 120
- BT, 122
- BT Connected World, 122

BTI (Battery Technology Inc), 122

Buck Knives Inc, 122

Budějovickým Budvarem NC
- Budweiser Budvar Brewery, 123

Budget Host Inns & Hotels, 123

Budget Rent A Car System Inc
- Budget Rent A Car, 123

Bugaboo International BV, 123

Bugatti Automobiles SAS, 123

BührmannUbbens, 124

Builder's Square Inc, 124

BuiltGreen, 124

Bulauto JSC, 124

Bulgari SpA, 125

Bull SAS, 125

Bulova Corporation
- Bulova Watches, 125

Bundesgartenschau (Federal Garden Expo), 125

Bunn-O-Matic Corporation, 126
- Bunn, 125

Buongiorno SpA, 126

Burberry Group plc, 126

Burbn Inc
- Instagram, 372

Bureau Veritas SA, 127

Burger King Holdings Inc, 127

Burgo Group SpA
- Burgopapers, 127

Burlington Coat Factory Warehouse Corporation, 127

Burlington Northern Santa Fe Corporation
- Burlington Northern Railroad, 128

Burton Snowboards Inc, 128

Bushnell Outdoor Products Europe
- Bollé, 114

BUT International, 128

Butterfly, 129

Buzzcocks, 129

C

C&A
- Palomino, 518

CAA (Canadian Automobile Association), 132

Cabela's Inc, 132

CablesOne Company, 132

Cable & Wireless Communications plc, 132

Cable & Wireless Worldwide plc, 132

Cadbury Adams USA LLC
- Dentyne, 203

Cadbury France
- Chocolat Poulain, 542
- Hollywood Chewing Gum, 357

Cadbury plc
- Vichy Pastilles, 702

Caesars Entertainment Corp

- Flamingo, 284

Caesars Entertainment Corporation
- Caesers Palace, 133

Cailler of Switzerland, 133

California Academy of Sciences, 134

California Department of Parks, 134

California Department of Transportation
- Caltrans, 135

California Federal Bank, 133

California Milk Producers Advisory Board
- Real California Cheese, 560

California Side Car Inc, 134

California Tree Fruit Agreement
- California Peaches, Plums, Nectarines, 134

California Water Service Group, 134

Callaway Golf Company, 134

Callon Petroleum Company, 134

Calloway Golf Company
- Ben Hogan, 106

Calvin Klein Inc
- Calvin Klein, 135
- ck Calvin Klein, 135

Camelot UK Lotteries Ltd
- The National Lottery, 657

Cameron International Corporation
- Ajax, 73

Campbell Soup Company, 135
- Franco-American, 296
- V8 Vegetable Juice, 694

Camper, 136

Campina Nederland BV
- Mona, 462

CAMPSA (Compañía Arrendataria del Monopolio del Petróleo SA), 136

Cam SpA, 135

Canada Post Corporation, 136

Canada Tsuga, 136

Canadian Airlines International Ltd, 136

Canadian Football League, 145

Canadian Natural Resources Ltd, 136

Canadian Pacific Railway Ltd, 137

Canadian Paediatric Society, 137

Candia, 137

C and J Clark International Ltd, 157

Candy Group, 137

Cannondale Bicycle Corporation, 137

Canon Inc, 137

Canson, 138

Canteen Vending, 138

Canterbury Ltd, 138

Caparol Farben Lacke Bautenschutz GmbH, 138

Capcom Co. Ltd
- Killer 7, 396
- Street Fighter II, 630

Cap Gemini SA, 138

Capital Partners
- Almaty Financial District, 79

Capitol Music Group
- Capitol Records, 138

Car & Boat Media SAS
- Caradislac, 138

Cardinal Health Inc, 138

Cardo Flow Solutions AB
- ABS, 58

Car-Freshner Corporation
- Little Trees, 422

Cargill Ltd, 139
- Dust-Off, 236

Cargolux International Airlines SA, 139

Cargotec Corporation
- Hiab (Hydrauliska Industri AB), 354

Carhartt Inc, 139

Caribbean Airlines-Air Jamaica Transition Ltd
- Air Jamaica, 72

Carlisle Companies Inc, 139

Carl Karcher Enterprises Inc
- Green Burrito, 334
- The Green Burrito, 656

Carlsberg A/S
- Tuborg Beer, 675

Carlsberg Group, 139
- Nevskoe, 485

Carlson
- T.G.I. Friday's, 651

Carlson Rezidor Hotel Group
- Country Inns & Suites, 175
- Park Plaza, 522

Carlton & United Beverages
- Victoria Bitter (VB), 703

Carl Walther GmbH, 715

Carl Zeiss AG, 41

Carl Zeiss Inc
- SOLA, 616

Carnegie Mellon University
- Digital Emoticon, 213

Carnival Corporation & plc
- Cunard Line, 182
- P&O Cruises, 516
- Princess Cruises, 545

Carolco Pictures Inc, 140

Carphone Warehouse Group plc, 140, 658

Carquest Corporation, 140

Carrefour SA, 140

Carrier Corporation, 140
- Payne, 523
- Totaline, 670

Cartier SA, 140

CASA International NV, 141

Casio Computer Co. Ltd, 141

Castle Investment Companies
- Castle Alternative Invest AG, 141

CA Technologies Inc, 132

Caterpillar Inc
- CAT, 142

Cava, 142

CBC (Canadian Broadcasting Corporation), 142

CBI Federal Credit Union, 178

CBR (Centraal Bureau Rijvaardigheidsbewijzen), 142

CBRE Group Inc, 142

CB Richard Ellis Group Inc
- Trammell Crow Company, 672

CBS Broadcasting Inc, 142
- The Twilight Zone, 660

CBS Corporation
- c|net, 160
- NCIS, 481
- Showtime, 603
- Star Trek, 626
- Star Trek - The Next Generation, 626
- Star Trek - Voyager, 626
- The Movie Channel, 657
- UPN, 689
- Westinghouse, 723

749

COMPANY INDEX

CBS Interactive
- c|net, 160
CBS Interactive Music Group
- MP3.com, 467
CBS Radio Inc
- MP3.com, 467
CBTE (Central Brasileira dos Trabalhadores e Empreendedores), 142
CCEBA (Centro Cultural de España en Buenos Aires), 142
CCTV (Chinese Central Television), 143
CDU (Christlich Demokratische Union Deutschlands), 143
CEA (Commissariat Energie Atomique), 143
CedarCrestone Inc
- Crestone International, 179
C. & E. Fein GmbH, 272
Celio, 143
Celtic plc, 143
CEMEX SAB de CV, 143
Centaur Media plc
- Marketing Week, 441
CenterParcs Europe NV, 143
Centerview Partners
- Del Monte Foods, 200
Centrais Elétricas do Norte do Brasil SA
- Electronorte, 246
Centrais Elétricas SA
- Furnas, 305
Central Bancshares
- Central Bank, 143
Centre national d'art et de culture Georges Pompidou, 144
Centrepoint, 143
Century 21 Real Estate LLC, 144
CEPP
- Porto Cruz, 541
CEPSA (Compañía Española de Petróleos SA), 144
Cequent Performance Products Inc
- Draw-Tite, 228
Cerner Corporation, 144
Cervecería y Maltería Quilmes
- Iguana Cerveza, 367
České dráhy AS, 144
Cessna Aircraft Company, 144
Cetursa Sierra Nevada SA
- Sierra Nevada, 605
CF Industries Holdings Inc, 145
CFP NV
- GVB Amsterdam, 343
C. Hahne Mühlenwerke GmbH & Co. KG, 346
Chanel SA, 145
Channel 5 Broadcasting Ltd, 146
Channel Four Television Corporation
- Channel Four Television Corporation, 146
- Film4, 279
- The Box, 653
Chaparral Boats Inc, 146
Charan Industries Inc
- ToyBiz, 671
Chaussures Eram SARL
- Eram, 254
C.H. Boehringer Sohn AG & Co. KG
- Boehringer Ingelheim, 113
CHC Helicopter, 146

Cheap Monday, 146
Checkers Drive-In Restaurants Inc
- Rally's, 557
Chelsea FC plc, 147
Chemical Industries Association, 147
Chemigate Oy, 147
Chemtura Corporation
- Great Lakes Chemical Corporation, 333
Cheung Kong Infrastructure, 157
Chevron Corporation, 148
- Caltex, 134
- Texaco, 650
Chicago Bulls, 148
Chicago Pneumatic, 148
Chicago Rawhide, 148
Chick-fil-A Inc, 148
Children's Miracle Network, 149
Children's Television Workshop
- The Electric Company, 655
Chilean Government
- Correos Chile, 173
China International Airlines Company
- Air China, 71
China Mobile Ltd, 149
China Ocean Shipping (Group) Company
- Cosco Pacific, 174
China Steel Corporation (CSC), 149
China Telecom Corp. Ltd, 149
China United Netcom (Hong Kong) Ltd
- China Unicom, 149
Chinon Industries Inc, 149
Chip Holding GmbH
- Chip Magazine, 149
Chiquita Brands International Inc, 150
Chodai Co. Ltd, 150
Choice Hotels International Inc, 157
- Comfort Inn, 166
- Comfort Suites, 166
- Rodeway Inn, 573
- Sleep Inn, 611
Choice Records, 150
C=Holdings BV
- Commodore, 166
Chris Craft Inc, 150
Christian Aid, 150
Christian Association), 738
Christian Dior SA, 214
Christian Reformed Church in North America
- Coffee Break Small Groups, 161
Christie Digital Systems USA Inc, 150
Christies Inc, 150
Christopher & Banks Inc, 150
C.H. Robinson Worldwide Inc, 151
Chrysalis Capital Partners
- Polartec, 539
Chrysler Group LLC
- Chrysler, 151
- Dodge, 219
- Dodge Viper, 219
- Jeep, 383
- Mopar, 464
Chubb, 151
Chubu Electric Power Co. Inc, 151
Chums Inc, 151

Chupa Chups SAU, 151
Church & Dwight Co. Inc
- Arm & Hammer, 91
- Trojan, 674
CIA (Central Intelligence Agency), 151
Cia Hering SA, 353
Cia. Tropical de Hotéis
- Tropical, 674
Ciba AG
- Chupa Chups, 151
Ciba Vision Corporation, 152
CIB (Commercial International Bank), 151
CIC (Crédit Industriel et Commercial), 152
Cicli Pinarello SpA
- Opera, 509
Cigna Corporation, 152
Cilag GmbH International, Division Greiter, 535
Cincom Systems Inc, 152
Cinema for Peace Foundation, 152
Cinergy Corporation, 153
Cineworld Group plc, 153
Cingular Wireless LLC, 153
Cintas Corporation, 153
CIPEC (Canadian Industry Program for Energy Conservation), 153
Circle Holdings plc, 153
Circle K Stores Inc, 154
Circus World Displays Ltd
- Electrohome, 246
Cirrus Logic Inc, 154
Cisco Systems Inc, 154
Citgo Petroleum Corporation, 154
Citibank, 154
CitiBus Ltd, 155
Citigroup Global Special Situations Group
- Red Roof Inn, 564
Citigroup Inc, 154
- Banamex, 99
- EMI, 249
- EMI-Capitol Music, 249
Citizen Holdings Co. Ltd, 154, 155
Citizens Bank of Canada, 155
Citrix Systems Inc, 155, 363
City & Guilds of London Institute, 155
City Hopper, 155
City National Corporation
- City National Bank, 155
City of Coteau du-Lac, 175
City of Dallas, 187
City of Hope National Medical Center, 156
City of Los Angeles
- Los Angeles Zoo, 426
City of Melbourne, 156
City of Tampa Department of Solid Waste & Environment Program Management
- Solid Waste, 616
City of Toronto
- Toronto Zoo, 670
City of Westminster College, 156
City University of New York, 156
Civitan International, 156
CJ Corp
- Baek Sul, 98
CJ Group, 157
C Joseph Lamy GmbH, 408
CKE Restaurants Inc
- Carl's Jr., 139

Claire's Stores Inc, 157
Clairtone Sound Corporation Ltd, 157
Clarion Co. Ltd, 157
Clearly Canadian Beverage Corporation, 158
CLIA (Cruise Lines International Association), 158
Cliché Skateboards, 158
Clinique Laboratories LLC, 158
Clopay Building Products Company Inc, 158
Closed Captioned, 159
Club Atletico Boca Juniors
- Boca Juniors, 113
Club Méditerranée SA, 159
CMAS (Confédération Mondiale des Activités Subaquatiques), 159
CMC Markets UK plc, 159
CMI Corporation, 159
CNA International Inc
- Magic, 437
CN (Canadian National Railway), 159
CNH Global NV, 486
Coach Inc, 160
Cobra USA Inc, 160
Coco's Bakery Restaurant Inc, 161
Codan Forsikring A/S, 161
Codarts, 161
CoffeeCompany BV, 161
Cofina Media
- Record, 562
Coflexip Stena Offshore, 162
Cofra Holding AG
- C&A, 132
- Palomino, 518
Cogeco Inc, 162
Cognac Gautier, 311
Cognos, 162
Coilhose Pneumatics, 162
Coinstar Inc, 162
ColArt Fine Art & Graphics Ltd
- Winsor & Newton, 728
Coldwell Banker Real Estate LLC, 162
Coleco Entertainment Corp, 162
Colegio de Arquitectos, 162
Coleman Company Inc, 163
Coles Supermarkets Australia Pty Ltd, 163
Colgate-Palmolive Company, 163
- Hill's, 354
- Palmolive, 518x
- Lady Speed Stick, 407
- Speed Stick, 620
Collective Brands Inc
- Keds, 392
- Shaq, 600
Collective Licensing International LLC
- Airwalk, 73
Colonial Life & Accident Insurance Company, 163
Colorado Group Ltd, 163
Colorado State University, 163
Colt Industries Inc, 164
Colt's Manufacturing Company LLC, 164
Columbia Pictures Industries Inc, 164
- Ghostbusters, 318
- S.W.A.T., 635

Columbia Sportswear Company, 164
- Sorel, 617
Columbia University
- Columbia Business School, 164
Comcast Corporation, 165
Comdial Corporation, 165
Comedy Partners LLC
- Comedy Central, 165
- South Park, 618
Comerica Inc, 165
Comet Group plc, 165
Comex Group
- General Paint, 316
ComfortMind, 166
Commerce One Inc, 166
Commerzbank AG, 166
Commodore-Amiga Inc, 166
Commodore International Ltd, 166
Commonwealth Bank of Australia, 166
Commonwealth Edison Company
- ComEd, 165
Compagnia Aerea Italiana SpA
- Alitalia, 77
Compagnie Financière Richemont SA
- Richemont, 568
- Vacheron Constantin, 694
Companhia Portuguesa de Hipermercados SA
- Jumbo, 389
Compaq Computer Corporation, 167
Compass Group USA
- Canteen, 138
Competitive Foods Australia Pty Ltd
- Hungry Jack's, 361
Computer Associates Inc, 132
ComputerLand, 167
COMTEK, 167
ComTrade Group, 167
Conad Soc. Coop, 168
ConAgra Foods Inc, 168
- Act II, 62
- David Sunflower Seeds, 193
- Hebrew National, 350
- Slim Jim, 611
- Van Camp's, 695
Conair Corporation
- Cuisinart, 182
- Waring Products, 716
CONALEP (Colegio Nacional de Educación Profesional Técnica), 168
Condé Nast
- Condé Nast, 168
- GQ, 330
- Mademoiselle, 436
- Self, 597
- The New Yorker, 658
- Vanity Fair, 696
- Vogue, 709
- Wired, 729
Condé Nast Digital
- reddit, 563
Condor Earth Technologies Inc, 168
Confiserie Leonidas SA
- Leonidas Pralines, 415
Conley Corporation, 169
Connectix Corporation, 169
Conner Peripherals Inc, 169
Conoco Inc, 169
- Conoco, 169
ConocoPhillips Company

COMPANY INDEX

- 76, 53
- Conoco, 169
- ConocoPhillips, 169
- JET, 384
- Kendall Motor Oil, 393
- Phillips 66, 532

Conseil général du Val-de-Marne, 204
Conservative Party, 169
Consolidated Edison Inc, 168
ConTel Corporation, 170
Continental AG, 170
Continental Tire North America Inc
- General Tire, 316

CONUS Communications
- All News Channel, 78
Converse Inc, 170
Cooling & Water Heating
- Ruud, 579
Co-operative Group Ltd, 654
- Coop Foodstore, 170
Coopers Brewery Ltd, 170
Cooper Tire & Rubber Company, 171
Coors Brewing Company
- Coors, 171
- Coors Light, 171
Copel (Companhia Paranaense de Energia), 171
Copenhagen Airports AS
- CPH, 176
Copperfield Publishing Inc
- Salt Lake City Weekly, 583
Cora SA, 171
Corbis Corporation
- Corbis, 171
- Veer, 698
Corby Distilleries Ltd
- Polar Ice Vodka, 538
Cordaid
- Stop Aids Now!, 629
CORE Business Technologies, 172
Corel Corporation, 172
Corlib Brand Holding Ltd
- Libby's, 418
Corning Inc, 173
- Corelle, 172
- Pyrex, 549
Corporate Express NV, 173
Corrugated Packaging Council, 173
CORSA (Corvair Society of America), 174
Corsair Memory Inc, 174
Cosmo Oil Co. Ltd, 174
Costco Wholesale Corporation, 174
Cotton Incorporated, 175
Coty US LLC
- Jövan, 388
Council of Ivy Group Presidents
- The Ivy League, 656
Country Music Television (CMT), 159
Covercraft Industries Inc, 176
Coverd Srl, 176
CPC International (Corn Products International Inc), 176
CPP Milan Srl
- Zagato, 740
Crafted With Pride in USA Council Inc, 176
Craigslist Inc, 177
Cramo Finland Oy, 177
Crane Co., 177
Crane Plumbing Corporation, 177

Cray Inc, 177
Crayola LLC, 177
- Silly Putty, 606
C.R. Bard Inc
- BARD, 102
CRC Industries Inc, 177
Cream Holdings Ltd, 177
Creative Commons, 178
Creative Technology Ltd, 177
Crédit Agricole SA, 178
Crédit du Nord SA, 178
Crédit Mutuel SA, 178
Credit Suisse Group AG, 178
Credit Union National Association
- America's Credit Unions, 85
Crem Helado, 178
CRKT (Columbia River Knife & Tool Inc)
- Crisco, 179
Croatian National Tourist Board, 179
Crocodile CR spol. s r.o., 179
Crown Corporation
- Canada Post, 136
- Petro-Canada, 530
Crown Holdings Inc
- Crown Cork & Seal Company, 180
Crown International
- Crown Audio, 180
- Crown International, 180
Crown Pacific Partners LP, 180
Crown Paints Ltd
- Hempel AS, 180
Cruise America Inc, 180
CSA Group, 181
CSC (Computer Sciences Corporation), 181
CSU CardSystem SA
- Market System, 441
C&S Wholesale Grocers
- Bruno's Supermarkets, 121
- Grand Union, 332
- Piggly Wiggly, 533
CSX Corporation Inc, 181
- CSX Intermodal, 181
CSX Intermodal Terminals Inc
- CSX Intermodal, 181
CTE Group
- Effer, 244
CT Financial Services Inc
- Canada Trust, 136
CTIC (Chicago Title Insurance Company), 181
CTP Donau, 223
CTT Correios de Portugal SA, 181
Cuauhtémoc Moctezuma Brewery
- XX Special Lager, 735
Cuauhtémoc-Moctezuma Brewery
- Tecate, 644
Cuban Red Cross
- Cruz Roja Cubana, 180
Culligan International Company, 182
Culver Franchising System Inc, 182
Cumberland Packing Corporation
- Sweet'n Low, 636
Cummins Inc, 182
- Onan, 508
Curtis Mathes Corporation, 183
Curves International Inc, 183
Cushman & Wakefield Inc, 183
CWS-boco International GmbH, 183

CXO Media Inc, 153
CYO (The Catholic Youth Organization), 183
Cypress Hill, 183
Czech Airlines (CSA), 183

D

D'Addario & Company Inc
- Evans Drumheads, 260
D&AD (Design & Art Direction), 184
Daemar Inc, 184
Daewoo Electronics, 185
Daewoo Motors, 184
Daewoo Shipbuilding & Marine Engineering Co. Ltd, 230
DAF Trucks NV, 185
DAF (Van Doorne's Aanhanwagen Fabriek), 185
Dagrofa AS
- Super Best, 633
Daiei Inc, 185
Daihatsu Motor Co. Ltd, 185
Dailymotion SA, 185
Daimler AG, 186
- Detroit Diesel, 206
- Mercedes-Benz, 450
- Orion, 512
- Smart, 612
Daimler-Benz Aerospace AG, 186
DaimlerChrysler AG, 186
Daimler Trucks North America LLC
- Freightliner Trucks, 298
Dainese SpA, 186
- AGV, 69
Dairy Crest Group plc, 186
- St. Ivel, 629
Daisytek Computers LLC, 187
Daiwa Bank Holdings Inc, 187
Daiwa House Industry Co. Ltd, 187
DAK-Gesundheit, 187
Daktronics Inc, 187
Daler-Rowney Ltd, 187
Dalis AS, 187
Dalum Papir AS, 188
Daman Albarn
- Gorillaz, 329
Damart, 188
Damiani International BV, 188
Danaher Corporation
- Tektronix, 645
Dana Holding Corporation, 188
Danfoss A/S, 188
Danisco A/S, 188
Danish Broadcasting Corporation, 227
Danish Crown AmbA, 189
Danish Ministry of Transport, 230
Danjaq LLC
- 007 James Bond, 50
Danko Emergency Equipment Co, 189
Danko Jones, 189
Danmarks Ishockey Union, 189
Danmønt, 189
Danske Bank A/S, 190
Dansk Squash Forbund, 190
Dansk Supermarked A/S
- Netto, 484
Dantex SA, 190
Dao Heng Bank Group Ltd, 190
DAP Products Inc, 191
Darden Restaurants Inc

- LongHorn Steakhouse, 424
Dark Dog, 191
Dark Horse Comics Inc
- Dark Horse Comics, 191
- Hellboy, 352
- Sin City, 607
- Rocket Comics, 572
Dashboard Confessional, 191
DAS Legal Expenses Insurance Company Ltd, 191
Dassault Group SA
- Le Figaro, 413
Dassault Systèmes SA, 192
Data General Corporation, 192
Datamax-O'Neil Corporation, 192
Datamonitor Group, 192
Daum, 193
David Briggs Enterprises Inc
- Fat Tuesday, 269
Davide Campari-Milano SpA, 135
- Cinzano, 153
- Frangelico Liqueur, 296
Davidoff & Cie SA, 193
Davis Entertainment, DaVita Inc, 193
Davos Destinations-Organisation, 194
Dayco Products LLC, 194
Days Inn Worldwide Inc, 194
D B Wilson & Co. Ltd, 195
dbx Inc, 195
DC Card Co. Ltd, 195
DC Comics Inc, 195
- Action Comics, 61
- Batman, 103
- Green Lantern, 335
- Superman, 634
- Superman: Ride of Steel, 634
- Watchmen, 717
DC Shoes Inc, 195
Dean Foods Company, 196
De Beers Group, 196
debitel AG, 196
Debrett's Limited, 196
de Buyer Industries SAS, 196
Decathlon
- Oxelo, 515
Decathlon SA, 197
Deceuninck NV, 197
Deckers Outdoor Corporation
- Teva, 650
De Dietrich Process Systems Group, 197
Dedon GmbH, 197
Deere & Company
- John Deere, 386
Deer Valley Resort, 197
Definitive Technology Inc, 197
Def Jam Recordings, 198
Deft Inc, 198
De Fursac, 198
Degussa-Hüls AG, 198
DekaBank, 198
Dekker Olifanta BV
- Protest Boardwear, 546
Dekra eV, 198
De La Rue plc, 198
DelElectronics Corporation, 198
Delcourt, 199
Delhaize Group SA/NV, 199
- Food Lion, 289
Dell Chemists (1975) Ltd, 200
Dell Inc, 199
- Alienware, 76
Dell'orto SpA, 199
Del Monte Foods

- Contadina, 170
Deloitte Touche Tohmatsu Limited, 200
DeLorean Motor Company (DMC), 200
Delta Airlines Inc, 200
- Comair, 165
Delta Card, 200
Del Taco Holdings Inc, 201
Delta Electricity, 201
Delta Faucet Company, 201
Delta Lloyd Group NV, 201
Demeco SAS, 202
DeNA Co. Ltd, 202
Dend Media Services, 202
De Nederlandsche Bank NV, 202
DenizBank AŞ, 203
Denny's Corporation, 203
Denso Corporation, 203
Department for Culture
- The Royal Parks, 659
Department for Regional Development
- Roads Service, 571
Department of Economic and Rural Development and Tourism
- Nova Scotia, 497
Department of Justice – Office of Justice Programs, 204
Department of the Treasury
- IRS (Internal Revenue Service), 376
De Persgroep NV, 204
Depom Depolama Loj.Hiz. Ltd.Şti, 205
De Post Group, 410
Depression Alliance, 205
Deputación de Pontevedra, 205
Der Grüne Punkt, 205
De Rigo SpA
- Police Sunglasses, 539
Derticketservice.de GmbH & Co. KG
- KölnTicket, 401
Descente Ltd, 205
Desert Group, 205
Design Exchange (DX), 206
Design Museum, 206
Design Museum Shop, 206
Design und Tuning GmbH
- Rieger, 569
Desnoes & Geddes Ltd
- Red Stripe, 564
DeTeMobil
- C-Netz, 160
Detroit Diesel Corporation, 206
Detroit Institute of Arts, 206
Detroit Red Wings, 207
Detroit Regional Chamber, 207
Deutsche Bahn AG
- DB (Deutsche Bahn), 194
- DB Schenker, 194
- S-Bahn, 580
Deutsche Bank AG, 207
Deutsche Börse AG, 207
Deutsche Bundespost Telekom AG
- C-Netz, 160
Deutsche Lufthansa AG, 429
Deutsche Messe AG, 207
Deutsche Nationalbibliothek, 207
Deutsche Post AG
- Deutsche Post AG, 207, 541
- Exel, 260, 261

COMPANY INDEX

- DHL Express, 209
Deutscher Motor Sport Bund eV
- DMSB-Streckensicherungs-Staffel, 219
Deutscher Paket Dienst GmbH & Co. KG, 226
Deutscher Sparkassen- und Giroverband eV, 620
Deutsches Zentrum, 208
Deutsche Telekom AG
- Telekom Deutschland, 647
- T-Mobile, 666
Deutz AG, 208
Devon Energy Corporation, 208
DeVry Inc, 208
Dexia NV/SA, 208
DFCG (Association Nationale des Directeurs Financiers et de Contrôle de Gestion), 208
DFL Deutsche Fußball Liga GmbH, 305
DGC (Directors Guild of Canada), 208
DGOF (Deutsche Gesellschaft für Online-Forschung eV), 208
Dia (Distribuidora Internacional de Alimentacion SA), 209
Diageo plc, 209
- Baileys Irish Cream, 98
- Gordon's Gin, 329
- Guinness, 341
- J&B, 380
- Johnnie Walker, 386
- Red Stripe, 564
- Smirnoff, 613
Dialogic Corporation, 209
Diamond Alloy, 210
DiamondCluster International Inc, 210
Diamond Foods Inc
- Kettle Chips, 394
- Pringles, 545
Diamondtraxx, 210
Diana Srl
- Gas Blue Jeans, 310
Diapar, 210
DICKIE Spielzeug GmbH & Co. KG
- Schuco, 591
Dickson-Constant Sarl, 211
Dictionnaires Le Robert
- Le Robert, 416
Diebold Inc, 211
Diehl Stiftung & Co. KG, 211
Diesel SpA, 211
DIF (Sistema Nacional para el Desarrollo Integral de la Familia), 212
Digg Inc, 212
Digimagen, 212
Digital Equipment Corporation, 212
Digital Radio Plus, 213
Digital River Inc, 213
Dillard's Inc, 213
Dilo Machines GmbH, 213
Dime (Dime Savings Bank of Williamsback), 213
Dimensional Fund Advisors, 214
Dimension Data Holdings
- Datacraft, 192
Dimension Data Holdings plc, 214
DIM SAS, 213
Diners Club International, 214

Dino Entertainment
- Pump Records, 549
Diósgyőr-Vasgyári Testgyakorlók Köre
- DVTK 1910, 236
Diplom-Is A/S, 214
Directbouw BV, 215
Direct Brands Inc
- Columbia House, 164
Direct Digital Television
- DD TV, 195
DirecTV Inc
- DirecTV, 215
- DSS (Digital Satellite System), 231
- GSN (Game Show Network), 339
Discovery Communications Inc, 216
- Animal Planet, 88
Discovery Communications LLC
- TLC, 666
Dish Network Corporation, 216
Disk Brakes Australia Pty Ltd, 194
DISK (Türkiye Devrimci İşçi Sendikaları Konfederasyonu), 216
Disney-ABC Television Group
- A&E Network, 54
- Disney Channel, 216
Disney Music Group
- Hollywood Records, 357
Disston Company, 217
Distress Centres of Toronto, 217
Distribuidora de Aceros Laminados SA de CV
- Dalsa, 188
Dive N' Surf Corporation
- Body Glove, 113
Divers Alert Network Inc
- DAN (Divers Alert Network), 188
Diversey Inc, 217
Diversified Business Communications
- International Boston Seafood Show, 373
Divo TV, 217
DivX Inc, 217
Dixons Retail plc, 218
DJ Litt Firearms Ltd
- Litt's Treetops Shooting Ground, 422
DKV (Deutsche Krankenversicherung AG, 218
D-Link Corporation, 218
DLR (Deutsches Zentrum für Luft- und Raumfahrt eV), 218
dm-drogerie markt GmbH & Co. KG, 218, 219
D&M Holdings inc
- Marantz, 441
D&M Holdings Inc
- Boston Acoustics, 116
- Denon, 203
DNA Oy, 219
DNB ASA, 219
DNV (Det Norske Veritas), 219
Do buckle up, 219
Doctor's Associates Inc
- Subway, 631
Doğan Sirketler Grubu Holding AS, 220
Dogs Trust, 220
Doimo Salotti SpA, 220
Do It Best Corporation, 220

Do-it-center, 220
DoKaSch GmbH, 220
Dolby Laboratories Inc, 220
Dolce & Gabbana, 221
Dole Food Company Inc, 221
Dollar Thrifty Automotive Group, 221
Dolphin Cruise Line
- Majesty Cruise Line, 438
Dometic Group, 222
Dominion Resources Inc, 222
Domino Foods Inc, 222
Domino's Pizza Inc, 222
Dommelsch Bierbrouwerij, 223
Donald Trump
- Miss Universe, 458
Dongfeng Motor Corporation, 223
Doorstep Dairy, 223
Doosan Group, 223
- Bobcat, 113
Dorel Home Furnishings, 223
Dorel Industries Inc, 223
- GT Bicycles, 339
- Roadmaster Bike, 571
Dorma Holding GmbH & Co. KgaA, 224
Douwe Egberts Koninklijke Tabaksfabriek-Koffiebranderijen-Theehandel NV, 225
Dover Corporation, 225
- Datamax-O'Neil, 192
Dovre-JBS A/S
- Dovre, 226
Dovrepeisen A/S
- Dovre, 226
Dow Jones & Company
- Factiva, 263
- The Wall Street Journal, 660
Dow Jones & Company Inc, 226
Downer EDi Ltd, 226
DQS Holding GmbH, 227
Dragon Alliance, 227
Draka Holding NV, 227
Drambuie Liqueur Company Ltd, 228
Draper Inc, 228
Dr. August Oetker KG
- Dr. Oetker, 229
- Radeberger, 556
Drayton Windows Ltd, 228
DreamWorks Animation SKG Inc, 229
- Shrek, 604
DreamWorks LLC
- Anchorman: The Legend of Ron Burgundy, 87
- Shrek 2, 604
Dresdner Bank, 229
Dreyer's Grand Ice Cream Holdings Inc, 229
Dronco AG, 229
Dr Pepper Snapple Group Inc
- 7 Up (USA), 52
- Canada Dry, 136
- Diet Dr Pepper, 212
- Diet Snapple, 212
- Dr Pepper, 230
- Orangina, 511
- Schweppes, 591
- Snapple, 614
- Squirt, 623
- Sunkist, 632
DRUCK & TEMPERATUR Leitenberger GmbH
- LTR Germany, 429
Drug Emporium Inc, 230
Dryden Flight Research Center, 230

DSA (Direct Selling Association), 230
DSP (Demokratik Sol Parti), 231
Dsquared2, 231
DSW Inc, 231
DTS Inc, 231
DTV Services Ltd
- Freeview, 298
Duales System Deutschland GmbH
- Der Grüne Punkt, 205
Duarig SA, 231
Dubai Cares, 232
Dubai Department of Tourism and Commerce Marketing, 232
Dubai Ports Authority, 232
Dubai Sports Council (DSC), 232
Dubbles, 232
Ducati Motor Holding SpA, 232
Duck Records Ltd, 233
Ducks Unlimited, 233
Dudson Ltd, 233
Duke Energy Corporation, 233
Duke Realty Corporation, 233
Dun & Bradstreet Inc, 233
Duncan Aviation Inc, 234
Dundee Corporation, 234
Dunhill Clothiers, 234
Duni AB, 234
Dunkin' Brands Group Inc
- Baskin-Robbins, 102
Dunkin' Brands Inc, 234
Dunlop Slazenger International Ltd
- Slazenger, 611
Duran Group GmbH, 235
Dusit International, 236
Dustbane Products Ltd, 236
DutchBird BV, 236
DVD FLLC, 236
DVD Format/Logo Licensing Corporation, 236
DVD+RW Alliance, 236
Dwindle Distribution
- Darkstar, 191
Dyflex Co. Ltd, 237
Dynamic Zone, 237
Dynamite Food Handelsgesellschaft mbH, 237
Dyneff SAS, 237
Dynegy Inc, 237
Dysan Corporation, 237
Dyson Ltd, 237

E

EA Digital Illusions CE AB
- DICE (Digital Illusions Creative Entertainment), 211
EADS (European Aeronautic Defence and Space Command NV), 240
EADS Space
- Astrium, 93
Eagle Broadband Inc, 240
Eagle Rock Entertainment, 240
Eastman Chemical Company, 240
Eastman Kodak Company
- Advanced Photo System, 65
- Kodak, 400
- Kodak Colorwatch system, 401
Easton-Bell Sports Inc, 240
East West Bancorp Inc, 240

Easy Aces Inc
- Fred & Friends, 297
EasyJet plc, 241
Eaton SRL, 241
EAT. The Real Food Co. Ltd, 241
Ebara Corporation, 241
eBay Inc, 241
- PayPal, 523
- rent.com, 566
EB Games
- Electronics Boutique, 246
ECCO Sko AS, 241
Eckerd Corporation, 242
Eckes-Granini Group GmbH, 332
Ecolab Inc, 242
ECR International
- Utica Boilers, 693
Eddy Merckx Cycles, 242
Edel AG, 242
Edelbrock LLC, 242
Eden Foods Inc, 242
EDF Group^, 242
Edinaya Rossiya/United Russia, 243
Edison International, 243
Éditions Marabout, 440
Éditions Mondadori Axel Springer
- Auto Plus, 96
Éditions Philippe Amaury
- Dakar Rally, 187
Editora Abril SA, 243
Editorial Andina, 243
Editorial Televisa
- Cinemania, 152
Edox & Vista SA, 243
Ed Tel (Edmonton Telephones Corporation), 243
Educación es camino, 243
Education First Ltd, 243
E! Entertainment Television, 243
Effer SpA, 244
Egidio Galbani SpA
- Galbani, 306
Egypt Air Holding Company, 244
Ehrmann AG, 244
E. I. du Pont de Nemours and Company
- 5 Star Service, 51
- Corian, 172
- DuPont, 235
Eiffage SA, 244
Eignarhaldsfélagið Fengur hf
- Iceland Express, 364
Eiki International Inc, 244
Einstein Noah Restaurant Group Inc
- Einstein Bros. Bagels, 244
Eircom Group Ltd, 244
Eizo Nanao Corporation, 245
Eker Süt Ürünleri Gıda San. ve, 245
Ekoland, 245
ELAC Electroacoustic GmbH, 245
Elan d.o.o., 245
El Corte Inglés SA, 245
Elco Vayonis SA, 245
E.Leclerc
- Leclerc, 412
Electricity Supply Board (ESB), 255
Electric Visual Llc, 245
Electrolux Hausgeräte Vertriebs GmbH
- Zanker, 740

752

COMPANY INDEX

Electrolux International Company
- Frigidaire, 300
Electronic and Information Technologies eV
- VDE, 698
Electronic Arts Inc, 240
- EA Games, 240
- EA Sports, 240
Electronics for Imaging Inc
- Fiery, 277
Elektra Entertainment Group Inc
- Elektra Records, 246
Elememt Skateboards
- Twigs, 676
Eletrobras Furnas, 305
Elevadores Atlas Schindler SA
- Atlas Schindler, 95
Eli Lilly and Company
- Lilly, 419
Elliott Aviation Inc, 247
Elmer's Products Inc, 247
- X-Acto, 734
e.l.m leblanc, 247
Elpida Memory Inc, 247
El Pollo Loco Inc, 247
ELSA Technology Inc, 248
Embarq Corporation, 248
Embassy Television, 248
EmblemHealth Companies
- GHI (Group Health Incorporated), 318
Embraer SA, 248
Embratur (Empresa Brasileira de Turismo)
- Brasil, 117
EMC Corporation
- Iomega, 374
- RSA, 577
Emco Maier GmbH, 248
EMD Chemicals
- Millipore, 456
EMD Millipore, 456
Emerald City Press, 248
Emerson Electric Co.
- Emerson, 249
- ISE – In Sink Erator, 377
- Leroy-Somer, 416
- Ridgid, 569
Emerson & Renwick Ltd Dixon Division
- Dixon, 217
EMI Group Ltd, 249
- Virgin Records, 705
EMI Records Ltd
- Abbey Road Studios, 56
Empire State Development Corporation
- I Love New York, 369
Empresa Nacional de Aeronavegación del Perú
- Aeroperú, 66
Empresas CMPC SA, 159
Empresas Polar
- Polar Pilsen, 539
Empresas Villares
- Villares, 705
ENAV SpA, 250
Endeavor Talent Agency, 250
Energie Thun AG, 250
Energis Communications Ltd
- Nevada Tele.Com, 485
Energizer Holdings Inc, 250
- Evans Drumheads, 260
- Playtex, 537
- Wilkinson Sword, 727
Energy Future Holdings Corporation
- TXU, 677

- TXU Energy, 677
Energy Trust of Oregon Inc, 251
Engen Petroleum Ltd, 251
English National Opera, 251
ENIC International Ltd
- Tottenham Hotspur Football Club, 670
Eni Lasmo plc
- Lasmo (London and Scottish Marine Oil), 411
Enkes Marine BV, 251
Enron Corporation, 251
Enterprise Holdings
- National Car Rental, 477
Enterprise Holdings Inc
- Alamo, 74
- Enterprise Rent-A-Car, 252
Enterprise Products Partners LP, 252
Environment Canada
- Environmental Choice Program, 252
E.ON AG, 252
EPA Neue Warenhaus AG, 252
E P Barrus Ltd
- Mariner, 441
Epilepsy Foundation of America, 253
E-Plus Service GmbH & Co. KG, 253
Equifax Inc, 254
ERA Franchise Systems LLC, 254
Ereğli Demir ve Çelik Fabrikaları TAŞ
- Erdemir, 254
Ergo Versicherungsgruppe AG), 218
Erie Insurance Group, 255
Ernst & Young Global Ltd, 255
Erreà Sport SpA, 255
ESAB (Electric Welding Limited company), 255
ESA (European Space Agency), 255
Escada SE, 255
ESPN Inc
- ESPN, 256
- X Games, 735
Esprit Holdings Ltd, 256
ESRB (Entertainment Software Rating Board), 256
Essar Group, 256
- Aegis Communications, 66
Esselte Corporation, 256
Essential Therapeutics Inc
- Maret, 441
Essilor International SA, 256
- Varilux, 697
Essve Produkter AB
- Fireseal, 281
Estée Lauder Companies Inc
- Clinique, 158
- Estée Lauder, 257
Esterline Technologies Corporation
- Duraswitch, 236
Estes-Cox Corporation
- Estes, 257
Estonian Tourist Board
- Estonia, 257
Etam Group, 257
Etex Group
- Wanit Fulgurit, 716
Etnies, 258
ETW Corporation
- Tiger Woods, 664
Eurazeo SA

- Europcar, 259
Eurocard International NV, 258
Eurocopter SAS, 258
Euroleague Basketball, 258
Euronics Group
- Gitem, 321
Europcar, 259
European Aeronautic Defence and Space Company NV
- Airbus, 70
- Eurocopter, 258
European Broadcasting Union
- Eurovision Song Contest, 259
- RDS Radio Data System, 560
European Economic Area (EEA)
- CE (Conformité Européenne), 143
European Patent Office, 259
Euro RSCG Worldwide, 259
Euro-Sportring
- Holland Cup, 357
Eurostar International Ltd, 259
EVA Airways Corporation, 260
Eveready Battery Company Inc
- Evans Drumheads, 260
Everex, 260
Evergreen Rehabilitation, 260
Evinrude Outboard Motors, 260
Exabyte Corporation, 260
Exel Inc, 260, 261
Exelon Corporation
- ComEd, 165
- PECO Energy, 524
Exercare Corporation, 261
Expedia Inc
- Expedia, 261
- Expedia.com, 261
Extra Space Storage LP
- Storage USA, 630
Exxon Mobil Corporation
- Esso, 257
- Esso Girl, 257
- Exxon, 261
- Mobil, 460
Eye Magazine Ltd, 261
Ezaki Glico Co. Ltd
- Glico, 322
E-Z Mart Inc, 261

F

Fabco-Air Inc, 262
Faber and Faber Ltd, 262
Faber Bygg A.S., 262
Faber-Castell AG, 262
Fabergé Ltd, 262
Fabric
- Matter, 445
Facebook Inc, 262
Facom SAS, 262
Factory Records, 263
Faena Hotel + Universe, 263
Fage SA, 019
FagorBrandt SAS
- Sauter, 588
Fagor Electrodomésticos S. Coop, 263
Fairchild Semiconductor Corporation, 264
Fair Isaac Corporation

- FICO, 276
Fairtrade Labelling Organizations International eV, 264
Fairwinds Credit Union, 264
Falck A/S, 264
FalconJet, 264
Falcon MFG, 264
Falken Tire Corporation, 264
Falken Tire Corporation HQ
- Ohtsu, 503
Fallen Footwear, 264
Family Dollar Stores Inc, 265
Family Inns of America Inc, 265
Family Motor Coach Association (FMCA), 265
Family Trust of Joe Ricketts
- Chicago Cubs, 148
Famous Brands Ltd
- Wimpy, 728
Fanatic Snowboards, 265
Fandango Corporation, 266
fapa (Friends and Player Alliance), 266
Fapinha Mini Veículos e Motores Ltda, 266
FaraEditore, 266
Fargo Electronics Inc, 267
Farmer John, 267
Farmers Insurance Group of Companies, 267
Farm Family Casualty Insurance Company, 267
Fashion Fair LLC
- Vantex, 696
Fassi Gru SpA, 268
Fast Company Inc, 268
Fastpuppy, 268
Fastsigns International Inc, 268
Fatboy Slim, 268
FatCow Inc, 269
Faurecia, 269
Favourite Website Awards, 305
FC Dallas, 269
FC Dietikon, 269
FC Dynamo Kyiv, 237
FDIC (Federal Deposit Insurance Corporation), 270
FDJ (La Française des Jeux), 270
FDR (Roosevelt-Campobello International Park), 270
FEAD (European Federation of Waste Management and Environmental Services), 270
Fechaduras Brasil, 270
Fedders Corporation, 271
Federación Nacional de Cafeteros de Colombia
- Café de Colombia, 133
Federal Bureau of Investigation
- Wanted by the FBI, 716
Federal Defence Forces of Germany
- Bundeswehr, 125
Federale Politie, 539
Federal Home Loan Mortgage Corporation (FHLMC), 270
Federal-Mogul Corporation, 271
- Champion, 145
- Fel-Pro, 273
- FP Diesel, 294
Federal National Mortgage Association (FNMA)

- Fannie Mae, 266
Federal Reserve Bank of Boston, 271
Federal Signal Corporation, 271
Federated Co-operatives Ltd, 170
Federated Department Stores Inc
- Burdines, 126
- Hecht's, 351
Federated Investors Inc, 271
FedEx Corporation
- Federal Express, 271
- FedEx Express, 271
- FedEx Home Delivery, 271
- FedEx Kinko's, 271
FedEx Office Print & Ship Services Inc, 271
Feed Nova Scotia, 272
Feintool International Holding AG, 272
Felina GmbH, 272
Felissimo Corporation, 272
Fellowes Inc, 272
Feminist Majority Foundation
- Ms., 468
Fenco Truck Accessories, 273
Fender Musical Instruments Corporation, 273
Fendi Srl, 273
Fenway Sports Group
- Liverpool Football Club, 422
- NESN (New England Sports Network), 483
Feodora Chocolade GmbH & Co. KG, 273
Ferco International SAS, 273
Ferma SA, 273
Fermax Electronica SAU, 274
Ferrarelle SpA, 274
Ferrari SpA, 274
Ferrero SpA, 274
- Estathè, 257
- Kinder, 396
- Nutella, 498
- Tic Tac, 663
Ferrioni SA de CV, 274
Ferro Corporation, 274
Ferrous Resources do Brasil, 274
Festina Lotus SA, 274
Festo AG & Co. KG, 275
FFBB (Fédération Française de Basketball), 275
FFS (Fédération Française de Ski), 275
FFT (Fédération Française de Tennis), 275
FGM/Dentscare Ltda, 203
F Group AS
- Fona, 288
FHC Holdings Ltd
- Fields Department Store, 277
F. Hoffmann–La Roche Ltd
- Roche, 571
Fiac (Foire Internationale d'Art Contemporain), 275
FiA (Fédération Internationale de l'Automobile), 275
FIAIP (Federazione Italiana Agenti Immobiliari Professionali), 275
Fiat Industrial SpA
- IVECO, 379
Fiat SpA, 275, 276
- Alfa Romeo, 76
- Lancia, 408
- Maserati, 444
- Scorpion, 592
- Weber, 718

753

COMPANY INDEX

Fida Film Yapim Dagitim Ve Reklamcilik AS, 276
Fidelity National Title Group
– Ticor Title, 663
Fidelity Southern Corporation, 276
Fidelstone Mortgage Company, 276
Fideuram Vita SpA, 277
Fido Dido Inc, 277
FIFA (Fédération Internationale de Football Association), 277, 278
Fila Ltd, 279
– Titleist, 666
Fil (Festival Intercâmbio de Linguagens), 279
Fill'er Up, 279
Film London
– Jarman Award, 381
Filmplus gemeinnützige UG, 280
Filmyard Holdings LLC
– Miramax Films, 457
– Miramax Home Entertainment, 457
FIM (Fédération Internationale de Motocyclisme)
– MX 1 – FIM Motocross World Championship, 473
Finance Ministry
– SHCP, 601
Findus Group, 280
Finlayson & Co. Oy
– Familon, 265
Finmeccanica SpA
– Agusta Westland, 69
Finnair Oy, 280
Finnish Road Administration, 281
Finnish Tourist Board
– Fine Living, 280
Fireman's Fund Insurance Company, 281
Fireye Inc
– Fireye, 282
First American Financial Corporation, 282
Firstar Bank, 282
First-Citizens Bank & Trust Company, 282
First Data Corporation, 282
– Cash Station, 141
– Star Networks, 625
– TeleCheck, 516
First Federal Bank of California, 282
FirstGroup plc, 283
First Hawaiian Bank, 283
First Horizon National Corporation, 283
First International Computer Inc of Taiwan
– Everex, 260
First Interstate Bancorp, 283
FirstMerit Corporation, 283
FirstRand Bank Ltd
– Rand Merchant Bank, 558
Fischer Sports GmbH, 283
Fisher & Paykel Appliances Ltd, 283
Fiskar Brands Inc
– Gerber, 317
Five Chefs, 284
Five Franklin Place (ffp), 284
Fixot, 284
Fjällräven AB, 284
Fjellman Press AB, 284
Fjordland A/S
– Bremykt, 118

Flap Jack Restaurants, 284
Fleetcor LLC
– Fuelman, 303
Fleet One Holdings LLC, 285
Fleetwood RV Inc
– Mallard, 439
FLENI (Fundación para la Lucha contra las Enfermedades Neurológicas de la Infancia), 285
Fletcher Building Ltd, 285
– Formica, 291
Flex-a-lite Consolidated, 285
Flextronics International Ltd, 285
FLIR Systems Inc
– FSI, 302
Florida Gulf Coast University, 286
Florida Ice & Farm Co, 286
Flos SpA, 286
Flowserver Corporation, 286
Flybe Group plc, 286
flyerwire GmbH, 287
FMC Corporation, 287
FMI Truck Sales & Service, 287
FMR LLC
– Fidelity Investments, 276
– Revlon, 567
Fnac (Fédération Nationale d'Achats des Cadres), 287
Foex Indexes Ltd, 287
Fog City Records, 287
Fokker, 287
FOLIATEC Böhm GmbH & Co. Vertriebs KG, 288
Folkpartiet liberalerna/ Liberal People's Party, 288
Fomento Económico Mexicano SAB de CV (FEMSA)
– Oxxo, 515
FONATUR (Fondo Nacional de Fomento al Turismo), 288
Fondation Abbé Pierre pour le logement des défavorisés, 288
Fondation de France, 288
Fontys University of Applied Sciences, 288
Food and Agriculture Organization of the United Nations, 289, 646
Food Lion LLC, 289
Food & Rural Affairs
– Foodland Ontario, 289
Foods Group LLC
– Nalley Foods, 475
Foot Locker Inc, 290
Forbes Media LLC, 290
Forbo International SA, 290
Force Financial LLC, 290
Ford Motor Company, 290, 291
– Lincoln, 419
Foreca Ltd, 291
Forest City Ratner Companies
– Building One at Atlantic Yards, 124
Forge Consulting LLC, 291
Forjas Taurus SA, 642
Formica Corporation, 291
Formula One Licensing BV
– FIA – Formula 1 World Championship, 292
– Formula 1, 291
Forney LLC, 292
Fortis NV/SA, 292

Fortum Oyj, 292
For us the living, 291
Fossil Inc, 292
Foster Electric Co. Ltd, 293
Foster's Group Ltd
– Foster's Group, 292
– Victoria Bitter (VB), 703
Foster Wheeler AG, 293
Fotbal Club Steaua Bucuresti, 270
Foundation Skateboard Company, 293
Four Winns LLC, 293
Fox Broadcasting Company
– The Simpsons, 660
Fox Entertainment Group Inc
– Fox Entertainment Group, 293
– 24, 52
– Fox Sports Net (FSN), 294
– Sun Sports, 632
FOX Factory Inc, 293
FOX Smart Estate Agency Network Ltd, 294
Fox Sports Interactive Media LLC
– Fox Sports Net (FSN), 294
Fox Sports Regional Networks
– Sun Sports, 632
Frabosk Casalinghi SAS, 294
Fram, 294
Framesi SpA, 294
Fram Group IP LLC, 294
FRAM Group IP LLC
– Prestone, 544
France Loisirs SAS, 295
France Telecom SA
– France Telecom SA, 295
– Orange, 510
– Wanadoo, 716
France Télé Numérique
– Tous au numerique!, 670
France Télévisions SA, 295
– France 2, 295
– France 3, 295
Franck dd, 295
Franke Artemis Management AG, 296
Franklin Covey Co., 296
Franklin Electronic Publishers Inc, 296
Frank Parsons Company, 296
Franz Schneider Brakel GmbH + Co KG, 302
Fraternal Order of Eagles International (F.O.E.), 297
Fraunhofer-Gesellschaft zur Förderung der angewandten Forschung eV, 297
Fred Meyer Inc, 297
Fred Perry Ltd, 297
Freemasonry
– 33rd Degree Masonic Emblem, 53
Freenet AG, 298
Freeview Australia Ltd, 298
Freidig Moto-Active GmbH, 298
French Connection Group plc, 270
French Government Tourist Office, 295
Fresenius Medical Care AG & Co. KGaA, 298
Freshfields Bruckhaus Deringer LLP, 299
Freudenberg & Co. KG, 299
Freudenberg Haushaltsprodukte KG
– Vileda, 704
Frico AB, 299

FriendFinder Networks
– Penthouse, 527
Friendly's Ice Cream LLC, 299
Friends of the Earth International, 299
Friendster Sdn. Bhd, 299
Frisch's Restaurants Inc, 300
Frís Vodka, 300
Frito-Lay North America Inc
– Cheetos, 147
– Cracker Jack, 176
– Doritos, 224
– Frito Lay, 300, 301
– Fritos, 301
– Lay's, 411
– Rollitos, 573
– SunChips, 632
– Walkers, 714
Fritz Hansen, 301
Frontier Airlines Inc, 301
Frontier Biscuits Factory Pvt Ltd, 301
Frontier Silicon Ltd, 301
Frost Bank, 301
Fruité, 301
FSC (Forest Stewardship Council), 302
FSG (Facility Solutions Group), 302
FTV BVI Ltd
– Fashion TV, 268
Fuchs Petrolub AG, 302
Fuji Co. Ltd, 303
Fujifilm Holdings Corporation
– Fujifilm, 303
Fuji Heavy Industries Co. Ltd, 303
– Subaru, 631
– Subaru/Fuji Heavy Industries, 631
Fuji Television Network Inc, 303
Fujitsu Ltd, 303
Fukuda Denshi Co. Ltd, 304
Full Sail University, 304
Funai Electric Co. Ltd, 304
Fundação CECIERJ
– Museu Ciência e Vida, 471
Fundación Alfredo Armas Alfonso, 304
Fundación Cultural de la Ciudad de México, 304
Funika Ltd, 304
Funke-Dr.N.Gerber Labortechnik GmbH, 305
Furniture Row LLC
– Denver Mattress Company, 204
Furukawa Industrial SA, 305
Fusion Retail Brands Pty Ltd
– Diana Ferrari, 210
Fußball-Club Bayern München eV, 269
Futbol Club Barcelona, 305
Futuremark Corporation, 305
FWT Studios, 305
F. W. Woolworth Company
– Woolworth, 730
FX Networks LLC, 305

G

G4S plc
– Group 4 Securicor, 337
Gadoua Bakery Ltd, 306
Gaffel Becker & Co. oHG, 306
GAF Materials Corporation, 306
Gaggenau Hausgeräte GmbH, 306
Gagosian Gallery, 306

Galardi Group Inc
– Wienerschnitzel, 726
Galaxy Microsystems Ltd, 306
Gallina Blanca Star SAU, 307
Gallup Inc, 307
Galp Energia, 307
Gambero Rosso Holding SpA, 307
GameStop Corporation
– Electronics Boutique, 246
Gammon Skanska, 308
Gannett Company Inc
– Gannett Co. Inc, 308
– USA Today, 691
Gap Inc
– Old Navy, 504
Gardner Denver Inc, 308
– CompAir, 167
Garmin Ltd, 309
Garrard Engineering & Manufacturing Company Ltd, 309
Gartmore Group Ltd, 309
Gart Sports Company, 309
GAS As Interface Co. Ltd, 309
Gascogne Wood Products SAS, 310
Gas Natural SDG SA, 310
Gas Supply Company of Thessaloniki SA
– Depa Fysiko Aerio, 204
Gateway Inc, 310
– Gateway, 310
Gateway Safety Inc, 311
GATX Corporation, 311
Gaumont Film Company, 311
Gaylord Container Corporation, 311
Gaylord Entertainment Company, 312
Gaz de France, 312
Gazprom JSC, 312
GDC Group Ltd
– Dimplex, 214
GDF Suez SA
– Lyonnaise des Eaux, 431
GEA Group AG, 312
Geberit International AG, 312
GEF (Global Environment Facility), 313
Gehl Company, 313
Geico Insurance Agency Inc, 313
GE Johnson Construction Company, 313
Gelco (General Equipment Leasing Corporation), 313
Gencorp Inc, 314
Genelec Oy, 314
Generac Holdings Inc
– Generac Power Systems, 314
General Atlantic
– Network Solutions, 485
General Cable Corporation, 314
General Cinema Corporation, 314
General Dynamics Corporation, 315
– Jet Aviation, 384
General Electric Company
– Datex Ohmeda, 192
– GE, 312
– Panametrics, 519
– Tungsram, 675
General Mills Inc, 315, 335
– Betty Crocker, 107
– Bisquick, 109
– Cheerios, 146
– Green Giant, 335
– Häagen-Dazs, 346

754

COMPANY INDEX

– KiX, 397
– Pillsbury, 533
– Pillsbury Doughboy, 533
– Trix, 674
General Monitors, 315
General Motors Company
– ACDelco, 59
– Buick, 124
– Cadillac, 133
– Chevrolet, 147
– Chevrolet Impala, 147
– Corvette, 174
– Courtesy Transportation, 175
– General Motors (GM), 315
– GMC, 324
– GMC Truck, 324
– Hummer, 360
– Oldsmobile, 504
– Opel, 509
– Pontiac, 540
– Saturn, 587
General Motors UK Ltd
– Vauxhall, 698
General Nutrition Centers Inc, 315
Genetic Skateboard Products, 316
Gentek Building Products Inc, 316
Gentry Living Color Inc, 316
Genuine Parts Company (GPC), 316
Geobra Brandstätter GmbH & Co. KG
– Playmobil, 536
Geobrugg AG, 316
George Weston Foods Ltd
– Don Smallgoods, 223
Georg Fischer Piping Systems Ltd, 316
Geox SpA
– Diadora, 209
Gepe Produkte AG, 317
Gerber Systems, 317
Gerry Weber International AG, 317
Getinge AB, 318
GetLiveMusic.com, 318
Getty Images Inc, 318
– Photodisc, 532
– The Image Bank, 369
Gianfranco Ferré SpA, 318
Gianni Versace SpA, 318
– Versace, 700
Giant Eagle Inc, 319
Giant Food Inc, 319
Giant Food Stores LLC, 319
Giant Manufacturing Co. Ltd, 319
Giant of Maryland LLC, 319
Gibson Guitar Corporation, 319
Gigabyte Technology Co. Ltd, 320
Gig Ant Promotion, 319
Giochi Preziosi SpA, 320
Giorgio Armani SpA, 320
– Armani Exchange, 91
– Armani Jeans, 91
– Emporio Armani, 250
Girl Scouts of the USA, 320
GIVI Srl, 321
GKN plc, 321
– Agusta Westland, 69
G&K Services Inc, 321
GLAAD (Gay & Lesbian Alliance Against Defamation), 321
Glacéau
– Vitaminwater, 706
Gladwork, 322

Glass Packaging Institute
– Glass Recycles, 322
GlaxoSmithKline plc, 339
Glendale Community College, 322
Glen Dimplex Group, 214, 465
Glengarry Highland Games, 322
Global Coffee Break
– Coffee Break Small Groups, 161
Global Crossing Ltd, 323
Global Reporting Initative (GRI), 323
Global System for Mobile Communications, 339
Global Van Lines Inc, 323
Globe International Ltd
– Enjoi Skateboarding, 251
Globetrotter Ausrüstung Denart & Lechhart GmbH, 323
Glock GmbH, 323
Glunz & Jensen A/S, 323
GM Holden Ltd, 356
GM Korea Company
– Daewoo Matiz, 445
GMPTE (Transport for Greater Manchester), 324
GMR Group, 324
GN ReSound Group, 324
Go Airlines, 325
GOAL (German Operating Aircraft Leasing GmbH & Co. KG), 325
Goaliath Kicker, 325
Godfather's Pizza, 325
Godiva Chocolatier Inc, 325
Goethe-Institut, 326
Go! General Overnight Service (Germany) GmbH, 325
Golden Corral Corporation, 326
Golden West Financial Corporation, 326
Gold Peak Industries (Holdings) Ltd, 326
Gold's Gym International Inc, 327
Gold Star Chili Inc, 327
Golfsmith International Holdings Inc
– MacGregor Golf, 434
Gol Linhas Aéreas Inteligentes SA
– Varig, 697
Gonera & Company Sp. z o.o., 327
Good Humor-Breyers
– Klondike, 398
Good Humor-Breyers USA
– Breyers, 118
Goodman Global Group Inc
– Goodman Manufacturing, 327
Goodrich Corporation, 328
– BFGoodrich Tires, 108
Goodwill Industries International, 328
Google Inc
– Android, 88
– Blogger, 111
– Gmail, 324
– Google, 328
– Google Chrome, 328
– Google Earth, 328
– Picasa, 533
– YouTube, 739
Goo Software Ltd, 328
Goshawk Insurance Holdings plc, 329

Government of Greenland, 335
Government of Japan
– JAS (Japanese Agricultural Standards), 381, 382
Government of Qatar
– Qatar Airways, 550
Government of Saskatchewan, 329
Government of South Africa
– South African Airways, 618
GO Voyages SAS, 325
Goya Foods Inc, 329
Graceland Universtity, 330
Gradiente Eletronica SA, 330
Graham Sourcing LLC, 330
GRAND-AM Road Racing, 331
Grand Banks Yachts Ltd
– Aleutian Class, 76
Grand Battery Technologies (Australia) Pty Ltd
– Grandcell, 331
Grand Eagle Companies Inc, 331
Grand United Order of Oddfellows, 501
Granite Hacarmel Invest Ltd
– Tambour, 640
Grant Thornton International Ltd
– Grant Thornton, 332
Gras Savoye SA, 332
Grayson Mitchell Inc, 333
Grease Monkey International Inc, 333
Great Eastern Group, 333
Greater Atlantic Financial Corporation, 333
Greater London Authority
– Transport for London (TfL), 672
Greater Toronto Airport Authority
– Toronto Pearson, 670
Great Southern Rail
– Indian Pacific, 371
Great Western Bank, 334
Great West Life Assurance Company, 334
Greek National Tourism Organisation (GNTO), 334
Green Hills Software Inc, 335
Greenlee Lighting Inc, 336
Greenlee Textron Inc, 335
Green Mountain Coffee Roasters Inc, 336
Green Mountain Energy Company, 336
Greenpeace, 336
GreenPoint Financial Corp., 336
Greenspun Media
– Las Vegas Magazine, 411
Greyhound Lines Inc, 336
Griffin Technology, 336
Griffin Thermal Products LLC, 336
Griffon Corporation
– Clopay, 158
GrindMedia LLC
– 411VM, 53
Grohe AG, 337
Groove Armada, 337
Group 4 Falck, 337
Groupama SA, 337
Group de Boeck, 196
Groupe 3 Suisses International
– 3 Suisses, 51
Groupe Arte

– Arte (Association Relative à la Télévision Européenne), 92
Groupe Auchan SA
– Auchan, 95
– Mammouth, 440
Groupe Bel
– La Vache quit Rit, 411
Groupe Bolloré
– IER, 366
– OCB, 501
Groupe Canal+
– Canal+, 137
– CinéCinéma Channel, 152
Groupe Canal+SA
– Direct 8, 215
Groupe Casino
– Casino Supermarkets, 141
Groupe Danone SA
– Dannon, 189
– Danone, 190
– Evian, 260
– Volvic, 710
Groupe Delta Dore, 201
Groupe Express-Roularta SA
– L'Express, 417
Groupe Flammarion
– Casterman, 141
Groupe Lactalis
– Galbani, 306
– Parmalat, 522
Groupe Lafuma, 407
Groupe Le Figaro
– Le Figaro, 413
Groupe M6, 434
– Paris Première, 521
Groupe Mellita
– Handy Bag, 347
Groupe Mulliez
– Auchan, 95
Groupe Pomona
– Polydor Records, 540
Groupe Rémy Cointreau
– Cointreau, 162
Groupe Royer SA
– Von Dutch, 711
Groupe SEB
– Moulinex, 466
– Rowenta, 576
– Tefal, 645
– T-Fal, 645
Groupe TF1
– Eurosport, 259
– TF1 (Télévision Française 1), 651
– TMC (Télé Monte Carlo), 666
Groupe Yves Rocher
– Petit Bateau, 529
Group Janssens, 337
Groupon Inc, 338
Groupo Sata
– Sata International, 587
Grubb & Ellis Company, 338
Grundfos Holding A/S, 338
Grundig AG, 338
Gruner+Jahr GmbH & Co. KG, 338
– Stern, 628
Grupo Abril, 243
Grupo Bimbo SAB de CV, 338
Grupo Clarin SA
– Multicanal, 470
Grupo Financiero Banamex SA de CV
– Banamex, 99
Grupo ICE, 364
Grupo Industrial Monclova
– Commsa, 167
Grupo Ken Construcciones SA de CV, 338
Grupo Keystone, 395

Grupo Modelo SAB de CV
– Corona Extra, 173
Grupo Munreco SL
– Viceroy, 702
Grupo Newsan
– Philco Argentina, 531
Grupo Petrópolis
– TNT Energy Drink, 666
Grupo Posadas SA de CV
– Fiesta Inn, 277
Grupo PRA SA, 338
Grupo Sanborns SA de CV, 584
Grupo Santander
– Abbey, 56
– Santander, 585
Grupo Tampico SA de CV, 339
Grupo Ultra
– Ultragaz, 681
Grupo Uniradio SA de CV, 339
Gruppo Editoriale L'Espresso SpA
– La Repubblica, 410
Gruppo Euromobil
– Zalf, 740
Gruppo SpA
– Columbus Tubi, 164
Gruppo Srl – Div. Cinelli
– Cinelli, 152
GS Yuasa Corporation
– GS Battery, 339
GTE Corporation, 340
GTL Infrastructure Ltd, 340
Guaranty Bank and Trust Company, 340
Guardian Media Group plc (GMG), 340, 656
Gucci Group
– Gucci, 340
– Stella McCartney, 628
GUD Automotive Pty Ltd
– Ryco Filters, 579
Guerlain SA, 340
Guess Inc, 341
GuideOne Mutual Insurance Company, 341
Gulf Air, 342
Gulf Oil LP, 342
Gullane Entertainment Inc
– My First Thomas & Friends, 473
G-Unit Clothing Company, 342
Gunnebo Industries AB, 343
Guoco Group Ltd, 343
Gustav Klauke GmbH, 397
Guy Cotten SA, 343
Guy Laroche
– Drakkar Noir, 228
GWDG (Gesellschaft für wissenschaftliche Datenverarbeitung mbH), 343
Gyproc
– Plâtres Lambert, 536

H

haacon hebetechnik GmbH, 346
Habitat Retail Ltd, 346
Hachette Filipacchi Médias SA
– Elle, 247
– Paris Match, 521
Hachette Livre
– Le Livre de Poche, 415
Hacı Ömer Sabancı Holding AŞ
– Akbank, 74

COMPANY INDEX

Hägglunds Drives AB, 346
Haglöfs Scandinavia AB, 346
Haier Group, 346
HAKOTOWI GmbH Berlin
– Ilmia, 369
Hakuto Co. Ltd, 346
Halliburton, 347
Hallmark Cards Inc, 347
– Crayola, 177
– Silly Putty, 606
Hamburg Messe und
Congress GmbH
– Nortec, 495
Hamilton International Ltd
(The Swatch Group Ltd),
347
Hamlet Holdings
– Caesars Entertainment, 133
– Caesers Palace, 133
Hammerson plc, 347
Hancock Holding Company
– Hancock Bank, 347
HanesBrands Inc, 347
– Champion, 145
– L'eggs, 414
– Wonderbra, 730
Hanjin Group, 347
Hankook Tire, 348
Hanley Wood LLC
– World of Concrete, 732
Haribo GmbH & Co. KG, 348
Harken Inc, 348
Harman International
Industries
– Crown Audio, 180
– Crown International, 180
Harman International
Industries Inc
– Deezer, 195
– JBL, 382
Harman Technology Ltd
– Ilford Photo, 368
HarperCollins
– HarperCollins Publishers, 348
Hasbro Inc
– Action Man, 61
– G.I. Joe, 320
– Hasbro, 349
– Kenner, 393
– MB (Milton Bradley), 446
– Micro Machines, 454
– Monopoly, 463
– Parker Games, 521
– Play-Doh, 536
– Playskool, 536
– Scrabble, 594
– Tonka, 669
Hästens, 350
Hauri Inc, 350
Havas, 350
Havells Sylvania, 637
Hawaiian Airlines Inc, 350
Hayward Industries Inc
– Hayward Pool Products, 250
Hazama Corporation, 350
HC Brill Company Inc
– Brill, 118
H-D Michigan LLC
– Harley-Davidson, 348
Head NV, 350
Hearst Corporation
– A&E Network, 54
– Cosmopolitan, 174
– Esquire, 256
– Redbook, 562
– San Francisco Chronicle,
585
Hearst Television Inc
– WCVB-TV Channel 5, 718
Hecho en México (Made in
Mexico), 351

Heidelberger Druckmaschinen
AG, 351
Heidmar Inc, 351
Heineken International
– Heineken, 351
– Pelforth, 525
– Sol, 616
Heineken NV
– Sagres Cerveja, 582
– Tecate, 644
Heineken Slovensko AS
– Corgon, 172
Helex Group
– Athens Stock, 94
Helgeland Holding A/S, 351
Helicopter Association
International (HAI), 351
Helicraft Ltee, 351
Hella KGaA Hueck & Co, 352
Hellenic Post SA, 352
Hellenic Telecommunications
Organization AE
– OTE, 514
Heller Joustra SA, 352
Hello, 352
Helvetia Group, 352
Henkel AG & Co. KGaA
– Dial, 209
– Fa Cosmetics, 263
– Persil, 528
– Pritt, 546
– Schwarzkopf, 591
Henkel Central Eastern
Europe GmbH
– Pattex, 523
Herbalife International, 353
Hercules Offshore Inc, 353
Herman Miller Inc, 353
Hermès International SA,
353
Hermes Real Estate
– Bluewater, 112
Hermle Uhrenmanufaktur
GmbH, 353
Hero Cycles Ltd, 353
Hero MotoCorp, 353
Heron. The coral Island, 353
Hertz Global Holdings Inc
– Advantage Rent-a-Car, 65
Hess Corporation, 354
Hettich Holding GmbH & Co.
oHG, 354
Hewlett-Packard Company
– 3Com, 50
– HP, 359
– HP OpenView, 359
Higashi-Nippon Bank Ltd,
354
High Performance
Industries Inc
– Road Demon, 570
High Speed Productions Inc
– Thrasher, 662
Hilding Anders Group
– Dunlopillo, 235
Hills Department Store, 355
Hill's Pet Nutrition Inc, 354
Hilti Corporation, 355
Hilton Worldwide
– Conrad Hotels, 169
– Embassy Suites Hotels, 248
– Hampton, 347
– Hilton Hotels & Resorts, 355
– Homewood Suites, 357
Hirobo Limited, 355
Hitachi Ltd, 356
Hitachi Maxell Ltd
– Maxell, 445
Hi-Tec Sports plc, 356
HIT Entertainment Ltd
(Fisher-Price Inc)

– Thomas & Friends, 661
Hivos
– Stop Aids Now!, 629
H. J. Heinz Company Inc
– Heinz, 351
– Ore-Ida, 511
HM Government
– Defra (Department for
Environment, Food and
Rural Affairs), 198
– Food Standards Agency,
290
H&M Hennes & Mauritz AB,
346
HMV Group plc, 355
Hobart Corporation, 356
HOBAS Engineering GmbH,
356
Hobie Cat Company, 356
Hoechst AG, 356
Holcim (Canada) Inc
– Dufferin Concrete, 233
Holley Performance Products
Inc, 357
– NOS, 497
HomeAway Inc, 357
Home Box Office Inc, 350
– Cinemax, 153
Home Credit BV, 357
Home Office
– Crime – Let's Bring It Down,
179
Home Retail Group plc
– Habitat, 346
Homer TLC Inc
– The Home Depot, 656
Home Satellite Sales &
Service, 357
Honda Motor Company Ltd
– Acura, 62
– Honda Automobiles, 358
– Honda Powersports, 358
– HRC (Honda Racing
Corporation), 359
Honeywell International Inc,
358
Hong Kong Dragon Airlines
Ltd, 227
Hong Kong Sports
Development Board, 358
Horizon Healthcare Services
Inc, 358
Hornby Hobbies Ltd
– Corgi, 172
Hornby plc, 358
Hoshino Gakki Co. Ltd
– Tama Drums, 640
Hoshino Gakki Group
– Ibanez Guitars, 362
Hostess Brands Inc, 730
– Butternut Breads, 129
– Dolly Madison Bakery, 221
– Drake's, 227
– Twinkie, 676
Hoya Corporation, 359
HP Software Division
– HP OpenView, 359
H&R Block Inc, 346
HSBC Finance Corporation
– HFC (Household Finance
Corporation), 354
HSBC Holdings plc, 359
HSLS (Hrvatska socijalno
liberalna stranka/Croatian
Social Liberal Party), 359
HTC Corporation, 359
Huawei Technologies Co. Ltd,
359
Hudson's Bay Company
– Designer Depot, 205
– Zellers, 741

Hudson's Bay Trading
Company LP, 360
Hugo Boss AG, 360
Hultafors Group
– Snickers Workwear, 615
Human, 360
Human Rights Campaign
Foundation (HRCF), 360
Human Rights Campaign
(HRCF), 360
Hungry Jack's Pty Ltd
– Hungry Jack's, 361
Hungry Tiger Press, 361
Huntington Bancshares Inc,
361
Hurricane Exploration plc, 361
Husky Energy Inc, 361
Husqvarna AB, 361
Husqvarna Consumer
Outdoor Products (HCOP)
– Weed Eater, 719
Hutchison 3G UK Limited
– Three, 662
Hyatt Corporation, 361
Hyatt Hotels Corporation
– AmeriSuites, 86
Hyster Company, 361
Hyundai Motor Company, 361

I

IAB (Interactive Advertising
Bureau), 362
IAC/InterActiveCorp
– Match.com, 445
IAFF (International
Association of Fire
Fighters), 362
IATA (International Air
Transport Association), 362
IATSE (International Alliance
of Theatrical Stage
Employees), 362
Iberia Líneas Aéreas de
España SA, 362
IBM, 363
– CrossPad, 180
– IBM Smarter Planet, 363
– Lotus Software, 427
ICA Group, 363
ICA (Institute of
Contemporary Arts), 363
ICA Sverige AB, 363
ICBC (Industrial and
Commercial Bank of China
Ltd), 363
ICC (Instituto Cidades
Criativas), 363
ICCO
– Stop Aids Now!, 629
IC Companys A/S
– Peak Performance, 524
Iceberg
– Gilmar SpA, 364
Icelandair Group ehf, 364
ICL (International Computers
Ltd), 364
ICOM Inc, 364
Iconix Brand Group Inc
– Eckō unltd., 242
– Op (Ocean Pacific), 509
– Starter, 626
ICS, 365
Idacorp Inc, 365
Idealease Inc, 365
Ideal Standard International,
365
IDEO Inc, 365
IDG
– Macworld, 435
IDG Enterprise

– Cinzano, 153
IDI (Industrial Developments
International) Inc, 365
IEA (Institute of Economic
Affairs), 365
IFAW (International Fund for
Animal Welfare), 366
IFIA (International Fence
Industry Service
Association), 366
IF (Instituto Federal Goiano),
366
iF International Forum
Design GmbH, 366
Ifor Williams Trailers Ltd, 366
Ifremer (Institut français de
recherche pour
l'exploitation de la mer),
366
IGA (Interessengemeinschaft
der Abschlepp- und
Pannendienstunternehmer
eV), 366
Igloo Products Corp., 367
IG Metall, 367
Igol France SA, 367
IHI Corporation, 367
IHK (Industrie- und
Handelskammer), 367
IHS Inc, 367
IIA (The Institute of Internal
Auditors), 368
IKEA International Group,
368
IKKS Group, 368
IKUSI – Ángel Iglesias SA,
368
Illinois Tool Works Inc
– Hobart, 356
– LPS, 428
illycaffè SpA
– Illy, 368
I Love New York More Than
Ever, 369
ILVA A/S, 369
Image Pro International Inc
– Shinko, 602
Imation Corporation
– Memorex, 449
IMAX Corporation, 369
IMI International, 369
Imperial Tobacco Group plc,
369
– Gitanes, 320
– John Player Special (JPS),
386
– Rizla+, 570
Imperial War Museum, 369
Impregilo SpA, 369
Imprensa Nacional-Casa da
Moeda SA, 370
Impresa Sociedade Gestora
de Participações Sociais SA,
370
Imprimis
– Piper Aircraft, 534
IMSS (Instituto Mexicano del
Segura Social), 370
Inco Ltd, 370
Independent Bank
Corporation, 370
Independent Grocers Alliance
– IGA Supermarkets, 367
Independent Insurance
Agents & Brokers of
America Inc, 370
Independent Pictures, 370
Independent Television
News Ltd, 378
Indesit Company, 370
INDITEX Group

756

COMPANY INDEX

- Zara, 741
Industrial and Financial Systems (IFS AB)
- IFS Defence, 366
Indústrias Romi, 574
Indústrias Vassallo Inc
- Vassallo, 697
Indy Racing League LLC, 371
Infineon Technologies AG
- SensoNor, 598
Infogrames Entertainment SA, 371
InfoWorld Media Group Inc (IDG), 371
Ingersoll Rand plc
- IR Bobcat, 375
Ingersoll-Rand plc
- Trane, 672
ING Groep NV, 371
Ingles Markets Inc, 371
Ingram Micro Inc, 371
Innocent Drinks Ltd, 372
In-N-Out Burgers Inc, 372
Innovative Dining Goup
- Luckyfish, 429
Insight Pharmaceuticals LLC
- Sucrets, 631
Insight Propaganda & Marketing Ltda, 372
Institute of Electrical and Electronics Engineers
- IEEE, 365
Instituto Cervantes, 372
Instituto de Turismo de España, 256
Instituto Terra e Memória, 372
Insurance Australia Group Ltd, 362
Intel Corporation
- Intel, 372
- Intel Inside, 372
- McAfee Security, 447
Interac Inc, 372
Interbrand/Omnicom Group
- Brand Channel, 117
InterContinental Hotels Group plc, 373
- Holiday Inn Express, 356
Interfilm-Berlin Management GmbH, 373
Intergamma BV
- Gamma, 307
InterMedia Partners LLC
- Vibe, 702
International Airlines Group
- bmi (British Midland International), 112
- Vueling, 713
International Business Machines Corporation (IBM)
- Lotus, 427
International Civil Defence Organisation (ICDO), 156
International Coffee & Tea LLC
- The Coffee Bean & Tea Leaf, 654
International Comfort Products LLC
- Tempstar, 648
International Consolidated Airlines Group SA
- Iberia Airlines, 25
- International Airlines Group, 373
International Dairy Queen Inc, 186
International Data Group (IDG)
- Computerworld, 167

International Equipment Solutions LLC
- Crenlo, 178
International Film Festival Rotterdam, 373
International Harvester Company, 373
International Ice Cream Association, 364
International Olympic Committee
- Olympic symbol, 506
International Paper Company, 374
- Champion International, 145
International Red Cross and Red Crescent Movement
- Red Crescent, 562
- Red Cross, 562
- Red Crystal, 563
- Red Star of David, 564
International Speedway Corporation, 194
International Tennis Federation
- Davis Cup, 193
Internet Brands Inc
- FlyerTalk, 286
Internet Initiative Japan Inc, 368
Interscope Geffen A&M
- Geffen Records, 313
Intershop Communications AG, 374
Interview Inc, 374
Intex DIY Inc
- Paint USA, 518
In the City Entertainment Inc, 374
Intramuros SA
- Intramuros (International Design Magazine), 374
Intuit Inc, 374
Invesco Ltd, 374
Invist
- Lycra, 431
Invista
- Cordura, 172
- Cordura Nylon, 172
- Stainmaster, 624
Iowa Public Broadcasting Board, 375
IPC Media
- What's On TV, 724
Ippon, 375
IPSSA (Independent Pool and Spa Association Inc), 375
IPWEA (Institute of Public Works Engineering Australia), 375
Iran National Airlines Corporation, 375
IRB (International Rugby Board), 375
IRFU (Irish Rugby Football Union), 376
Irisbus IVECO, 376
Irish Dairy Board
- Kerrygold, 394
Iris Ohyama Inc, 376
Irma A/S, 376
I.R.S. Records (International Record Syndicate), 376
Irving Convention & Visitors Bureau
- Irving Texas, 376
Irving Oil Ltd, 376
Irwin Financial Corporation, 376, 377
Irwin Toy Limited, 377

Isetan Mitsukoshi Holdings Ltd, 459
Islands of Peace ASBL, 368
ISN (Instituto de Servicios a la Nación), 377
Isocor, 377
ISO (International Organization for Standardization), 377
Israel Chemicals Ltd (ICL Fertilizers)
- Dead Sea Works Ltd, 196
Israeli Ministry of Public Security
- Israel Police, 377
ISSF (International Shooting Sport Federation), 378
ISS (International Service System), 378
ISS World Services A/S, 377
Ista, 378
Isuzu Motors Ltd, 378
Italian Institute for Foreign Trade (ICE), 378
Itaú Unibanco Holding SA
- Unibanco, 683
ITC (Incorporated Television Company), 378
I Teach Nyc, 378
ITT Corporation, 379
ITV plc
- Freesat, 298
- Yorkshire Television, 739
ITW Heller GmbH, 352
Iauv University of Venice, 379
Ivar's Inc, 379
IVECO SpA, 379
Iwatsu Electric Co. Ltd, 379

J

Jack Daniel Distillery
- Jack Daniel's, 380
Jack in the Box Inc, 380
Jackson Hole Realty, 380
Jack Wolfskin GmbH & Co. KGaA, 380
Jacobson Group
- Gola, 326
Jacuzzi Inc, 380
JAG Footwear
- Anne Klein, 89
Jaguar Cars Ltd, 381
Jaguar Land Rover Group
- Land Rover, 409
Jaguar Land Rover plc
- Rover, 576
Jamie Hewlett
- Gorillaz, 329
Jamie Oliver Enterprises Ltd, 381
Jams Music Center, 381
Janus Capital Group Inc, 381
Japan Airlines Co. Ltd, 381
Japan Industrial Design Promotion Organization
- Good Design Award, 327
Japan Information Processing Service Ltd, 381
Japan International Cooperation Agency, 385
Japan National Tourism Organization, 381
Japan Railways Group, 388
Japan Securities Finance Co. Ltd, 388
Japan Telecom Co. Ltd
- J-Sky, 388
Japan Tobacco Inc, 388
Jarden Consumer Solutions
- Mr. Coffee, 468

Jarden Corporation
- Adio Footwear, 64
- Coleman, 163
- KEM Playing Cards, 393
- Rawlings, 559
- Sunbeam, 631
- Völkl, 710
Jatronic A/S, 382
Jayco Inc, 382
J/Boats Inc, 382
J C Bamford Excavators Ltd, 382
JCB Co. Ltd, 382
J.C. Penney Company Inc
- JC Penney, 383
- Liz Claiborne, 422
Jeanne Lanvin SA
- Lanvin, 409
Jean Paul Gautier, 383
Jeep, 383
Jeppesen Sanderson Inc, 384
Jersey Mike's Franchise Systems Inc
- Jernbanaverket, 384
Jessica Cosmetics International Inc, 384
Jet Airways (India) Ltd, 384
JetBlue Airways Corporation, 384
Jewson Ltd, 385
Jiffy Lube International Inc, 385
Jiffy Products International BV, 385
Jil Sander AG, 385
JJF Management Services
- Rent-A-Wreck, 566
J&J Snack Foods
- Arctic Blast, 90
JK Harris & Company LLC, 385
JNC Datum Tech International Ltd
- Yashica, 737
Johannesburg Stock Exchange Ltd, 388
John D. Brush & Co
- SentrySafe, 598
John Dickinson & Co. (WI) Ltd, 386
John F. Kennedy Presidential Library and Museum, 386
Johnny Loco International BV, 386
Johnny's Pizza House Inc, 386
John Sands (Australia) Ltd, 386
Johns Manville, Berkshire Hathaway Inc, 386
Johnson Controls Inc, 387
- York, 739
Johnson & Johnson
- Alza, 81
- Band-Aid, 99
- Listerine, 421
- Neutrogena, 485
Johnson & Johnson Consumer, 387
Johnson & Johnson Healthcare Products
- Visine, 706
Johnson & Johnson Santé Beauté France SAS
- Le Petit Marseillais, 415
- RoC, 571
Johnson & Johnson Vision Care Inc
- Acuvue, 62
Johnson Outdoors Inc
- Scubapro, 594

Johnson Publishing Company Inc
- Ebony, 241
- Vantex, 696
Jones Lang LaSalle Inc, 387
Jonny Cupcakes Inc, 387
Josef Seibel Group
- Romika, 574
Jøtul AS, 388
Journal Register Company
- The Oakland Press, 658
JPMorgan Chase Bank
- Chase, 146
J-POWER Electric Power Development Co. Ltd, 388
J. Sainsbury plc
- Sainsbury's, 582
JSC AvtoVAZ
- Lada, 407
JSC Baltika Breweries
- Nevskoe, 485
JSC Mafka, 437
Jungheinrich AG, 389
Junker Group, 389
Junkers Flugzeug- und Motorenwerke AG (JFM)
- Junkers, 389
–
JVC Kenwood Holdings Inc
- JVC, 389
- VHS (Video Home System), 701

K

Kagawa Bank Ltd, 390
Kahala Corporation
- Blimpie, 110
Kamaz Inc, 390
Kambly SA Spécialités de Biscuits Suisses, 390
Kampgrounds of America Inc, 400
Kamps GmbH, 390
Kaneka Americas Holding Inc, 390
Kanematsu Corporation, 390
KangaROOS International Ltd, 390
kangolstore.com
- Kangol, 391
Kansai Paint Co. Ltd
- Alesco, 75
Kantar
- Millward Brown, 456
KAO Brands Company
- Ban, 99
Karl Lagerfeld, 408
Karl Lagerfeld Retail BV, 391
Karsten Manufacturing Corporation
- PING, 533
Kashi Company, 391
Kaufland Warenhandel GmbH & Co. KG, 391
Kaupthing Banki HF, 391
Kawasaki Heavy Industries Ltd, 391
Kawasaki Steel Corporation, 391
Kazanci Holding
- AKSA Energy, 74
KCD IP LLC
- Craftsman, 176
- DieHard, 211
Keane Inc, 392
Keeneland Association Inc, 392
KEF Electronics Ltd, 392
Keiper Group, 392
Keiyo Bank Ltd, 392

COMPANY INDEX

Kellogg Company
- Gardenburger, 308
- Keebler, 392
- Kellogg's, 392
Kendi Droujestvo S Ogranitchena
- Supra Vit, 635
Ken Garff Automotive Group, 393
Kenko Ball
- Nagase-Kenko Corp., 393
Kennametal Inc, 393
Kensington Computer Group, 393
Kent Nutrition Group Inc
- Kent Nutrition Group, 394
- Blue Seal, 111
Kenwood Corporation, 394
KENZO SA, 394
Kerr-McGee Corporation, 394
KESA Electricals plc
- Darty, 191
Kesko Corporation, 394
KeyCorp
- KeyBank, 394
Keyence Corporation, 395
Kia Motors Corporation, 395
Kidp (Korean Institute of Design Promotion), 395
Kikkoman Corporation, 396
Kimberly-Clark Corporation, 396
- Huggies, 360
- Kleenex, 398
Kimberly-Clark Worldwide Inc
- Pull-Ups, 548
- Scott Products, 593
Kimco Realty Corporation, 396
King's Seafood Company Inc
- 555 East American Steakhouse, 53
Kingsway Exhibitions, 396
Kintek Srl, 396
Kirch Group
- Taurus Film, 642
Kiss, 396
Kitaco Co. Ltd, 397
Kiwi, 397
KKR & Co. LPO
- Del Monte Foods, 200
Klabin, 397
Klipsch Group Inc, 398
- Energy, 250
K&N Engineering Inc, 399
K'Nex LP Group, 399
Knight Frank LLP, 399
Knights Franchise Systems Inc, 399
KNIPEX-Werk C. Gustav Putsch KG, 399
Knirps Licence Corporation GmbH & Co. KG, 399
Knoll Pharmaceuticals, 399
Knowing Science LLC
- Kid Knowledge, 395
Knowledge Network Corporation, 400
Kobe Sportswear Inc, 400
Kobe Steel Group
- Kobelco, 400
Koch Industries Inc, 400
- Cordura, 172
- Cordura Nylon, 172
- Dixie Cup, 217
- Georgia-Pacific LLC, 317
- Lycra, 431
- Stainmaster, 624
Koç Holding AŞ
- Koçbank, 400

Kodak Digital Product Center Japan Ltd
- Chinon, 149
Kohlberg & Company LLC
- Trico, 673
Kohl's Corporation, 401
Ko-Ken Tool Co. Ltd, 401
Kokuyo Co. Ltd, 401
Kolon Industries Inc, 401
Komatsu Ltd, 401
Komenda AG
- Cresta Swiss Bike, 179
Konami Corporation, 402
Kone Oyj, 402
Konica Corporation, 402
Konica Minolta Business Solutions USA Inc
- Danka, 189
Konica Minolta Holdings Inc, 402
König-Brauerei GmbH
- König Pilsener, 402
Koninklijke Ahold NV
- Ahold, 69
- Stop & Shop, 629
Koninklijke DSM NV, 230
Koninklijke FrieslandCampina NV
- FrieslandCampina, 299
Koninklijke Friesland Foods NV, 300
Koninklijke Grolsch NV
- Grolsch, 337
Koninklijke KPN NV
- Hi, 354
Koninklijke Luchtvaart Maatschappij NV
- KLM Royal Dutch Airlines, 398
Koninklijke Philips Electronics NV
- Compact Disc, 167
- DAB (Digital Audio Broadcasting), 184
- Direct Stream Digital (DSD), 215
- Norelco, 494
- Philips, 532
- PYE, 549
- Wide-Lite, 725
Koninklijke Wegener NV
- Wegener, 719
Kookaï SA, 402
Korea Gas Corporation
- Kogas, 401
Korean Air Lines Co. Ltd, 403
Korg Corporation, 403
Kosovo ICT Association
- Stikk, 629
Kowloon Motor Bus Company Ltd
- Kmart, 398
KP & ABTCO Siding Products
- ABTCO, 58
KPARK SAS, 403
KPMG, 403
KPS Capital Partners LP
- Wedgwood, 719
Kraft Foods
- Cadbury, 132
- Carambar, 138
Kraft Foods Deutschland
- Jacobs, 380
Kraft Foods Inc
- Chips Ahoy!, 149
- Côte d'Or, 175
- Dentyne, 203
- Jell-O, 383
- Kool-Aid, 402
- Kraft, 403
- Kraft Foods, 403

- LU (Lefèvre-Utile), 430
- Maxwell House, 446
- Milka, 455
- Nabisco, 474
- Nilla Wafers, 491
- Oreo, 512
- Oscar Meyer, 513
- Philadelphia Cream Cheese, 531
- Planters, 535
- Planters mascot (Mr. Peanut), 535
- Ritz Crackers, 570
- Royal, 576
- Stimorol, 629
- Tang, 640
- Toblerone, 667
Kraft Foods Italia Srl
- Fonzies, 289
Kraft Inc
- Velveeta, 698
Krispy Kreme Doughnuts Inc, 403
Kroenke Sports Enterprises LLC
- Colorado Mammoth, 163
Krohne Messtechnik GmbH, 404
Krüger GmbH & Co. KG, 404
Krups, 404
Krylon Products Group, 404
K-Swiss Inc, 404
KTM Sportmotorcycle AG, 404
Kubota Tractor Corporation, 404
Kubotek USA Inc
- KeyCreator, 394
Kumutu Inc, 404
Kungsörnen AB, 405
Kuno Moser GmbH, 405
Kuoni Group, 405
Kurita Water Industries Ltd, 405
Kuwait Petroleum Corporation
- Q8, 550
KYB Corporation, 405
Kyocera Corporation, 405
- Direct Print, 215
Kyocera Document Solutions Corporation
- Mita, 459
Kyodo Credit Service Co. Ltd, 405
Kyosho Corporation, 405
Kyowa Hakko Kirin Co. Ltd, 405

L

Labatt Brewing Company Ltd
- Labatt Blue, 406
- Labatt Ice, 406
- Labatt's, 406
Labels, 406
Laboratoire Nuxe
- Nuxe, 498
Laboratoire Oenobiol SA, 502
Laboratoires Decleor SAS, 197
Laboratoires Guigoz SAS, 341
Labour Party, 406
Labrador Records, 406
Labtec Inc, 406
Lachmann, 406
LaCie Ltd, 406
Lacoste, 407
LADWP (Los Angeles Department of Water and Power), 407

Lafarge SA, 407
La Flor del Itapebí Editorial, 407
Lagardère Active
- Elle, 247
- Paris Match, 521
Lagardère Publishing
- Hachette Livre, 346
L'Air Liquide SA
- Air Liquide, 72
L'Alco Grandi Magazzini SpA
- Altasfera, 80
Lalique, 408
Lambretta Consortium, 408
Lambretta Srl, 408
La Nacion, 408
Lancel Sogedi SA, 408
Lancia Automobiles SpA, 408
Land O'Lakes Inc
- Purina, 549
Lanover, 409
La Poste, 410
La Poste SA, 409
La Prairie Group, 410
Larry Flynt Publications
- Hustler, 361
Läse 2007, 410
La Sept (Société d'édition de programmes de télévision), 410
LaserVision Association
- LaserDisc, 410
Laurent-Perrier Group SA, 411
La Vie-Le Monde Group
- Le Monde, 415
LA X...Press, 411
Leading Edge Hardware Products Inc, 411
Leaf Sverige AB
- Malaco, 439
League Inc
- Massachusetts Credit Union, 444
LeapFrog Enterprises Inc, 411
Lear Corporation, 412
Learning Curve Brands Inc
- Johnny Lightning, 386
Learning Tree International Inc, 412
Le Bon Marché Maison Aristide, 412
Le Coq Sportif, 412
Le Cube, 412
Lee Cooper Brands, 413
Lee's Sandwiches International inc, 413
LeFooding.com, 289
Legal & General Group plc, 413
Legal Sea Foods, 413
Legambiente (League for the Environment), 414
Lega Nazionale Professionisti Serie AP
- Serie A, 599
- Serie A TIM, 599
Legendary Pictures Inc, 414
Legrand Group SA, 414
- Bticino, 122
Leha GmbH, 414
Lehman Brothers Holdings Inc, 414
Leica Camera AG, 414
Leiner Health Products Inc, 415
Lem Motlow
- Jack Daniel's, 380
Lend Lease Europe Ltd
- Bluewater, 112
Lend Lease Retail Partnership
- Bluewater, 112

Lenovo Group Ltd, 414, 415
Lenoxx Electronics Corporation, 415
Le Petit-Fils de LU Chopard & Cie SA, 150
Leprino Foods Company, 415
Les Brasseurs du Nord
- Boréale, 115
Lesjöfors AB, 416
Les Moteurs Reunis SA
- Behrmann Motors, 105
L'est Républicain
- Le Progrès, 416
Les Yeux Wines
- Polo Sur, 539
Lete SpA, 416
Letraset Ltd, 416
Leucadia National Corporation, 416
Levi Strauss & Co
- Levi's, 417
- Levi's Store, 417
Levitz Furniture Inc, 417
Lexjet Corporation, 417
Lexmark International Inc, 417
LFP (Ligue de Football Professionnel), 417
LG Corporation, 417
LG Electronics
- Zenith Electronics, 741
Libbey Glass Inc, 417
Libération, 418
Liberty Ltd, 418
Liberty Media Corporation
- QVC, 553
Liberty Mutual Group, 418
Librairie Générale Française
- Le Livre de Poche, 415
Lidl Stiftung & Co. KG, 418
Liebherr-International Deutschland GmbH, 418
Lieken Brot- und Backwaren, 418
Light, 419
Lightstorm Entertainment Inc, 419
Lillian Vernon Corporation, 419
Limited Brands
- Victoria's Secret, 703
Linde Group
- AGA, 68
Lindt & Sprüngli AG, 420
Lineas Aéreas Costarricenses SA,
- Lacsa, 407
Linens 'n Things Inc, 420
LinkedIn Corporation, 420
Linkin Park, 420
Linotype GmbH
- Linotype, 420
Linux
- Linux mascot, 420
- Linux Powered, 420
- Linux Professional Institute, 420
Lion Capital LLP, 280
Lionsgate Entertainment Corporation, 420
Lippert-Unipol GmbH, 421
Liquid Audio Inc, 421
Liqui Moly GmbH, 421
Lita, 421
Little, Brown & Company, 421
Little League Baseball Inc, 422
Little Red Door Cancer Agency, 422
Live Aid, 422
Live Nation Entertainment Inc
- Ticketmaster, 663

COMPANY INDEX

Liverpool LFC, 422
LKAB (Luossavaara-Kiiru-navaara Aktiebolag), 423
L!–Lance!, 423
LL Bean plc, 423
Lloyd's of London, 423
Lloyds TSB
– Access Credit Card, 59
Lloyds TSB Bank plc, 423
Local authority of the city of Almere, 313
Local authority of the city of Breda, 314
Local authority of the city of Uden, 314
Lockheed Martin, 423
Loctite Corporation, 424
Lofthouse of Fleetwood Ltd
– Fisherman's Friend, 284
Logica plc, 424
Logitech International SA, 424
– Color QuickCam, 163
– Labtec, 406
Logorama, 424
Lokomotiv Yaroslavl, 424
London Eastern Railway Ltd
– One, 508
London Stock Exchange plc, 424
Lonely Planet Publications Pty Ltd, 424
Lone Star Brewing Company
– Lone Star, 424
Long John Silver's Inc, 425
Lonsdale Sports Ltd, 425
Look Cycle International, 425
Loon Mountain Resort, 425
Looptroop Rockers, 425
Lord Abbett & Co. LLC, 425
Lord Corporation, 425
L'Oréal Group
– Garnier, 309
– Kiehl's, 395
– SkinCeuticals, 609
– Softsheen-Carson, 615
L'Oréal SA
– L'Oréal, 425
– Biotherm, 109
– Lancôme Paris, 409
– Maybelline New York, 446
– Redken, 563
– The Body Shop, 652
– Vichy Laboratoires, 702
Lorillard Tobacco Company Inc
– Newport, 486
Los Angeles Dodgers, 426
Loterie Nationale, 426
Loto, 426
Lotto (Deutsche Lotterie), 427
Lotto (Lotterie Nationale), 427
Lottomatica Group SpA, 427
Lotto Sport Italia SpA, 427
Lotus Cars Ltd
– Lotus, 427
Lotus Group plc
– Lotus, 427
Louis Dreyfus Holding BV, 427
Louisiana-Pacific Corporation, 428
Louvre Hotels Group
– Campanile, 135
Lowe and Partners
– Lowe, 428
Löwenbräu AG, 428
Lowe's Companies Inc, 428

Lowe's Food Stores Inc, 428
LPS laboratories, 428
L&Q Group (London & Quadrant Housing), 428
LQ Management LLC
– La Quinta Inn, 410
– La Quinta Inns & Suites, 410
LSB Industries Inc
– International Environmental, 373
LSI Corporation, 428
Lucasfilm Ltd, 429
– Star Wars, 626
– Star Wars – The Empire, Strikes Back, 626
– THX, 662
Lucas Oil Products Inc, 429
Lucent Technologies Inc, 429
Lufthansa AirPlus Servicekarten GmbH
– AirPlus International Ltd, 72
Luigi Lavazza SpA, 411
Lund International, 430
Lund International Inc
– Deflecta-Shield, 198
Lustucru Frais SAS, 430
Luxair SA, 430
Luxo ASA, 431
Luxottica Group SpA, 431
– Oakley, 500
– Persol, 528
– Ray-Ban, 559
– Revo, 567
LVMH Moët Hennessy Louis Vuitton SA
– Bulgari, 125
– DKNY (Donna Karan New York), 218
– DKNY Eyes, 218
– Fendi, 273
– Givenchy, 321
– LV Louis Vuitton, 431
– LVMH, 431
– Tag Heuer, 638
– Veuve Clicquot Ponsardin, 701
– Zenith, 741
Lyonnaise des Eaux SA
– Lyonnaise des Eaux, 431
Lysoform Disinfektion AG
– Lyso+Form, 431

M

MacAndrews & Forbes Holdings Inc
– Revlon, 567
MacGregor Golf, 434
Mackenzie Financial Corporation, 434
– Saxon Mutual Funds, 588
Mack Trucks Inc
– Mack Trucks, 435
MacLaren, 435
Macmahon Holdings Ltd, 435
Mac Papers Inc, 435
Mac Publishing LLC
– Macworld, 435
Macromedia Inc
– Macromedia, 435
– Macromedia Flash 5, 435
Macy's Inc, 436
– Bloomingdale's, 111
– Bullock's Department Store, 125
– The Cellar, 653
Made in America, 436
Made in USA Brand LLC, 436
Madison Square Garden Inc, 436
Maersk Group, 436

Maestrani Schweizer Schokoladen AG, 436
Magen David Adom
– Red Crystal, 563
– Red Star of David, 564
Magic Software Enterprises Ltd, 437
Magimix, 437
Mag Instruments Inc
– Mag-Lite, 437
Magneti Marelli Powertrain SpA
– Weber, 718
Magneti Marelli SpA, 438
Magnet Magazines BV
– Dag Allemaal, 185
Magnum Magnetics Corporation, 438
Mahle GmbH, 438
Major League Baseball, 438
Makita Corporation, 438
Mako Marine International Inc, 438
Maldives Marketing & Public Relations Corporation (MMPRC), 439
Mali (Museo de Arte de Lima), 439
Malmö Högskola, 439
Malta Tourism Authority, 439
Malt Shovel Brewery Pty Ltd
– James Squire, 381
Mammut Sports Group AG
– Mammut, 440
Mango Group, 440
Manila Electric Company
– Meralco, 449
Mannesmann Mobilfunk
– D2 Privat, 184
ManpowerGroup, 440
MAN SE, 440
– Renk, 565
Mantilla Ltd
– Dolphin Square, 221
Manufacture des montres Vulcain S.A.
– Vulcain, 713
Manulife Financial Corporation, 440
Mapal Inc, 440
Mapei SpA, 440
Mapfre SA, 440
Marathon Ashland Petroleum LLC
– SuperAmerica, 633
Marathon Equipment Comapany, 441
Marathon Petroleum Corporation, 441
Marchesan Implementos e Máquinas Agrícolas TATU SA, 441
Marc Jacobs International LLC, 441
Marcus Corporation
– Marcus Theatres, 441
Maret Pharmaceuticals Inc
– Maret, 441
Margarete Steiff GmbH, 628
Marks & Spencer plc, 442
Marlette Homes, 442
Marmitek BV, 442
Marmon Group
– Wells Lamont, 721
Marmot Mountain LLC, 442
Marquee Holdings Inc
– AMC Theatres (American Multi-Cinema), 82
Marriott International Inc, 442
– Fairfield Inn, 264

– Residence Inn by Marriott, 566
Marshall Amplification plc
– Marshall, 443
Marshall Field & Company
– The Cellar, 653
Marshalls Inc, 443
Marshall University
– Marshall Thundering Herd, 443
Marsh Supermarkets, 443
Mars Inc, 442
– Bubble Tape, 122
– Dove, 225
– Maltesers, 439
– Mars, 442
– Milky Way, 455
– M&M's, 434
– Royal Canin, 576
– Skittles, 609
– Snickers, 615
– Uncle Ben's, 682
– Whiskas, 724
– Wrigley's, 732
Mars Supermarkets Inc, 443
Martinair Holland NV, 443
Martini & Rossi, 443
Marui Co. Ltd, 443
Maruti Suzuki India Ltd, 443
Marvel Worldwide Inc
– Marvel Comics, 444
Mary Kay Inc
– Mary Kay Cosmetics, 444
Maryland-National Capital Park and Planning Commission (M-NCPPC), 444
Masco Corporation, 444
– Delta Faucet, 201
MAS-DAF Makina Sanayi AŞ, 185
Maserati SpA
– Maserati, 444
Massachusetts Institute of Technology (MIT)
– MIT Press, 459
Massive Music BV, 444
MasterCard Worldwide, 444
– Cirrus, 154
– Maestro, 437
– Mondex, 462
Matrox Electronic Systems Inc, 445
Matsushita Electric Industrial Co. Ltd, 445
Mattel Inc, 445
– Barbie, 101
– Fisher-Price, 284
– Hot Wheels, 358
– Matchbox, 444
Mavi, 445
MAW (Masters at Work), 445
Maxis (Electronic Arts Inc)
– The Sims Online, 660
Maxtor Corporation
– Matchbox, 446
Maya Ediciones, 446
Maybach-Motorenbau GmbH, 446
May Cheong Group
– Bburago, 104
MayDream Inc
– AdForum, 63
Maytag Corporation, 446
Mazda Motor Corporation, 446
MBG International Premium BrandsGmbH
– Effect Energy Drink, 244
MBK Europe, 446
MBT Holding AG, 447

McAfee Inc
– McAfee Security, 447
MC Appliance Corporation
– Magic, 437
McCain Foods Ltd, 447
McCormick & Company Inc, 447
– Schwartz, 591
McCulloch Motors Corporation, 447
McDonald Corporation
– McDonald's, 447
– McDonald's Drive Thru, 447
McDonalds Corporation
– Ronald McDonald, 574
– Ronald McDonald House Charities, 574
McDonnell Douglas Corporation, 448
McEvoy Group
– 7x7 San Francisco, 52
– Chronicle Books, 151
MCI Inc, 448
McIlhenny Company
– Tabasco, 638
MCI WorldCom
– UUNET, 693
McKesson Corporation, 448
– US Oncology, 692
McNeil-PPC Inc
– o.b., 500
– Visine, 706
Measurex Corporation, 448
Meat and Livestock Commercial Services Ltd
– MLC Services, 460
MECA Group, 448
Meccano, 448
Meccano/Erector Sets
– Erector, 254
Mechel, 448
Mecom Group plc
– Wegener, 719
Media and Sport
– The Royal Parks, 659
Mediacontech SpA
– Mikros Image, 455
Media Saturn Holding
– Saturn, 587
Mediaset SpA
– Italia 1, 378
Media Temple Inc
– Virb, 705
Medima GmbH, 448
Medtronic Inc, 449
MEE Direct LLC
– Eckō unltd., 242
MEF (Maskinentreprenørenes Forbund), 449
Mega Brands Inc
– Mega Bloks, 449
Megadyne Group, 382
Meiji Dairies Corporation, 449
Melitta Kaffee GmbH, 449
meneba BV, 449
Mercedes-Benz
– Mercedes-Benz, 450
Merck & Co. Inc, 450
– Coppertone, 171
Merck KGaA, 450
– Millipore, 456
Mercosur (Mercado Común del Sur), 450
Mercury Insurance Group, 450
Mercury Records
– Vertigo, 700
Meredith Corporation, 451
Merlin Entertainments Group Ltd

759

COMPANY INDEX

- Madame Tussauds, 436
Merrill Lynch & Co. Inc
- Merrill Lynch, 451
Mervyns LLC, 451
Merz Pharma GmbH & Co. KGaA, 451
Messe Berlin GmbH
- ICC Berlin (Internationale Congress Centrum Berlin), 364
Messerschmitt AG, 451
Metallica, 451
Metal Manufactures Ltd
- MMEM (MM Electrical Merchandising), 460
MetLife Inc, 451
Metro AG
- Makro, 438
- Metro Cash & Carry, 451
- Real,-, 560
- Saturn, 587
Metro-Goldwyn-Mayer Inc
- Stargate SG-1, 625
Metro Inc
- Food Basics, 289
- Loeb, 424
Metro International, 451
Metropolitan Transportation Authority of the State of New York (MTA), 469
Met-Rx Inc, 452
Mexico Tourism Board, 452
Meyer Corporation, 452
- Farberware, 267
Meyer Products LLC
- Diamond Snow Ploughs, 210
MGA Entertainment Inc
- Little Tikes, 422
MGI Luxury Group SA
- Ebel, 241
MGM Holdings Inc
- Metro-Goldwyn-Mayer, 452
- United Artists, 686
MG Motor UK Ltd
- MG, 452
MGM Resorts International
- MGM Grand, 452
MHM Holding GmbH
- Huber Gruppe, 360
Michelin North America Inc
- Uniroyal, 685
Michelin SA
- TCi Tire Centers, 643
Michelin SCA, 453
- Michelin XAS, 453
- Riken, 569
Michelin Tyre plc
- Kleber, 398
Microchip Technology Inc, 454
Micro Focus International plc
- Borland, 115
Micron Technology Inc, 454
Microsoft Corporation, 454
- Bing, 109
- HDCD (High Definition Compatible Digital), 350
- Internet Explorer, 374
- MSN, 468
- Skype, 610
- Windows, 728
- Windows 1.0, 728
- Windows 3.0, 728
- Xbox, 734
- Xbox 360, 734
- Zune, 743
Micro-Star International Co. Ltd
- MSI, 468
Midas International Corporation, 454
Midland Bank

- Access Credit Card, 59
Midwest Airlines, 454
Miele & Cie KG, 454
Milca Soda Roja, 455
Milk, 455
Milk Producers Cooperative Dos Pinos RL, 224
MillerCoors LLC, 455
Miller Electric Mfg Co, 455
Milton Bradley Company, 446
Milwaukee Electric Tool Corporation, 456
Mind, 456
Mind the Gap, 456
Mineralbrunnen Überkingen-Teinach AG
- Afri Cola, 67
Mini, 456
Ministério da Saúde, 456
Ministero dell'Istruzione dell'Università e della Ricerca
- Stazione Zoologica Anton Dohrn of Naples, 627
Ministry of Culture, 370
Ministry of Tourism
- Argentina, 91
Minor League Baseball Properties
- Durham Bulls, 236
Minuteman Press International Inc, 457
Miracle-Ear Inc, 457
Miramax Film Corporation, 457
Miro Marketing + Service GmbH, 457
Miss America Organization, 458
Mission Foods Corporation, 458
Miss Universe Organization, 458
Mister Minit, 458
Mistral International BV, 458
Mistral Paints sro, 458
Mita Industrial Co. Ltd
- Mita, 459
Mitek Corporation
- MTX Audio, 469
Mitel Networks Corporation, 459
MIT (Massachusetts Institute of Technology), 458
Mitre Sports International Ltd, 459
Mitsubishi Chemical Corporation, 459
Mitsubishi Group, 459
- AGC, 68
Mitsubishi Motors Corporation
- Ralliart, 557
Mitsubishi Pencil Co UK Ltd
- Posca, 541
Mitsui Sumitomo Insurance Group, 459
Mitsukoshi Ltd, 459
Mitsumi Electric Co. Ltd, 459
Mitutoyo Corporation, 459
Mizuno Corporation, 460
MK2, 460
MKE Ankaragücü, 460
MLB Advanced Media LP
- Cleveland Indians, 158
- Columbus Clippers, 164
MLS (Multiple Listing Service), 460
Mmm! Sarl
- Fooding, 289
Moblime Muebles, 461

Moderatera samlingspartiet, 461
Modern Products Inc
- Gayelord Hauser, 311
Modern Times Group MTG AB, 461
- Viasat, 701
Modo Papers
- Data Copy, 192
Moen Inc, 461
Moët & Chandon, 461
- Dom Pérignon, 223
Mohawk Industries Inc, 461
Moldavkabel ZAO, 461
Moleskin Srl, 461
Molinos de Nicaragua SA
- Pollo Rico, 539
Molson Coors Brewing Company, 455, 461
- Coors, 171
Momo Srl, 462
Monarch Group, 462
Moncler Group, 462
Mondex International Ltd
- Mondex, 462
Mondi Group, 462
Mondragon Corporation
- Fagor, 263
Moneo Payment Solutions, 462
Monotype Imaging Inc
- Linotype, 420
Monster Cable Products Inc, 463
Monster Worldwide Inc, 463
Montblanc International GmbH, 463
Montecatini Edison SpA, 463
Montreal Transit Corporation, 464
Moog Music Inc, 464
Moore Wallace Inc, 464
Morellato SpA
- Sector No Limits, 596
Morel Ltd, 464
Morgan Stanley, 464
Moriwaki Engineering Co. Ltd, 464
Morningstar Inc, 464
Moroccan National Tourist Office, 465
Morphy Richards, 465
Mosaid Technologies Inc, 465
Mothercare plc, 465
Mothers Polishes Waxes Cleaners Inc, 465
Motion Picture Association of America Inc (MPAA)
- Restricted (MPAA Movie Rating), 566
Motion Picture Association of America Inc (MPAA), 465
- PG - Parental Guidance Suggested - MPAA Movie Rating, 531
Motobecane USA, 465
MotorCities National Heritage Area, 466
Motor Components LLC
- Facet, 262
Motor Entertainment GmbH, 466
Motorola Inc, 466
Motorola Mobility Inc
- Netopia, 484
Motown Record Corporation, 466
Motul SA, 466
MountSnow, 467
Mozilla Corporation, 467

- Firefox 3.5, 281
- Thunderbird, 662
Mozilla Foundation, 467
MRC Polymers Inc, 468
Mr. Jardinage, 468
Mrs. Fields Famous Brands LLC
- TCBY (The Country's Best Yogurt), 643
Mrs. Fields' Original Cookies Inc, 468
MSA (Mine Safety Appliance) Corporation, 468
MSAS, 468
MSG Holdings LP, 468
MSHK Group Ltd
- Ministry of Sound, 457
MSNBC.com, 469
MSNBC Interactive News LLC, 469
MTD Products Inc
- Yard-Man, 737
MTV Networks
- Comedy Central, 165
- MTV, 469
- MTV2, 469
- Nickelodeon, 489
- South Park, 618
- The Box, 653
- TV Land, 676
- VH1, 701
MTV Networks Europe Inc
- Viva, 707
Multicanal SA
- Multicanal, 470
Municipality of Quito, 553
Munster Simms Engineering Ltd
- Whale, 723
Murata Manufacturing Co. Ltd
- Murata, 470
Murphy Brewery Ireland
- Murphy's Irish Stout, 470
Murphy Oil Corporation, 470
Muse, 470
Musée d'Orsay, 471
Musée Olympique (Olympic Museum), 471
Museo de Palpa, 471
Museon, 471
Museum für Film und Fernsehen, 471
Museum of Arts and Design, 472
Museum of Chinese in America, 472
Museum of Modern Art
- MoMa (Museum of Modern Art), 461
- LOVE, 428
Museum of Sex, 472
Museum of the Moving Image (MoMI), 472
Museuminsel Berlin, 472
Music for All Inc
- Bands of America, 99
MUSIC Group IP Ltd
- Behringer, 105
Mustang Survival, 472
Mute Records, 472
Muzak Holdings LLC, 472
Mylan Inc, 473
MYOB Ltd, 473
My Tiny Planets Ltd, 665

N

NAA (North American Aviation), 474
Nabisco

- Chips Ahoy!, 149
- Nilla Wafers, 491
- Oreo, 512
- Ritz Crackers, 570
Nady Systems Inc, 474
NAHB (National Association of Home Builders), 474
NAHI (National Association of Home Inspectors Inc), 474
NAIT (The Northern Aberta Institute of Technology), 474
Nakamichi Corporation Ltd, 474
Naked Music Recordings, 474
Nalco Holding Company, 474
Namco Bandai Co. Ltd
- Bandai, 99
Namco Bandai Games Inc
- Pac-Man, 517
Namco Bandai Holdings Inc
- Bandai, 99
Nampak Ltd, 475
Nanni Diesel, 475
Nanya Technology Corporation, 475
NARPM (National Association of Residential Property Managers), 475
NASA (National Aeronautics and Space Administration), 476
NASCAR (National Association for Stock Car Auto Racing), 476
Nasha Gazeta, 476
Nathan's Famous Inc, 476
National Arts Centre (Ottawa), 476
National Association for Stock Car Auto Racing (NASCAR)
- Whelen, 724
National Association of Broadcasters
- RDS Radio Data System, 560
National Association of Realtors
- Realtor, 561
National Automotive Parts Association (NAPA), 475
National Bank van België (National Bank of Belgium), 476
National Baseball Hall of Fame and Museum, 476
National Basketball Association
- Detroit Pistons, 207
National Broadcasting Company (NBC), 481
National Cable Satellite
- C-SPAN (Cable-Satellite Public Affairs Network), 181
National Captioning Institute
- Closed Captioned, 158
- National Captioning Institute Inc, 477
National Center for Missing and Exploited Children (NCMEC)
- National Car Rental, 477
National Emergency Number Association (NENA)
- Call 911 Emergency, 134
National Express Group plc, 477
- One, 508

COMPANY INDEX

National Fire Protection Association (NFPA)
- NFPA International, 488

National Gallery of Art, 477

National Geographic Society, 478

National Institute of Food and Agriculture (NIFA)
- 4-H, 51

National Instruments Corporation, 478

National League of POW/MIA Families, 543

National Leasing Group Inc, 478

National Library of Australia, 478

National Linen and Uniform Service LLC, 478

Nationallotterie, 478

National Lottery Commission, 478

National Mutual, 478

National Notary Association (NNA), 478

National Oceanic and Atmospheric Administration
- Sea Grant Oregon, 595

National Park Foundation (NPF), 479

National Park Service (NPS), 479

National Railroad Passenger Corporation
- Acela Express, 60
- Amtrak, 87

National Rifle Association of America (NRA), 479

National Safe Place, 581

National Safety Council
- Green Cross for Safety, 334

National Semiconductor Corporation, 479

National September 11 Memorial & Museum
- 9/11 Memorial, 52

National Sign Systems, 479

National Stonewall Democrats, 479

National Stores Inc
- Factory 2-U, 263

National Trust for Historic Preservation
- The Glass House (The Philip Johnson Glass House), 655

National Westminster Bank plc
- Access Credit Card, 59
- NatWest, 480

Nationwide Building Society, 480

Nationwide Mutual Insurance Company, 480

Natixis, 480

NATSN (North American Truck Stop Network), 480

NaturFoods, 480

Nautibel vzw, 480

Navimo Group
- Plastimo, 536

Navistar International Corporation, 480, 481
- International Trucks, 374

Navitair Inc, 481

Navy Federal Credit Union, 481

Naya Waters Inc, 481

NBA Media Ventures LLC
- Los Angeles Lakers, 426

NBA (National Basketball Association), 481

NBC (National Broadcasting Company)
- Scrubs, 594

NBC Universal LLC
- 13th Street Universal, 52
- Miss Universe, 458
- The Weather Channel, 661

NBCUniversal LLC
- E! Entertainment Television, 243
- Fandango, 266
- Sci-Fi Channel, 592
- Syfy, 637
- Universal Studios, 688

NBCUniversal Media LLC
- Bravo, 118
- CNBC, 160
- Telemundo, 647
- USA Network, 690

NCC AB
- NCC Construction, 481

NCR Corporation, 482

NCR Netkey Inc, 484

NDR (Norddeutscher Rundfunk), 482

Neal's Yard Remedies, 482

NEC Corporation
- NEC, 482

Nedlloyd, 482

NeilPryde Ltd, 482

Nelvana Ltd, 482

Nemi Forsikring A/S, 482

Neo Corporation
- Neo Synthetic Oil, 483

Neos SpA, 483

Nerco Inc, 483

Nertdecisions Group, 484

Nestlé Nespresso SA
- Nespresso, 483

Nestlé SA
- After Eight, 67
- Buitoni, 124
- Carnation, 139
- DiGiorno Pasta, 212
- Dreyer's Grand Ice Cream, 229
- Friskies, 300
- Gervais, 317
- Herta, 353
- Kit Kat, 397
- La Laitière, 408
- Maggi, 437
- Mövenpick, 467
- Nescafé, 483
- Nestlé, 483
- Nestlé Crunch, 180
- Nestlé Food Services, 483
- Nestlé Waters, 483
- Perrier, 528
- PowerBar, 542
- S.Pellegrino, 621
- Thomy, 662
- Vittel, 707

NetApp Inc, 484

Netflix Inc, 484

Netgear Inc, 484

Netherlands Government
- Nederlandse Spoorwegen, 482

Netigy Corporation, 484

Netopia Inc
- Farallon Computing, 267

Netscape Communications
- Netscape, 484

Net Serviços de Comuni-cação SA (Organizações Globo)
- NET, 484

Network Appliance Inc, 484

Network Solutions LLC, 485
- Network Solutions, 485

Neutrogena Corporation
- Neutrogena, 485

Nevada Bell Telephone Company
- Nevada Bell, 485

Neways International, 485

New Balance Athletic Shoe Inc, 485

Newcastle United FC Ltd, 485

Newell Rubbermaid Inc
- Foohy, 290
- Graco, 330
- Irwin Tools, 377
- Paper Mate, 520
- Parker, 521
- Rolodex, 574
- Rotring, 576
- Rubbermaid, 578
- Sanford, 584
- Sharpie, 601
- Waterman, 718

New Era Cap Co, 486

New Jersey Cardinals, 486

New Line Cinema
- Fine Line Features, 280

New Line Film Productions Inc

New Line Home Entertainment, 486

New Man, 486

New National Theatre Tokyo, 486

Newport Boats, 486

News Corporation, 486
- 20th Century Fox, 52
- HarperCollins Publishers, 348
- New York Post, 487
- Star Gold (US), 626
- The Wall Street Journal, 660

News International Ltd
- News of the World, 487
- The Sun, 660

News Ltd
- The Daily Telegraph, 654

Newsvine Inc, 487

New Swiss Hutless International AG
- Swiss Hutless, 636

Newton Investment Management, 487

New York City Ballet (NYCB), 487

New York Giants, 319

New York Life Insurance Company, 487

New York State Department of Economic Development
- I Love New York, 369

Nexans SA, 487

NeXT Software Inc, 488

NFB/ONF (National Film Board of Canada/Office national du film du Canada), 488

NFL (National Football League), 488

NFL Players (National Football League Players Association), 488

NGA (National Gallery of Australia)
- NFPA International, 488

NGA (National Glass Association), 488

NGK Spark Plug Co. Ltd, 488

NHRA (National Hot Rod Association), 488

NHS Blood and Transplant, 477

NHS Inc

- Santa Cruz Skateboards, 585

NHS (National Health Service), 488

Niasi Indústria de Cosméticos Ltda., 489

NIBCO, 489

Nichirei Corporation, 489

Nicoletti, 489

Nidar, 489

Nidwaldner Kantonalbank, 489

Niederösterreichische Schneebergbahn GmbH, 590

Nihon Bussan Co. Ltd
- Nichibutsu, 489

Niigita Institute of Technology, 489

Nike Inc
- Air Jordan, 72
- Air Max, 72
- Cole Haan, 162
- Just Do It, 389
- Nike, 490
- Umbro, 682

NIKI Luftfahrt GmbH, 490

Nikkei Business Publications, 490

Nikkei Inc, 490

Nikko Co. Ltd, 490

Nikon Corporation, 490

Nilfisk-Advance A/S, 491

Ninja Tune Records Ltd, 491

NIN (Nine Inch Nails), 491

Nintendo Co. Ltd
- Game Boy, 307
- Nintendo, 491
- Nintendo 64, 491
- Super Famicom, 633
- Super Mario Bros (Mushroom Kingdom), 634
- Super Nintendo Entertainment System, 634
- Wii, 726

Nippon Carbide Industries
- Nikkalite, 490

Nippon Express Co. Ltd, 491

Nipponkoa Insurance, 491

Nippon Life Insurance Company
- Nissay, 492

Nipponpaint Co. Ltd, 491

Nippon Sanso, 492

Nippon Takkyu Co. Ltd
- Nittaku, 493

Nirvana, 492

Nissan Motor Company Ltd
- Infiniti, 371
- Nissan, 492

Nissin Brake Ohio Inc
- Nissin, 492

Nissin Foods Holdings Co. Ltd
- Nissay, 492

Nitrous Oxide Systems Inc
- NOS, 493

Nitta Corporation, 492

Nitto Denko Corporation, 493

Nixxo Telecom, 493

NKK Group, 493

NMMA (National Marine Manufacturers Association), 493

NOBI (Norsk Betongindustri), 493

NOK Corporation, 493

Nokia Corporation, 493

Nolte Küchen GmbH & Co. KG, 494

Nomaï SA, 494

Nomura Holdings Inc, 494

Noranda Inc, 494

Norbert Dentressangle SA
- Norbert Dentressangle, 494
- TDG, 643

Nordica
- Rollerblade, 573

Nordic Aluminium Oyj, 494

Nordisk AS
- Novo Nordisk, 497

Norges Dykkeforbund, 494

Norges Elektriske Materiellkontroll
- Nemko, 482

NorgesGruppen ASA, 494

Norges Ischockeyforbund, 495

Noritake, 495

Nor Lines AS, 495

Norman ASA, 495

Norquip, 495

Norske Skogindustrier ASA, 495

Nortel Networks Corporation, 495

North American Van Lines Inc, 495

North Atlantic Treaty Organization (NATO), 480

Northeast Utilities, 495

Northern & Shell Network Ltd
- 5* (Five Star), 51
- Channel 5, 146

Northern Trust Corproation, 496

North Marine Group, 496

Northpine Ltd, 496

Northrop Grumman Corporation
- Litton Industries, 422

Northstar California
- Northstar at Tahoe, 496

Northwest Airlines Inc, 499

NorthwesTel Inc, 496

Norton Motorcycles Ltd, 496

Norton Villiers Triumph
- Norton Triumph, 496

Norwegian Diving Federation, 494

Norwegian National Rail Administration
- Jernbanaverket, 384

Norwest Corporation, 496

Norwich Union, 497

Novartis AG
- Ciba Vision, 152

Novartis International AG
- Maalox, 434

Novell Inc
- Novell, 497

NSA (National Speakers Association), 497

NSB Group, 497

NSI (National Service Industries), 497

NSTA (National Safe Transit Association), 497

NTPC Ltd, 498

NTT Communications Corporation
- NTT Verio, 498
- NTT Communications (Nippon Telegraph and Telephone) Corporation, 498

NTT DoCoMo Inc, 498

Nuance Communications Inc
- OmniPage Pro, 507

Nuclear Energy Institute
- National Academy for Nuclear Training (NANT), 476

Nucor Corporation, 498

Nutrition & Santé
- Céréal, 144

761

COMPANY INDEX

Nuvelo Inc, 498
NV Energy Inc
- Nevada Power Company, 485
Nvidia Corporation, 499
NV Nederlandse Gasunie, 310
NYC & Company Inc, 499
Nykredit Holding A/S, 499
NYLC, 499
NYSE (New York Stock Exchange), 499

O

Oakley Inc, 500
Oakwood Worldwide, 500
OAO Severstal, 600
Oase GmbH, 500
Oasis Merchandising Ltd, 500
Obayashi Corporation, 500
ÖBB-Holding AG (SBB)
- S-Bahn, 580
Oberalp SpA AG
- Salewa, 583
Obey Giant, 500
Oblicore Inc, 501
Occidental Petroleum Corporation (Oxy), 515
Oceanário de Lisboa, 421
Oceanico Group, 501
Ocean Spray Cranberries Inc, 501
Océ NV, 501
Octagon Motorsport
- Silverstone, 607
Octanorm Vertriebs GmbH, 501
Ocura Hotels & Resorts
- Nikko Hotels International, 490
Oddrane, 501
Odell Brewing Co., 502
Odyssey Ltd, 502
Oerlikon Corporation AG, 502
Office Depot Inc, 502
Office Depot International Ltd
- Viking, 704
Office of Fair Housing and Equal Opportunity (U.S. Department of Housing and Urban Development), 254
Offley Porto, 502
Offshore Logistics Inc, 502
of Graphic Arts), 70
Öhlins Racing AB, 503
OJD Quick Brake ApS, 553
OJSC Lukoil, 430
OJSC Siberia Airlines
- S7 Airlines, 580
OJSC SUN InBev
- Sibirskaya Korona, 605
Okamura Corporation, 503
Okasan Securities Group Inc, 503
Oki Electric Industry Co. Ltd, 503
Okuma Corporation, 503
OK Used Cars,
Oldcastle Inc, 504
Old Dutch Foods Ltd
- Humpty Dumpty, 360
Old Mutual plc
- Skandia, 609
Olidata SpA, 504
Olin Corporation, 504
Olivetti SpA, 505
Olivine Group BV
- greenSand, 336
Oloid AG, 505
Olympic Airways, 505

Olympic Games Tokyo 1964, 505
Olympic Games Mexico 1968, 505
Olympic Games Los Angeles 1984, 505
Olympic Games Barcelona 1992, 505
Olympic Games Atlanta 1996, 505
Olympic Games Sydney 2000, 506
Olympic Games Athens 2004, 506
Olympic Games Beijing 2008, 506
Olympic Games London 2012, 506
Olympic Winter Games Salt Lake City 2002, 506
Olympic Winter Games Torino 2006, 506
Olympic Winter Games Vancouver 2010, 506
Olympique de Marseille SASP, 507
Olympus Corporation, 507
Olympus Hospitality Group
- Park Inn International, 521
Omaha Paper Company, 507
OMC Card Inc, 507
Omega SA, 507
Omer DeSerres Inc, 507
Omnicom Group
- BBDO, 104
Omni Hotels Corporation, 507
OmniSky Corporation, 507
Omron Corporation, 508
OMS Online Marketing Service GmbH & Co. KG, 508
OMV Petrol Ofisi AS, 538
OMV Petrom SA, 530
OMX Inc
- OfficeMax, 502
O'Neill Inc, 508
One Laptop per Child Foundation, 508
One Little Indian Records
- Björk, 109
Oneok Inc, 508
Onex Corporation
- Allison Transmission, 78
Onkyo Corporation, 509
Ontario Ministry of Agriculture
- Foodland Ontario, 289
Onward Manufacturing Company Ltd
- Broil King, 120
Oops! Inc, 509
OpenText Corporation,
Oprah Winfrey, 510
Optimal AG & Co. KG, 510
Optimist International, 510
Oracle America Inc
- Sun Microsystems, 632
Oracle Corporation, 510
- Java, 382
- MySQL, 473
Orange County Convention Center (OCCC), 510
Orange Julius of America Inc, 511
Orange SA
- Wanadoo, 716
Orangina Schweppes France
- Pulco, 548
Orbea S. Coop, 511

Orbis Tecnología Eléctrica SA, 511
Oreck Corporation, 511
Ore-Ida Potato Products Inc, 511
O'Reilly Automotive Inc, 512
Organizações Globo
- Rede Globo, 563
Oriental Brewery Co. Ltd
- OB Lager, 501
Orion Pictures Corporation, 512
ORIX Corporation, 512
Orlando Museum of Art (OMA), 513
Oscar de la Renta, 513
OSCE (Organization for Security and Co-operation in Europe), 513
Osco Drug
- Sav-On Drugs, 588
OSG Tap & Die Inc, 514
OshKosh B'gosh Inc, 514
Osotspa Co. Ltd
- Shark Energy Drink, 600
OSRAM AG, 514
Osuna Nursery, 514
Otis Elevator Company, 514
OTP Bank,
Ottakringer Brauerei AG, 514
Otto Fuchs KG, 302
Outokumpu Group, 515
Owens Corning Corporation
- Overture Services, 515
Owens Illinois Inc, 503
Oxfam Novib
- Stop Aids Now!, 629
Oxiteno, 515
Oxxio, 515
Oy Karl Fazer AB
- Fazer, 269

P

Pabst Brewing Company, 516
- Lone Star, 424
- Old Style Beer, 504
- Stroh's, 630
Paccar Inc, 516
- DAF, 185
- Peterbilt, 529
Pacific Bell
- Nevada Bell, 485
Pacific Bell Telephone Company
- Pacific Bell, 516
Pacific Brands
- Mooks Clothing Co., 464
Pacific Cycle In
- Roadmaster Bike, 571
Package Industries Inc, 516
Packard Bell BV
- Packard Bell, 517
Pacon Corporation, 517
Pactiv Corporation
- Hefty, 351
Pac West Distributing Inc
- Rush, 578
Paddington Basin
- Paddington Walk, 517
PADI (Professional Association of Diving Instructors), 517
Pago International GmbH, 518
Pakistan International Airlines Corporation, 518
Palace Amusement Co. (1921) Ltd, 518
Palitoy Ltd
- Action Man, 61
Pall Corporation, 518

Pallinghurst Resources Ltd
- Fabergé, 262
Palm Inc, 518
PalmOne Inc, 518
Pan American World Airways
- Pan Am, 519
Panasonic Corporation, 519
- Technics, 644
Panavision Inc, 519
Panda Embroidery, 519
Panda Restaurant Group Inc
- Panda Express, 519
Panda Security
- Panda Software, 519
Panini SpA, 519
Pantech Corporation, 519
Paper Products Design GmbH, 520
Papier Recyclé, 520
Papyrus AB, 520
Paramount Pictures Corporation
- Grease, 333
- Grease 2, 333
- Indiana Jones, 371
- Paramount Pictures, 520
- The Godfather, 655
- The Warriors, 661
- Transformers: Revenge of the Fallen, 672
Parexel International, 521
Parex Group
- Klaukol, 397
Parfümerie Douglas GmbH, 225
Paris Saint-Germain Football SASP, 521
Parken Sport & Entertainment AS
- F.C. København, 270
Parker Hannifin Corporation, 521
Parker Pen Company, 521
Parmalat SpA
- Parmalat, 522
Partek Oy Ab, 522
Parti Socialiste, 522
Pathé Records, 522
Pathé SA, 522
Pato Pampo, 523
Patta, 523
Paulaner Brauerei GmbH & Co. KG, 523
Paul Jaeger GmbH & Co. KG, 380
Paulmann Lighting, 523
Paul Smith Ltd, 523
Pax Cultura
- Banner of Peace, 101
PayPal
- PayPal, 523
PBS (Public Broadcasting Service), 523
PCC (Power Corporation of Canada), 524
Peace Corps
- Peace Corps, 524
Peace Symbol, 524
Pearl Musical Instrument Company, 524
Pearson Education
- New Riders Publishing, 486
Pearson plc, 524
- Dorling Kindersley (DK), 224
- Puffin Books, 547
- Que Publishing, 552
Peavey Electronics Corporation, 524
PECSA, 525
Pediatric Palliative Care Institute, 525

Peerless Tyre Co, 525
PEFC International, 525
Pelforth Brewery, 525
- Pekao Leasing, 525
Pelikan Holding AG, 525
Pemsa International, 526
Pen Club Venezuela, 526
Penguin, 526
Penguin Group
- Dorling Kindersley (DK), 224
- Gotham Books, 329
- Puffin Books, 547
Penn, 526
PennWell Petroleum Group
- Oil & Gas Journal, 503
Penske Corporation, 526
Pentax Ricoh Imaging Coporation, 526
Pentel Co. Ltd, 526
Pentland Group plc
- Pentland Group, 459
- Speedo, 620
Peoples Gas
- Peoples Energy, 527
Pepe Jeans SL, 527
Pepsi Center (aka The Can), 527
PepsiCo Inc
- 7 Up (International), 52
- Cheetos, 147
- Cracker Jack, 176
- Doritos, 224
- Frito Lay, 300, 301
- Fritos, 301
- Gatorade, 311
- Lay's, 411
- Looza, 425
- Mountain Dew, 467
- Pepsi, 527
- PepsiCo, 527
- Pepsi-Cola, 527
- Quaker Oats, 551
- Rollitos, 573
- SoBe Grape Grog, 615
- SunChips, 632
- Tropicana, 674
- Walkers, 714
Perfetti Van Melle SpA
- Chupa Chups, 151
- Mentos, 449
- Smint, 613
Performance Sailcraft Pty. Ltd
- Laser, 410
PerkinElmer Inc, 528
Perma Press AB, 528, 532
Pernod Ricard SA, 528
- Absolut Vodka, 58
- Malibu Rum, 439
- Seagram's, 595
- V&S (Vin & Spirit), 694
Peroni Brewery, 528
Perricone MD
- Super by Dr. Nicholas Perricone, 633
Perry Ellis International Group Holdings Ltd
- Munsingwear, 470
Perry Sport BV, 528
Persgroep NV
- Dag Allemaal, 185
Pershing LLC, 528
Personal Care Group Inc
- Diaperene, 211
Petco Animal Supplies Inc, 529
Peterbilt Motors Company, 529
Peter Kaiser GmbH, 529
Peter Paul Candy Manufacturing Company, 529

COMPANY INDEX

Peterson Manufacturing Company, 529
Petro-Canada
- Petro-Canada, 530
PetroChina Company Ltd, 530
Petróleo Brasileiro SA
- Petrobras, 529
Petróleos de Venezuela SA
- Petróleos de Venezuela, 530
- Citgo, 154
Petróleos Mexicanos
- PEMEX, 525
Petroliam Nasional Berhad, 530
Petroplus Holdings AG, 530
Peugeot SA, 530
- Talbot, 639
PEZ, 530
Pfizer Inc, 531
- Advil, 65
- Dristan, 229
- Wyeth, 733
PG&E Corporation, 516
Pharmacia Corp, 531
Philco Argentina SA, 531
Philip Morris International
- Marlboro, 442
- Philip Morris International (PMI), 532
Philippine Stock Exchange, 532
Philips Electronics North America Corporation
- Magnavox, 437
- Philco US, 531
Phillips-Van Heusen Corporation
- Arrow, 92
- Van Heusen, 696
PHLX (Philadelphia Stock Exchange), 532
Phoenix Brands LLC
- Ajax, 73
Piaggio & Co. SpA
- Gilera, 320
- Moto Guzzi, 465
- Vespa, 700
Picard Surgelés, 532
Picture Licensing Universal System
- Plus, 537
Piedboeuf Brewery
- Jupiler, 389
Pier 1 Imports Inc, 533
Pierce Manufacturing Inc, 533
Pikolin SA, 533
Pilot Corporation, 533
Pininfarina SpA, 534
Pink Floyd, 534
Pinnacle Foods Group LLC
- Van de Kamp's, 695
Pinterest Inc, 534
Pioneer Corporation, 534
- LaserDisc, 410
Piper Aircraft Corporation
- Piper Cub, 534
Piper Aircraft Inc, 534
Piperlime, 534
Pirelli & C. SpA, 534
Pitney Bowes Inc, 535
Pivovary Staropramen a.s.
- Staropramen, 626
Pixar Animation Studios, 535
- A Bug's Life, 58
- Buy 'N Large, 129
Pizza Hut Inc, 535
PKN Orlen SA, 513
Planar Systems Inc
- Vidikron, 703
Plan B Skateboards, 535

Planet Hollywood International Inc, 535
Plannja AB, 535
Plastics USA, 536
Platinum Equity
- U.S. Robotics, 692
Plaxo Inc, 536
Playboy, 536
Play Ltd
- Play.com, 536
Playskool Corporation, 536
Playtex Products Inc, 537
PLR IP Holdings LLC
- Polaroid, 538
Plus Retail BV
- Plus, 537
Ply Marts Inc, 537
PMC-Sierra
- Adaptec, 62
PMU, 537
PocketCard, 538
Pohang Iron and Steel Company (POSCO), 541
Pohjola Insurance Ltd, 538
Point.P, 538
Pokémon Company, 538
Polar Electro Oy, 538
Polaris Industries Inc
- Polaris Industries, 538
- Victory Motorcycles, 703
Polaroid Corporation, 538
Polartec LLC, 539
Pôle emploi, 539
Police Fédérale, 539
Polish People's Party (PSL), 547
Polizei Hamburg, 539
Polskie Linie Lotnicze LOT SA, 427
Polskie Radio SA, 540
PolyGram Filmed Entertainment
- Gramercy Pictures, 331
Polyphony Digital Inc
- Gran Turismo, 332
Pomare Inc
- Hilo Hattie, 355
Pont-Aven School of Contemporary Art, 540
Poron SA (Groupe Zannier)
- Absorba, 58
Porsche Automobil Holding SE, 540
Porter-Cable, 540
Port-O-Let International Inc, 541
Porto Seguro Seguros SA, 541
Postal Instant Press Inc, 534
Postbank NV, 541
Post Danmark A/S, 541
Posten AB, 541
PostgreSQL Global Development Group, 542
Post Holdings Inc, 541
PostNorden AB, 541
Post Office Ltd, 542
Potlach Corporation, 542
Powell Peralta, 542
Powerflush Ltd, 542
PowerPC, 543
Pöyry PLC, 543
PPG Architectural Finishes Inc
- Olympic Paints & Stains, 505
PPHE Hotel Group Ltd
- Park Plaza, 522
PPP Group
- Gucci, 340
PPR SA
- Le Point, 415

- Yves Saint-Laurent, 739
Prada SpA, 543
- Miu Miu, 460
Praktiker Bau-und Heimwerkermärkte Holding AG, 543
Pramac Group SpA, 543
Prandium Inc
- Chi-Chi's, 148
Preciosa AS, 543
Precision Locker Company, 544
Premier Cruise Lines
- Dolphin Cruise Line, 221
Premier Cruises, 544
Premier Farnell UK Ltd, 268
Premier Research Group, 544
Prestone Products Corporation, 544
Pret A Manger (Europe) Ltd
- Pret A Manger, 544
Prevent Child Abuse America, 544
Primark Stores Ltd, 544
Primedia Ltd, 544
Prince Sports Inc, 545
Princeton University
- Princeton University Press, 545
Princeton University Art Museum
- Princess Cruises, 545
Principal Financial Group Inc, 545
Prinsel, 545
Private Post Secondary Education Commission
- PPSEC Accredited, 543
Procter & Gamble Co
- Clairol, 157
- Cover Girl, 176
- Crest, 179
- Dawn, 194
- Duracell, 235
- Gillette, 320
- Glad, 322
- IAMS, 362
- Ivory, 379
- Mr. Clean, 467
- Old Spice, 504
- Oral-B, 510
- Pampers, 518
- P&G, 516
- Tampax, 640
- The Gillette Company, 655
- Tide, 663
- Vicks, 702
- Vidal Sassoon, 703
- Vizir Ultra, 708
- Wella, 720
- Zest, 742
Procter & Gamble GmbH
- Oil of Olaz, 503
- Wick, 725
profine GmbH
- KBE Fenstersysteme, 392
Progress Energy, 546
Progressive Waste Solutions Ltd
- BFI Canada, 108
Prometheus Global Media
- ADWEEK, 65
- Billboard, 109
Promoción y Operación SA de CV
- Carnet, 139
Prop. Inc
- Jack Daniel's, 380
ProSiebenSat.1 Digital GmbH
- ProSieben, 546
ProSiebenSat.1 Media AG

- Kanal 5 Danmark, 390
- ProSiebenSat.1, 546
- Sat.1, 587
Prospect Park Alliance, 546
Protective Life Corporation, 546
Proton Holdings Bhd, 546
Province of Nova Scotia, 497
Prudential Financial Inc, 547
Prudential plc
- Bluewater, 112
PSA Peugeot Citroën, 155
- Citroën Picasso, 533
- Faurecia, 269
PT. Bank Danamon Indonesia, 188
PT Garuda Indonesia (Persero) Tbk, 309
PT Miwon Indonesia
- Miwon, 460
PT Telekomunikasi Indonesia Tbk, 648
- Perumtel, 529
PTT Post, 547
Public Broadcasting Service (PBS)
- Reading Rainbow, 560
Public Enemy, 547
Publicis Groupe, 547
Publix Super Markets Inc, 547
Puget, 547
Pukka-Pies Ltd, 547
Pulp, 548
Puma AG
- Cobra Golf, 161
Pumas de la UNAM (Club Universidad Nacional AC)
- Pulsar, 548
Puma SE
- Pulsar, 548
Pumper Nic
- Pulsar, 548
Pure Fishing Inc
- Abu Garcia, 58
- Fenwick, 273
Purina Mills LLC
- Purina, 548
Purolator Courier Ltd, 549
Putoline Oil, 549
Putzmeister Concrete Pumps GmbH, 549
PVH Corp
- Calvin Klein, 135
- ck Calvin Klein, 135
- Tommy Hilfiger, 668
- Van Heusen, 696
Pye Ltd, 549
PZ Cormay SA, 173
PZ Cussons Ltd
- Original Source, 512

Q

Qantas Airways Ltd
- Qantas, 550
Qatar Airways QCSC, 550
Qatar Investment Authority
- Harrods, 349
Qiagen NV, 550
Qinetiq Group plc, 550
Qisda Corporation
- BenQ, 106
QLogic Corporation, 550
QSC Audio Products LLC, 550
QSound Labs Inc, 551
Quadriga, 551
Quaker Oats Company
Quaker Oats, 551
Qualcomm Inc, 551
Qualibat, 551

Quality Hotel, 551
Quantum Corporation, 551
Quark Inc, 552
Quarto Group Inc
- Rockport Publishers, 572
Quasar Electronics Inc, 552
Quebramar, 552
Queen, 552
Queensland Government
- QR Queensland Rail, 550
Quelle GmbH, 552
Que Publishing, 552
Quercetti & C. SpA, 552
Questar Corporation, 552
Quick Chek Food Stores Inc, 553
Quick meals, 553
Quik Print, 553
Quiksilver Inc, 553
QVC, 553
Qwest Communications International Inc, 553

R

Rabigh Refining & Petrochemical Co., 530
Rabobank Groep NV, 556
RAC plc, 556
Radiator Specialty Company
- Gunk, 343
Radioactive (Hazard symbol), 556
Radiomovil Dipsa SA de CV
- Telcel, 645
Radio Popular
- COPE (Cadena de Ondas Populares Españolas), 171
Radio-Québec, 556
RadioShack Corporation, 556
Radura, 556
RAF (Red Army Faction), 556
Rail Corporation New South Wales
- CityRail, 156
Rainforest Alliance, 557
RAI (Resource America Inc), 557
Raisio Group, 557
Ralcorp Holdings Inc
- Mueller's, 470
Ralf Bohle GmbH
- Schwalbe, 591
Ralliart Inc, 557
Ralph Lauren Corporation
- Polo Jeans Company, 539
- Ralph Lauren, 557
Ram Golf Corporation, 558
Rammstein GbR, 558
Ramones, 558
Randstad Holding NV, 558
Randy's Donuts, 558
RATP Group (Régie Autonome des Transports Parisiens), 558
Rautaruukki Oyj
- Ruukki, 579
Ravensburger AG, 558
Rawlings Sporting Goods Company Inc
- Rawlings Sporting Goods Company Inc, 559
- Worth, 732
Rayovac Corporation, 559
Raytheon Company, 559
RBC Financial Group, 559
RBS (Royal Blind Society), 560
RCA Corporation
- RCA, 560
RCA Music Group

763

COMPANY INDEX

- Jive Records, 385
RCapital Partners LLP
- Little Chef, 421
RCA Trademark Management SA, 560
RCS MediaGroup SpA
- Corriere della Sera, 173
Reading Matters, 560
RealChat Software, 560
Real Madrid Club de Fútbol, 561
RealNetworks Inc, 561
Realogy Corporation
- Century 21, 144
Realty World Inc, 561
Rearden Commerce Inc, 561
Rebublic Steel, 561
Reckitt Benckiser LLC
- Frank's RedHot, 296
- Spray 'n Wash, 623
Reckitt Benckiser plc, 561
- Dr. Scholl's, 230
- Durex, 236
- French's, 298
- Harpic, 349
- Lysol, 431
Reclaim the Media, 562
Recording Industry Association of America
- RIAA, 568
Recording Industry Association of America (RIAA)
- Parental Advisory Explicit Content, 520
Record Makers, 562
Recreational Equipment Inc
- REI, 565
Recycle, 562
Recycling Symbol, 562
Red Bull GmbH, 562
Red Diamond Holdings Sàrl
- Lee Cooper, 413
red dot GmbH & Co. KG
- red dot design award, 563
Red Group Ltd
- VPAR, 712
Red Hat Inc, 563
Red Lion Hotels Corporation, 563
Redman Homes Inc, 563
Red River Supply Inc, 563
Reebok-CCM Hockey Inc
- CCM, 142
Reebok International Ltd
- RBK, 559
- Reebok, 564
Reed Business Information
- Variety, 697
Reed Elsevier plc/NV
- Variety, 697
Reed Specialist Recruitment Ltd
- Reed, 564
Refco Inc, 564
Refractarios Basicos SA de CV
- Rebasa, 561
Regional Express Pty Ltd
- Rex Regional Express, 567
Regional News Network Company, 570
Regions Financial Corporation, 564
Registers of Scotland
- ros.gov.uk, 574
Reifen Gundlach Inc
- Com4Wheels, 165
Reitangruppen AS
- Rema 1000, 565
Reliance Group, 565

Reliance Life Insurance Company, 565
Remington Arms Company LLC, 565
Renault Deutschland AG
- Dacia, 184
Renault SA, 565
Renfe Operadora, 565
Renk AG, 565
Reno-Depot Inc
- The Building Box, 653
Rent-2-Own, 565
Rent-A-Wreck of America Inc, 566
Reprise Records
- Green Day American Idiot, 335
Repsol YPF SA, 566
Republican Party, 331
Republic Services Inc, 566
Republic Technologies International Company
- Zig-Zag, 742
Research In Motion Ltd (RIM)
- BlackBerry, 110
Retail Motor Industry Federation (RMI), 566
Revell-Monogram Inc
- Monogram, 462
- Revell, 566
Revigrés Lda, 567
Revlon Inc
- Almay, 79
- Revlon, 567
- Revlon Professional, 567
Rexel
- Selga, 597
Rexel Group, 567
Reynolds American Inc
- Kool, 402
- Winston, 729
Reynolds Group Holdings
- Reynolds Metals Company, 567
RFM, 567
RFU England Rugby, 567
Rheem Manufacturing Company, 568
Rhiga Royal Hotels, 568
Rhino Entertainment Company, 568
Rhodia SA, 568
RIA Novosti
- RT (Russia Today), 577
Ribogojstvo Goričar d.o.o., 568
Ricard SA, 568
- Clan Campbell, 157
Richard-Pontvert SA
- Paraboot, 520
Richmond Gear & Machine Co. Inc
- Lock-Right, 423
Ricoh Americas Corp
- IKON Office Solutions Inc, 368
Ricoh Company Ltd, 568
- Savin, 588
RICS (Royal Institution of Chartered Surveyors), 568
Rieber & Søn Danmark AS
- K-Salat, 404
Rieger Kfz-Kunststoffteile, 569
Rieker Holding AG, 569
Rietze Automodelle GmbH & Co. KG, 570
Rīgas Piena kombināts JSC, 569
Rimowa GmbH, 569
Rio Offices, 569

Rip Curl International Pty Ltd, 569
Rita's Franchise Company, 569
Rite Aid Corporation, 570
- Fay's Drug, 269
Rivella AG, 570
R. J. Reynolds Tobacco Company
- Camel, 135
- Doral, 223
- Winston, 729
RKO Pictures (Radio-Keith-Orpheum), 570
R.L. Drake Holdings LLC, 227
RMN (Réunion des Musées Nationaux), 570
R.M. Williams Pty Ltd, 570
Roadmaster Drivers School, 571
Robert Bosch GmbH
- Bosch, 116
- Bosch Service, 116
Robert Bosch LLC
- Telex, 648
Robert Bosch Tool Corporation
- Skil, 609
- Vermont American, 700
Roces Srl, 571
Rochdale, 571
Roche Bobois International SAS, 571
Roche Group
- Genentech Inc, 314
Roche Holding AG, 571
Rock and Roll Hall of Fame and Museum, 571
RockBottomGolf.com
- Ray Cook Golf, 559
Rockford Corporation
- Rockford Fosgate, 572
Rock 'n' Roll High School, 572
Rock Oil Ltd, 572
Rockstar Games Inc
- Rockport Publishers, 572
- Vice City (Grand Theft Auto:, Vice City), 702
Rockwell Automation, 572
Rockwell Collins Inc, 572
Rockwell International, 572
Rocky Brands Inc, 573
Röd Press, 573
Rogers Broadcasting Ltd
- Citytv, 156
Rogers Communications Inc, 573
- Citytv, 156
- Omni Television, 508
- Toronto Blue Jays, 669
Rogers Media Inc
- OLN, 505
Rohm and Haas Company
- Rohn and Haas, 573
Roland Corporation, 573
- Boss, 116
Roland Meinl Musikinstru-mente GmbH & Co. KG
- Meinl Percussion, 449
Rolex SA, 573
- Tudor, 675
Rollei GmbH, 573
Rollins Inc
- Orkin, 512
Rolls-Royce Group plc, 574
Rompetrol Group NV
- Dyneff, 237
Roots Canada Ltd, 574
Ropa Siete Leguas SA de CV, 574

Roskilde Bank, 575
Rotary International, 575
Rotel, 575
Ro Theater, 575
Roto Frank AG, 575
Rotork plc, 575
Roto-Rooter Group Inc
- Roto-Rooter, 575
Rotovision, 576
Rotring, 576
Rovi Corporation
- DivX, 217
Rovio Entertainment Ltd
- Angry Birds, 88
Royal Air Force, 576
Royal Bank of Canada
- Banque Royale, 101
Royal Canin SAS, 576
Royal Caribbean Cruises Ltd, 576
Royal Dutch Football Association
- KNVB, 400
Royal Dutch Shell plc
- Rain-X, 557
- Shell, 601
- Shell Helix, 601
- Slick 50, 611
Royal KPN NV, 403
- Oppo, 509
- Telfort, 648
Royal Life Saving Society, 576
Royal Mail Holdings plc
- Royal Mail, 577
Royal Talens BV (Sakura Color Products Corporation)
- Talens, 640
Royal Unibrew A/S
- Thor, 662
Royal Wear, 577
RR Donnelley & Sons Company
- RR Donnelley, 464
- Bowne, 116
RSA Insurance Group plc
- More Th>n, 464
RTL Group
- RTL, 577
- RTL 4, 577
- RTL 7, 577
RTL Group SA
- RTL, 577
- RTL Group, 578
- RTL Z, 578
- Vox, 712
RTL Nederland
- RTL, 577
- RTL 4, 577
- RTL 7, 577
RUAG Ammotec GmbH
- RWS Rotweill, 579
Ruger & Company Inc
- Ruger, 578
Rundfunk Berlin-Brandenburg
- RBB, 559
Run-D.M.C., 578
Rural Centro, 578
Russell Brands LLC
- Russell Athletic, 578
- Spalding, 619
Russell Hobbs Inc
- George Foreman, 317
Russell Stover Candies Inc
- Whitman's, 725
Russian Football Union, 578
Russian International News Agency
- RT (Russia Today), 577
Russian Post, 578

Russian Railways, 579
Ruud Heating
- Ruud, 579
RWE AG, 579
RWE Dea AG
- DEA (Deutsche Erdöl AG), 195
Rx, 579
Ryanair Ltd, 579
Ryba Ve Vodě, 579
Ryobi Ltd, 579
Ryohin Keikaku Co. Ltd
- Muji, 470

S

Saab Automobile AB
- Saab, 580
Saab-Scania AB, 580
Saatchi & Saatchi plc, 580
Sabena World Airlines, 580
SABMiller plc, 455, 580
SA Brain & Co. Ltd
- Brains, 117
SAC Philco
- Philco Brazil, 531
Saeco International Group SpA, 581
Safeco Insurance Company of America, 581
Safescan, 581
Safety-Kleen Systems Inc, 581
SafeWay Hydraulics Inc, 581
Safeway Inc, 581
- Randalls, 558
- Vons, 711
SAGEM (Société d'Applications Générales de l'Électricité et de la Mécanique), 582
SAIC Group
- MG, 452
SAIC (School of the Art Institute of Chicago), 582
SAI Global Ltd, 582
Saint-Gobain Abrasives Inc
- Norton Bear-Tex, 496
Saint-Gobain Construction Products Belgium NV SA
- Plâtres Lambert, 536
Saint-Gobain SA, 582
Säkerhetspartner AB, 582
Saks Inc
- Saks Fifth Avenue, 582
Saku Õlletehase AS, 583
Saldus Celinieks Ltd, 583
Salisbury House of Canada Ltd, 583
Salitos Brewing Company
- Salitos Tequila, 583
Sallie Mae Inc, 583
Salling Bank A/S, 583
Salomon Group, 583
Salton Appliances (1985) Corp, 583
Salvatore Robuschi & C. Srl, 584
SAM Group Holding AG, 584
Samro SA, 584
Samsøe & Samsøe, 584
Samsonite Corporation, 584
Samsung Group, 584
SanDisk Corporation, 584
Sandro Magli & C. SAS
- Di Sandro, 215
Sandryds Handel AB
- The Pirate Bay, 659
Sanford Limited, 585
Sanford LP, 584
- Foohy, 290

COMPANY INDEX

- Paper Mate, 520
San Francisco Municipal Transportation Agency
- CultureBus, 182
Sanistal, 585
Sanitarium (Australian Health and Nutrition Association Ltd)
- Up & Go, 689
Sankyo America Inc, 585
Sanmina-SCI Corporation
- Viking Components Inc, 704
Sanrio Co. Ltd
- Hello Kitty, 352
Sansui Electric Co. Ltd, 585
Santa Fe (The Atchison, Topeka and Santa Fe Railway), 585
Sanwa Bank, 585
Sanyo Electric Co. Ltd, 586
São Paulo Alpargatas SA
- Havaianas, 350
São Paulo Petróleo, 586
SAP AG, 586
SAPEC Agro SA, 586
Sapling Foundation
- TED (Technology Entertainment and Design), 644
Sappi Ltd, 586
Saputo Inc, 586
SA Quick Restaurants, 552
Sara Lee Corporation, 586
- Ball Park, 98
- Douwe Egberts, 225
- Hillshire Farm, 355
Sarar Giyim Sanayii Fabrika, 586
Sargent Aerospace & Defense Inc, 587
Sarotti, 587
SA Spadel NV
- SPA, 619
SAS WD
- 64, 53
Sata, 587
Satellite Television Asian Region (STAR)
- Star Gold (US), 626
Saturn LLC
- Saturn, 587
Saudi Arabian Airlines, 587
Sauer Danfoss, 587
Savin Corporation, 588
Saxo Bank, 588
SBAC (The Society of British Aerospace Companies), 588
Sbarro Inc, 588
SBB CFF FFS (Schweizer-ische Bundesbahnen), 589
SBC Communications Inc, 589
SCA Indústria de Móveis Ltda, 589
SCALA Inc, 589
Scanbox Entertainment Group A/S, 589
Scandale, 589
Scandinavian Airlines
- SAS, 587
Scania AB, 589
Scarlets Regional Ltd, 590
SCA (Svenska Cellulosa Aktiebolaget), 589
Schaeffler Gruppe
- LuK, 429
Schaeffler Technologies GmbH & Co. KG
- FAG, 263
Schenker AG
- DB Schenker, 194

Schering-Plough Corporation, 590
Schibsted ASA
- Aftenposten, 67
Schindler Management AG, 590
Schlumberger Ltd, 590
Schmidt Beer, 590
Schnucks, 590
Schöffel Sportbekleidung GmbH, 591
Schott Boral dd, 591
Schüco International KG, 591
Schunck GmbH & Co. KG, 591
Schwan-Stabilo Group
- Schwan, 624
Schweizer Fernsehen, 591
Schwinn Bicycle Company, 592
Science Museum, 592
Scientific and Cultural Organization
- UNESCO, 683
S.C. Johnson & Son Inc
- Baygon, 104
- Drano, 228
- Glade, 322
- OFF!, 502
- Raid, 557
- SC Johnson Wax, 592
- Ziploc, 742
Scottish Arts Council, 593
Scottish Citylink Coaches Ltd, 593
Scottish Equitable plc, 593
ScottishPower PLC, 594
Scotts Miracle-Gro Company
- Scotts Lawn Products, 594
- Scotts Lawn Service, 594
Scott Sports SA, 593
Scouts Canada, 594
Scripps Networks Interactive
- Fine Living, 280
- TV Food Network, 676
Scripps Networks LLC
- Travel Channel, 672
SD Card Association, 594
Seagate Technology LLC
- Seagate Technology, 595
- Maxtor, 446
Seagram Company Ltd, 595
Sealed Air Corporation, 595
Sealy Corporation, 595
Sears Holdings Corporation, 595
- Big Kmart, 108
- Kmart, 398
Seat SA, 596
Seaway Foodtown Inc
- Food Town Supermarkets, 290
SeaWorld Parks & Entertainment
- Discovery Cove, 216
- SeaWorld, 596
Secom Co. Ltd, 596
Secretaría de Desarrollo Social
- Vivir Mejor, 708
Securitas AB, 596
Securitas AG, 596
SEDESOL
- Vivir Mejor, 708
Seed Media Group LLC, 596
See's Candy Shops Inc, 596
See Your World LLC
- Life, 418
SEGA Corporation, 597
- Dreamcast, 228
- SEGA Saturn, 597
SEGD (Society for Environmental Graphic Design), 597
Seiko Epson Corporation, 253
Seiko Holdings Corporation
- Seiko, 597
- Seiko Instruments, 597
Seiko Instruments Inc, 597
Seiko Watch Corporation
- Lorus, 426
Seiko Watch Corporation of America (SCA)
- Pulsar, 548
Selectour Voyages, 597
Selfridges Retail Ltd
- Selfridges & Co, 597
Selkirk Corporation, 597
Semcon AB, 597
Seminole Tribe of Florida
- Hard Rock Café, 348
Sempra Energy
- SDGE (San Diego Gas & Electric), 595
- Southern Californian Gas Company (SoCalGas), 618
SEM Products Inc, 597
Senco Brands Inc, 598
Seneca Foods Corporation, 598
Senior Corps, 598
Sennheiser Electronic GmbH & Co. KG, 598
SensoNor A/S, 598
Senstar Stellar, 598
Sentry Group, 598
- Sentry Insurance, 598
Sequent Computer Systems Inc, 598
Serta Mattress Company, 599
Service de police de la Ville de Montréal
- SPVM, 623
Servior, 599
ServiStar, 599
Servpro Industries Inc, 599
Sesame Workshop
- Sesame Street, 599
SES SA, 599
- Astra, 93
SETI Institute (Search for Extra Terrestrial Intelligence), 599
Seven & I Holdings Co. Ltd
- 7-Eleven, 52
Severin Elektrogeräte GmbH, 600
SEV-Marchal, 441
Sex Pistols, 600
SFMOMA (San Francisco Museum of Modern Art), 600
SFR SA
- Joe Mobile, 385
SGL Carbon AG, 600
SGPS SA, 641
Shanghai Automotive Industry Corporation
- MG, 452
Sharp Corporation, 601
Shaw Communications Inc
- Global Television Network, 323
- Shaw Communications, 601
Shaw Media
- Historia, 355
Shelter, 602
Shenzhen Science and Technology Company
- HYT Radios, 361
Sherwin-Williams Company, 602
- Krylon, 404

Shikoku Electric Power Co. Inc
- Yonden, 738
Shimadzu Corporation, 602
Shimano Inc, 602
Shinkin Central Bank (SCB), 602
Shinko Shoji Co. Ltd, 602
Shinsegae Corporation, 602
Shinsei Bank Ltd, 602
Shiseido Americas Corporation
- NARS Cosmetics, 475
Shoney's North America Corporation, 603
Shopko Stores Operating Co. LLC, 603
Shoppers Drug Mart Corporation, 603
Shop-Vac Corporation, 603
Showa Corporation, 603
Showtime Networks Inc, 603
- The Movie Channel, 657
Shueisha Inc
- Dragon Ball Z, 227
Shure Inc, 604
Shutterstock Images LLC, 604
Shu Uemura Cosmetics, 604
Sia Abrasives Industries AG, 604
Siam Tyre Phra Pradaeng Co Ltd, 604
SIA (Securities Industry Association), 604
Sichuan Changhong Electric Co
- Changhong, 146
Sidney Harman
- Newsweek, 487
Siebe plc, 605
Siemens AG, 605
- Acuson, 62
Siemens Nixdorf Informationssysteme AG, 605
Sierra Wireless, 605
SIGG Switzerland AG, 605
Sigma Corporation of America, 606
Signal Iduna Group, 606
SIIA (The Software & Information Industry Association), 606
Silicon Graphics International Corporation
- SGI, 600
Siligom SAS, 606
Simca (Société Industrielle de Mécanique et Carrosserie Automobile), 607
Simmons Bedding Company, 607
Simon Property Group Inc
- Franklin Mills, 296
Simon & Schuster Inc
- Scribner, 594
Sinclair Oil Corporation, 607
Singapore Airlines Ltd
- Singapore Airlines, 607
- Virgin Atlantic Airways, 705
Singer Sewing Company, 607
Sinochem Group, 608
Sirius XM Radio Inc
- Open Road, 509
- Sirius Satellite Radio, 608
- Sirius XM Radio, 608
- XM Satellite Radio, 735
- SIRVA Inc
- Allied Van Lines, 78

Sistema de Transporte Colectivo, 452
SITA, 608
Six Flags Entertainment Corporation
- Superman: Ride of Steel, 634
Sixt, 608
Skandia International
- Skandia, 609
Skandia International (Old Mutual plc)
- Skandia, 608
Skanska AB, 609
Skate America, 609
SKF AB, 609
Skillbond Direct Ltd, 609
Skis Rossignol SA, 575
- Lange, 409
Skoal Tobacco, 609
Škoda Auto, 610
- Škoda, 610
SKS Germany, 610
Skullcandy, 610
Skype Communications Sàrl, 610
SkyTeam, 610
SkyWest Airlines Inc, 610
Slim-Fast, 611
Sloggi, 611
Slovakia Tourist Board, 612
Slovnaft as, 612
Slow Food, 612
S-Mart, 612
Smart & Final Inc
- Smart & Final, 612
Smeg Group SpA, 612
SMG Television
- STV (Scottish TV), 631
Smithfield Foods Inc
- Farmland Industries, 267
SmithKline Beecham plc, 613
Smith & Nephew plc, 613
Smiths Group plc, 613
Smithsonian Institution, 614
Smith & Wesson Holding, 613
SMM/Hamburg Messe und Congress GmbH, 614
Snapixel, 614
Snap-on Inc, 614
SNCF Geodis
- Calberson, 133
SNCF (Société Nationale des Chemins de fer français), 614
SNCM (Société Nationale Maritime Corse Méditerranée), 614
SNC Nova
- Mamie Nova, 439
Snickers Workwear, 615
Sobey's Inc, 615
SOCEMIE (Société Opératrice de la Chaîne Européenne Multilingue d'Information Euronews)
- Euronews, 258
Social Democratic Party of Croatia (SDP), 595
Socialistische Partij (SP.), 619
Socialist Party, 522
Socialist Party (SP.), 619
Sociedad Central de Cervejas e Bebidas SA
- Sagres Cerveja, 582
Sociedad Estatal Correos y Telégrafos SA, 173
Sociedad General de Derechos Audiovisuales SA
- Filmax, 279
Societatea Româna de Televiziune

COMPANY INDEX

- TVR (Televiziunea Română), 676
Société Bic
- Tipp-Ex, 665
Société BIC
- BIC, 108
Société CMC
- agnès b., 68
Société de transport de Montréal, 464
Société Générale SA
- SG Cowen, 600
Société Nautique de Genève
- Alinghi, 76
société Unowhy
- Qooq, 550
Socijaldemokratska Partija Hrvatske (SDP), 595
Sodexo SA, 615
Sofegi Filtration SpA
- Filtri Tecnocar, 280
Softub Inc, 615
Sogo Co. Ltd, 615
Sokkia Co. Ltd, 616
Solectron Corporation, 616
Sole Technology Inc
- Emerica, 249
Solidarnosc, 616
Solomon R. Guggenheim Foundation (SRGF), 341
SO Luxury HMC Sarl
- Sofitel, 615
SOMFY SAS, 616
Sonatrach SpA
- Naftal Algerie, 474
Sonion A/S, 616
Sonjangol EP, 616
Sonofon Holding A/S, 617
Sony Computer Entertainment Inc
- Gran Turismo, 332
- Guerrilla Games, 341
- PlayStation, 537
- PlayStation 2, 537
- PlayStation 3, 537
Sony Corporation, 617
- Aibo, 69
- Aiwa, 73
- Cyber-shot, 183
- DAT (Digital Audio Tape), 192
- Digital 8, 213
- Digital Data Storage (DDS), 213
- Direct Stream Digital (DSD), 215
- Discman, 215
- DV (Digital Video), 236
- i.LINK, 368
- It's a Sony, 617
- MD Walkman, 448
- MiniDisc, 456
- Vaio, 694
- Walkman, 715
- Wega, 719
Sony Corporation of America
- Sony Music, 617
Sony Ericsson Mobile Communications AB, 617
Sony Music Entertainment Inc
- American Recording, 85
- Epic Records, 253
- Legacy Recordings, 413
- RCA Records, 560
- Sony Music, 617
Sony Pictures Entertainment Inc
- Columbia Pictures, 164
- Screen Gems, 594
- Sony Pictures, 617
Sony Pictures Television Inc

- GSN (Game Show Network), 339
- Sony Entertainment Television, 617
- Who Wants to be a Millionaire?, 725
SOPUS Products
- Pennzoil, 526
- Rain-X, 557
- Slick 50, 611
Sosland Publishing Co.
- FoodBusiness News, 289
Sotheby's International Realty Affiliates LLC, 617
Source Records, 618
South African Tourist Board, 618
South Beach Beverage Company
- SoBe Grape Grog, 615
Southern Company, 618
- Georgia Power, 317
Southern Family Markets
- Bruno's Supermarkets, 121
- Piggly Wiggly, 533
Southern States Cooperative Inc
- AGWAY, 69
SouthTrust Corporation, 618
Southwest Airlines Co, 618
Southwestern Bell Telephone, 619
Soy Kaas Inc
- Soya Kaas, 619
Soyuzplodimport
- Stoli Razberi, 629
Spalding Sports, 619
Sparco SpA, 619
Spar International, 619
- EuroSpar, 259
Spar Nord Bank A/S, 620
Spartan Stores Inc
- Family Fare Supermarkets, 265
Speakman Company, 620
Specialized Bicycle Components Inc, 620
Specific Media LLC
- Myspace, 473
- MySpace, 473
Spectrum Brands Inc
- George Foreman, 317
- Lady Remington, 407
- Remington, 565
Speedo International Ltd
- Speedo, 620
Speedway Motorsports Inc
- Texas Motor Speedway, 651
Speedy Muffler King, 620
Spencer Gore Developments (Pty) Ltd, 621
Spescom Ltd, 621
Spies Hecker GmbH, 621
SPIN Media LLC, 621
Spitfire, 622
spol. sr.o.
- TDS Tele Data System, 643
Sporoptic Pouilloux SA
- Vuarnet, 713
Sport Club Corinthians Paulista
- Corinthians, 173
Sports Car Club of America (SCCA), 622
Sportswear Company SpA
- Stone Island, 629
Spotify AB, 622
Spotify Ltd, 622
Spot LLC, 622
Spring Window Fashions LLC
- Graber, 330

Sprint Nextel Corporation, 623
- Boost Mobile, 115
- Nextel Communications, 488
SPX Corporation
- OTC, 514
Square Enix Holdings Co. Ltd, 623
SRG SSR, 623
Sri Lanka Tea Board
- Ceylon Tea, 144
SSAB Swedish Steel AB
- SSAB, 623
SsangYong Motor Company, 624
- Rexton, 567
SSL International plc
- Dr. Scholl's, 230
SSP Group Ltd
- Upper Crust, 689
SSTL India
- MTC, 469
Staedtler Mars GmbH & Co. KG, 624
Stagecoach Group plc
- Coach USA, 160,
- Stagecoach Group plc, 624
Stage Entertainment Group
- Holiday on Ice, 357
Standard Bank Group, 624
Standard Chartered Bank, 624
Standard Life plc, 625
Standard Oil of Ohio
- Boron Gas Station, 115
Standard & Poor's Financial Services LLC
- Standard & Poor's, 625
Standards Australia
- Type Tested, 677
Stanley Black & Decker Inc, 625
- Black & Decker, 110
- DeWalt, 208
- Facom, 262
- Mac Tools, 435
Staples Inc, 625
- Corporate Express, 173
Star Alliance Services GmbH, 625
Starbucks Corporation
- Seattle's Best Coffee, 596
- Starbucks, 625
Star Channel, 625
Star Communications Holding
- P4 Ogilvy, 516
Starkey Laboratories Inc, 626
Starline Inc, 626
Star Networks Inc, 625
- Cash Station, 141
Starwood Hotels and Resorts Worldwide Inc, 602
- W Hotels, 725
Starz Entertainment LLC, 627
State Bank of India, 627
State Farm Mutual Automobile Insurance Company, 627
State Oil Company of Azerbaijan Republic
- SOCAR, 615
Statoil ASA, 627
STCP (Sociedade de Transportes Colectivos do Porto), 627
Steelcase Inc, 627
Steel Dynamics Inc, 627
Steel Recycling Institute, 627
Stefanel SpA, 628

Steinberg GmbH, 628
Steinway & Sons, 628
Stella Travel Services Pty Ltd
- Jetset Travel, 384
Stellican Ltd
- Chris-Craft Boats, 150
Stena AB, 628
Stena Metall AB, 628
Stepgrades Motor Accessories Ltd
- Viking Tyres, 704
ST Ericsson, 628
Sterling Drug Inc
- Diaparene, 211
Stichting Pensioenfonds ABP
- ABP, 58
STIHL Ges.m.b.H
- Viking, 704
Stile Bertone SpA
- Bertone, 107
STMicroelectronics NV, 624
STM (Société de transport de Montréal/Montreal Transit Corporation), 629
Stockade Companies LLC
- Sirloin Stockade, 608
StockLogos, 629
Stoll Giroflex AG, 320
Stork BC, 630
STP, 630
StrategicNova Inc, 630
Strukton Groep, 630
Studio Ghibli Inc, 630
StumbleUpon Inc, 630
Sturm
- Ruger, 578
Stüssy Inc, 630
Sulake, 631
Sümerbank, 631
Sumitomo Group
- NEC, 482
Sumitomo Rubber Industries Ltd
- Dunlop Tyres, 235
Sumo + Compal SA, 631
Sunbeam Products Inc, 631
Suncor Energy Inc, 632
Sunflower Children, 632
Sunkist Growers Inc, 632
- Sunkist, 632
Sunoco Inc, 632
Suntory Holdings Ltd
- Orangina, 511
SunTrust Banks Inc, 633
Suomi Mutual, 633
Super 8 Hotels Inc, 633
Superdry
- Superdry, 633
Superga SpA, 634
SuperGroup plc
- Superdry, 633
Superior Essex Inc, 634
Super Rifle SpA, 569
Supervalu Inc
- Sav-On Drugs, 588
SuperValu Inc, 634
- Cub Foods, 182
- Osco Drug, 513
- Shaw's, 601
Supreme, 635
Surcouf SAS, 635
SureFire LLC, 635
Suzuken Co. Ltd, 635
Suzuki Motor Corporation, 635
- Maruti Suzuki, 443
Svit (Swiss Real Estate Association), 635
Swann-Morton Ltd, 635
Swarovski AG, 635
Swedish Automobile NV

- Saab, 580
Swisscom AG, 636
Swiss International Airlines AG, 636
Swiss Life Ltd, 636
Swiss National Tourist Office, 637
Swiss Paraplegic Centre, 636
Swiss Paraplegics Foundation, 636
Swiss Reinsurance Company Ltd
- Swiss Re, 637
Swiss Travel Fund (Reka), 565
Symantec Corporation, 637
- ACT!, 61
- Norton Antivirus, 496
- Norton Utilities, 496
Syms Corporation
- Filene's Basement, 279
Syngenta AG, 637
Synovus Bank
- Athens First, 94
SYQT Inc
- SyQuest, 637
Sysco Corporation, 637
Systemax Inc
- CompUSA, 167
Système U, 680

T

TACA SA, 638
Tact Precision Industrial Co. Ltd, 638
taggen4life, 638
Taishin Financial Holding Co. Ltd
- Taishin Bank, 639
Taishin International Bank, 639
Taisho Pharmaceutical Co. Ltd, 639
Taisho Pharmaceutical Holdings
- Taishin Bank, 639
Taiwan Business Bank Co. Ltd, 639
Taiwan Cooperative Bank, 639
Taiwan Tourism Bureau, 639
Tajan SA, 639
Takara Bio Inc
- Takara Bio, 639
Takara Holdings Inc
- Takara Bio, 639
Takeda Pharmaceutical Company Ltd
- Takeda, 639
Take-Two Interactive Software Inc, 639
- Rockstar Games, 572
TalkTalk Telecom Ltd, 640
Tallink Silja Oy
- Silja Line, 606
Tambour Ltd, 640
Tamiya Inc, 640
Tamron Co. Ltd, 640
Tandem Computer Inc, 640
Tandy Corporation, 640
Taniguchi Ink Corporation of America, 641
Tapflo AB, 641
TAP Pharmaceutical Products Inc, 641
Target Corporation, 641
Tarra Group, 216
Tartan Yachts, 641
Tartex + Dr. Ritter GmbH
- Tartex, 641
Tata Motors Ltd

COMPANY INDEX

- Jaguar, 381
- Land Rover, 409
- Rover, 576
Tata Steel Ltd, 641
Tate, 642
Tate & Lyle plc, 642
Tatneft, 642
Tatonka GmbH, 642
Tatra AS, 642
Taurus International Manufacturing Inc, 642
Tax Free Shopping, 642
Taylor Label, 642
TaylorMade-Adidas Golf Company, 642
Taylor Wimpey plc
- Bryant Homes, 121
TBC Corporation
- NTB (National Tire & Battery), 497
TBN (Trinity Broadcasting Network), 643
TCF Co. LLC
- The Cheesecake Factory, 653
Tchibo GmbH, 643
Tci Tires LLC, 643
TCL Corporation
- GoVideo, 325
TD Bank Financial Group, 643
TDK Corporation, 643
Teac Corporation
- Tascam, 641
TEAC Corporation, 643
Teachers Insurance and Annuity Association – College Retirement Equities Fund (TIAA-CREF), 663
Tecatel SA, 644
Tech Data Corporation, 644
Technicolor Motion Picture Corporation, 644
Technicolor SA, 644
- RCA, 560
Techtronic Industries Company Ltd
- Dirt Devil, 215
Tecnica Group
- Rollerblade, 573
Tecnica Group SpA
- Nordica, 494
Tecumseh Products Company, 644
TED Conferences LLC, 644
Teijin Limited, 645
Tein Inc, 645
Tekman Group Ltd
- Tact Precision, 638
Teksid SpA, 645
Tektronix Inc, 645
Tele 2 AB, 645
Tele Atlas NV, 645
Telecom Italia SpA, 646
- TIM (Telecom Italia Mobile), 664
Telecom New Zealand Ltd, 646
Tele Data System
- TDS Tele Data System, 643
Teledyne Technologies Inc, 646
Teleflora LLC, 646
Telefonaktiebolaget LM Ericsson
- Ericsson, 254
Telefónica SA, 646
- Terra Networks, 649
Telefónica UK Ltd
- O2, 500
Telefunken Licenses GmbH, 646, 647

Telegraph Media Group
- The Daily Telegraph, 654
Telekom Malaysia Berhad, 666
Telekom Slovenije dd, 647
Telekom Srbija ad, 647
Telemarketing SA
- Telemarketing Store, 647
Telenor Group, 647
- djuice, 218
Televisión Autonómica de Madrid SA
- Telemadrid, 647
Telewest Communications plc, 648
Telewizja Polska SA
- Telewizja 3 Krakow, 648
- TVP, 676
Telfort BV, 648
Telkom SA Ltd, 648
TelkomVision, 648
Tellabs Inc, 648
Telstra Corporation Ltd
- TradingPost, 671
Tenneco Inc
- Fonos, 288
- Tenneco Inc, 649
- Walker Exhaust Systems, 714
Tennis Australia, 649
Tenzing Communications Inc, 649
Tequila Cuervo SA de CV
- José Cuervo, 387
Teradyne Inc, 649
Terasaki Electric Europe Co. Ltd, 649
Terex Corporation
- Genie, 316
Termingnoni SpA, 649
Ternium SA, 649
Terra Networks SA
- Terra Networks, 649
Terremark Worldwide Inc
- Data Return, 192
Terumo Corporation, 650
Tesa SE, 650
Tesco Corporation, 650
Tesco plc, 650
Tesla Motors Inc, 650
Tetra Laval
- Tetra Pak, 650
Teuco Guzzini SpA, 650
Texas Instruments Inc, 651
Texas State Aquarium, 651
Textron Inc, 651
- Cessna, 144
- Klauke, 397
Tex-Tryk A/S, 651
T-Fal USA, 645
TFM LLC
- The Franklin Mint, 655
T.G.I. Friday's Inc, 651
Thai Airways International, 651
Thales SA, 651
Thames & Hudson Ltd, 651
Thames & Kosmos LLC, 651
Thames Valley Housing Association, 652
Thames Water Utilities Ltd, 652
The Affiliated Auxiliaries of the Knights of Columbus
- Columbiettes, 164
The Allstate Corporation
- Allstate Insurance, 79
- Allstate Motor Club, 79
The Anchor Hocking Company
- Anchor Hocking, 87

The Attachmate Group
- Novell, 497
The Bank of New York, 652
The Bank of New York Mellon Corporation
- Pershing, 528
The Bank of Tokyo-Mitsubishi UFJ Ltd
- BTMU, 122
The Barn Markets, 652
The Bear Stearns Companies Inc
- Bear Stearns, 104
The Beatles, 652
The Black Book Inc, 652
The Black & Decker Corporation
- Porter-Cable, 540
The Blackstone Group
- Conrad Hotels, 169
- La Quinta Inn, 410
- La Quinta Inns & Suites, 410
- SeaWorld, 596
- The Weather Channel, 661
The Body Shop International plc, 652
The Boeing Company
- Boeing, 113
The Bond Market Association, 653
The Brand Distillery Ltd, 653
The Burton Corporation
- Analog Clothing, 87
The Canadian Football League
- Hamilton Tiger-Cats, 664
The Carlson Rezidor Hotel Group
- Park Inn, 521
- Radisson Hotels, 556
The Carlyle Group LP
- Allison Transmission, 78
The Chamberlain Group, 145
The Charles Machine Works Inc
- Ditch Witch, 217
The Charles Schwab Corporation, 146
The Chemical Brothers, 653
The Cherokee Group, 147
The Child Accident Prevention Foundation of Australia
- Kidsafe, 395
The Children's Medical Center of Dayton, 654
The Chocolate Skateboard Company Inc, 150
The City of New York Mayor's Office of Film, Theatre & Broadcasting
- Made in NY, 436
The Clash, 654
The Clorox Company, 158, 654
- Glad, 322
The Coca-Cola Company
- Bonaqua, 114
- Cherry Coke, 147
- Coca-Cola, 161
- Coke, 161
- Dasani, 191
- Del Valle, 201
- Diet Coke, 212
- Fanta, 266
- Glacéau, 321
- Minute Maid, 457
- Powerade, 542
- Sprite, 623
- TaB, 638
- Vitaminwater, 706
The Colomer Group

- Revlon Professional, 567
The Cooper Union for the Advancement of Science and Art, 654
The Dannon Company
- Dannon, 189
The Denver Public Library, 654
The Dial Corporation, 209
The Dorchester Collection, 654
The Dow Chemical Company, 226
- Biohazard, 109
- Rohn and Haas, 573
- Union Carbide, 684
The Driving Force Inc
- Driving Force, 229
The Duchossois Group
- Chamberlain, 145
The Dutch Film Distributors' Association
- NVF, 499
The Economist Group, 654
The Emirates Group, 249
- Fly Emirates, 286
The Evergreen Group
- Eva Air, 260
The Finals, 655
The Football Association Premier League Ltd, 544
- Barclays Premier League, 102
The Football League, 655
The Frye Company (LF USA), 302
The Fuji Bank Ltd, 303
The Game Manufacturers Association, 307
The Gap Inc, 308
- Banana Republic, 99
The Garlock Family of Companies, 308
The Glad Products Company, 322
The Global Fund to Fight AIDS, 655
The Goldman Sachs Group Inc, 326
The Goodyear Tire & Rubber Company, 328
- Dunlop Tyres, 235
The Goodyear Tire & Rubber Company,
- Dunlop Tyres, 235
The Great Atlantic & Pacific Tea Company
- A&P, 54
The Greater Boston Food Bank, 655
The Greene Turtle, 656
The Green Hornet, 656
The Guardian Life Insurance Company of America, 340
The Gunica Company, 342
The Hain Celestial Group Inc
- Westbrae Natural, 722
The Hartford Financial Services Group Inc, 656
The Hershey Company, 353
- Almond Joy, 79
- Mounds, 467
- Peter Paul, 529
The Hertz Corporation
- Hertz Rent-A-Car, 354
The Hillshire Brands Company
- Ball Park, 98
The Hoover Company, 358
The Huffington Post Media Group, 656

The Ink Well, 656
The Japan Research Institute Limited, 657
The Jewel Companies Inc, 385
The J.M. Smucker Company
- Jif, 385
The J.M. Smucker Company
- Crisco, 179
- Folgers Coffee, 287
- Hungry Jack, 361
The John F. Kennedy Center for the Performing Arts, 657
The Jones Group Inc
- Anne Klein, 89
The Jonsson Group, 387
The Karlsberg Group, 391
The Kroger Company, 404
- Ralphs, 557
The Lego Group
- Duplo, 235
- The LEGO Group, 414
The Lincoln Electric Company, 419
The Linde Group, 419
The Little Tikes Company
- Little Tikes, 422
The Livestock & Meat Commission of Northern Ireland
- Farm Quality Assured Northern Ireland, 268
The Lung Association, 657
The Mac Store, 657
The McGraw Hill Companies
- Standard & Poor's, 625
The Mennen Company,
- Lady Speed Stick, 407
- Speed Stick, 620
The Merisant Company
- Canderel, 137
The Metropolitan Opera, 657
The Momiji Financial Group
- Momiji Financial Group, 461
The Monsanto Company, 463
The Nasdaq Stock Market Inc, 476
The National Trust for Places of Historic Interest or Natural Beauty, 479
The Nelson-Atkins Museum of Art, 657
The New York Currency Exchange
- NYCE (New York Cash Exchange), 499
The New York Times Company
- The New York Times Company, 658
- The New York Times, 658
The Nishi-Nippon Bank Ltd, 492
The North Clothing, 658
The North Face Inc, 658
Theo Klein GmbH, 398
The Open University, 658
The Opus Group, 510
The Pep Boys – Manny, Moe & Jack, 527
The Philadelphia Phillies, 532
The Pickup Guy, 658
The Pillsbury Company
- Pillsbury, 533
- Pillsbury Doughboy, 533
The Plastic Lumber Company Inc
- Simple Signs, 607
The Public Theater, 659
The Reinalt-Thomas Corporation

767

COMPANY INDEX

- America's Tire Co., 86
- Discount Tire Co. Inc., 215

The Ritz-Carlton Hotel Company LLC, 570
Thermax Ltd, 659
Thermo Electron Corporation, 659
Thermo Products LLC
- Thermo Pride, 659

Thermos LLC, 659
The Rolling Stones, 659
The Royal Bank of Scotland plc
- Access Credit Card, 59
- Coutts & Co, 176

The Royal National Theatre, 479
The Ryland Group Inc, 659
The Sage Group plc
- ACT! by Sage, 61
- Sage, 581

The Salvation Army, 660
The Schindler Group, 590
The Schwan Food Company, 660
The Shaw Group Inc, 601
The Sherwin-Williams Company
- Martin-Senour Paints, 443
- P&L (Pratt & Lambert), 516

The Smead Manufacturing Company Inc, 612
The Sperry and Hutchinson Company Inc
- S&H greenpoints, 580
- S&H Green Stamps, 580

The Standard Bank of South Africa Ltd, 624
The Stop & Shop Supermarket Company, 629
The Store Corporation Bhd, 660
The St Paul Companies Inc
- USF&G, 691

The Swatch Group
- Omega, 507

The Swatch Group Ltd
- Swatch, 635
- Tissot, 665

The Timberland Company, 664
The TJX Companies Inc
- AJ Wright, 74

The Toro Company, 669
The Travelers Companies
- Travelers Insurance, 672

The United States Government
- The White House, 661

The United States Playing Card Company
- KEM Playing Cards, 393

The University of Mississippi
- Southern Miss Golden Eagles, 618

The Upjohn Company
- UpJohn, 689

The Victorian Institute of Chemical Science, 660
The Vons Companies Inc
- Vons, 711

The Walt Disney Company
- A Bug's Life, 58
- Buy 'N Large, 129
- Disney Channel, 216
- Walt Disney Pictures, 715
- Walt Disney Records, 715

The Waltham Centre for Pet Nutrition
- Waltham, 715

The Washington Post Company, 661
The Wattyl Group, 718
The Wendy's Company
- Wendy's, 721

The Western Union Company
- Western Union, 722

The Who, 661
The Williams Companies Inc
- Williams, 727

The World Bank, 731
Thimble Sourcing, 661
Thomas Cook Group plc, 661
- Condor Flugdienst, 168

Thomson Reuters Corporation, 566, 662
Thomson SA, 662
Thrivent Financial for Lutherans
- Lutheran Brotherhood, 430

Thule Group, 662
THX Ltd, 662
ThyssenKrupp AG, 663
Ticketmaster LLC, 663
Tieto Oyj, 663
Tiffany & Co., 663
Time Inc
- Fortune, 292
- People, 527
- Real Simple, 561
- TIME, 664
- What's On TV, 724

Time Out Group Ltd, 664
Time Warner Inc, 664
- Action Comics, 61
- Cartoon Network, 140, 141
- Cinemax, 153
- CNN (Cable News Network), 160
- DC Comics, 195
- Friends, 299
- HBO, 350
- HLN (Headline News), 356
- MAD, 436
- Sports Illustrated, 622
- Sports Illustrated for Kids, 622
- Superman, 634
- Superman: Ride of Steel, 634
- TIME, 664
- Time Inc, 664
- TNT (Turner Network Television), 666
- Turner, 675
- Warner Brothers, 717
- Watchmen, 717

Time Warner Cable, 664
Timex Group BV, 665
Timex Group USA Inc, 665
Tim Hortons Inc, 665
Tine SA, 665
Tirol Milch Wörgl GmbH, 665
Tishman Speyer Properties
- Rockefeller Center, 572

Tissot SA, 665
TITAN Technology Ltd
- Data Cooler, 192

Titoni Ltd, 666
TK Techniker Krankenkasse, 666
TMC Distributing Ltd
- Co-op, 170

T-Mobile International AG
- T-Mobile, 666

TNT NV, 666
Tochigi Bank Ltd, 667
Todini Costruzioni Generali SpA, 667
Toei Co. Ltd
- Changeman (Dengeki Sentai Changeman), 145

Tofutti Brands Inc, 667
TOGU Gebr. Obermaier OHG, 667
Tohatsu Corporation, 667
Tokio Marine Holdings Inc, 667
Toko-Swix Sport AG, 667
Tokyo Dome Corporation, 667
Tokyo Electric Power Co. Ltd
- TEPCO, 649

Tokyo Electron Ltd, 668
Tokyo Gas Co. Ltd, 668
Tokyo Steel Co. Ltd, 668
Tokyo Stock Exchange Group Inc, 668
Tokyu Group
- Tokyu Hotels, 668

Tokyu Hands Inc, 668
Tombow Pencil Co. Ltd, 668
Tom Ford International LLC, 668
Tomkins Ltd
- Gates Corporation, 310

Tommy Hilfiger Licensing LLC
- Tommy Hilfiger, 668

Tom Tailor GmbH, 669
Tom Tailor Holding AG
- Tom Tailor, 669

TomTom NV, 669
Tomy Co. Ltd, 669
Toothfriendly International, 669
Topcon Positioning Systems Inc, 669
Toshiba Corporation, 670
Tosoh Corporation, 670
Total SA, 670
- Elf Service Stations, 247
- Fina, 280
- Minol, 457

Toupargel-Agrigel SA
- Agrigel, 68

Tourism Ireland Ltd, 375
Towa Corporation, 671
Tower.com Inc
- Tower Records, 671

Townsville City Council
- Ross River Parkway, 575

Toy Machine Blood Sucking Skateboard Company, 671
Toyobo Co. Ltd, 671
Toyota Motor Corporation, 671
- Lexus, 417
- Scion, 592

Toys "R" Us-Delaware Inc, 671
TracFone Inc
- TracFone, 671

Tragon Corporation, 672
Trane Inc
- Trane, 672

Transamerica Corporation, 672
Transelec
- Conelsur, 168

Transportes Aéreos Portugueses (TAP), 641
Transport for London (TfL), 683
Transport International Holdings Ltd
- KMB (Kowloon Motor Bus), 398

Transworld Corporation
- TWA (Trans World Airlines), 676

Trans World Entertainment Corporation
- Record Town, 562

Trappey's Fine Foods Inc, 672
Travel Channel International Ltd, 672
Travel of America, 673
Travis Perkins plc, 673
Trebruk AB, 673
Trek Bicycle Corporation, 673
- Gary Fisher, 309

Trekstor GmbH & Co. KG, 673
Tribune Company, 673
- Chicago Tribune, 148
- Los Angeles Times, 426

Trico Corporation, 673
Trinity Ltd, Li & Fung Group
- Cerutti, 144

Triple-S Management Corporation, 673
Tri Star Energy LLC
- Daily's, 186

Triton Systems of Delaware LLC, 673
Triumph Global Sales AG, 673
Triumph Motorcycles Ltd, 674
Troika, 674
Tropicana Looza Benelux BVBA, 425
Tropicana Products, 674
T. Rowe Price Investment Services Inc, 674
Truck Accessories Group LLC
- Leer, 413

True Value Company, 674
Trust Co. Ltd
- GReddy, 334

Trusted Choice Inc, 674
TRW Automotive Holdings Corp
- Lucas, 429

Tryg plc, 674
TSE (Turkish Standard Institution), 674
TSRC Inc
- Frank Parsons, 296

TSX (Toronto Stock Exchange), 675
TTI Floor Care North America
- Dirt Devil, 215

Tuberculosis and Malaria
- The Global Fund, 655

TUI AG, 675
TUI.com GmbH
- Robinson, 571

Tumblr Inc, 675
Tumi Inc, 675
Tune Group Sdn Bhd, 675
Tupperware Brands Corporation, 675
Turespaña, 256
Turkish Airlines, 675
Türkiye Denizcilik İşletmeleri AŞ, 203
Turner Broadcasting System Inc, 675
- Cartoon Network, 140, 141
- CNN (Cable News Network), 160
- HLN (Headline News), 356
- TNT (Turner Network Television), 666
- Turner Classic Movies (TCM), 676

Turner Digital Basketball Services Inc
- Los Angeles Lakers, 426

Turtle Rock Studios
- Left 4 Dead, 413

TV2 Cultura São Paulo, 676
TV Guide Online Holdings LLC, 676

TVR Motors Company Ltd, 668
Twentieth Century Fox Film Corporation, 293
- 20th Century Fox, 52

Twitter Inc, 677
Tyco International Ltd
- ADT Security Services, 64
- Tyco Electronics, 677

Type Directors Club (TDC), 677
Tyr Sport Inc, 677
Tyson Foods Inc, 677

U

UBM Aviation
- OAG, 500

UBM LLC
- NetWorld Interop, 485

UBS AG, 680
UCB SA, 680
UCLA (University of California, Los Angeles), 680
UCSF (University of California San Francisco), 680
UEFA (Union of European Football Associations)
- UEFA Champions League, 680

UFA Film & TV Produktion GmbH, 681
- UFA, 681

UGC Cinémas, 681
U-Haul International Inc (AMERCO), 681
Uher informatik GmbH, 681
UHU GmbH & Co. KG, 681
UK Film Council (UKFC), 279
UK Government
- Crime – Let's Bring It Down, 179
- Fire Kills, 281
- The Land Registry, 657

U&lc. (Upper and lower case), 680
UL International Demko A/S, 202
Ülker Bisküvi Sanayi AŞ, 681
Ultragaz, 681
Ultralink Products Inc
- XLO Electric, 735

Ultrapar Participações
- Oxiteno, 515

UMAX Technologies Inc, 682
UMB Financial Corporation, 682
UMP (Union for a Popular Movement), 682
UMWA (United Mine Workers of America), 682
UNCF (United Negro College Fund) Inc, 682
Under Armour Inc, 682
Underwriters Laboratories Inc
- UL Classification Mark, 681

UNDP (United Nations Development Programme), 683
União Cervejeira SA
- Super Bock, 633

União de Bancos Brasileiros SA
- Unibanco, 683

Unibank, 683
UNICEF Ecuador
- Museo del Niño, 471

Unicer

COMPANY INDEX

- Super Bock, 633
UniCredit SpA
- UniCredit Banca Mobiliare (UBM), 684
- UniCredit Group, 684
Unifrutti, 684
Unilever plc/NV
- AdeS, 63
- Amora, 87
- Axe, 97
- Ben & Jerry's, 106
- Blue Band, 111
- Breyers, 118
- Brut, 121
- Cif, 152
- Domestos, 222
- Dove, 225
- Good Humor, 327
- Klondike, 398
- Knorr, 399
- Langnese, 409
- Lipton, 421
- Lipton Ice Tea, 421
- Lux, 430
- Magnum, 438
- Maille, 438
- Marmite, 442
- Miko, 455
- Persil, 528
- Pond's, 540
- Royco, 577
- Signal, 606
- Skippy, 609
- Slim-Fast, 611
- Sunsilk, 632
- Timotei, 665
- Unilever, 684
- Vaseline, 697
- Wish-Bone, 729
Unimed, 684
Union Bank of California, 684
Union Carbide Corporation
- Union Carbide, 684
Union Central
Union Central Life Insurance Company
- Union Central, 684
Unión de Rugby del Uruguay, 685
Unione di Banche Italiene ScpA
- UBI Banca, 680
Union Pacific Railroad Company, 685
UNIQA Versicherungen AG, 685
Uniqlo Co. Ltd, 685
UniSA (University of South Australia), 685
Unisys Corporation, 685
Unitau (Universidade de Taubaté), 685
United Airlines Inc
- Shuttle by United, 604
United Air Lines Inc, 686
United Artists Corporation
- United Artists, 686
United Artists Music and Record Group (UAMARG), 686
United Continental Holdings Inc
- Continental Airlines, 170
- United Airlines, 686
United Dutch Breweries BV
- Oranjeboom, 511
United Financial Group, 686
United Fire & Casualty Company, 686
UnitedHealth Group Inc

- PacifiCare, 516
United International Pictures BV, 686
United Kingdom Warehousing Association (UKWA), 681
United Nations
- World Health Organization (WHO), 731
United Nations Children's Fund
- UNICEF, 683
United Nations Educational
- UNESCO, 683
United Nations (UN), 686
United Overseas Bank (UOB) Ltd, 689
United Pageant International Corporation, 687
United Paramount Network
- UPN, 689
United Parcel Service (UPC) Inc, 690
United Rentals Inc, 687
United Space Alliance (USA), 687
United States Air Force, 690
United States Army
- 82nd Airborne Division, 53
United States Cellular Corporation, 691
United States Civil Defense, 156
United States Coast Guard (USCG), 687
United States Department of Commerce, 204
United States Department of Defence
- DHCC (Deployment Health Clinical Center), 209
United States Department of Defense
- America Supports You, 86
United States Department of Energy, 204
United States Department of Health and Human Services
- National Institutes of Health (NIH), 478
United States Department of Health & Human Services, 204, 270
United States Department of the Interior
- National Park Service (NPS), 479
United States Environmental Protection Agency
- Green Chemistry Challenge, 334
United States Figure Skating, 691
United States Government
- Peace Corps, 524
United States Lines, 687
United States Military Academy at West Point
- Army Black Knights, 92
United States Postal Service
- U.S. Mail, 692
United States Postal Service (USPS), 687
United States Sailing Association, 692
United States Satellite Broadcasting Company Inc, 693
United States Space Foundation, 687

United States Steel Corporation (USS), 692
United Technologies Corporation
- Carrier, 140
- Pratt & Whitney Canada, 543
UNited Technologies Corporation, 687
United Telecom, 687
United Utilities Group plc, 688
United Way of America, 688
Universal Cooperatives Inc
- Farm Bureau Co-op, 267
Universal Music Group
- A&M Records, 54
- Def Jam, 198
- DreamWorks Records, 228
- Fiction Records, 276
- Geffen Records, 313
- Island Records, 377
- Mercury Records, 450
- Motown Records, 466
- Polydor Records, 540
- Uni records, 685
- Verve, 700
Universal Music UK
- Vertigo, 700
Universal Pictures
- Gramercy Pictures, 331
- Jurassic Park, 389
Universidad Central de Venezuela
- AAAA (Arte, Arquitectura, Antropologia y Autoritarismo), 54
University Games Corporation
- Colorforms, 163
University of Cambridge, 688
University of Iowa
- Iowa Hawkeyes, 375
University of Louisville
- Louisville Cardinals, 428
University of Oxford, 688
Universum Film AG
- UFA, 681
Univision Communications Inc, 688
Unocal Corporation, 688
Unternehmensgruppe Theo Müller, 470
Unum Group, 688
- Colonial, 163
UPC (Universitat Politècnica de Catalunya, 689
UPM-Kymmene Oyj, 689
Uponor Oyj, 689
UPSA (Union Pharma-cologique Scientifique Appliquee) Laboratories, 690
Uralita
- URSA, 690
Urban Decay Cosmetics, 690
Urban Outfitters Inc, 690
URSA Insulation, 690
USA Cycling, 690
US Airways Inc, 690
USA Partnership LP
- Storage USA, 630
US Bancorp
- U.S. Bank, 691
USB Implementers Forum Inc, 691
U.S. Boiler Company Inc
- Burnham, 128
U.S. Chemical Storage LLC
- FIREloc, 281
- Superloc, 634

US Concrete Inc, 691
US Democratic Party, 202
U.S. Department of Agriculture
- SNAP (Supplemental Nutrition Assistance Program), 614
U.S. Department of Commerce
- Dolphin Safe, 221
- Sea Grant Oregon, 595
- U.S. Grade A, 692
U.S. Department of Energy
- Energy Star, 250
U.S. Environmental Protection Agency, 252
- Energy Star, 250
US General Services Administration, 339
US Government
- Senior Corps, 598
Usiminas SA, 692
U.S. Office of Personnel Management, 272
US Oncology Inc, 692
U.S. Patent and Trademark Office, 564
USRobotics Corporation, 692
US Smokeless Tobacco Company
- Skoal, 609
U.S. Space & Rocket Center
- Space Camp, 619
USTA (United States Tennis Association), 693
USWC (Union Sky Wine Company Limited)
- Pop, 540
USX Corporation, 693
Utah Office of Tourism, 693
UTA (United Talent Agency), 693
UTC Fire & Security Company
- Fireye, 282
Utz Quality Foods Inc, 693

V

V2 Music Ltd, 694
V33 Group, 694
VAASAN Group
- Finn Crisp, 280
Vagle Elektro Installasjon A/S
- Vagle Elektro, 694
Vaillant GmbH
- Saunier Duval, 588
Vaja Corp., 694
VAK, 694
Val d'Isère Tourist Office, 695
Valentino Fashion Group SpA
- Hugo Boss, 360
Valeo SA, 695
Valero Energy Corporation
- Diamond Shamrock, 210
- Ultramar, 682
Vallourec SA, 695
Valmont Industries Inc
- Valley Irrigation, 695
Valspar Corporation, 695
Valve Corporation, 695
- Left 4 Dead, 413
Van Halen, 696
Van Hool NV, 696
Vans Inc
- Pro-tec, 546
- Vans, 696
- Vans "Off the Wall", 696
Vänsterpartiet/Left Party, 696
Vantaa
- Pöyry, 543

Vårdförbundet, 696
Varefakta Kontrolleret, 697
Variflex Inc, 697
Varta Microbattery GmbH, 697
VatOil, 697
Vattenfall AB, 697
Vaude Sport GmbH & Co. KG, 698
Vauxhall Motors, 698
VBB (Verkehrsverbund Berlin-Brandenburg), 698
VDE Association for Electrical
- VDE, 698
Vectorpile.com, 698
Velbon Tripod Co. Ltd, 698
Venturi Automobiles SA, 699
Veolia Environnement SA, 699
Verband der Schweizerischen Gasindustrie (VSG)
- Erdgas/Natural Gas, 254
- Natural Gas, 480
Verbatim Americas LLC, 699
VeriFone Holdings Inc, 699
Verio Inc, 699
- NTT Verio, 498
VeriSign Inc.
- Network Solutions, 485
Veritas Software Corp, 699
Verizon Business
- UUNET, 693
Verizon Communications Inc, 699
- Data Return, 192
- MCI Worldcom, 448
Verkade, 699
Verlagsgruppe Handelsblatt GmbH & Co. KG
- Wirtschaftswoche, 729
Vermeer Corporation, 700
Vertu, 700
Verve Records
- Verve, 700
Veryeri Makina, 700
Vestar Capital Partners
- Del Monte Foods, 200
Vestax Corporation, 700
Vetropack Holding Ltd, 701
VF Corporation, 701
- Eastpak, 240
- Lee, 412
- Riders, 568
- The North Face, 658
- Vans, 696
- Wrangler, 732
VF Europe BVBA
- Kipling, 396
VGH Versicherungen, 701
Viacom Inc, 701
- Comedy Central, 165
- MTV, 469
- MTV2, 469
- Nickelodeon, 489
- South Park, 618
- The Box, 653
- VH1, 701
Viacom International Inc
- Spike TV, 621
Viacom Networks Europe
- Viva, 707
Via Rail Canada, 701
Vice Media Inc, 702
Vickers plc, 702
Vicson Bekaert, 702
Victor Company of Japan Ltd
- JVC, 389
- VHS (Video Home System), 701
Victor Hasselblad AB, 349

769

COMPANY INDEX

Victoria & Albert Museum (V&A), 694
Victorinox AG, 703
Victorinox Swiss Army Brands Inc
– Swiss Army Brands, 636
Video Technology Ltd
– Vtech, 712
Vienna Beef Inc, 703
Vienna University of Technology, 703
Viessmann Werke GmbH & Co. KG, 703
Viking Group Inc
– Viking, 704
Viking International
– Viking Tyres, 704
Viking Range Corporation
– Viking, 704
Viking Technology
– Viking Components Inc, 704
Vileda GmbH, 704
Villeroy & Boch AG, 705
Villeroy & Boch Gustavsberg AB, 343
Vimeo LLC, 705
Vincenzo Zucchi SpA
– Bassetti, 103
Vinci Group
– Eurovia SA, 259
Vinci SA, 705
Vinex International Wine Fair, 705
Virb LLC, 705
Virgin Group Ltd
– Virgin Atlantic Airways, 705
Virgin Records
– Daft Punk, 185
Visa Inc, 706
– Plus, 537
Visit Britain, 119
Visit Denmark, 203
Visit Estonia, 257
Visit Finland, 280
Visit Scotland, 593
Vistakon
– Acuvue, 62
Visteon Corporation, 706
Vitkovice Inc, 706
Vitra AG, 706
Vittoria SpA, 707
Viva! Experiências, 707
Vivantes, 707
Vivendi SA
– Activision, 61
– Canal+, 137
– CanalSat, 137
– CinéCinéma Channel, 152
– DJ Hero, 218
– Guitar Hero, 342
– Vivendi SA, 707
– Vivendi Universal Games, 707
– Zenji, 741
Vivienne Westwood Ltd, 707
Vivitar Corporation, 708
VKR Holding A/S
– Velux, 698
VM (Veenkoloniaal Museum in Veendam), 708
VNB (Vermont National Bank), 708
VNG (Vereniging van Nederlandse Gemeenten), 708
VNU Exhibitions Europe BV
– VIV América Latina, 707
VNU Group, 708
Vodafone Group plc, 708
Vodafone Romania

– Connex, 169
Vodavi Technology Inc
– Vodavi, 708
Vogelzang International Corporation, 708
Voith GmbH, 709
Vola A/S, 709
Volaris, 709
Volcom Stone Inc, 709
VolgaTelecom OJSC, 709
VolkerWessels NV, 709
Völkl Group, 710
Volksbank AG, 710
Volksbühne am Rosa-Luxemburg-Platz, 710
Volkswagen AG, 713
Volkswagen Group
– Audi, 95
– Audi NSU, 95
– Bentley, 106
– Bugatti, 123
– Škoda, 610
Volontari della Sicurezza
Volunteers of America, 710
Volvo GM Heavy Truck Corporation, 710
Volvo Trademark Holding AB
– Volvo, 710
Von Dutch Originals LLC
– Von Dutch, 711
Von Roll Holding AG, 711
Voortman Cookies Ltd, 711
Votorantim Group, 711
Vox Footwear, 712
VRG Linhas Aéreas
– Varig, 697
VR Group, 712
– VR Cargo, 712
V&S Group
– Absolut Vodka, 58
– V&S (Vin & Spirit), 694
VSM Group AB
– Pfaff, 531
VTG-LEHNKERING AG, 712
VTR Banda Ancha (Chile) SA, 712
Vulcan Materials Company
– Vulcan, 713
Vulco Développement SA
– Vulco, 713
Výtahy VMC s.r.o., 713

W

Wachovia Corporation, 714
– First Union, 283
Wacom Co. Ltd, 714
Wagner Brake Products, 714
WAGNER-Group, 714
Walden Book Company Inc, 714
Walgreen Co., 714
Wallace Mills Architect, 456
Wall of Sound, 715
Wall-Thürmer A/S
– Wallkö, 715
Wal-Mart Stores Inc
– Hiper Bompreço, 355
– Walmart, 715
Walt Disney Motion Pictures Group
– Touchstone Home Entertainment, 670
Walter's Produce Inc, 715
Wander AG, 716
Wang Laboratories Inc, 716
Warburg Pincus LLC, 716
Warner Bros. Entertainment Inc
– Fine Line Features, 280
– Friends, 299
– Harry Potter, 349

– Warner Brothers, 717
Warner Bros. Pictures
– 300, 53
Warner Chilcott plc, 717
Warner-Lambert Company
– Actifed, 61
Warner Music Group
– Atlantic Records, 94
– East West Records, 241
– Elektra Records, 246
– Reprise Records, 566
– Sire Records, 608
– WEA (Warner-Elektra-Atlantic), 718
– Rhino Records, 568
Warn Industries Inc, 716
Warp Records Ltd, 717
– Boards of Canada, 112
Warren Unilube Inc
– Coastal, 160
Warteck Invest AG, 717
Wasabröd AB, 717
Washington Mutual Inc, 717
Washington Redskins, 564
Waste Management Inc
– WM Waste Management, 729
Watabe Wedding Corporation, 717
Waterman SA, 718
Wausau Paper Corporation, 718
Wawa Inc, 718
W.C. Bradley Co.
– Zebco, 741
WD-40 Company, 718
– 3-IN-ONE, 50
Weathermatic Inc, 718
Weber-Stephen Products LLC
– Weber, 718
Wega Srl, 719
Wegmans Food Markets Inc
– Wegmans, 719
WEG SA, 719
Weight Watchers International Inc, 720
Weiler Corporation, 720
Weil-McLain Inc, 720
Weinbrenner Shoe Company Inc, 720
Weiss Umwelttechnik GmbH, 720
Wella AG, 720
Wellcraft LLC, 720
– Scarab, 590
Wells Fargo Bank NA
– Wells Fargo, 720
Wells Fargo & Company
– Wells Fargo, 720
Wembley National Stadium Ltd
– Wembley Stadium, 721
Wenger Corporation, 721
Wenner Media LLC
– Rolling Stone, 573
Werkraum Wartek PP, 721
Werner Co., 721
Wernli AG, 721
WeSC (We are the Superlative Conspiracy), 721
Wesfarmers Curragh Pty Ltd
– Curragh, 182
Wesfarmers Ltd, 721
– Coles Supermarkets, 163
Wessanen Group
– Tartex, 641
West Bend Housewares LLC, 722
Westbound, 722
Westbridge Hospitality Fund LP

– Red Roof Inn, 564
West Coast Choppers Inc (WCC), 722
Western Digital Corporation, 722
Western Properties Trust, 722
Westfalia, 722
Westfield Group, 722
Westinghouse Electric Company LLC
– Westinghouse, 723
Weston Foods (Canada) Inc, 723
Westside Concrete Materials, 723
Wetterau Incorporated, 723
Weyerhaeuser Company, 723
WGBH Educational Foundation
– WGBH-TV, 723
Wham-O Inc, 723
Whataburger Restaurants LP, 724
Whatcom Museum, 724
Whirlpool Corporation, 724
– Jenn-Air Brand Home Appliances, 383
– KitchenAid, 397
– Maytag, 446
White Castle Management Co., 724
Whitesnake, 724
White Spot Ltd
– Triple O's, 673
Whitman's Candies Inc
– Whitman's, 725
Whole Foods Market IP LP, 725
WHSmith plc, 725
Wickes Inc, 725
Wide Span Sheds, 725
Wielton SA, 725
Wienerberger AG, 726
Wieners der Kaffee-Röster GmbH, 726
Wiener Städtische Versicherung AG, 726
Wiesbauer Holding AG, 726
Wiha Werkzeuge GmbH, 726
Wihuri Oy, 726
WIKA Alexander Wiegand SE & Co. KG, 726
WikiLeaks, 727
Wikimedia Foundation Inc, 727
Wild Side Vidéo, 727
William Grant & Sons Ltd, 727
Williams Grand Prix Engineering Ltd
– BMW Williams F1, 112
Williamson-Dickie Manufacturing Company
– Dickies, 211
William Wrigley Jr. Company
– Bubble Tape, 122
– Freedent, 297
– Juicy Fruit, 388
– Skittles, 609
– Wrigley's, 732
Willys AB
– Willy:s, 727
Wilson Sporting Goods Company, 727
Wilton Industries Inc, 727
Winchester Repeating Arms, 728
Wingate Inns International Inc, 728
Winn-Dixie Stores Inc, 728
Wintershall Holding AG, 729
WinWay Corporation, 729
Wipro Unza Holdings Ltd

– Unza, 689
W.L.Gore & Associates Inc
– Gore-Tex, 329
– Windstopper, 728
WMF AG Geislingen/Steige, 729
WNBA Enterprises LLC
– Indiana Fever, 370
Wolford, 730
Wolf's Head Oil Company, 730
Wolters-Noordhoff BV, 730
Wolverine World Wide Inc, 730
Woolrich Inc, 730
Woolworths Group plc, 731
Woolworths Ltd, 730
WordPress Foundation, 731
WorldCom Inc, 731
World Customs Organization (WCO), 731
World Federation of the Sporting Goods Industry (WFSGI), 731
World Hockey Association (WHA)
– Calgary Cowboys, 133
World Industries Inc
– Flame Boy, 732
– Wet Willy, 732
World Kitchen LLC
– Revere Ware, 567
World Smile Corporation
– Smiley, 613
Worlds of Wonder (WoW) Inc, 732
World Wide Fund for Nature (WWF), 733
WPP plc, 732
– Millward Brown, 456
Wright Tool Company, 732
Wrigley Company
– Life Savers, 418
Writers Guild of Canada, 733
WSP Group plc, 733
WTA Tour, 733
Wu Tang Clan, 733
W. W. Grainger Inc, 330
Wyeth, 733
Wyndham Hotel Group
– Days Inn, 194
– Super 8 Motels, 633
Wyndham Worldwide Corporation
– Knights Inn, 399
– Wyndham Hotels & Resorts, 733
Wyse Technology Inc
– Wyse Technology, 733
– Qume, 553

X

Xantech LLC, 734
Xantrex Technology USA Inc, 734
Xaos Tools Inc, 734
Xerox Corporation, 734
XL Group plc, 735
XO Holdings Inc
– XO Communications, 735
X-Rite Inc
– Pantone, 520
– Pantone Hexachrome, 520
XV Pan American Games Rio 2007
– Rio 2007, 569
XXX Energy Drink Inc, 735
Xypex Chemical Corporation
– Xypex, 735

COMPANY INDEX

Y

Yacco SA, 736
Yahoo! Inc
- AltaVista, 81
- flickr, 286
- Overture Services, 515
- Yahoo!, 736
Yakka Apparel Solutions, 736
Yale Materials Handling, 736
Yale University
- Yale University, 736
- Yale University Press, 736
Yale University Athletics
- Yale Bulldogs, 736
Yamaguchi Bicycles Inc, 737
Yamaha Corporation, 737
Yamaha Motor Corporation USA
- Yamalube, 737
Yamaha Motor Europe NV
- MBK, 446
Yamaichi Electronics Co. Ltd, 737
Yamanouchi Pharmaceutical Co. Ltd, 737
Yamato, 737
Yankee Global Enterprises LLC
- New York Yankees, 487
Yara International ASA, 737
Yaskawa America Inc
- Yaskawa, 738
Ybrant Digital Ltd
- Lycos, 431
Yellow Book USA Inc
- Yellow Book, 738
Yellow Pages, 738
Yellow Worldwide Inc
- Yellow Freight, 738
Yildiz Holding
- Ülker, 681
Yıldız Holding
- Godiva Chocolatier, 325
YMCA (Young Men's), 738
Yogen Früz
- I Can't Believe It's Yogurt (ICBIY), 363
Yokogawa Electric Corporation
- Yokogawa, 738
Yokohama Rubber Company Ltd
- Yokohama, 738
Yonex Co. Ltd
- Yonex, 738
Yoplait Marques International SAS
- Yoplait, 738
Yoppi Hungary kft
- Yoppi, 738
Yoshimura R&D of America Inc
- Yoshimura, 739
Yoshinoya Holdings Co. Ltd
- Yoshinoya, 739
YouSendIt Inc, 739
YouTube LLC, 739
YPF
- Full, 304
Y&R (Young & Rubicam), 739
Yukos Oil Company, 739
Yum! Brands Inc, 739
- KFC, 395
- Pizza Hut, 535
- Taco Bell, 638
Yupo Corporation, 739

Z

Zale Corporation, 740
- Zales, 740
Zalman Tech Co. Ltd
- Zalman, 740
Zanello SA, 740
Zapata Corporation, 740
Zaragoza Municipality
- DWP (Digital Water Pavilion), 237
ZDF (Zweites Deutsches Fernsehen), 741
ZD (Ziff Davis Inc), 742
Zebra Technologies, 741
Zeeman textielSupers BV
- Zeeman, 741
Zenetti Wheels, 741
Zenitel NV
- Stentofon, 628
Zenith Electronics, 741
Zentraler Kreditausschuss
- Electronic Cash (EC), 246
Zeppelin, 742
Zero Skateboards, 742
ZF Electronics Corporation
- Cherry, 147
ZF France SAS
- Zadig & Voltaire, 740
ZF Sachs AG
- Sachs, 581
Zhejiang Geely Holding Group
- Volvo, 710
Ziff Davis Holdings Inc
- MacWEEK, 435
Ziff Inc
- PC Week, 524
Zimmer Inc, 742
Zippo Manufacturing Company
- Ronson, 574
- Zippo, 742
Zirh International, 743
Zix Corporation, 743
Zodiac International SASU
- Zodiac Marine & Pool, 743
Zoomp, 743
Zott SE & Co. KG
- Monte, 463
Zurich Financial Services AG
- Zurich, 743
Zwillings J. A. Henckels, 743
Zylab Technologies BV
- ZyLAB, 743

Design Index

#
3Deluxe, 265
75B, 373, 575
999 Design, 298

A
Abdullah, Rayan, 95
abold, 278
Acer, 517
A&Co Paris, 670
ADSA, 278
Aicher, Otl, 429
AID, 254
Aishima, Miho
– johnson banks, 592
Aldridge, Alan, 348
Alexander, Henry, 738
Alex Gonzales, 684
Allah Mathematics, 733
Allen, Ernie
– Tatham-Laird & Kudner, 467
Allied International
 Designers, 57, 75
Aloof Design, 653
Ampersand Design, 162
Amster Yard, 499
Ana Couto Branding &
 Design, 406
Anderson, Gary, 562
Anderson, Ian
– The Designers Republic, 717
Andersson, Rasmus, 622
Angelvuo, Renne
– Priority Advertising, 473
Anspach Grossman Portugal, 154
Apeloig, Phillipe, 379
Appia, Louis, 562
Apple, 434
Arbiter, Ivor, 652
Arcade Agency, 360
Armored AutoGroup Inc, 630
Arnell Group, 168, 218, 310, 527, 559
Arnell, Peter
– Arnell Group, 218
Arnold Saks Associates, 75
Ascender Corporation, 88

Ash, Stuart
– Gottschalk+Ash, 151
Associati, Robilant, 408
Astbury, Paul
– Minale Tattersfield, 369
Atelier Works, 156
Attik, 115
Axiom, 643
Ayer, N.W., 156
Aykroyd, Dan, 318
Ayres, Will, 237
Azuca Ingenio Gráfico, 446

B
Backes, Lutz, 548
Bailey Lauerman, 168
Baker, Eric, 329
Baker, Scott, 454
Ball, Harvey, 613
Ballmer, Walter, 505
Banks & Miles, 120
Bardou-Jacquet, Antoine
– H5, 53
Barnes, Paul, 656
Barney, Gerry
– Design Research Unit, 120
Baron, Fabien, 211
Bartholomew, Robert, 174
Bass, Saul, 217, 313, 320, 482, 551, 572, 686, 717, 726
– Yager & Associates, 94
Baumann & Baumann, 76, 472, 729
BBC, 560
BD+A Design, 188
Beatman, Josh
– Brainchild Studios, 195
Beattie, Trevor
– TBWA, 270
Behrens, Peter, 65
Belk Mignogna Associates, 226
Bell Canada, 105
Beltrán, Félix, 180
Benson, Oscar Herman, 51
Berkman, Justin, 457
Bernhardt Fudyma Design
 Group, 474

BETC Design, 530
Beth Singer Design, 84
Bhang, Dave, 696
Bierut, Michael
– Pentagram, 164, 325, 362, 365, 472, 652
Biles, Anthony
– Turner Duckworth, 82
Bilheimer, Chris, 335
Bizjak, Borut, 568
Blackburn, Bruce
– Chermayeff & Geismar, 85
Blackburn, Tim, 458
Blok, Irina, 88
Boguslav, Raphael, 392
– Lippincott & Margulies, 487
Boldrini & Ficcardi, 539
Boot, Jesse, 115
Bos, Ben
– Total Design, 558
Bosch, Robert, 116
Bostock & Pollitt, 373
Bowman, Brian
– Digital Kitchen, 356
Brahm, 456, 560
Brainchild Studios, 195
Brand Advisors, 383
Brandia Central, 181
Brandimage, 71
Brand Integration Group, 400
BrandLogic, 572
Brand New School, 141
BrandSinger, 152
Brink, Gaby
– Templin Brink Design, 381
Browne, Dik, 150
Browne, Tom, 386
Bruce Dunlop & Associates, 631
Brunazzi & Associati, 634
Brunazzi, Giovanni
– Brunazzi & Associati, 634
Build, 206
Bulletproof, 721
Buster Design, 339
Byron Osterweil Associates, 387
Bysted, 335, 499

C
Cannon, Brian
– Microdot Creative, 500
Carbone Smolan Agency, 93
Carpenter, Tad
– Design Ranch, 600
Carrá, Luxon
– Deskey Associates, 690
Carra, Vince
– TrueBrand, 499
Carré Noir, 614, 707
Carter, Matthew, 458
Carter Wong Tomlin, 291, 428, 607
Cartoon Network, 141
Casado, John, 256
– Apple, 434
Cassandre, A.M., 739
Cato, Ken, 96
Cazadamont, Rachel
– H5, 63, 374
CB'A, 80
CDT, 251
Cefai, Jon
– KentLyons, 381
Chanel, Coco, 145
Charles S. Anderson
 Design Co., 151
Chermayeff & Geismar, 85, 88, 102, 348, 377, 386, 421, 450, 460, 470, 478, 479, 481, 523, 545, 572, 594, 603, 614, 647, 653, 688, 723
CHI & Partners, 120
Chu, Sylvia
– FutureBrand, 372
Chute Gerdeman Retail, 603
Chyliński, Henryk, 513
Cleary, Bill, 241
Cobb, Rebecca
– FutureBrand, 372
Code & Theory, 644
Coiner, Charles T., 156
Colani, Luigi, 138
Collins, Brian, 455
Concrete, 142, 633
Conran Design Group, 467
Cook, Sandy, 110
Cooley, Helen

– The Partners, 381
Cooper, Muriel, 459
Corey, Tom
– Fred/Alan Inc, 489
Cornet, Baer, 501
Cornwall Design, 550
Corporate Branding, 97
Corporate Edge, 97, 309
Corrales, Diego, 377
– Azuca Ingenio Gráfico, 446
de Coubertin, Pierre, 506
Courtes, Alexandre, 562
Creature, 596
Creed, Trevor
– SVP Design, 151
Cuban Council, 262
Curt Swan, 634

D
Dalí, Salvador, 151
Danne & Blackburn, 476
Danne Design
– Danne Design, 395
Danne, Richard, 395
Darwin, 627
Davidson, Carolyn, 490
DDB Worldwide, 133
de Dreux, Alfred, 353
Deepend, 372
Dell Global Creative, 199
Dempsey, Mike
– CDT, 251
Dennis, Ian, 479
Design Bridge, 120
Design Collaborative, 476
Design & Image
 Communications, 627
Design Ranch, 600
Design Research Unit, 120, 235, 368
Designworks, 646
Deskey Associates, 690
DeSola Group, 699
Deveria, Achille, 127
DG Design, 173
Dieffenbach, John
– TrueBrand, 499
Digital Kitchen, 356

DESIGN INDEX

Dinkins, Benny, 403
Dior, Jerry, 438
Diseño Shakespear, 113
DMC Group, 559
Dompierre, Fred, 355
Donner, Hans, 563
Douglas, Dave, 135
Doyle Partners, 654
Dragon Rouge, 430
Drake, Theodore "Ted" W., 148
Dream On, 666
Dual, 305
Duffy & Partners, 380, 457
Dufour, Guillaume-Henri, 562
Dumbar, Gert, 482
Dunant, Henry, 562
Dunmore, Laurence, 241
Dunning Eley Jones, 88, 591
Dunning Penney Jones, 623
Dupla Design, 569
Duszek, Roman, 427
Dwyer, Toni, 160

E

Edenspiekermann, 351, 556
eg.design, 419
Eiber, Rick, 113
Elmwood, 132
English & Pockett, 676
Enorm, 208
Enterprise IG, 100, 178, 355, 553, 596, 708
Erickson, Ralph, 517
Ernstberger, Matthias
- Sagmeister Inc, 596
Ervin, Don
- Sandgren & Murtha, 139
Esquer, Rafael, 436
Essex Two, 422, 510, 525
Euro RSCG, 430, 651
Ewing, Larry, 420

F

Fahlman, Scott, 213
Fairey, Shepard, 500
Fanstone Group, 394
Farkas, Kiko, 117
Farnham, Kevin
- Organic, 736
Faydherbe & De Vringer, 471
Fernández, Juan Carlos
- Ideograma, 709
Ferriter, Roger
- Herb Lubalin Associates, 414
Ferrone, Joanna, 277
FFL, 258
FHA Image Design, 506
FHK Henrion, 479
Fick, Hans, 63
Figtree, 359
Finocchiaro, Joe, 154
Fleming, Allan, 159
Fletcher, Alan, 184, 694
Foakes, Kevin, 491
Foley, Jack
- WGBH-TV, 159
Fonseca, Mario, 243
Fontana, Rubén, 304, 408
Forsman & Bodenfors, 352
Forssell, Carl
- Ideograma, 709
Fortuné, Fleur
- H5, 198
Franco, Jesús Emilio, 530
Franke, Craig
- Franke+Fiorella, 139
Franke+Fiorella, 139
Frankfurt Balkind, 497

Fred/Alan Inc, 489
Frehley, Ace, 396
Frog Design, 424, 586
Fry, 419
Fujita, S. Neil, 655
Fukuhara, Hiroshige, 715
Funimation Productions, 227
FutureBrand, 57, 66, 67, 71, 103, 339, 372, 492, 646, 649, 688, 690
FutureBrand BC&H, 515, 711
Future Farmers, 262

G

Gabriela Rodríguez Studio, 304
GAD, 158
Garrett, Malcolm, 129
Geismar, Tom
- Chermayeff & Geismar, 688
Geissbuhler, Steff
- Chermayeff & Geismar, 88, 102, 377, 450, 470, 481, 647, 653, 688
Geldof, Bob, 422
Genesis, 403
Gentile, Antonio, 535
Gentleman, David, 479
George, Robert, 407
Gericke, Michael
- Pentagram, 278, 597
Giambarba, Paul, 538
Gibson, Jim, 724
Gifford, Luke
- Wolff Olins, 440
Giglio Jr, Louie Floyd, 148
Giovanni Bianco Studio 65, 231
Glaser, Milton, 195, 369
Glazer, 456
Glover, Linda, 700
Godson, Suzi, 504
Golden, William, 142
Gonzalez, Ana
- FutureBrand, 372
Goodby Silverstein & Partners, 690
Google, 324
Google Creative Lab, 328
Gorman, Pat
- Manhattan Design, 469
Gottschalk+Ash, 142, 151, 299
Graphèmes, 275
Graphic Thought Facility, 206
Graven Images, 593
Gravy (aka David Streek), 372
GRFX/Novocom, 577
Groening, Matt, 660
Grossman, Gene, 423
- Anspach Grossman Portugal, 154
- BrandLogic, 572
- Enterprise IG, 355
Grube, Ben
- Digital Kitchen, 356
Grupo Oxigeno, 168, 173
Gucci family, 340
Guenoun, Joël, 416
Guillermo Brea & Associates, 91
Guo Chunning, 506
Gyro:HSR, 644

H

H5, 53, 63, 150, 198, 210, 374
Haglind, Jörgen, 650
Hallmark, 347
Hambly & Woolley, 670
Handler, Elliot, 445

Happy F&B, 352
Hardy Design, 274
Hardy, Mariana
- Hardy Design, 274
Harris, Dale, 660
Harvey, Matthew
- TBWA\Neboko, 669
Hatfield, Tinker, 72
Hayman, Luke
- Pentagram, 284, 652
Heckler Associates, 625
Heckler, Terry
- Heckler Associates, 625
Helou Design, 208, 461
Henrik Nygren Design, 99
Henrion, 398
Herb Lubalin Associates, 414
Herrainco, 155
Hetfield, James, 451
Hewlett, Jamie, 329
Hibbard, Angus S., 105
Hick, Jon
- The Iconfactory, 281
Hicks, Jon, 328
Hidy, Lance, 421
Hinrichs, Kit
- Pentagram, 182
Hoet & Hoet, 121, 539
Hoffmann, Julia
- Pentagram, 657
Holder, Randell
- BrandLogic, 572
Holloway, Rob
- The Partners, 196
Holtom, Gerald, 524
de Homem-Christo, Guy-Manuel, 185
Horlander, Stephen
- The Iconfactory, 281
Hosokawa, Mitsuo, 405
Houplain, Ludovic
- H5, 150
Howard, Kenny (aka Von Dutch), 711
Huerta, Gerard, 59, 636, 664, 677, 714
Hughes, Tom
- Apple, 434
Hunt, Robert, 229
Hurley, Chad, 523, 739
Hyland, Angus
- Pentagram, 332, 526

I

ICG, 155
ico Design, 221, 517
IDEO, 670
Ideo Comunicadores, 471, 661
Ideograma, 709
IE Design+Communications, 193
Imaginary Forces, 165
Indiana, Robert, 428
Interbrand, 50, 59, 94, 181, 356, 403, 444, 448, 530, 637, 647, 651, 662, 677, 731, 734
Interbrand Newell & Sorrell, 91, 93, 119
Interbrand Zintzmeyer & Lux, 102, 456, 637, 666, 675, 680
Irons, Rick, 358
Irvin, Rea, 658

J

Jaggi, Fredy
- BrandLogic, 572
Janiszewski, Jerzy, 616

Janoff, Rob
- Regis McKenna Advertising, 89
Jan Sabach Design, 579
Jerry Kuyper Partners, 152
johnson banks, 150, 464 592, 602, 705
Johnson, M.B., 226
Johnson, Michael
- johnson banks, 592
Johnston, Edward, 683
Jorgensen Quint, 539
Jung von Matt, 579

K

Kamat, Shekhar, 627
Kamekura, Yusaku, 449
Kapaz, Ronald
- OZ Design, 456
karlssonwilker, 472
Kass, Milt
- Byron Osterweil Associates, 387
Katona, Diti
- Concrete, 633
Katz, Geoff
- Organic, 736
Kawagoi, Takuya, 617
Kedar, Ruth, 328
Keen, Quo, 439
Kellogg, Will Keith, 392
Kennard, Bill, 56
KentLyons, 318, 381
Kidd, Chip, 389
Kiedis, Anthony, 563
Kiku Obata & Co, 82
King, Ben
- Pentagram, 652
King Casey, 451
Kirkpatrick, Janice
- Graven Images, 593
Kitschenberg, Lisa
- Pentagram, 103
Klaus Koch Corporate Communications, 720
Kleefeld, Hans
- Stewart & Morrison, 100
Klein, Barry, 574
KMSTeam, 587
Kobrow, Peta
- KMSTeam, 587
Koch, Claus, 78, 104, 207, 229
Kontrapunkt, 541
Kosa Jr, Emil, 52
Kraft, 403
Kral, Joe
- Cuban Council, 262
Kramer, Burton, 157
Kraus, Audrey
- Chermayeff & Geismar, 450
KSDP, 666
Kudos, John
- Pentagram, 341
Kuhr, Barbara, 729
Kuroki, Yasuo, 617
Kurpershoek, Theo, 87
Kuyper, Jerry, 154
- Yager & Associates, 94

L

Laboratório Secreto, 279
La fe ciega studio, 152
Lambie-Nairn, 500
Lambie-Nairn, Martin, 104
Landor Associates, 52, 57, 58, 75, 93, 117, 119, 132, 136, 152, 155, 156, 167, 195, 200, 219, 221, 233, 271, 295, 301, 354,

361, 379, 395, 403, 464, 482, 488, 499, 505, 522, 527, 531, 556, 565, 580, 585, 595, 637, 699, 706, 733, 734
Langer, Helmut, 125, 270, 401, 705
Langhus, Luke, 383
Larghero, Marcos, 407
Lark Publicité, 421
Larrea, Vicente, 372
Latinbrand, 243, 471
LaVerge-Webb, Anne-Marie, 133
Lawrence Pierce, 508
Leader, Lindon, 350
- Landor Associates, 152, 271
Lea, Ed, 258
Ledoux, Mathias, 410
Leegi, Mariana
- Ideograma, 709
Lee, Sid, 629
Leo Burnett, 533
Leow, Linda
- Future Farmers, 262
Lester Beall Associates, 374
Leuvelink, Gert-Jan, 482
Lichtenstein, Roy, 228
Liechtenstein, 355
Linck, Connie, 227
Lindström, Per, 317
Lintas, 384
Lippincott, 83, 84, 99, 107, 115, 223, 235, 241, 321, 387, 451, 545, 553, 618, 625, 638, 704, 715, 728
Lippincott & Margulies, 54, 87, 102, 105, 148, 151, 154, 161, 170, 487, 535, 584, 649, 655
Lippincott Mercer, 200, 371, 623, 652, 664
Lipson Alport Glass & Associates, 516
Lloyd Northover, 98, 465, 522
Locke, Andy
- Moon Brand, 659
Loewy, Raymond, 151, 261, 358, 429, 430, 486, 601, 619, 676, 687, 692
Louis Vuitton, 431
Loyalkaspar, 672
Loža A5, 676
Lubalin, Herb, 680
Ludlow, Chris
- Henrion, Ludlow & Schmidt, 398
Ludlow & Schmidt, 398
Ludwig, Yve
- Pentagram, 472
Luna, Alejandro
- Guillermo Brea & Associates, 91
Lundquist, Oliver Lincoln, 686
Lupi, Italo, 152

M

MacGregor, Elena Rivera, 506
Machbar, 325
Magalhães, Aloísio, 51, 419, 529
Le Mahec, Patrick
- Plan Créatif, 242
Maher, Steve, 422
Makita, 438
Manhart, Toni, 650
Manhattan Design, 469
Marek, Bruno
- KMSTeam, 587
Marianek, Joe
- Pentagram, 652
Markatos, Peter

773

DESIGN INDEX

- Cuban Council, 262
Mars & Venus, 100
Martinez, Marcelo
- Laboratório Secreto, 279
Martino, Cauduro, 574, 676, 705
Martinowicz, Michelle
- Design Ranch, 600
Martins, Ruben, 57, 674
Maserati, Mario, 444
Matsuo Yasamura & Associates, 308
Matza, Robert
- Chermayeff & Geismar, 647
Mauk, Mitchell, 234
McLaughlin, Donal, 686
M&C Saatchi, 582
Meilin, Han, 71
Meistrell, Bill, 113
Ménard, Nicolas, 355
Mendell & Oberer, 605
Mercury, Freddie, 552
Messerli, Joe, 660
MetaDesign, 113, 166, 218, 584, 599, 636, 713
Metahaven, 727
Metschan, Philip
- Wikimedia Foundation, 727
Microdot Creative, 500
Microsoft, 468
Mignola, Mike, 352
Mikalef, Carolina
- Guillermo Brea & Associates, 91
Miller, Abbott
- Pentagram, 92, 341
Miller, Frank, 53
Minale Tattersfield, 112, 349, 369, 621
Miró, Joan, 256
Mitchell, Greg, 158
Mitchell, Joseph
- Wolff Olins, 325
M/M Paris, 275, 618
Modarelli, James, 476
Moon Brand, 488, 659
Moon, Richard
- Moon Brand, 488, 659
Moore, Peter, 63
Moore, Terry
- AID, 254
Moving Brands, 636
MTV Networks Europe, 707
Müller-Brockmann, Josef, 589
Munger, Curt
- Interbrand, 677
Muren, Dennis, 229
Mussfeldt, Peter
- Versus, 99, 434

N

Nash, Scott
- Fred/Alan Inc, 489
Neal, Paul, 346
Neumann, Bert, 710
Newlyn, Miles, 358, 610
- Wolff Olins, 140, 684
Nies & Partners, 314
Nitro Group, 403
Nitsch Design, 207, 209
Nodell, Martin
- Leo Burnett, 533
Noorda, Bob
- Unimark, 68
Norges Kreative Fagskole, 226
North, 556, 657
Norton, James Lansdowne, 496
Nude, 137

O

Oestreich, Peter J., 400
Office, 139, 328
Ogilvy, 363
OH&CO, 60, 87
Olinsky, Frank
- Manhattan Design, 469
Oliver, Vaughan
- V23, 51
Open, 118
Oppenheimer, Brent
- OH&CO, 87
Opperman, George, 94
Organic, 736
Orth, Lisa, 492
Ossott, Isabella
- FutureBrand, 372
Ove Design and Communications, 670
Owen, Steve
- The Partners, 381
Oxley, Simon, 677
OZ Design, 456

P

Pągowski, Andrzej
- Studio P, 540
Paisley, Michael
- The Partners, 196
Pappas Group, 485
Paprika Communications, 488
Parker, Trey, 618
Parkinson, Jim, 487, 573
Pasche, John, 659
Paul, Art, 536
Pearce, David
- Tatham Pearce, 409
Peavey, Hartley, 524
Peloton Design, 690
Pennzoil Quaker State Company, 551
Pentagram, 52, 55, 74, 79, 84, 92, 103, 104, 107, 124, 134, 154, 156, 164, 182, 201, 206, 224, 241, 248, 262, 278, 284, 318, 325, 332, 334, 341, 362, 365, 378, 411, 423, 429, 445, 471, 472, 487, 508, 515, 526, 534, 537, 540, 545, 547, 566, 567, 582, 589, 597, 652, 654, 655, 657, 659, 663, 672, 707
Perfect Day, 169
Perz, Rudy
- Leo Burnett, 533
Peter Schmidt Group, 72, 419, 539, 587, 591, 690
Petrie, Rob, 177
Pettersson, Göran, 317
Phillips, Jim, 585
Pike, Brian, 661
Pintos, Ariel, 526
Piraino, Anthony
- The Iconfactory, 281
Pirtle, Woody
- Pentagram, 201
Plan Créatif, 242
Plunkett, John, 729
Poelvoorde, Raymond
- Lippincott & Margulies, 148
Pol, Santiago, 54
Popp, Franz Josef, 112
Porkka & Kuutsa, 69
Porter, Mark, 656
Poulton, Neil, 406
Princess Feodora, 273
Priority Advertising, 473
projectGRAPHICS, 629
Publicis, 707
Push, 513
PVDI Design, 587

Q

Quark, 552
Quinton, Greg
- The Partners, 381

R

Rademacher, Paul, 207
Rand, Paul, 56, 163, 182, 234, 251, 316, 363, 365, 376, 464, 488, 503, 693, 723, 736
Razorfish, 109, 216
RDYA, 694
Red Design, 506
Redhouse, Diana, 86
Regis McKenna Advertising, 89
Reid, Jamie, 600
Reiwald, Jean, 275
de la Renta, Oscar, 513
Reuterswärd, Carl Frederik, 580
Reznor, Trent, 491
Rice, Suzy, 626
Richard Runyon, 271
Richardson, Gardiner, 562
Ridenhour, Carlton Douglas (aka Chuck D), 547
Rijven, Martin, 74
Ritz, Cesar, 570
Robert Miles Runyon Associates, 505
Robial, Étienne, 410, 521
Robilant Associati, 76, 276
Robinson, Frank M., 161
Roerich, Nicholas, 101
Rogoff, Patti
- Manhattan Design, 469
Rose, 184
Rosenquist, James, 368
Rose, Sue, 277
Roth, Richard, 104
Rovio, 88
RR Donnelley, 574
Rudolph, Dirk, 558
Runyon, Richard, 271
Runyon, Robert Miles, 181
Rushworth, John
- Pentagram, 654

S

Saatchi & Saatchi, 580, 708
Saffron Brand Consultants, 74, 132, 713
Sagmeister Inc, 596
Sagmeister, Stefan
- Sagmeister Inc, 596
Sakamoto, Manabu, 537, 694
Salzberger, Claude
- FutureBrand, 71
Sämann, Julius, 422
Samenwerkende Ontwerpers, 73, 733
Sandgren & Murtha, 139
Sandstrom Design, 146
Saroglia, Francesco, 730
Sato, Kashiwa, 685
Saul Bass & Associates, 97, 105
Saunders, Jason
- Scenario Communications, 496
Savignac, Raymond, 108
Saville, Peter, 263
SBG Partners, 690
Scandinavian Design Group, 219, 627
Scarfe, Gerald, 534
Scenario Communications, 496

Schäfer, Ole
- MetaDesign, 113
Schecter Interbrand, 90
Schecter & Luth, 395
Scher, Paula
- Pentagram, 103, 154, 487, 566, 657, 659
Schindler, Jim, 447
Schindler Parent Identity, 186
Schlagheck & Schultes, 68
Schmittel, Wolfgang, 118
Schnapp, Ira R., 61
Schulpig, Karl, 78
Schwartz, Christian, 656
SEA Design, 381
Sedley Place, 95
Segura, Carlos
- Segura Inc, 171, 538
Segura Inc, 171, 538
SEK & Grey, 280
Selame, Joseph, 328
Sender, 101
Sequel Studio, 132
Serio, Sean
- Peloton Design, 690
Shelepov, Alexey, 553
Shen, David
- Yahoo!, 736
Shimizu, Yuko, 352
SicolaMartin, 552
Sidie, Ingred
- Design Ranch, 600
Siegel+Gale, 50, 113, 417, 481, 495, 499, 531, 547, 690, 693
SightTwo, 722
Sign*, 196, 410
Silveria, Greg, 706
Silverstein, Rich
- Goodby Silverstein & Partners, 690
Sim, Daniel
- Interbrand, 677
Di Simone, Dean
- Tender, 632
Sims, Phil, 177
SlooDesign, 521
Smith, Leslie, 382
Sockeye Creative, 258
Söderqvist, Rune, 55
SoDesign, 115, 269, 400, 499, 571
SomeOne, 259
Sonderegger, Michelle
- Design Ranch, 600
Sonnhalter, 732
Sony, 537
Sotillo, Álvaro, 55, 162, 304
Spalinger, Peter, 589
Specter, 68
Spiekermann, Erik
- United Designers Network, 116
Spielberg, Steven, 229
Spunk Design Machine, 114
Sridhar, KV
- KV Sridhar, 384
Staedtler, 624
Stankowski, Anton
- Stankowski & Duschek, 207, 703
Stankowski & Duschek, 207, 414, 703
Stanley, Robert
- Lippincott & Margulies, 151
Starbucks in-house design team, 625
Stebbing, Timothy
- Frog Design, 424
van Steelandt, Vanessa
- Plan Créatif, 242
Steiner, Henry, 359

Sterling Brands, 127, 398
Stevens, Andy, 346
Stewart & Morrison, 100
- Kleefeld, Hans, 71, 72
Stockholm Design Lab, 350, 587, 696
Stone, Matt, 618
Stone Yamashita, 360
Strohl, Eric, 329
Struck, 643
Studioa, 439
Studio Dumbar, 403, 509, 541
studio FM milano, 237
Studio Intraligi, 363
Studio P, 540
Stun Creative, 339
Stussy, Shawn, 630
Stylus Design, 337
Suiter, Tom
- Brand Advisors, 383
Sundblom, Haddon, 551
SViDesign, 712
SVP Design, 151
Szoeke, Andrew
- Hallmark, 347
Szylinski Associates, 76

T

Tabano, Ray, 67
Tallon, Roger, 614
Talpas, Gary, 491
Tatham-Laird & Kudner, 467
Tatham Pearce, 409, 574
Tatil Design, 506
Tattersfield, Brian
- Minale Tattersfield, 349
TAXI Toronto, 79
TBD, 132, 292
tbd agency, 502
TBWA, 270
TBWA\Neboko, 669
Tchérakian, Sophie
- Sophie Tchérakian, 242
Team Créatif, 137
TEArk, 350, 587
Technicolor, 644
Tecnopop, 471
TelDesign, 124
Templin Brink Design, 381
Templin, Joel
- Templin Brink Design, 381
Tender, 632
Teo, Keshen
- Wolff Olins, 647
The Brand Union, 73, 91, 97, 101, 200, 664
The Designers Republic, 112, 717
The Gate Worldwide, 688
The Iconfactory, 281
The Lab, 165
The Partners, 196, 290, 381, 480, 651, 719
The Watt Group, 289
The Workroom, 561
Tholön Kunst, 263
Thonik, 619
Tloupas, Yorgo, 110
- H5, 210
Toet, Andre
- Samenwerkende Ontwerpers, 73
Total Design, 558
TracyLocke, 52
Trias, Josep Maria, 505
Troika Design Group, 56, 666
Trollbäck & Company, 82
TrueBrand, 499

774

DESIGN INDEX

Tudball, Kath
- johnson banks, 592
Turner Duckworth, 82, 161, 220, 482, 518, 599

U

Uderzo, Albert, 93
Uehling, Kass, 328
Ulf Nilson, Greger, 99
Underware, 186
Unimark, 68
Unimark International, 383
United Designers Network, 116
Unreal, 55
USTA, 693

V

V23, 51
Vår, 146
VBAT, 648
Vega, Arturo, 558
Vellozzi, Eric, 193
Venturethree, 165, 421, 735
Versus, 99, 434
Vignelli Associates, 111, 582, 686
Vignelli, Massimo, 82
Vincenti, Laurent
- A&Co Paris, 670
Virgin Atlantic, 705
Visa International Brand Management, 706
Visual Design Association, 144
Vivarelli, Carlo L., 246
Vogt, Armin, 275
VSA Partners, 153, 282

W

Wallace Church, 551
Wangsillapakun, Tnop
- Segura Inc, 538
Warhol, Andy, 374
Warnock, Marva, 64
Washam, Ben, 108
Watt, Don, 715
Wayne, Ronald, 89
W&Cie, 79, 362, 615
Webber, Ceri
- Moon Brand, 659
Weidemann, Kurt, 194, 450
Weinberger, David
- FutureBrand, 688
WGBH-TV, 159
Whitestone, 278
Widmer, Jean
- Visual Design Association, 144
Wieden, Dan, 389
- Wieden+Kennedy, 389
Wieden+Kennedy, 379, 389
Wikimedia Foundation, 727
Wilkin III, William Graham, 543
Williams Murray Hamm, 101
Wilsson, Christian, 622
Winkreative, 318, 628, 636, 639
Wolf, Arnold, 382
Wolff Olins, 74, 85, 86, 122, 140, 146, 178, 209, 218, 312, 325, 364, 370, 440, 499, 506, 510, 550, 613, 641, 642, 647, 684, 714
Wollner, Alexandre, 270, 397, 409, 586, 681
Woodhouse, Marc, 457

Woods, Mo
- Pentagram, 182
Woody Pirtle, 280
Woolley, Barbara
- Hambly & Woolley, 670
Wyman & Cannon, 718
Wyman, Lance, 452, 505
- Wyman & Cannon, 718
Wyndham Worldwide Corporation, 399

X

Xin, Shao, 71

Y

Yager & Associates, 94
Yahoo!, 736
Yello, 299
York, John, 101
Yoshimara, Rei, 446, 737
Youngblood, Margaret
- Landor Associates, 522
Young & Rubicam, 308, 552

Z

Zbrożek, Andrzej, 427
Zena, 523
Ziner, Zeke, 466
Zip, 337

IMPRINT

TASCHEN

Editor
Julius Wiedemann

Editorial Coordination
Daniel Siciliano Bretas

Editorial Assistant
Nora Dohrmann

Design
Daniel Siciliano Bretas, Nora Dohrmann

Layout
Daniel Siciliano Bretas, Nora Dohrmann
Jon Cefai, Lucinda Ireland (KentLyons)

Production
Stefan Klatte

English Revision
Chris Allen

German Translation
Egbert Baqué, Ursula Wulfekamp

French Translation
Aurélie Daniel for Delivering iBooks & Design

Logo Data Research
Chris Mizsak

Picture Credits
Page 17: © Edward Burtynsky, courtesy Nicholas Metivier, Toronto & Stefan Röpke, Köln
Page 20: © 2012 The Andy Warhol Foundation for the Visual Arts, Inc./Artists Rights Society (ARS), New York
Page 21: © Ed Ruscha, courtesy of the artist
Page 23: © 2012 Yale University Art Gallery/Art Resource, NY/Scala, Florence. VG Bild-Kunst, Bonn
Page 36: © Louis Vuitton/Stéphane Muratet
Page 44: © 2012 The Andy Warhol Foundation, Inc./ARS, New York/Trademarks, Campbell Soup Company. All rights reserved.
Page 45: © 2012 The Andy Warhol Foundation for the Visual Arts, Inc./Artists Rights Society (ARS), New York

All trademarks and images that appear or are related to the artwork featured in this book belong to their respective artists and/or companies that commissioned the work and/or feature herein.

Printed in China
ISBN 978-3-8365-3413-0

H5

Acknowledgements
Special thanks to Denis Assor, Antoine Bardou-Jacquet, Laurence Basset, Matthieu Büchsenschütz, Charlotte Camille, Rachel Cazadamont, Tiphaine Diaconu, Sabine Houplain, Stephane Kooshmanian, Matthieu Lelièvre, Gilles Lipovetsky, Sandrine de Monte, Raphael Naccach, Maurice Prost, Nicolas Rozier, Aline Schneider, Yorgo Tloupas, Isabelle Wekstein and all TASCHEN crew, Daniel Siciliano Bretas, Nora Dohrmann and Julius Wiedemann.

Collaboration
Aline Schneider

Cover and Endpaper Design
H5: Ludovic Houplain, Matthieu Lelièvre

Cover and Endpaper 3D Design
Denis Assor

© 2013 TASCHEN GmbH
Hohenzollernring 53, D-50672 Köln
www.taschen.com

To stay informed about upcoming TASCHEN titles, please request our magazine at www.taschen.com/magazine or write to TASCHEN, Hohenzollernring 53, D-50672 Cologne, Germany, contact@taschen.com, Fax: +49-221-254919. We will be happy to send you a free copy of our magazine which is filled with information about all of our books.